MILTON BERLE'S PRIVATE JOKE FILE

Also by the Author

Milton Berle: An Autobiography
Earthquake
Laughingly Yours
Out of My Trunk
B.S. I Love You

MILTON BERLE'S PRIVATE JOKE FILE

Over 10,000 of his best gags, anecdotes, and one-liners

by Milton Berle

edited by Milt Rosen

THREE RIVERS PRESS
NEW YORK

Published by Three Rivers Press, New York, New York.
Member of the Crown Publishing Group.

Random House, Inc. New York, Toronto, London, Sydney, Auckland
www.randomhouse.com

THREE RIVERS PRESS is a registered trademark and the Three Rivers Press colophon is a trademark of Random House, Inc.

Printed in the United States of America

Library of Congress Cataloging-in-Publication Data
Berle, Milton.
  Milton Berle's private joke file / by Milton Berle. Edited by Milt Rosen.
  1. American wit and humor. I. Rosen, Milt. II. Title. III. Title: Private joke file.
PN2287.B436A25   1989   818'.02—dc20

ISBN 0-307-29033-6

*This one is for
Moses Berlinger, who was the
best Moses Berlinger there could be.*

This book is also
dedicated to the funny men and women
who make comedy,
the nice people who laugh at it,
and my wife, whose special humor
deserves its own book.

contents

Z

Tricks of the Trade

acknowledgments

Jokes can work, as can the internal desire for audience reaction. Sometimes, however, these two elements aren't enough. If raw material and hunger for guffaws could get the job done, all people would be as funny as all other people. The fact is, however, that some people are funnier than others.

To narrow the gap, reinforcements can be brought in. (Me and my mixed metaphors!) To the *art* of bringing laughter, generally, can be added the *carpentry* of making laughter. There are tricks to the trade.

These shortcuts, hints, opinions, systems, and methods aren't etched in stone. They are only the conclusions reached by a man who has been offering himself to audiences for seventy-five years.

Eighty, if you count baby parts.

To my attorney, Paul Schreibman, and my agent, Arthur Pine, who made sure there was a bottom line to sign; to the mechanics and repairmen who kept my machinery running, and my doctors, who kept *me* going; to the many hands and fingers who stroked the keys that inscribed the words on paper; to my editor, Mark Gompertz, who took time off from fatherhood to aid in the delivery of this baby; to my family, for tiptoeing past my office during working hours; to Ruth, for tuna or sardine sandwiches and the endless supply of bottled water; to my friends, fellow Friars, performers, and even the strangers who said a million times, "Have you heard this one?" and proceeded to tell it to me: to all of these and many who will go unsung, I give my total thanks.

introduction

My mother's plans for me were not to be questioned. Her eyes flashing, she announced again and again, to one and all, whether they wanted to hear it or not, that I was going to be a world-famous dramatic actor. Broadway and London's West End would belong to me. My name would become a household word, etched forever in the hearts of men. Edwin Booth, David Garrick, and Maurice Barrymore might just as well take up other lines of work.

All of the previous dicta were ordained while I was still in my mother's womb. Some of them probably predated her first meeting with my father.

After my birth, further instructions were issued to Fate: This boy-child would someday receive the first Nobel Prize for Acting. Also, he would surely be the first Jewish Pope.

Thus spake Sandra Berle; thus listened the gods in their heavens. Thuslier they quivered in their winged sandals and let her have her way. They were smart gods. They knew that my mother's mouth had the best right hook in town.

Of the hundred and six goals set for me, my mother managed to effect close to a hundred. A few, like my marrying into British royalty and starting a Berlinger/Berle dynasty were tough even for her.

But she had one hell of a batting average.

Plan A was to infiltrate serious theater with my incredible ability to cry on demand. By the time I was two, I could out-sob Niagara Falls. Since there was no shortage of roles for those able to play orphans, bastard children, or waifs about to lose one or more parents, most often to evil whiskey, my ability to dampen an agent's rug won many an audition. Drama was in my stars. It would have remained there, but my neighborhood and my older brother Phil teamed up to switch the tracks almost as neatly as I just switched metaphors.

My neighborhood appreciated funny people. Already in kid revues, Georgie Jessel, later to become the Toastmaster General of the United States and confidant of presidents, was a block idol. Another laughmaker, Eddie Cantor, could have run for office in our part of Harlem and won easily, although he was only about ten years old. People cheered when the comedians blessed them with their words.

As a serious Thespian, *I* didn't rate one little "rah."

I decided to do battle for a place in the sun. I was about four when I tossed off my first ad lib. My Uncle Charlie was at the dinner table with us. My Uncle Charlie had a unique way of going at chicken soup. In his hands, the soup spoon was a baton. The golden globules of fat in the steaming broth were notes to be tossed out in all directions. On this occasion, my mother cautioned Uncle Charlie to eat neatly, saying, "If you get one stain on that shirt I'll kill you."

I chimed in. I said, "Momma, you better kill Poppa. It's his shirt!"

My brothers laughed. Uncle Charlie laughed. My father laughed. My mother debated a comeuppance but decided what the hell, and she laughed too.

My mother laughed at me and with me for the rest of her life. Once when I was playing the Hippodrome in Baltimore, she even led the audience in Milton appreciation under trying circumstances. A man sitting next to her started to get fresh. She refused to acknowledge his advances and kept laughing until my act ended. As soon as the applause ebbed, she turned to the sex fiend, swatted him with her purse, and had the manager deport him to Siberia before the next show.

That, of course, was a long time after the brilliant dinner-table ad lib and my first foray into comedy.

My "shirt" joke led to other jokes. Soon I was telling jokes garnered from the four corners of Broadway to anybody who'd stop and listen. Often I told jokes to people who didn't want to listen.

In those formative days I didn't repeat jokes. I made a funny and moved on. It never occurred to me to save my ad libs. There were plenty more where those came from.

Enter my older brother Phil. Until I first displayed my comic muse, Phil wasn't thrilled with me. He would have traded me gladly and quickly for a penny jawbreaker. However, as my reputation grew, and along with it my popularity, Phil started to look at me in a new way. He was never one to let opportunity go by without trying to pick one of its pockets. He knew that I'd be bankable yet. At the moment he wasn't sure how, but he knew deep in his heart that he'd be able to cash in, and therefore, it would be necessary to keep me hot. For my sixth birthday, brother Phil gifted me with a copy of *Dill's Delites*.

Forgotten today, like so many unsung greats, Joe Dill, a reporter, published on his own a four-page booklet once a month. Each issue contained stories, humorous comments, and, infrequently, a real knee-slapper. Dill offered the material for use by vaudevillians and public speakers to freshen up their acts and lives. The depth and scope of the humor can be gauged from a reading of an actual joke that appeared in my first copy:

Salesman to farmer: I've got some soap for your pigs.

Farmer to salesman: That's a lot of hogwash!

I used that joke in a hillbilly sketch fifty years ago. It evoked a big laugh, followed by a long groan, and several death threats.

Unbeknownst to Phil, his *Dill's Delites* unleashed an insatiable hunger in his younger brother. Like a comedic Oliver Twist holding out his porridge bowl, I had to have more. More. And more!

I was and will be forever grateful to my brother Phil. My brother Frank also earned my gratitude by introducing me to *Laff-A-Minute, Jim Jam Jems,* and many of the more expensive humor magazines: *College Humor, Judge, Life* (then purely out for laughs), *Captain Billy's Whiz Bang,* and the *Calgary Eye Opener.*

Soon I was compiling files filled with humorous excerpts from newspaper columns and adding, once in a while, jokes told by comedians onstage. Of course, in the days of vaudeville, it wasn't uncommon for a performer to "borrow" a joke from another performer. Etiquette demanded only that the borrower add to the joke and make it his own. Bert Williams, a star of the Ziegfeld Follies, pilfered a story about fish and added enough laughs to turn it into a classic fifteen-minute routine. Naturally, that routine happens to be in my file.

Over the years I added several thousand joke and humor books, material written for me by many great writers, several hundred thousand ad libs, and let the concoction simmer for seventy-five years. One morning I woke to discover that I'd amassed six and a half million jokes. The count is conservative. After six million, what's a hundred thousand either way?

Time has eroded some of the humor. I have, for example, jokes about forgotten mayors of New York. Jokes about the Palace Theater fill thirty pages. Unless the Palace makes a comeback, these jokes are in deep trouble.

Surprisingly, most of the jokes remain funny and fresh. Besides, nothing funny is old. Nothing's old if it's funny. A joke first used in 1890 illustrates these truths. One member of a two-man team tells a joke. The other says, "That's one of my father's jokes." The first man asks, "What are you—one of your mother's?"

A sure laugh-getter a hundred years ago, the same lines, down to the exact words, were used in 1988 by a ventriloquist at the Universal Amphitheater in Los Angeles and evoked the biggest laugh of a generally funny evening.

The matter of longevity aside, there was no problem in finding solid material for this compilation. There was, in fact, too much to choose from. I have ten thousand "ugly" jokes. This volume can carry about a hundred before tipping over. I had to inform some of my favorites that I still cared and would add them to my next collection. They cried, curled up, and went back to sleep in my computer. One did manage to sneak back into contention when I wasn't looking: I called her my melancholy baby. She had a shape like a melon and a face like a collie!

This joke, written in 1948, was finally voted in and can be found leading the parade.

My darling wife Ruth, of whom it has often been said and rightfully too, suggested that I put my vast cache of jokes on computer. She felt that my office was beginning to look cluttered, and, more important, she needed the closet space for the clothes she doesn't have any of. Ruth also pointed out that computerization would enable me to end up with a tiny disk that didn't have to be dusted. Ruth was concerned with dusting. Once she was laid up for a month after dusting a bowl of plastic fruit.

Faced with the task of putting six and a half million jokes into a computer, many secretaries abandoned ship. Three quit before the first coffee break. Finally, two brave souls, one a young man, went to work. For their efforts, both secretaries will be placed on permanent exhibit at the Smithsonian early next year. They'll be the poor souls with the swollen fingers.

What follows is the best of my private file. It's possible that I sneaked in one or two that do show their age, but I feel that they served me well and deserve recognition.

By and large, my mother would have felt that this was the best collection of jokes ever put between covers. Moreover, she would have believed that my comments on performance and technique that introduce many of the categories—a bonus added at no extra cost to the buyer—were at least brilliant. They could make a comedian of anybody. There would be no doubts in her—this is an amazing and remarkable work.

Who am I to argue with my mother?

MILTON BERLE
Beverly Hills, California

JOKES
FROM A to Z

aa

If you ask my computer to print out "drunk" jokes, it can keep going until the printer starts to hiccup. There are a few, however, that concern Alcoholics Anonymous specifically, starting off naturally with the one about the fellow who wanted to drink half as much, so he joined A.

A man who has a little too much to drink staggers into an AA meeting. A member asks, "Are you here to join?"

The drunk says, "No, I came in to resign!"

A drinking man explains to a friend about his peculiar relationship with Alcoholics Anonymous, "I send in my empties and they give me credit."

AA made a new man out of him. In fact, after two meetings he came home sober and his dog bit him!

A man joins AA, attends a meeting, and disappears. After backsliding for twenty years he returns for a second meeting and is greeted with great warmth and affection. People hug him, kiss him, and overwhelm him with their friendliness. He looks at them and says, a little puzzled, "You'd think I'd never been here before!"

There's a new organization for people who want to give up drinking while they're driving. It's called the AA AAA!

Alcoholics come up with the weirdest excuses to justify their falling off the wagon. At Alcoholics Anonymous, for example, they have a ritual for those who remain sober. After a member enjoys a year's sobriety, a small cake with a lit candle is handed to the lucky person. One alcoholic rationalized his falling off the wagon after eleven months with, "I don't like sweets!" Another used as his excuse, "I can't stand heat!"

Talk about rats. This guy stands outside of AA meetings with a smile and hiccups!

This boozer went to an AA meeting. When he came out he felt like a new man. The trouble was that the new man wanted a drink!

aaa

My son Billy has an old heap. I think it's a Canhardly. He can hardly get it out of the driveway! He refuses to take off the old AAA decals. They're the only thing holding the car together!

Talk about a lonely soul. He joined the AAA for its dances!

An auto club tow truck is summoned for roadside repairs. The ailing vehicle is in terrible shape. The engine coughs, the sparkplugs are filthy and miss, the battery is dead, the oil filter leaks, and the radiator is a sieve. The owner of the car asks fearfully, "Is there anything we can do?"

The tow truck operator says, "Sure! Repeat after me—Our Father who art in Heaven..."

On a busy street, a man jumps into a cab and says, "Follow the car in front of you."

"I have to," says the cabbie. "He's towing us!"

A man called the auto club for emergency repairs. Hours went by without the arrival of the tow truck. As the truck finally arrived, the motorist feigned a smile and asked, "Did the man who was supposed to come leave a next of kin?"

After hours of patient waiting, the same motorist could have as easily said when the tow truck operator arrived, "I was expecting a much older man!"

aardvarks

A few jokes about anteaters belong in every repertoire, especially since anteaters and aardvarks come up in almost every conversation. These jokes are crucial for people who show pride in their sense of humor. And who knows, somebody can call you up at four in the morning and ask for an aardvark joke. Without knowing those that follow you'd be marked down as a dull fool without the slightest funnybone. Aardvarks, in addition, are among the few animals that deserve a category of their own.

An aardvark reports to another about his discovery of a field of ants. "I'm telling you," he says, "you could have a picnic."

Aan aardvark is aan aanimal like aan aanteater.

Two aardvarks meet at a small anthill.

Albert Aardvark says, "Look, if we both go at this hill, neither of us will have a decent meal. There's only enough ants for one. Why don't we fight it out. The winner gets it all."

Anthony Aardvark agrees. At the count of three they start to battle. In a tenth of a second, Albert has Anthony by the snout, bangs him up and down against the ground, whips him around, and finally tosses him fifty feet into the air. Another aardvark watching the fight is amazed. Turning to another nearby, he asks, "What kind of aardvark is that Albert?"

The second aardvark answers, "Well, before he got that nose job he was an alligator!"

A male aardvark starts his mating ritual by sidling up to this female and rubbing his long snout against hers. In a while, the male feels that the female is aroused. He says, "Let me kiss you on the lips."

The female purrs, "Fine, but tell me when you get there."

A pair of aardvarks are planning their marriage and family. The female says, "First thing, we have to put away a hundred dollars for the plastic surgeon."

The male asks, "Why a hundred for the plastic surgeon?"

The female says, "In case the baby is born with a small nose."

Then there's the kid who says there's an anteater in his family—his uncle!

abortion

Good jokes on this subject are hard to come by. The following are the only ones I've found that aren't in terrible taste.

A woman goes to her physician for her fourth abortion. Puzzled, the physician asks, "Is this the same fellow?"

"Why do you ask?"

"Well, I thought I'd suggest that you marry the guy."

"Never! He doesn't appeal to me!"

"What do you think of the abortion bill?"
"I think we should pay it!"

A woman comes to a doctor. After having four children, she wants to abort the fifth. The doctor asks, "Why not have the fifth?"

The woman answers, "It's like this. The first two were from my first husband. The second two were from my second husband. The fifth I did on my own!"

A woman has eight children and is pregnant with a ninth. She goes to a doctor and asks for an abortion, explaining, "I just found out my husband never loved me."

The doctor says, "Can you imagine what would have happened if he did?"

absentmindedness

Oh, yes . . . what is this category?

"What's Joe's last name?"
"Joe who?"

The absentminded professor and his wife are having dinner. The wife asks, "Will you pass the salt?"

The professor answers, "How fast is it going?"

An acquaintance, not knowing any better, asks the absentminded professor, "Do you know that in California a man is run over every half hour?"

The professor shakes his head sadly and says, "Poor fellow!"

One absentminded gent slammed his wife and kissed the door good-bye.

Elephants can't be absentminded. An elephant never forgets, but what does he have to remember?

Talk about an absentminded man—yesterday he cut his finger and forgot to bleed!

As this absentminded professor is about to leave the house, his wife asks, "Darling, are you sure you've forgotten everything?"

Then there was the absentminded professor who lit a match to see if he'd put out the candle!

Then there was the absentminded wife of the absentminded professor. She was going to have a baby but forgot to bring it up!

There was an absentminded professor who saw a sign on his door that said, "Back in thirty minutes." So he sat down to wait.

After many years of bachelorhood, this gent, on in years besides, finds and marries a beautiful young lady. On their honeymoon night she slips into a sheer negligee and a comfortable bed as he goes into the bathroom to prepare himself for glory. Five minutes go by. Ten minutes go by. Concerned, the bride goes into the bathroom, where she finds her husband masturbating. She smiles and says, "You're married now. You don't have to do that anymore."

Her husband says, "I know. But I keep forgetting!"

The ladies can be flaky too. A very pretty lady had the kind of charms that would smite a man. In this case, one of the smitten asked, "Could I have your phone number?"

The pretty lady said, "It's in the telephone book."

"Great! What's your name?"

"Oh, that's in the phone book too!"

accents

When I was a kid, my mother took me to every audition, no matter what the requirements were. One agent wanted an Italian kid. I became an Italian kid two weeks off the boat from Sicily. A week later I was Russian or Irish. One time we waited for this agent to get off the phone. It seems that he was looking for a trained dog. When he hung up, my mother said, "Milton, bark for Mr. Samuels."

An elderly Jewish couple attended a séance and attempted to contact the husband's older brother. They concentrated, heard some weird noises, then suddenly a voice filled the room. "Al, Evelyn, this is Harry."

"My God!" Evelyn said. "Is that really you, Harry?"

"Yes, Evelyn," the voice answered.

"You're really in heaven?" Al asked.

"That's right, Al."

"Have you seen anybody else up there?"

"The whole family—Uncle Morris, Aunt Ruth, everybody."

"I have another question," Al said. "When did you learn how to talk such a good English?"

All girls who win the Miss America contest have a sweet Southern drawl. One entrant didn't talk Southern and she almost lost her citizenship!

Then there was the Southern announcer who couldn't announce a baseball game one Sunday. His interpreter didn't show up!

The first thing that strikes an out-of-towner in New York is the accent. The second is generally a taxi!

A perfect American English accent can be mastered in a week. My Japanese gardener does it in the week before Christmas!

A doctor in a London hospital asks a Cockney, "What about this ear?"

The Cockney says, "This 'ere what?"

The word is out that English will soon be the most popular language in the world. Now if somebody would only tell Brooklyn!

A Japanese visitor went to an American eye doctor. After an examination the doctor said, "You have a cataract."

The Japanese visitor shook his head. "Oh no. I have a Rincoln!"

accidents

People thrive on stories about pain. Describe a horrible agony inflicted on another, and the laughter rolls in waves. It's probably a way of thanking God that the agony has been inflicted on some other poor soul. Steve Allen, a student of the mechanics of comedy, once wrote, "Comedy is tragedy plus time." Why debate with Steve Allen, a nice man?

A man on a trip goes to the local barber in this small town for a shave. After being cut a dozen times, the man asks, "Pal, do you happen to have an extra razor?"

The barber says, "Certainly. Do you want to do your own shaving?"

"No, I thought I might be able to defend myself!"

Two teenagers visit a museum where there's an exhibit of Egyptian artifacts. Beneath one of the mummies is a card that says, "3218 B.C." The first teenager wonders out loud what the card means.

The second teenager answers, "Must be the number of the car that hit him!"

This woman failed her driving test because of one slight mistake. She ran over the man giving her the test!

A barber was shaving a customer. About ten strokes in, the barber asked, "Did you have catsup for lunch?"

The customer answered, "I haven't had lunch."

"Well, then I think I cut your throat!"

"This man fell off an eave on his house and was killed."

"That's what he gets for eavesdropping!"

"My kid brother accidentally swallowed a frog."

"Did it hurt him?"

"He's liable to croak any minute!"

A man is sightseeing all over the country. In the Sioux country of the Dakotas, he meets an old-timer who tells him one of the legends about the nearby caverns. It seems that many years ago, to avoid the gold miners, some of the beautiful maidens of the tribe had hidden in these caves. If a man hears a "woo-woo" come from one of them, he is to strip off his clothes and rush into the cave from which the sound came.

The traveler makes light of the story, but that night as he is walking he hears a faint "woo-woo" from a cave. Tearing off his clothes, he rushes into the cave.

The next morning they find his nude body. Nobody can explain why he was hit by a train coming through the tunnel!

Recently a woman went through three red lights in a row. They were on the truck in front of her!

At an alligator farm, Joe Dumb was told that an alligator would eat off his hand. He tried it and it did!

I went to a tough school. After the first football practice we counted four broken arms, two broken legs, and a broken neck. And those were just the cheerleaders!

"Which would you rather be in—an explosion or a collision?"

"In a collision, anytime."

"Why?"

"Well, in a collision, there you are. In an explosion, where are you?"

A man was brought into the emergency room at the local hospital. He had drunk from a bottle marked "poison." The physician asked, "Why would you drink from a bottle marked 'poison'?"

The man answered, "Underneath, it said 'lye,' so I didn't believe it!"

A railroad engineer wakes up one morning on the worst side of the wrong side of the bed. Because his alarm didn't go off, he's almost an hour late. He can't shave because the water heater burst in the night. Breakfast has to be a gulp of orange juice because none of the appliances work. Naturally, the juice is filled with sour pits. He can't get his car started. The cabbie who runs him to the railroad yard overcharges him by five dollars. He gets into the cabin of the train and manages to start it up, but just as the wheels start to turn, he sees another train on the same track, heading for him at ninety miles an hour. He turns to his fireman, shakes his head, and says, "Did you ever have one of those days?"

"I almost got killed twice today."
"Once would have been enough!"

Mr. Parker came home unexpectedly and saw the telltale signs of hank-panky in the house. He searched the house, but, finding nothing, started to scream at his wife. His anger grew, and he picked up the refrigerator and heaved it out of the window. A stranger was walking by innocently when the icebox landed on him and killed him.

A few days later, the stranger, now in heaven, meets another man. They discuss their fates. The first stranger says, "It's amazing, but you never know when you'll buy it. I was walking down the street and I got hit by a refrigerator." Then the first man asks the second, "What happened to you?"

The second man says, "I don't know. There I was—sitting in this refrigerator..."

A man went hunting and accidentally shot himself in the groin with a whole charge of shotgun pellets. He was rushed to a doctor. After working on him for hours, the doctor managed to get all the buckshot out. Then the doctor cautioned, "If I were you, I'd go to a music teacher and take clarinet lessons."

"Why?"

"Well, somebody is going to have to teach you how to finger that thing without peeing all over your hand!"

A young man runs into a friend, who notices that the young man has a beautiful shiner. "How'd you get that?" the friend asks.

"It was like this. I was at the movies the other night and I picked up this cute girl. One word led to another, and before long we were in her living room, listening to the stereo and dancing. Then her father came in. He's deaf and didn't hear the music!"

A man is walking his dog when it gets away from him and attacks a woman on a nearby lawn. She rushes in and sends out her husband. The dog owner is beside himself. He says, "Sir, how about a settlement? Will twenty-five dollars do?"

The husband says, "Sure. And if you come around next week, I'll give you more!"

A man falls out of a seventy-story building. As he descends, at each floor he says to onlookers, "Don't worry. I'm not hurt—yet!"

Two addicts shared an eighth-floor apartment until one sad morning. That day, one of the addicts was found in the alley between their building and the next. It was obvious that he'd fallen to his death. The police questioned the survivor, who said, "We had a little grass, when all of a sudden he said he was going to Mexico. He opened the window and took off."

A policeman asked, "Why didn't you try to stop him?"

"Man, I thought he could make it!"

A young man fills out an application for a job and does well until he gets to the last question, "Who should we notify in case of an accident?" He mulls it over and then writes down, "Anybody in sight!"

A man broke a mirror, but he didn't have seven years' bad luck. Fate was with him. He died two days later!

A man falls down a flight of stairs and somebody rushes over to him and asks, "Did you miss a step?"

"No," he answers, "I hit every one of them!"

A born genius put his hand in a lion's mouth to see if the lion had any teeth. The lion closed his mouth to see if the man had any fingers!

A young man was bemoaning his brother's fate: "He had a bad accident. His horse was ailing and the veterinarian gave him some powder to put in a tube and blow it into the horse's stomach."

"Didn't it work?" a friend asked.

"He did what the vet said, but the horse blew first!"

For potential disasters, this pessimist carries a card in his wallet that says, "In case of accident, I'm not surprised."

Reporting on her third accident in a week, Mrs. Smith explains indignantly to her husband that she's blameless. "A drunk was driving the other car. He came over to my side of the road and banged into me."

"How could you tell he was drunk?"

"He had to be. He was driving a tree!"

Ninety percent of accidents occur in the kitchen. And my wife cooked quite a few of them!

A man falls out of a tenth-story window. As he lands, another man rushes over and says, "What happened?"

The fallen man says, "I don't know. I just got here myself!"

You can tell when a man worries too much about accidents. He puts a safety mat in the birdbath!

A boy of ten calls into the house, "Mom, which would you rather have happen—I fall out of the big oak tree or I tear my pants?"

The mother answers, "Naturally, I'd pray that you tore your pants."

The kid says, "Your prayers have been answered!"

A young man comes to work an hour late. At the door he's greeted by his employer, who asks angrily, "What happened that you're an hour late?"

The young man explains, "I had a terrible accident. Some guy sideswiped me."

The employer asks, "That took an hour?"

A man is hit by a car while crossing a Beverly Hills street. A woman rushes to him and cradles his head in her lap, asking, "Are you comfortable?"

The man answers, "I make a nice living!"

This unlucky gent had a terrible accident. He threw a lit cigarette down an open manhole and then stepped on it!

Mr. Brown, an attorney, and Dr. Jones crashed into one another on a slick street. Both were shaken up, so Mr. Brown took a small bottle of whiskey out of his glove compartment and gave Dr. Jones a drink. Thanking him, Dr. Jones said, "Why don't you have a belt too?"

"Don't worry, I will," the attorney answers. "Right after the highway patrol shows up!"

A body-shop man tells a potential client, "Let me give you the *good* news first. Your glove compartment and sun visor are in good shape!"

A woman jumps out of her car a second after a slight run-in with a male driver. Indignantly she says, "What gave you the right to assume I had my mind made up?"

"**W**ith all those bandages, you look as if you had a terrible accident."
"Well, I tried to climb a tree in my car."
"Why'd you do that?"
"I tried to oblige this lady driver. She wanted to use the street!"

A man fell off a ferry into the ice-cold water of the bay. Not being able to swim, he yelled, "Somebody save me. I'm the father of eight!"
Another passenger said, "He sure picked a hell of a time to brag!"

A magician had a terrible accident while he was doing a trick that involved sawing his girl assistant in half. The assistant left the act and moved to Dallas and Tulsa!

A wino weaved his way out of a liquor store and started to cross the street. A car came along and knocked him down. Feeling wetness on his chest, he put up his hand and said, "I hope it's only blood!"

"**W**hat happened to the car?"
"I hit a cow."
"There was a cow in the middle of the road?"
"No, I had to chase it into the barn!"

A woman was telling of her trip to Niagara Falls. "My husband's face dropped a mile when he saw the falls."
Her listener asked, "He was that disappointed in the sight?"
"No, he fell over the rim!"

One day while puttering around the house, doing things he shouldn't have been doing, a boy of six found a bullet. Typically curious, he swallowed the bullet. His mother rushed him to the emergency room at the hospital. The doctor said, "Give him this strong laxative. But be sure that for the next few hours you don't point him at anybody!"

A Hollywood tycoon threw a party at his beachfront Malibu home. While the party was in progress, a giant tidal wave swept ashore, pulled the guests into the sea, and destroyed much of the house, knocking out the tycoon. The tycoon came to and started to search for survivors. In the guest bathroom he found one guest. The guest said, his voice quivering, "Frank, I swear, all I did was pull the handle!"

Two assassins are hired to kill a South American tyrant. They study his habits and discover that each day at exactly noon he comes out on his patio, stretches for five minutes, and reenters the building.
The assassins set up shop across the street. They get their gunsights adjusted to the nth degree. They sit down to wait. Noon comes, but the dictator doesn't. Ten minutes go by. No dictator. A half hour goes by. No dictator. Finally, one assassin says to the other, "Gee, I hope nothing happened to him!"

He recently recovered from a bad car accident. He followed a white line and it turned out to be a skunk!

Her husband was killed by hard drink. A cake of ice fell on him!

He's the kind of guy who always hits the nail squarely on the thumb!

accountants

The following may not be the first one-liner I ever told, but it's surely among the first half-dozen: My uncle is a CPA—Cleaning, Pressing, and Alterations! I used this joke a week ago. That proves one of two things. Either I'm in a rut, or people like to hear jokes that flail accountants.

An accountant tells his client, "We can get your books to balance if you'll strike oil on the way home!"

I have some accountant. What he doesn't know about taxes could fill a prison cell.

Panicked by a letter telling him that an IRS audit is upcoming, a man calles his accountant, who responds, "Don't worry. I have all the bills and papers. I've got every receipt. But let me give you one word of caution. When you show up there, dress like a derelict—torn jacket, torn shirt, old shoes. If the auditor sees you're poor, he won't come down hard on you."

Still concerned, the man phones his attorney and explains the situation. The attorney says, "I'm sure your accountant has everything under control. You'll do fine. But one thing—dress well. The auditor will see that you look nice, you're respectable, and obviously a man of responsibility. Surely you wouldn't lie on your tax returns. He'll give you a break."

More mixed up than ever, the man goes to his minister and again explains the difficult problem. The minister says, "I have the same problem with marriages. The mother of the bride wants her to dress like an old-fashioned girl. She wants her daughter to look nice on her honeymoon, but not wild enough to bring out the beast in her groom.

The bride's father, on the other hand, wants her to be provocative. He wants her to wear something revealing. I tell the bride, 'What you wear doesn't matter. You're going to get screwed!'"

It's a thrill to read *Fortune* and find out that your accountant is one of the dozen richest men in the country.

The company accountant is shy and retiring. He's shy a quarter of a million dollars. That's why he's retiring.

If you become successful, you owe part of it to your accountant. After that, you owe it all to the IRS.

My accountant must work with Washington. Every time I make a few dollars he turns it into Capitol gains.

A private detective is hired to find a company accountant, and asks, "Is he tall or short?"

The boss answers, "Both!"

All of the company's accounts must be Russian. The terms are always thirty days *nyet!*

I know an accountant who gave his clients a great tax break. He put all their money in his name.

I have a CPA who's brilliant. They just named a loophole after him.

Old accountants never die. They just lose their balance.

"My company is looking for a new accountant."

"Didn't you hire one last week?"

"We did. He's the one we're looking for!"

My accountant just went into business with General Motors. They make the cars, he's making the license plates.

Then there's the accountant who told his client sadly, "I've got awful news for you. Last year was the best you've ever had!"

A simpleton thought he could get along at an audit without an accountant, so he showed up at the IRS with all of his records—the Beatles, the Rolling Stones, Bruce Springsteen . . .

I'm confused. The national anthem tells us that this is the land of the free. My accountant tells me it isn't!

Last year my accountant deducted for all of Bulgaria. I told him that was wrong. He said, "Why not? Do you know anybody else who's deducting for Bulgaria?"

acknowledgments

When called upon to receive an award or some kind of kudos for services well rendered, people sometimes find themselves unable to offer the sparkling thank-you the occasion warrants. Only later, much later, does the recipient think of fascinating remarks he or she could have made, words diamond-like in their brilliance. The following lines will turn all who use them into masters and mistresses of repartee, and recipients par excellence.

You've obviously been here for a long time and are now in obvious pain. As anybody knows, there's no better painkiller than: Thank you and good night!

You make me feel important. Until now I felt that the whole world was a tuxedo and I was a brown shoe!

The timing of this award is perfect, although while the last speech was being made I thought I might have to get it posthumously!

Please laugh fast. My time is short.

It's more than a thrill for me to get this award. It's an inconvenience!

I won't take long. This suit is due back in forty minutes!

I enjoy being with smart, exciting, and decent people. I also enjoy groups like this!

I'm not certain that I deserve this token of your gratitude, but what's my opinion against hundreds?

Thank you very much. I could make a long speech now, but I'd rather be a little schizophrenic and say, "Let's split!"

I don't deserve this wonderful honor, but then I don't deserve bursitis either!

This gift is a token of your kindness, friendship, and good taste!

As the cow said to the farmer, "Thanks for the warm hand!"

I'd tell you some jokes now, but you'd only laugh!

Lock the doors. This is one group I won't let get away!

This is a very nice scroll, but to tell you the truth I could have used a car payment!

This gift means a great deal to me. I'll remember it until . . . I get to my car!

I'd like to share this with all the people who helped me. But since there aren't any, I'll keep it for myself!

Listening to all the glowing things said about me puts me in mind of what the male skunk said after making love to the female skunk for hours: "I've had about as much of this as I can stand."

I'm not going to bore you with a long thank-you. I think I'll bore you with a short one!

I'll never forget this affair . . . no matter how hard I try!

I'm as nervous as a mailman at a dog show!

I'm not the type to exaggerate my accomplishments, but I do my best!

I wish I had as much fun today as my wife thinks I'm having!

You've just been listening to that great Chinese speaker—On Too Long!

Thank you for that wonderful round of indifference!

actors and actresses

We often sit at the Round Table of the Friars Club and tell stories on or about our peers. We are governed by a rule that prohibits kindness and charity. All ends well because this week's victims are next week's destroyers.

An actor, Penrose Garth, is standing on Broadway, leaning against a building, when he hears a commotion coming from people on the street. He looks up to see an agent who has accidentally fallen out of a tenth story window. At about the seventh floor, the agent sees the actor and starts to scream, "Penrose, catch me! Catch me!"

Penrose looks at him and says bitterly, "Did you catch *me* last month in *King Lear?*"

An actor was hired to play the role of a millionaire. When the deal was signed, the actor said to his agent, "Lend me a buck. I want to feel the part!"

Then there was this actor whose landlord babied him. The landlord carried him longer than his mother did!

An actor was known along Broadway as a great dresser. His suits were handmade and of the finest fabrics. Unfortunately, he never paid his tailor. One of the tailor's friends suggested that the actor was a total deadbeat. "The bum probably doesn't have a penny to his name," the friend said.

"He must have money," the tailor answered. "Look at the way he dresses!"

An actor walked into a decrepit restaurant for a quick cup of coffee. He noticed another actor busing dishes. "My God," the first actor said, "what is this? A man with your talent, slaving in a greasy spoon like this?"

The other actor retorted, "At least I don't *eat* here!"

A ham actor spent most of his career playing Lincoln. Year after year he toured as Lincoln. After thousands of performances, a fellow player told him, "You're obsessed with Lincoln."

"I am not."

"You are. You are. If you're not, why don't you do *Hamlet* next?"

The actor said, "Not until I'm assassinated!"

Invited to a performance by a third actor, two actors met at the bar next to the theater during the intermission. One actor said, "This is an awful show."

The second one said, "We can't knock it too much. We're in on passes."

The first actor said, "I think I'm gonna *buy* a ticket, then you'll really hear something!"

An actor who was considered by his peers to be the worst actor of all time goes out on the road with a Shakespearean company. The first night in Cleveland, as he starts Hamlet's first speech, the audience starts to groan. Then they start to talk back to him, telling him what he can do with his acting ability. He presses on, and as soon as he begins another crucial scene, the audience throws things at him. First the programs, then peanuts, and finally cups of soda pop. The actor steps forward and says, with great aplomb, "What the hell do you want from me? I didn't write this crap!"

A young actress had a rather plaintive comment about the producer of her show: "His hands should have search warrants!"

An actor and his wife, a well-known actress, attempted a miniseries on television. After the first episode was screened for them, the couple started to discuss their performances. The actress said, "We've killed our careers. You televise without lips and I come out looking a hundred years old, ugly as sin, my feet are huge, my lisp is accentuated, and my wardrobe looks as if it came from the Salvation Army!" The tears started to roll down her cheeks.

The actor mused, "No lips, you say?"

There's an actress around town who's a real Cinderella story. Regularly, at the stroke of midnight, she turns into a motel!

A producer invited a budding young actress up to his lavish suite overlooking New York's Central Park. On the walls of his bedroom were all the indications of a kinky sex life—whips, chains, studded leather gear, and an occasional torture rack. The actress gulped and asked, "What are you planning to do with me?"

The producer said, "Don't worry, I'm going to make love to you."

The actress sighed in relief, "Thank God!"

A young actress, eager to get a part in an upcoming play, shared some of her charms with the stage manager. He arranged for her to audition. A few days later she was passed on to the assistant to the producer. This resulted in a job as an understudy. The director seemed to show some interest in her, so she reciprocated. After spending a weekend away with the director, she was given a small part with lines. The producer's turn came, and the actress squeezed out a few more lines. The rehearsals began. The cast worked sixteen hours a day, seven days a week. Not satisfied with the results, the director reduced even the few hours of sleep and leisure allowed the cast. The performers found no time to eat, sleep, or even write a letter home. Worn out, the young actress asked another female performer, "Who do you have to screw to get out of this play?"

AGENT: Leave your number. I'll call you when an old man's part shows up.
ACTOR: I'm a young man.
AGENT: By the time I call, you'll be old.

A famous actor's son was asked to write a composition in school. The topic was "poor people." The child wrote, "Once there was a poor family. The father was poor. The mother was poor. The children were poor. The butler was poor. The maid was poor. The chauffeur was poor..."

An actor auditioned for the part of an impoverished man. The reading went well, but the director wanted somebody who had really known poverty. The actor insisted that he came from the humblest of backgrounds.

The director asked, "Was your family indescribably poor?"

The actor said, "We had no clothes, no food, no heat. My mother was ill, my father was dying. The only one who could move was my eighty-year-old grandmother, who stood in the snow all day and sold pencils for a nickel."

"And I'll bet she stood in the fierce cold, begging for people to buy a pencil. She'd stand there for ten, twelve hours, and maybe sell one pencil. Is that how it was?"

The actor said, "Yes, that's exactly how it was."

"If she hadn't sold that pencil, you could have had this job!"

A producer is smitten by a beautiful but less than brilliant young actress. He asks for her hand in marriage. She doesn't quite grasp what he's saying. He adds, "You don't understand. I want you to be the mother of my children."

The actress asks, "Really? How many do you have?"

Before walking down the aisle, an actress told her husband of her previous indiscretions. Three others leanred of this move and were more than surprised. One said, "What amazing confidence she has." The second said, "What faith she has." The third said, "What a memory she has!"

He was an actor who really moved the audience. Everybody left at the end of the first act!

A play opened the other night. Nobody came to the first performance, but after that business fell off a little.

A ham actor was appearing in a melodrama. Late in the first scene, the actor made a speech that ended with, "The villain is coming. It's time to act!"

A member of the audience yelled out, "I think so too!"

This actor spent three years in stock, but the cattle finally objected!

An actor joins a company opening a small theater. When he inquires about the facilities, the owner says, "We have only one dressing room."

"Do you expect both men and women to dress in one room?"

"Why not? Are they mad at one another?"

The audience saw his play under unfortunate circumstances—the seats faced the stage!

adages

There's a wise saying to cover almost all occasions. Unfortunately, the right one avoids you when needed. The best one was over a mirror in a vaudeville house in Altoona, Pennsylvania. There, scratched into the dull red brick, were these words: You'll think of something!

Today is the tomorrow you worried about yesterday, but not enough.

Don't trust the advice of a man in trouble.

A woman's place is in the home, and she should go there right from work.

If at first you don't succeed, your sky-diving days are over.

If at first you don't succeed, try again. She's expecting it.

Many people can't stand prosperity. Most don't have to.

The only real argument for marriage is that it remains the best way of getting acquainted.

The only place where two heads are better than one is on a ship.

Experience is what you have after you've forgotten her name.

Hard work never killed anybody. But then, relaxing is responsible for very few casualties.

If you want to get a sure crop, sow wild oats.

Pity costs nothing and is worth it.

Repartee is what you wish you'd said.

If at first you don't succeed, find out if there's a prize for the loser.

Nice guys finish last, and so do the folks who read and follow instructions.

Man is owned by the company nobody knows he's keeping.

You can catch more flies with honey than with vinegar. But who wants a lot of flies?

A woman's word is never done.

A journey of a thousand miles begins with leaving the trip tickets on the dresser.

No work is impossible without a committee.

A clean tie will always attract the soup of the day.

Getting into hot water keeps you clean.

Caution is when you're scared. Cowardice is when the other guy is scared.

A liberal is a man who leaves the room when the fight begins.

Two is company. Three is poor birth control.

The early bird would never catch the worm if the dumb worm slept late.

Poverty is not a disgrace, but it's terribly inconvenient.

People who have a baby can't sleep like one.

Nostalgia is longing for a place you'd never move back to.

Just when you're about to make both ends meet, somebody comes along and moves the ends.

Two can live as cheaply as one. But not as long.

A cynic is one who looks down on those above him.

Cockiness is the feeling you have just before you know better.

The way to a woman's heart is through a Porsche.

Popularity is the small change of glory.

It's hard to save your money for a rainy day, because it always keeps on raining.

All the world loves a lover, except her husband.

Don't try to meet trouble halfway. It goes faster than you do.

Better get interested in your future. That's where you're going to spend the rest of your life.

Most people who fall in love with themselves have no rivals.

He who laughs last probably had it explained to him.

The future isn't what it used to be.

The best way to get rid of somebody is to tell him something for his own good.

If you tell the truth, sooner or later somebody's going to find you out.

People who live in glass houses don't have much of a sex life.

You can lead a man to Congress, but you can't make him think.

True love never runs smoothly. It pulls over to the side and parks.

A hole is nothing at all, but you can sure break your neck in it!

Most of us aren't young enough to know everything.

It's hard to plan your future when you're busy repairing all the things you did yesterday!

If you can keep your head about you when all others around you are losing theirs, you're probably the cause of it all!

If you think things improve with the years, attend a class reunion.

You can fool some of the people some of the time and some of the people all of the time. That's usually enough.

Never try to teach a pig to sing. You'll be wasting your time and bugging the pig.

Love at first sight saves a lot of time.

If ignorance is bliss, why aren't there more happy people?

Life may not begin at forty, but that's when it begins to show.

A little's a lot if that's all you've got.

People who say the first hundred years are the hardest never knew about love.

Temptation comes easy. Opportunity takes a little longer.

Nothing lasts forever except a bad play.

School days are the happiest of your life, but only if the children are old enough to attend!

A woman's work is never done—thanks to soap operas!

Behind every man is a woman who keeps telling him he's not so hot.

If at first you don't succeed, failure may be your thing.

What you don't owe won't hurt you!

Many a man who spends a lot of time in the doghouse may end up in the cathouse.

Isn't it a greater life if you weaken a little?

Worry is the interest you pay on trouble before it's due.

Be moderate in all things, especially moderation.

Let him among us who is the fastest throw the first stone!

A cocktail party is a get-together where olives are speared and acquaintances stabbed!

It's great to live with the saints in heaven, but it's hell to live with them on earth!

No man would listen to another talk if he didn't know it was his turn next.

Scientists say that animals laugh. They could hardly resist it if they watched human beings act!

A leader of men is one who sees which way the crowd is going, and steps in ahead.

Think twice before you speak, and then you might be able to come up with something more aggravating than if you had spoken right out.

It is easy enough to restrain our anger when the other guy is bigger.

adam and eve

Paradise seemed like a great idea. Why the Lord put humans in it cannot be explained except by the fact that He was tired by then.

Adam and Eve, it is reliably reported, had the first rib joint.

Because Adam had come home late, Eve started to berate him, "You've been unfaithful to me!"
Adam looked at her, puzzled. "With whom?"

Adam and Eve must have been the first bookkeepers. They invented the loose-leaf system.

Eve was God's *second* mistake!

A Sunday-school class is in session. The youngsters are showing off before a visiting bishop and are reeling off the answers to questions they've been asked a thousand times by the teacher. Because of the bishop's presence, the children are a little withdrawn. To jog their memories, the teacher punctuates each question by stabbing at a child with a pin. The teacher gets to the question, "What did Eve say to Adam?" and pricks a child. The child answers, "Hey, don't stick that thing in me!"
The bishop never came back!

Adam loved the time of day when Eve was falling.

The story of the missionary position is

written between the lines. Adam came home from dinosaur hunting one evening. He was dead tired. Eve, meanwhile, had been doing nothing all day and felt kittenish. She said coyly, "Let's make love."

Adam said, "You're putting me on."

She did, and it was the birth of the missionary position.

God was wise in making Adam before Eve. If he'd made Eve first, he'd still be working on Adam.

Adam couldn't wait for autumn, because that's when the leaves fall.

It wasn't the apple on the tree that ruined everything. It was the pair on the ground!

God made Eve. He gave her a wonderful figure. He gave her a beautiful face, lovely lips, a luscious mouth, and then He put a tongue in it and ruined the whole thing!

A Sunday-school lesson on Genesis is in session. "Who made you?" the teacher asks.

"God," a youngster answers. Then he excuses himself, as he has to go to the bathroom.

The class goes on and the teacher asks another youngster, "Who made you?"

The child responds, "Adam and Eve."

"No," the teacher says, "God made you."

"Nope. The kid God made just went to the bathroom!"

Johnny and Mary were walking to Sunday school. Mary carried a large, juicy apple for a snack. As they walked, Johnny said, "Let's play Adam and Eve."

"How do you play Adam and Eve?" Mary asked.

"You try to tempt me with the apple and I'll give in."

When Eve said that she had nothing to wear, she meant it!

A young boy came home from a Sunday school sermon about Adam and Eve. He sat down in a corner and counted his ribs, then walked over to his mother and said, "Mom, I think I'm having a wife!"

Adam and Eve must have been Communists. They had no clothes, no shoes, no roof over their heads, ate only an apple, and thought they were in paradise!

Eve returned from a stroll in the woods, wearing an outfit she'd never worn before. Adam looked at her and seemed to feel that something was different. Finally, Eve let him in on the secret: "I just turned over a new leaf!"

Adam and Eve had a great marriage. Adam couldn't bring up his mother's cooking, and Eve couldn't talk about the man she was supposed to marry!

Adam blamed Eve. Eve blamed Adam. But the snake didn't have a leg to stand on!

God made Adam and then He rested. He made Eve, and since then nobody's rested!

adultery

My grandmother used to say, "In somebody else's bed you can't find happiness!" But you can come up with a lot of laughs.

A man comes home and finds his best friend in bed with his wife. The man throws up his hands in disbelief and says, "Joe, I have to, but you?"

"Zeke, you must have a gal friend."

"I do not."

"You must, because you've washed your feet three times this week!"

Many men are discouraged from fooling around with women during the morning because they don't know what they can run into later in the day!

Farmer Jones returned home from a trip to the city, only to find his wife in bed with a traveling salesman. Taking the safety off his shotgun, he ordered the salesman out of bed in the altogether and pushed him into the barn. There he took a delicate part of the salesman's anatomy and placed it in a vise. A half-dozen turns, and the vise was clamped tight. The salesman panicked. "You're not going to cut it off, are you?"

Farmer Jones handed the salesman a sharp knife and answered, "No. I'm just gonna set fire to the barn. *You're* gonna cut it off!"

A woman goes to a doctor who examines her and says, "You need a rest. Is it possible that you and your husband can stop having relations for about a month?"

The woman says, "Sure. The mailman can take care of me for that long!"

"If my husband was built any bigger, I swear I couldn't take it."

"Don't think I could either!"

"Listen. I'm having an affair."

"Really? Who's catering it?"

A man is in bed with a woman when there's the sound of the front door opening. The woman says, "That must be my husband. Go faster, I'm coming."

The man says, "Kiss my ass. I'm going!"

A man comes home and sees a cigar butt in the ashtray. He asks his wife, "Where did that cigar come from?"

The closet door opens and a nude man pops out and says, "Cuba!"

Pete and Joe were returning from a night at the bowling alley. Pete suggested that they stop off and get a beer. "I know this new joint," he said, "where you can have some fun. When you come in, they give you a number. If your number is called, you can go into the back and have sex."

Joe asked, "Did you ever get your number called?"

Pete said, "No, but my wife won four times last week!"

The whole world dies and an endless line waits to get into heaven. Suddenly there's a loud roar from the front of the line. A man in the back calls out, "Why are they cheering?"

Somebody in front yells back, "They're not counting adultery!"

Mr. Jones has to work late in the office. His head starts to throb, so he asks his secretary, Sonia, if she has any aspirin. She looks around and can find none. She suggests, "I know I have some in my apartment. It's only two blocks from here. Let's go there."

They go to her apartment, where Sonia gets him his aspirin. Then she asks him if he wants a drink. He nods. They have a drink. They have two drinks. Three. The drinks lead to cuddling. Before long, they end up in bed together.

Mr. Jones looks at his watch after a while and is aghast. It's very late. He must rush home. Before he goes, however, he asks Sonia, "Do you have some talcum powder?"

"Of course."

He rubs the powder on his hands and

heads home. As soon as he walks into the house, Mrs. Jones greets him with less than warmth. She is also puzzled because he has his hands behind his back. She says, "Where were you?"

Mr. Jones proceeds to tell her the truth, that he went to his secretary's apartment and they made love.

Mrs. Jones doesn't believe him. "Let me see your hands," she says. He won't bring them forward. "I want to see your hands!"

Reluctantly, he brings them forward. Mrs. Jones studies them, then explodes. "You son of a bitch, you've been bowling again!"

A rather simple soul is chuckling as he walks along the street. A friend comes along and asks the reason behind the wide grin. The simple soul says, "I just found out the guy next door pays my wife ten dollars to make love to her, and I get it for nothing!"

A man comes home at five in the morning and finds his wife in the middle of a love bout with another man. The wife looks daggers at him and asks, "Where were you until five in the morning?"

The husband asks, "Who is this man?"

The wife says, "I asked first!"

A husband catches a naked milkman in the house with his wife. Fast as lightning, the milkman says, "I'm going to tell you one more time, lady, if you don't pay your milk bill, I'll pee on your floor!"

A husband comes home in the wee hours of the morning. As he undresses, his wife sees that he doesn't have his jockey shorts. She asks, "Where's your underwear?"

The man looks down and says, "My God, I've been robbed!"

A man, suspecting his wife of blatant infidel-ity, hires a private detective to follow her. The detective makes his report: "At eight o'clock your wife sauntered into a bar. A man bought her three drinks. They seemed to be having a great time. After the third drink they got into the man's car and drove to a motel. They went into room 112 and remained there for three hours. When they came out, your wife was disheveled and her hair was a mess."

The man nodded when the report was over and sighed. "Doubts," he said. "Always those doubts!"

The Fromans go to court for a divorce. "I want to unload this bum," Mrs. Froman demands.

"I can't live with this monster," Froman says.

The judge asks, "How many children do you have?"

Froman says, "Three."

"Stay married another year," the judge suggests. "Have another child, then you'll be able to take two apiece."

Froman says, "With my luck, we could have twins."

Mrs. Froman says, "Twins he's gonna have! If I depended on him, *these* three wouldn't have been here!"

A man meets another in a bar and starts a round of small talk as men are wont to do. The man explains that he's a newlywed, having only two weeks before married the manicurist at the hotel barbershop.

The other man reacts, "Wow, buddy, you are crazy! That little gal has been had by every guy in town. On her lunch break I used to take her into the hotel office and screw the hell out of her."

The newlywed calls over to the bartender, "Give my buddy here a drink. Friend of the wife!"

"Hey, Bubba, you got yourself new pants and a shirt."

"My wife got them for me."

"Must have been a surprise."

"Sure was. I come home and there they were on a chair in the bedroom!"

A young married woman was discussing her sex life with a girl friend. The girl friend asked, "Do you talk to your husband when you're making love?"

The young married woman considered the question a moment and then said, "No, but I could if I wanted to. I have his office phone number!"

"How come you never tell me when you're having an orgasm?"

"You're never home!"

The din of the fire engine swinging into action caused Herman at the local bar to stir. He put money down and said, "Time for me to get going."

The bartender asked, "What's your rush? You're not in the fire department."

Herman said, "My girl friend's husband is!"

Alex was an accountant. Even though it wasn't tax season, he felt worn out. He went to his doctor for a checkup. The doctor asked, "How often do you have sex?"

"Every Tuesday, Thursday, and Saturday."

"I suggest you eliminate Thursday."

"That's impossible. It's the only night I'm home!"

A salesman returns from a long trip to his many accounts all over the country. His wife confesses an infidelity. "Who was it?" the salesman bellows. "It must have been my friend Tommy."

"No, it wasn't Tommy."

"My friend Alex? My friend Steve?"

"No, it wasn't your friend Alex or Steve."

"Then it was my friend Willie!"

"What's wrong with you?" the wife roars. "Don't you think I could have friends of my own!"

Thompson and his wife went to a doctor because they seemed to be having trouble with their sex life. It seemed that the missus was misfunctioning. The doctor listened to their story, ordered the missus to remove her clothes and lie down on an examining table. The doctor also disrobed and started that noble act that involves penetration. Thompson watched for a while and said, "If it weren't for that diploma on the wall, Doc, I'd swear you were making love to my wife!"

A man suspects his wife of adultery and asks a friend of his to check up for him. The friend follows the wife one afternoon and reports that the husband's suspicions are justified. "I saw her and this guy go into the park and go at one another right then and there."

The husband asks, "Do you have any idea of how long this has been going on?"

The friend answers, "From the freckles on his ass, it looks like it's been going on all summer!"

Sy Collins was fearless enough to confess to his wife. When she came into the office one afternoon, he admitted that the receptionist was his mistress. Pointing to another girl in the office, he went on, "The girl in the Xerox room is my partner's mistress."

Sy's wife looked at one girl and then the other. Nodding after a moment, she said, "I like ours better!"

It happened in Montana. An Idaho cowboy was passing through and found himself a pretty young lady. They went over to her place and had some sport. While they were resting, the cowboy told about his days on the range and, finally, his great hope: "When I go, I want to die with my boots on."

Suddenly there was the sound of a car coming into the garage. The woman said, "Better get your boots on. That's my husband!"

By the time she was eighteen, Mary Jane had had eight husbands—two of them her own!

"My wife is such a liar."
"What did she do?"
"She came home at dawn and said she'd spent the night with Alice."
"How do you know it was a lie?"
"Because *I* spent the night with Alice!"

A man comes home to find his wife in a mad embrace with another man. The husband starts to bellow. The wife looks up and says, "Bigmouth is home! Now everybody'll know!"

A man comes home to find his wife in bed with another man. The husband starts to berate the couple, who continue their love-making. Throwing up his hands, the husband says, "At least you could stop while I'm talking to you!"

A wife was dying. She called her husband to her bed and said softly, "Gary, I must confess. I've been unfaithful."

Gary answered, even with more softness, "I know. That's why I poisoned you!"

Some people were discussing a friend who happened to be a writer. One said, "He'd be in great shape if his books had half the circulation his wife does!"

Two men meet in heaven. After discussing the food and accommodations, they start to talk about life on earth and how they ended up on a cloud. The first explained that he froze to death. The second went on to describe what had happened to him. "I had a rough time. I was very suspicious of my wife. One day I returned home from a trip a day early so I could catch her. I ran into the house. I had the feeling that a man was there somewhere. I looked in every room, every closet, under every bed. I got so excited I had a heart attack and I died."

The first man said, "It's a shame you didn't look in the freezer. We'd both be alive today!"

Marie's funeral is a sad one as she goes to join her departed husband. Standing near the casket, a mourner keeps repeating, "At last they're together. At last they're together."

A mourner whispers, "Why are you making such a tumult? She was a tramp even when Nick was alive. What's with this nonsense—at last they're together!"

The first mourner says, "I'm talking about her *legs!* At last they're together!"

He went out with a perfect 36. Then his wife showed up with a .45!

advertising

Modern advertising makes the world go round. They've even started advertising condoms on television, a strange development if there ever was one, because cigarette advertising is taboo. It has gotten so that a person can walk into a drugstore and order condoms at the top of his or her voice, but has to whisper a brand of cigarettes.

Unforgettable newspaper advertisement:

Wanted—Man to understudy human cannonball. Must be willing to travel!

An ad appears in *Soldier of Fortune* magazine. It asks for "a man who speaks French, German, Chinese, and Swahili. Must be willing to travel to dangerous places and be knowledgeable about weapons."

Two days later, Mr. Cohen, a man in his late seventies, appears at the address given and asks for Mr. Thompson. Mr. Thompson, obviously an ex–Green Beret, asks, "Have you come about the ad?"

"I have, most certainly."

"Do you speak all the required languages?"

"I can hardly speak English."

"Do you want to travel?"

"I get seasick in the bathtub."

"Can you shoot Uzis and other guns?"

"The noise from soda pop scares me."

"Then what are you doing here?"

"I came to tell you that you can't count on me!"

Some magazine ads are incredible. One insists that lemon rinse is the best thing in the world. I don't know too many people with an urge to rinse lemons!

A man buys a horse from an ad saying that the horse is a fine animal. Angrily, the man returns to the horsetrader. "The horse you sold me is practically blind."

"The ad said he was a fine horse. It didn't say he saw too well!"

"Does advertising pay for your company?"

"It certainly does. Yesterday we put in an ad for a night watchman, and we were robbed!"

Thanks to advertising, our streets aren't safe to walk on, our homes are scary places to be, the air around us is poisoned, but under our arms we've got complete protection!

A schoolboy, eager to boast, pees a message on the wall of the school: "Johnny Jones is built like a horse." The teacher orders him to remain after school. His friends hang around until the punishment is carried out. At five o'clock, Johnny comes out whistling and says, "It pays to advertise!"

If you don't think advertising works, remember that there are a lot of peaks in Colorado higher than Pike's Peak, but try to name them!

Samson must have had the right idea about advertising. He took two columns and brought down the house!

A country storekeeper turns down an advertising salesman's offer for some good rates on the local radio station. "No, sir," the storekeeper says. "The last time I did that people came in and bought me out of everything I had!"

Padded bras are not truth in advertising!

How can they advertise that certain headache tablets can give relief in seconds, when it takes an hour to get out the cotton?

The advertising campaign to get people to quit smoking isn't all good. Some of the people who gave up smoking got their taste buds back and found out they've been eating things for years they can't stand!

One advertisement in magazines doesn't make sense. It tells you to take a certain laxative and stay in bed!

The advertising business is known for its worship of youth. A newcomer can work his way up an important position in a short time. In one agency a lad of tender years signed on. Bright and a good worker, he went from the mailroom to the executive suite in no time at all. One day the boss called him in and said, "Johnny, you are now a vice-president. Aren't you happy?"

Johnny answered, "I've never been so happy. I can't wait to go home and tell my mommy!"

A recent ad appeared in a large newspaper: "Wish to sell secondhand tombstone. Real bargain for person named Olson!"

Advertising is effective. One young boy goes to bed every night with a simple prayer: "Dear Lord, please take care of Mommy. Please take care of Daddy. Please take care of my sister. And thank you for giving us our daily, slow-rising, butter-crusted, vitamin-enriched bread!"

You know you're getting on in years when the commercial for hair restorer is more interesting than the show.

They have commercials for disposable douches today. Who'd want to keep them?

Hard ad to explain: Ears pierced. We pick up and deliver!

aerobics

For a birthday gift this year, one of my friends gave me a video tape to which I could exercise. It was packed in that heavy shrink wrap so common today. As soon as I can get the tape out of the wrapper, I hope to play it!

They have a new organization called Aerobics Anonymous. When you get the urge to exercise you call somebody and he comes over and sits on you until the urge passes.

I do aerobic reading. I move my lips as I go down a page.

After six months of aerobics I can touch my knees without bending the floor.

I have all the aerobic tapes. Next month I plan to get a VCR.

In aerobics class I start slow and then I taper off.

I like my flab. I don't have to exercise to keep it on.

agents

Any jokes about agents work because it's impossible to malign an agent. I know because I've tried!

Show business agents are hard workers. They come in to work on Tuesday and tell one another, "Have a nice weekend!"

A rich kid wanted a Mickey Mouse outfit, so his father bought him a theatrical agency.

One famous show-business agency is noted for the small stature of its agents. It's almost impossible to get a job at that agency if you can see over the top of the desk. One day, one of the agents became a father. He looked at the infant and said, "He's only two hours old, but look how short he is already!"

An agent's heart is perfect for transplants, because it's never been used.

An agent is generally bitter because you get ninety percent of his salary!

One actor has an agent with branches overseas. Now the actor is out of work in sixteen countries.

aging and the aged

In my seventies, I was invited to be the president of the American Longevity Association. I accepted with pleasure. Whenever possible and wherever I could find a platform, I promoted the idea that calendar years do not senility make. Age is purely a state of mind.

In a volume dedicated to humor, a restatement of the notion is extremely pertinent. Look around, and you'll see a lot of comedians well along in years. One has already signed to play Las Vegas on his hundredth birthday. His motto, and mine, is simply, "I want to die at the age of a hundred and twenty from a bullet wound inflicted by a jealous husband!"

The mature do not necessarily want to abandon the myriad jokes about the elderly that focus on diminished performance. We like to laugh at and with the jokes. We enjoy them because we have a few secrets that can make a teenager blush!

Joe Thomas still enjoyed chasing girls when he got to be seventy. His wife was asked if she minded. She answered, "Why should I be upset? Dogs chase cars, but they can't drive!"

Aging isn't all bad. Think of the trouble many of us would be in if wrinkles hurt!

A young boy looked at himself in the mirror as he peeled off some skin where he'd been tanned during the summer. Shaking his head, he mused, "Five years old and I'm wearing out already!"

Aging is a wonderful experience. What a thrill it is to learn that Polident isn't a beat-up parrot!

Klein, a man of eighty, goes to a doctor and complains, "I can't pee."
    The doctor asks, "How old are you?"
    "I'm eighty."
    "You've peed enough!"

"I hear that Joe has a penchant for chasing young girls."
"His company pays him for that?"

There's a simple secret for long life—get to be a hundred and then be careful!

"How does an eighty-year-old man like you get a gorgeous twenty-year-old bride?"
"I told her I was ninety!"

Two elderly gents were sitting on a bench in Santa Monica, California, enjoying the warmth. One says, "I bet I can tell you how old you are."
    The other says, "You're crazy."
    "I guarantee you."
    "Okay, what do I have to do?"
    "Take down your pants."
    "What?"
    "You heard me. Take down your pants."
    The second man finally drops his pants. The first one studies the wrinkled rump for a moment and says, "You're eighty-one years old."
    "You're a genius! How can you know my age by looking at my rear end?"
    "It's easy. You told me yesterday!"

He's at that age where he won't take yes for an answer!

They're having an age problem. He won't act his, and she won't tell hers.

A man of eighty-one yells with joy as the nurse comes in and tells him that his twenty-year-old bride just gave birth to a baby. The man muses, "I wonder if I could do it again."

Another expectant father answers, "What makes you think you did it the first time?"

You're getting older when it takes you more time to recover than it did to tire you out.

A man of indeterminate age checked with a doctor to see if the doctor could tell him how old he was. After a quick examination, the doctor said, "According to the examination, I'm alone in this room!"

"The girl on the fourth floor is suing Mr. Brown for breach of promise."

"He's ninety-two, what could he promise?"

An older man states his intention to marry a girl of twenty. A friend says, "Such a marriage could be fatal."

The man answers, "So she'll die!"

An older man explains his interest in young women: "Just because there's snow on the roof doesn't mean there's no fire in the house!"

"Do you think there's as much love as there used to be?"

"Certainly, but there's a different bunch doing it!"

I'm saving up for my old age—arthritis, bursitis, cataracts . . .

"The girl next door gave my grandpa something great for his seventy-ninth birthday."

"What was it?"

"An erection!"

He's at that age where everything about him is starting to click—his knees, his elbows, his neck . . .

You know you're getting old when your idea of an early-bird dinner is lunch!

DOCTOR: You should live to be eighty.

PATIENT: I'm eighty-five.

DOCTOR: See—what did I tell you!

An elderly lady fills out the registration form at a doctor's office. After the address, the form asks for "Zip." She writes, "Not bad for my age!"

Aging asks some unanswered questions: Why is it we spend half of our lives with our fingers crossed because we don't have arthritis, and the other half with our fingers crossed because we do?

A woman along in years applied for a job. Where the application asked "Age?" she put down "Nuclear!"

"Grandpa, why don't you get a hearing aid?"

"Don't need it. I hear more now than I can understand!"

A reporter who specialized in feature articles interviewed a man one year shy of the century mark. At the end of the interview the reporter said, "I'd love to come back and see you when you reach a hundred."

The man answered, "Don't see why not. You look healthy enough!"

If you don't wear your specs when you look in the mirror, you'll eliminate wrinkles!

Two nice elderly ladies were sitting together in the coffee shop of a Miami Beach hotel. One asked, "What are your plans for to-night?"

The other said, "I have a date with Al Kemp."

The first one said, "Al Kemp? He's an animal. He'll get you up to his place, tear off your dress, and make love to you. How do you like that!"

The other said, "I'm glad you told me. I'll wear an old dress!"

Mr. Thompson hit seventy and decided he wanted to live a long time. He started to diet and exercise, and gave up smoking. He lost his gut, his body firmed up, and, to make the picture complete, he bought a toupee to cover his bald scalp. Then he walked out in the street and was hit by the first car that came along. As he lay dying, he called up, "God, how could you do this to me?"

God answered, "To tell you the truth, I didn't recognize you!"

"To what do you attribute your old age, Wilbur?"

"I was born a long time ago!"

Aging is when you've come a long way, baby, and you just ran out of gas.

A girl of five and her brother, seven, are both in the nude. She starts to cry because she wants a certain part of the male anatomy not shared by the female gender. She keeps jumping up and down. "I want one of those! I'll hold my breath till I get one of those!"

Her mother tries to calm her. "If you're a nice girl, when you grow older you'll get one of those."

Her brother adds, "And if you're bad you'll get a lot of them!"

Two youngsters, both aged six, decide to get married. The boy goes to his father and tells of his plans. His father asks, "How will you support her?"

"I get fifty cents a week allowance, and she gets an allowance too."

"But what if there's a baby?"

"Bite your tongue, Pop, so far we've been lucky!"

They call them the good old days. The old days weren't so good, they weren't so old, and they must be talking about the nights!

If Youth only knew, and Age could!

A man of seventy-five applied for a job as a lifeguard. The head lifeguard asked him, "Can you swim fast?"

The man answered, "I can't swim, but I wave good!"

An elderly woman wrote to one of the advice columns: "I think I made a mistake with my third marriage. My new husband is eighty but he's a sex fiend. He won't leave me alone. He comes after me twenty-four hours a day. I could be in the shower, making dinner, and even when I'm bending down to turn on the television set. What can I do? Oh, please excuse the jerky handwriting."

Older women have a sense of humor about their mature husbands. One was telling her friend about her husband's unexplained and mysterious disappearance: "I haven't seen him for a week," she said. "I went to the police to describe him and told them all about him—he'd lost his hair, his eyesight was gone, he didn't have one tooth. In fact, I told them that most of him was missing before he was!"

She insisted that she'd just turned forty, but she must have made a U-turn somewhere!

Mrs. Clay and her friend go to the police to let them know that Mr. Clay has disappeared. Mrs. Clay describes him as being six-two, a hundred and eighty pounds, wide-shouldered, brown-haired, and the closest thing to a forty-year-old lifeguard. As they walk out, her friend says, "What kind of description is that? Your husband is seventy-two. He's bald. He doesn't have a hair on his head."

Mrs. Clay says, "Who wants that one back?"

Mr. Daggett was ninety-six when he married Amelia, his twenty-five-year-old nurse. For a week the couple was happy, then Mr. Daggett died. It took the undertaker seven days to wipe the smile off his face!

"Even though he was seventy, he was a great lover."
"At that age?"
"Age meant nothing. He always made love to me by the sound of the bells from the church next door. If that goddamn fire-truck hadn't passed by he'd be alive today!"

Mr. Foster wanted a transplant. The hospital explained that they no longer made the parts!

"You're an old man!"
"I'm old? When you were young, the Dead Sea was only sick!"

They called their water bed the Dead Sea!

They made love almost every day—almost Monday, almost Tuesday, almost Wednesday . . .

He has a slight problem. The girls he goes out with are younger than his dentures!

He can't go out with girls his own age because there aren't any!

A woman in her late eighties went to a doctor to complain about her husband's impotence. The doctor heard her out and asked, "How old is your husband?"
"Eighty-eight."
"When did you first notice his waning enthusiasm and inability to perform?"
"Well, the first time was last night, and again this morning!"

Poor man. His pilot light went out now that he's got money to burn!

For someone up in years, weightlifting consists of standing up!

The oldest man in the county was asked how he managed to reach a hundred. He answered, "I stayed away from women till I was twelve!"

One ninety-year-old man married a woman of the same age. They spent their honeymoon trying to get out of the car!

At his age, when something comes up he's proud!

An old man went to a doctor because of a strange condition. "I have a little leak in my penis."
The doctor examined him and asked, "When did you have sex last?"
The old man said, "About nine months ago."
The doctor said, "That's what it is. You're having the orgasm!"

airports and air travel

What a parlay! If one doesn't get you, the other will. The comedy literature about the big birds is constantly growing. Advances in technology have dated some of the jokes. I recall proudly a joke about flying before the pressurized cabin came into existence: "I just flew in from Europe. When we got on the plane the hostess gave me a stick of gum and a wad of cotton. The cotton was delicious, but I can't get the gum out of my ears!" Then there is the standard of the 1940s: "I just flew in from Chicago. Are my arms tired!" Well, maybe we're better off with the pressurized cabin and the great new subject matter.

A UFO landed at Kennedy Airport the other day. The aliens were safe, but they lost their luggage!

On El Al Airlines they have two stewardesses. One passes out the food. The other says, "Eat, eat!"

You can always tell an Italian airplane. It has hair under the wings!

I just flew in on a no-frills airline. Before we took off, the stewardess told us to fasten our Velcro!

Two gents were traveling across the country on a plane that made many local stops. At the first stop, a little white wagon drove up to the plane and fueled it. At the second stop, another white wagon fueled the plane. At about the tenth stop, one passenger turned to the passenger next to him and said, "We're making good time, aren't we?"

The other passenger answered, "That white wagon isn't doing bad either!"

You have to be in trouble when you approach the airport and read a sign that says "Terminal."

On some airlines the seats are very narrow. Turning the other cheek isn't a virtue, it's a necessity!

Airlines are mean. They send your luggage to places you can't afford to go!

"Could you please send this valise to Chicago and send that two-suiter to Minneapolis and the garment back to Miami."
"We can't do that."
"Why not? You did it last month!"

With all the weather instruments on planes today, one flight was canceled because of clear visibility!

You have to worry at the airport when you see that the insurance machine is sold out!

It was a no-frills airline. Twenty minutes before the flight the passengers got together to elect a pilot!

It was a no-frills airline. The rate was good, but at the end of the flight you had to steal back your luggage!

It was a no-frills airline. Before the flight, the captain asked the passengers to chip in for gas!

The airport has sped things up lately. Each company has an express line for flights with six ticket prices or less!

Most airports make passengers walk a long way to get to the plane. That's so the luggage can get a head start!

The Lord must have loved airline fares. He made so many of them!

Some of the airlines from Third World countries fly the latest aircraft, like the 747.

But it takes some getting used to. The planes have more bathrooms than the countries!

We were going to fly this no-frills airline, but they pulled the steps away and the plane fell over!

Today people go over to a ticket counter of a no-frills airline and say, "Can I have two chances on your six-fifteen flight?"

The other day a plane was hijacked. A passenger put a gun to the pilot's head and demanded to be taken where his luggage was going.

In Peru, scientists have found ancient, strange, lost airfields. They've also found ancient, strange, lost luggage!

More and more crews are being made up of women lately. Soon they won't be able to call it the cockpit anymore!

By mistake, a captain forgets to disconnect the intercom from the cockpit and is overheard by the passengers as he tells the copilot, "The first thing I'm going to do is take a crap and then I'm going to grab this new stewardess." Hearing this, the stewardess rushes forward toward the cockpit. A nice old lady stops her and says, "Don't rush. He hasn't gone to the toilet yet!"

Two gents were sitting on a park bench discussing their likes and dislikes. Ken said, "I'm scared to fly. I don't believe planes are safe."

"That's dumb," said Pete. "Do you think trains are safe? Last week there was a great big train wreck and almost four hundred people were killed."

"No kidding, what happened?"

"A plane fell on it!"

"How often do those big jets crash?"
"Once, I imagine!"

It was a small airline. You couldn't get on the plane unless you had the exact change.

All the airlines are cutting back. One no-frills airline has eliminated movies. Passengers just pass around pictures of their kids.

You can become a little upset when you go to the airline counter to complain about lost luggage and the ticket agent is wearing your clothes!

If the Lord had wanted people to fly, he would have made it simpler to get to the airport!

After a harrowing flight, a passenger went over to the ticket agent and said, "If I were you, I would tell the pilot to keep that little red light off. Every time he puts it on, it gets bumpy!"

On a recent flight, three engines went out. Wearing a parachute, the pilot appeared in front of the passengers and announced, "We've got a lot of problems, but don't worry—I'm going for help!"

Always supportive, the pilot on one flight announced, "Ladies and gentlemen, I have some bad news and some good news. The bad news is that we're lost. The good news is that we have a strong tailwind!

About an hour after the flight started, the pilot announced, "Ladies and gentlemen, I'm afraid we'll have to slow down because of the loss of our number-one engine. A few minutes later, the second engine went out and a similar announcement was made. The plane would have to slow down more. Then the third engine went out. A passenger turned to the man next to him and said, "If that last one goes, we'll be up here all night!"

On Air India they have a unique way of feeding the passengers. They give the people in second class a bowl and let them beg in first class!

On the Chinese airline they serve you lunch . . . to go!

It's a hell of an airline. Each plane has two bathrooms and a chapel!

Before the flight, the pilot had one request: he wanted to go by bus!

When we landed, I ran over and kissed the wing. It must have been glad to have landed, because it kissed back!

The in-flight movie was so bad the passengers walked out!

Nairobi Airlines isn't bad either. In first class, for dinner they give passengers the people in second class!

On a recent Lufthansa flight, the plane was forced to ditch. In his most reassuring manner, the captain addressed the passengers: "Those of you who are good swimmers, please exit the plane through the escape hatch and stand on the right wing. Those of you who can't swim will stand on the left wing. Now, those of you on the left wing start swimming. Those on the right wing, let me thank you for flying Lufthansa!"

Many a stewardess thanks you for flying United, but she won't!

They didn't need a movie on that flight.

Every ten seconds your life passed before your eyes!

Then there's Gypsy Airlines. It has the lowest fares in the country, but when you land your wallet will be gone!

A sensitive and rather withdrawn man had the bad luck to be seated next to a six-foot Texan with wide shoulders and a roaring voice that indicated a vile temper. After the flight had been in the air for an hour, the Texan dozed off. The sensitive soul, a charter member of the white-knuckle club, up-chucked his lunch right onto the Texan's shirt. Grabbing half a box of Kleenex, the sensitive man started to clean up the mess. This woke the Texan, who asked, "What the hell is going on here?"

The sensitive man said, as he wiped, "There, there, you'll feel better in a minute!"

One airline had to send one stewardess in for further training. When passengers departed, she had kept saying, "Nice to have had you!"

A plane was experiencing great turbulence. Fearful that their lives were endangered, a passenger turned to a priest sitting next to him and said, "Do something religious!"

The priest started to call Bingo.

There's Vatican Airlines. The escape instructions are in Latin so that the Catholics can get off first!

The tower called the pilot of one flight and asked, "What is your height and position?"

The pilot answered, "I'm six-one and I'm in the cockpit!"

A nervous passenger fidgeted from the minute he boarded the plane. After a while, he looked out the window and said to the passenger next to him, "We must be miles up in the air. The people look like ants."

The other passenger said, "Those *are* ants. We haven't taken off yet!"

The first black pilot, a young man from a rural Southern town, was about to take off on his first solo flight for a major airline. As is usual, the pilot got on the intercom when the passengers were seated and said, "Welcome, ladies and gentlemen, to Flight 206. We are flying the latest Boeing 787 jet, a plane equipped with four Pratt & Whitney 6AR4Z engines, each of which gives a thrust of six hundred thousand fifty pounds. We shall cruise at forty thousand feet to avoid the turbulence of the cumulonimbus clouds off to the east. Now, if you'll sit back, I'll try to get this mother off the ground!"

You can worry about hijacking if you're flying Confederate Airlines and the pilot's name is Mohammed!

You can worry about being hijacked if your filet mignon is served in pita bread.

alimony

This category is proof that jokes can make some people laugh and others cry! For those who are merciless, Divorce will be a category of its own.

Alimony has an advantage for an ex-husband. He doesn't have to bring his paycheck home. He can mail it.

Alimony is like feeding a dead horse.

Alimony is like putting gas into another guy's car.

Marriage is a weird business. It's the only one that pays off when it fails.

Alimony is a deal that enables a woman to profit from her mistakes!

No man knows how short a month can be until he has to pay alimony.

Some women know how to rub it in. They keep reminding their husbands that they spend less money than their alimony would be.

Alimony is man's cash surrender value.

"Is there a way to avoid alimony?"
"Sure, stay single or stay married!"

One fellow recently made an alimony settlement. He and his wife split the house. He got the outside!

One fellow got a great deal. When his wife moved away, he got to keep what fell off the back of the moving van!

A woman was given a divorce because her husband had only spoken to her three times in all their years of marriage. The husband had to come up with child support for the three kids!

A man offered his wife a fortune in alimony if she'd give him a divorce. She refused, saying, "After all these years, why should I make him happy?"

Alimony is like paying installments on a car after you've totaled it.

Alimony is proof that two can live more cheaply as one.

Alimony is the high cost of loving.

After hearing all the evidence in a divorce proceeding, the judge said to the wife, "I'm going to give you six hundred a month alimony."

The husband jumped up and said, "I tell you what, Your Honor. I'll throw in a couple of bucks myself!"

Recently it has become fashionable for husbands to demand alimony too. The young husband of a famous star demanded twenty thousand a month in alimony because he didn't want to change his life-style.

The wife refused to pay him and said, "The fact that he got out of bed this morning is proof that he's already changed his life-style!"

The best gift you can give a divorced man is a recording that says, "Yes, dear, the check is in the mail!"

alligators and crocodiles

I wouldn't dare keep these beauties from having their own category.

"In Florida they use alligators to make shoes."
"It's amazing what they can get alligators to do!"

"What can you do with alligator skins?"
"Keep alligators in them!"

"What do you get when you cross a crocodile with a Shetland pony?"
"A crockoshet!"

A bellhop asks an alligator if he can carry his suitcase. The alligator replies, "Certainly, but be careful. It's my wife!"

"Will an alligator hurt you if you carry a torch?"
"Depends on how fast you carry the torch!"

A university professor is lecturing a class, the subject for the day being the mating habits of the alligator. The professor says, "The female alligator lays three million four hundred thousand eggs at one time. The male alligator eats three million, three hundred and ninety-five of those eggs."

From the back of the room, a student raises his hand and asks, "Sir, why does the male alligator eat all those eggs?"

The professor answers, "Because if he didn't, we'd be up to our asses in alligators!"

At a Florida alligator farm there is a daily show in which the keeper displays great bravery. One day, two gays are sitting in the bleachers watching the act. After a few minor tricks, the keeper presents his awesome closing trick. The largest alligator on the farm is brought out. To a fanfare of recorded music, the keeper embraces the alligator and starts to kiss him intensely. After several minutes of hugging and kissing, the keeper takes a big bow.

One gay says to the other, "Do you think you could do that?"

The other gay says, "If you get the alligator out of there, I'll try it!"

One alligator tried to get rid of his wife. She was an old bag!

Then there was the baby alligator who walked over to a shoe and asked, "Are you my mommy?"

ancestry

A nice hobby, tracing the family tree, but not much fun if you find out that your family is better dead than alive!

A young Harvard graduate applied for a job with a large brokerage house. During the interview with the personnel manager, the young man explained that he was descended from people who'd come over on the Mayflower. He was even able to trace his ancestry back to William the Conqueror. The manager thanked him and said, "Young man, your family tree is quite the thing, but we're interested in you for selling stock, not breeding!"

He looked up his family tree, and they were still living in it!

"I'd like a dog I can be proud of."
"This one's a beaut."
"Does he have a pedigree?"
"Lady, if he could talk, he wouldn't speak to either one of us!"

A rabbi and a priest were arguing about their religions. It was the priest's contention that the rabbi had no future. He could remain a rabbi and that was that. The priest could become a bishop, then a cardinal, and even a Pope.
The rabbi said, "And that's as far as you can go?"
The priest said, "What do you expect after Pope? You want me to become God?"
The rabbi said, "Why not? One of our boys made it!"

Thrift is a great virtue, especially in your ancestors!

A man was being challenged about his social graces by another, who said, "I'll have you know that my family came over on the Mayflower."
The man, only twenty years in America, said, "When I came over, the immigration laws were much stricter!"

A girl of ten asks her mother, "Mom, where'd I come from?"
The mother answers, "God sent you."
"Where did you come from?"
"God sent me."
"How about Grandma and Grandpa?"
"God sent them."
"Gee, nobody in this family has had sex in a hundred and fifty years!"

"Why doesn't the Lord come down to earth anymore?"
"The last time he was here, he knocked up this Jewish girl and we never heard the end of it!"

A Boston Brahmin was boasting about his fancy neighbors. "I understand," he said, "that their family was the first to come across."
The man listening said, "I'm their butcher, and I can tell you, they're the last to come across!"

A fancy Boston lady was sitting at tea with a friend, discussing their status. She said, "Can you imagine—if Jesus came to Boston he couldn't have belonged to our club. His father was a carpenter."
The other said, "Yes, but he had good connections on his mother's side!"

"Pa, what are ancestors?"
"Son, your grandfather is an ancestor. So am I."
"No kidding? Then why is everybody always bragging about them?"

"My family records go back ten centuries. How about yours?"
"They were lost in the Flood!"

A society lady goes to a florist and says, "I need about ten dozen roses for my daughter's coming-out party."

The florist says, "It's none of my business, but what was she put away for?"

A person of breeding is someone who doesn't get to a party until everybody is there.

A fancy gentleman went to an old Jewish tailor to have a suit fitted. As the tailor worked, the fancy gent bragged about his ancestry: "One of my ancestors signed the Declaration of Independence."

The tailor looked up at him and said, "One of mine signed the Ten Commandments!"

A very proper British gentleman happened to share seats with a typical American as they flew across the ocean. The subject of ancestry came up. Taking out a coin, the Englishman said, "My great-grandfather was made a duke by the man on this coin."

The American took out an Indian penny and answered, "The guy on this coin made my great-grandfather an angel!"

There was a young person named Smarty
Who sent out invites for a party.
So exclusive and few
Were the friends that he knew
That no one came to the party but Smarty!

Some people are just born with their faces lifted.

One fellow checked on his family tree and learned that his grandfather died of Dutch elm disease!

Two hillbillies were discussing their families. One said, "I can trace my family tree way back."

The other said, "'Tain't hard. Only two things live in trees—monkeys and birds. And I don't see no feathers on you!"

I know a gal who was descended from a long line her mother fell for!

Two young prep-school boys were talking about their ancestors. One said, "I can trace my family back to biblical days. My family was probably on the Ark with Noah."

The other retorted, "My family had a boat of its own!"

You can't choose your ancestors. Chances are they wouldn't have chosen you either!

I can trace my ancestry back to Washington. I also have a cousin in Baltimore!

A recently arrived Jewish refugee and his family decide to picnic in their new city of Los Angeles. They pack up and head for the park. They end up on the green of a hole on a golf course. A butler type rides up in a golf cart and says in a veddy-veddy British accent, "Sir, do you know that you are on the green of the eighteenth hole of the Brentmawr Golf Club?"

The refugee shrugs his shoulders.

The butler type goes on, "This is the most exclusive club in California. To belong, you must be able to trace your ancestry back two hundred years. The initiation fee is one hundred thousand dollars. The monthly dues are five thousand dollars. So take your family and all this trash and leave immediately!"

The refugee motions for his stuff to be packed up, then looks up slowly. "Mister, with an attitude like you got, how do you expect to get new members!"

A lady of pedigree revealed it one day when she returned from her first subway trip. She announced to her family, "You never saw so many people. They were crowded in like caviar!"

The best part of his family tree is underground!

anecdotes

Anecdotes are the first cousins of fables. Generally, an anecdote, like the fable, makes a point at the expense of the high and mighty. The hero or heroine of the anecdote always manages to give a swift kick in the rump to some deserving snob, ingrate, or pompous fool. Among the most famous anecdotes is the one in which Lady Astor, after trying to match wits with George Bernard Shaw, bellowed, "If you were my husband I'd give you poison." Mr. Shaw said pleasantly, "If I were your husband I'd take it."

From this less-than-humble origin, this particular anecdote has gone on to be associated with everyone from Stalin to Yogi Berra, stopping briefly at Winston Churchill, John Barrymore, and Dwight D. Eisenhower. That's one of the nice things about an anecdote: you can populate it with any persons of your choice. Thus, for the would-be public speaker, famous anecdotes can be borrowed whole or in part and used to make a point.

As with great purely fictional jokes, anecdotes can be personalized for the occasion. A story told about a guest of honor or someone at the next table is always funnier than the story in abstract.

Telling an anecdote isn't difficult. We all do it when we capture people and show them pictures of the children or grandchildren, and relate the brilliant things Junior or Juniorette came up

with last Sunday. What to say to people who pull out their wallets or purses and force baby pictures on you is another department!

A senator from Ohio was famous for his ability to talk endlessly on any subject. One day another senator told Senator Daniel Webster that the first senator was going deaf. Senator Webster said, "It's not from lack of practice!"

At the start of his career, the great attorney Clarence Darrow was involved in a trial during which the other attorney kept calling him "this beardless youngster" in an obvious attempt to discredit the young man.

When Darrow's turn came, he told the jury a story about the king of Spain: The king sent a young emissary to the king of France to discuss important matters. The French king was livid. "Does the Spanish king think so little of France," he screamed, "that he sends a beardless boy to us?" The emissary answered, "Your Highness, had my sovereign known that you imputed wisdom to a beard, he would have sent a goat!"

For a while, Ulysses S. Grant shared a military command with another general. Grant was planning to send a note to Washington asking that the other general be sent somewhere else. One of Grant's aides advised caution. "You may be underrating the man. He's been through ten campaigns." Grant answered, "So has that mule over there, but he's still a jackass, isn't he?"

President Franklin D. Roosevelt was about to send some special legislation to Congress that was bound to cause some problems. They could affect the President's plans to run for reelection. One of his aides suggested that the politics be considered. It might not be an easy campaign. The aide said, "Wendell Wilkie has his eye on the President's chair." Roosevelt answered, "Yes, but look what *I've* got on it!"

A Southern congressman from a remote parish in Louisiana was interviewed on his birthday by a reporter from a Northern newspaper. The reporter asked, "You've been in Congress for a long time, haven't you, sir?"

"About twenty-five years."

"You've seen some mighty big changes, haven't you?"

"Yes, sir. And I've been against them all!"

George S. Kaufman, the brilliant playwright and wit, walked into the office of Jed Harris one day. Harris, a producer, was a man of unique habits. On this occasion he was seated nude at his desk. Without batting an eyelash, Kaufman said matter-of-factly, "Jed, your fly is open!"

In addition to being a war hero and later the President of France, General Charles de Gaulle was a rather vain gentleman. One day, an actor told of an adventure that morning. While escorting friends on a tour of Paris, he had seen General de Gaulle at the Cathedral of Notre Dame, praying. The great actor Jean Gabin asked, "To whom?"

For years, the Stork Club in New York City was posh and stuffy, but still the place to go at night. The owner, an ex-bootlegger, was less than brilliant and rather bigoted. He especially disliked dark-skinned people. A great raconteur and vaudeville star, Georgie Jessel, came into the Stork Club one evening, escorting the beautiful but dark-skinned Lena Horne. Billingsley, the owner of the club, rushed over and asked, "Who made your reservations?" Jessel replied, "Lincoln!"

At a fancy dinner party where the hostess was an important businesswoman, Winston Churchill was asked, "Have you ever met any professional women?" Churchill answered, "I never met any amateur ones!"

Marv Throneberry was one of those ballplayers who seemed to have an aversion to catching balls hit at or thrown to him. His manager and a baseball legend, Casey Stengel, was presented with a birthday cake one day. Throneberry pouted and said, "I had a birthday the other day. Why didn't somebody give me a cake?" Stengel answered, "We would have, but we was afraid you'd drop it!"

During a tour of Oklahoma, President Teddy Roosevelt went to see an old friend, Quanah Parker, the chief of the Comanches. Parker showed Roosevelt around and pointed out all the concessions he'd made to living like a white man. His children even attended the white man's school. Roosevelt was appreciative but said, "Look, dear friend, why don't you set your people a better example? A white man has only one wife. You live with five squaws. Give up four of them and live with the fifth. That would really be living as the white man does." The chief mulled over the notion, then said, "I will do as you suggest on one condition. You choose the one I am to live with, then you go tell the other four!"

Two British politicians met in a corridor of the House of Commons. One, John Wilkes, had been expelled from Commons several times. The other, Lord Sandwich, was the force behind the expulsions. Angrily, Lord Sandwich said, "Sir, you will come to your end either upon the gallows or of a venereal disease!" Wilkes answered, "I should say that depends upon whether I embrace your principles or your mistress!"

During a dinner party at a small Montmartre café, Ernest Hemingway was boring the hell out of the other diners with a long story about Pamplona, a story he'd told a dozen times before. Seated against the wall, Gertrude Stein said, "My dear, my leg has fallen asleep. Do you mind if I join it?"

Napoleon died, and one of the British king's ministers wanted to be the first to break the news. He rushed into the king's boudoir and said, "Sir, your bitterest enemy is dead!" The king said, "Is she, by God?"

Mahatma Gandhi was on an important mission to London, one of those occasions when the British tried to bargain the pacifist out of another fast. Leaving the first session, Gandhi was greeted by a dozen reporters. One of them asked, "What do you think of western civilization?" Gandhi answered, "I think it would be a good idea!"

Robert Benchley, the humorist, loved to send telegrams. From Venice once, he wired to an actor friend, "Streets full of water. Advise!"

A truly funny lady, Dorothy Parker, went to San Francisco, where she happened to meet two lesbians. They were considering marriage. Parker listened to them for a while and said, "Of course, you must have a legal marriage. The children have to be considered!"

The performance was brilliant and the ovation overwhelming. A lady from the inner circle rushed backstage to the conductor, Serge Koussevitzky, and said, "Maestro, you are God!" "Yes, madame," the conductor answered, "and it's such a responsibility!"

For our century and probably for many to come, Jascha Heifetz is the gauge by which violinists are measured. One winter's night, Heifetz was scheduled to play a hall in Cleveland. The weather was atrocious. Roads were closed. Streets were impassable. Came the time of the recital, and only one couple sat in the audience. The theater manager delayed the curtain for a half hour. Still no more concertgoers. Finally, Heifetz stepped in front of the curtain. He announced that the concert was called off. The man of the couple appealed, "Sir, we came fifty miles from Dayton for this. Please. Please sing one number!"

It was the shank of the evening. The guests were leaving one by one. At the door, a departing guest shook the hand of Chico Marx, the host, and said, "I would like to say good-bye to your wife." Marx said, "Who wouldn't?"

animals

For some reason we ascribe to humans many of the characteristics of animals: a person has a memory like an elephant, eats like a horse, is as fat as a pig, and can be as sly as a fox. Since turnabout is fair play, we have managed to lay a few trips on animals by giving them human characteristics. To compound the felony, we have given animals our voices. Somehow, when animals speak for us, it's funnier. It's safer too!

A bear approached a trapper in the woods and asked what he was looking for.

"I'm after a nice fur coat for myself," the trapper said. "How about you?"

"I'd like a nice breakfast. I tell you what, let's go into the cave and discuss it."

They went into the bear's cave and everything worked out. In a half hour the bear had his breakfast and the trapper was in a nice fur coat!

A man walked into a bar and ordered, "A bourbon for me and a vodka for my pal." When the drinks were served, the man swallowed the bourbon and poured the vodka in his pocket. After five rounds, the man became a little rambunctious. The bartender asked him to leave. Slurring his words, the man stood up and said, "I know when I'm not wanted. You can go to hell!"

A little mouse stuck his head out of the pocket into which the vodka had been poured and said, "And that goes for your goddamn cat too!"

A lady opened her refrigerator only to see a rabbit inside. "What are you doing in there?" she asked.

"This is a Westinghouse, isn't it? Well, I'm Westing!"

An ape is the only other animal that kisses.

A caterpillar looked up at a butterfly and said, "You'll never get me up in one of those!"

A mother mouse and her baby were walking in a cave when a bat flew by. The baby mouse said, "Look, Ma, an angel!"

One kid ended up with two dozen hamsters because his hamster's sister turned out to be a himster.

Two minks meet one morning and exchange a few words. Then, as he moves on, one mink says, "I'll see you tomorrow in temple!"

A scientist crossed a raccoon with a skunk. He got a dirty look from the raccoon!

A boy of six is watching two monkeys in a cage make love. He asks his father, "How long does it take to make a baby monkey?"

The father answers, "Nine months."

The kid says, "So what's their hurry?"

Two fleas meet in the street. One says to the other, "Do you want to walk or catch a dog?"

At a large zoo where animals are kept in open compounds so that visitors can mingle with the beasts, a woman tickles a kangaroo. The kangaroo jumps once and takes off at eighty miles an hour. The keeper comes over and asks the lady, "What happened?"

The lady says, "I tickled that kangaroo and it took off."

The keeper says, "You better tickle me in the same place, lady, because I have to catch it!"

A man sees a lion in the jungle. The man falls to his knees and starts praying. Lo and behold, the lion goes down on his knees next to him and also starts to pray. The man says, "It's a miracle."

The lion says, "Please don't talk while I'm saying grace!"

The flood ends. Noah tells all the animals to leave. "Go forth and multiply," the patriarch says. Two snakes lag behind. Noah asks why they don't go off. The snakes answer, "We can't multiply. We're adders!"

A man walks into a doctor's office. On his head is a bright green frog. The doctor asks, "What's the problem?"

The frog answers, "I'd like to have this wart on my ass removed."

Three turtles sit around their compound at the zoo. A new zookeeper puts their fruit allotment into the wrong receptacle, about twenty feet from where they're seated. A vote is taken and Elmer, the oldest turtle, is chosen to go after the food.

Three hours go by. The remaining turtles become a little antsy and they look around. Elmer is about a foot away. They berate him for taking so long. Elmer says, "If you keep that up, I'm not going!"

Turtles are helping science. Not long ago, the heart of a turtle was put into a man. The man walked out of that hospital one week later, and six weeks later he reached his car!

A scoutmaster saw one of his young charges playing with a squirrel. The kid had taken out his Swiss Army knife and was about to commit mayhem on the helpless squirrel. The scoutmaster asked, "What are you planning to do to that squirrel?"

The scout said, "I was thinking of castrating him."

"Really? Let me tell you something: whatever you do to that squirrel I'll do to you."

"Well, in that case, I think I'll just kiss his ass!"

We may not be descended from monkeys, but we may be heading that way!

A woman in Pennsylvania looked at her shadow on Groundhog Day and predicted six weeks of dieting!

One skunk said to another, "So do you!"

A mother skunk told a friend, "Junior just keeps rambling. He makes no scents!"

A kid stared at an organ-grinder and his monkey for hours and finally turned to his mother and said, "Isn't it awful the way our ancestors had to beg for money!"

A man complained to a friend, "My wife didn't know what she wanted. I got her a fox. That wasn't it. I got her a beaver. Then a mink. Now the house is filled with animals!"

"I work like a beaver."
"Why? Who needs dams?"

A boy sees a female camel and says, to the chagrin of his mother, "Look, Ma, a mother-humper!"

I know a parent who wouldn't take his kids to see *Bambi* because it was a stag movie!

A man explained to a friend that he grew up in a sanitary home. In the top drawer of the dresser, for example, they kept cheese. In the bottom drawer, mice. The other man asked, "What was in the middle drawer?"

"Cats!"

A kid sees a baby kangaroo stick its head out of the mother's pouch and says, "I always knew those Cesareans leave a nasty scar!"

One woman refused a leopard coat. It spotted too easily!

There is, of course, the laughing hyena. He eats once a day, moves his bowels once a month, and mates once a year. What does he have to laugh about?

The male porcupine said to the female, "I do love you, but I can't stand to be hurt again!"

The day came and Noah brought the Ark to a standstill on Mount Ararat. The animals debarked. Two elephants walked off. Two lions. Two tigers. Then four gnus came down the gangplank. A spectator was surprised to see four animals of one kind. Noah explained, "You see, first there's the good gnus and then there's the bad gnus!"

A male rabbit says to a female rabbit, "This is fun . . . wasn't it?"

Then there was the time two rabbits got on a plane. Six hours later, two rabbits got off the plane. They were *brothers!*

A lovelorn worm said, "I can't live without you. Marry me."
  "Oh, shut up! I'm your other end!"

A male hyena brought some food home to his mate and said, "Don't you ever take anything seriously?"

Strolling through the woods one day, a female hyena was grabbed by a young male leopard who had his way with her. A male hyena passed by and disregarded the activity. When the leopard was satiated and had taken off, the female asked the male hyena, "Why didn't you help me?"
  The male answered, "The way you were laughing, I thought you were enjoying it!"

One day it was so hot a leopard stood around the zoo with his spots on the ground!

The luckiest man in the world is a fisherman who marries a woman with worms!

A worm tries to make love to a centipede. The centipede crosses her legs and says, "No, no, a hundred times no!"

Then there was the small octopus who was just a crazy, mixed-up squid!

One gent crossed a praying mantis with a termite. He got a bug that said grace before it ate his house!

Two worms were crawling on the ground. One stopped and the other crawled on!

A camel can go five hundred miles without water. Science ought to find out how far it could go *with* water!

"What does a bat do in winter?"
"It splits if you don't oil it!"

Then there was this porcupine who made love to a hairbrush!

Eskimos have a great saying: Never pet a bear unless it's a rug.

A cat may have nine lives, but a bullfrog croaks every time!

A keeper at the zoo was asked by a young girl, "Do these giraffes ever catch cold from standing there with their feet wet?"
  The keeper answered, "Yes, but not until the following week!"

There was once a young lady who said she'd do anything for a mink. Now she can't button it!

Up in the frozen wastes of the Yukon, a young polar bear asked its mother, "Mommy, am I your natural child?"
  "Certainly."
  "You mean, it was you and Dad and the whole thing. I'm the result. Right?"
  "Right. Why don't you discuss it with your father?"
  The youngster waited until his father returned from a day's fishing with dinner, then asked, "Am I your real son, Pop?"

"Of course."

"A natural son and all of that?"

"Yes. Yes. Why do you ask?"

"Because to tell you the truth, Pop, I'm freezing!"

Then there was the female deer who was always worried about a buck!

Then there was the sex-crazed mouse. Pussy got him!

Then there's Indian roulette. You sit down next to a snake charmer with six cobras, one of which is deaf!

There once was a prince named Montezuma
Who had an affair with a puma.
The prince said, "Sit."
The animal bit.
Just an example of animal huma!

In the middle of a love bout, the female porcupine whispered, "Pull it out deeper, it hurts so good!"

A snake went to a psychiatrist and claimed that all of his friends kept sticking out their tongues at him.

Pity the poor nearsighted snake who tried to rape a rope.

A female baboon wanted a baby badly, but couldn't arouse her male companion. Finally, the zookeeper volunteered his services. He had one condition: the baby had to be brought up Catholic.

His house was in such bad shape the termites ate out.

There were once two weevils. One worked hard and became very rich. The other did nothing and became the lesser of two weevils.

"Do you think I'm going to wear this squirrel coat for the rest of my life?"

"Why not? The squirrel did!"

Desirous of a new thrill, a woman decided to sleep with a man who had never had a woman. Her search brought her to Australia, where she found a man who, having spent his life in the outback, hadn't even seen a woman in thirty years. The lady brought the man back to her hotel room. He looked around and said, "This room isn't big enough."

The woman said, "It seems large enough to me."

The man said, "I never slept with a woman, but if it's anything like a kangaroo, we'll need all the room we can get!"

A man brought a dyed skunk coat to his wife. She asked, "How can such a pretty coat come from such a foul-smelling animal?"

The husband answered, "I don't expect gratitude, but I do deserve a little respect!"

Many a man who says, "I'll be a monkey's uncle," is one.

A lady in Tibet rushed home to her stove and saw her dinner going up in smoke. She said, "Oh, my baking yak!"

One fellow chased down a zebra and made a coat for his brother in jail!

A man was camping in Yellowstone National Park when he saw a huge bear coming at him. The man ran toward a tree and ended up on a limb thirty feet off the ground. The man's companion came by and was amazed. "Don't tell me you jumped so high you could catch that limb?" he asked.

The man answered, "No, but I did get it on the way down!"

One woman wanted to see something in a fur, so her husband took her to the zoo!

They crossed a tomcat with a turtle. Now they have a snapping pussy!

As a reward for winning a race, a young stallion was put in a compound with a beautiful female zebra. As the next day dawned, the keeper ran to see how the horse had made out, and was chagrined to see the horse leaning up against a tree. His mane was disheveled, his body covered with welts from angry hooves, and he had two giant black eyes. Astounded, the keeper asked what had happened.

The horse said, "I spent the whole night trying to take off her pajamas!"

anniversaries

I forgot mine... once!

It is the eve of the Collinses' twentieth wedding anniversary. Mrs. Collins says, "Don't you think we should do something?"

"I certainly do," Mr. Collins replies.

"How do you suggest we celebrate it?"

"How about two minutes of silence?"

They just celebrated their tin anniversary—six years of eating out of cans.

A doctor sent a deadbeat patient a copy of a bill, saying, "This bill is a year old."

The deadbeat wrote back, "Happy anniversary!"

A couple were celebrating their twenty-fifth wedding anniversary with a lavish party at a fancy restaurant. Everybody was having a great time except the husband, who sat off in a corner with a tear in his eye. The family attorney came over to him and asked what was wrong. The husband said, "Remember when we were first married and I couldn't stand her? I hated her."

The attorney said, "I recall those days."

"I hated her with every bone in my body. I wanted to kill her, remember?"

"I remember."

"You wouldn't let me. You said I'd get twenty-five years in jail for the crime."

"That was a long time ago. Why are you so sad?"

"Because today I would have been a free man!"

On the phone, a man is given instructions on how to get to an anniversary party. The host explains, "You get to Sunburst Avenue and it's the second house on the left. When you get to the door, try ringing the bell with your elbow."

"Why my elbow?"

"Well, with the gift you'll be carrying, you won't be able to use your hands!"

On the eve of their thirtieth wedding anniversary, a man tells his wife how they'll celebrate. "Tonight," he says, "we'll act just like we did on our honeymoon. Everything goes. We'll have a wild time."

The next morning they sit at the breakfast table, and the wife asks, "Oh, yeah, how did you make out last night?"

A couple celebrate their fortieth wedding anniversary by checking into the hotel where they honeymooned. In the honeymoon suite, the wife says, "Remember that first night? You couldn't wait for me to get my stockings off."

The husband says, "The way I feel now, you could knit a pair."

Farmer Brown and his wife are about to have their twentieth wedding anniversary. Mrs. Brown asks, "Should I kill a chicken for tonight?"

Farmer Brown says, "Why blame a bird for something that happened twenty years ago?"

A silver wedding anniversary is proof that twenty-five years of happy married life are over!

A young couple, newly married, moved into the home of the bride's parents and were put up in a bedroom adjoining that of the parents. The walls were paper-thin. On the first wedding anniversary, the youngsters were a little more amorous than usual and went to bed early. Before long, the parents went to bed. They were unable to sleep because of the noise from the bedsprings in the other bedroom. The sounds stirred up something in the mother, who turned to the father and suggested that they make love too. Not averse to pleasure, the father gladly accepted the situation. An hour went by, and once again there was the sound of springs creaking from the next bedroom. The mother looked at the father. "Would a second helping be out of order?" The father obliged. A third lullaby of the bedsprings was heard an hour after that. At the mother's look, the father shrugged his shoulders and made the attempt. One moment later, he fell back in a dead faint. The mother banged on the wall and yelled, "Stop celebrating, you're killing your father!"

Then there was the actress who couldn't remember if it was her fourth wedding anniversary with her fifth husband or her fifth with her fourth!

A married pair went to their honeymoon hotel to celebrate their fiftieth wedding anniversary. Only this time the *groom* went into the bathroom and cried!

antiques

I never dreamed that the stuff in the house I grew up in was antique. I just thought it was old. Somehow, it led to a joke I used for years: "I walked into an antique dealer the other day and he rapped me in the mouth. I shouldn't have asked, 'What's new?'" That was a partner of another joke about the guy who used to go into the funeral parlor and ask if they had any used boxes... (In a section on antiques, what's wrong with a few antique jokes?)

"My father has a Louis XIV bed."
"That's nothing. My father has an Adam's apple."

I bought a statue of the Venus de Milo real cheap because it was an irregular. It had both arms!

An antique shop always makes me feel as if I'm walking around in my wife's purse!

An antique is something you pay too much for, and don't need or want.

The stuff in my house is all antique. The table is 1492. The chairs cost a few bucks more.

A woman brought an old book into a store specializing in old volumes. The dealer studied the book and said, "This is a rare find, a Gutenberg Bible. It's worth a fortune!"

The woman says, "I had two of them, but I threw the other one out. Some guy named Martin Luther had written all over it!"

A woman browsing through an antique store sees a cat drinking milk from a saucer. She recognizes the saucer as a rare antique piece. Trying to be clever, she says to the lady running the store, "How much do you want for that cat?"

The woman says, "Ten dollars."

The buyer goes on, "While I'm at it, could I give you another dollar for the saucer? The cat seems to enjoy drinking from it."

The shopkeeper shakes her head. "Sorry, ma'am, but I've sold nineteen cats from that one saucer!"

Sylvia and Edith are sitting in the kitchen finishing their morning brunch when a dozen roses arrive for Sylvia. The card expresses her husband's love for her. Sylvia says, "Oh, now I'll have to spend a week with my legs up in the air."

Edith says, "You don't have to. I'll lend you my antique vase!"

A customer was raving about the price of an antique. "Two thousand for that piece! Absurd! I came in last week and you only wanted fifteen hundred!"

The dealer said, "You know how the cost of labor and materials have gone up!"

"That credenza goes back to Louis XIV."
"That's nothing. If I don't come up with a
   payment, all my furniture goes back to
   Penney's the thirtieth!"

ants

If I put these with the animals, they're so small they'd get lost.

A football game was being held between a team of ants and a team of elephants. On the first play, one of the ants started to run around the end for a touchdown. An elephant stomped on him and killed him. Angrily, the referee ran over and accused the elephant of very unsportsmanlike conduct.

The elephant answered, "I was only trying to trip him!"

A male fly made love to a beautiful female elephant. When he was done, he leaned over and asked, "Was it good for you too?"

A male gnat was making love to a female elephant. In the heat of the romantic bout, he leaned over and asked, "Am I hurting you?"

An ant fell in love with a lovely female giraffe, but soon called off the affair. He explained, "First, kiss, and then, pump. Then, kiss, and then, pump. It was wearing me out!"

apartments

My family lived in what they called a railroad flat. It was an apartment made out of a foyer. There were four apartments on each story, but only one bathroom at the end of the hall. We were unlucky because one of our neighbors was a long reader!

It wasn't a bad apartment. On a clear day you could almost see through the windows!

Apartment buildings aren't put up as well as they were in the past. Recently a landlord put up a six-story building. As soon as the scaffolding was removed, the building fell. The landlord came running to the foreman of the building crew and yelled, "I told you—the scaffolding doesn't come down until the wallpaper is up!"

As part of spring cleaning, they threw out a lot of useless things. They started with some of their relatives!

Looking at an old Roman building, a traveler reads, "'This building is exactly as it was when built. Not a stone has been changed, nothing has been replaced.'" The tourist shrugs and says to another tourist, "Must have the same landlord I do!"

A prospective tenant complained to the building manager who was showing him around that the walls were thin. The manager became indignant. The tenant said, "This is the flimsiest apartment I've seen."

"Flimsy? This is flimsy? Let me show you something." The manager went to the apartment next door and called out a few words, saying at the end, "Can you hear me?"

"Every word."

"But you can't see me, can you?"

"No."

"Well, with walls like this, how can you say this apartment is flimsy!"

Some landlords don't maintain their buildings. In one I know about, a tenant slipped on the ice—in front of the bathtub!

He doesn't have to move to a fancier place now. The owner raised the rent on his old place!

A prospective tenant wondered about some stains on the walls of the kitchen. "The man who lived here before," the rental agent said, "was an inventor. He mostly worked with explosives."

"Oh, so those stains are some of the stuff that went wrong?"

"No, those are the inventor!"

When I was a kid, we were evicted so often we had to buy curtains to match the sidewalk!

"Where have you been?"

"I moved."

"Where?"

"To a new place."

"Where's the new place?"

"Across the street from the old place."

"Where's the old place?"

"Across the street."

"From where?"

"The new place."

"Forget it!"

They had a nice apartment overlooking the park until they made a mistake. They overlooked the rent!

"We moved into a new apartment recently."

"Do they ask a lot for the rent?"

"Five times last month!"

An actor is slightly behind in rent and the landlord hints that he'd like to have it paid. The actor says, "Just think. Ten years from now you'll be able to point to this place and tell people a great actor used to live here."

The landlord replies, "I can start saying it tomorrow."

He got a new apartment. It had hot and cold running mice!

The apartment was so small, when you put in the key to open the door, you broke the window!

His apartment has hot and cold running water—without turning on the faucets!

"I wonder if they take kids in this place."
"They must. The rooms are too small for grownups!"

One nice thing about those economy apartments. You have no room for complaints!

The walls were so thin I could watch two TV sets—mine and the neighbor's!

One tenant broke his alarm clock. He never bothered to get it repaired. He merely started to play his trumpet whenever he wanted to know the time. One of his neighbors would always yell, "Hey, don't you know it's two-fifteen in the morning!"

Then there was the fellow who was thrilled when the landlord said that he was raising his rent. The fellow was having a hard time raising it himself!

I love living in a penthouse. It's nice to have a roof under my feet!

In some apartment buildings they don't want children. One woman loves her place so much, she's in her eighteenth month!

appearances

How you appear to others is important in life and business, they say. But I don't know. I saw a one-legged man put his best foot forward and he fell down! They say you can't judge a book by its cover. I saw a cover showing a nude man and woman intertwined on the grass. I opened the book and it was dirty. Maybe you can judge some books by their covers!

There are many laughs waiting to be culled by the person able to turn a neat phrase about a person's appearance. The remark should be based on feeling rather than on vision. In a play, the author calls a young lady "a candy store of a girl." We know exactly what she looks like. The impression is what counts.

"Was that your wife I saw you with last night?"
"That was my new son-in-law, and I think I'll kill myself!"

He's living proof that stuffed shirts come in all sizes!

He should live down evolution!

He's a born-again cretin!

He's not a good artist, but he draws flies!

He went right from puberty to adultery!

He looks like an unmade bed!

She's not photogenic, especially in person!

He just went on a crash diet. That's why he looks like a wreck!

He's lucky he doesn't have to pay taxes on his appearance!

He's the shifty type. If he went on jury duty, they'd find him guilty!

She should have a newspaper column: Dear Shabby!

He's carried away with his own importance, but not far enough!

When he was born, his folks got together and gave him a dirty look!

She's not all here, and everybody's grateful!

Her face looks like it's going down for the third time!

He's such a miserable specimen it looks as if he was made in Hong Kong!

He's got an angry look. He probably goes to gypsies to have his *fist* read!

Every time he looks in the mirror he takes a bow!

Her face is proof that you can have a hit-and-run accident without having a car!

She must have gone to the prom at the school of hard knocks!

She's in the prim of life!

He looks as if life has put him on hold!

He doesn't think much of himself, but next week he's leaving to pose for a wall at the Vatican!

He's underfed, undernourished, and over-wifed!

When she walks, from the rear it looks like two puppies fighting!

He looks like death warmed over—in a microwave oven!

His neck is so dirty, when he sweats he has swamp around the collar!

He's a sloppy tobacco chewer. Someday he'll die from cancer of the beard!

His hair is so long Moses couldn't part it.

A man went into a diner. Sitting at the end of the counter was a young man with long hair, the last of the hippies. The man kept staring. The hippie walked over to him and said, "What's bothering you, pal?"

The man said, "I didn't mean to stare. But twenty-five years ago I made love to a buffalo and I was wondering if you were my kid!"

It's great to be rich and let other guys keep up appearances!

His hair is so long, other men won't undress in front of him!

He's so conceited that a week after he checks out of a motel, the mirror is still warm!

He'd make a great death wish!

He used to be humble, but he broke himself of the habit!

He's hostile, and nobody knows the reason. What should a short, fat, stupid, ugly guy have to be hostile about?

God should have mercy on his soul. He didn't have any on the rest of him!

She looks like she was rode hard and put away wet!

He's a real snapdragon. He's got no snap, and everything's draggin'!

His picture is in the dictionary under "Slob"!

She's discovered a new use for old clothes—she wears them!

The largest room in his house is for improvement!

He comes from a prim and proper town. The town slut is a nun!

She hovers over you like a helicopter.

Take away his bearing, his mien, his *joie de vivre*, and what have you got—the same him!

He keeps his nose to the grindstone, his shoulder to the wheel, and his ear to the ground. And what does he have—the world's worst posture.

When he goes to a wax museum, he has to have a note to get out.

He clicks with everybody he meets. His dentures don't fit!

By comparison, she loses!

Even with ragweed behind each ear, she's nothing to sneeze at!

The way he dresses, he should be allowed to use handicapped parking spaces.

arabs

The people of the desert are lucky. They get to be the first ethnic group about which my computer can wax funny. But then, in case of fire, Arabs would be lucky if everyone left alphabetically.

"I saw a lot of Arabs in the desert."
"Bedouins?"
"Bedouins, goodouins. Both, I imagine."

In the desert the men form a circle and dance with one another. Sort of sheik to sheik!

An Arab sold me a plain terrycloth towel. He said it was a no-frills flying carpet!

An Arab is having one of those days. He wakes up to find that his camel is gone. He is out of water, and wanders around looking for any kind of help. He wanders everywhere and is soon lost. He prays, then after a day he finds an oasis with a small stream. Another Arab offers him a drink of water from a small cup. The thirsty man asks, "Did you rinse it first?"

An Arab, his camel having perished in the heat, wandered around looking for an oasis. The sun beat down on him as he went first one way and then another. Finally he spied a man in the distance and ran toward the figure. The man stood in the middle of the desert with an open valise on a stand in front of him. The wanderer asked for a drop of water. The man said, "I don't have water. I'm selling ties. Would you like to buy a tie?"

The wanderer blinked and said, "What am I going to do with a tie?"

The vendor said, "What do you want from me? I sell ties, that's all."

The wanderer took off and started a more desperate search. As the heat grew fiercer, he again searched in all directions. Just when the sun was at its highest, he saw a restaurant in the distance. It was almost certainly a mirage, but he didn't care. He ran toward it and arrived at the front door to discover that it was a real restaurant. He started in. A doorman stopped him.

"Sorry, sir, you can't get in without a tie!"

An Arab walked into a typical New York delicatessen and asked the price of a corned-beef sandwich. The owner looked at him with disdain and, wishing to discourage him, said, "A sandwich is nineteen dollars."

The Arab said, "Let me have two."

The next day the Arab showed up again, asked the price of a pastrami sandwich, and was told that pastrami sandwiches cost thirty-two dollars. He ordered six.

The day after that, the Arab asked about tongue sandwiches. The owner told him, "Tongue is fifty-eight dollars each."

The Arab said, "Let me have sixteen of them."

The next day there was a large sign on the front door: "No Jews allowed!"

There is also the oo-oo bird of Arabia. It lays an egg directly on the burning sands, which sometimes reach a temperature of a hundred and thirty degrees. And every time the bird lays an egg, it says, "Oo, oo!"

A rich Saudi Arabian started a collection of miniatures. He recently picked up Dubai and Kuwait!

An Arab looked at his land. It was barren, not a drop of water or even a cloud in sight. The Arab said, "Allah is good. Allah is great. But Allah doesn't know anything about farming!"

An Arab sat in his tent sharpening the blade of an ax. A traveler happened by and asked the reason for the ax. The Arab said, "I am Mustapha, the greatest hewer of trees in Arabia. I can chop down a tree in the time it would take another to have one sip of coffee."

"But look around. There are no trees. This is a desert."

And Mustapha replied, "*Now* it's a desert!"

Mr. and Mrs. Faulkner, a pious couple, visited the Middle East and stopped off at places of deep meaning to Christians. An Arab boatman, hoping to guide them for the day, pointed to a spot of blue-green water on which Jesus had walked and said that he could take them over to it for a small fee. He wanted only fifty dollars. Mr. Faulkner shook his head and said, "Fifty dollars? No wonder Jesus walked!"

A sheik can have three hundred wives. It must be a thrill to have six hundred stockings drying in the bathroom!

arithmetic

When I first took dancing lessons, Mr. Sherblock, the teacher, made us count steps by the numbers: one, two, three, four, five, six, seven. Whenever I goofed, he'd look at me and say scornfully, "And you got an 'A' in arithmetic!" On one occasion, some of the class was in early. Before Mr. Sherblock arrived, one of the boys started to kid around with a crazy dance that was half ballet and half you-name-it. Unnoticed, Mr. Sherblock arrived and asked, "What kind of dance is that?" I said, "Algebra!" Not too bad for a boy of seven!

Two youngsters are left alone by their mother, who has to run to the supermarket for a few moments. The older child, a girl of seven, is left in charge. She'll be the mother until the real one returns. Bugged, the five-year-old son says to his sister, "Okay, if you're the mommy, how much is three times six?"

The sister replies, "Wait till your father comes home!"

"How much is $5q$ plus $5q$?"
"$10q$."
"You're very welcome!"

A football coach and his assistant feel out a potential candidate for the team. Concerned that the young man might have trouble with the college entrance exam, the coach probes, "How much is three and three?"

The player answers, "Five."

The coach turns to his assistant and says, "He'll do fine. He only missed it by three!"

In the school cafeteria, several college students were talking about their various courses. One said, "Calculus is the toughest course in the world."

A second said, "You're crazy. Trigonometry is ten times harder."

The third, a football recruit, said, "You guys must be kidding. You ever hear of something called subtraction?"

"**P**a, I can't find the greatest common divisor."

"Are they still looking for that, son? They couldn't find it when I was a kid either!"

A young boy came home with a 98 on a math test. His father wanted to know who had gotten the other two points.

A teacher asked, "If you had five apples and I asked for one, how many would you have left?"

A boy answered, "Five!"

A teacher asked, "What is one-half of one-half?"

A student answered, "I don't know exactly, but it ain't much!"

The teacher came up with a good problem. "Suppose," she asked the second-graders, "there were a dozen sheep and six of them jumped over a fence. How many would be left?"

"None," answered little Norman.

"None? Norman, you don't know your arithmetic."

"Teach, you don't know your sheep. When one goes, they all go!"

"**I**f a farmer," the teacher asks, "has two thousand bushels of corn and gets a dollar a bushel, how much will he end up with?"

A farm boy answers, "Nothing. He wouldn't even cover the bank loan!"

"**S**uppose you had fifty cents in one pocket and fifty in the other, what would you have?"

"My hands in my dad's pockets!"

Then there were the two little rabbits who couldn't wait to get to school. The teacher was going to teach multiplication!

army

If army jokes were taken out of circulation, there'd be a lot of silence in the world. The same jokes work in every war. The following joke was used in three movies about World War II and in at least that many about World War I:

Sergeant: Fire at will!
Soldier: Which one is Will?

I mentioned the joke during one of my college seminars. A student, familiar with the area, had traced the same joke to magazines during the Civil War and joke books of the nineteenth century. Along came a college professor who worked the joke back to England in the seventeenth century. I'm certain somebody will trace it to the Norman Conquest and possibly the Roman legions. The glorious thing is that the joke was used on television any number of times and always worked. Due to my desire to be fair, the navy has its own category.

The commanding officer bragged about the base's power. "From here we can hit any target in Dallas, Denver, and Los Angeles."

A congressman asked, "What about Russian targets? Can you knock *them* out?"

The officer said, "Of course. As long as they're in Dallas, Denver, and Los Angeles!"

"The guy who designed that Alamo should give back the money."
"Why?"
"No back door!"

A mess officer was bugged because too much bread was being left over. Some of the soldiers complained that it was too hard. The mess officer said, "If Napoleon's troops had that bread, they'd have eaten it down to the last crumb."

A young soldier said, "I believe that, sir. But it was fresh then!"

The sergeant was in a rare mood as he finished drilling his company. He barked out a final order: "All right, you idiots, fall out!"

The men fell out, but one rookie stood firm. The sergeant stared as the rookie smiled. "There were a lot of them, weren't there, Sarge?"

The Vietnam War was at its height when Joe Taylor received his draft notice. It requested his presence and a urine sample. To con the draft board, Taylor filled a bottle with urine samples from his father, his sister, and the family dog.

At the draft board, Taylor waited to see what they would come up with. A doctor finally came out with a computer printout and said, "Your old man has diabetes, your sister is pregnant, your dog is in heat, and you're in the army!"

A master sergeant strode into the enlisted man's barracks and said, "Fellows, I have some good news and some bad news for you. The good news is that you all get a change of underwear tomorrow. The bad news is—Bobby Joe, you change with Bubba, Billy Bob, you change with Hank..."

I tried to put on my old army outfit the other day. I had to let out the tie!

When they landed on the beach at Normandy, he was the only guy in sight with a blanket and tanning lotion.

In a Swiss café, an American soldier on leave happened to sit next to another uniformed man who spoke with a thick Tyrolian accent. The American started to ask questions: "Would you take up arms to defend this country?"

The other man said, "Never."

The Yank pressed on. "How about your buddies at the next table—would they fight?"

"No, sir."

"And the two at the next table?"

"Nope."

"Why wouldn't you fight for your country?"

The uniformed man answered, "Because we're with the band!"

How can any place be good where the bed is a bunk and the kitchen is a mess?

He was stationed where the bullets were thickest—a munitions depot!

He owed his life to an Oriental girl who hid him in a cellar for two years. They were in San Francisco at the time!

He wanted to join the army as an 8F. In

case of an enemy invasion, they'd send him overseas!

It was a brilliant idea to make army fatigues and army food the same color!

A squad of recruits went out to the rifle range for a try at marksmanship. At two hundred yards, they fired. All missed. There wasn't a hit at a hundred yards. Or fifty. Finally the sergeant yelled, "Fix bayonets and charge! It's your only chance!"

The army jacket they issued to me was so long it came with shoelaces!

"How does your new uniform fit, soldier?"
"The coat is fine, but the pants are a little loose around the armpits!"

The army has a brand-new tank that costs two and a half million. The radio and heater are extra.

A veteran was entertaining his small son with stories of his wartime experiences. After the tenth anecdote, the child asked, "Pop, what'd you need the rest of the army for?"

As the regiment moved off, the crowd cheered. A youngster asked, "Who are all those cheering people?"
A veteran answered, "Those are the ones who aren't going!"

In my outfit, company punishment was seconds!

The general addressed the troops, "Keep on fighting, men. Never say die. Never quit. Never give up fighting, even if your ammunition is gone. When you run out of bullets, throw rocks. Only then should you run. I'm a little lame, so I'll start now!"

Everything issued was olive drab. One soldier fainted on the barracks lawn and they didn't find him for two days!

The sergeant looked at the new recruits and gulped unhappily. "Men," he bellowed, "I have a real easy job for the laziest guy in this outfit. Step forward!"
All the men stepped forward except for one rookie.
"How come you didn't step up with the others?" the sergeant asked.
"Too much trouble."

DRAFTEE: My name's Wright and you spelled it wrong twice. Two wrongs don't make a right.
COMPANY CLERK: That's right.
DRAFTEE: But it's wrong.
CLERK: If it's wrong, it can't be right.
DRAFTEE: You don't understand. My name's Wright.
CLERK: How do you write it, Wright?
DRAFTEE: That's not right.
CLERK: Then you don't write it Wright?
DRAFTEE: Right.
CLERK: Next!

After indulging a little too much at a local bar, two soldiers got into a slight brawl. The first pushed the second to the ground and pulled back his arm to deliver a blow, but was stopped by another soldier, who asked, "You wouldn't hit a man when he's down, would you?"
The first soldier answered, "What do you think I got him down for?"

"Why are you running away from the firefight?"
"'Cause I can't fly!"

Army shoes are leakproof. When it rains not a drop comes out!

The army is trying to become more attractive to recruits. In the mess hall now they have strolling violin players.

A draftee was being questioned by an army psychiatrist. "What do you think of the army?"

"I love it," the young man said. "I want to wear the uniform proudly and learn all about soldiering. Write that down."

The psychiatrist went on, "Will you be a capable soldier?"

"Sir, give me a gun and I'll show you. I'll shoot until the gun melts. If I can't get another weapon, I'll pick up a stick and go at the enemy with that. Then I'll go at them barehanded. I'll bite them if I have to. Write that down."

The psychiatrist said, "You sound a little crazy."

"Write that down!!"

A draftee was complaining, "Twenty years ago I went to a department store and asked Santa for a soldier's outfit. *Now* he gives me one."

A soldier writes home to his mother, "Dear Mom, I miss you, I miss Pa, but most of all I miss the little potty under my bed."

An answer came some time later: "Don't worry, son. You used to miss it when you were home too!"

A cowardly soldier was convicted and sentenced to be shot. As he and his execution team marched off through the mud and rain to a spot far from camp where the sentence would be carried out, he started to feel sorry for himself. The sergeant in charge of the detail said, "What are you complaining about? The rest of us have to walk back!"

The sergeant was in one of his rare moods as he lectured the recruits. "Let me ask you a simple question—what is fortification?" There was no response. Nor did any of the rookies answer when he repeated the question. Walking up to the new man who looked closest to normal, the sergeant barked right into his face, "What is fortification?"

The soldier gulped and managed an answer, "Two twentifications, Sarge!"

A recruit asked the supply sergeant, "Tell me the truth. This uniform fits me perfectly. Am I deformed?"

A friendly Vietnamese farmer who spoke some English spied a paratrooper. He said, "Much trouble for you to have to parachute down in such bad wind."

The paratrooper replied, "Man, I didn't come down in a parachute. I went up in a tent!"

GIRL: How were you wounded?
SOLDIER: A shell, miss.
GIRL: Did it explode?
SOLDIER: No. It crept up close and bit me!

A new recruit couldn't understand why they called him private. He slept in a room with eighty other guys!

A young soldier wrote his mother a note saying, "As I write this, there are shells flying overhead, bullets are zooming by, and everywhere I look there's bazooka fire."

A few weeks later he received an answer from his mother: "Don't butt in!"

FIRST PRIVATE: Got a pen I can borrow?

SECOND PRIVATE: Sure.

FIRST PRIVATE: Got some paper?

SECOND PRIVATE: Yup.

FIRST PRIVATE: Going past the mail room later?

SECOND PRIVATE: Sure thing.

FIRST PRIVATE: Wait till I finish this letter.

SECOND PRIVATE: Fine.

FIRST PRIVATE: One more thing—what's your girl's address?

It was the age when knighthood was in flower. A young lady was pounding away at a piece of iron with a sledgehammer. Another young lady saw her and asked, "What are you doing?"

The first one answered, "I'm making socks and a sweater for some soldier boy!"

A Frenchman ran into another Frenchman who had become a British citizen. The Frenchman berated the turncoat, ending up by asking him bitterly, "What did it get you, becoming an Englishman?"

The turncoat answered, "Well, for one thing—I won the Battle of Waterloo!"

On a brief holiday in town, a soldier met a young lady. One minute later he told her, "I don't know whether you're going to believe this or not, but I fell in love with you at first sight."

The young lady asked, "Are you sure?"

The soldier answered, "It has to be love at first sight. I only have a four-hour pass!"

A Southern soldier was trying to sidle out of camp unnoticed, but was seen by the guard. The guard asked him for his pass. The soldier said, "Look, buddy, I don't have any old pass, but that don't bother me none. I have a date with my girl in town. I'm fixing to keep it."

The guard stopped him. "If you try to get past this gate, I'm afraid I might have to shoot you."

The soldier shrugged his shoulders and replied, "I've got a mother up in heaven, a daddy down in hell, and a gal in town. And I'm going to see *one* of them tonight!"

A detachment of paratroopers was practicing in a rural area. One jumper started down on the property of an old mountain man and his very large family. One of the kids saw the chute floating down and yelled out to his father, "Pa, bring your shotgun. The stork is bringing them full-grown now!"

A recruit who wasn't really meant to soldier went out to the rifle range for the first time. He missed every target and most of the hills behind them. Despondent, he said to the sergeant, "I think I'll just go and shoot myself."

The sergeant said, "Better take a couple of extra bullets!"

"Why do you keep scratching yourself, soldier?"

"I'm the only one who knows where it itches, sir!"

The army is great. Where else can you sleep until four in the morning?

Some recruits love the sound of the bugles in the morning. It reminds them that the birds aren't sleeping later than they are.

My cousin was rejected by the army because he has an impediment in his back—he can't get off it!

A young soldier was making his first parachute jump. The corporal explained the procedure: "You count to ten and pull the first ripcord. If the chute doesn't open, pull the second. That should do it. Then, after you land, there'll be a truck waiting to pick you up."

The soldier checked his gear, called out the customary "Geronimo!" and jumped out of the plane. He counted to ten and pulled the ripcord. The chute failed to open. He pulled the second ripcord and the chute still didn't open. As he plummeted downward, he said, "I'll bet that goddamn truck won't be there either!"

A veteran out of the service for only a few days applied for a job at a large corporation. The application contained a line asking questions about work experience. One question asked, "What was your last job?" The veteran filled in, "U.S. Army." The next question asked, "Reason for leaving job." The soldier wrote, "Won the war!"

Pity the French soldier today. With AIDS everywhere, they can't win the Croix de Guerre because they can't find a general who'll kiss them!

One young soldier destroyed five bridges, blew up an ammo dump, and wiped out an important military installation. Fortunately, after that, they sent him overseas!

"Halt, who goes there?"
"You wouldn't know me. I'm new here!"

At the height of the Battle of Britain, an English pilot was shot down. Because of the camaraderie of men who fly, he was treated with great kindness by the Luftwaffe. His many wounds were attended to immediately. After examining him, the German doctor said, "Lieutenant, I'm afraid I have terrible news for you. I must amputate your right arm."

The pilot answered, "If you must, you must, sir. However, I would appreciate it if on your next bombing raid you'd be kind enough to drop my arm over England."

The request was carried out. A few days later, the German doctor said, "I have dreadful news—your left arm must be taken off. Awful gangrene."

The pilot made a request similar to the first, and his left arm was dutifully tossed out over England on the next raid.

Several days passed. The German doctor reported that the right leg was in trouble and would have to go. The pilot said, "If it must, it must. But please throw my leg out over England."

The German doctor studied him for a moment and said, finally, "Lieutenant, are you trying to escape?"

"Beg pardon, General, but the troops are revolting."
"Well, Captain, you're pretty repulsive yourself!"

If people think that old soldiers fade away, they ought to try to get into an old army uniform!

A recruit, a veteran of several hours in the army, was awakened by the barracks noncom at four in the morning. The recruit said, "Pal, better get to bed. We have a big day tomorrow!"

To cool his ardor, a soldier was given saltpeter in 1943. It's just beginning to work on him!

He was a country boy in a labor battalion, who had no mind for war or hard work. As he broke some rocks, he said to another soldier, "The next time they has a war, there's two of us ain't gonna be in it—me and the guy they send for me!"

An officer asked a soldier, "Why are you moving back? Didn't I tell you they were four to our one?"

The soldier said, "Well, I got my four!"

art

I come from a long line of painters. I have an uncle who painted walls. I have another uncle who painted MEN *on one door and* WOMEN *on the other. The fact is, I'm knowledgeable about art. I don't have any Old Masters, but I have an agent who bosses me around a lot!*

An artist stops painting for a moment, gapes at his nude model, and starts to hug and kiss her. Flushed, he says, "You're the first model I ever kissed."

"How many models have you had?"

"Three. Some flowers, a plate of fruit, and you!"

An artist specialized in paintings that showed hurricanes, violent storms at sea, and towns ravaged by typhoons. A visitor, studying the many paintings, said, "It's a shame you always have such bad weather!"

An artist painted a picture of a canary and thought he could sell it by calling it "Mother's Whistler!"

Then there's the showoff who bought a painting for fifty thousand dollars and framed the canceled check!

A couple is visiting a mansion in Newport. The host shows them dozens of paintings of his ancestors. When the host goes off for a minute, the man's wife asks, "Are those genuine Gainsboroughs?"

The husband answers, "They aren't even genuine ancestors!"

Then there's the absentminded sculptor who put his model to bed and started chiseling on his wife!

There was an old sculptor named Phidias,
Whose knowledge of art was invidious.
He carved Aphrodite
Without any nightie,
Which startled the purely fastidious.

"I'd like to give my artwork to a worthy charity."

"Try an institute for the blind."

Two children visiting a museum arrived at a copy of the Winged Victory. One child said, "She doesn't have a head."

The other one answered, "That's art. She doesn't need one!"

A country gent had a farm in Bucks County. An artist guest, having nothing to do one afternoon, painted a picture of the rural hideaway. The country gent liked the painting and paid the artist a thousand dollars for it.

Hearing about the transaction, the farmer next door laughed, "I'd have sold him my farm for five hundred!"

A modern artist, looking at a portrait he did of a client, is obviously upset. Another artist comes by and asks, "What's the matter?"

The first artist says, "Well, I did this portrait of Parsons and he wants me to fix the nose a little."

"Why don't you?"

"I can't find it!"

FIRST ARTIST: How's business?

SECOND ARTIST: Not bad. Johnson wants me to paint his children very badly.

FIRST ARTIST: You're the guy for the job!

"That painting cost me fifty thousand dollars."
"For *one* coat?"

"That painting is a wow."
"It's more than that. It's the wowsiest painting I ever saw."

One artist paints a complete canvas in a day and a half and thinks nothing of it. Nor does anybody else.

"What do you think of my painting?"
"It could be worse."
"I resent that."
"Okay, it couldn't be worse."

A girl reported to her friend that she'd met an artist the day before. She said, "He took me up to his apartment and showed me his etchings. Then he sold me two hundred dollars' worth!"

My uncle is sort of an artist. He draws welfare!

A sculptor needed a nude model. He interviewed several. The last was exactly what he'd been searching for, but she wanted fifteen dollars an hour. The sculptor was unwilling to go that high. He offered five dollars an hour. The model turned him down.

In desperate need of a model, the sculptor enlisted the services of his wife, who was stumpy and shapeless. As he did his best, the model happened by, peeked in his half-open door, and saw the wife. The model shook her head sadly and said, "See what you get for five dollars!"

A woman complained about her husband's virility: "He's like a modern painter. Two strokes and he's done!"

A famous abstract artist, lost in thought, was knocked down by a hit-and-run driver. To help the police find the culprit, the artist drew a sketch of the driver. In two hours, the police arrested the Statue of Liberty, a nun, and a hotdog stand!

"That painting is supposed to be of a ship on the ocean."
"Why isn't it?"

The model ascended the ladder
As Titian the artist had bade her.
The position, to Titian,
Suggested coition,
So he climbed up the ladder and had her!

An artist was weary of working, so when his model showed up for the day, he suggested that they merely have a glass of wine and talk.

As they sipped their claret, the artist heard a car arriving outside. He jumped up and said, "It's my wife! Quick, take off your clothes!"

He wanted to paint her in the nude, but she demanded that he keep his clothes on!

One artist used a strange medium. He painted everything on an empty stomach!

A good artist draws the line somewhere!

Auctions are weird. You can't pick anything up unless it's been knocked down first!

VIEWER: That doesn't look any more like a donkey than I do.
ARTIST: It couldn't.

A sculptor explained his art form: "You take a block of marble, a hammer, and a chisel, then you knock off all the marble you don't want!"

artificial birth

Getting to be the "in" topic. Read on and be ready for it.

People who make babies in glass tubes have it glass backwards!

It's a new thing—conception is now a spectator sport!

At a leading university, an eighty-year-old professor has come up with a pill that can make a woman pregnant. He's eighty. What does he care!

Do test tubes need foreplay?

One woman refused to have a test-tube baby because she didn't think the test tube would respect her in the morning.

They're trying to make artificial birth sexier. They now have a test tube with a mirror on the ceiling!

He has so many test-tube babies, on Father's Day he gets a card from Corning!

He wanted to have a test-tube baby, but the test tube told him it had a headache!

A little girl came running to her mother and asked, "Mommy, was I a test-tube baby?"
Her mother pats her on the head and answered, "No, my dear. You were a regular baby. Now get some Windex and wipe your face!"

In the works they have a robot able to bear babies. Unfortunately, they haven't been able to solve one drawback—what do they do when the robot gets morning malfunction?

She was such a fat baby, the test tube had stretch marks.

astronauts

I think about space a great deal. That comes from my genes. You've heard of flying saucers. My Uncle Charlie used to make the cups for them!

Two young astronauts were discussing the space program. One says, "Why do we have to go to the moon or Mars? Why don't we go straight to the sun?"
The other astronaut says, "If we come within ten million miles of the sun, we'll burn up."
"So we'll go at night!"

When starting their training, astronauts are given one caution, "Don't look down!"

Two astronauts land on the moon. They search the horizon for signs of life and see some movement far off. Getting on their ATV, they drive for hours, finally arriving at an area where two older men sit in the dust, working at sewing machines. One of the tailors looks up and asks, "Who are you?"
"We're astronauts."
The tailor says, "Astronauts they send us. We need pressers!"

Astronauts never get athlete's foot. They suffer from missile toe!

Two astronauts are deep in outer space. One exits the capsule for some testing. When he is finished, he tries to get back in, but the door is locked. He starts to knock on the door.
Inside the capsule, the other astronaut hears the rapping and asks, "Who's there?"

Two astronauts are hurtling through interplanetary space. Suddenly, on the video monitor in front of them are a dozen weird creatures with green skin, tails, and long antennae. One astronaut says, "My God, it's just like 'Star Trek'!"

The other says, "It *is* 'Star Trek.' You forgot to turn off the TV set!"

Two astronauts are deep in space. Suddenly, framed in front of them in the large observation window are a whole mass of strange creatures with squiggly antennae, pointed ears, and two sets of lips. One astronaut says, "It's just like 'Star Trek'!"

The other says, "Yeah, but I think it's a rerun!"

They should never send up three astronauts in one capsule. Sooner or later they'll start arguing about who gets the seat by the window!

It was dinnertime. One astronaut took his packaged meal and started through the escape door. The other astronaut asked, "Where are you going?"

The first astronaut answered, "I'm going to eat out!"

atlantic city

I'm glad that there are two places for gambling jokes. It was always unfair to pick on Las Vegas mercilessly, as did every performer who played there. Now, to paraphrase an ex-President, you have Atlantic City to kick around!

A gent takes the train to Atlantic City, goes to his room to change, heads for the casino, and spends the next forty-eight hours at the craps table. His last penny gone, he walks away from the table and mumbles, "This is the last time I'll ever spend in the country!"

Years ago, people went to Atlantic City to get tanned. Now they go to get faded.

Some people go to Atlantic City to get away from it all, but most of the time it all gets away.

Where else but in Atlantic City? An entertainer arrives in his private jet, puts on an outfit that costs ten thousand dollars, works with sixty musicians, eight backup singers, and opens his show with "I Gotta Be Me."

He took a nine-to-five job in Atlantic City. He didn't like the work, but the odds were nice.

People can gamble everywhere in Atlantic City. One fellow went into a laundromat and lost his laundry!

There's a great way to beat Atlantic City. When you're driving down and see a sign that says "Gas," take it!

One guy flew into Atlantic City and didn't lose a penny. He walked into the plane's engine.

Atlantic City is one of the few places where you can enjoy yourself without having a good time!

A man was playing at Trump's and beating the table. After his tenth roll, he said to his wife, "Honey, tonight you're going to sleep with the richest man in Atlantic City."

He played on and started to lose. After his last hundred went on the line, his wife said, "Tell me. Is he going to my room or do I go to his?"

Having lost every penny in a casino, a man walks out and decides to end his life in the ocean. As he nears the water's edge, he sees something flicker in the sand. The shiny object is a dime. A voice says to him, "Go back to the casino."

Back in the casino, he puts the dime in a slot machine. The jackpot is fifteen dollars. The voice says, "Go to the blackjack table."

At the blackjack table, he plays for ten minutes and amasses fifty dollars. The voice moves him on to roulette, then on to the dice table. He is winning ten thousand dollars and is about to pocket it when the voice says, "Let it ride." Dutifully, he rolls the dice again and loses. The voice says, "You can go back to the ocean now."

A man loses his stake and is walking the streets aimlessly when he runs into a friend who is counting a thick wad of bills. The friend explains, "Before I go in to gamble, I stop off at the Catholic church two blocks away and pray. After that, I can't lose."

The first man is impressed. On his next junket to Atlantic City, he gets off the train and goes right to a church. He prays with incredible fervor. A few minutes later he heads for a gambling palace. Three rolls of the dice and he's busted.

Again he walks the streets and runs into the other fellow, who has another wad of money. The loser says, "I did what you told me to do. I got off the train and went right to pray. Then I walked into Resorts International and got murdered."

The winner asks, "Which church did you go to?"

"St. Joseph's, down the block."

"No wonder you lost. St. Joseph's is for Trump's!"

What they need in Atlantic City is a good detour!

The best throw of the dice is to throw them away.

A wino put a quarter in an Atlantic City parking meter and said, "How do you like this? I won an hour!"

A gambler and his wife checked into a fancy Atlantic City hotel. While the wife dressed for dinner, the man went to the gaming tables. In fifteen minutes he had won thousands. Leaving the money on the table, he threw the dice again and made a seven. The pressure was too much for him, his heart gave out and he slumped to the ground, dead.

One of the pit bosses went up to the room, knocked on the door, and, when it was opened, told the woman, "Madam, your husband dropped dead!"

"No!" she shrieked.

The pit boss said, "Would you like two-to-one odds on it?"

attorneys

My attorney threatened to sue me if I put jokes about lawyers in this book. The threat didn't bother me. He's never won a case yet.

My attorney is brilliant. He didn't bother graduating from law school. He settled out of class!

Most attorneys practice because it gives them a grand and glorious feeling. Hand them a grand and they feel glorious!

A law office was held up recently. The stickup man lost two hundred dollars!

A wall between heaven and hell fell down. Saint Peter called over to the Devil, "Send over an engineer to get this wall back up."

Satan answered, "My men don't have time for that."

"If you don't, I'll sue you."

Satan asked, "Where are you going to get a lawyer?"

A tough case was being argued in court. The defense attorney, feeling that he was in trouble, sent the judge a bottle of hundred-year-old brandy. The defendant was fit to be tied.

"The judge'll kill me. Trying to bribe him! We're dead!"

"I don't think so," his attorney told him. "I sent it in the other lawyer's name!"

A doctor, a dentist, and an attorney were in a boat together when a wave came along and washed them overboard. Unable to get back into the boat, they decided two would hold on and the third would swim to shore for help. The doctor volunteered.

The dentist said, "There are hundreds of sharks between here and the land. You'll get killed."

Without further discussion, the attorney took off. As he swam toward the shore, the sharks moved aside. The dentist said, "That's a miracle!"

The doctor said, "That's professional courtesy!"

One lawyer's client believed in reincarnation. In his will he left everything to himself!

A gangster was being coached on his appearance in court.

"You will tell the truth," his attorney said. "Just the plain and simple truth."

The gangster said, "I'll try anything once!"

One thug was having a tough time getting an attorney. Each time a lawyer learned that he hadn't stolen the money, the lawyer quit!

A man walks past a grave and reads the writing on the tombstone. It says, "Here lies an attorney and an honest man."

The man muses, "How did they get two of them in one grave?"

A lawyer says to a witness on the stand, "Now, sir, did you, or did you not, on the date in question or at any time, say to the defendant or anyone else that the statement imputed to you and denied by the plaintiff was a matter of moment or otherwise? Answer me, yes or no."

"Yes or no, what?"

"Law is crazy."
"Why's that?"
"They swear a man to tell the truth."
"So what?"
"Every time he starts to, some damn lawyer objects!"

One lawyer said to the other, "You're a cheat." The other said, "You're a liar!"

The judge rapped with his gavel. "Now that both sides have identified one another, let's go on with the trial!"

Only a lawyer could write documents with more than ten thousand words and call them briefs!

"Ma'am, have you ever been a witness in a suit like this?"
"No, sir. The only time I was in court I wore a blue outfit!"

A funeral was being held. A latecomer sidled in and sat down next to a man who happened to be an attorney. Hearing the minister start to talk about Jesus, the latecomer asked, "What stage are we in?"

The lawyer answered, "He just opened for the defense!"

We should bless all the lawyers. If we didn't have them, who would get us out of the trouble they got us into?

He was a brilliant attorney. The other day he got a parking ticket reduced to second-degree manslaughter.

A lawyer comes in handy when a felon needs a friend.

Fresh from school, the lawyer finished a glowing summation for the defense. Then he turned to the judge and asked, "Your Honor, will you charge the jury?"

The judge said, "I don't think so. They don't look too well off, so I'll let them keep what they make on the side!"

"Your honor, must I be tried by a jury of twelve women?"
"Why not?"
"I can't fool my wife. How am I going to fool twelve of them?"

A young girl explains her field trip to a court. "The judge made a speech, some other men made a speech, then they put twelve of them into a dark room to be developed!"

"Do you believe in capital punishment?"
"Only if it's not too severe!"

Only in Ireland. The judge asked a defendant, "Do you wish to challenge any members of the jury?"

The defendant said, "I'm not in very good shape, Your Honor, but I think I could handle those two in back!"

authors

Having written a dozen books, I have learned to take the barbs thrown at me. Of the book previous to this one, a comedian said, "He's written another book. Now if he would only read one!"

AUTHOR: I once got ten dollars a word.
FRIEND: How was that?
AUTHOR: I talked back to the judge!

Salome made Oscar Wilde.

A kid in school was a little shaky on his English literature when he wrote, "William Shakespeare was born in 1564, supposedly on his birthday!"

"Name two ancient sports."
"Antony and Cleopatra!"

"What was one of the greatest dates in history?"
"One of them must have been Romeo's with Juliet!"

"My husband writes fiction."
"My husband speaks it."

"I just got money for my last novel."
"Which publisher?"
"No publisher. UPS—they lost it!"

He must be a good writer. Even his dog poured over his last book!

He recently finished his last book. At least people hope it is!

He has often been compared to great writers of the past—and unfavorably too!

The wife of a successful writer hired a maid. Day after day, the maid saw the writer around the house at all hours. Worried about her job, she went to her employer and said, "You pay me a hundred a week. I'm willing to work for less until your husband finds a job!"

"How'd your novel come out?"
"Well, it proved beyond a doubt that it wasn't one of those trashy best-sellers!"

Then there's the Hebrew mystery writer who gave up. He always revealed the killer on the first page!

"How are you going to paint a true picture of life in Tibet? You've never been there."
Neither have any of my readers!

"How are you getting on with your magazine writing?"
"I'm holding my own. They send me back as much as I send them!"

A writer ran into an astute critic one afternoon and they sat down for a cup of coffee. The writer said, "I can't understand it—I'm a big seller now, yet my work isn't nearly as good as it was in the beginning."
The critic answered, "Your work's just as good as it ever was. Your taste is getting better!"

He wanted to be an author in the worst way, and he made it!

His books sell like wildfire. Everybody burns them!

"Do you write for money?"
"In every letter."

He started to make some money writing. He started with bad checks!

He wrote something that was accepted recently by a magazine—a check for a year's subscription!

A wife complained about her husband, "He's writing a novel. I don't know why. For three dollars he can buy one!"

A play opened and closed on Broadway in one night. One critic said, "I hear the playwright worked six months on this drama. It's a shame. All work and no play!"

He started out by writing dime novels. He became famous. Now he gets fifteen cents a novel!

One man spent thirty years writing a book about jail. In fact, it took him twenty years to finish one sentence!

There was a young writer named John
Whose pornographic works turned me on.
For those who will read,
That's as good as the deed,
Once your get-up has got up and gone!

One writer spent all of his time in jail writing escape literature!

He got the plot of his latest novel from the movie version of the one before that!

automobiles

Man's greatest love used to be for the little woman. Then he fell in love with his car. He's in trouble because both talk back to him now! The next move is for a car to get a headache!

The other day he lost control of his car. He couldn't keep up his payments!

A man took his wife and mother-in-law for a Sunday drive. The women were sitting in the back seat and were the worst backseat drivers of all time. Do this. Do that. Don't turn here. Stay closer to the right. The ladies wouldn't shut up.

After a while they reached a railroad crossing, and as luck would have it, the car stalled in the middle of the tracks. In the distance a train approached. The husband said, "I got my end across, girls. Let me see what you can do with yours!"

Who can forget the auto mechanic who celebrated his tenth wedding anniversary by bringing in his wife and trying to get the worn-out parts replaced!

Some cars have things that'll last a lifetime—payments!

A car is something your kid manages to get into the garage on the last drop of gas!

A wife told her husband, "Be an angel and let me drive." He did and he is!

I have a five-passenger car. One drives and four push.

The only thing that works on my car is the clock.

Two nuns were on a Sunday sortie into the countryside when they ran out of gas. The only container in the car was a chamber pot that was used when youngsters were taken on picnics.

The nuns went up to a nearby farmhouse and begged enough gas to get them to the next town, a few miles away. The farmer gave them as much gas as the chamber pot could hold.

Returning to the car, the nuns started to put the gas into the tank. A farmhand, not far off, looked and said, "Wow, do they have faith!"

Some of the new minicars stop on a dime. They can't get over it!

A man in Chicago accidentally put a Canadian dime in a parking meter. The next day he got a ticket from the Mounties!

I have a baby car. It goes everywhere with a rattle!

The new minicars have a special heater. It's called the cigarette lighter!

Some new cars come with a silencer. It fights right over her mouth!

For some reason, since the cops have gotten lady drivers, they don't have unmarked cars anymore!

He took the phone out of his car the other day. It was too much trouble running out to answer it all the time!

The way things go wrong with cars today, the ideal second car is a tow truck!

The Rolls-Royce can't be much of a car. Very few people drive them!

The trick is to drive so that your license expires before you do!

A man returned to the dealer who'd sold him a brand-new car and complained, "Whenever I get up to any speed, it makes a noise like a hundred castanets playing. What can I do?"

The dealer said, "Hum 'La Cucaracha'!"

A man in his beat-up old car drove up to a toll booth. The toll collector said, "Two dollars."

The owner said, "Sold!"

Car manufacturers spend years designing cars with smooth, sleek lines. Then they sell you a ski rack so you can put two tons of junk on top!

What the world really needs is a windshield wiper that won't hold parking tickets!

He always had trouble finding a parking place, so he bought a parked car!

One Texan never bothers with air-conditioning for his Cadillac. He keeps six of them in his freezer!

Some cars are expertly designed. One of them has a place to hold your ownership papers, a pack of gum, and a box of Kleenex. It's called the trunk!

"The engine seems to be missing, dear."
"Forget it. It doesn't show!"

There used to be a time when opportunity knocked and engines didn't!

"What part of the car causes the most accidents?"
"The nut behind the wheel!"

The doctor told me that he'd have me on my feet in no time. It worked. To pay his bill I had to sell my car.

Don't drive as if you owned the road. Drive as if you owned the car!

A man came over to me one day and asked me if I wanted to get screwed. I told him yes, so he sold me an Edsel.

Why do auto mechanics carry rags when they have perfectly good seatcovers to wipe their hands on?

American cars are going to be around for a long, long time. I'd bet my Kaiser on it!

I have one of those new subcompacts. It has an extra powerful gear for getting off gum!

The best time to buy a used car is when you're moving. The new neighbors'll think you bought it new!

I know a fellow who put a beard on his Ford and told everybody it was a Lincoln!

B

babies

No audience in the world can resist jokes and stories about babies. Julius Caesar would have lived to a ripe old age had he greeted his fellow Romans at the Senate door with, "Fellows, would you like to hear what my kid did today?" Or, "I have a nephew about three months old. Have you ever heard the expression, 'I'll be a monkey's uncle'? Well, I am!"

On second thought, it's possible that Brutus and the guys would have given Julius the shiv earlier. As Caesar said to Brutus, "Et tu?" And Brutus answered, "No, I only ate one!"

"It must be time to get up, dear."
"How do you know?"
"The baby's fallen asleep!"

To improve his virility, an older man went to Europe and had an implant of monkey glands. In time, and after many attempts, his wife became pregnant and ultimately went into labor. After an endless wait in the reception room, the father was thrilled to see the doctor appear. "Congratulations," the doctor said. "You're the father of a fine baby."
"Is it a boy or a girl?"
"We don't know yet. It won't climb down from the chandelier!"

NURSE: Sir, you've just become the father of twins.
MAN: Don't tell my wife. I want to surprise her!

A baby brightens up a home. Since ours came, the lights have been on all night!

Don't all babies look just like the richest uncle in the family?

The hospital resident was making the rounds of the maternity ward. Stopping at a bed, he asked the expectant mother, "When are you expecting?"
"On the eighth."
At a second bed, he repeated his question and was answered, "On the eighth."
After getting the same answer at a half-dozen beds, he finally came to one in which the expectant mother was napping. He turned to the woman in the next bed, "Do you know when she's expecting?"
The woman answered, "It can't be the eighth, because she didn't go on that picnic!"

A young lady, new to the game, was in the middle of labor. After much work and pain, she was delivered of the baby. The mother said to the nurse, "Will you do me a favor?"
"Certainly."
"Will you go down to the waiting room and ask for Al?"
"What is the message?"
"Tell him that if this is what married life is like, our engagement is off!"

"My nurse used to drop me a lot."
"What did your mother do?"
"She got me a shorter nurse!"

A baby is an addition that becomes a deduction.

Every baby born in America is endowed with life, liberty, and owes about a quarter of a million toward the national debt!

"I hear you have a new baby at your house."
"Yup."
"Is he going to stay?"
"I think so. He took all his clothes off!"

"My sister is expecting a little stranger."
"Oh, they'll get to know each other!"

One woman got bruise marks in her womb from the baby holding on until after the wedding!

"My sister is going to have a baby."
"Did you call her up?"
"I don't have to. She knows about it!"

Our baby is a member of British royalty—the Prince of Wails!

The day my kid was born, he cried like a baby!

The doctor who'd deliver the Bryant baby said to Mr. Bryant, "That'll be three thousand dollars."
  Mr. Bryant said, "I'll pay you next month."
  "Nothing doing. *Your* father still hasn't paid me for *you!*"

"My baby brother was born yesterday, and he's in the hospital."
"No kidding! Sick already?"

They had a baby buggy and they used to keep their dog in it. When the baby came, they put the baby in the buggy. Now they have not only a baby buggy, but a buggy baby!

There is always the sad story of the baby who was born gray-haired and remained that way until somebody discovered that the mother had bad eyesight and was always powdering the wrong end!

A Martian listened to an earthling describe how babies were made. The Martian laughed and said, "Amazing! That's how we make bicycles!"

A new mother was overanxious about the welfare of her new baby. Nobody was allowed near the child without first putting on a surgical mask. After a few months the baby started to act up and a neighbor thought that it might be teething. "Put your finger in the baby's mouth," the neighbor said, half-smiling, "but I think maybe you ought to boil it first!"

When I was born it was pouring rain. The stork refused to budge. A sea gull had to bring me!

A man was away when he received a wire from his wife. It said, "Twins born today." The man was thrilled until he read the bottom of the wire. It said, "More to come."

A telephone operator became the proud mother of twins. From force of habit she even gave her husband the wrong number!

An unwed mother was delivered of a baby with bright red hair. The mother's hair was black as a raven. The doctor asked, "What was the color of the father's hair?"

The mother said, "I have no idea. He never took off his hat!"

One of the tricks of being a happy parent is to fall asleep when the baby isn't looking.

What I can't understand is why people with kids and people without kids both feel sorry for the other.

A man stood in front of the large glass window beyond which all the new babies were on display. Father O'Hara, the padre of the hospital, which happened to be Catholic, saw the happy look on the man's face and asked, "Is this your firstborn?"

The man said, "No, sir. This is my fifth."

"Oh, and what parish do you attend?"

"I'm a Baptist."

The padre feigned a smile and moved on. Reaching the nurse's station, he whispered to the nurse on duty, "Keep your eye on that man over there. There's a good chance he's a sex fiend."

Off the coast of Maine, a lobsterman pulled up to a boat in which Enos, another lobsterman, was pulling in his traps. The lobsterman called out, "Thought you'd like to know that your wife just gave you a baby son."

"How much did he weigh?" Enos asked.

"Four pound ten."

"Don't seem much of a deal. Hardly got my bait back."

Mother's milk is the best thing for babies. It's nutritious, cheap, satisfying, and doesn't make crumbs!

A woman had a baby about six months after her marriage. The father asked the doctor, "How does that happen?"

"Don't let it bother you," the doctor answered. "This can happen with the first child, but never again!"

A busy executive received a phone call from a nurse at the hospital. The nurse informed him that he was the father of a fine young son. The executive answered, "Why call me about it. My wife always takes care of those matters!"

A doctor delivered a fine male baby who had a wide grin on his face. After the usual smack on the fanny, the baby continued to beam. The doctor turned to the nurse and shrugged his shoulders. He had no idea what could have caused such glee. The nurse pointed to the baby's tightly clenched fist. Prying it open, the doctor saw a birth-control pill in the baby's palm.

When they have a baby, most women worry about getting their figures back. My mother worried about getting my father back!

Two women, Mrs. Selden and Mrs. Cabot, delivered at about the same time, so both were in the hospital. As they walked off a typical hospital lunch, Mrs. Cabot, a woman given to toniness, told her companion, "When our first child was born, my husband bought me a floor-length mink coat."

Mrs. Selden nodded and said, "That's nice."

"When our second child was born, my husband bought me a beautiful white Rolls-Royce."

"That's nice."

"Now that we have our third child, my husband just bought me a sixty-carat diamond ring."

"That's nice."

"Does your husband do anything for you?"

"Certainly. He sent me to charm school."

"Charm school?"

"Yes, because I used to say 'Bullshit.' Now I say 'That's nice.'"

"I hear that God has sent you two more brothers and a sister?"

"Yup, and He knows where the money's going to come from. I heard Pop say that!"

"Do the twins make a lot of noise at night?"

"Well, I can't be sure because one of them screams so loud we can't hear the other one!"

A woman is well into her pregnancy, as is obvious from her roundness. Wishing to involve her six-year-old son in the birth process, she asks, "What would you rather have—a boy or a girl?"

The boy says, "If it wouldn't get you out of shape too much, how about a pony?"

babies (insults)

A good way to seal friendships and win elections (and even get killed, if the guy who showed you the baby's picture in his wallet is bigger than you).

The police are still looking for the stork who brought him.

On her birthday, his folks go to the zoo and throw rocks at the stork.

She was so ugly, the stork who brought her waited around until dark.

She was so ugly, her parents put out a contract on her.

He was such an ugly baby, his folks sued the sperm bank.

He was such an ugly baby, his father went to court to have his vasectomy made retroactive.

She was so ugly when she was born, for six months her folks diapered the wrong end.

She was so ugly, when she was born the doctor slapped her mother.

He was so ugly when he was born, his mother was arrested for littering.

A woman boarded a bus with her baby and sat down next to a man. Because the baby kept making baby noises, the man's attention was drawn to it. He said to the mother, "That's the ugliest baby I ever saw! I mean, that's an ugly baby! Ugly!"

When the bus stopped, the woman rushed to the driver and complained. Angrily she demanded that the unchivalrous gent be thrown off the bus. The bus driver tried to soothe her, telling her that some people are born rude and will remain rude forever. He added, "Calm down, lady. Everything will be fine from here on in." Then he reached into his lunchbox and said, "And here's a banana for your monkey!"

He was such an unwanted baby, they bought him sandpaper diapers!

His parents spent a year looking for a loophole in his birth certificate.

He became a father recently. They must have lowered the requirements!

His father was an electrician and he was his first shock!

When she was born, they didn't know whether to buy a crib or a cage!

He was a war baby. As soon as they saw him, his parents started fighting!

Is that a girl? Is that a girl? That's what everybody kept asking—"Is that a girl?"

The stork who delivered him flew backwards so it wouldn't have to look at his face!

Her mother was naïve. When somebody asked her if she knew the baby's formula, she said, "Sure. Two hickeys, some music, and turn out the lights!"

He fell out of his crib when he was brought home, but he didn't get hurt. Luckily, he fell on his head!

She was named after her father—Army!

It was easy to explain her birth. Her father's car stalled, but her mother didn't.

Her mother was so flat-chested, the baby had to nurse through a straw!

He was such a big baby, the doctor was afraid to slap him when he was born!

His parents were too poor to have children. A neighbor had him!

When his mother asked the father to change the baby, he wasn't sure they'd give him another kid!

His bath toys should have been a toaster and an electric clock!

They must have found him in the bottom drawer of the Missing Persons Bureau!

When he was born, his father tried to collect on his accident insurance!

He's descended from a long line his mother listened to.

The stork who brought him resigned the next day and went into wading.

She was so ugly, it looked as if the stork had made a crash landing.

People looked at her and wondered where the organ grinder was.

She was such an ugly baby, the stork had her sent by mail.

It's possible that the doctor who came up with test-tube babies had an ugly wife.

He was an unwanted child. When his folks gave him a rattle, it was still attached to the snake.

When she was a baby, she bawled all night. Now only the spelling has changed.

He's the son his father never had.

He must be of noble birth. He screws everybody royally.

Most babies come out of the womb. He must have come out of another place, because he's a turd.

She should have named her baby Bonus. She got him from the boss.

They should have called him Napoleon, he has so many bony parts.

She should have named her baby Target, because everybody had a shot at it!

She was pregnant for twelve months, but then she always carried things too far.

When he was born, the doctor slapped him because he had no right being up there.

He was born old. When he was a teenager, his acne had liver spots.

He was an unloved baby. When he was missing, his folks tried to get his face *off* milk cartons.

She accused her husband of being unfaithful because he wasn't the father of the baby.

He was such an unwanted baby, he was breast-fed by his father.

When the doctor who delivered her walked out of the delivery room, he was arrested for leaving the scene of a crime.

When he was born, his parents willed him to the Missing Persons Bureau!

When he was born, his mother went into hard labor. Now his father's serving it!

His folks refused to have him circumcised. They were afraid of brain damage!

His mother didn't want him. She didn't have her first child until six years after he was born!

His mother never knew she was giving birth. She thought the doctor was just lancing a boil.

She was born in the year God knows when!

He cried a great deal when he was a baby. His mother wasn't bothered. She wouldn't change him for a million in gold. The father said, "Change him. Maybe he'll stop crying!"

She was born in the crash of '29. That was the year the doctor dropped her!

He was an only child, and he still wasn't his father's favorite!

When he was born, his father went around showing people the kid's picture that came with the wallet!

He was born at home. His mother took one look at him and *then* she went to the hospital!

In the hospital, his father looked at him and then took a turn for the nurse!

He looked as though he was born into a wall at fifty miles an hour.

When he was born, two nurses jumped on chairs.

When he was born, his mother started to sing "Melancholy Baby," because he had a shape like a melon and a face like a collie.

He was born an only twin.

When he was born, the doctor sent a bill and a condolence card.

He was born of passion and a condom that had been in his father's wallet too long!

He was a premature baby from an ejaculation of the same name!

It was a beautiful scene: His father and mother got into a taxi and his father said, "City Hall, then Doctor's Hospital, and go like crazy!"

The stork brought him and then went right to confession!

baby-sitters

My mother-in-law moved in with us. My wife felt that we could save a lot of money on baby-sitters. Then one day I realized we didn't have any kids! Eventually we got a son. My mother-in-law wouldn't sit. She said that she already had access to the refrigerator anyway!

The lady of the house had to let the baby-sitter go . . . because her husband wouldn't!

A baby-sitter is somebody who feeds the baby at twelve, two, and four. She feeds herself at one, three, and five!

We found a great baby-sitter—an Eskimo girl who lived in a refrigerator anyway!

Our last baby-sitter got the layout of the house immediately. Right off, she knew that the way to every room was through the fridge!

Little Harold was seven and liked to be pampered. Marie, his baby-sitter, carried him everywhere. If he wanted to go to the kitchen from the den, Marie would hold him to her bosom and bring him there. An hour after the sitting assignment began, Marie received a visit from her mother, who had popped in to see if everything was going well. Seeing that Marie was carrying the boy everywhere, the mother said, "He's seven. Why are you carrying him around like that?"

Harold turned from where his head had been buried in the girl's ample bosom and said, "Lady, am I bothering *you?*"

They found a great way for the sitter to keep watching the baby. They put the kid in the refrigerator!

The house had a big TV, a VCR, a dozen movies, and tons of food in the refrigerator, but the sitter turned down the job because the people wanted to leave the kid home!

The baby-sitter couldn't find the baby for hours, but she looked away from the TV and there it was!

They called their baby-sitter Mary Poopins. The slightest thing was too much for her!

A husband and wife returned from a night out to see the living room in a shambles. Candy wrappers were strewn all about. An inch of cookie crumbs covered the carpeting. The coffee table was wet with spilled milk and sodas. Getting the baby-sitter's attention from where she was watching a movie, the lady of the house said, "Look at this place! It's a pigsty! You told me you were intelligent and you knew how to take care of a child. But look at this room!"

The sitter answered, "I never said I was neat!"

Mrs. Grayson divorced Mr. Grayson. Mrs. Grayson got the house and Mr. Grayson got the baby-sitter—about two years before the divorce. Which was why Mrs. Grayson divorced him.

After a night of baby-sitting, fifteen-year-old Marsha was rushed to the hospital for immediate surgery. They had to remove a phone from her ear!

A woman calls an agency and asks, "Do you have a baby-sitter who knows the martial arts?"

The lady from the agency asks, "Is your child that rough?"

The woman answers, "The kid's a pussy-cat. The sitter will have to know some martial arts later, when my husband drives her home!"

A couple returns home from a dinner party to see their small son and the baby-sitter pooped out on the couch from having devoured a large box of candy, a huge bowl of potato chips, and pounds of peanuts. The wife says, "This makes me ill!"

The boy says, "That'll give you an idea of how *we* feel!"

A recent baby-sitter asked us for references. I wrote a note saying that she was a good sleeper and had a terrific appetite!

We have a baby-sitter who loves bananas. All evening long she eats bananas. But we keep her because I don't have to drive her back home. She just swings through the trees to her house!

Our baby-sitter does her homework while we're away. The other night we came home and found her on the couch with her boy-friend doing a sex education assignment!

The younger generations live with television. We had a sitter over last week, when the TV set was broken. She went into the auxiliary room and watched laundry.

A couple return from a night out and find the house in a shambles. The husband starts to berate the baby-sitter, who looks at him indignantly and says, "I'm going home to Mother!"

We break even with baby-sitting. We give our sitter a dollar. At about ten o'clock, the baby refuses to go to sleep until the sitter gives him a dollar. When we get home, we won't promise to get a sitter the next night unless the kid give *us* a dollar!

We keep looking for a sitter with an impediment in her reach!

bachelors

A man doesn't know what it means to give up his bachelorhood until he's married. But then it's too late! Let's face it—things went pretty well for Adam when he was single!

A bachelor is a man who doesn't have anybody to share the trouble he'd have if he was married.

A bachelor is a man who prefers to have loved and lost to getting up for the 2:00 A.M. feeding.

A bachelor believes that one can live as cheaply as two.

A bachelor never forgets that he's a thing of beauty and a boy forever.

His marriage vow is never to take one.

He'd rather have a woman on his mind than on his neck.

A bachelor is a guy who hasn't let a woman pin anything on him since he wore diapers.

I visited a bachelor buddy the other night. He was standing in the kitchen washing his dish.

To a bachelor, planned parenthood means living with his folks.

He who hesitates is lost—unless he's a bachelor.

A bachelor wants a gal in his arms, but not on his hands.

It's easy to pick out the bachelors in a laundromat. They're the ones stuffing their clothes into the video machine!

A nice old gent in Miami Beach met a woman only a year or two younger than he. They became fast friends. Every night they'd go up to her apartment, have tea and cookies, and engage in pleasant chatter. One day the old gent ran into a friend who asked, "Why don't you marry the lady?"

The old gent said, "Then where would I spend my evenings?"

Many wives hate it when their husbands go out on the town with their bachelor buddies. The husbands always come home so depressed!

A bachelor is a man who thinks before he acts, and then doesn't act.

A bachelor is a man who never makes the same mistake once.

A bachelor is a man who has found the secret of happiness and will stay that way.

A bachelor is a man who's crazy to get married, and he knows it.

A bachelor is a man who doesn't want to; a bigamist *has* two.

A bachelor is a man who doesn't have any children to speak of.

A bachelor is a man who believes in life, liberty, and the happiness of pursuit.

A bachelor is a man who can get into bed from either side.

Bachelors know more about women than married men do—which could explain why they're still single.

Most bachelors are never lonesome. They spend a lot of time listening to the troubles of their married friends.

She was an ideal thing for a bachelor—an overnight bag.

bad debts, bankruptcy, and deadbeats

Somebody once said, "Neither a borrower nor a lender be—but if you have to be one or the other, be a borrower!" With some people I know, the previous statement is the Eleventh Commandment, and the only one to which they adhere.

A collection agency called a gent who owed a fair amount of money. He was indignant at the call and said, "Look, your bill came this morning and I put it on top of all the bills on my desk for early consideration. At the end of thirty days I put the top bill on the bottom of the stack and it stays there. If you don't stop annoying me, I'll throw your bill out altogether!"

A lucky deadbeat found a wallet. In a matter of days he used the American Express card to run up a large bill. He was arrested and brought before a judge. After hearing the evidence, the judge became furious and said to the defendant, "To make sure you know the severity of your crime, I'm going to fine you two thousand dollars!"

The deadbeat said, "Okay, Your Honor. But can I put it on my MasterCard?"

He owes so much money, his will is made out to the small claims court!

I light my cigars with hundred-dollar bills. Some are a year overdue, some are two years overdue.

"Who should we pay first—the gas company or the doctor?"
"The gas company. What can the doctor turn off?"

"Here's a new outfit I bought for a song, dear."
"Send in the guy who sold it to you and I'll sing for him!"

I just burned a hundred-dollar bill. It's easier to burn them than to pay them.

Bankruptcy is when you plan on early retirement but your company beats you to it!

A fellow says, "I'm not too thrilled to hear that we're in a depression. I still owe a quarter of a million from the boom!"

A man took a whole stack of bills and tossed them into the trash with a contented sigh, saying to a friend, "It's a pleasure not to have to hold on to those bills anymore."

The friend said, "Did you pay all of them?"

"I didn't pay any. But all the duplicates are so I can throw these out!"

"I came up with something to keep my bills down."
"What's that?"
"A paperweight!"

One gent came up with a brilliant idea for people to whom he owed money. He puts some of them on his "preferred" list. They would know in thirty days that they weren't going to get paid. Regular clients wouldn't know for six months!

A man called his creditors together and told them, "I owe you about a million. My assets come to twelve hundred dollars. You can divvy that up. If not, you can just cut me up into small pieces and divide those."

One client said, "If we do that, can I have his gall?"

One fine gent took a cab to bankruptcy court and named the cabbie as a creditor!

When he borrows money, he says, "I'll be eternally indebted to you." And he means it!

He's always postdating checks. His tombstone will probably read, "He died June first, as of the twentieth!"

He owes a lot to his tailor!

A collection agency was hired to collect from a deadbeat. After many months, the original creditor called the agency and said, "Look, I detest that guy. I'd move heaven and earth to go after him."

The agency man answered, "It won't do you any good. He's not in either place. He died last week!"

badges

I'm an honorary sheriff in eight places. I have some wonderful badges. One of them looks official, although I really never knew what I could do with it. One day I managed to go fifty in a twenty-mile-per-hour zone and was stopped by a traffic cop. As a hint, I showed him the badge, and he told me what I could do with it!

A man was made the police chief in a nudist colony. He liked the life, but putting on the badge was murder!

There's a town in the West that's very poor. The posse has to ride out two to a badge!

A Boy Scout wanted to earn a merit badge, so he started to help old ladies cross the street. The first day, it took him five hours to help three old ladies across the street. Two of them didn't want to go!

In one town in the Midwest the police are notoriously corrupt. Even their badges are in the shape of a pretzel!

bad luck

I put a horseshoe over my door for good luck. I came home last night and it fell on me. I believe that "bad luck" jokes are good for you. People laugh because they're glad it didn't happen to them. It also evokes pity, which is a good dynamic for jokes if you don't have too much talent!

A man started off with a great deal of good luck. One morning he learned that he'd inherited a million dollars. From that moment on, however, his luck went sour. One of the codicils of the will said that in order to accept the money, he'd have to live in either Italy or France. He chose France. In France he had to choose again, this time between getting his fortune in red wine or white wine. He chose white. A glut of white wine wiped out the price. Red wine tripled in price. His money gone, the man sold his possessions and bought an airline ticket. This time he had to choose between New York and Atlanta. He chose Atlanta. One hour into the flight, the plane started to shake. Knowing how unlucky he was, the man went into the cockpit and told the pilot, "If I stay aboard this plane, you'll crash. Let me jump out and save all these innocent passengers."

The pilot said, "All right, but you'll have to take one of our dual parachutes. They come in yellow or white."

The man chose white, strapped on the parachute, and bailed out over the Alps. Falling, he was unable to decide which ripcord to pull first. Closing his eyes, he pulled the one on the left. Disused for many years, the handle gave way and no chute opened. He pulled the other handle and this failed to open the chute. As he tumbled down, he called out, "Saint Francis, save me!"

A hand seemed to grip the man's arm and a voice said, "Which Saint Francis—Xavier or Assisi?"

Here's luck for you: A fellow worked for a large company. Each week he skimmed money from the earnings and salted them away. After years of skimming, he put the money, almost a million dollars, in a valise and took off for parts unknown. But in the airport somebody stole his luggage.

I bought a stock at fifteen. It went down twenty points.

If I didn't have hard luck, I wouldn't have any luck at all.

A man spent years perfecting his employer's signature. Sure of himself after all that practice, he forged the employer's name on a check. It came back marked "insufficient funds."

He's so unlucky, he always meets up with accidents that start out happening to somebody else.

bad times

They say that things can always get worse. What a thrilling thought!

Times are so bad, stores are getting returns from shoplifters!

Business is so bad, people who don't expect to pay aren't buying!

Things are so bad, I could put on my socks from either end!

"What will people be wearing next year?" "The clothes they wore last year!"

So many farmers are being thrown off their farms, they're buying drapes to match the dust.

I have a lot of things that money can't buy— stacks of unpaid bills!

I've saved up enough money to last me the rest of my life—unless I want to buy something!

Times are bad when a penny for your thoughts is considered a good deal.

There's an advantage to going broke. It's not expensive.

You know things are bad when you forget how to swallow.

All you get when you pick my pocket is practice.

Times are bad when Must Get Rid Of becomes a brand name.

Times are bad when they start to cut the wages of sin!

Times are so bad, hitchhikers are offering to go either way!

Times are bad when you go to the park and see the pigeons feeding people!

I know somebody who found a new use for stale old food—he eats it.

Times are bad when counterfeiters start to make pennies.

Times are bad when "dollars to doughnuts" is even money.

Times are bad when "Nuts to you" is a great offer.

Times are tough when you open your refrigerator and a roach tries to pull you in.

People are going to the dogs, but the dogs are holding out for a better offer.

A man carrying a cigar box ran into a friend. The friend said, "Look at this. Times are tough, and you're walking around with a box of fancy cigars."
   The other man said, "I'm moving. This is my luggage!"

It used to be news when a man bit a dog. Now it's news when a man bites a sandwich.

Times are so bad, parents are writing to their kids in college to send money home.

Poverty isn't a disgrace, but that's about all that can be said for it.

This may not be a depression, but it's the worst boom year in history!

"There isn't a bite of food in this house."
"Then what are all those mice doing?"
"They just room here. They eat out!"

Things are so bad, the mice only use my house for a short-cut!

A blind man tells a friend about how bad things are. He hasn't even sold one pencil and goes on, "I haven't got a penny, I'm crippled, I'm blind, and I have eighteen kids at home."
    The friend asks, "How do you end up with eighteen kids?"
    "I'm blind. Can I see what I'm doing?"

People are trying to make ends meet any way they can. In one Los Angeles apartment building, an inspector recently found four families living in one room of one apartment. Chalk lines marked the property of each family. The inspector asked, "How can you live this way?"
    One of the dwellers answered, "It wasn't bad until last year. Then the guy over there started taking in boarders!"

I beat the recession last year. I went broke two years ago!

bagels

We used to buy day-old bagels. They were so hard we had to hammer the butter on. Then my uncle came up with a brilliant idea. He went to Israel and made a fortune selling Cheerios as bagel seeds. If you believe either of the previous, there's some border property along the Golan Heights I'd like to sell you!

A Texan eats bagels and lox for the first time. He enjoys this ethnic specialty with gusto. But after the meal he turns to his host and says, "This here stuff is dee-lishus, but can you tell me something—which is the bagels and which is the lox?"

Bagels have been around for centuries, the ones I bought yesterday even longer!

One enterprising gent made a fortune in South America selling bagels as halos for shrunken heads.

People who attack bagels and lox at midnight often find that at two in the morning they attack back.

baldness

My family was cursed with nice heads of hair, so I got a late start with "bald" jokes. I made up for my tardiness in due time. In vaudeville my favorite was to point to someone in the audience and say, "Sir, will you put on your hat. Your head is shining in my eyes!" That was and is followed by, "Is that your head or are you sitting upside down?"

He never worried about his baldness. He was born that way!

"Dad, are you getting taller?"
"Why do you ask?"
"Your head seems to be growing through your hair!"

He wore his hair departed on both sides.

The best thing about being bald is—when her folks come home, all you have to do is straighten your tie.

Whatever else you say about baldness, it's neat.

His hair is getting thinner—but who wants fat hair?

It's not that he's bald. It's just that his part won't quit.

A religious sect for baldies—Hairy Krishna.

One good thing about being bald—when you find a hair in your soup, you know it isn't yours.

He knew he'd be bald. People said that he'd come out on top.

Science has found that only one thing can prevent baldness—hair!

He's so bald, his head keeps slipping off the pillow when he goes to bed.

Her hair is so long it grows all the way down her back. It might look better if it grew on her head.

Few people know that baldness comes from the Lord. God made billions of people, and those he's ashamed of he covers with hair!

A young man knows a dozen women who'd tear the hair out of their heads for him. But who wants to go out with baldheaded women!

A child asks his mother, "What did Daddy look like a long time ago?"
The mother answers, "He had long dark hair with natural waves."
The kid said, "Well, who's the old baldheaded coot who lives with us now?"

He's sensitive about his hair. That's odd, because he doesn't have any!

He isn't really baldheaded—he just has a tall face!

A baldheaded man asks a druggist for some hair restorer. The druggist offers him a very expensive concoction, but he wants to know if it really works. The druggist says, "Does it work? I accidentally spilled some on my comb, and now it's a brush!"

His hair was as white as snow, but somebody shoveled it off!

"Since I've started to lose my hair, you should charge me less for a haircut."
"On the contrary, I should charge you more for looking for it!"

The raiding party is over. The Indians are taking scalps. One brave comes on a baldheaded victim and says, "Nobody ever told me neatness counted!"

The most useless move in history—one of Custer's men getting a haircut the day before the Battle of the Little Bighorn.

He once had very wavy hair. Now he's only got beach left.

A hair-restorer salesman bragged, "One bald customer bought a bottle of my hair restorer. He took it home, put on two drops, rubbed them in, stepped back to see what happened, slipped, fell out of the window of his apartment on the sixth floor, and lived. He landed on his head and his hair saved him!"

One woman nagged her bald husband so much his scalp turned gray.

A baldheaded man met a baldheaded woman. When they put their heads together they had to wear a bra.

I was in Las Vegas once and went into a casino barbershop for a haircut. The barber, bald as a golfball, kept telling about a lotion he sold that would grow hair. I asked, "How come you're baldheaded?"
    He said, "It's a shill!"

Not long ago there was a robbery at a pharmaceutical house. Everything was taken except the hair pomade and the birth-control pills. Now the police are looking for a baldheaded Catholic!

His hair is a new color—platinum bald.

Forty is the age when a man starts to get thin at the top while his wife starts to get fat at the bottom.

Look at the bright side—suppose your hair was like teeth and had to be pulled out one at a time.

A real optimist is a man who goes into a drugstore and buys a bottle of hair restorer *and* a hairbrush.

He's not bald; it's just that he finds it easier to polish his hair!

The advantage of having a toupee is that you can go see a movie while your hair is being shampooed!

banking and banks

Banks and savings institutions used to be fun when they gave toasters and radios to new customers. One small bank in Mississippi never got it right. When you brought in a toaster or radio, they gave you money. I pick on Mississippi because I once got a speeding ticket there. It's hard not to get a speeding ticket in Mississippi. If you're from out of town you don't even need a car!

A man went into a bank and, almost on hands and knees, begged for a loan. He needed the money desperately to feed his family. The banker okayed the loan and in no time at all handed the borrower a check in the amount of the loan. The banker said, "I'd suggest you go right out and buy some food."
    The borrower looked at the banker indignantly and answered, "Don't tell me what to do with my money!"

"I hear you're really going after the guy who robbed the bank yesterday."
"You bet. If he wanted to steal, why didn't he work his way up in the bank like I did!"

You're solvent if you don't have to smooth down your hair and straighten your tie when you go into the bank for a loan!

Two spinsters were in a bank when a half-dozen armed men burst in and ordered all of the people in the bank to lie down on the floor. One of the armed men started to pat down the customers to see if any were armed. As one spinster was being patted down, the other said to the robbers, "You shouldn't be doing that!"

The other spinster said, "Quiet, Genevieve. *They're* robbing this bank, not you!"

Some banks charge incredibly high interest rates. You can tell those because the TV camera that takes pictures of robbers is aimed at the loan officer.

Banks are very much concerned with the best interest of the town. And they get it!

"I tried to open an account in the bank yesterday, but they turned me down."
"Why?"
"I wanted to open a charge account!"

After receiving a notice of overdraft from her bank, a woman called up, indignant. "How much did I have in the bank last month?"

The bank officer said, "Two hundred dollars."

"Did I send *you* a letter?"

A bank is a dignified institution that was established for people to have a place to keep the government's money until tax time.

The first drive-in bank was established so that people could show their cars who really owned them.

You can tell when you're in trouble—the bank sends somebody to repossess your toaster!

They now have a microwave bank—it's for those who want to go through their money faster!

A computer manufacturer called his bank and informed the loan officer that he needed an extension on his loan. The loan officer said, "We need it today. We can't wait till next Monday."

The manufacturer asked, "Were you ever in the computer business?"

"No."

"You will be next Monday!"

A rural gent went to the big city and got himself a job as a gardener on a large estate. Happy enough to have all the pleasures of the estate, he never took time off, but spent his days off around the gardens and grounds he loved so much. His pay was sent back to the small bank in his hometown. Not once in ten years did he as much as draw a ten-dollar check.

One day he decided to take some time off and go into the large city nearby. For the first time he wrote out a check.

In the city he had himself a grand old time. He returned to the estate to find that his check had come back marked "insufficient funds." Angrily he wrote a letter to the bank. He was sore as all hell and wanted an explanation. The bank wrote back, "Dear Sir: When one of your checks comes back marked 'insufficient funds,' it doesn't mean that *you* don't have any money. It could also mean that *we* don't have any money!"

Why are there bank robbers? Bank ads make it seem that it's easier to just walk in and get a loan.

"I'm here to speak to the loan arranger."
"He's not here."
"Well then, can I talk to Tonto?"

I must have a dishonest face. The bank asks me for identification when I deposit money!

A man went into the bank for a loan. The loan officer said, "I'll have to have a statement from you."

The applicant said, "Certainly. How's this: A rolling stone gathers no moss!"

A bank is a hock shop with manicures and vests.

A little old lady walked into the bank, cashed a small check, and started out. Passing the armed guard, she smiled and said, "You can go home now."

I received a letter from my bank the other day, telling me, "This is the last time we're going to spend a quarter to tell you that you have fifteen cents!"

"I was a cashier in a bank for a while, but
   then I went on to something else."
"What was that?"
"Jail!"

A young college grad applied for a job with a bank. The personnel officer asked, "What kind of job do you want?"

   "I'll take vice-president for a start."

   "We already have twelve vice-presidents."

   "That's okay. I'm not superstitious."

A man stopped a young man and asked for directions to the Second National Bank.

   The young man said, "Will you give me a dollar?"

   The man said, "That's a lot of money."

   "Not for a bank director it isn't!"

He was an infielder in a bank. He used to catch checks on the first bounce!

Nowadays, when you go to a bank and hear talk about redemption and conversion, you have to look twice to see if you're in church!

A banker was returning to the marina in his boat when he lost his bearings. He called the coast guard. The monitoring guardsman asked, "What is your position?"

   The banker answered, "I'm the loan officer at Security Federal!"

A man told his wife that her last check had just come back. She was thrilled and asked, "What can we buy with it now?"

For me, banking is like a Western shootout, but it's my wife who beats me to the draw!

If bankers can count, how come they always have ten windows and two tellers!

There was a bank in a bad neighborhood that had three windows—one for deposits, one for withdrawals, and one for bank robbers.

A holdup man walked into a bank in the Chinese section of the city. Aiming a gun at the teller, he said, "Give me all your money."

   The teller said, "To go?"

In the old neighborhood we didn't have a bank. The loan shark gave out toasters!

I like to take out bank loans. That way I know somebody's going to write to me!

A banker was interviewed about his start in the banking business. He explained that upon arriving in the town forty years before, he'd put up a sign that said "Bank." The next day somebody came in and gave him fifty dollars. Later that day, another man came by and gave him a hundred dollars. A third put in two hundred. "By then," the banker said, "I had so much faith in the place I put in a few bucks of my own!"

Banking is just like our government—a system of checks and balances. If you want to cash a check, you have to have a balance.

A woman came up with a great idea for her husband, telling him, "Why don't we borrow a little money every month and set that aside?"

A new employee was counting money rapidly. The bank president was impressed and asked, "Where did you learn your math?"
    The employee said, "Yale."
    "That's good. And what is your name?"
    "Yohnson."

He must have some inner ear trouble. He went into a bank and lost his balance.

A woman walked into a bank and said, "I want to open a joint account with somebody who has money!"

I just went partners with the bank. They own half of my car.

A banker fell out of his pleasure boat and called for help. A nearby boat owner said, "Can you float alone for a while?"
    The banker said, "How do you like that? I'm drowning and he wants to talk business!"

A bank employee took fifty thousand dollars from the vaults, stole a car, and ran away with his best friend's wife. The town had a tough time trying to find someone who could teach his Sunday-school class.

A man went to a bank for a loan, saying he wanted it only until he could get a credit card.

One bank did well with its Christmas Club accounts. It decided to try a New Year's Eve account for drunks who wanted to plan ahead!

A young man became interested in, and then married, a young lady because he'd heard that her father owned a bank and his health was failing. Then the young man learned that the father was healthy. It was the bank that was failing!

A bank recently came up with instant credit. You just add money.

A bank called a man and asked him to return money he'd borrowed. The man replied, "I can't. I haven't finished with it yet."

My bank charges very high interest. When its TV camera takes your picture, a voice says, "Smile, you're on Bandit Camera!"

A man wanted something for a rainy day, so a friend gave him a rubber check!

A woman walks into a bank to cash a check. The teller says, "You'll have to identify yourself." The man looks in the mirror and nods. "It's me, all right!"

If George Washington was such an honest man, why do they close the banks on his birthday?

A woman spent some time with her banker. Then she went to her doctor and said, "I found a way of paying your old bill. Now I have another problem!"

He's a retired banker. A local judge retired him.

A woman tries to cash a check but has no identification. However, the security guard knows her and confirms that she is who she says she is. When she leaves, the teller asks how long the guard has known the woman. He answers, "For about a year. Ever since I caught her stealing."

A derelict walks into a bank and says, "I have a hunch that you won't cash this check."

The teller says, "If I had hunches like that, I'd do nothing but bet on horses!"

"I wouldn't cash a check for my own brother."

"Well, you know your family better than I do!"

One bank opened a branch near a cemetery. In the window the president put a sign that read, "You can't take it with you when you go, but here's a chance to be near it!"

When I moved into this small town, everybody greeted me, "Hello, pardner." Wherever I went, it was "Hello, pardner." Then I went into the bank to cash a check, and it was "Howdy, stranger!"

Broke, a bank closed its doors to shut out a rush of its depositors. One man stood in front of the large glass doors and yelled for all to hear, "They ought to throw the bank president in jail. They ought to take the whole board of trustees and hang them from the nearest tree. Every person who works in that bank should be tarred and feathered and run out of town!"

A policeman asks, "Is your money in that bank?"

The man says, "If I had money in that bank, would I be taking it this lightly?"

A man goes into a bank to open an account and is asked to fill out the usual form. He puts his name down. He gets to the third line and puts down his father's name and next to that his mother's name. The next line asks, "Introduced by?" He writes, "A bellhop."

Jesse James told his brother Frank, "Tomorrow we rob the Second National Bank."

Frank said, "We'd better not. That's where we keep *our* money!"

Banks have fallen on hard times. Many are closing. That things are tough is reflected by this banker who goes into a hardware store and buys a hundred shovels at six dollars each. Three days later he returns for another hundred shovels. The storekeeper says, "It's none of my business, but I'm curious. What do you do with all those shovels?"

The banker says, "I sell them for three dollars each."

"Three dollars? They cost you six!"

The banker nods and says, "It's better than banking!"

One dumb guy thinks a pole vault is a bank safe in Warsaw!

baptists

They're nice folks if the water isn't too cold!

The revival is going full force. After hours of Hallelujah, the minister exhorts all of the flock to have their souls washed as white as snow. One old codger refuses to come up as do all the other people. The minister asks, "Brother, don't you want a soul as white as snow?"

The old codger says, "I've been washed."

"Where?"

"The Congregational Church."

"Brother, your soul hasn't been washed. It's been dry-cleaned!"

The baptism was going along at full steam. Came the time to immerse Jed Parker. The minister exhorted forgiveness for poor Jed and dipped him. Another member of the flock said, "That dip won't do any good. With his drinking and carousing, you'd have to let Jed soak all night!"

The Sunday school teacher asked the class, "Can you name two things that are necessary for a baptism?"

Little Jenny answered, "Water and a baby!"

An old-time preacher summed up his sermon with, "Maybe you can't avoid your mouth watering at somebody else's melon patch, but you sure can run!"

One Baptist minister decided to cut the length of his sermons. He didn't mind when his flock looked at their watches. But when the members held the watches up to their ears to see if they were still going, he decided it was time to pare down his words!

"Are the people in this town Baptists?"

"Nope. We have to haul water too far!"

barbers

My old barber was a beautiful man. He smelled of a dozen lotions and perfumes. I can also still smell the fresh starch of his barber's coat. He never once cut me. He knew when I wanted or needed silence and he knew when he could prattle on. He didn't want a tip. He asked only two things—a tip on a horse and a joke about a barber. I gave him many tips on horses, which *may explain why he had to keep cutting hair until he was eighty. But the jokes made him happy.*

A young man, new to town, walked into a hotel barbershop and asked for the works. As he was being shaved, he tried to make time with the manicurist. He suggested dinner and dancing.

The manicurist said, "I don't think I should. I'm married."

The young man laughed. "Ask your husband. He wouldn't mind."

"Ask him yourself. He's shaving you!"

A dog, the barber's pet, stared at the man whose hair was being cut. The man said to the barber, "That's a funny dog. He likes to watch haircuts."

The barber said, "That's not it. You see, once in a while I snip off an ear."

The barber was far from proficient, knicking the customer more than once with his sharp razor. After the shave, the customer asked for some water.

"Are you thirsty, buddy?" the barber asked.

"No. I just want to see if my face leaks!"

That's a great barbershop. I used to go there for a shave and an overcoat!

A hippie walked into a barbershop and asked, "Are you the barber who cut my hair the last time?"

The barber answered, "No, I've only been here two years!"

A hippie walked into a barbershop and asked, "Do I need a haircut?"

The barber said, "Is that what it is? I thought you were wearing a fur coat!"

One barbershop in town put up a sign attacking the fancy salon down the block. The sign said, "Why pay twenty dollars? We give haircuts for two dollars."

The salon got even by putting up a sign of its own that said, "We repair two-dollar haircuts!"

The barber college had a football team, but it always got penalized for clipping!

One barbershop had a sign that read SIX BARBERS. CONTINUOUS DISCUSSION.

I like to aggravate barbers. When one shows me my finished haircut in the mirror and asks, "Do you like it?" I always answer, "No, a little longer in the back!"

There's a razor that its manufacturer claims can shave the fuzz off a baby chick. It's called a Chicken Schick!

When one barber shaves another, who does the talking?

A man tells the barber, "Don't put any sweet stuff on me. My wife'll think I've been to a whorehouse."

Another customer in a nearby chair says, "You can put as much as you want on me. My wife has never been to a whorehouse!"

Sign outside an opera house: THE BARBER OF SEVILLE. 2,000 SEATS. NO WAITING.

A barber cuts a man while shaving him. To assuage the man's anger, the barber says, "Can I wrap your face in a hot towel?"

The man says, "No. I'll just carry it home under my arm!"

A hippie walks into a barbershop and says, "Take a little off the hips."

He used to wear his hair long, but it kept getting caught in things—like his toes.

My barber isn't the best. When I go in for a shave, I ask for ether!

"Your hair is getting gray."
"Try cutting a little faster!"

A young man went to barber college. He couldn't get the knack of shaving people and would nick them all the time. To stop the flow of blood, he'd put on a small piece of paper. He finally graduated and two months later he got a job—as a paperhanger!

"What do you do for falling hair?"
"Rake it up and burn it with the leaves!"

A barber suggested a certain lotion for a balding customer. The customer rubbed in the lotion night and day for three years. At the end of that time his head was still completely bald, but he had to shave his fingers twice a day.

I know why they call it a crewcut. It looks as if it was cut with an oar!

One barbershop took out insurance against the opinions of the barbers not agreeing with those of the customers!

You have to worry about a barber who orders one bottle of hair lotion and two dozen styptic pencils!

One barber cut customers so often his family crest consisted of two crossed tourniquets!

I go to a shop with more than one barber. I like panel discussions!

My barber is so bad he cuts himself with a towel!

If you've ever been shaved in a barbershop, you're sure to have wondered why they call Santa Claus "Saint Nick"!

I once knew a barber who quit because he couldn't stand the sight of whole skin!

The greatest frustration there is: being a deaf-mute barber who has to use sign language to talk!

bars and bartenders

Pity the poor bartender. He's forced to listen to the sad stories of men whose wives don't understand them, whose bosses don't appreciate them, and whose dogs bark at them when they come home. Whom can the bartender complain to?

A man walked into a posh café and sat down at the bar. He was greeted by a bartender with a severely hunched back. The bartender asked, "What'll it be?"

Afflicted with a lisp, the man asked the price of a Scotch.

"Nine dollars."

"How much ith a thcrewdriver?"

"Ten dollars."

"And how much ith a beer?"

"Nine and a half."

The lisping man ordered a Scotch and sat back. When the drink was brought to him, he said, "Thank you very much for not making fun of my affliction."

The bartender said, "You didn't make fun of my hunched back."

The man said, "Oh, the pritheth in thith

plathe are tho high, I thought it wath your ath!"

Ex-prizefighters often open up bars. If the drinks are mixed wrong, who'll complain?

Two men met at a bar and had a great evening together. They promised to meet at the same bar a year from that day. One of the men returned at the exact moment and found the other sitting, waiting for him.

"When did you get here?" the man asked.

The other said, "Who left?"

A man comes into a bar and has a drink. Looking around for companionship, he sees a woman at the other end of the bar and calls, "Hey, douchebag, want a drink?"

The woman looks at him disdainfully and then turns to the bartender and says, "I've never been so insulted in my life."

The bartender agrees with her and tosses the uncouth man out of the bar. Returning, the bartender says to the woman, "I'm sorry about that. Let the house buy you a drink."

"That'll be nice."

"What'll you have?"

"Vinegar and water."

One bar has a midget bartender to make the drinks look bigger.

A bartender had acquired a strange means of adding to his income. For every dollar he'd put into the cash register, he'd manage to drop another for himself in his shirt pocket. This one evening he passed on the cash register with some money, and dropped two dollars in his shirt pocket. The boss asked, "What's the matter? Aren't we partners anymore?"

A man walked into a bar and ordered a martini with an olive. Two minutes later he ordered another. After about a dozen, the bartender asked him, "Don't you think the little woman'll be upset?"

"Nope. She's the one who sent me out for a jar of olives."

A woman walked into a bar and marched straight at her husband, who was feeling no pain as he sat on his barstool. The woman took a sip of the booze he'd been drinking and spat it out in disgust. "It tastes awful," she said.

The man answered, "And you think I'm having a good time every day!"

One bar has a sign over the register that says, IF YOU DRINK TO FORGET, TRY PAYING IN ADVANCE.

Bill and his pal Jan met in the street just as Bill came out of a bar. Bill said, "Jan, old buddy, I've got a real winner for you. The bartender in that bar is a flake. He doesn't remember anything. When he asked me for money for my beer, I told him that I'd paid him already. He believed me."

Immediately, Jan went into the bar, ordered a drink, and waited for the bartender to broach the cost, which he did after a while. "That'll be a buck," the bartender said.

Jan said, "What are you talking about? Will you give me my change and let me get out of here!"

A giant wrestler sits down at a bar next to a dwarf about three feet tall. After watching the little fellow belt down a dozen martinis, the wrestler asks, "Where do you put them, buddy?"

The dwarf turns and pinches the wrestler on the cheek.

"Hey!" the wrestler says. "Don't do that."

The dwarf pinches him again.

"Do it again and I'll flatten you."

A third time the dwarf pinches the wrestler's cheek. The wrestler picks up the dwarf, hits him with a dozen karate chops, dropkicks him in the groin, bouncing him off the wall, and sums up the beating with three more kicks in the groin. Nothing seems to affect the dwarf, who shakes his head and then proceeds to beat up the wrestler. He bounces the giant off the floor like a rubber ball. Finished, he drapes the wrestler over the barstool.

Ten minutes later, the wrestler comes to. He walks over to the midget, who prepares for action. The wrestler shakes off the thought of doing battle. "Look," he says, "I don't want to fight. I just want to know why you didn't die when I kicked you in the groin. It must be painful."

The dwarf says, "I'm from another planet. We have nothing under our belts."

"Well, how do you have sex?"

The dwarf leans over and pinches the wrestler again!

A man sitting in a bar lets out a giant belch. Nearby, a man looks at him and says angrily, "How dare you belch before my wife?"

The belcher says, "I didn't know she wanted to go first."

A man approaches a woman at a bar. He buys her a drink, and after a sip or two she lets him know that she's a lady of the evening. She'd gladly go to a nearby motel with him. The man starts to explain, "There are three reasons I won't go to a motel with you. The first is that I have no money."

The woman interrupts, "You can shove the other two reasons!"

A man walked into a bar and sat down. There didn't seem to be a bartender. After a few moments, from the door at the back of the bar, a horse came out. Tying an apron around its waist, the horse asked the man if he wanted a drink. The man stared. The horse asked, "Why are you staring? Didn't you ever see a horse before?"

The man answered, "Well, I didn't think the cow would sell the place!"

A man walked into a small country bar and was delighted to see the rustic decor, especially the sawdust on the floor. As he drank a beer, he said to the bartender, "What a nice idea—putting sawdust on the floor."

The bartender said, "That's not sawdust. It's last night's furniture!"

Identical twins sauntered into a bar and laughed as one of the barflies started to gawk at them. One of the twins said, "Don't worry, the booze hasn't affected you. We're twins."

The man said, "No kidding, all four of you?"

The new barmaid was endowed beyond belief. Moreover, she wore a blouse that revealed much of her splendors. For some strange reason, the first ten boozers in ordered milk. The next one ordered a pair of Scotch.

A wino made a nuisance of himself so the bartender picked him up and tossed him out into the street. A minute later, the wino was in again. Again the bartender heaved him out. This happened a half dozen times. Finally the wino said, "Do you work in every joint on this block?"

baseball

I live in California and have suffered with the L.A. Dodgers through thin and thinner. At least once a year I am the toastmaster at a Dodgers

victory dinner. We celebrate a great and winning season. Then, the next day, the season starts. When I lived in New York it was much better. I had three losing teams to root for!

After a terrible half-inning, the pitcher came back to the dugout. Before sitting down, he kicked at the bat rack. The coach said, "Don't do that. You'll break your leg and we'll never be able to trade you."

Life isn't fair. When I tried out for baseball, I couldn't hit a curve. Now I play golf and I can't stop hitting them!

That team has been in the cellar so long it's damp!

Our team just doesn't have the game down. One of our players slid into home plate last week, and he was just coming to bat!

Some of our hitters are so bad they can strike out on two pitches!

The young man and his cute lady arrived at the game almost an hour late, when the game was in the sixth inning. The cute lady asked, "What's the score?"

A patron said, "There's no score yet."

The lady said, "How nice. We haven't missed anything yet!"

In spring training, a rookie was asked the size of his cap. He said, "I don't know. I'm not in shape yet."

A man knows when he's cut from the team if he comes to the clubhouse and they tell him visitors can't come in!

There's one minor-league team that's so poor it doesn't have a team bus. It has a team bike!

One ballplayer was having trouble hitting the ball. The batting coach gave him some special practice. The coach started with a clue: "Study the pitch when you swing."

The ballplayer said, "I can't swing and think at the same time!"

Players made a lot of money this year. One time the coach called the bullpen and got an answering service!

He's a lucky pitcher. He always pitches on days the other team can't score a run.

It's thrilling to see the best pitcher on your team raise a cup of water to his lips and miss!

One baseball team found itself in a terrible batting slump. The coach held a special batting practice session. It seemed to be of no value. The players could only dribble the ball on the ground or, after a healthy swing, pop it about twenty feet in the air.

The coach grabbed a bat, ran out of the dugout, and said, "Let me show you guys what I want." The pitcher threw the ball. The coach missed by a mile. After a dozen swings in which he didn't manage to hit one ball with authority, he threw the bat to the ground and said, "That's what you've been doing. Now get up there and *hit* the damn ball!"

They were a pair of baseball girls—they were thrown out at home!

The team looked awfully good on paper, so they took out the grass and put in Astropaper!

A catcher, new to the team, didn't seem too bright. That may have been because nobody had told him about a mask for five years.

UMPIRE: If the pitcher threw a rhino, you couldn't hit it!

PLAYER: If he threw a rhino, you couldn't call it!

One umpire hates night games. The lights make it hard to sleep!

It was cold and windy, not a fit night out for man or beast, but the game was being played. Half-frozen, the manager ran out on the field to dispute a play and got thrown out of the game. He called the umpire every name in the book, and some that were too obscene for the book. Finally the umpire said, "Yell your head off. If I have to be out here, so do you!"

The kid struck out so many times in Little League that his father traded him!

A ballplayer passed a burning building. A woman stood in a window on the second floor with a baby in her arms. The ballplayer shouted to her to drop the baby. She did, and he caught the infant. Then he whirled and threw it to first base!

With a shortstop like that, the routine ground ball has become obsolete!

"I thought I had good stuff today," the pitcher said.

"The batters on the other team liked it," replied his manager.

The team was negotiating with one of its star players. The ante was up to an insurance policy worth ten million, an annuity when he retired of six million a year, and four million dollars if he led the league in hits or runs batted in. After hours of negotiating, it seemed as if an agreement had been reached. Suddenly the deal exploded. One owner asked a partner, "What killed a great deal like this? We're offering twenty million."

The other owner said, "He also wants a hundred dollars cash!"

We've lost so many games, when it rains we have a victory party!

If diamonds are a girl's best friend, why does my wife get sore when I go to a ballgame?

One ballplayer has just finished his first book. He will now try to read a second one!

It was spring training. A horse ambled over to the manager of the team and said he wanted to try out for the team. In desperate need of players, the manager figured that he had nothing to lose. He told the horse to grab a bat and try to hit a few. No matter how hard the pitcher threw, the horse slaughtered the ball. He hit it out of the ballpark without even trying.

The manager became a little more interested. He told the horse to get a glove and catch some grounders. The horse did so and was brilliant. Not one ball passed him.

Really excited now, the manager said, "All right, get on first. We'll see how fast you can run."

The horse answered, "Who can run? If I could run, I'd be in the Kentucky Derby!"

He's working on a new pitch. When he has it down pat, it'll reach the plate!

Ballparks are religious places. I keep hearing, "Sit down, for Christ's sake!"

A scout reported that he'd discovered a great pitcher. "In last night's game," he reported by phone to the manager, "he struck out all twenty-seven men on the other team. What's more, he got all of them on three pitches, except for one guy who hit a foul."

The manager said, "Get the name of the guy who hit the foul. We need hitters!"

One vendor at the ballpark was fired. They found him heating the franks!

At one game, a lady kept up a steady flow of threats at the umpire. No matter what was happening on the field, she kept yelling, "Kill the umpire!" This went on for an hour. Another patron said, "Lady, the umpire hasn't done anything wrong."

The woman said, "He's my husband and he came home last night with lipstick on his collar. Kill the umpire!!"

One team was so poor the players didn't have numbers. They had fractions!

The purest water there is—a ballpark Coke!

He wore the number 8. That was three points higher than his batting average.

He has baseball eyes—two-baggers!

He can't pitch, catch, or field. So they put him in a league by himself!

Having imbibed a little too much the previous evening, a pitcher was called on to start a game. His inability to focus got him into trouble. Soon the other team had men on all bases. The pitcher wound up and threw as hard as he could to what he thought was the plate. Instead he'd thrown it to third and picked off the baserunner on that base. Another windup, and this time he threw to second base, getting that man too. His third pitch went to first, and that was the third out. Walking to the dugout, the pitcher said to a teammate, "And they keep saying you can't drink and play!"

Sinus trouble kept us from playing pro ball. No one wanted to sign us!

A woman is standing completely nude in the large picture window of a large condo building. Six stories below, on the street, a man is standing. The woman signals him by touching her bosom and then her groin. She touches her bosom and groin. In answer, the man touches his rear end and his groin. The woman touches her bosom and groin. The man touches his rear end and groin. A policeman walks by and is amazed by what's going on. Afraid that it's some kind of obscene behavior, he asks the man what is happening. The man explains, "That woman is my wife. She's touching her bosom and groin because she wants me to go to the supermarket and get milk and meat. And I'm telling her, 'Kiss my ass. I'm going to the ball game!'"

The team is in real trouble. This afternoon, the pitching machine threw a no-hitter!

They once got two hits in a row. The ball was sent out for drug analysis!

bathing

This may be the oldest joke of all time: One man says, "Did you take a bath?" The other answers, "Why, is there one missing?" If one is older, it's the one about a man checking into a small hotel. The desk clerk says, "I have a room, but you'll have to make your own bed." He hands the man a hammer and nails! I prefer the bath joke because cleanliness is next to godliness!

"Do you like bathing beauties?"
"I don't know. I never bathed any!"

"Draw me a bath."
"Why? Don't you know what one looks like?"

A man returns from work to find his wife modeling a mink coat. He asks where she got it. She says, "I won it playing bingo." The next night the man returns to find his wife sitting and staring at a huge diamond in a platinum setting, sparkling against her finger. The man asks the source of the diamond ring. The wife says, "I won it playing bingo." The next day the man doesn't get the chance to come into the house. His wife is sitting behind the wheel of an expensive car. She repeats, "I won it playing Bingo. Now go upstairs and draw my bath."

The woman comes into the bathroom a few minutes later to find only an inch of water in the tub. She says, "I thought I told you to draw my bath. There's only an inch of water in the bathtub."

The man says, "I know. I didn't want you to get your bingo card wet!"

A mother gave her young son a bath and then started to dry him. The boy asked, "Mom, don't you love me?"

"Of course I do."

"Then why are you trying to erase me?"

It was a hot desert country, where the desert sands clung to everything. A nomad found his way to an army post and was handed over to two young soldiers. They were ordered to bathe him. Undressing the poor soul, they bathed him for two hours. Along came their officer, who asked, "Why is it taking so long?"

One of the soldiers said, "Well, we scrubbed him for an hour and a half, then about thirty minutes ago, we found out he was wearing another outfit!"

A tenant complained that the faucet didn't produce enough water to fill the bathtub. The landlord had the tub moved under a hole in the roof!

beaches

We'd pack a lunch and take the train to Coney Island. The lunch was gone by the time we arrived. The next three hours were spent trying to find an inch of beach without a body on it. By the time we found space, it was time to go home. I never did get to taste the Atlantic. I got even by making jokes about it.

It was a nude beach with lots of action. The tide started to come in, blushed, and went out again.

She was rather plump. She didn't have to go to the beach. She *was* a beach!

I went to the beach the other day. I held my stomach in so much I threw out my back!

A Midwesterner who didn't know much about the ocean and tides watched as a very fat man jumped up and down in the water. As the tide started to roll the water closer and closer to the Midwesterner, he yelled at the fat man, "Stop jumping up and down. You'll get me wet!"

A fat woman is having a merry old time in the water. Two children arrive and one says, "Let's go in."
    The other says, "I don't think we can while that lady is using it!"

Bikinis at the beach are great. They either show a girl off or up.

A bikini is the closest thing to a barbed-wire fence—it protects the property without obstructing any of the view.

About the only place figures don't lie is in a bikini.

Her body was so bad she had to wear a prescription bathing suit!

She was real thin. Every time she went to the beach, a dog buried her!

beasts

The Ark was about the only place that could contain all the animals. A section on animals can't possibly do justice to all the beasties. You may even find some more under "Critters." But then there can never be too many stories about animals; they make great points in speeches.

A lion is by the river. A female baboon saunters up and the lion makes mad love to her, although she protests. When the attack is over, the baboon runs off. Exhausted, she arrives at a native village. She puts on a straw skirt, sits down outside a hut, and pretends to read a newspaper. After a while the lion walks up and asks, "Did you see a female baboon go by?"
    The female baboon says, "Do you mean the baboon who was violated by the lion?"
    The lion says, "Don't tell me it's made the papers already!"

Two rabbits are beset by wolves. One rabbit asks, "Shall we stay here and outnumber them?"
    The other answers, "We'd better make a run for it. We're brothers!"

A bigot is telling a friend about his trip to Alaska. "I spent months alone."

The friend asks, "What did you do for companionship?"

"There were a few female polar bears. Thank heaven, they were all white!"

A mouse goes "Ruff, ruff!" and the cat runs away. The mother mouse says, "See the advantage of a second language?"

Noah watches the animals debark on Mount Ararat. Two by two they saunter off. Then two cats move off, followed by a dozen kittens. The tomcat says, "I bet you thought we were fighting?"

The Bible says the Lion will lie down with the lamb. But you have to understand that the lamb won't get too much sleep.

A man was roasting a chicken on a barbecue spit in his backyard. A drunken neighbor looked over from his side of the fence and said, "Not only can't I hear a note of what your organ is playing, but your monkey's on fire too!"

A man is shipwrecked on a desert island with a pig and a dog. Every time he tries to go near the pig, the dog barks and keeps him away. One day a beautiful woman is swept ashore. She says, "I'll do anything you want."

The man says, "Will you hold that damn dog!"

A tomcat says to a female cat, "For you I would die."

The female asks, "How many times?"

"What comes in quarts?"
"An elephant!"

A rabbit and a lion went into a small restaurant. The rabbit ordered some lettuce and a carrot.

The waitress asked, "What'll the lion have?"

The lion said, "Nothing. I'm not hungry."

The rabbit said, "If he was hungry, do you think I'd be here?"

"Do you know it takes a half dozen sheep to make a sweater?"

"I didn't even know they could knit!"

An elephant decided to make love to a female mouse. The female mouse was rather frightened. The elephant said, "Don't worry. I'll wear a golf bag."

Then there was the young female dinosaur who became a woman. She had her first century!

Then there was the hotel room that only looked small because the mice were so big.

A hunter hid in a tree so no one would take him for a deer. It worked. He was shot for a bear!

"Where do you find an elephant?"
"That depends on where you left him."

The only way to keep an elephant from charging is to take away his credit cards!

"How do you make an elephant fly?"
"First you take about three feet of zipper..."

A cop sees a man walking with an elephant. He asks, "Where are you going with that elephant?"

The man answers, "To have her bred."
"Where?"

The man picks up the elephant's tail and points: "Right there!"

A lion walks into a bar, gulps down a drink, and roars, "I'm a lion and I'm the mightiest creature on earth!" A fox, sitting at the other end of the bar, looks up annoyed, then turns back to drinking. The lion gulps down a second drink and repeats his announcement. The fox is a little more annoyed. When the lion gulps down his tenth drink and roars, "I'm a lion and I'm the mightiest creature on earth!" the fox gets up, walks over to the lion, and hits him in the stomach with a right hook. The fox says, "What do you say to that?"

Nursing his pain, the lion says, "Don't you know you're never supposed to hit a lion in the stomach?"

A baby porcupine says to a hairbrush, "Is that you, Mama?"

A female monkey says to a bull elephant, "Look, if it doesn't fit, don't force it!"

A donkey in school had an IQ of 156 but no friends. Nobody likes a smartass!

A young cat came home late and her mother bawled her out. The young cat finally said, "Why can't I lead one of my own lives?"

ELEPHANT: I fill my trunk with peanuts.
HIPPO: No kidding? Where do you keep your clothes?

A female squirrel in a tree is teasing a male on the ground. He starts to run around in circles like a madman. The female becomes more coquettish. The male whirls around faster and faster. A rabbit going by asks the male squirrel, "Why don't you climb the tree and get her?"

The male says, "Did you ever try to climb a tree in my condition?"

beauty parlors, mud packs, and lady things

A beauty parlor is the best birth-control device in the world. After she's had her hair done, no woman lets a man come within ten feet of her! The same goes for wet fingernails. Any woman who lets a man near her after having her hair and her nails done is a nymphomaniac!

A woman was unhappy that she was starting to look like a little old lady. She rushed to a beauty parlor, where the usual magic was performed. When she emerged, she no longer looked like a little old lady. She looked like a little old man!

When she went to a beauty parlor, she had to use the emergency entrance!

Some women go to a beauty parlor for years. After a while it doesn't seem to help. They probably have built up an immunity.

She was so ugly she went to the beauty parlor out of memory.

When she came into the beauty parlor, the staff would start to hum "The Impossible Dream."

Most women make a reservation at the beauty parlor, but she was committed!

In some beauty parlors, it's the gossip, not the stylist, that curls the customers' hair!

This woman wanted to go back to her

natural color, but she couldn't remember what it was!

One old lady was so worried about growing old that she turned blonde overnight!

One woman went to the beauty parlor and got a poodle cut. It hasn't helped her looks, and she still can't do any tricks!

A man complained, "My wife is still as pretty as she used to be. It just takes her longer now!"

A sign at a local beauty parlor reads: TEN YEARS OFF FOR CASH.

One woman went into a beauty parlor and came out looking twenty years younger. Her twenty-year-old sister went to the same beauty parlor and disappeared altogether.

A woman went into a beauty parlor. She wanted to reroute her eyebrows.

His wife came back from the beauty parlor looking gorgeous. But three days later the mud wore off.

Some beauty parlors do a great job. One young man followed a young woman for twenty blocks. Then he found out it was his grandmother.

Twin sisters had different lives. One went to the beauty parlor weekly. One day she ran into her sister and was astonished. "I never realized my hair was that gray!"

My wife went to a beauty parlor, where they worked on her hair. They dyed it, pushed it, pulled it, teased it, cooked it, fried it, and singed it. When she came home I ran my fingers through her hair and lost three of them!

She has a real bleaches-and-cream complexion!

She's on the two hundred and tenth day of a fourteen-day beauty plan!

A furrier lost his business and became a hair stylist. One day the boss asked him why he kept blowing in the clients' hair. He said, "Once a furrier, always a furrier!"

A man called a beauty shop and said, "Kindly send me up two beauties, please!"

My brother makes up jokes. He works in a beauty parlor!

My wife keeps putting on oils and lotions at night. She has so much grease on her she keeps sliding out of bed!

A child walks over to a hair stylist and says, "Mommy says you're a fairy. Will you show me your magic wand!"

My wife lost five pounds today. She took off her makeup!

She goes to a real cheap beauty parlor. They put her finger in a live socket to make her hair curly.

A thing of beauty is a job forever.

My wife goes to the beauty parlor for an estimate!

At night my wife puts on oil for her elbows, oil for her lower arms, oil for her upper arms, ear oil, eyebrow oil . . . The other evening, two Arabs broke into our house!

A woman looked at herself after the beautician got through and said, "This doesn't do me justice."

The beautician said, "You don't need justice. You need mercy!"

Cosmetics are a woman's way of keeping a man from reading between the lines!

beginners

As the fly said when it was about to eat its first meal from a chunk of cowflop, "Everybody has to begin somewhere." But then I suppose that after his first moment of romance with Eve, Adam said, "So far you're the best!"

A young bride and her husband were about to consummate their marriage. The groom asked, "Darling, am I the first?"

The bride responded, "Why does everybody ask me that question?"

MASTER CARPENTER: You really hit those nails like lightning.
APPRENTICE: Am I that fast?
MASTER CARPENTER: No, you never strike twice in the same spot!

MASTER CARPENTER: You really hit those nails like lightning.
APPRENTICE: Am I that fast?
MASTER CARPENTER: No, you're half-fast!

I feel sorry for the poor mosquito. When he goes to a nudist colony he doesn't know where to begin!

An expectant father paced nervously. When the doctor passed, he said, "This is my first baby. I'm so nervous."

The doctor said, "*You're* nervous? This is my first delivery!"

The farmer's daughter came running to her father. "Daddy, Elmer, the new hired man, just broke my maidenhead."

The farmer said, "He's got to learn to be more careful. This morning he broke the plow!"

The most famous question after the first time—Was it good for you too?

A man came to a large theme park and asked for a chance to perform an incredible feat. "I will climb that hundred-foot pole," he said, "and then I'll dive off into a damp sponge."

"How long have you been doing that trick?" the manager asked.

"It'll be the first time."

"Oh, then I couldn't let you risk your life like that."

"It's my life. Let me try it. If it works, millions will come to see me."

The manager agreed. A test was scheduled. Later in the day a damp sponge was placed in a shallow dish. The diver climbed the hundred-foot pole, pretended that the band had just played a fanfare, and dove off the top of the pole. There was a slight thud as he landed on the damp sponge. The manager ran to him and was relieved to see that the man was still alive. Ecstatic at the result, the manager offered the man a huge salary. The man shook his head from side to side. "I don't think I want to do that again."

"Why not?"

"To tell you the truth, it gave me a headache!"

beverly hills

That's where I live, so be nice! These jokes also apply to Grosse Point, the Hamptons, Greenwich, Palm Beach, and any town where you can buy a basket with a swimming pool!

In Beverly Hills the phone company has an unlisted number.

In Beverly Hills the police department has an unlisted number.

In Beverly Hills the fire department has an unlisted number.

In Beverly Hills the lottery has unlisted numbers.

I met a man in Beverly Hills who has a rowing machine that sleeps eight.

Two Iranian businessmen meet in Beverly Hills. One greets the other in Farsi, the language of the Iranians. The other says, "You're in America now. Speak Spanish!"

One Beverly Hills gent traded in his forty-foot boat. It got wet!

One Beverly Hills mogul just built a new house. It's in four area codes!

I met a kid in Beverly Hills whose skateboard sleeps eight.

I met a man in Beverly Hills who has no air conditioning in his Mercedes. He just keeps six others in the freezer!

One Beverly Hills gent refused to play on a golf course because it had holes in it.

One Beverly Hills kid won a prize for having the most parents at a PTA meeting.

Two Beverly Hills kids were arguing. One said, "My father can lick your father!"

The other one answered, "Your father *is* my father!"

Two Beverly Hills matrons meet. One says, "I'm having an affair."

The other one says, "Who's catering it?"

Beverly Hills is famous for three great lies: "The Rolls-Royce is paid for"; "The mortgage is assumable"; "It's nothing but a cold sore!"

bible

This section should be treated with reverence. Oh, yeah?

A man checks into a hotel, making certain he gets the rate for single occupancy. Soon after registering, he calls a waiting friend in the lobby and gets him up to the room. Later that evening the original guest is called by the desk clerk. The hotel knows there are two men sharing the room and it will have to charge double. The guest says, "All right, but in that case, send up another Bible!"

An out-of-towner becomes friendly with Thelma, the waitress in a hotel coffee shop, and invites her up to his room. She is indignant. The man says, "Don't get excited. This is all in the Bible." Thelma is appeased.

After Thelma is finished working, they go to a café and have some drinks and a few dances, and the man again invites Thelma to his room, and again she is angry. The man explains, "It's in the Bible."

An hour later they are in the man's hotel room. He suggests that they undress and have some fun. He assures Thelma that it isn't sinful, since it's in the Bible. Thelma says, "Where? Where does it say that?"

Taking the Gideon from the nightstand, the man opens it and shows the inside cover, where someone has written, "Thelma the waitress puts out."

A man checks into a hotel and sits down to get some solace from the Gideon Bible. After reading a few pages he sees, printed neatly on the inside of the back cover, a handwritten message that says, "If you are worried about that old demon rum and crave alcohol, call 555-5557."

The man watches television for a while, reads a little more, and then finds himself craving a drink. He rushes to the Bible and opens it to the back cover. Quickly he dials the number in the message. From the other end a voice answers, "Smith's Liquor Store."

One passage in the Bible dictates that a married man should never let his mother-in-law move in with him. It's the part that says, "No man can serve two masters!"

A traveler checks into a hotel. Glancing at the Gideon Bible, he reads on the front page, "If you are sick at heart, read page 124. If you are unsure of your journey, read page 144. If you are very lonely, read page 188."

Being very lonely, the man reads page 188. At the bottom of the page, scribbled in ink, he finds a message: "If this page hasn't worked, call Martha at 555-8910."

A minister told his congregation, "Next week I plan to preach about the sin of lying. To help you understand my sermon, I want you all to read Mark 17." The following Sunday, as he prepared to deliver his sermon, the minister asked for a show of hands. He wanted to know how many had read Mark 17. Every hand went up. The minister smiled and said, "Mark has only sixteen chapters. I will now proceed with my sermon on the sin of lying."

"The Bible tells us that we should love our neighbors."
"Did the Bible mention that they'd have a kid who plays drums?"

A minister went to an asylum to give the inmates some moments of biblical solace. A few minutes after his arrival, he ran into an inmate who said he was God. Trying to make light of the matter, the minister said to the inmate, "If you're the Lord, I would love to ask you some questions. In the Bible you say that you created the world in six days. Were those twenty-four-hour days, or did you have a different kind of day in mind?"

The inmate answered, "You'll have to forgive me, but I don't like to talk shop."

bigamy

By definition, a bigamist is somebody with one marriage too many. There must be a lot of bigamists in the world.

A bigamist is a poor soul who makes his second mistake before he tries to correct his first.

A man is brought up on charges of bigamy. After hearing the testimony, the judge frees him and says, "You can go home to your wife now."

The man says, "Which one?"

"A bigamist is a man who makes the same mistake twice at the same time."

There once was a man of Lyme
Who married three wives at a time.
When asked, "Why a third?"
He replied, "One's absurd,
And bigamy, sir, is a crime!"

A man was brought up on charges that he'd married six women.

The judge said, "How could you do a thing like that?"

The man answered, "I was only trying to find a good one!"

A woman was brought up on charges that she'd married two soldiers at the local army post. She said, "I could never resist a uniform."

The judge gave her sixty days and she was led off by the court guard. The following week, she married the court guard!

birds

Until I was six, I thought they were "boids."

The ostrich is the biggest bird alive. It's also the biggest bird dead.

Several pigeons flew over the Superdome in Miami as an important game was in progress. One pigeon said, "Sure is a big crowd down there."

The other pigeon said, "Takes the fun out of it, doesn't it?"

A man walks into a pet store and asks how to tell the difference between a male and a female canary. The clerk says, "It's easy. You put down a male worm and a female worm. A male canary will go after the male worm, a female after the female worm."

"How can you tell a female worm from a male worm?"

"Oh, for that you'll have to go to a worm store!"

An ostrich arrived near the watering hole and saw all the other ostriches with their heads in the sand. Puzzled, the newly arrived ostrich said, "Where did everybody go?"

Talk about drunks. I know a man who's two hundred swallows ahead of Capistrano.

A woman went into a bird store for a canary that would sing. Luckily, the store owner had one bird that sang magnificently. He was willing to let it go for a handsome price. The woman paid and took the bird home. Later that day she returned very agitated and said, "This bird is lame!"

The store owner said, "Make up your mind, ma'am. Do you want a singer or a dancer?"

A bird in the hand is worth two in the bush, but that's not the way the birds look at it.

The bad thing about being the early bird is that you have to make your own breakfast.

"Do you have a peacock?"
"What do you think—I squirt it out of my navel?"

Two can live as cheaply as one, if one is a horse and the other a sparrow!

Then there were two horny roosters—one made it to the henhouse in the rain and the other made a duck under the porch!

A rooster saw a whole slew of dyed Easter eggs. After thinking about it for a minute he said, "When I find him, I'm going to beat the hell out of that peacock!"

A farmer and his wife were blessed with sixteen children. A traveling salesman stopped by the farmhouse and saw a rather strange-looking bird roaming about. The salesman said, "That's a strange-looking chicken."

The farmer said, "That's not a chicken. It's a stork with his legs worn off!"

A baby chick said, "I want my mommy. I want my mommy."

The rooster told him, "You don't have a mommy. It was a lamp!"

A young man checked into a hotel for a few hours of pleasure with a girl from the office. The young man turned on the bath. Occupied with a romantic interlude, he neglected to turn off the water in time, and a flood ensued. From the room below, a man yelled up, "You dumb son of a bitch! Turn off the goddamn water!"

The young man asked, "What kind of language is that? I happen to have a young lady in my room!"

The man from below answered, "What do you think I have down here—a duck?"

As the rooster said to the hen, "How do you want your egg today?"

A rooster came out of the henhouse grinning and said, "Well, that's one piece Colonel Sanders won't get!"

Once there were some pigeons who wanted to buy a house. They didn't have the money, so they put down a deposit.

A canary was given a sip of whiskey. One minute later, it ripped two bars out of its cage and chased the cat around the block.

Then there was the man who had the job of throwing fish to the pelicans. Not a great job, but it filled the bill.

A young wiseguy said to his girl, "Did you ever see an owl with a Beatle haircut?"

"No."

He said, "Let me unzip my pants and show you!"

Two ducks are flying over an area used as a gunnery range for naval antiaircraft. As the ducks float along, several bursts of antiaircraft flak explode in front of them. One duck says, "Those guys must be terribly hard up for meat!"

Two birds are flying over Boston. Below them a regatta is taking place. One bird asks, "Who's racing?"

"Yale and Harvard."

"Who's winning?"

"Yale."

"Well, I think I'll put my all on Harvard!"

"If storks bring regular babies and larks bring babies that aren't legitimate, what kind of bird doesn't bring babies at all?"

"Swallows!"

There's a bird called the whiffsenuff. It eats onions and garlic, so one whiff's enough!

There's a bird called the oo-oo bird. It weighs two ounces and lays an egg of ten ounces. When it lays an egg it goes "Oo-oo!"

There's an ah-bird. It lays a square egg, and when it's finished it says, "Ahhhhh!"

One pigeon in the park ate so many breadcrumbs it laid a roll.

A man was proud of his favorite homing pigeon. It flew home, no matter where he released it. The man bragged so much that another pigeon fancier decided to teach him a lesson. A bet was made that the pigeon wouldn't come back from a place this other pigeon fancier could take him to. The pigeon fancier took the bird across the country. Arriving at the coast three thousand miles from the pigeon's home, the fancier cut the pigeon's wings.

Six months later, the bragging pigeon owner was sitting in his house when there was a knock on the door. He opened it to find his pigeon standing there. The man swept the pigeon up in his arms and started to kiss him. The pigeon said, "Be careful. My feet hurt!"

A man shot a woodpecker one day. A friend asked why he'd done such a dastardly deed. The man answered, "I got tired of saying 'Come in'!"

"Why do ducks have flat feet?"
"To stamp out forest fires."
"Why do elephants have flat feet?"
"To stamp out burning ducks!"

A woodpecker goes on a journey. As is his way, he starts to peck at a tree. At that moment a bolt of lightning splits the tree in half. The woodpecker looks at the damage and says, "You never know how strong your pecker is until you leave home!"

There's a wowee bird. It mates every thirty years, and when it does—wowee!

Then there was a male quail who went off on a lark!

Two eagles see a jet flying by. One says, "That bird is certainly in a hurry."
    The other says, "You'd be moving too, if your rear end was on fire!"

A flock of birds is flying south for the winter. One asks, "Why do we always have to follow Murray?"
    Another bird answers, "Because he has the map!"

A pigeon invited a friend from out of town to the top of the World Trade Center in New York. The friend said, "It's a very nice view."
    The host pigeon said, "And it also shows you how far a turd can go in this city!"

Two birds met. One was all frayed and beat up. The other asked, "What happened to you?"
    The frazzled one answered, "I got caught in a badminton game!"

black jokes

Ethnic jokes won't go away. If only one or two groups were picked on, the discrimination would be unfair and probably immoral. The fact is, however, that no ethnic group has escaped comedy probing. In parts of China, jokes are made about "whites." "Browns" in Malaysia make fun of the Chinese. The rich go after the poor, and the poor after the rich. Canada picks on its Newfoundlanders, Louisiana on Cajuns and "Coonasses," and the Southwest on Chicanos. One of my friends, a comedian whose television shows have been very successful, did a sketch about a hate group with two members, one of whom wants to quit. To make the piece work, an ethnic group hatable by the members of the sect had to be found. Group after group was dismissed as being too volatile. The network would get letters. Finally the writers decided to use Eskimos. The fictional hate group had such slogans as "A Nation in Mukluks Is a Nation in Chains!" and "Bicycles, Not Icicles!" Who in the world could dream that the sketch was trying to make a serious point about Eskimos? Yet, two weeks after the performance the show received a letter. In it was part of the front page of an Indianapolis newspaper. The headline read, ESKIMO STABS WOMAN. Printed over it in a firm hand was, "You're so right!" Nevertheless, ethnic is and will be. My litmus test for my personal use of ethnic jokes is a simple one: Use only if you're not angry, seeking revenge, or trying to inflict pain! And you aren't immune to fun at your own expense!

A young, uneducated black applied for a job in an office. After the interview, he left and joined some neighborhood friends. One asked, "How'd you make out?"
    The black answered, "The first part was darn good. But then she said she wanted to see my testimonials. I showed them, and there went that job!"

A black is in heaven. He's hanging around when he sees the Lord. Walking over, he says reverentially, "God, can I ask you a question?"

God says, "Certainly, my child."

"Look, we've had a Polish Pope. Do you think we'll ever have a black Pope?"

God answers, "Of course, my son. But not while I'm God!"

A young black calls up to heaven, "Lord, Lord, can you straighten me out?"

"What troubles you?"

"Well, can you tell me why you gave me black skin?"

"There's a simple reason, child. I wanted your skin to be able to reflect the burning hot rays of the sun at the Equator."

"And why did you give me such long legs?"

"So you could outrun the animals of the jungle."

"And why did you give frizzy hair?"

"I didn't want you to catch in the thick underbrush of the jungle."

"I have one more question, God."

"What is that?"

"What the heck am I doing in Cleveland?"

A young black arrived on a small-town bus. Holding his worn valise, he went over to a man lounging in the bus station and asked, "Do you know if there's a Jim Brown living in this town?"

"Never heard of a Jim Brown. I've lived here forty years and I never saw, sniffed, or laid my eyes on a Jim Brown."

The young man said, "Good, this is where his new son-in-law gets off!"

The football team gathers at the entrance to the field house so all can board the bus for the game. The coach says, "There's been some talk of my being unfair to people of different-colored skins. That's a lie. To me there's no black skin, there's no white skin.

To me you are green. Now I want you to get on the bus. Light green guys in front and dark green in back!"

The coach of a major college football team finally broke the racial barrier at the school. For the first time, a black player joined the team. A brilliant runner, he would no doubt help the team to a championship.

The afternoon of the first game found the team gung-ho and ready to play. The other team had several black players. After the kickoff, the first team went on the offense. On the first play the ball was given to the black back. He ran into the other line and was pulled to the ground by a black tackle. Then two other black linesmen piled on him. The coach jumped up and yelled, "What are those nigras doing to our black man?"

A black man in a small Southern town told of his attempt to join a white Baptist church that was in the middle of a brotherhood campaign. He said, "I was welcomed with open arms. They gave me one hallelujah after another. Then we went down to the river and the reverend said some words over me and then he dipped me in the water, and come to think of it, that's the last thing I remember!"

"How do you stop five blacks from mugging you?"

"Throw them a basketball!"

A black came to a small Southern town. Forced to be there on business, he went to the nearest church on Sunday morning. It happened to be an all-white congregation, and he was refused admission. The minister said to him, "Why don't you go to your own church, about six blocks from here?"

The black did so. Sitting in the church, he started to talk to the Lord. "God," he said,

"I feel so bad that I couldn't get into that white church on the other side of town."

God answered, "Don't feel bad, son. I've been trying to get into that church for years!"

"Good morning," said the soft, warm voice, and went on, "You have called the Sacred Abode of Divine Meditation. My name is Kareem and I am one of the meek followers of the Swami Maharapet, the sacred leader of our sacred temple. May I help you? Do you wish to have words with the omnipotent Maharapet?"
The voice at the other end of the line said, "I certainly do. Go tell him his mother's calling from Mississippi!"

busts, bosoms, and bazooms

Although the bosom loses its function as a food supply, many men remain obsessed with it all their lives. It's not a terrible obsession unless a man dreams about being alone on a desert island with a Sumo wrestler!

Her measurements were 55-46-44. Her other breast was just a little smaller.

Her bra was so padded, one day she threw it down and it bounced out of the bedroom window.

Her bust was so large, she had to back up to ring a doorbell.

She wore a bra, out of hope.

She had a living bra that died.

Her boobs were so big they had to let out the windshield of her car.

Her boobs were so small she had to carry her nipples in her pocket.

One day the doctor felt a lump in her breast—it was her shoe.

One day she tried to shoot herself in the breast. She blew off her kneecap.

She was so flat, her hope chest was a training bra.

"I heard your wife went without a bra the other day."
"She certainly did."
"Did you notice anything?"
"Her legs straightened out!"

She was so flat-chested, she had to hold up her bra with suspenders.

She was so flat-chested, she had "This Side Up" written on her chest in case of rape.

She used to rub her chest with pollen and pray for bees.

"My girl has no boobs."
"That's nothing."
"Oh, you've seen her!"

It's a good thing for her that a bra can't laugh.

Ashamed of her gigantic bosom, a woman went to Halmar the faith healer. He studied her for a while and said that faith could move mountains. She paid him a large sum of money and he started to pray. For hours he prayed, and, lo and behold, her bosom grew smaller. Her breasts became beautiful, but now she has two giant lumps on her ass!

Each time she met a man, she'd heave her bosom. He'd heave it back!

She's so flat-chested, she got a job in a hardware store modeling walls!

bosses

The best way to get the crowd on your side is go after and make fun of authority. Going after the boss's wife is risky. One second after she arches her eyebrow, your career is over. Yet, if the authority figure is a woman, feel free to take on her better half. The trick is to know how far you can go. When two security guards come after you and toss you out of the room, it's possible that you've gone a mite too far.

"Mary, I know we had a fling, but who told you that you could come to work when you pleased?"
"My lawyer!"

One company had two bosses. One boss, Witherspoon, went on a vacation, leaving Blake, the other, to run the business. Clients calling the firm would hear from the receptionist, "I'm sorry, but Mr. Blake is tied up." After hearing this a dozen times, one client said, "He can't be tied up all day."
The receptionist answered, "All week. When Mr. Witherspoon leaves town, he ties Mr. Blake up!"

A boss is a man who is all thumbs, with a hireling under each.

A young businessman had just started his own firm. He'd rented a beautiful office and had it furnished with antiques. Sitting there, he saw a man come into the outer office. Wishing to appear busy, the young business-man picked up the phone and started to pretend he had a big deal working. He threw huge figures around and made giant commit-ments. Finally he hung up and asked the visitor, "Can I help you?"
The man said, "Sure. I've come to install the phone!"

For some reason, the man most likely to succeed is the boss's son!

A modern boss is one who would replace people with a computer, if he could find one that cringes!

My boss made it the hard way. He was nice to his father!

It's not easy to fire an employee who does the most insignificant chores. How do you let someone know he's flunked "flunky"?

A man finally achieved the goal of a lifetime—he became the boss of his own company. Asked if it was all he'd expected it to be, he said, "Let me put it this way. The building code tells me what kind of plant to put up. The union tells me what the salaries and the hours should be. The government makes me deduct from paychecks. My sales-men tell me what they can sell and what I should make. And on top of that, last month I got married!"

A good boss is one who makes a raise effective as soon as the employee is.

Yesterday my boss fired me. I started to cry. He said, "I can't watch a grown man cry." So he took off his glasses.

It's always easy to see who's the boss. At the company party, he always gets the cringing ovation.

When he got booted off his last job, his boss said, "You've been like a son to me—loud, rude, and insolent."

"The boss gave his secretary a beautiful mink coat."
"That should keep her warm."
"He hopes it'll also keep her quiet!"

boston

Boston is a great city—I spent a month there one night. But it did give us the Boston Tea Party when they threw all the bags overboard. I knew one of the bags they threw overboard!

A traveler was going through the desert when he happened on a decrepit lean-to. The land around it was barren of life. The heat was unbearable. The traveler was puzzled but was about to move off when a grizzled old prospector came out of the lean-to. The traveler said, "How can you live in a place like this?"

The prospector said, "Well, I was in Boston one weekend, and anything since has been good by comparison!"

Boston's a great town, but I wish Paul Revere hadn't warned them!

Boston society women really walk around with their noses up. The other day it rained and three of them drowned.

Boston still has those great beans—at last reports!

boxing and boxers

I have a sneaking suspicion that I'd trade fame and fortune for the chance to own all or part of a great fighter. I've been involved with some who took a large chunk of my fortune, but never a champion. I did have one fighter who came close. He had a hundred fights and won all but ninety-nine of them! The previous may have been a joke, although I did have a light-heavyweight who came close to that record. It was a moral victory when we got him into the ring!

For three rounds he was battered by a barrage of rights and lefts, uppercuts, and jabs. When he sat down between rounds, however, his manager kept saying, "He hasn't laid a hand on you. He hasn't touched you."

After the fourth round, one in which the pounding was merciless, the fighter sat down exhausted, only to hear his manager say, "He hasn't laid a hand on you. He hasn't touched you."

The fighter gasped for air and said, "You better keep your eye on the ring, because *somebody* is beating the crap out of me!"

"You said you could beat him hands down."

"He doesn't want to keep his hands down!"

One fighter ruined his hands in the ring. The referee kept walking on them!

He once had the champ on one knee. The champ bent down to see if he was still breathing!

A couple of fight managers were discussing the upcoming match between their fighters. One manager said, "I think your boy ought to go down in the second round."

The other said, "The fifth round is better. We don't want the crowd to feel cheated."

Two fighters went through the motions, hardly touching one another. They danced around and around. Finally the referee got them in a clinch and said, "I don't mind your dancing around like that, but dipping is out!"

He was a colorful fighter—black and blue and blood.

He had a great way of leading with his chin and feinting with his nose.

"Should I keep swinging even if I'm missing him?"

"You bet. The draft might give him pneumonia!"

The two fighters were playing it safe. They circled one another for two minutes, each refusing to throw a blow. Finally a voice from the crowd said, "Hey, black trunks, hit him one. You got the wind with you!"

He fought like a baseball pitcher—at the end of the fight he had a no-hitter.

"A big crowd is going to see me fight tonight."

"Yup, and they'll know the result ten seconds before you do!"

He had a great rabbit punch, but the commission wouldn't let him fight rabbits.

He was on his back so often they thought he was a hooker.

A fighter was getting clobbered by his opponent's right hand. When he sat down between rounds, his manager said, "Let him hit you with his left for a round. Your face is crooked!"

A punch-drunk fighter ran into a fight promoter and demanded a fight, saying, "I can beat the stuffings out of Tiger McGraw."

The promoter said, "You *are* Tiger McGraw!"

One boxer who got knocked out a lot made a fortune. He sold advertising space on the bottoms of his shoes.

A lot of people want to see him fight. That's why they get there early.

The bout was obviously crooked. The blow that had put Bull Roberts on the canvas couldn't have cracked an egg. To show that he understood what had happened, the referee didn't stop counting at ten. He kept going till twenty and then on to twenty-one, twenty-two.... Bull looked up and said, "I know you're trying to be helpful, but I'm through for the night."

boy scouts

I never made it in the Scouts. I know I wanted to, because Molly Kamen loved men in uniform. She now goes with a guy who's serving life.

Tim, a young Boy Scout, fell madly in love with little Jane. He bought her ice cream and candy, and took her to the movies, but she wouldn't let him kiss her. She wanted his Boy Scout knife. Too much in love to be rational, Tim came over to Jane's house. In his hand was his knife. He handed it to her. Opening a footlocker against the wall of her room, Jane placed the knife among dozens and dozens of other Boy Scout knives. Bewildered, Tim wondered why she had all the knives. Jane explained, "Right now I'm a cute little girl and I can get anything I want. But what'll happen if I grow up and I become ugly and gruesome? Do you know what a Boy Scout will do for one of these knives?"

Until he's about fifteen, a young fellow is a Boy Scout. Then he becomes a girl scout!

Mr. Klein, the scoutmaster, took his troop for an overnight in a park not far from the area in which most of the youngsters lived. After the usual night of giggling and kidding around, the boys were still up at dawn. Mr. Klein prepared a breakfast of tepid orange juice, fried eggs burned at the bottom and runny cold in the middle, and toast that passed for charcoal.

The boys gulped down the food and asked, "Gee, Mr. Klein, how'd you learn to cook like that?"

Mr. Klein answered, "Those were my wife's recipes!"

One boy scout spent all of his time making knots. He knew every knot, and knotted everything he touched. One day he watched his mother making dough for bread. He picked up a piece and invented the pretzel!

brides

"Bride" jokes work, I believe, because they are titillating by nature. Somehow, the notion of the bride conjures up a picture of a pale beauty being deflowered. It's not an easy picture to form nowadays, because people live together for about ten years before they skip down the aisle. One actress I knew announced that she was finally going to marry the man she was living with. My mother, always funny, said, "She started to practice her honeymoon six years before she got married!"

If you are called upon to speak at a tribute to a co-worker or friend, a few bride and honeymoon jokes, tailored to the target, are infallible. Since the jokes are pure fiction, the target won't really know whom you're discussing. The target will laugh anyway. If not, hit them with a few "dumb" or "dull" jokes.

Nowadays they're marrying young. I went to a wedding where the bride's mother wouldn't let her have any wedding cake until she finished her vegetables.

The bride murmured, "Do you think of me? Do you think only of me?"

The groom said, "Once in a while I think of the furnace, or we'd freeze!"

One bride who'd eloped wrote a letter to the justice of the peace: "Thank you for the wonderful way in which you brought my happiness to a conclusion."

Because your bride has been given away, don't imagine that she's going to be cheap.

She's been a bride so often, her wedding gown is her native costume!

If there are so many beautiful brides, where do all the ugly wives come from?

The bride wore blue—her veins!

She was such an ugly bride, the hotel gave the couple the honeymoon sour.

A man wakes to find that he is sharing a bed with the ugliest woman of all time. He jumps out of bed, starts to dress, and reaches in his pocket for some money. He puts a twenty on the nightstand next to the sleeping creature. Swearing that he'll never drink himself into ending up with anything like this woman again, he starts out. As he passes the open bathroom door, he sees, doing her ablutions, a hag uglier than the other. Through the mirror she has seen him awaken. Smiling, she asks, "Nothing for the bridesmaid?"

Niagara Falls is a bride's second greatest disappointment.

She was such an ugly bride, instead of a wedding ring, the groom gave her a setting for her wart.

She was such an ugly bride, on the honey-

moon the groom insisted on separate beds
. . . in different hotels . . . in different cities!

bridge

*The game, not the engineering feat. The last
time I played bridge I lost four rubbers, three
friends, and the use of my shins from the
swelling caused by my wife kicking me!*

Bridge was invented so that women could
have a thing or two to think about while
talking!

Once upon a time there was a couple who
hated one another. Along came another
couple who hated one another. The four of
them sat down and invented bridge!

At a recent homicide, the police report read,
"Deceased: Male. Forty years old. Six foot
two. Cause of death: Doubling three
spades."

I know a man who likes to play bridge
tourniquets—anything to stop the bleeding!

A woman nagged her husband for bridge
lessons. All of their friends played. After ages
of being nagged, the husband gave in and
said, "All right, I'll teach you the game, but
you have to learn it slowly."
    "That's all right with me."
    "Okay, now there are fifty-two cards in
the deck."
    "Fifty-two."
    "Great. Now come back tomorrow and
I'll give you another lesson."

The action was fierce and the bidding excited. At one bid from his wife, a man
jumped up, bellowed for a good three minutes, then stormed out of the room. One of
the other players asked, "Is that your husband?"

The woman answered, "Would I be *living*
with a creep like that?"

britain and the british

*Only one word of caution here: don't expect the
British to laugh on the same day that they hear a
joke. In certain parts of England they're just
beginning to snicker at jokes told during World
War II.*

The headmaster of a fancy British school
was lecturing his students on etiquette. He
said, "In moments of stress or agitation, you
must count to twenty before you speak up."
    One student raised his hand: "Nineteen,
twenty, your pants are on fire!"

An American performer entertained at a
large café in London. His act over, he was
greeted with a ten-minute ovation. He had
to take a dozen bows. After the last bow, he
took a break backstage, where he turned to a
stagehand and asked, "What do you think of
that crowd?"
    The stagehand said, "They seem friendly."

It's easy to see why they drink so much tea
in England. Just taste their coffee!

A Londoner was punting down the Thames
when his oar slipped out of his hand. He
drifted aimlessly when his path crossed that
of a rowboat. In the rowboat were a man
rowing and two young women facing him.
The punter called over, "Sir, will you lend
me one of your oars?"
    The rower was furious and answered
sharply, "They're not 'ores! They're my two
sisters!"

An American was in a pub, bragging about
the good old States. He said, "We're a real

melting pot. I have Indian, Greek, Irish, and German blood in me!"

The bartender answered, "That was rather sporting of your mother."

An elderly Jewish gentleman had spent a life of backbreaking work in a small tailor shop in a poor section of London. His endless days and nights of toil had helped him to amass a fortune. He decided to become a gentleman, and went to the fanciest men's shop on Savile Row, a street famous for quality, history, and high prices. A salesman showed the elderly man many fine fabrics and helped him pick out a half-dozen colors and stripes. Accessories were added, as were the two final pieces worn by British gentlemen—a bowler and an umbrella.

The old man came in for a fitting a few days later. The first of the cutaways was put on. With his bowler and umbrella he was the quintessential Brit. After looking at himself in the mirror for a few moments, he started to cry.

The salesman asked, "Why are you crying?"

The elderly Jewish man said, "Ve lost India!"

A British destroyer was on patrol in the Atlantic. A German U-boat circled it from a distance. The British captain decided to bide his time. The German radioman came on the radio and proceeded to curse the Empire and call the Royal Family all kinds of names. The British captain remained patient. After a while he looked through his field glasses. There in the distance he saw the surfaced U-boat. A German sailor finished a chore, then turned around and spit. Immediately the British captain ordered battle stations. In one minute he gave orders to rush at the submarine and blow it out of the water. His mate asked, "Why are we attacking now?"

The captain said, "I don't mind the blighter cursing the Empire. Or insulting the Royal Family. But when he spits in our ocean, that's a bit much!"

Lord Favisham woke one morning at his country estate. He was in an agitated sexual state. His butler asked, "Shall I call Lady Favisham?"

Lord Favisham said, "No, just get my knickers. We'll try to smuggle this one through to London!"

brothels (whorehouses, cathouses, and houses of ill repute)

Cross my heart, this is true: A famous madam wrote a book about her work entitled A House Is Not a Home. *The madam sent me an autographed copy. Receiving it, my wife glanced at the cover and said, "You don't know anything about home repairs. Let's give this to somebody who does."*

She worked in a brothel for five years and then had a nervous breakdown. She found out the other girls were getting paid!

An outfit of American soldiers was offered a weekend pass, but for only one man. The men selected a farmer from Kansas as their representative. He was given every penny in the outfit and told to go to Bangkok and have a weekend they'd all be proud of.

After hitching a ride on an army plane, Jimmy, the boy from Kansas, went to the Purple Grotto, which was the most famous brothel in the world. He walked in to find the most opulent setting he'd ever seen. Describing it to the other men after his return, he said, "I never saw anything like we had in Kansas. There were silk drapes blowing in the breeze. There was incense.

All around were beautiful women. I never saw anything like that in Kansas. Then they gave me the most delicious drinks and they made me sit on cushions. I had two drinks, and down the steps came this absolutely beautiful woman. I never saw anything like her in Kansas. Her eyes glistened. Her lips were soft and moist. She came over to me, took my hand, and led me up the marble steps. I never saw anything like it in Kansas. Then we went into this room. A beautiful room."

A half-dozen of the men couldn't contain themselves. "What happened? What happened?"

Jimmy said, "From then on it was just like Kansas!"

A married man feels like having a little romance. Unfortunately, his wife is asleep. Putting on his hat and coat, he goes to a nearby brothel. As luck would have it, his son is there. The son looks at him aghast. "Dad, how could you come to a ten-dollar whorehouse?"

The father answers, "For ten dollars I didn't want to wake your mother."

"Why do you always ask for Mamie?"
"She's got something I like."
"What's that?"
"Patience!"

"What do you call a whore's children?"
"Brothel sprouts!"

A man, new to town, goes to the best brothel in the city. Choosing a succulent morsel, he retires to a large and well-appointed bedroom, where a most pleasant sexual interlude takes place. Satiated, the man asks the madam, "How much do I owe you?"

The madam motions for him to put away his money. Taking fifty dollars from a silk purse dangling between her breasts, she gives him the money. She fends off any request for an explanation.

Naturally, the man returns the following evening. Again, he sports in an opulent bedroom and again he is given fifty dollars.

The third night, he finishes a pleasant love bout and goes down to the madam. She says, "That'll be seventy-five dollars."

The man says, "Wait a minute. Wait a minute. I came in the first time and you gave me fifty. The second time you gave me fifty. Now you want to get paid. Why?"

The madam answers, "Tonight you're not on television."

Several Catholic women live across the street from a local bordello. This gives them something to do all day—they watch the door of the bordello and remark on everyone entering or leaving. One day they arrive at their station later than usual. They start to watch. The second person to emerge is the town's Baptist minister. One woman says, "I told you the Baptists were bums."

A minute later, a priest emerged. Another of the women said, "There must be somebody sick in there!"

A couple is engaged in a most private embrace on the second floor of the local brothel. Their passion is unbounded, and the couple is bounced up and down and finally out the window to the ground, thirty feet below. Both are dead. A wino comes by, looks at them, and rings the doorbell of the whorehouse. When the madam opens the door, he says, "Lady, your sign fell down!"

The police make one of their periodic roundups of ladies of the evening. In the courtroom, the judge asks the first, "Are you a prostitute?"

"I was only taking a walk. I'm a secretary."

The second also responds, "I'm a secretary." The first dozen have the same response. The last girl saunters up to the bench. The judge asks her, "What do you do for a living?"

She answers, "I'm a hooker."

"How's business?"

"It would be great if it wasn't for all these damn secretaries!"

The girls in that place were so nice. They all called their mother "Madam."

A hooker became ill. Her doctor ordered her to stay off her back for a week.

budgets

My wife never spends more than I earn. Although I didn't know it, last year I must have earned $1,000,310,000.

A budget is a systematic way of living way beyond your means.

A budget is just another name for a family quarrel.

We never worry about keeping up with the Joneses. We passed them years ago!

One day the wolf came to our door. I showed him my budget. He gave me five dollars and left.

Thirty percent of my income goes to food, thirty to rent, thirty for insurance and cars, ten percent for doctor bills. The rest I spend foolishly.

Last week I made a terrible mistake. I blew all my money on rent.

I do earn well. My problem is that there's too much month left after my money.

My wife and I misuse money so badly we're allowed to use handicapped parking.

My wife makes the budget work. We go without a lot of things I don't need.

My wife has low estimates in her budget for her food. She is reasonable when it comes to clothing and the beauty parlor. She's very tight with beverages, theaters, and eating out. But she's got a "miscellaneous" that could choke a horse!

My wife just blew fifty dollars by having her car overhauled. It was overhauled by a traffic cop.

I figured out a great way of having money to spend. I charge everything. When my accounts are close to the limit, I go to the post office, get a change-of-address card, send it out, and then I don't move!

Our budget is a mass of red ink. That's why we're going broke—I have to keep buying red ink.

bugs

We must be coming to a new understanding about bugs. Once they were universally disliked. Take the roach, for example. We used to detest it. Now if you go into a supermarket you can buy a Roach Motel for them!

Killer bees attack everything they see. It's understandable when you consider the fact that we call their leader a queen.

To us, a bee is a pain. To a flower it's Don Juan!

Mosquitoes grow big in Texas. Recently a man found one with six ticks on it.

A Jersey mosquito once bit a bus, and the vehicle couldn't get through the tunnel to New York.

In Jersey the mosquitoes show up on radar.

Louisiana mosquitoes grow pretty big. I was bitten by one the other day, and it left footprints on my arm!

Bees travel thousands and thousands of miles. When they arrive at their destination, they're ready to kill. Most of us have had flights like that!

An experiment took place at the college lab. A young student studied the fly. To get to know the fly's motor capabilities, he tore off two of the legs and said, "Jump!" The fly jumped. After tearing off the next legs and repeating the order, the young man saw the fly jump again. The student removed all of the fly's legs and yelled, "Jump!" The fly didn't budge. The student reported a great scientific find. If all of a bug's legs are removed, it loses the ability to hear.

A moth wanted to get away, so he spent the winter in a tropical worsted suit!

The weather was foul. Two men waited in the cold and wet for a bus. One said, "Isn't this the worst goddamn weather?"

The other answered, "It must be. I haven't seen a butterfly since I got here!"

A mosquito is like a kid. When he stops making noise, he's on to something.

Insects must have brains. How else would they know that you're going on a picnic?

My hotel room was so small I had to go out every hour to let my bug bites swell.

"What's the best way of preventing infections from biting insects?"
"Don't bite any."

"I want something for fleas."
"How about a dog?"

A city slicker, riding with a farmer on a horse-drawn wagon, is bothered by a mosquito. He asks what it is. The farmer says, "That's a horsefly. He hangs around the rear end of a horse."

The city slicker said, "Do I look like the rear end of a horse?"

The farmer said, "You could fool me, but you can't fool a horsefly!"

Two flies flew out to the city garbage dump. Hovering over it were about a quarter of a billion other flies. The first fly asked, "Who else knows about this?"

Then there was this termite who dreamed that he lived in marble halls.

There were two flies. Both felt great because they were down in the dumps.

bulls and cows

They go together. If they didn't, we'd never have calves or "bick" jokes. Along with several friends, I was part of a syndicate that owned a farm in Petaluma, California. We had ninety-nine cows and one bull. The manager decided to sell the bull, but the cows wouldn't let him. The part about the farm is true. My ownership lasted for ten thousand dollars.

In a rural town the school day has started. One student is late. The teacher asks him why and he explains, "I had to bring the bull to cover the cow."

"Couldn't your father do that?"

"No, ma'am. You gotta have the bull!"

A salesman was trying to sell a motorcycle to a farmer, hinting that it would get him around faster. The farmer said, "I'd rather buy me a cow."

"The motorcycle'll save you time."

"Yup, but I'd sure look dumb trying to milk it."

A country boy and girl were walking through the fields when they happened to witness a bull mounting a cow. The country boy said, "I'd sure like to be doing that."

The girl said, "Why can't you? It's your cow."

Seeing a lovely cow in the next pasture, a young bull snorted and tried to jump the barbed-wire fence. Misjudging the height, he zoomed over a little low. When he landed, he shook his head and asked, "How now, brown cow?"

There was a knock on the door. Little Hazel opened it to see a man standing there. She said, "If you've come about the bull, it's a hundred dollars and we got all the necessary papers."

The man said, "Little girl, I want to talk to your father."

"If it's about the bull, I can handle it. It's a hundred dollars."

The man said, "It's not about the bull. It's about your brother Andrew. He's gotten my daughter in a family way!"

The little girl said, "Gee, you'll have to come back. I don't know what we get for Andrew."

Two young soldiers find themselves trapped by an enemy patrol. The only escape route is across a pasture in which cows are grazing. Looking around, the soldiers find a cowhide drying on the barn door. Putting it on quickly, one in front and one in back, they start across the pasture. Suddenly, the one in front says, "Brace yourself. Here comes the bull!"

It was so cold I saw a cow go into a drugstore and buy six ChapSticks.

There are lessons to be learned. One time a large cougar jumped a small bull, killed him, and ate his share of the good red meat. Filled, the puma roared to let the world know what he'd done. The rancher came by and killed the puma with one shot. The puma should have known—If you're full of bull, keep your mouth shut!

A farmer comes home with a lively young bull. His two old bulls have fallen on sad days. He's letting them hang around for old times' sake. The minute the new bull is put into the pasture, he starts servicing the cows. At about the fourth cow, one of the old bulls starts to paw the ground and snort. The other asks, "Why are you doing that?"

The old bull answers, "I don't want him to think I'm one of these cows!"

A frisky young bull and an old one are looking down on a peaceful pasture full of pretty cows. The young bull says, "Let's run down there and take care of one of those cows."

The older bull says, "Let's walk down slowly and take care of all of them."

bums and hoboes

Nonworking people run in my family. I have one brother who hired a private detective to find out what he did for a living. I have another brother who signed up for trade school so he'd know what kind of work he was out of. My third brother almost destroyed my "brother" routine by getting a job. Fortunately, he quit at lunch. It was the longest he'd ever held a position.

A bum called at a house and asked for a small handout. The lady of the house, a nice woman in crinoline, asked, "How would you like a nice chop?"

The bum answered, "It all depends. Is it lamb, pork, or wood?"

"Mister, will you give me a buck for a
    sandwich?"
"Let me see the sandwich!"

A beggar walked over to a man in the street. "I haven't had a bite in three days." So the man bit him!

A beggar walked up to a man in the street and said, "I haven't had food in so long I've forgotten what it tastes like."

The man said, "Don't worry. It still tastes the same."

A beggar walked up to a man in the street and said, "Could you spare a hundred and forty dollars for a cup of coffee?"

The man said, "Coffee's a quarter."

The beggar said, "I know, but I couldn't go into a restaurant dressed like this."

Mrs. Jones was working in her kitchen when a beggar appeared at the kitchen door. "Ma'am, I'd love to have some food."

Mrs. Jones said, "Would you like some of yesterday's soup?"

"I'd love it."

"Good. Come back tomorrow."

A beggar stood in front of a department store, trying to raise some money for a pint. An elderly woman exited the store, stopped when she saw him, rummaged through her purse, and came up with a penny. Dropping it in his hat, she said, "My poor man, how did you get in this condition?"

"Well, ma'am, I was just like you. I gave away vast sums to those in need."

A bum stops at a house to beg some food. The lady of the house says, "Why don't you go out and get a job?"

The bum answers, "What for? To support a bum like me?"

Two bums were brought to court for vagrancy. The judge asked the first, "Don't you have a home?"

The bum said, "I live in the fields and the countryside. Sometimes I just lie down on some beach."

The judge turned to the second bum. "Where do you live?"

The second bum answered, "Next door to him."

"Are you really happy, just walking around and begging for money?"

"No. Once in a while I wish I had a car."

"Ma'am, I haven't eaten a thing for two
    days."
"I wish I had your willpower!"

"Could you spare five nickels for a cup of coffee?"

"Why not a quarter? Why five nickels?"

"I like drip coffee."

"Can you spare three hundred dollars for a
    cup of coffee?"
"Three hundred dollars?"
"For a plane ticket to Brazil. I like it fresh."

A man stood in front of a restaurant with an extended cap in each hand. Another man asked, "Why do you have two caps?"

The beggar said, "Business is so good, I've opened a branch office."

"You should be ashamed of yourself, begging for money."

"I'm only practicing my hobby."

"What's that?"

"Coin collecting."

"I haven't eaten in three days."

"Force yourself!"

A bum gets a piece of chicken from a lady, who insists, however, that he eat it outside. The bum says, "Don't feel bad about the request, ma'am. When I left the house this morning I told my butler that I was eating out."

A beggar says to a man, "I've seen better days."

The man answers, "I haven't got time to talk about the weather."

A hobo knocked on the back door of a house. Opening it, the lady of the house asked, "Hasn't anyone ever offered you a job?"

The hobo said, "Only once. Outside of that, I've met only with kindness."

A beggar meets another on Broadway in New York. He asks, "Don't you usually go on Park Avenue?"

The other answered, "I got married a month ago, and I gave my wife Park Avenue as a wedding present."

"Hasn't it ever occurred to you that you'd have more if you were in some other line of business than begging?"

"Oh yes. I'd love to open a bank, but I don't have the tools."

A bum goes over to a rabbi and asks for a dime or so. A few minutes later, the bum goes over to another bum across the street. The second bum asks, "How much did you get from the rabbi?"

The first bum says, "Get? I ended up giving him a dollar for the temple building fund!"

A train stopped at a watering station for a refill. Checking the boxcars, a railroad detective found a hobo hidden under some straw. He gave the hobo ten seconds to get off the train. The hobo begged him to be kind. "I'm going to my daughter's wedding. I have no money for fares. I just have a few dollars to buy her a gift. Please let me stay."

Grudgingly, the detective agreed to let the hobo stay on. A few feet down, in another pile of straw, the detective found another hobo. The hobo said, "Don't look at me. *He* invited me to the wedding!"

business

Since about half of all dinners, banquets, gatherings, and roasts are somehow involved with business, a few well-chosen barbs about the business can help to solidify your reputation as a master or mistress of the bon mot. The barbs can also get you fired. If you're the boss, you don't have to worry about getting laughs with your jokes. Fear gets the job done!

We're beginning to worry about our accounts receivable. Last week we had to add antifreeze to our cash flow.

When it comes to playing hard-to-get, you can't beat profits.

At our last stockholders' meeting, a slight problem showed up. In the yearly statement, one item read, "Cash flew—$200,000." I brought the attention of the company president to the error. I said, "That should be 'cash flow.' The accountant is in error."

The president said, "It's 'cash flew' all right. And the accountant is in Rio!"

I just don't have an instinct for business. I'm the kind of guy who would open a day-old salad bar!

I don't know the first thing about business. If I were a florist, I'd close for Mother's Day!

Why is it that a generally bright businessman will ignore his assistant's advice and pay a consultant two hundred an hour for the same thing?

In front of the giant skyscraper, old Alex could be found every day, hawking his pencils for a quarter. For twenty years, a customer, Mr. Carling, gave him a quarter each day, but never accepted a pencil. Curiosity got the better of old Alex, and one day he finally asked, "Mr. Carling, how come you never take the pencil?"

Mr. Carling said, "It's a simple story. The first day I gave you a quarter and didn't take the pencil. I went up to apply for a job. Our little transaction was lucky for me. Today I'm the president of the company."

Alex mulled it over, then said, "Okay, in that case, starting tomorrow pencils are fifty cents!"

The boss was furious. He called over his plant manager and said, "I just found out that you've been getting huge kickbacks from our suppliers, making our costs just about double what they should be. I know that you sold our new designs to another company who'll have the products on the shelves a month before us, and I understand that last month you fooled around with my wife. Believe me when I tell you this: one more thing and out you go!"

"Doctor, remember how you told me to take a vacation from my business, get some girls, and have some fun? Remember you told me that?"

"I remember."

"Now tell me one more thing—How do I get my business back?"

One outfit became very upset with another store on the same block that advertised a "going out of business" sale. The resentful outfit put up a huge sign that said, WE'VE BEEN GOING OUT OF BUSINESS LONGER THAN ANYBODY ON THIS BLOCK.

A man started a business on a shoestring. In six months he tripled his investment. Now what is he going to do with the other shoestring?

You know you're in trouble with a businessman if he thinks Dun & Bradstreet is an intersection!

Two merchants were discussing their businesses. One said, "What a September I had! Not ten dollars came in! October, I could have shut my doors. And November was worse than the others."

The other man said, "What are you complaining about? I just found out my son is a homosexual and my daughter is a lesbian and my wife goes both ways. What could be worse than that?"

The other man answers, "December!"

JUDGE: You say the unwritten law could have justified you in killing Mr. Daniels? Yet you didn't fire? Why?

MR. BROWN: He asked me how much I wanted for the gun. How can you kill a man when he's talking business?

"How much do you think I made last year?"

"Half!"

butchers

And anybody else who has a thumb that weighs a pound and a half!

I'm beginning to question my butcher's accuracy. The other day a fly landed on his scale. It weighed four pounds eight ounces!

Meat prices are so high, I bought a steak the other day and I keep it in an unnumbered Swiss freezer.

The butcher trade is the only one in which it's good to be all thumbs.

A woman comes into a butcher shop and asks for a Long Island duckling. The butcher offers her one. She insists on looking at it. She holds it up to the light, looks through the rear end, and says, "I'm sorry. This duckling is not Long Island. It looks like it comes from Delaware or Maryland."

The butcher hands her another duckling, which she also examines. Looking in its rear end, she decides, "This is from the South. Georgia, I'm pretty sure."

She goes through a dozen ducklings and can't find a proper one, even though the butcher swears that they're Long Island ducklings. After the last, the woman says, "Are you some kind of clown? Where are you from, mister?"

The butcher drops his pants, turns around, and says, "Suppose you tell me!"

Butchers are sure putting a lot of fat into their hamburger nowadays. I bought a pound the other day with a new color—white!

A woman goes into a butcher shop and complains that the turkey she'd bought didn't have a wishbone. The butcher says, "Our turkeys are so contented they have nothing to wish for!

cabs and cabbies

The men behind the wheels of our taxis are largely unsung. To many, they are arrogant and vicious, but to some, like me, they can also be loudmouthed, ugly, mean, and nasty. Yes, a taxi may be hard to find when it's pouring, but you will concede that when you get one, it's always going the other way!

He loves being a cabdriver. He goes to work every day in a taxi.

The cabbie whizzed around corners like a demon. His lady passenger said, "The way you make turns, you must pray a lot."

The cabbie said, "Nah, I just close my eyes!"

With airline fares plummeting, it now costs as much to get to the airport as it does to fly somewhere!

The cabbie was being very quiet as his two women passengers debated the easy life of taxi drivers. One said, "The worst part is that they make so much money. They have homes in the country. They take trips."

The other added, "They send kids through college. But they don't spend a penny on their taxis. Look, this one doesn't even have an ashtray."

The cabbie leaned back and said through clenched teeth, "Drop your butts on the floor, ladies. Once a week, I get a girl in to clean!"

A man asked a cabbie to take him to an address on the west side of town. The cabbie started the journey by darting into traffic, making impossible one-wheeled turns, and cutting in and out, changing lanes a dozen times a minute. After one hair-raising turn, the passenger said, "Please be careful. I have ten kids at home."

The cabbie answered, "You have ten kids, and you're telling *me* to be careful?"

A man with a hearing aid stepped into a cab. After taking off, the cabbie tried to make small talk. "I notice you're wearing a hearing aid. Help you much?"

"I'd be dead without it."

"Must be tough to be deaf. But then, everybody's got some problem. Look at me—I can't see a foot in front of my face!"

A cabbie in Washington, D.C., had himself a victim on a cold winter's day. Instead of driving the passenger directly to his hotel, he circled and backtracked and circled again. After seeing the Lincoln Memorial for the tenth time, the passenger asked, "How many Lincoln Memorials are there?"

The cabbie answered, "I don't know for sure, but he was a biggie!"

She was so bowlegged she could get out of both sides of a cab at the same time!

A cabbie takes on a fare in wintry Washington. Driving at a snail's pace to put as much as possible on the meter, the cabbie seems to be in absolutely no hurry. Finally the passenger says, "If you're trying to do me a favor by waiting for the cherry blossoms to bloom, I've seen them!"

A woman gets into a cab and goes on a twenty-dollar jaunt to the edge of town. Upon arriving, she says, "I have no money."

The cabbie says, "I want to get paid."

She raises her dress and says, "Will this do?"

The cabbie says, "Don't you have anything smaller?"

A well-dressed man waited in front of a Brooklyn apartment. Surrounding him were a dozen pieces of luggage. Eventually a taxi came along. The driver placed the luggage inside neatly. He started to drive to the docks without hitting a bump. The passenger said, "You're very gentle. I have a suggestion that might interest you."

"Sure."

"Well, as you can see, I'm taking a cruise. I'll be away six months and no doubt will see every major port in the world. In each port I'll have to hail a taxi. Most of them will be dismal, most of the drivers uncouth."

"It happens."

"I was thinking perhaps you'd like to come along. I don't care about the cost."

"That could run into a fortune."

"I told you, I don't care. Naturally, I'll also pay all of your expenses."

The cabbie pondered the offer and decided to take it up. When they arrived at the Manhattan dock, the cab was loaded onto the ocean liner. The gentleman made all the necessary arrangements. Two hours later they were under way.

For six months they traveled the world. Dutifully, in each city, the cabbie and his cab debarked, drove the passenger around, returned, and then went aboard again.

The trip ended. They arrived in Manhattan at ten in the evening. The cabbie had left the meter running, as was agreed upon, and it read $42,653.80. True to his word, the passenger wrote out a check, which included a handsome tip. Then he said, "Now take me home to Brooklyn."

The cabbie said, "Brooklyn at night? Forget it. I always have to come back to Manhattan empty!"

A man stops a stranger on the street and asks, "How do you get to Carnegie Hall?"

"Practice!" the stranger answers.

During the Vietnam War, a reporter tried to make a few dollars on the side with his expense account. He put down a figure of one hundred fifty dollars for taxi fares. Aware that the reporter was on an aircraft carrier all of this time, the newspaper's accountant wrote him asking how he could explain the expense of cabs on a carrier. The reporter wrote back, "It's a damn big carrier!"

It's not the job of being a cabbie that he likes. It's the people he runs into.

A drunk sank into the passenger seat of a Manhattan cab and asked to be taken to his hotel. En route the taxi went past the library at Forty-second and Fifth Avenue, in front of which there are two stone lions. Dancing around the maws of the lions were the usual pigeons. The wino leaned forward and asked the cabbie, "Don't they feed them beef, like most lions?"

A rabbi, a minister, and a cabbie arrived in heaven at the same time. There being room for only one that day, Saint Peter turned down the men of the cloth. Opening the door wide for the cabbie, he said, "You've scared more hell out of people with your cab than they did with their Bibles!"

A passenger got into a taxi and said, "Take me anyplace."

The cabbie said, "I'm not going that way!"

Rain is weird—it makes flowers emerge and taxis disappear.

They knew he was going to be a cabbie. In math class at school he could never find the shortest distance between two points.

Traffic was bad in Los Angeles one day. A cabbie, who'd had a long wait between rides, was ready to chew live meat. Obviously in a hurry, his passenger barked, "Can't you go any faster?"

"I can go a hell of a lot faster," the cabbie said, "but I'm not allowed to leave the taxi!"

A cabbie avoids hitting a pregnant woman and says, "Lady, be careful. You can always get knocked *down!*"

"Three dollars. You can't fool me. I haven't ridden in cabs for years for nothing!"
"I bet you tried!"

Clouds must give off some kind of radio waves. The minute one appears, the "off duty" sign on all cabs goes on!

Cabbies are always on the spot, even if it's where somebody's standing!

"**Y**ou are a vicious, cold-blooded killer," the judge yelled at the cabdriver on trial. "You deliberately drove miles out of the way to a secluded spot and murdered your passenger. Do you have anything to say on your behalf?"

The cabbie said, "I didn't keep the meter running!"

A cabbie knocked down a pedestrian and was bawled out by a cop on the corner. "What kind of driver are you? You must be blind!"

"Blind? Didn't I hit him?"

Cabbies drive like they own the road, when they don't even own the cab!

These new small cabs are dangerous. Signaling left turns with his hand, one cabbie has desexed eight cops!

A cabbie went on vacation to England. While in London, he was taken to many of the historic places. Finally he was shown the statue of Lord Nelson in which a leg has been shot off. He was told, "This is where Nelson was hit."

The cabbie said, "Were there any witnesses?"

A gent walks over to a parked New York cabbie and asks, "Can you tell me where the Guggenheim Museum is, or should I go screw myself?"

cajuns

Nothing spices up a party more than jokes about how dumb or simple other people are. Meanwhile, back at the ranch, the other people are talking about you. Along the Mississippi, the "others" are Cajuns and "Coonasses." When Cajuns hear a joke about another Cajun doing something dumb, they laugh louder and longer than anybody. They don't know who you're talking about, because the bayou folk can skin a city slicker so fast he won't know it until his bones fall in a heap!

A Cajun left his small town in the backwater and went to New Orleans for a vacation. He arrived just as Mardi Gras was getting under way. Aware that accommodations wouldn't be easy to find, what with the mob that descends on the city during the festival, he went to a hotel and asked for a room. The desk clerk laughed and laughed. "My Cajun friend, every hotel in New Orleans has been sold out for a week. Some people make reservations a year early."

"I'll take any room. I don't care if it got a 'gator in it."

"There are no rooms."

"Hold it, brother. You mean to tell me that if the Pope were to come for Mardi Gras and he didn't have no reservation, you wouldn't have a room for him?"

"Of course we would."

"Well, he ain't coming, so you can give me *his* room!"

A Coonass found himself with a paid lady of easy virtue in his hotel room. After having sex with her, he said, "I like you, girl. Tell you what I'm going to do. I'm fixing to take a nap now, but I want you to hold on to my right hand while I'm napping and I'll give you extra money."

Not adverse to extra money, the young lady did as requested. When the Coonass woke from his nap, another love bout occurred. He explained that he needed some time to refresh himself with a nap again. Would the young lady hold his right hand as before?

Four times the Coonass napped, and four times the young lady held his right hand for some extra money. Finally, curiosity got the better of the young lady. She asked, "Why do I have to hold your hand while you're napping?"

The Coonass said, "Well, the last time I had a woman in the room and I took a nap, she stole my wallet!"

Two Cajuns went fishing in the bayou. The perch couldn't wait to jump into the little rowboat the men shared. Soon the Cajuns got tired of hauling in the fish. They decided to call it quits. One said, "But before we go, we should mark this here spot."

The other said, "I got the agreement with you."

They put an *X* in the middle of the boat and were about to move away when the first Cajun started to shake his head sadly.

The other was puzzled and asked, "Why are you shaking your head?"

The head-shaker said, "You know something? If we don't get this same boat, how we going to know where to fish next time?"

A Cajun's wife had just baked the thickest sweet potato pie of all time. Her young daughter watched as she stuck in a knife to see if it came out clean, showing that the pie was ready. The knife came out like new. The daughter said, "That knife sure is clean, Mama. Let's put in all the other dirty knives!"

A pretty young lady was driving into the backcountry to shop for some antiques. It was warm and she stopped at a pond to wet her face. The water seemed very pleasant, so she decided to take a little swim. Undressing, she got into the water and was enjoying herself very much when a Cajun of just about her age happened by. He stopped to enjoy the view. After a moment the young girl emerged from the water and saw him. It was too far to run for her clothes on the bank, so she looked around for some cover. Seeing a rusty old frying pan in the sand, she picked it up and placed it in front of her strategically. The young man smiled. She said accusingly, "Don't you dare do anything, whatever you're thinking!"

The Cajun said, "I wasn't thinking nothing. But I know what you're thinking. You're thinking that pan has a bottom to it!"

A new priest came to this small bayou town. His first Sunday, he stood and preached against the use of the Pill. Jacques Ribot, a member of the parish, yelled at him, "Padre, if you don't play the game, don't make the rules!"

A Cajun was drafted into the army. After basic training he was sent to Europe and eventually ended up in France. As his outfit moved farther and farther inland, he saw terrible scenes of desolation. Everywhere he saw the French without homes, little food, and in ragged old clothes. Another soldier said to the Cajun, "It's a shame what the French have had to go through."

The Cajun said, "I don't feel sorry for the French. They never should have left Louisiana in the first place!"

Three men—a Yank, a Texan, and a Coonass—were all struck ill during a stay in New Orleans. After a thorough examination, the doctor said that all three men had come down with a virulent kind of swamp fever. They had six months to live and they should all do what they had always wanted to do. The Yank said he wanted to go on a world cruise. The Texan said he wanted to ride the range of Texas. The Cajun said, "I want another doctor!"

Pierre LaPorte was famous because he'd

saved two women—one for himself and one for his brother Jacques!

A New Orleans social worker was doing a survey of conditions in the bayou country. She arrived at one shack where she saw a woman feeding a baby. The meal consisted of rabbit drippings and brick-hard bread. The social worker said, "That isn't good food for a baby. Breast-feeding is the best way to feed a baby."

The mother pointed to a burly man cleaning some fish. His shoulders were wide and his muscles rippled through his shirt. "That's my oldest boy," the mother said. "He didn't have a tit in his mouth till the day he got married!"

A Coonass went to his first movie. It turned out to be a mushy love story. The Coonass watched a love scene. The hero kissed the girl on her hand, on her arm, and then on the neck. The Coonass turned to the man in the next seat and said, "The damn fool don't know where to kiss a girl!"

Driving through bayou country, a snoopy tourist saw a child sitting on a rotted porch. His face was filthy and his clothes barely rags. The tourist asked, "Where's your mother?"

"Don't have one."

"How about your father?"

"Don't have one of them either."

"That's terrible—both parents dead."

"I didn't say that, ma'am. I never had any."

"That's impossible."

"No it isn't. Some Yankee tourist played a dirty trick on my aunt!"

california

Some states are maligned because their natives have certain characteristics that the general popu-lation finds unappealing. That can't be the reason California is joked about. California has every characteristic, and some nobody else has ever heard of. California also has every kind of weather, sometimes in the same place at the same time. If anything is truly Californian, it's the account of a recent year's July Fourth weekend. California manages to lead the nation in every-thing. It is always number one in highway fatalities. In the year under scrutiny, California wasn't even in the top ten when the Department of Transportation announced its first statistics. One of the California bigwigs had to go on television and exhort the people to try harder. By Monday morning, California led the nation again in highway fatalities!

Californians are incredible. They sit around their pools and spend hours discussing water conservation.

There are about ten million hair dryers in California. Then there are some also owned by *women.*

Californians all have a great tan. It comes from snorting shoe polish.

You can always tell a California car. It doesn't have a muffler under it. It has a pedestrian!

Californians march to their own drummers. To them, "too far out" is a breast measure-ment.

A Californian was bragging, "We have the most fertile land in the world. We had an orange at the state fair last year that was so big, fifty men could have stood under it."

The gent he was bragging to, a simple soul from West Virginia, said, "That's nothing. We make glass in our neck of the woods.

We make glasses so big, it takes fifty men to heat-fuse them together and one man can't see where the other man is putting his seam."

The Californian asked, "Why would anyone want a glass that big?"

"To hold the juice from that orange of yours!" answered the mountaineer.

A fellow, born in California, was asked how he'd left the state. He answered, "I was drugged and carried out screaming!"

A Californian went to Texas for a funeral. Unfortunately, no one was willing to speak for the deceased. Nobody had a kind word for him. After a long period of silence, the Californian got up and said, "If nobody's going to say anything about that bugger, I'd like to say a few words about California."

Visiting one of the local farmers' markets all over California, a Floridian picked up a watermelon and asked, "Is this as big as your kiwi fruit grows?"

The produce man answered, "Don't squeeze too hard, you'll bruise that raisin!"

Saint Peter stopped a new arrival at the gate. "Excuse me, but you're supposed to go to hell."

The Californian he'd stopped said, "I know. But I'm from California, and the change had better be gradual!"

A couple of Floridians were visiting relatives in California. Complaining of the August heat, one said, "This California weather is impossible!"

The other said, "Dear one, you have to remember we're thirty-five hundred miles from the ocean!"

A mind reader relocated in California. In two weeks he almost died because he had nothing to do!

Rain is a rare commodity in California. They have "dew." The other day a man slipped coming up the street to his house, and to find him they had to drag the dew for three hours!

California has some of the richest towns in the country. In one town near Hollywood at Christmas, they bring baskets of food to people with only one Mercedes!

A nun, famous for her total dedication to spiritual matters, came to California on a fund-raising drive. After a month, a man called her to pledge some money and got her answering machine. It said, "Hi, there. This is Sis. I'm not in right now . . ."

A couple were worried about an earthquake, so they sent their kids to live with an aunt in the East. Two weeks later, they got a wire from the East: "Returning kids. Send earthquake."

Once in a while you hear about a dry spell in California. I know it's true because I got a letter from my cousin—the stamp was attached with a pin!

If you feel a tremor in California, you should do two things: get under a doorway, and make sure the doorway is in Cleveland.

California has the spiffiest dressers. I know a guy who puts shoe trees in his tennis shoes.

In California, the eye of a hurricane would wear contact lenses!

California is loaded with condos. One kid was asked by his teacher, "What happened in 1492?"

The kid answered, "How would I know? I live on the twelfth floor!"

camp

The greatest pleasure trip of all time—driving your kid to camp! We sent my son Billy to camp every year, but they kept sending him back! Camp jokes can be curved slightly and serve as great insults. The reverse is also true—scratch an insult and you may have a good camp joke.

My wife and I had a great summer, relaxed and restful. In fact, this morning I said, "Camp is over. Billy's coming home."
  She said, "Who?"

A kid wrote home, "Please send me some food. All they serve here are meals!"

Their son returned from camp. He looked six inches taller. Then they washed his feet.

Next year we're going to save money. We're sending my son to Camp Grandparents.

Camp counselors are always about seventeen. You wouldn't trust them with your car, but you let them have your kids.

A camper found himself bothered by mosquitoes during the first day at camp. At night he saw some fireflies and said, "Now they're coming after me with flashlights!"

My son came home from camp yesterday with a six-week stack of dirty clothes. That's surprising, because it was only a two-week camp.

My son's camp laundry wasn't hard to clean, once the Roto-Rooter man got the stuff separated.

A counselor was helping his charges put their stuff away on their first morning in camp. He was surprised to see that one youngster had an umbrella. The counselor asked, "Why did you bring an umbrella?"
  The kid answered, "Did you ever have a mother?"

A woman gave the counselor some last-minute instructions. "At no time," she said, "should you hit my son Jeff. If Jeff does something bad, just hit the boy next to him. That'll scare Jeff!"

My kid ate so much spaghetti in camp, one day he went into the heat and starched himself.

Last year my son set a record. He came home from camp with a hundred eighteen unmatched socks! They went with his one hundred eighteen unmatched shirts.

Some of the kids wanted to get away from the camp, so they touched some poison ivy and broke out!

My ten-year-old daughter got so many bug bites that when she came home from camp she wore a 42D bra.

The counselor called and told us that our son was sleeping with a stray dog. "What about the smell?" we asked.
  The counselor answered, "The dog seems to be getting used to it."

candles

Nobody notices them until the icing of your birthday cake starts to sag in the middle. Or you begin to sag in the middle. Or both of the above!

He's getting pretty old. If you lit all the candles on his birthday cake, you could bury an unknown soldier behind them!

Two old maids go into a candle shop. They see a special sale on candles at three for a dollar. One says, "Let's buy three of them. We can always *light* one!"

She's so old she tried to blow out the candles on her cake, but the heat drove her back!

He must be getting on in years. Instead of candles, last year they built a bonfire in the center of his cake.

One day the candle factory burned. It took the firemen six hours to blow out the flames.

Jack be nimble, Jack be quick,
Jack jumped over the candlestick.
Jack didn't go as high as he could get,
So now Jack's name is Juliet!

She decided they'd have a romantic dinner. She lit the candles. The candles lit the drapes. The drapes lit the wall. The wall lit the propane tank. The propane tank exploded. It turned out to be romantic anyway, because for the first time in years they went out together.

If you put the right number of candles on his cake, it would be a fire hazard.

Her last birthday cake looked like a prairie fire.

The last time she lit the candles on her birthday cake, she barbecued the ceiling.

She's so old, a hook-and-ladder company comes with her cake.

She's so old, they put all the ingredients for a cake in a pan, and when they add the candles, it bakes itself.

She's so old, at her party the candles cost more than the cake.

cannibals

How can you resist people who love their fellow man?

The cannibal king sat back and said, "I like those relaxed moments when the meal is over and everybody's eaten!"

The cannibal wiped his mouth daintily and said, "My wife makes great soup. But I'll miss her!"

A cannibal extends an invitation to another cannibal. "Why don't you come over for dinner tonight? We're having my mother-in-law."
The other says, "I don't like your mother-in-law."
The first one says, "Okay, then, just come over for coffee and dessert."

A cannibal mother pointed out a downed airliner to her small child and said, "It's like seafood. You just eat what's inside."

A cannibal student was thrown out of school one day for buttering up his teacher.

Once there was a very hip cannibal—he ate three squares a day.

Most people don't like drunks, but it takes a cannibal to like somebody stewed.

She was so ugly, when she was captured by

cannibals, they threw her away and cooked her clothes.

A cannibal is a man who loves his fellow man—with gravy.

A cannibal king and his son were hunting in the jungle. After a while they came to a small waterfall, under which a beautiful young girl was bathing. Her body glistened in the sun. Her curves hugged the droplets of water that bathed her dark skin. The son said, "Ah, Pop, we've finally found breakfast. I'm starved."

The king said, "We will not eat her."

"You're kidding. I'm famished."

"No, we will not eat her. I will crawl up to her. When I capture her, we'll go home and eat your mother!"

One cannibal asked another, "Have you seen the dentist?"

The other answered, "Yep. He filled my teeth at dinner!"

The cannibals stopped eating missionaries because of indigestion. They had a lot of trouble keeping a good man down.

A cannibal is somebody who lives on other people.

My relatives must be cannibals. They've been living off me for years!

"**T**hrow him in the pot. We'll eat him."

"No, no. I'm not what I'm cooked up to be!"

A cannibal chief captured a newspaperman. The newspaperman cried, "I can do you good. I'm an editor."

The cannibal said, "Good. Tonight you'll be editor-in-chief!"

A cannibal is a guy who goes into a restaurant and orders a waiter.

One cannibal had a bad case of hay fever. He ate a grass widow.

A cannibal ate a missionary because he wanted a taste of religion.

Some missionaries wandered into a cannibal village. The next thing they knew, they were in a flying stew!

He used to be the pride of the islands, then one day the natives swallowed their pride.

Two cannibals, father and son, captured a stranger and, as is their way, cooked the gentleman. When he was done, the father said, "Let's eat him this way—you will start with his toes and I'll start with his head. We'll meet in the middle."

The son agrees and starts chomping on the delicious toes. After a few minutes, the cannibal father asks, "How are you doing, son?"

The son says, "I'm having a ball."

The father says, "You're eating too fast!"

cards

As a kid, I learned many card tricks from magicians in vaudeville. I became so good at it that I wasn't allowed to deal in a social game of any kind. I was allowed to play and hold cards, but not deal. One day in New Orleans, I found a poker game in which I was offered a seat and the right to deal. It turned out that four of the players were local cardsharps. One of them, from Abbeville in bayou country, finally said, "This is the crookedest game I ever been in. Ain't nobody playing the cards I dealt them!"

The card game was going full steam. As a hot deal was being played out, one of the players keeled over dead. The others carried him to the bedroom and put him on the bed. One said, "What do you think we ought to do?"

Another player said, "Out of deference to old Steve, let's finish this hand standing up!"

A kibitzer stands behind a gin rummy player and watches him for hours. The player says, after a dozen games, "Why don't you try your hand?"

The kibitzer answers, "Not me. I don't have the patience!"

Playing poker with a one-eyed man is considered bad luck. That didn't seem to matter to the fellows, because they needed a man to complete the game. One-eyed Carl was the only man around.

The game went on for hours. One-eyed Carl was winning a fortune. His turn to deal came again. As he dealt out the cards, another player noticed the flash of one card. One-eyed Carl was dealing from the bottom of the deck. The player whipped out a derringer and said, "I think we're going to start to deal this hand again. Not that I'm accusing anybody of cheating or being dishonest, or in any fashion not playing legitimately. Remember, I'm not accusing a soul of being crooked. It could be anybody here if it has been happening. Any man among us, so I won't be accusatory. However, if that son of a gun cheats again, I'll shoot out his other eye!"

You can tell a truly religious man—he holds four aces and still prays to God.

An out-of-towner came into Reno and looked for a nice card game. At one casino he found a table at which there were five players. One of them was a beagle. The man said, "Sure is something, a dog playing cards."

Another player said, "He's not so good. When he's got a good hand, he wags his tail."

A group of women are playing poker. In one hand the betting was furious. Finally, all the money was in the pot with only two players left. Marsha said, "What have you got?"

Gloria said, "Jacks."

"How many?"

"One."

"Good. I thought you were bluffing."

A kibitzer watches a poker game all night. As dawn creeps up outside, he looks at his watch and says, "Fellas, win or lose, in ten minutes I'm going home."

They didn't mind his marking the cards, but one day somebody came in early and saw him marking his sleeves.

A group of men are playing poker at Sid's house. A kibitzer rushes in and says, "Sid, Tommy's in the kitchen making love to your wife."

Sid says, "That's it. Guys, this is positively the last deal!"

The usual crowd is playing poker when Greg rushes in from the outside and says to one of the players, "Your wife just died of a heart attack."

The player says, "Wait till this deal is over. You guys are going to see a fellow start crying."

"Don't tell me you've been up all night with a sick friend, holding his hand."

"If I'd been holding his hand, I'd have made a lot of money!"

They named a card game after him—rummy!

"Last night, Ed had four kings. But this other guy had five aces."
"What happened?"
"They held an inquest over the guy with the five aces."

Life is a poker game—it takes a pair to open. He shows her diamonds. She calls his bluff. They end up with a full house!

My wife does great card tricks when she shops—she can make the jack disappear.

He's a conservative player. When he opens the pot, you can throw away four kings.

"I have four aces."
"You win. I only have three aces."

A game is going hot and heavy, in which each of the players is a man of the cloth. At about midnight a policeman bursts into the room. "All right, break it up!"
One clergyman says, "Break what up?"
"Come on. I know you've been playing cards." The policeman looks the priest square in the eye. "Have you been playing poker, Padre?"
The priest says, "Of course not."
"How about you, Reverend Cagle?"
The Lutheran minister shakes his head. "Me, play cards?"
Rabbi Stein also denies playing, as do two of the other men. The policeman asks the Baptist minister, the last man left, "How about you, Reverend? Have you been playing cards?"
The Baptist minister says, "With whom?"

"Do you want to have a friendly game of cards?"
"No, let's play bridge!"

cars

The difference between a car and an auto is about twenty thousand dollars.

He's wanted a Chevy ever since 1970. He finally realized his dream. Last week he bought a 1970 Chevy.

They have a fuel today that combines a little gasoline with a lot of alcohol. The other day the cops stopped a guy and made his car blow up a balloon.

He has the kind of car he shouldn't stop. The minute he does, people think it's an accident!

Watch out for children on the road. They're terrible drivers.

Most men have a big problem—how do they get the car started in the morning and their wives at night?

He bought one of these new sub-sub-compacts. It saves him a fortune in gas—he can't get into it.

I'm having awful car trouble—the car won't start and the payments won't stop.

I'm so far behind in my car payments, the company wants to repossess. But what will they do with a Reo?

I have a used car with a quarter of a million miles on it. It belonged to a little old lady with grandchildren at the South Pole.

I saw a fancy convertible with sheepskin seat covers. It looked nice, but you couldn't park it in the country. Rams kept attacking it.

The best way to stop the noise in your car is to let her drive.

I just bought a device that keeps the inside of your car quiet. It fits right over her mouth.

I won't say my car is a lemon, but once a week I take it to a carwash to have it peeled.

Remember those ancient days when a backseat driver had room to sit there?

I was hit by one of those foreign compacts. I had to go to the hospital to have it removed.

catastrophes (man-made and natural)

But not including my act!

It was the worst rainstorm of the century. Half the valley was gone. Agitated, a man called the rescue hotline. "Help me. I'm standing in two feet of water!"
   The rescue monitor said, "That's not exactly a flood emergency around here."
   The man said, "No? I'm calling from the fourth floor!"

It's going to be a rough winter. I just saw a squirrel bury four acorns and a can of Sterno!

We have to worry about the weather bureau. When Noah started to build the Ark, the weather bureau said it would be partly cloudy.

It was real windy the other day. One hen laid the same egg six times.

"How close did the lightning come to you?"
"Don't know for sure, but my cigarette wasn't lit before!"

I never worry about tornadoes or hurricanes. The mortgage on my house is so heavy nothing could budge it.

We have special rules that go into effect during a catastrophe like a storm. For example, your house can turn right without making a stop first.

A farmer went through a terrible tornado. His insurance agent asked, "Much damage to the house and the barn?"
   The farmer said, "Don't know. I haven't found them yet!"

One fellow got into trouble during a hurricane. The cops got him for going ninety miles an hour in his bedroom.

It was the worst cold spell of the last ten years. Turkeys were begging to be roasted, and it was still four weeks to Thanksgiving!

Freddie, a boy of seven, was in no mood to eat his Brussels sprouts. His mother insisted, warning him, "If you don't eat your Brussels sprouts, God will be angry."
   The boy toyed with his sprouts but was unable to get them down. He managed to hide most of the mangled vegetables under the fat from his meat.
   That night, Freddie went to bed. Just as he was about to fall asleep, a flash of lightning lit his room. A moment later a clap of thunder shook his room. Freddie ran to the window and said, "You're sure making a fuss about three Brussels sprouts!"

It was a terrible storm. Six inches of rain had fallen in the first twenty-four hours. Eight had fallen on the second day. The entire town was flooded. Over at the Bronson house, little Jimmy Bronson, eight years old, sat at the window of his upstairs room and stared outside. He was looking at a sun hat that was floating in one direction for a while, then seemed to get caught up and start to float back toward the house. The process went on for hours. Jimmy's uncle came by the house to see if all was well, and saw his nephew staring. He started to look too, and couldn't understand why the hat kept moving up and back, up and back. Finally he asked Jimmy, "What's going on down there?"

Jimmy said, "That's Pa. Last week he said, 'Come hell or high water, I'm going to mow the lawn Saturday!'"

The skies opened and the rain poured down. Noah looked up and said to his son, "I knew I shouldn't have washed the Ark this morning!"

The volunteer fire and emergency department has the right idea. When you hear the disaster signal, you jump out of bed and touch the wall. If it's cool and still standing, you go back to bed.

cemeteries

In my college seminar there comes a touchy moment when I declare that some of the grimmest subjects can be funny. Cannibalism can be funny. Otherwise students wouldn't laugh when I ask how long fingers should be cooked. Death and cemeteries can be great fun. Try an Irish wake for size.

Thinking about anything but his work, a gravedigger managed to dig a hole from which he couldn't emerge. He kept clawing at the sides of the hole, but the dirt wouldn't hold enough weight for him to be able to pull himself up.

The day wore on. The evening chill fell on the cemetery. The poor gravedigger's teeth chattered as he sat waiting for someone to rescue him. He kept calling for help. His cries went unheard until a drunk happened by. The drunk looked in and surveyed the situation. The gravedigger begged, "Please help me out. I'm freezing."

The drunk started to kick dirt back into the grave and said, "I wouldn't be surprised. You don't have any dirt on you!"

A man placed some flowers on the grave of his departed mother and started back for his car, parked on the cemetery road. His attention was diverted to a man kneeling at a grave. The man seemed to be praying with profound intensity, and kept repeating, "Why did you die? Why did you die?"

The first man approached him and said, "Sir, I don't want to interfere with your private grief, but this demonstration of hurt and pain is more than I've ever seen before. For whom do you mourn so deeply? Your child? A parent? Who, may I ask, lies in that grave?"

The mourner answered, "My wife's first husband! Why did you die? Why did you die?"

At a woman's funeral, the family boarder carries on without end. He was her lover for years, and is unable to hold back his tears. Things become so miserable, the husband has to walk over to him and say, "Don't worry, Pete. I'll get married again."

A man puts down flowers on each of three graves and stops to sob tenderly at each.

Another man walks over to him and asks, "Who are these three people to give you so much grief?"

The man says, "Those are my first three wives. The first one died from eating poisoned mushrooms. The second died from eating poisoned mushrooms. The third died from a broken skull."

"How was her skull broken?"

"She wouldn't eat the poisoned mushrooms!"

This town is so healthy they had to shoot a visitor to start a cemetery.

A man belonged to a group that asked its members to join the group's cemetery plot. Most of the men joined. One man who joined, however, wasn't the swiftest payer in town. After ten years, the treasurer of the group asked him to come up with some money. The man said, "Why should I have to pay? I haven't used it."

The treasurer said, "Who stopped you?"

A sentimental widow put up a lovely marble stone for her late husband. Its wording read, REST IN PEACE—UNTIL WE MEET AGAIN.

Joe's mother-in-law had died, and Joe was at the mortuary to make plans for her disposition. The official asked, "Which should we do—cremate her, embalm her, or merely bury her?"

Joe answered, "All three. Let's not take any chances!"

Pat's wife had died, or so it seemed. As the funeral procession moved toward the cemetery, the hearse hit a bad bump in the road. This loosened the piece of food that had lodged in the wife's throat. Suddenly the woman sat up.

There was general glee, except, of course,

on the part of Pat, whose life had been made miserable by the lady.

Time went by, and once again Pat's wife received the last rites. This time she really expired. As the funeral procession went down the same road, Pat said, "Careful, boys, watch that bump this time!"

Two lifelong buddies went on an ocean cruise. On the fifth day out, Marshall became ill and died. A burial at sea was ordered. The general pattern for burials at sea is to load the casket down with heavy shot so it'll sink. There being no shot on this ship, a large chunk of coal was put in the casket. As Marshall was lowered to his eternal sleep, his friend cried out, "Marsh, I knew you were never going to make it to heaven, but I never dreamed you'd have to bring your own fuel!"

A funeral procession was winding its way down the main street of the town. A stranger asked the man next to him, "Whose funeral is it?"

The man answered, "The guy in the first car."

A man is carrying on beyond belief at his wife's funeral. No one can comfort him. He can't be consoled. "My life is empty. I'm a lost soul."

A friend says, "What are you talking about? You're a young man. You'll meet another woman. In a year or so you'll get married again."

The man says, "Sure. But what am I going to do tonight?"

A great actor meets another as both return from the funeral of a woman star. The other actor says, "I couldn't believe you. In the mortuary you carried on, you made a spectacle of yourself."

The great actor says, "Didn't you catch me at the grave?"

"Why do widows wear black garters?"
"In memory of those who have passed beyond."

The wife dies and the husband has her cremated. Then he mixes her ashes with marijuana. He explains to a friend, "This is the best she ever made me feel!"

cheapness

This is a good section to mark. You'd be surprised how much fun "cheap" jokes can generate at a function. Also, they are generally true. I have a list of fifty movie stars who still have the first dollars they ever made. I know one who's so tight that when he winks, his kneecaps move!

You can recognize him in any restaurant. He's always sitting with his back to the check.

He's a man of rare gifts. Nobody ever got one from him.

He's so cheap he wouldn't lend a videocassette to a blind man.

She said she wanted to see the world—he bought her a map.

His idea of being forced to commit an unnatural act is to pick up a check.

He has an impediment in his reach.

He's the kind of cheap bastard who'd buy himself a wind-up pacemaker.

He throws money around like a man without arms.

He's got low pockets and short arms.

He'd give you the sleeves off his vest.

When the home for the aged came to him for a donation, he gave them his mother and father.

At dinner he sits as if the check were going to reach out and hit him!

He keeps his wife's teeth with him so she can't eat between meals.

He's so cheap, he had Baggies sewed into his pockets so he could take soup home from the restaurant.

He's so cheap, he wouldn't give a rabbi a tip at a circumcision.

He gives until it hurts—but he's extremely sensitive to pain.

He never gave her a present—he figured a past was enough.

The drinks he serves are so weak they wouldn't even stain the tablecloth.

He thinks nothing is too good for her. That's what he gives her—nothing!

He buys his wife the cheapest clothes. Yesterday her coat shrank two inches, and it was only cloudy outside!

He builds castles in the air because the rent is cheap.

He believes that a friend in need is a friend you stay away from.

If he saw a spastic in his swimming pool, he'd throw in soap and laundry.

He deducts for charitable contributions to the widow of the unknown soldier.

Some people want to make money fast. He wants to make it *last.*

He always remembers the poor. It doesn't cost him anything.

He keeps divorcing ugly wives. It's cheaper than sending them to the beauty parlor.

He just bought his wife a fifty-two-piece dinner set—a box of toothpicks.

She wanted a foreign convertible, so he bought her a rickshaw.

He's a real sport. You furnish the ship, he'll furnish the ocean.

When they got married she didn't have a rag on her back. Now she has nothing but!

He's a ladykiller—he starves a date to death.

When there's a call for charity, he's the first one to put his hand in his pocket—and leave it there.

He's made an art of avoiding picking up checks. You have to hand it to him.

His drinks look sick—he nurses them for hours.

He likes to go to singles bars, because that's about all he spends.

He's got a great way of saving money—he forgets who he borrowed it from.

He pays his bills with a smile. Most of his creditors would prefer cash.

He's so cheap, when he doesn't feel well, he doesn't go to the doctor for X rays—he goes through the luggage X ray at the airport.

He's the carefree type. He doesn't care as long as it's free.

He'll never go to outer space. He only goes where he can stay with a relative.

He's so tight you can hear him squeak when he walks.

He lives near a nuclear plant so he can read by the light from his wife.

He's so cheap, when his girl wants to go dancing he takes her to the Hare Krishnas at the airport.

He spent his entire life scrimping and saving. Eventually it became too much for him. Borrowing a gun from a neighbor, he went into a fancy haberdashery and ordered the clerk to bring him a fancy suit. Afraid for his life, the salesman brought over a magnificent garment that cost nine hundred dollars. The cheapskate studied the suit and said, "Don't you have something a little cheaper?"

He wants to die with his boots on. He has holes in his socks.

He bought his daughter a dollhouse with a second mortgage on it.

He's always trying to pass the buck—except when it has Washington's picture on it.

He could squeeze pennies out of a nickel.

He's the last of the big spenders. He orders asparagus and leaves the waiter the tips.

He talks through his nose to save wear and tear on his teeth.

He wouldn't buy a round of drinks at an AA meeting.

He's so cheap, he hypnotized his wife into believing she was a canary so she'd eat birdseed. When that worked, he made her believe she was a sparrow so she'd go out and dig up her own food!

He loves to take things for gratis.

He'd sell herring with measles as trout.

His checks bounce so much, his bank book has to be retreaded.

He takes things easy, and from anybody.

He gives gifts that keep on giving—like a pregnant cat.

If he found a corn plaster, he'd go out and borrow tight shoes!

In this country you can be anything you want to be. He wanted to be cheap.

He's got a great gift for the woman who has everything—him!

He wouldn't buy a Christmas seal because he thought he'd have to feed it.

He's miserable because he has only one mouth.

He knows that the Lord giveth, so he taketh and runneth.

He's so cheap he went on his honeymoon alone.

He wants to go places, but he doesn't want to share expenses with himself.

He's so cheap he puts slugs in his penny loafers.

He doesn't have to go to a shrink. He's small enough already.

When he got run over by a liquor truck, it was the first time the drinks were on him.

His pants have one-way pockets.

He's so cheap he soaps up in the rain.

He's so cheap—to save on his water bill, he soaks up rain!

He's living on borrowed time, and a lot of borrowed cash!

He's so cheap he once sprained his ankle emptying a tube of toothpaste!

He was too cheap to buy talcum powder. He'd rather rough it.

He always gives her money for the table. After all, how much can a table eat?

His heart would be great for a transplant. It's never been used.

The things he does for people can be counted on his missing finger.

He wouldn't have any milk of human kindness if he drank a cow.

He's such a cheapskate his family thinks meat is a fad diet.

He's so cheap he even goes to massage parlors on standby.

He's one cheap boss. When a worker is there for twenty-five years, the company gives him a testimonial coffee break.

He's so cheap his money speaks with a stutter.

He's so cheap he got sore because he got better before his medicine was gone.

He left everything to an orphanage—his kids!

cheating

This is the poor man's adultery. The extremely rich believe that both are sports much too good for the masses.

Two men met and started to drink at a bar. One asked, "Do you like fat women who have warts with hair growing out of them?"

The other man said, "Who could look at a woman like that?"

The first one said, "Well, how come you're having an affair with my wife?"

"Did you hear about Bud getting shot when Sy found him in bed with his wife?"
"It could have been worse."
"How?"
"It could have been me the day before!"

Most men cheat in America. The rest cheat overseas!

A woman, obviously in widow's weeds, is sitting in a corner of a café. Seeing her grief, a man walks over and asks, "What's the matter?"

The woman says, "I'm going to miss him. I'm going to miss him."

"Your husband?"

The woman nods and continues her litany. "I knew he was no good and fooled around, but I'm going to miss him. I know he spent every penny we had on women, but I'm going to miss him."

The man asked, "When did he die?"

The woman answered, "Tomorrow morning."

A man came down with the flu and was forced to stay home one day. He was glad for the interlude because it taught him how much his wife loved him. She was so thrilled to have him around that when a delivery man or the mailman arrived, she ran out and yelled, "My husband's home! My husband's home!"

There were still a few minutes left before the flight. Bronson was thanking Kemp for being such a good host. "My room was great. The food was terrific. You didn't bug me. And, more than anything else, thanks for letting me sleep with your wife. She was the best I ever had!"

Boarding was announced. Kemp waved good-bye and left. A stranger walked over to Bronson and said, "Pardon me, but did I just hear you thank that man for letting you sleep with his wife? And that she was the best you ever had?"

Bronson said, "She really wasn't, but Sam Kemp's such a nice guy!"

A man found his wife in bed with another man. Angrily he asked, "What the hell are you doing?"

The wife looked at him with disgust and

said to the strange man, "Didn't I tell you he was stupid?"

"I know you're cheating on me, Sam. I know with whom. I know where. But what I don't know is—with what!"

He told his girl that more people drown in bathtubs than in the ocean. That night he came home and found her in the bathtub with a lifeguard!

A wife ran into her husband's mistress and said, rather bitchily, "My husband has told me so little about you!"

His wife had a catered affair. She carried on with the guy from the delicatessen.

A man came home to find his wife in the arms of the milkman. His wife asked, "What are you going to do?"

The man answered, "When I figure out something, I'll leave you a note in a milk bottle!"

Bill Carter wired his wife that he'd be home a day earlier than planned. Arriving at the house, he discovered his wife in bed with another man. Bitterly, Carter stormed out of the house, checked into a hotel, and planned a course of action. His thoughts were interrupted by a call from his mother-in-law. She believed that there was no doubt a good explanation for her daughter's behavior. Carter told her to buzz off.

The next day his mother-in-law called again. "Did I tell you?" she said. "Did I tell you there was an explanation? I just got through talking to your wife. She never got your telegram!"

A man comes home to find his wife in bed with a midget. His face turns red as he screams, "You promised you'd never cheat again!"

The wife says, "Look, don't you see I'm tapering off?"

Mrs. Brown was having lunch with her friend, Mrs. Klein. After a nervous sip of coffee, Mrs. Brown said, "I have the feeling that my husband is having an affair with a girl in his office."

Mrs. Klein answered, "You're only saying that to get me jealous!"

Lord Farnsworth was about to get into his pajamas when his valet rushed in. "Sir, I thought I should tell you. I just passed Lady Farnsworth's room and saw her having sexual relations with another man."

Lord Farnsworth went to his gaming closet and took out a hunting rifle. Proceeding to Lady Farnsworth's chambers, he found her still in congress. He raised his gun and pulled off one shot, getting the other man. His valet applauded gently and said, "Always a sport, sir. You got him on the rise!"

I have a friend with brains. He just hired a private detective to trail his wife. He doesn't suspect her of cheating, but he wants to know where she is when *he's* cheating!

A man says unhappily to his friend, "My wife has cut me down to sex twice a week."

The friend answers, "Don't feel too bad. I know a guy she cut out completely."

A man comes home to find his wife in bed with a friend of theirs. Bitterly, the husband says, "You're sleeping with my wife. Just for that, I'm going over to your house and sleep with yours."

The other man says, "Go ahead. You can probably use the rest!"

children

I just have the feeling that when God came up with the idea of children, he wasn't sure about it. But he didn't have anybody to show the plans to. So we got them!

My son is planning on becoming an astronaut. He sits at home taking up space.

A few days ago I was working on the roof and fell off. Torn and bloody, I managed to make it back into the house. My son said, "What did you bring me?"

The family was moving to New York City. The last night before leaving the old home, little Louise said her bedtime prayers: "God, take care of us tonight and give us pleasant dreams. And, God, you won't be hearing from me anymore. We're moving to New York!"

The father was only slightly annoyed when he said to his inquisitive son, "You never stop asking questions. All day long you ask questions. Where would I be if I asked questions like you?"

The son answered, "You might be able to answer some of mine!"

A little boy asked one of his sister's beaux, "How come you show up every night to see my sister? You have one of your own!"

I always wanted to spend more time with my son. Then one day I did!

MINISTER: Why did Joseph and Mary take Jesus with them to the temple?
KID: They couldn't get a sitter!

I asked my wife the other day, "Would you like some martinis until our son grows up?"

An old man saw a young boy sitting on a curb, crying. The old man asked, "Are you all right, little fellow? Lost?"

The kid said, "It's worse than that. My mother gave up on Dr. Spock an hour ago and started using her own judgment!"

I just gave my son a hint. On his room door I put a sign: CHECKOUT TIME IS 18.

A salesman rings the doorbell of a pleasant-looking home in the suburbs. The door is opened by a boy of eight with a long cigarette in his mouth. The salesman asks, "Is your mother home?"

The boy takes a puff and says, "What the hell do you think?"

A boy of seven spends a lot of time cursing. He looks at his breakfast and calls it "damn crap." His mother tells him to do a chore, and he responds, "Screw you!"

A little sick of his behavior, the mother says, "If you say one more bad word, you can pack your stuff and get out of this house."

A few minutes later, the boy sits down to watch television and says, "This new remote control is a pain in the ass!"

With that, his mother throws a small valise at him and orders him to pack and leave. He does so. His mother tells him, "I don't care where you go, just get out!"

Two hours pass. The mother becomes a little concerned and decides to check up on the kid. As she opens the front door, there he is, standing with the valise at his side. The mother says, "I told you to get out of here because of your cursing!"

The kid says, "Where the hell could I go?"

We should have had three children so that the other two could support the genius we do have!

Two children, a boy and a girl of about seven, were playing house. Naturally, she was the wife and he was the husband. As a married couple, they decided television was boring. They would visit a friend. Off they went to Suzie's house. Suzie's mother beamed at the game they were playing and, even though Suzie was away, invited them in for refreshments. After their fifth chocolate chip cookie, the little girl said, "I'm afraid we have to go now."

Suzie's mother said, "Stay. Suzie will be home soon."

The little girl said, "We can't. My husband just wet his pants!"

Children cannot understand adult logic. Why does a kid have to go to sleep when Mommy's tired?

A girl of seven talked into her mother's bedroom and asked her mother to tell her a bedtime story. The mother wasn't thrilled with the request. She said, "It's almost four in the morning."

"I know, Mommy, but I'd love to hear a story."

The mother said, "Lie down in bed with me. We'll wait for your father and he'll tell us both one!"

"It's nice to see you so quiet while your Dad naps."

I'm just waiting for his cigarette to burn his fingers!

A boy of seven woke up after midnight and started to cry. His mother rushed in. "What's the matter, darling?"

"I have to make a tinkle."

"I'll take you."

"No, I want Grandma."

"Why would you want Grandma?"

"Her hand shakes!"

"You failed history? When I was your age, it was my best subject."

"When you were my age, what had happened?"

The dentist came back with the X rays and told little Henry he'd have to have a filling. "What kind of filling would you like?" he asked.

"Do you have chocolate?"

"Pop, does ink cost a lot of money?"

"No. Why?"

"Ma wanted to kill me because I spilled some on her new rug!"

Having kids is like eating half a grapefruit. No matter what you try, you end up with a little squirt!

A small boy asked the girl next door, "Are you the opposite sex, or am I?"

"How many children do you have?"

"None."

"What do you do for aggravation?"

children (insults)

Learn every one of the following by heart. They'll come in handy after a weekend with your sister's four kids or one afternoon with the two angels from next door. This is a "must" category for those who want to participate in a roast.

His family adored him. On Saint Patrick's Day they always gave him a four-leaf poison ivy.

One day his folks played hide-and-seek with him. Five years later he found them in a house eight hundred miles away.

Even as a Boy Scout he was mean. He only walked elderly women halfway across the street.

She was stood up at the father-daughter dance.

He was so unpopular they had to tie a porkchop around his neck so the dog would play with him.

His mother loved children. She would have given anything if he'd been one.

When she was a kid, her mother had to buy her back twice a week from the dogcatcher!

It's a shame his parents didn't have any children.

He was pretty dumb. He didn't know he was twelve until he was fourteen.

His folks hated him so much they hired another kid to play him in home movies.

He was so hated he had to be his own buddy in camp.

As a kid, he was so thin the teacher kept marking him absent in school.

He was a little Greek boy but he left home. He didn't like the way he was being reared!

He ran away from home when he was a kid. His parents never found him. They never even looked for him.

He spent his whole youth behind the eight ball. His mother liked to shoot pool!

He was a precocious child. He was already eating solids when he was two months old—crayons, paper, pencils, erasers . . .

When they took him to the zoo, they needed two tickets for him—one to get in and one to get out.

When he was a kid, he got paddled so often he thought he was a canoe.

He went right from puberty to adultery.

As a kid, he used to help his sister sell Hitler Youth cookies!

Even when he was a kid, they knew he'd go far. They chased him.

He's not the missing link, but he's one of the weakest.

He was such a poor kid, he only had rickets in one leg.

He was such a miserable specimen as a kid, he thought he was made in Hong Kong.

The Boy Scouts in her hometown made her an honorary Boy Scout because she went along with the one good deed they wanted.

She not only had pigtails—she oinked!

When he met her, it was puppy love. Then it became a dog's life.

He was so skinny he had to stand next to his brother to have a shadow.

She ate a lot of Wonder Bread. Her body grew in twelve ways.

As a kid, he knew he could be anything he wanted to be. He wanted to be an idiot.

He wasn't always Jewish, but one day he went swimming and ran into a swordfish!

He was so poor as a child, he couldn't afford to go through puberty.

When he was a kid he swallowed a spoon, and he hasn't stirred since.

He was a born rat. When he was a kid, he used to hide his grandpa's bedpan in the freezer.

His folks kept him in the closet for years. Until he was fifteen, he thought he was a suit.

The kids in school used to call him "Bighead." All day long they called him "Bighead." He ran home crying to his mother and said, "Ma, the other kids say I have a big head."

His mother said, "They're wrong. You have the same size head as any other child. It's not big at all. Now run down to the market and get me ten pounds of potatoes."

"Where'll I carry them?"

"In your hat, dummy!"

When he went to see *The Wizard of Oz*, he rooted for the witch.

He was so fat as a child—when it rained, they made him come in so the lawn could get wet.

"She has a face that only a mother could love."

"Not necessarily. I'm her mother!"

She was such an ugly child that one day her father took her aside—and left her there.

She had so many pimples, the kids played connect-the-dots on her face.

Her family had a pet name for her because she looked like one.

She was so ugly they had to feed her with a whip and a chair.

Every day he prayed that his brother would live. Otherwise he'd be the ugliest man in the world.

She was so fat as a child, when she got off a merry-go-round the horse limped.

"What a strange-looking young man."

"That happens to be my daughter."

"I'm sorry, I didn't know you were her father."

"I'm her mother!"

china and the chinese

Without them, what would the rest of us eat?

The Stones returned from a trip to the Orient. Mrs. Stone, a bit of a showoff, bragged about the number of fancy restaurants they'd eaten in. A friend asked her, "Did you get to see the pagodas?"

Mrs. Stone answered, "*See* them? We had lunch with them!"

It was dinnertime at the Yangtse restaurant, the only kosher Chinese restaurant in town. At one table the Chinese waiter took the order in Jewish, making small talk in that language with the customers as they studied the menu. The meal over, the customer paid at the desk and remarked to the Jewish owner, "I never saw a Chinese man talk Jewish. That waiter did great."

The owner said, "Shh. He thinks he's learning English."

A poker game was going hot and heavy in Hong Kong, an American playing against six Chinese. Toward the shank of the evening, the American remained in one expensive hand, hoping to draw to a flush in spades. He drew a heart, which made the hand valueless. He fumed, "Ah, fooey!"

Immediately all the Chinese threw away their cards, enabling him to win the hand. A kibitzer behind him said to the puzzled Yank, "Shrewd move, buddy. Your million-dollar bet bluffed them out of the pot!"

"What do you think of Red China?"
"You have to have the right tablecloth!"

Where do the Chinese go when they want to eat out?

Chinese is a tough language. A quarter of a million words, and not one in English.

chins

This is an age of specialization!

She had so many chins, she had to jack up her face to wash it!

She had a space between her chins—for her knees.

His chins were like a serial—to be continued.

He had so many chins that when he drooled, people honeymooned nearby.

He had so many chins he had to put a bookmark in his mouth.

"Your wife has a double chin."
"Yeah, it was too much for one!"

She had more chins than Shanghai.

When the minister said, "Come to the fold," he meant her.

She's neat. Every chin is in place.

She had so many chins her neck limped.

christmas

It's the season to be mellow. I'll always cherish the memory of the Christmas tree and getting up to see everything lying under it—my wife's family! I do remember a real Christmas morning. I was playing Altoona, Pennsylvania. This was still in the not-so-good days. My mother and I shared a hotel room for a dollar fifty. For breakfast we shared an orange and two crusty rolls. After this huge repast, I was standing in the small lobby waiting for my mother to dress upstairs. Looking at the small Christmas tree in the corner, I must have made a wry face with a touch of sadness in it. The owner of the hotel said to me, "Why are you hanging around? You want a present or something?"

Our dog loves the Christmas tree. He looks at it and it brings tears to the floor.

I gave my wife a twenty-five-dollar gift certificate. She used it as a down payment on a mink coat.

I can't get a Christmas gift my wife likes. Last year I gave her a hundred-dollar gift certificate. She exchanged it.

Our tree was so puny we used orthopedic bulbs.

Our local department store had two Santas—one for regular kids and one for kids who wanted ten toys or less.

My son has a big Christmas problem—what do you buy for a father who has everything and you're using it?

Talk about cheap—on Christmas Eve, my neighbor shoots off three blanks and tells his kids Santa Claus just committed suicide.

My son gave me a nice bottle of cologne—Eau de Owe.

My sister-in-law found a real surprise in her stockings—my brother!

A man walked into the lingerie section of a store and asked the salesgirl for a nice bra.
"What size?" she asked.
"Seven and three-quarters."
"How did you measure it?"
"With my hat!"

It's always consoling to know that today's Christmas gifts are tomorrow's garage sales.

"Mommy, is it true that Santa brings us presents?"
"Yes."
"The stork brings babies?"
"Yes."
"The police protect us? The fire department puts out fires?"
"Yes, yes."
"What do we need Daddy for?"

At Christmas you can get real bargains. I saw one item marked down ten dollars. It was a yacht!

A young soldier sat in the bus station waiting for his bus and feeling sorry for himself. A man nearby said, "Cheer up, young fellow. It's Christmas. You know, Santa, ho-ho-ho."
The soldier said, "Let him go ho-ho-ho himself! When I was ten, I asked him for a soldier suit. This year I got it!"

At the last Christmas party, the secretary with the long red hair ate three pickles, and four salesmen panicked.

Even though it was the Christmas party, I should never have asked the receptionist for what I wanted by its generic name!

The TV news people keep saying that this could be the greatest Christmas we ever had. I kind of thought the first one was.

I had a great Christmas. I received a lot of presents I can't wait to exchange.

Do you want to feel insecure? Count the number of Christmas cards you sent out, and then count those you received.

One of those Christmas songs says, "You better not shout, you better not cry, you better not pout." How's my wife going to get along?

My wife wants something foreign—like a Mexican divorce!

My wife and I were shopping for the whole family. In the music department my wife said, "Let's get your nephew a set of drums. That's what your brother did to us last year!"

I made a terrible mistake last Christmas. My wife made me swear that I wouldn't give her a fancy gift. And I didn't.

I bought my kid an educational toy to help him make it through life. No matter how you put it together, it's wrong.

I bought my son a bat for Christmas. On New Year's it flew away.

I bought a Christmas tree for twenty dollars. When I came home the next day, my wife was wearing it in her hair.

I bought my son an indestructible toy. Yesterday he left it in the driveway. It broke my car.

War toys are scary. They have a rocket launcher with a bayonet attached, in case you miss.

My wife can't figure out what to buy me. What do you give a man who's had everything up to here?

I just bought a great gift for my boss—a leaky ant farm.

Santa is having a hell of a time this year. Last year he deducted eight billion for gifts, and the IRS wants an itemized list!

I bought my mother-in-law a beautiful chair for Christmas, but she won't let me plug it in.

I wanted to get the guy who works next to me in the office something he really wants, but how do you wrap up a saloon?

She wanted an Italian sports car—with the sport still in it.

For Christmas they just came out with a battery-operated battery. But the batteries aren't included.

In the suburbs it's hard to buy your Christmas gifts early in the year. You never know who your friends will be in December.

I was in a department store and I saw a weird-looking gadget. I asked the young saleslady what it was. She answered, "It doesn't do anything. It's just a Christmas gift!"

This man's wife told him, "For Christmas, surprise me." On Christmas Eve he leaned over where she was sleeping and said, "Boo!"

I gave my wife a gift certificate for Christmas. She ran out to exchange it for a bigger size.

They've got plastic Christmas trees now. They're hard to tell from the real aluminum ones.

I bought an ideal gift for my mother-in-law—a battery-operated mouth.

My son asked for very little: a kickstand—with a motorcycle attached.

Every year my boss used to give me a bottle of expensive brandy because I'd told him that my doctor suggested a drink once in a while. This year my boss gave me the name of a new doctor.

There are a lot of things money can't buy. Not one of them is on my son's list.

The post office is very careful nowadays. When they get a package marked "Fragile," they throw it underhand.

church

A Congregationalist minister in Chicago, a good friend, once told me, "When you get to a town, the best buy is the church!"

The new minister was a spellbinder. One woman in the gallery was so taken with his words that she fell out. Her fall was stopped by the big chandelier above the pews. Unfortunately, her dress was also caught and tore in several unchurchlike places. The minister said, "Any man in the congregation who looks up will be blinded by the Lord."

The sermon went on. After a minute or two, one of the men in the congregation shrugged his shoulders. Starting to look up, he said, "I'll risk one eye!"

The minister was vehement in his attack on adultery. He called down the wrath of the Lord on every man who dared to leave his own nest and look for happiness in the bosom of a neighbor's wife. At that point, one of the men got up and started out of church. "Where are you going, brother?" the minister asked.

The man answered, "I just remembered where I left my hat!"

A man went to church for the first time in ages. The minister was eloquent and the morning passed quickly. After the end of the service, the man walked over to the minister and said, "That was one hell of a sermon."

The minister said, "I appreciate what you said, but there's no need for profanity in God's house."

The man said, "I had to tell you. I was so impressed I gave a thousand dollars to the charity fund."

The minister said, "No shit!"

The little boy returned from his first experience in church and was asked how it went. He said, "The music and singing were nice, but the commercial was too long."

The minister prayed, "Protect us from members of this church who, when it comes to giving, stop at nothing."

A minister made a home visit to one of his congregation, a deaf lady. She was apologetic at having missed his sermon. He said, "That's all right. You didn't miss anything."

"That's what I heard."

A Catholic and a Jew met at a local café. As they drank together, the matter of religion came up. The Catholic said, "Father Mulcahy knows a lot more than your rabbi."

The Jew said, "I wouldn't be surprised. You tell him everything."

A topless dancer tried to get into the church for the Sunday service. The sexton stopped her. The dancer was furious. "You can't keep me out. I have a divine right!"

The sexton said, "Both of them are divine, but you'll have to put something on!"

The church was conducting its annual fund drive. One member of the congregation said, "I give ten dollars." Just then, a piece of plaster fell from the ceiling and landed on his head. He spoke up again quickly. "I give a thousand dollars!"

The minister said, "Lord, hit him again!"

The sermon had been going on endlessly. Finally the minister's voice cracked and said, "What more can I say?"

One parishioner yelled, "How about 'Amen'!"

One minister had a great way of making sure the church didn't empty out fifteen minutes into his sermon. He'd say, "The whole first half of my sermon will be for the sinners among you. The other half will be for the saints."

A minister was telling the congregation about his recent trip to Africa. Most of his sermon was aimed at the children, in the hope that the contributions would be heavier than usual. The minister said, "In Africa there are millions of children. Sundays they can't go to church. You must save up your pennies and nickels and dimes, and do you know what you should do with them?"

A young voice from the rear answered, "Yup. We should buy a ticket for Africa!"

One thing about a church—you're never too bad to come in and you're never too good to stay out.

"I'm just a poor Baptist minister."
"I know. I've heard you preach."

A truly good person is a guy who can sell his parrot to the town gossip without moving away.

The priest was exhorting the parishioners to do good deeds because there was no telling when something might cut their lives short. "Yes," he said, "somebody in this parish will die today."

A man in the back sighed with relief and said, "Thank the Lord I'm not from this parish!"

A gossip came up to the minister and said, "I'd like to place my tongue at the service of the Lord."

The minister said, "Won't work out. Our altar's only twenty feet long."

"What did the minister speak about?"
"Sin."
"What did he say?"
"He was against it!"

The minister studied the poor showing at the service and shook his head sadly, then said, "There will come a time when every man, woman, and child in this town will be on trial for being a Christian. I'm afraid there isn't enough evidence to convict one of you."

A minister from the other side of town came to the West Side to preach on the sorry causes of the fire that had burned down the West Side church. He blamed it on the lack of faith in the hearts of all the members of the congregation. He was about to damn them when the sexton leaned over and whispered, "I'd suggest that you temper it, sir. There's smoke coming from over your way."

The Sunday-school teacher said, "Quiet down. I want it so quiet I could hear a pin drop."

The class became still and one youngster called out, "Okay, let her drop!"

A wandering preacher came to a town, set up a tent, and conducted a powerful service. After he'd saved a hundred souls and damned a few others, he passed his hat around. When it was returned to him, there wasn't one thin dime in it. The preacher said, "Let us pray. Most of all, let us thank the Lord that my hat came back!"

A man won a million in the lottery. His family was afraid to tell him, as he had a bad heart condition. They asked the parish priest to break the glad tidings.

The priest went to the park where the man spent his afternoons and told him that he'd won a million. The man said, "Thank the Lord. For that I'll give half to the church!"

The priest dropped dead!

The priest told about the power of prayer. Paul and Amy, a middle-aged couple, had been having marital problems of late, so they decided to pray.

The next day, Amy visited the priest and said, "I have an amazing story to tell you, Father. You know that Paul and I haven't been getting along too well. Our desire for sex was about as low as could be. Well, yesterday we prayed. In the afternoon I was bending over a sack of potatoes and Paul came at me like a bull."

The priest said, "Yes, prayer can be powerful."

The next day, Paul came in and told the same story. "You wouldn't believe it, Father, but when I saw her bending over that sack of potatoes, my heart started to pound. I couldn't wait another minute. But it has me worried. Is this going to get us thrown out of the church?"

The priest said, "Of course not. Why do you ask?"

"Because it got us thrown out of that supermarket!"

The congregation went to the minister. The spokesman said, "Reverend, you're only getting a pittance. We'd like to show our appreciation of what you've done. From now on, instead of three thousand a year, you're to get four thousand."

The minister said, "That's a noble deed, but I must decline. Getting that extra thousand into the collection box would kill me!"

cigarettes and cigars

You can always tell if I'm in the neighborhood. Look around, and if you see a group of men sitting around in a cloud of smoke, it's me and my friends. We're the old fogeys puffing away on good cigars as we discuss the recent passing of doctors who told us to stop smoking!

They now have something called Nicotine Anonymous. When you have the urge to light up, you call somebody. He comes over and then you go out and get drunk together.

A man walked into a liquor store and asked for a certain brand of cigarette. The clerk asked, "Soft pack or crushproof box?"

"Crushproof."

"Regular or king-size?"

"Regular."

"Filter tip or plain?"

"Plain."

"Menthol or mint?"

"Mint."

"Pack or carton?"

"Forget it. I just broke the habit!"

"Does your wife smoke after sex?"

"No, she just sizzles a little."

There's a new smoker's toothpaste. It looks nice, but it's so hard to light . . .

Some people think drinking vodka keeps them breathless. They ought to try smoking!

A newly engaged young lady went into a shop to plan her trousseau. The saleslady said, "As soon as you're married, start training your husband. Don't let him get away with a thing. Five years ago, when I was married, I ordered my husband to quit smoking and boozing."

"Did he?"

"I don't know. I haven't seen him in five years!"

Thank the good Lord for the cigarette cough. It gives some people the only daily exercise they get.

I know a man of great faith. He decided one day that his wife had given up cigarettes, because he'd come home and found a cigar butt in the house.

One thing I do know—smoking definitely causes reports.

It's easy to stop smoking. You only need a little willpower and a pack of wet matches.

There's a new cigarette on the market with a two-pound filter. When you inhale you don't get any tar, but you do get a hernia.

I watch some of those ballplayers chewing tobacco. The stuff keeps dripping out. One day we'll read about a player who died of cancer of the uniform.

She was a heavy smoker. One night they made love, and as they did, she started to wheeze deeply. She forced out an explanation: "That's my smoker's asthma."
   The man said, "I'm so glad. I thought at first it was an opinion."

The first morning after you quit smoking is the worst. I found myself going outside and inhaling car exhaust.

"Joey, what would your mother say if she saw you smoking?"
"She'd blow her stack. They're her cigarettes!"

There was a cigar manufacturer whose chemist presented him with a brand-new kind of cigar. The manufacturer was thrilled, and went around giving everybody a baby!

There was a man whose wife presented him with quintuplets. He went around giving everybody a trip to Havana!

circuses

They're going, going, and almost gone now. Shame. Now kids who dream have no place to run away to.

The circus wasn't doing well. Not enough money had come in by the end of the tour to pay the entire cast and crew. For some strange reason, the first three paid off were Yarko the Strongman, Sasha the Knife Thrower, and Corbo the Human Alligator!

Then there's the story of the man on the trapeze who caught his wife in the act.

The tattooed lady at the circus married the India Rubber Man. By the end of the honeymoon night he'd erased her altogether.

The Dudleys did a unique act in circus history. Mrs. Dudley would place a square of concrete on her head. To the music of the "Anvil Chorus," Mr. Dudley would hit his wife on the head until the concrete was smashed to smithereens.
   The act did well for years until one day Mrs. Dudley quit. Most people thought it was because the act gave her headaches. The truth was that it broke down her arches!

One of the roustabouts had a severe case of insomnia, so he married the tattooed lady. When he can't sleep at night, he stays up and watches pictures!

The tightrope walker had an awful accident. One night he was tight, but the rope wasn't.

The midget at the circus married the tall lady. When they returned from a brief honeymoon, the strong man asked the midget, "How was the romance?"

The midget said, "Okay, but there was nobody to talk to!"

Two visitors to the back part of the circus were being shown around by the owner. They passed a roustabout with one arm who was working on some ropes. The owner pointed out the roustabout and said, "He used to be a lion tamer."

One of the visitors said, "I'll bet he lost his arm putting it in the lion's mouth."

The owner said, "No. Trying to take it out!"

The knife swallower finally solved his cholesterol problem. He stopped swallowing butter knives!

A boy was asked what he had done on the weekend. He explained, "Sunday I went to the circus, because one of us kids had to take Dad!"

A man was desperate for work. He read an ad in which the circus playing the town needed somebody for an important job. After a brief interview as to his character and background, the man was accepted. His job was to put on a tiger's skin and work the tightrope in imitation of a real tiger.

During his debut performances, he became frightened and fell into a cage in which a lion pranced. The lion came at him, roaring. The man-tiger tried to roar back, failed to get a sound out, and started to run around the ring. The lion caught up with him after a moment and said, "Don't be such a fraidy-cat. You're not the only guy who needed a job!"

citizenship

It's great to be an American. That's why I wear Italian suits, eat French food, drive a Japanese car, and on holidays put out an American flag made in Korea!

A Frenchman spends years trying to become a British citizen, and finally succeeds. Another Frenchman asks, "What good has all this done you?"

The ex-Frenchman answers, "For one thing, I have now won the Battle of Waterloo!"

An Italian and his wife emigrated to America and, after years of preparation, became American citizens. Returning from the ceremony, the husband said, "Maria, Maria, at last we are Americans!"

The wife tied an apron around him and said, "Great. Now *you* wash the dishes!"

The border between Russia and Poland was always being changed. One week the Russians held sway, the next week the countryside came under Polish domination. But one thing was always certain. In winter, the weather was foul.

Came a day when the Poles took over the territory. Podoloski said, "Thank God! No more of those rotten Russian winters!"

A Jewish couple in Moscow fought for exit visas so that they could go to live in Israel. They finally were awarded the proper papers. They took the next flight to Tel Aviv. Four days later they were back in Russia. Again they struggled for an exit visa, and again they finally went to Israel. They did this four times. On the fifth time, a friend said, "You fight for an exit visa, you get on a plane, you head to Israel, and a minute later you go back to Russia—what is this?"

The refusenik said, "Tell you the truth—we love the food on the plane!"

clothes

In 1987 I was chosen one of the ten best-dressed men in America. True, honest? The news came to me as I was having lunch at the Friars Club. A call came from one of the news services. A friend, sitting at our booth, asked, "Milton, is that before or after you've had lunch?"

"Joey, you have your shoes on the wrong feet."
"Teach, these are the only feet I have!"

His pants were so tight he couldn't get them on unless he trimmed his toenails first!

He had the worst taste in clothes. One day a moth flew into his closet and threw up.

The owner of a haberdashery store came in from lunch one afternoon, only to be greeted by one of his salesmen wrapped in bandages, his skin bruised and scratched. The owner asked, "What happened here?"
    The salesman said, "Remember that purple suit with the light green stripes and the little yellow checks?"
    "Yes."
    "Well, I sold it."
    "But what about the bandages?"
    "The guy's seeing-eye dog didn't like it!"

"Pardon me, are you Al Dvorak?"
"No."
"I only asked because that's his coat you're putting on."

That's a nice suit. When did the clown die?

He keeps a diary of what he's eaten. It's called a tie.

An older man in Miami Beach was complaining about his wife's use of her clothes. When she wanted to hide anything, she poked it down her dress. When she wanted to get at it, it was always in her stocking.

Virgin wool comes from the sheep that can run the fastest.

A top model came home from a hard day's work on a magazine cover. Because she and her live-in boyfriend were going to a fancy dinner, she put on a new outfit. She was pooped and said, "I can't make it tonight. Call them up and give them our apologies."
    The boyfriend said, "Fine. Put something on and we'll go to bed."

She looks as if she threw something on and missed!

She looks as if she was poured into her dress but forgot to say "when."

Kids outgrow clothes fast. One kid started to lace up his shoes, and when he got to the top he'd outgrown them!

It was an awful night. Somebody else was wearing the same outfit she was—her date!

He's worn that suit so long it's been in style six times!

A man won a million in the lottery. He called home and told his wife, "I want you to pack all your clothes."
    "Winter or summer?"
    "All of them. I want you out of the house in an hour."

That's a nice suit. Don't you ever throw anything away?

The meanest thing you can do to a woman

is buy her fifty hats and put her in a room without a mirror.

They have a right to call it high fashion. Just look at the prices!

"You ought to buy a coat. It's getting cold."
"I don't need it. I just think of the price of my wife's mink and I start to sweat!"

He wears sad pants—de-pressed!

He has a suit made of material you can wear in the rain. It shrinks, but you can wear it in the rain!

"When I came home last night, my wife greeted me with a triple strand of natural pearls around her neck."
"Choker?"
"No, but I wanted to!"

The old-fashioned girl used to stay home when she had nothing to wear.

"Where'd you get that nice sportcoat?"
"A surprise from my wife. I came home early the other night, and it was on a kitchen chair."

You can tell he hasn't bought any clothing in a long time. His bathing suit comes with spats.

On some ladies, stretch pants have no choice.

Women should buy right now. I heard that dresses were going up.

Her clothes never go out of style. They look just like that year after year!

I wear a very special size—38 baggy.

She was wearing a low-cut gown, but you could tell her heart wasn't in it.

The other day a suit salesman said to me, "Shall I measure your waist, or would you rather not know?"

I bought a nice-looking Italian silk suit last week. The tailor made some money on it. The guy who sold him the fabric made money. The guy who raised the silkworms made money. Isn't it great—so many people make a living from a suit I haven't paid for!

Clothes that make a woman can break a man!

My new pants are one hundred percent virgin wool. They have to be—the legs keep trying to cross.

Why do we need training bras? What can we teach them?

They're making clothes out of new kinds of fabrics. They just made some men's pants out of wood. No more flies—swinging doors!

His pants were so tight he wore them out from the inside.

His pants were so tight, one time he crossed his legs and he had to go to the hospital.

coats

A few goodies that belong on the bargain rack!

"Why did you give that hatcheck girl such a big tip?"
"Did you see the coat she gave me?"

I saw a sign in a restaurant: WATCH YOUR HAT AND COAT! So I did, and somebody stole my dinner!

His coat is so old the only things holding it together are the buttonholes!

"She got a beautiful mink coat yesterday."
"Oh yeah? What did she have to do for it?"
"Just shorten the sleeves."

I felt a man's hand in my coat pocket. I said, "What the hell are you doing?"
He said, "I'm making change and I didn't want to bother you."

She's so hairy she doesn't need a coat. She *is* a coat!

coffee

There's nothing like a cup of coffee. Then I taste what my wife made and I'm sure there's nothing like a cup of coffee. Someday I hope to have one!

Coffee is a pretty powerful stimulant. I had a friend who drank twenty cups a day at work. He died last month, but a week later he was still mingling in the company lounge.

I tried giving up coffee in the morning, but I noticed something—when I woke up, I didn't!

A man walked into a greasy spoon, sat down, and ordered coffee. As he sipped it, he looked out the window and said, "It looks like rain."
The girl at the counter said, "No, it's coffee!"

They should call him Sanka. He has no active ingredient in his bean.

"Waiter, take this coffee away. It tastes like mud."
"It should. It was ground this morning."

I never make fun of my wife's coffee. I may be old and weak myself someday!

He tried to swallow the darn liquid, but couldn't. He called over the waitress and said, "This coffee is funny. It tastes like cocoa."
The waitress took one sip, made a face, and said, "No wonder. I gave you tea!"

"Do you drink coffee?"
"Every day."
"Doctors say it's a slow poison."
"It must be. I'm eighty-five!"

"This gentleman says this coffee isn't fit for a pig."
"Take it away and bring him some that is."

cold

Someday I'm going to come out with a book of jokes beginning, "It was so cold that..." or "It was so hot that..." or "It was so something-or-other that..." It's an easy formula with which to practice and hone your joke-writing talent.

It's been freezing all week. Last night I was in a poker game where we played strip poker—for keeps.

It was so cold I saw a thirty-third-degree Mason drop ten degrees.

Somebody gave me a hotfoot and I kissed him!

It was so cold this morning, I saw a robin eating a thermal worm.

How does a priest start his car on a blistery cold day? "Darn" and "Drat" won't do it!

It's going to be cold this winter. My next-door neighbor Noah just started to build a furnace four hundred cubits long and eighty cubits high.

It was so cold, hens were laying eggs from a standing position.

She's grateful for the cold. The goose pimples give her a shape.

It was so cold I advertised for a girl with a high fever to be my roommate.

TOURIST: I've come here for the winter.
CALIFORNIAN: You've come to the wrong place. We don't have one here!

It was so cold I saw a politician with his hands in his own pockets!

It was so cold I saw freeze-dried coffee hitching a ride back to Brazil.

It was so cold, when you spoke, words froze in midair. You had to bring them in and thaw them out at the fire to hear what people were saying.

It was so cold people were putting things in the refrigerator to keep them warm.

It was so cold, in the morning you'd get up and have a chunk of coffee.

It was so cold you had to part your hair with an ax.

It was so cold I saw a polar bear wearing a grizzly.

college

Until this generation, no one in my family went to college. One thing kept me from going to college—high school! Just a joke. Now all the young people in the family are in college, and it looks as if that's where they're going to stay! We worry about high prices. I have a nephew who's costing my brother a hundred and fifty dollars a pound!

When I lecture at colleges, I enjoy being on campus. It's a special world. I also get a ton of material.

The average college student goes through 210 books in four years. About ten percent aren't bank books.

My son is a great spender. He's the only college student who ever overdrew an unlimited expense account.

You can call it college. I think of it as remedial high school.

The doctor was lecturing a class on sex. He asked, "Do you know what the first oral contraceptive was?"
A coed said, "No."
The doctor said, "Exactly!"

A guest lecturer on sex was explaining some of the sexual phenomena. He asked, as part of an area he was covering, "What is there in the human male that swells to ten times its original size during sexual excitation?"
One coed stood up and said indignantly, "You have no right to talk about that!"
The lecturer said, "Let me tell you something, young lady. The cornea of the eye grows to ten times its original size during

sexual stimulation. And let me tell you one more thing—you're in for a lot of disappointments in life!"

My son ran out of clean clothes to wear. Last week he tried to wire home his laundry.

A college commencement is when the real world beckons to the graduate—but not always with the right finger!

My son is adorable. Last Valentine's Day he sent his mother a heart-shaped box of laundry.

My kid went to a fine academic college. He can write on toilet walls in three languages.

It was an advanced class in biology. The lecturer, a woman in her forties, was engaging in a diatribe against premarital sex. "Would you," she asked, "risk your future for an hour of pleasure?"

One young lady in the back row raised her hand and asked, "How do you make it last an hour?"

"When your son gets out of college, what will he be?"
"About forty-five."

My son came home one day and said that he'd flunked a test—but he'd gotten a high F!

My son is just as smart as the kid next to him—who also failed.

My son saved me a fortune in books this year. He flunked out last year!

A salesman of technical supplies finished his day's work at a major Southern university. Rather than drive home at night, he checked into a hotel. Sitting in the bar, he remarked to a burly man, obviously a native, that the whole student body of the school consisted of young hookers and football players.

The native put down his beer and turned slowly to the salesman, saying, "I heard that. I'd like you to know that my daughter goes to this university."

The salesman smiled. "No kidding? Which position does she play?"

A professor asked a student to remain for a few moments after class. Holding out the young man's assignment, the professor said, "Did you write this poem all by yourself?"

The student said, "Every word of it."

The professor said, "Well, then, I'm glad to meet you, Mr. Poe. I thought you were long dead!"

"You've a faculty for making love."
"No, just a student body."

Money may not be everything, but it sure keeps the kids writing to you!

A professor sidled into class and waited as the class buffoon regaled the other students. After a while the professor coughed to call attention to his presence, saying, "When the person who's making a jackass of himself is through, I'll start."

One college kid wrote home, "Dear folks, I've been worried sick because I haven't heard from you. Please send me a check so I'll know you're okay."

The coach was miserable after his team lost again. He complained to the trainer, "For a bunch of college kids, they play like amateurs."

Many schools lower their test requirements because they have a specific end in mind. And a few tackles and halfbacks.

Many a student worked his way through college. His father is the man he worked!

One young fellow wrote home saying that he wanted a liberal education, but his dad wouldn't increase his allowance by a dime.

A college student wrote a letter home: "Dear folks, I feel miserable because I have to keep writing for money. I feel ashamed and unhappy. I have to ask for another hundred, but every cell in my body rebels. I beg on bended knee that you forgive me. Your son, Marvin. P.S., I felt so terrible I ran after the mailman who picked this up in the box at the corner. I wanted to take this letter and burn it. I prayed to God that I could get it back. But I was too late."

A few days later he received a letter from his father. It said, "Your prayers were answered. Your letter never came!"

"Will you love me forever?"
"I'd like to, but I have a nine-o'clock class in the morning."

A girl with brains can go to the head of a professor's class. A girl with class can go to the head of the professor.

The professor was irate. The entire class had flunked an exam he'd given. He asked one student, "Jones, why didn't you prepare for the test?"

Jones answered, "I was holding hands with Gilda last night."

"Mr. Allison, why didn't you prepare?"

"Sir, I was necking with my girlfriend Alice."

The professor bellowed, "You're both suspended for a week!"

Young Mr. Kemp stood up and started out of the room. The professor said, "Where do you think you're going?"

Young Mr. Kemp said, "See you next semester, Prof!"

A coed you can read like a book is generally a circulating library!

A college student calls up his parents. "I need another two hundred dollars."

At the other end, his father says, "I can't hear you."

The boy shouts, "Two hundred. I need two hundred!"

"I can't hear you."

The operator cuts in, "*I* can hear him."

The father says, "Good. *You* send him the money!"

They called her Alma Mater because she educated a lot of guys!

This test will be conducted on the honor system. Please take seats three apart and in alternate rows.

I'm making a fortune today—I manufacture maternity graduation gowns!

commandments

The best ten one-liners ever written.

We ought to count our blessings. What if Moses had been a doctor and written down the Ten Commandments by hand? Every time we wanted to read one, we'd have to go to the drugstore.

Moses came down from Mount Sinai with the Ten Commandments. It wasn't easy for him—writing them down with a ballpoint chisel!

What people really wanted from Moses was for him to get another Commandment that said, "Disregard the other Commandments!"

commercials

This will be the first era described by its commercials. Future scientists will spend long hours trying to figure out why we squeezed toilet paper or wore watches underwater or shot pens at targets to prove they could still write afterward. Scientists will wonder why a product that was already perfect in June was new and improved six months later.

I think about strange things. Where are the germs that cause *good* breath?

They now sell disposable douches. Who'd want to keep them?

You have to watch out for those vitamin ads. I took an iron supplement for a month. I had to stop it. Every time I yawned and stretched my arms, I slowly turned to point north!

One new product contains no sugar, no preservatives, no additives, and no chemicals. For a dollar and a half you get an empty box!

Local used-car dealers are on TV at all hours. One of them swears that he stands behind every car. With their brakes, he'd better!

I hate cosmetic ads. After watching an evening of those beautiful women, it takes me six hours to get used to my wife again!

After watching those beautiful models in cosmetic commercials, I start conversations with my wife, "Sir..."

The car companies are going all out to get you to buy their new mini-sub-compacts. You have to buy two—one for each foot!

One car company gives you a thousand in cash if you buy one of their cars. I went in and told them, "Give me five hundred and keep the car!"

I have the feeling that you couldn't show on TV what four out of five doctors *really* prefer.

They now have a headache pill for masochists. It won't come out of the bottle.

One company shows how to get fifty shaves out of one razor blade. The company also makes bandages.

common sense

What we all have so much of, and can't understand why everybody else doesn't have any.

Julia was downcast as she told her secret to her father. She was pregnant by Mr. Williams, the bank president. Her father flew out of the house, ran to the bank, and accosted Mr. Williams. "You animal! Beast! No good son of a—"

Mr. Williams interrupted him. "Sir, what is this all about?"

"My daughter Julia is carrying your child."

"There's no need to panic. I'm honorable. If she has a daughter, I'll settle three hundred thousand dollars on the baby. A son will get four hundred thousand."

Julia's father asked, "What if she loses the baby? Can she have another chance?"

"If the Panamanians don't start behaving, we can get even with them."
"What'll we do?"
"We'll take the canal out of there and move it."
"What'll it connect?"
"Utah and Nevada."
"They're already connected."
"Not by water!"

A soldier was brought to an army hospital. He'd been hiding out in a cave, nursing awful wounds. He looked more dead than alive, and the doctor said so. The soldier said, "At times I felt as if I were dead, but I knew I was alive. My feet were freezing and I was starving. I knew that if I was hungry I couldn't be in heaven, and if I was dead my feet wouldn't be that cold!"

A man of ninety complained to a friend that the woman who cleaned his apartment once a week was suing him for breach of promise. The friend asked, "No kidding? But what could you promise?"

Hotels are getting ready for the political convention. They're putting their Gideon Bibles on chains!

computers

I have a lot of jokes about computers, but my computer won't print them. It's like making fun of your own family. My computer will gladly print up jokes about typewriters or quills, but not computers. The following slipped through before the machine knew what was happening.

A computer salesman came into a company and showed the president how his computer was more efficient than their old one. The president said, "Yours is a heck of a deal, but we can't get rid of the old one. It knows too much!"

She loves computers. She always has a Wang in her hand.

One computerized bank got itself into trouble. One day it received a card that said, "This is a stickup." The next day the computer mailed the robber a hundred thousand dollars in unmarked bills.

Our company has a giant abacus under glass. It's for emergencies in case the computer breaks.

A computer arrived at a business concern on the third floor of a building. The computer was too large for the elevator. Nor would it fit through any window. The problem seemed insurmountable. The deliveryman didn't bat an eyelash. He plugged the computer in and let it solve the problem by itself.

A politician was waxing poetic. He said, "You have to reelect me because I am the watchdog of your rights. I won't stand by and let computers take over. That day is coming. Someday soon, computers may even be programmed to try to take away the jobs of politicians."
A man in the back yelled, "Impossible! How do you get a computer to break promises?"

They've finally come up with the perfect office computer. If it makes a mistake, it blames another computer.

Our company has an old computer. It runs on candles.

A young male computer and a female

computer met at a computer show. The female computer offered the male an Apple. The male asked, "Is your name Eve?"

We have one man who runs programs for computers. Last week he ran *Dumbo*, and the week before, *Fantasia*.

Our computer is down so often it has canvas burns.

The company I work for is so stressful our computer has an ulcer.

A computer salesman is justly proud of his new product, and tries very hard to sell it to the vice-president of a company. The veep is insecure about investing so much money. To egg him on, the salesman invites the young man to ask the computer any question. The young man prints out: WHERE IS MY FATHER?
  The machine responds in a tenth of a second: YOUR FATHER IS IN MICHIGAN.
  The young vice-president says, "This machine is a lot of crap."
  "Try asking the same question in another way."
  The young man types: WHERE IS MY MOTHER'S HUSBAND?
  The machine answers: YOUR MOTHER'S HUSBAND HAS BEEN DEAD TEN YEARS. YOUR FATHER IS IN MICHIGAN AND JUST LANDED A TEN-POUND TROUT!

conceit

This is a human condition I'm not familiar with. Being sensitive, bright, ebullient, and incredibly funny, I can afford humility.

He'd gain twenty pounds if he swallowed his pride!

He has the only head in town with stretch marks!

He's a very humble man, and he's got a lot to be humble for!

He has been compared to many great men . . . and unfavorably too!

He's the kind of guy who'd ask the Venus de Milo for elbow room!

He's sure that Nature is doing better work than it used to!

When he checks out of a hotel, three weeks later the mirror is still warm!

In high school he looked in a mirror and knocked himself up!

He runs around in circles, so he thinks he's a big wheel!

He was born with a silver spoon in his mouth—but it had somebody else's initials on it!

On his birthday he sends his mother a basket of applause!

He's so vain he won't let his answering machine take messages!

He doesn't sign his checks—he autographs them!

Her head is so swollen it has a waist!

Her head is so big it has its own Zip Code!

Her head is so big it applied for membership in the UN!

He's leaving tomorrow to pose for a wall at the Vatican!

He recently had a boat accident. One hit him while he was taking a walk on a lake!

He doesn't think he's God, but he likes to spake unto people!

Under duress, he'll admit he's wonderful!

cooking

I have two volumes of cooking jokes. I used to have a third, but my wife cooked it!

My wife's cooking comes in handy. Sunday morning I patched a tire with one of her hotcakes!

My wife hurt herself preparing dinner yesterday—frostbite!

They say that coffee is habit-forming. They've never tasted my wife's!

Always be wary of recipes that tell you to add two heaping tablespoons of anything!

Her idea of a hot meal was when the house burned down!

My girl uses all the modern gadgets in the kitchen. She even has a microwave grease fire!

For the first two years I was married, I thought the only flavor was charcoal!

My wife's T-bones aren't bad, once you tenderize the gravy!

My wife gives our leftovers to our cat. The vet says that the cat only has four lives left!

I cast my bread upon the water tonight. Of course, my wife said it was soup!

My wife is a religious cook. Everything she makes is a sacrifice or a burnt offering!

My wife is making a fortune with her cooking. Indians come from the Amazon to dip their arrows in it!

Every night, my wife calls me to dinner in the same way. She yells out, "Dinner's on the table. Come and guess it!"

I bought my wife a microwave oven. She now scares the food to death!

I bought my wife a foreign cookbook. Now she complains that she can't get parts for our dinners.

She's a terrible cook. This afternoon she burned her shopping list.

In my house we have Mylanta on tap!

My wife is an old-fashioned cook. She still makes radio dinners!

I broke my dog of the bad habit of begging for food at the table. I let it taste my wife's cooking!

My wife found a new way to keep dishes and silver spotless. We eat out!

In our house the garbage disposal is the dining room centerpiece!

I came home the other night. My wife was in tears because the dog had eaten one of her chicken pot pies. I said, "Stop crying. I'll buy you another dog."

She made orange juice every day for her husband, until one day she lost the recipe!

The trouble is, when I meet a girl who

cooks like my mother, she looks like my father!

She has to be a bad cook. Betty Crocker once threw a rock through her window!

I love TV dinners. I also like them warmed up!

My wife's coffee is real strong. I have to use two hands to dunk a doughnut!

She always makes something delicious for dinner—reservations!

He misses his wife's cooking—every chance he gets!

They have a great marriage. He brings home the bacon and she burns it.

One day he brought home fifty pounds of ice. His wife cooked it and drowned the dog!

He knows when there's salad for dinner—he doesn't smell anything burning!

The morning after they were married, she made burnt toast, cold eggs, and rotten coffee. Then he realized that she couldn't *cook*, either!

She found the wolf at her door and invited him in for dinner. The poor critter starved to death!

She used to serve him dehydrated food, right out of the package. One day he went out in the rain and put on a hundred and fifty pounds!

She's always making salmon for him—salmon croquettes, salmon steaks, salmon salad. Twice a year he has to fight the urge to go north and spawn!

She must be half-Irish and half-Italian. The other day she made potatoes and mashed them with her feet!

She's a mean cook. For punishment, she gives seconds!

He doesn't say much about her cooking, but it keeps coming up!

What she doesn't know about cooking would fill a cookbook!

He had a bad can of alphabet soup the other day, and his name came up!

His wife must be a great cook. During the day there's always a truck parked in front of the house.

The other day she cooked her spaghetti too long—four feet.

She's a religious cook. Every meal tastes like the last supper.

She's such a bad cook, she can't even bring her husband to a boil!

She's so bad in the kitchen, she has an arson cookbook!

Where there's smoke—she's cooking!

Her cooking is so bad, even her cornflakes have to be marinated!

She gives him a lot of health food, so he always has natural gas!

Her soup is so thick—when she stirs it the room goes around!

When she makes chicken, it tickles her palate. She forgets to take off the feathers!

The other day it took her three hours to stuff a bird. She got so angry she could have killed it!

We eat a lot of leftovers. That's what they are at the end of the meal!

My wife has a grease fire with three settings!

My wife's an imaginative cook. She wraps spaghetti around meatballs and calls them "hot yo-yos"!

She just doesn't understand the kitchen. The other day she tried to defrost the stove!

courage

When I do my act, they say I have a lot of this. I wonder what they mean.

A mild-mannered gentleman missed his ride out to the suburbs. To work out a plan that would get him home, he went into a nearby bar and allowed himself a few belts. He emerged after the fifth drink, and decided he'd head for the train station, where there might be a late train. Because he was unfamiliar with the area, he lost his way and ended up in the zoo. Sleepy by now, he got into the lion's cage and managed to end up with his head on the lion's chest. He slept peacefully through the night.

The next morning, after searching half the city, his wife came upon him asleep on his leonine pillow. She rushed up to the cage and said, "Come out of there, you coward!"

A young man and his date were walking through the park when they came across a snarling dog. The young man started to beat a wise retreat. The young lady said, "Henry, you always swore you would face death for me."

Henry said, "I would, but that damn dog ain't dead!"

"Who led the regiment in that last battle?"
"I did."
"I thought it was General Radcliffe."
"It was I who saved all those lives. He led them going forward. I led them coming back!"

During World War II, he led a thirty-mile retreat. Of course, he was in Philadelphia at the time.

He didn't want to join the army because of his religion—he was a devout coward.

During World War II he was hidden in a cellar for a year by an Italian girl. They were in Minneapolis at the time!

He'll fight anything or anybody, living or dead—preferably dead!

He doesn't know the meaning of the word *surrender*. There are a lot of words he doesn't know the meaning of!

He was with the navy in Kansas during World War II. He did a bang-up job, too. While he was there, not once was Kansas attacked by an enemy ship!

When he was called to take a physical for the army, he put on a dress and high heels. The army didn't take him in, but the doctor took him out.

courts and court cases

How I laughed the first time I heard this one:

JUDGE: Order! Order in the court!
DEFENDANT: I'll have a ham sandwich!

The secret of much humor lies in an attack on authority. You'll be at your funniest when you attack giants.

A judge asked a locksmith who'd been apprehended in the back of a grocery store, "What were you doing in that place when the cops arrived?"

The locksmith said, "I was making a bolt for the door!"

"Can't this case be settled out of court?"
"Your Honor, that's what we were trying to do when the cops arrested us!"

JUDGE: Do I understand that you're trying to show contempt for this court?
ATTORNEY: No, Your Honor. I'm trying to hide it!

A man who had never been in a court of law before was put on the stand as a witness. The court stenographer recorded every word he said. The man started to talk faster. The stenographer's fingers flew across her keyboard. The man spoke even faster, but finally came to an abrupt halt and said, "Miss, will you stop writing so fast? I can't keep up with you!"

You have to be shaky if you're on trial. Your fate is in the hands of a dozen people who aren't smart enough to get out of jury duty!

It was the trial of the year in the county. The defendant's evidence consisted of pistols, sawed-off shotguns, rifles, axes, and a dozen combat knives. The plaintiff's arsenal had in it a sharp razor, a pitchfork, a bazooka, and a pit bull terrier.

After days of hearing evidence, the jury retired to the jury room and debated the outcome. Finally it returned with a verdict:

"We, the jury, would have given twenty bucks apiece to see that fight!"

"What," the judge asked the defendant, "were you doing when the police came?"
"Waiting, sir."
"For what?"
"For money."
"Who was supposed to give you money?"
"The man I'd been waiting for."
"What did he have to give it to you for?"
"For waiting."
"Enough of this garbage! What do you do for a living?"
"I'm a waiter!"

The jury finally returned to the courtroom. The judge asked the foreman if a decision had been reached. The foreman said, "Yes, sir. In our opinion, we don't think he did it because we don't believe he was there. But we think he'd have done it if he'd had a shot at it!"

Five dice players were in court, waiting to be arraigned. The judge said, "Will the dice players come forward?" Six men stepped to the bench. The judge said to the sixth man, "Why are you up here?"

The man said, "What's the matter? Isn't my money good?"

Esmeralda emptied a load of buckshot into a neighbor who'd been trying to get next to her. She admitted guilt, so the judge couldn't let her off scot-free. He fined her two dollars for shooting an Elk out of season!

My uncle went to court and got a client suspended. They hung him!

The DA stared at the jury, unable to believe its verdict. Bitterly he asked, "What possible excuse could you have for acquitting this man?"

The foreman answered, "Insanity."

The attorney said, "All twelve of you?"

This is the only country in the world where they lock up the jury and send the guilty man home!

The judge faced the defendant and said, "This is not an ordinary case and it must be argued very carefully, so I'm going to let you have four lawyers."

The defendant answered, "Instead of four lawyers, sir, could you hunt up just one good witness?"

A woman says to the judge, "That's my side of the story. Now let me tell you his!"

The judge was firm. "I sentence you to eighteen months for breaking into a house during the night."

The defendant said, "Your Honor, the last time I was here, you put me away for eighteen months for breaking in during the daytime. If I can't do it at night or in the daytime, when am I supposed to make a living?"

"This is the fifth time I've had you in this court. Aren't you a little ashamed?"

"Your Honor, haven't I seen you five times? Do I criticize you?"

A prosecuting attorney said to the lady defendant, "Why did you shoot your husband with a bow and arrow?"

She answered, "I didn't want to wake the children!"

"You've been convicted five times for this offense. Aren't you sorry?"

"No, sir. I never apologize for my convictions!"

cowboys

What can you say about guys who walk around in high heels?

An old cowpoke and his lazy son were sitting in front of a warm fire, drinking some home brew and stretching their legs every hour or so. The cowpoke heard something on the roof of the shack and said, "Son, will you take a gander outside and see if it's raining?"

The younger and lazier man said, "Pa, why don't we just call in the dog and see if his pelt's wet?"

A cowhand had a pair of boots made for him. The bootmaker had taken measurements of his feet and suggested that he order a size bigger than the one requested. The cowhand insisted on the smaller size and explained, "I want them tight like I said. You see, I spend the whole damn day on that freezing range. I chase after dogies all day and sometimes I end up in all that curd they make. I get back and the foreman gives me what-for. Dinner'll be enough to sicken a soul, 'cause we got the worst cook in cattle country. That's why I want those boots. When I take them off, I'm gonna feel good!"

A sheepherder took his son to the zoo in a large Western city. They stopped at the baboon's cage and the youngster asked what the critter was. The sheepman said, "I reckon it's a cowboy. The seat of his pants is worn off!"

Two cowboys met in a large outhouse. As one prepared to use the facilities, he loosened his trousers, only to have a five-dollar bill fall out of his pocket into the hole below. Seemingly unperturbed, the cowboy reached into his pocket, found some more paper money, and dropped that down into the hole too. The other tenant asked, "Why'd you do that?"

The cowboy answered, "Well, I ain't going down there for five dollars!"

credit (credit cards and charge accounts)

My wife only ran up a lot of monthly bills because she wanted us to have something that'll last a lifetime. When you practice telling jokes about credit and charges, don't try them out on women. Women find nothing funny about them. Shopping is a tough and dirty job, but somebody has to do it! You can't lose with an audience if you start by saying, "My wife has a black belt in shopping." The last has a good frame for any kind of overage—"My wife has a black belt in Mouth," "My husband has a black belt in Shirt Staining," and so on. Ruth said that I have a black belt in doing switches on women having black belts.

Credit is a wonderful gimmick that lets you start at the bottom and then dig yourself into a hole!

A sign in a shop read: WE HONOR MANY CREDIT CARDS, BUT WE ONLY ACCEPT CASH.

A new man is brought into cell 102. Already there and obviously a long-time resident is a worn-out, frazzled, gray-haired man who looks to be a hundred years old. The new man looks at the old-timer inquiringly. The old-timer says, "Look at me. I'm old and worn out. I'm like an old dirty torn shirt. You'd never believe that I used to live the life of Riley. I wintered on the Riviera, had a boat, four fine cars, the most beautiful women, and I ate in all the five-star restaurants of France."

The new man asked, "What happened?"

"One day Riley reported his credit cards missing!"

After Sam had missed a few sessions at the club bar with the fellows, one of the men went to Sam's home to check. At first, Sam's wife was reluctant to talk. Finally she caved in and told the truth: "Sam never made much money, but he was always under pressure to keep up with you men. Last month he cracked. He stole a Mercedes 350 and got caught. He'll be in jail for three years."

The man was aghast. "Why?" he asked. "Why? Why couldn't he buy one and not make the payments like the rest of us?"

A man ordered and ate the most expensive dishes in the restaurant, topping them off with the finest wines. When the check was brought, he told the waiter, "I haven't any money."

The waiter said, "That's not terrible. We'll write your name on the wall. You can pay the next time you come in."

"Everybody'll see it."

"I don't think so. Your overcoat will be hanging over it!"

There's only one problem with buying on time. When you get sick of something, you finally own it.

Every time my kid wants to quit school, I explain how important education is. If we couldn't sign our names, we'd have to pay cash!

Nowadays, if somebody pays cash, you worry that his credit is no good.

A man went into a shop and tried to establish credit with the young manager. The manager asked, "Do you have any references?"

The man answered, "Certainly, I owe every store in town!"

crime

I've known a few criminals. Most of them were decent misunderstood people. The gun being held to my ribs has nothing to do with my statement. I knew some beauties. Al Capone, the biggest we've had, once sent his brother to invite me to cut the ribbon for the opening of one of his nightclubs. I went because I was twenty years old and I wanted to see twenty-one. My favorite criminal, not Big Al, was a petty hoodlum in our neighborhood in Manhattan who met an accidental death—he walked into a knife fifteen times with his back! I will say one thing for those outside the law—most of them enjoyed a joke at the expense of the illicit. Should you be planning to entertain some men with flat noses and cauliflower ears tonight, a sampling of the following may get you laughs and longevity!

A man visited some friends in a rather sordid part of town. When the evening was over, he decided to walk to the subway, some blocks away. His friends cautioned him, "This is a tough neighborhood. Don't dawdle. Start running as soon as the door is closed, and don't stop till you get to the subway."

The next day his friends learned that he was in the hospital. They went to visit him and saw him beaten black and blue. "What happened to you?" one of them asked.

The man explained, "You told me to run. Well, I ran and I ran and I ran, and I caught up with a mugger!"

A man found life with the woman he'd married unbearable. He fantasized a dozen ways of killing her. He even asked his doctor for a powerful poison. The doctor, a friend and sympathetic, said, "You'll go to jail for life. Do you need that?"

"But I can't stand her," the man said.

"All right, let me help you. Give her this medicine. It's a powerful aphrodisiac. You'll be able to love her to death without being concerned about the law. How can you convict a man for loving his wife to death? She'll be gone in a month!"

The man blessed the doctor, went home, and started the treatment with the powerful love elixir.

A month later, not having heard from him, the doctor visited his patient and friend. He found the man sitting in a rocking chair on the porch, his body wrapped in blankets. His face was gaunt and pale. The doctor asked, "What happened?"

The man said, "I followed your advice to the letter."

At that moment the wife appeared from inside the house. Dressed in tennis clothes, she looked the picture of health and was off to play a dozen sets of tennis. As she lowered herself into her new sports car, her husband cackled and said to the doctor, "Look at that crazy lady. She doesn't know she has only a couple of days to live!"

"How long will Fred be in jail?"

"Thirty days."

"What's the charge?"

"No charge. Everything's free!"

Some mobsters are efficiency itself. I know one who sends out get-well cards a week before they're needed!

A man asked a prisoner, "What did you do?"

The prisoner answered, "I shot my wife."

"How long will you be in jail?"

"A month."

"A month in jail for killing your wife?"

"Right. Then I get hung!"

I have a brother with the FBI. They caught him in Texas.

Talk about tough neighborhoods. Where I live, nobody asks you the time. They just take your watch.

It was always fists, fists, fists. He was fourteen before he knew he had fingers!

A policeman was checking up about a robbery in a home. The policeman asked the lady of the house, "This is the messiest room I ever saw. You should have reported the robbery right away."

The woman said, "I didn't know it was a robbery. I thought my husband had been looking for a clean shirt!"

Mrs. Ramirez went to the mayor and begged for her husband to be let out of the hoosegow.

"Why is he in prison?" the mayor asked.

"He stole a loaf of bread."

"Is he a decent father?"

"He's rotten. He drinks, he hits the kids, he gambles."

"Why do you want him back?"

"We're out of bread again!"

A bad guy was taken by the police during a crime. A judge put him away for ten years. After about six years in prison, he managed to escape. His escape was the lead item on the six-o'clock news. Because he had to be careful, the bad guy worked his way home slowly, taking side streets, dark alleys. Eventually he arrived at his apartment. He rang the bell. His wife opened the door and bellowed at him, "You're a good-for-nothing bum. Where have you been? You escaped six hours ago!"

A gangster was scheduled to be rubbed out.

As he walked down a dark street, a rain of bullets from a passing car cut him down. Crawling and coughing up blood, he managed to make it to his mother's house. It took all of his energy to knock on the door. His mother opened the door and saw him writhing in pain. He managed to gasp, "Ma, I've been shot."

His mother said, "We'll talk later. Eat something first!"

One local store put up an interesting sign: IF YOU'RE INTERESTED IN FINDING OUT IF THERE'S LIFE AFTER DEATH, TRY ROBBING THIS STORE.

There's a factory in my neighborhood that manufactures burglar alarms. Yesterday it was robbed!

Talk about tough places. My high school newspaper used to have a recess twice a day to carry out the wounded!

Maybe the trouble is we have ten million laws to enforce the Ten Commandments!

The other day I was walking down a dark street when a man walked up to me and said, "Sir, could you spare me the price of a meal? I have no job, no home, no clothes. All I have in the world is this knife."

A counterfeiter went to work on a bill that would fool the best eye. After working for twenty years, he came up with his masterpiece—an eighteen-dollar bill. When he realized his mistake, he got into his car and drove to a remote section of the country. Going into a general store that looked as if it was out of the eighteenth century, he passed off his bills. He returned to the city a rich man. In his pockets he had a hundred and fifty seven-dollar bills and twenty nines!

Where I live, we don't worry about crime in the streets. They make house calls!

I know a counterfeiter who made almost perfect five-dollar bills. His one mistake was to make Lincoln blinkin'!

A fellow walked up to me the other day and said, "Have you seen a cop around here anywhere?"

I said, "No."

He said, "Great. Stick 'em up!"

Crime is getting so bad where I live, muggers travel in pairs.

I'll give you an idea of how crime-ridden our neighborhood is. The other day I saw half a cop!

critters

Animal stories are like grits. You can't stop them from coming. They may even show up as "Four-legged Friends."

A mother skunk was always in a panic because she couldn't keep track of her two tiny ones. One was named Out and the other In. When Out was in, In was out. One day she saw Out but couldn't find In. She told Out to go out and bring In in. In about twenty seconds, Out brought In in. Surprised, the mother skunk asked, "How did you find him so fast?"

The tiny skunk answered, "It was easy— In stinct!"

A weekend farmer bought a small farm in Bucks County, the garden spot of Pennsylvania. Eager to populate it, he went to a nearby farm and asked if the farmer had any livestock for sale. The farmer said he had a horse, but there was one caution: "This here horse likes to sit on apples."

"He really sits down on apples?"

"Yup. He's a fine horse, but he sees an apple and he squats."

The neophyte farmer had no apple trees on his farm, so he decided to take a chance. He bought the horse and started home with it. On the way, they had to cross a shallow stream. Midway across the stream, the horse sat down. The new owner rushed the horse back to the original owner and said, "You said he liked to sit down on apples. We were heading home and he sat down in the stream."

The farmer said, "I forgot to tell you—he also likes to sit on fish!"

Two ants were on a box of cereal when one of them started to run fast. The other asked, "Why are you racing like that?"

The other ant said, "It says, 'Tear along the dotted line'!"

Two goats were nibbling at the trashbin. One of them found and chewed up a dog-eared book. The other asked, "Did you like that?"

The chewer answered, "Actually, I liked the movie better!"

A bear was just about to enter his winter's cave, but stopped for a moment to remind his friend, the woodpecker, "Remember— you have to wake me at half past April!"

A female fly went to Hollywood and started a great career—She passed the screen test!

As the mother turkey said to her playboy son, "If your father could see you now, he'd turn over in his gravy!"

A roach ran into another roach who was nibbling at a discarded cracker. The newcomer said, very excited, "I just came from a new restaurant. It's beautiful. The kitchen is all stainless steel. There's not a drop of grease on anything. No fat drippings! It's all spick-and-span."

The other one said, "Cut it out! Can't you see I'm eating?"

A young male octopus and a female married in a twelve-ring ceremony. Then they went through life hand in hand in hand in hand in hand in hand . . .

This woman had two chickens. One became ill, so she killed the other to make chicken soup for it!

A farmer woke one morning to find his pet rooster lying on the ground, legs in the air, looking as dead as a bird can look. The farmer said, "I told you this would happen. You can't run around after every chicken day and night."

The rooster motioned the farmer to quiet down and said, "When you're romancing a buzzard, you've got to play it right!"

crossed eyes

Where would we be if we couldn't make fun of the problems of others? The fact is that I've only met two or three cross-eyed people in my life. One of them, and this is the absolute truth, did a knife-throwing act. His assistant was a very nervous lady. It's true, honest!

She's so cross-eyed—when she rolls her eyes she hits her ears.

She was so cross-eyed—when she cried, tears rolled down her back.

She was so cross-eyed—when she opened one eye, all she could see was her other eye.

She had a cross-eyed nanny. The nanny would put her on the table and powder the kid next door.

There must be something about her left eye. Her right eye keeps looking at it!

She was so cross-eyed she could read pretzels.

crossing two objects

Fads come and go, but the game of mating one object with another of unmatchable genes seems to be persistent. I know that when I was no more than six I crossed a parrot and a gorilla. I ended up with a parrot that said, "Polly wants a cracker—now!" The other kids laughed. My reputation remained secure for the rest of the day.

I once crossed a waiter with a tiger. I don't know what I got, but I tip him big!

I once crossed a rooster with another rooster. I got a very angry rooster!

cruises

A good way to get an audience on your side is to make yourself the victim. A small routine about your problems on a cruise you've just finished is a good example. Because you'll be describing moments of great pain, the audience will love it. From the brief routine you can segue into the matter at hand. Segues are always available. You can also, if roasting someone, fib a little and say that the two of you, or couples, or a mob, spent two weeks on a cruise. You simply have to tell the audience about this great seaman it is honoring.

On my last cruise I became so ill I was afraid to yawn!

A man and his wife went on a four-day luxury cruise. The wife was slightly more than gregarious. In fact, she never shut her mouth. She talked at breakfast, while they were lounging on deck, at lunch, at play, and all through the night. On the fourth morning, the man and his wife were standing at the bow of the ship when a lurch caused the wife to fall overboard. Seeing her bobbing up and down in the water, a crew member ran to the husband and said, "Your wife is overboard!"

The husband said, "Thank God. I thought I was going deaf!"

The ship was sinking. The captain called the passengers and crew together and asked, "Is there anybody here who can really pray?"

One passenger said, "I pray all the time."

The captain said, "That's terrific, because we're short one life preserver."

A passenger was under the weather and spent most of his time leaning over the rail, upchucking almost continuously. As he went into his tenth round of seasickness for the day, the ship hit an iceberg and started to sink. The captain yelled, "Don't give up the ship!"

The passenger said, "I can't. I haven't eaten it yet!"

It was a great ship. I think it was called the SS *Deadly!*

When we arrived at the dock to board, the captain looked at my wife's luggage and said, "You should have told me. I would have brought a bigger ship!"

A young girl took a pleasure cruise. Because she was pretty and traveling alone, she was invited to the captain's table. After a fine dinner, the captain invited her to his stateroom. There he said that he wanted to make love to her. She refused. He said, "If you don't let me make love to you, I'll sink this ship."

The next day she called her mother and said, "Ma, last night I saved nine hundred passengers!"

At a dance for mature people, a woman of forty-five started to dance with a man. As they tripped the light fantastic, she told him about her life. She explained that she'd lost her husband at sea.

The man said, "Wow, you must have encountered a tidal wave or something."

The woman said, "No tidal wave. He met a redhead on a cruise to Ensenada!"

cures

Medical science makes great strides every day. This morning they announced three new cures for which we don't have diseases yet!

Al had the worst toothache of his life. He rushed to his dentist, who took X rays and checked out his mouth. The bad tooth was too far gone to be saved. Procaine was administered, and the dentist started to extract the tooth. When he had extracted the culprit, it slipped out of his instrument and fell down into Al's throat. The dentist shook his head and said, "Sorry. I can't do any more for you. You'll have to go to an ear, nose, and throat man."

Al rushed off to the specialist, who examined him immediately. In trying to extract the tooth, the doctor accidentally pushed it down farther. The doctor said, "I'm awfully sorry. It's a stomach man's job now."

Al raced to a stomach specialist. Unfortunately, the specialist had an emergency and Al was forced to wait. Four hours later, the doctor was able to see him. By now the tooth had worked its way through the intestines and was now lodged near the anal opening. The specialist said, "Okay, let's take a look at this pain you're having. Bend over."

Al bent over, the doctor looked, and said, "There's a tooth up there. You'll have to go see a dentist!"

Recently a man tried to treat himself with a cure in one of those magazines that cure everything monthly. Something wasn't right, and the man died of a typographical error!

Mr. Pinckney's most prized possession had lost all of its power. Limp was hardly the word for his condition. A famous urologist said to him during an examination, "There's one cure that might work. In Nairobi they're doing interesting things with transplants from the trunks of baby elephants."

"I'll get one."

"They're expensive."

"I'll pay what I have to pay."

Arrangements were made and the operation performed. A month later, Mr. Pinckney went to the doctor for a checkup. "How's it going?" the doctor asked.

"Incredibly. You saved me from shame."

"Any side effects?"

"Well, it's possible that there's a connection—when we go to somebody's house and we're sitting around having a snack, it keeps reaching for cookies on the table!"

"**H**ow do you feel?"

"Awful. My throat is killing me."

"When I get a sore throat, I suck on a Life Saver."

"That's easy for you. You live near the beach!"

D

dancing and dancers

Mostly, in my day, I liked to dip. That's generally about all a fellow got. If your knee didn't keep tingling for hours after a date, all the money spent on food, the movies, and the coffee afterward was wasted!

The girl who turns you down for a dance probably knows her bunions.

Why do ballet dancers dance on their toes?

Why doesn't the company just hire taller dancers?

They started to dance. As they spun around, he noticed that his partner was growing shorter. Asked what was happening, the girl explained, "I've got a wooden leg and you keep turning me the wrong way!"

Greatest sound ever made—a flamenco danced by a man with false teeth.

They met at the school dance and spent the whole evening together. As midnight approached, she said, "Take me to your place."

He laughed and asked, "What's in it for me?"

She said, "Only a little dust from dancing!"

A small town is where a girl dances with a man who's old enough to be her father—and he is!

There was a fire in the chorus girls' dressing room in a Las Vegas hotel. It took an hour to put out the fire. It took six to put out the firemen!

Strippers should go to Washington. They could put some great motions before the House.

She used to be a bubble dancer. One night her career blew up in her face.

She was a go-go dancer. Men looked at her face and said, "Go! Go!"

I saw a unique thing the other night. A Jewish orchestra was playing and the Spanish were dancing!

I knew a fellow who didn't want to dance because he felt that he had two left feet. Then he found out his feet were fine. It was the two left shoes that bothered him.

"How's your wife doing at ballet?"
"Improving by leaps and bounds!"

An elderly couple tried to check into a hotel. All the rooms were gone except the bridal suite. The husband said, "What are we going to do with the bridal suite? We've been married forty-one years."

The desk clerk said, "I could rent you the main ballroom. Does that mean you have to dance?"

You know you've been discoing too much when your shorts and your socks wear out from the inside!

I think I'd like ballet, but no matter where I sit, I can't hear a word they're saying.

The dance scene is getting wilder. At one club they've had to ban premarital dancing!

He led her closely as they moved around the dance floor. After the fifth time he'd stepped on her toes, he said, "I can't understand it. I never danced so badly before."

"Oh," she said, "you've danced before?"

Today the young kids dance so far apart, they know they're out on a date, but they don't know with whom.

The aging Russian ballerina, now plump and leaden-footed, made a comeback in New York. Another dancer watched her attempt to leap and said, "She reminds me of Grant's Tomb in love!"

I'd be a great dancer except for two things—my feet!

She was an ugly stripteaser. When she started to dance, men yelled, "Up in front!"

A young man approached a girl at the club dance and asked if she would care to dance. She said, "I don't dance with a child."

The young man said, "If I'd known you were in that condition, I wouldn't have asked!"

She was a novelty dancer, her gimmick being that she had her costume painted on. Men used to sit at the club all night, waiting for the novelty to wear off!

An elderly man went to a dance at the senior citizens' center. An attractive woman spotted him. With a few flutters of the eyelashes she got him on the dance floor. As they danced, they exchanged bits of information about their backgrounds. He was a widower, retired with a large pension from a company in which he still owned much stock, and the owner of a fancy condo. The woman listened, then said, "You remind me of my third husband."

"Really? How many marriages have you had?"

"Two!"

There's a beautiful song: "I'm Dancing with Tears in My Eyes Because the Girl in My Arms Is My Brother."

A comedian was talking about his background in Las Vegas girlie shows: "It developed my timing, my feel for an audience, and my eyesight!"

My wife said, "Let's go discoing."

I said, "Against whom?"

It's hard to describe today's music, but the other day I was in a restaurant where a waiter dropped a tray of dishes, and six people got up to dance.

Joe Jones went off to a stag party being thrown for a friend who was about to marry. Before leaving the house, Joe had to swear to his wife that it would be an all-male party.

He arrived at the party to see a cake brought in. From its decorated center, out came a beautiful nude woman who proceeded to dance sensuously. A dutiful husband, Joe went to the phone, called his wife, and said, "It's not all men here. There's a gorgeous nude girl shaking and writhing and dancing all around. What should I do?"

The wife said, "If you think you can do anything, come right home!"

dating

When my son was six years old, he fell in love with a girl who lived around the corner. On Valentine's Day he sent her some flowers with a note that said, "To Linda, with all my allowance!" They saw one another the following week at a birthday party. She said, "Flowers are stupid!" My son never recovered. That's one of the risks you have to take in the dating game!

He found it impossible to make a date. He'd start to talk to a girl, and his tongue would twist up like a pretzel. He went to a bookstore and looked for a volume that might help him overcome his timidity. On a nonfiction rack he saw a book titled *Ways to Women*. Blowing his whole allowance, he bought the book, rushed home, and discovered that he'd bought volume ten of the encyclopedia!

He was bowlegged and she was knock-kneed. When they stood together, they spelled the word "ox"!

"My daughter is getting married."

"Who is the boy?"

"Alex, the boy she's been going with. I hope she makes him as happy as she's making my husband!"

"Don't you love driving?"

"Well, usually I stop first!"

I'll never forget this one girl I met. I got such a lump in my throat. She was a karate champ!

Sir, you'll have to excuse me for coming to the door to get Amy, but my car horn isn't working!

The father said, "Young fellow, aren't you spending too much money on my daughter?"

"Yes, sir," the young man said. "I wish you'd talk to her about that!"

They were walking toward a movie house when a gust of wind attacked her miniskirt. He started to giggle. She said, "You're not a gentleman."

He said, "I can tell you aren't either!"

There was an old monk of Siberia
Whose life grew drearier and drearier.
He burst from his cell,
Gave out a yell,
And eloped with the Mother Superior!

A young man wrote, "Dear Sybil, please forgive me but I'm becoming forgetful. I proposed to you last night, but forgot whether you said yes or no."

Sybil wrote back, "Dear Fred, so glad to hear from you. I know I said no to somebody last night, but I forgot who it was!"

"What should I do to keep from falling in love?"

"Try pricing houses!"

Nothing's more expensive than a girl who's free for the evening.

A father asked his daughter's date, "Can you give my daughter the luxuries she's accustomed to?"

The date said, "Sure. I'm the guy who accustomed her to them!"

A father asked the young man who'd been seeing his daughter about his finances. "What will be your yearly income?" the father asked.

"Fifty thousand," the young man said.

"Not too shabby. When you add my daughter's forty thousand, that'll be decent enough."

"Oh, I already counted her in the fifty!"

Alex and Marian were walking along the shore, their souls intertwined in great love. Alex gazed out to the sea and said poetically, "Blue ocean, roll out to the setting sun!"

Marian clasped his hand tighter. "Oh, Alex," she said. "it's doing it!"

She kept throwing out tiny hints. When it was warm, she fanned him with a marriage certificate.

Her first date with a man is so wonderful he won't spoil it by asking her out again.

She thinks she's a jinx date. Every time she goes out with a guy, he runs out of gas.

A young beau said to Marjorie, the family pride, "I'd like to see more of you."

Marjorie answered, "There isn't any more of me!"

He never wears his glasses on a date. That way the girls look better to him.

She must be a pilgrim. Each time they go out, he makes a little progress.

Before she goes out, her mother tells her to play easy to get.

She's the kind of girl a fellow likes to take home to smother.

He's a real great date. He never puts gas in his car. He just takes his girl out for a push!

The cure for love at first sight is to take another look.

"Let's get married."
"Who'd have us?"

They weren't really compatible. She was twenty-eight and he was poor.

Going steady is like a tourniquet. It stops your circulation.

She must be descended from Abraham Lincoln. Everybody has taken a shot at her in the balcony.

When you go out with her, it's cafeteria-style—you help yourself.

She has boyfriends by the score, and most of them do.

In school, she was chosen as the girl most likely to.

daughters

Young sons are awkward. They evoke pity, not humor. Most of all, they're not as delicious as daughters. Daughters don't cause any problems. I can say that, since I've never had a daughter!

One girl put an ad in a matrimonial magazine in which she painted a glowing picture of herself. She received one response—from her father.

"Mother, John has given me every single thing I've asked for."
"You're not asking for enough!"

What did I know? Until I was sixteen, I thought my sister was a soft boy!

"What did your daughter do last summer?"
"Her hair and her nails!"

A daughter is a young lady who always marries a man of much lower mental capacity than she does, and yet manages to have utterly brilliant children.

I have a niece who is a *prima* slob. I went into her room one day and saw a roach running with one leg over its eyes!

I wouldn't go into a daughter's room without a whip and a chair!

I wouldn't go into her room without a tetanus shot!

My niece finally decided to clean up her room. Her phone rang and she couldn't find it.

This teenage girl decided to run away from home. She got as far as the door, then the phone rang!

"Don't play with boys. They're too rough."
"But, Mother, I think I found a smooth one!"

This man's daughter broke up with her boyfriend. She sent back his candy and books of poetry, but kept the jewelry for sentimental reasons.

Margie wasn't home, and it was awfully late. Not knowing their phone numbers, her mother wired Margie's four best friends asking them if they knew where Margie was. By midnight she'd gotten back four wires, each of which said, "Don't worry. Margie is staying with me!"

Do you want to send a great gift on Mother-in-Law Day? Send her her daughter!

The businessman's daughter married a young man who didn't seem to be qualified to do anything. To enable him to take care of his new bride, the manufacturer gave the young man half of his business. He then asked the young man if there was anything else he could do to make life easier for the newlyweds. The young man said, "Yes. Buy me out!"

"What is your daughter taking in college?" "Everything I've got!"

A woman comes home and finds her daughter in a hot embrace on the couch. The woman says, "I never!"

The daughter answers, "Oh, Mother, you must have!"

A year ago, the daughter's boyfriend asked, "Can I change your name to mine?"

"Yes," said the daughter.

Since then he's been calling her Fred!

A young man's career can be destroyed by a mere quirk of fate—the boss doesn't have a daughter!

Her mother was on a girl's softball team, and she was her first error!

Little Ellen was sitting with some of the ladies of her mother's bridge club, waiting for her mother to finish getting ready for a game. One woman looked at Ellen and said to the ladies, "Not too P-R-E-T-T-Y."

Ellen said, "No, but awfully S-M-A-R-T!"

A visiting aunt watched little Carol learning to write. The aunt asked, "Where is the dot over the *i*?"

Carol answered, "It's still in the pen!"

MOTHER: Do you know where bad little girls go?

DAUGHTER: Certainly. They go everywhere!

The six-year-old daughter came back from her first day at school. Her father asked, "What did you learn today?"

The child said wearily, "Nothing. I have to go back again tomorrow!"

Little Anna saw a cat carrying its newborn kitten by the nape of the neck. Alice scolded the cat, "You aren't fit to be a mother. You're not even fit to be a father!"

"Darling, I'd like to marry you."

"Have you seen my father?"

"Lots of times, but I still want to marry *you*!"

A young lady came home from a date, rather sad. She told her mother, "Jeff proposed to me an hour ago."

"Why are you sad?" her mother asked.

"Because he also told me he was an atheist. Mother, he doesn't even believe there's a hell."

Her mother said, "Marry him anyway. Between the two of us, we'll show him how wrong he is."

A young man sitting in a bus depot turned to a middle-aged man nearby and asked him for the time. The middle-aged man said, "I'm not going to give you the time."

"Why not?"

"I'll tell you why. If I gave you the time you'd thank me. I'd concede that you had manners, so I'd probably start talking to you. We'd keep talking on the bus, and by the time we got to Philadelphia we'd be more than mere acquaintances. I might even ask you to come to my house for dinner. You'd meet my lovely daughter. You'd start taking her out. After a while, you'd fall in love and you'd propose and she'd say yes. So I won't tell you the time because I don't want a son-in-law who doesn't even have a watch!"

When she wears a sweater, she's just itching to meet a man!

Nowadays a girl wears less in the street than her mother wore in bed!

She's one for the books and she's in everybody's!

Her boyfriends worship the ground her father left her!

deafness

I'm at that age where people have to start repeating. My answering machine starts each message with "What was that?" One of these days I may get a hearing-aid dog!

A woman returned home after having her tenth child, left the baby with a nurse, and rushed off to the nearest hearing-aid store. The doctor took down her medical history and general information. He was stunned that she had ten children. She said, "That's why I want the hearing aid."

"I don't understand," the doctor said. "What does a hearing aid have to do with babies?"

"In my case, everything. You see, I make my husband dinner and we sit down to watch television and read a little. Then, after the eleven-o'clock news, he asks, 'Do you want to watch more television or what?' I can't hear him, so I say, 'What?' That's why we have ten kids!"

"I understand Phillips is now in the Complaint Department."
"The perfect place for him since he lost his hearing!"

A gynecologist is the only doctor who has to read lips.

A man worked in a boiler factory and suffered from the condition called "Boilermaker's deafness." He was unable to hear normal conversation unless it was accompanied by the noise from the heavy banging of hammers. One afternoon he was taking a nap in the company lounge during his break when a power failure brought a halt to the work and the noise. He jumped up from his nap and said, "What was that?"

A man, worried about his hearing, went to a doctor who examined him and said, "Your hearing loss is a reflection of your general condition. Do you smoke?"

"Three packs a day."
"You'll have to quit."
"Fine."
"Do you drink?"
"Three martinis at lunch. A six-pack when I get home."
"Quit."
"Okay."
"You'll also have to give up sex."
"What for—so I can hear a little better?"

A deaf man couldn't afford a hearing aid. Instead, he went to a hardware store and bought some wire. Fashioning it into a small coil, he put it behind his ear. He ran into a friend, who noticed the contraption and was curious about it. The deaf man explained what it was. The friend asked, "Does it really work?"

"No," the deaf man said, "but everybody talks louder!"

I found a perfect marriage—she's blind and he's deaf.

Aware that he wasn't hearing too well, a man went to an ear doctor. After giving him a thorough examination, the doctor told him that he'd have to give up drinking or risk total deafness. The man left, seemingly inspired by the doctor's admonition. Some months passed. The doctor happened to come out of a shop next to a bar. He stopped as his patient staggered out of the bar. The doctor said, "You'll be as deaf as a post if you don't cut this out."

The patient said, "Tell you the truth, Doc. What I'm drinking is a heck of a lot better than what I'm hearing!"

Two deaf men met in the street. One was also physically handicapped. He had only one arm, and that was little more than a stump. The first man signed, "It's great seeing you."

The one-armed deaf man signed back, "That's easy for you to say!"

Three well-bred Englishmen, one of them hard of hearing, were sipping drinks slowly in the outer bar of a fine London restaurant as they waited for their dinner reservation to be honored. In walked two middle-aged Americans who had also made reservations. The Americans ordered a drink. As they sipped, one started to reminisce about his war days near Oxford. He started to tell about an English girl named Guinevere, saying, "She had beautiful red hair and a little beauty mark right under her left eye. And she was wild. She loved to tumble all day. They had this great big manor house and she used to sneak me into her bedroom, and, wow, what we did under that canopy! I mean, she would swing from the chandelier and jump down right on me." He paused to take a drink.

The hearing Englishmen couldn't avoid his excited description and had started to listen. The deaf Englishman knew he was missing something. He asked impatiently, "What did he say?"

One of the Englishmen spoke directly into his ear. "He knows Mother!"

A man, suffering from a terrible itching, was on his way to the doctor's office. In the elevator he was joined by a deaf man and a companion. Smiling a greeting, the itcher started to scratch himself all over. He finished just as he reached the right floor and left. The deaf man turned to his companion and signed, "I wonder what he meant by that!"

death

There's only one per customer, so it must be a real bargain!

The doctor had just been buried. The last words of the service over, his friends and family started toward their cars. However, they stopped because a strange, eerie sound suddenly was heard from the grave. As the guests looked around, a colleague of the deceased said, "It's nothing, just his beeper."

The priest was preparing a man for his long day's journey into night. Whispering firmly, the priest said, "Denounce the devil! Let him know how little you think of his evil!"

The dying man said nothing. The priest repeated his order. Still the dying man said nothing. The priest asked, "Why do you refuse to denounce the devil and his evil?"

The dying man said, "Until I know where I'm heading, I don't think I ought to aggravate anybody."

Do you realize that very few people die after a hundred years of age?

One of my friends had a very rich uncle. When the uncle passed away he left my friend his entire fortune. My friend sent out a card saying, "On the seventh of May, my uncle, Harry Gray, and I passed on to a much better life."

"I miss Al so much."
"Why?"
"Because I married his widow!"

I looked at the obituaries the other day and I realized something—everybody dies in alphabetical order!

Peterson's wife was dead, and he was inconsolable. He cried through the first day of his loneliness without stopping even to have a cup of coffee. Two days later, a friend came to see him and found him with the maid sitting on his lap. Peterson and the pretty Swedish girl were having a great time. The friend said, "Pete, your wife has been dead two days. What the heck is going on?"

Peterson answered, "In my grief, I don't know what I'm doing!"

A man lay dying. His voice hardly a whisper, he called over his best friend and said, "I can't go to my Maker without telling you all. I have to confess. Remember that hun-

dred thousand that was missing when we owned the carpet store?"

The friend and ex-partner said, "I remember."

The man said, "I stole it. I also told your wife that you were fooling around with the blonde at the switchboard. And speaking of your wife, I was her lover for two years. Then—"

His friend interrupted, "You don't have to tell me any more. I know everything. That's why I poisoned you."

An older man died during sex. At the funeral, his wife explained, "He came and he went."

"How much did Phil leave when he died?"
"Everything!"

He used a lot of liver vitamins. Two days after he died, they had to beat his liver to death with a stick.

The man who came up with the phrase "you can't take it with you" must have known about the price of coffins.

An old man is dying and smells the delicious aroma of fresh-baked cookies. He says to his wife, "Can I have one of your cookies?"

The wife answers, "Absolutely not. You know they're for the wake!"

Two lawyers met. One said, about a third, "Did you hear about Carl Henry? He died last week."

The other lawyer asked, "What did he have?"

"Two personal injury cases and a divorce!"

His four children were gathered around Mr. Staley's deathbed. As the eighty-year-old man seemed to doze off in a blissful sleep, the children started to discuss the final funeral plans. One wanted to spend a hundred dollars for a coffin, a second thought a plain wooden box would do, and the third was even ready to dump the remains into a paper sack. All agreed there was no reason to spend much money, as their father would never know the difference.

Mr. Staley stirred. Having heard every word, he thought it was time to set the record straight. "Children," he said, "I've never told you this and never wanted to, but I can't go to my final resting place with this burden. My darling children, your mother and I were never married."

His oldest son was aghast. "You mean we're—"

Mr. Staley said, "Yup. And cheap ones too!"

debts

I decided to make sense of all my bills. I went out and bought a filing cabinet in which I filed every one of my bills. The next day a bill came for the filing cabinet, and I was off and running again!

A company sent me a notice that my bill was a year old, so I sent them a birthday card!

He has more attachments on him than a vacuum cleaner!

He has an all-electric home—everything's charged.

"Don't worry about the money you owe me."
"Why not?"
"There's no need for both of us to worry."

A millionaire was walking into the giant building he owned, when a man came over to him and said, "Mr. Bronson, you may not remember me, but twenty years ago on this very spot, when you were only a clerk with the company, I came over and asked if you could lend me ten dollars. You whipped out ten dollars and handed the bill to me. I've never forgotten that."

The millionaire said, "Now, twenty years later, you came to pay me back!"

"Not exactly. I was just wondering if you've got another ten."

He believes in the hereafter. He's always here after a few dollars!

He has the first dollar he ever earned. He got it yesterday.

You have to give him a lot of credit. He has no cash.

He has a great system for paying bills—he calls it "tomorrow."

He's pretty snappy—just like his checks.

He owes money that hasn't been minted yet!

He doesn't owe everybody, but he's getting there.

His idea of Cloud Nine is Chapter Eleven.

He tried to commit suicide the other day. He jumped off last week's bills.

To him, a debt is a gift you didn't know about right away.

His owings aren't quite as big as our national debt, but he didn't get today's mail yet.

delicatessens

What foods these morsels be!

A customer was admiring the business at a delicatessen. The line for lunch wound halfway around the block. The customer remarked to the owner that the place was a gold mine. The owner said, "Now it's a gold mine. It's a gold mine because I have brains and know how to do business. How do I get brains? I eat a lot of fish—herring, salmon, lox."

Before leaving, the customer loaded up with fish. He returned a week later and told the owner, "That fish isn't working."

"It works."

"All right, I'll try it for a while longer. But I'm not going to buy it here. The delicatessen around the block is cheaper on every kind of fish."

The owner said, "See how much smarter you are already?"

One counterman in a small delicatessen was fired because they found him putting meat in a sandwich.

"I don't like the color of this corned beef."
"Wait until four o'clock. A painter is coming in!"

A man came into a delicatessen and ordered a meal, but warned the waiter, "I love bread. I don't care about the rest of the meal, but I have to have a lot of bread."

The waiter left, returning a few minutes later with a salad and, in a straw basket, two pieces of bread. The customer started to eat, but repeated his admonition about bread. He wanted more bread. Serving the soup, the waiter put four pieces of bread in the straw basket. The customer gulped down the soup and chewed up all the bread. Eight slices were served with the main course. Before he had started on the main course, the customer ate all the bread. Seeing him, the waiter took a foot-long loaf of bread, sliced it lengthwise, and brought it over to the table. The customer looked and said, "Why'd you go back to two slices?"

A customer complained, "There are fingerprints all over this glass."

The waiter said, "What other part of the body do you want it washed with?"

A customer sat down, looked at the menu, and said, "I'll start with a mixed salad."

The waiter said, "Forget the salad. The lettuce is wilted. Take the chopped liver instead."

"All right. I'll take the chopped liver. Then I want the chicken-and-rice soup."

"It's yesterday's. Take the lima bean."

"Okay, I'll take the lima bean soup. For the main dish I'd like the stuffed veal."

"No you wouldn't. Take the brisket."

"You win again. I'll have the brisket. Which vegetables do you suggest?"

"Pick your own. I don't have time to make suggestions."

Anytime a person goes into a delicatessen and orders pastrami on white bread, somewhere a Jew dies.

dentists

Another prime example of how closely related pain and comedy are. It may even be the best example. Of course, my dentist is the exception. He's painless. He's worked on my teeth for forty years and never once had any pain!

"My teeth don't fit."
"I checked them ten times."

"They don't fit."

"All right, put them in your mouth and I'll look."

"In my mouth they're fine. They don't fit in my *glass!*"

A Texas wildcatter went to his dentist one afternoon. After a thorough examination the dentist said, "Your teeth are in great shape. I can't think of a thing to do."

The Texan said, "Drill anyway. I feel lucky today!"

A dentist is a man who pulls lots of silver out of your pocket by putting silver in your teeth!

A dentist was asked, "How come you spend so much time on your wife's teeth?"

He replied, "It's the only time her mouth is open and I'm talking."

A dentist examined a lady and said, "You need a lot of work."

The woman said, "Believe me, I'd rather have a baby."

The dentist said, "Make up your mind before I finish adjusting this chair."

Two good ways to keep your teeth: Brush after meals and keep your mouth shut.

I wouldn't mind being a dentist sometimes. I could tell a woman to shut her mouth and get away with it.

"I don't know how to tell you, but the tooth you pulled wasn't the one that hurt."

"Don't be impatient. I'm getting to it!"

A dentist met a patient who owed him some money. The patient was angry because the dentist kept dunning him. Listening for a moment, the dentist finally said, "Don't gnash my teeth at me!"

A very busty lady had terrible teeth. The dentist couldn't get close enough to drill!

Coming out of a restaurant, a man met his dentist on the way in. The man asked, "Listen, what should I do about my yellow teeth?"

The dentist said, "Wear brown."

A dentist was working on a young woman patient, and kept telling her to open her mouth wider and wider. Finally she asked, "Aren't you planning to stand outside?"

I go to a poor dentist. Instead of cleaning your teeth, he just brushes the tartar under your gums.

I have so many cavities, I talk with eight echoes.

An orthodontist is a guy who braces the kids and straps the parents.

A man came into a dentist's office with his wife and said to the dentist, "Look, I want you to pull this bad tooth, but we haven't got a lot of time, so forget the novocaine or the laughing gas."

"You've got guts," the dentist said. "Which is the tooth?"

The man said, "Marie, show him the tooth that hurts!"

He goes to the dentist twice a year—once for each tooth!

"How much to have this tooth pulled?"

"Forty dollars."

"For two minutes' work?"

"I'll work slower!"

Do you call a gay dentist a tooth fairy?

Our dentist is an investment adviser. He put all our money in precious metals—we got braces for the kids!

Two longtime friends were catching up with the goings-on in their families. One father related that his son was studying to be a dentist. The other man said, "Your son wanted to be a proctologist. How come he switched to dentistry?"

"When we were having a chat one day, I pointed out that people have thirty-two teeth but only one rear end!"

A dentist was working hard on a new patient and finally finished preparing a cavity, asking, "Are you sure this tooth has never been filled before?"

"Never. Why?"

"There are some gold flecks on my drill."

"Maybe you hit the clasp on the back of my necklace!"

The Marquis de Sade used to go to his dentist and say, "Pick one!"

"Did you have a good time at the dentist?"
"It was a scream!"

My dentist saves me a lot of money. When my X rays show a lot of cavities, he touches them up.

My dentist said to me the other day, "I have bad news and good news for you."

I said, "What's the bad news?"

"You need root-canal work."

"What's the good news?"

"I birdied two holes yesterday!"

Happiness is listening to your dentist promise that it won't hurt, then watching him stick himself with a drill.

They recently got a dentist to remove the thirty-pound tusk of an elephant. The hard part was trying to get the elephant to spit in the little sink!

My dentist charges ten dollars a cavity. I give him ten dollars, and he gives me a cavity.

The dentist was just about to start drilling when the patient reached down and grabbed him below the belt. The dentist said, "What the heck are you doing?"

The patient said, "We're not going to hurt one another, are we?"

I went to my dentist the other day. My cavity was so deep he sent me to a chiropodist!

A dentist married a manicurist. They keep fighting tooth and nail!

A dentist came home to find his wife in a sheer negligee. Feeling frisky, he reached over and goosed her. His wife looked at him almost angrily and said, "For God's sake, you've had your hand in people's mouths all day!"

A local orthodontist recently perfected a great technique—he can remove your life's savings through your kid's mouth.

When my dentist gets through doing a canal, you don't know whether it's root or Panama.

I love to go to the dentist. Where else can you read *Collier's* today?

My dentist isn't too bright. He took a girl out for a ride the other day. When he ran out of gas, he gave her a local.

My dentist's assistant has giant boobs. After she leans over me for a while, I hate it when he puts in *his* fillings!

Joey's mother didn't want her son to become the typical boy who keeps chasing after girls. She concocted a story about the most intimate part of a woman's body having teeth. They could inflict great damage on a man and his virility.

The brainwashing worked. Joey grew up in total ignorance of female anatomy. Being able to concentrate on his studies, he became a dentist, graduating first in his class. Not long afterward, fate intervened. Joey met a young lady and fell in love. Wishing to share herself with him, the young lady invited him up to her apartment. A drink or two later, she offered him some pleasure. Joey said, "I can't. I don't want to get hurt."

The young lady said, "Why would it hurt?"

"Because you have teeth there."

"Teeth? I want you to look. There are no teeth."

Joey proceeded to examine the anatomy under discussion and said, "You're right. No teeth, but you have a terrible gum condition!"

My dentist just put in a tooth to match my other teeth. It has three cavities!

A woman comes into her dentist husband's office as he bends over a pretty patient, enjoying a brief sexual interlude. The wife says, "I hope for your sake that she's got a very deep cavity!"

She has so much bridgework, a man pays a toll to kiss her.

My dentist died last week. At the funeral I cried because he was filling his last cavity.

My dentist doesn't even have an X-ray machine. Instead, on a sunny day you come in and stand against the window!

My dentist is always giving out free samples. But last week he got into trouble because of free samples. His wife came in and found him getting one!

They say that being exposed to too many X rays can make you impotent. I was going to ask my dentist about it the other day, but he was too busy trying on new heels!

My dentist got into trouble for drumming up business. Last week they found him putting two root canals back into a patient!

A dentist said to a gorgeous patient, "We can't go on meeting like this. You have no more teeth left."

department stores

My wife has a daily route of four department stores. If she misses two days in a row, they send Get-well cards!

A woman walked over to a clerk in the men's section of a department store and asked for a pair of shorts. The clerk asked about the price range. The woman said, "The cheapest you got. They're for a corpse!"

The new clerk in the men's department was a great salesman. A woman came in for a suit in which to bury her husband, and the clerk sold her one with two pair of pants.

The clerk showed the lady customer just about every blanket in the bedding department. The lady customer said, "I was looking for a friend."

The clerk said, "If you think she's in there, I'll gladly go over them again!"

There's a new science-fiction movie out. It's about a customer in a department store who gets waited on.

A customer examines himself in the tenth coat he's put on, decides it's the right one, and says he'll take it. As he's waiting to pay at the register, one of the two clerks who waited on him says, "I walked over and sold him in a minute."

The other clerk said, "But who made him dizzy first?"

I won't say the service is slow, but every morning somebody comes in and dusts the sales clerks!

A kleptomaniac had been caught for the fifth time. Rather than go through the rigmarole of police reports and trials, the manager tried to reason with the shoplifter. "Look," the manager said, "there's another department store in this town. Why don't you go to them?"

The thief answered, "You give a better value for a dollar!"

A young lady goes to the perfume counter and asks for an audacious scent. The salesgirl tests a new one on her and says, "This is one perfume you don't use if you're only bluffing!"

People who go shopping in the shoe department always put their foot in it.

"What size shoe do you take?"
"Six is my regular size, but six and a half feels comfortable, so I wear a seven."

A woman had tried on every pair of shoes on the shelves. Disappointed, she said to the clerk, "Are those all you have?"

The clerk said, "Yup, except if you want to try on the pair *I'm* wearing!"

A woman was trying on a floor-length mink coat, admired herself in it, and said to the clerk, "If my husband doesn't like it, will you promise me that you'll *refuse* to take it back?"

A department store had to call off its special summer sale in August because of a conflict—its Christmas sale was beginning two days later.

When I was touring years ago, I worked at a large hotel in New Orleans. I went into a major department store and bought a suit. It needed some alterations. The clerk assured me that they would be done before my departure from the city.

Because a sudden opportunity presented itself in Hollywood, I left New Orleans hurriedly, without picking up my suit.

Years went by. I was in New Orleans again, for a roast. I suddenly recalled my suit. I went to the department store, saw the same clerk, older but still attentive, and asked about my suit. He retreated to the back and returned a minute later, saying, "It'll be ready tomorrow!"

A small shopkeeper found himself wedged between two branches of major department stores. The one to the right of him announced a giant clearance sale. A huge sign, hanging down six stories, announced THE BIGGEST SALE IN OUR HISTORY!

Not to be outdone, the other department store, to the left of the small shop, declared it was holding the most gigantic sale ever.

The owner of the small shop decided that he couldn't compete in grandeur, so he put up a sign that said, ENTRANCE TO THE SALE.

One department store held its fantastic fire sale last month. The sale was widely successful. In the first four hours of the sale, the store sold eighteen fantastic fires!

depression

I like the government's definition: a recession is merely a downward trend of a sliding tendency!

Things are so bad, Snow White laid off three dwarves!

A dress manufacturer ran into a friend at a restaurant. The friend started to discuss some of the other manufacturers they both knew. One had lost a million through a poor season, another had lost three million, and a third had lost three and a half million. The dress manufacturer started to smile and said, "And I thought this was going to be a bad year!"

Things are so bad, the Mississippi is only running two days a week!

Things are so bad, one store had a pre-fire sale!

Two computer manufacturers, their companies shaky, were flying back to New York from a huge convention in Las Vegas. They sat side by side silently for two hours, when one finally spoke up, saying, "You're telling me!"

The depression came at a bad time. Everybody was out of work.

This year will go down as the year that went down.

Things are so bad, the wages of sin have been reduced!

A presidential candidate said, "I am very optimistic about the future."

A reporter asked, "Then why do you look so worried?"

"I'm not certain my optimism is warranted!"

Today even Siamese twins can't make both ends meet.

Depressions never bothered my brother. He was a failure during the boom!

A recession is when you have to tighten your belt. A depression is when you *have* no belt!

They say that our present depression doesn't compare to the one in 1929. They're not giving us a chance!

We haven't reached rock bottom yet, but we'll get there—we're still climbing!

They just announced the top ten industries in the country. Begging is up to seventh!

designer jeans

Someday, somebody will explain to me why I pay extra so that some designer can advertise his jeans on my rear end!

His jeans are so tight, he crossed his legs and they had to take him to surgery!

In her jeans, from the back she looks like two puppies fighting!

They told him to let out his crotch. It came home at four in the morning!

One designer had such bad handwriting they'd only sell his jeans in drugstores.

One designer was very timid. He signed his jeans in pencil.

I won't say it's been a long time since my son had his jeans cleaned, but I opened his closet the other day and found two pairs standing by themselves.

One thing about signed jeans—they've made youngsters read better!

One thing we can be sure of—this year women will still be wearing the same old things in jeans.

Her jeans were so tight she had to wear her skin on the outside!

Some men's jeans are so tight in the crotch, you can tell their religion!

determination (perseverance)

I once met an oil billionaire. I asked him how'd he made so much money. He said, "I just kept digging holes!"

Never give up. Look at what would have happened to the chemist who only got to Preparation G!

The man who concocted the formula never would have forgiven himself if he'd stopped at 6-Up!

Hooray for the songwriter who didn't stop at "Tea for One"!

He had come up with it—the wheel! Unfortunately, it was square. It wouldn't turn. No matter how hard the slaves pulled the wagons, the wagons wouldn't move an inch.

Determined, he sat down again and for fifty years studied the matter. Day and night, night and day, he sat at his drawing board in a dark cave and worked out a thousand designs. Then, finally, in the fifty-first year, he came up with the answer. He invented the whip! Those wagons sure did move!

If at first you don't succeed, try again. Then quit. There's no reason to make a darn fool of yourself.

Be sure you're home when opportunity knocks. Or it may steal your TV set!

He worked his fingers to the bone for years. Now he has bony fingers.

For years he thought he was a failure. They told him to be positive. Now he's positive he's a failure.

Every problem can be solved, except maybe how to refold a road map.

Even a subway conductor shouldn't marry below his station.

Keep trying. Look at the man who put a hole in a Life Saver and made a mint!

I just started on my second million. I gave up on the first!

diagnosis

If not the catalyst for more jokes than any other subject, doctors come close. Which is more than I can say for their diagnoses! The goings-on in a doctor's office, if laid end to end, would make some malpractice suit!

"What's wrong with me, Doctor?"
"You're too fat, you smoke like a chimney,

you huff and puff, and you're in the wrong office. I'm a lawyer!"

A lady ear, nose, and throat specialist examined a client, found out what was wrong immediately, and decided to paint the patient's throat. Then she went crazy trying to decide on a color!

A man went to an internist and complained of listlessness, especially when it came to matters of sex. After an examination, the doctor said, "You ought to try hormones."

"Like they give women?"

"Everybody uses hormones. They even give them to racehorses."

The patient agreed to take a hormone injection. Three weeks later he returned to the doctor who asked, "Did the shot work?"

The patient said, "You bet."

"Your sexual ardor is back?"

"No, but yesterday morning I ran six furlongs in one-ten!"

The doctor examined a woman and said, "You're anemic."

She said, "I'd like a second opinion."

The doctor said, "You're ugly too!"

"My right foot hurts."

"It's old age."

"How come my left foot doesn't hurt? It's the same age!"

"Doc, what do I do for a broken leg?"

"Limp!"

A doctor said to a beautiful young patient, "So far I don't see anything wrong with you. Keep undressing!"

He was a great diagnostician. He could tell your condition by feeling your wallet!

A doctor said to an old woman patient,

"You need a physical. Get undressed."

The woman said, "Doctor, you first!"

A doctor told an old woman patient to undress. She said, "I'll do it, Doctor, but I want you to know—you're playing with fire!"

The patient asked, "How do I stand, Doctor?"

The doctor answered, "I'll be damned if I know! It's a miracle!"

A patient said to the doctor, raising his left arm, "It hurts when I do that."

"Okay," the doctor said, "don't do that."

"You're coughing easier today."

"I practiced all night!"

I feel very nervous. The doctor examined me today and said I was as sound as a dollar!

The patient was telling the doctor his symptoms. "After climbing the first flight of stairs," he said, "I start to feel a little dizzy. After the second it's hard to breathe. After the third I can hardly move."

The doctor said, "Why don't you stop after the second?"

The man said, "How can I? I live on the third!"

The doctor gave me three days to live, but not consecutively.

A patient complained to a doctor, "I've been to three other doctors and they don't agree with your diagnosis."

The doctor said, "Wait till the autopsy. They'll see I'm right!"

A doctor examined a man and said, "I don't like the looks of him."

The man's wife said, "I know, but he's so good to the pets!"

He's a careful doctor. A patient came in with the german measles. The doctor gave him two shots—East and West.

A nervous man, accompanied by a nagging wife, was examined by the doctor. Studying the man's chart, the doctor nodded to himself and wrote out a prescription for a powerful sedative. The man asked, "When do I take them?"

The doctor said, "They're not for you. They're for your wife!"

A patient asked a doctor, "Do you like rich foods?"

The doctor said, "No, but I'm grateful to them!"

Then there's the unethical allergist. He keeps a dead cat in his desk drawer!

"Mrs. Klein, your husband will never be able to work again."

"I'll tell him. That'll cheer him up!"

The patient came into the doctor's office, suffering from amnesia. The doctor asked, "Have you ever had it before?"

A man complained to the doctor that his sexual ardor was gone. The doctor told him, "Your body is out of tone. You have to get in shape. I want you to run ten miles a day."

At the end of a week, the patient called the doctor and said, "I'm seventy miles out of town. What do we do now?"

My doctor has started a discount medical practice. For five dollars you can come into the office and read the issue of *Reader's Digest* with your cure in it!

diamonds

A girl's best friends, unless you include legs!

A woman showed another a magnificent diamond in a platinum setting and explained, "My husband died last month, but just before he breathed his last, he told me about some money in a bank vault. He told me to buy a stone with it. This is the stone!"

A richly dressed lady meets another at a fancy spa. She shows off her huge diamond ring. The other woman is impressed and says, "That's the most beautiful diamond I ever saw."

The rich woman says, "It is nice, but it comes with the Montague curse."

"Who's Montague?"

"My husband!"

A woman was having her portrait painted. Before she sat down to pose, she put two huge diamond rings on her fingers. Close up, they looked as shabby as what they were— penny imitations. The artist asked her why she had put on the jewelry. She responded, "My husband is younger than I. When I die, he'll get married again. I want his next wife to go crazy looking for these rings!"

Two women basked in the sun of Florida. One asked, "Do you have the time?"

The other answered, "It's two rubies past four diamonds!"

The potentate of an Eastern kingdom came to New York and checked into the biggest suite of the fanciest hotel. The potentate spoke no English. As he worked with an interpreter on a speech, a noise from the other room diverted their attention. Before they could make a move, two masked bandits stormed in, guns in their hands. They demanded the potentate's famous jewels. The interpreter translated their demands. In his native tongue, the potentate told the bandits to go to hell. He had no jewels. One of the bandits said, "We know he has jewels. We're going to count to three. If we don't get the jewels, we're going to shoot him!"

The interpreter conveyed the message to the potentate, who said in his own language, "I don't want to die. Tell them that the jewels are hidden in the chandelier in the outer room."

The interpreter said to the bandits, "He said he'd rather die than tell you where the jewels are!"

A couple walked along the street. They stopped to look in the window of a famous jewelry store. She said, "I'd love that little diamond pin in the window."

He took a brick out of his pocket, broke the window, and handed her the pin.

They walked on and came to another jewelry store. She liked the diamond earrings. He took another brick out, broke the window, and handed her the earrings.

They walked on and reached a third jewelry store. She said, "I'd love to have that diamond ring."

He said, "What is this with you? You must think I'm made of bricks!"

diet

Eat, drink, and be merry, for tomorrow we diet!

The second day of a diet is always easier than the first. By the second day you're off it.

I had a forty-four-inch waist, so I started to drink low-fat milk. Now I have forty-four-inch knees!

With exercise, I've managed to work all the fat from my stomach. It's all behind me now!

Here I am in the flesh. When I say "flesh" I'm speaking loosely.

A husband and wife were waiting for a clerk in a drugstore. Seeing a scale, they walked over and the lady got on. A moment later, a card came out. It said, "You are warm-hearted, lovable, understanding, and an excellent cook."

Peeking over his wife's shoulder, the husband said, "It didn't get your *weight* right either."

I'm always on a diet. If I'd come down from Mount Sinai instead of Moses, the two tablets would have been saccharin.

As part of a diet, I took up exercising by riding horses. It worked. In three weeks the horse lost eighteen pounds!

I don't know. Diet just seems to take the starch out of me!

I knew I had to slow down on my eating. I'd started to put mayonnaise on aspirins!

It took a lot of willpower, but I finally gave up dieting!

When you start on a diet, the first thing you lose is your patience.

I can see why America is called a melting pot—everybody's dieting!

We *lived* a diet when I was a kid. Some of our dinners were so small I used to burp from memory.

I was so heavy I couldn't touch my toes. I went on a diet. Now I touch my toes all the time. I fall down a lot!

You meet a woman and put her on a pedestal. Ten years later you put her on a diet!

If my wife doesn't go on a diet soon, we're going to have to let out the couch!

I went on a diet that allowed me to drink wine and eat vegetables. In ten days I lost five pounds and my driver's license.

Diets are for people who are thick and tired of it!

"Was your wife's diet a success?"
"It was perfect. She disappeared last week!"

I know a woman who went on a diet of coconuts and milk. She didn't lose an ounce, but she sure can climb trees!

I knew somebody who used only sugar substitutes. After a few years he died of artificial diabetes.

The doctor told me to think thin. I did, and lost four inches around my head.

I went on a drinking man's diet once. In three weeks I lost twenty-one days!

I know somebody who eats the same every day—three giant bowls of cereal in the morning, four hamburgers for lunch, and at dinner a two-pound steak and french fries. He still weighs what he weighed ten years ago—four hundred and ten pounds.

I tried the drinking man's diet. I lost five pounds and the location of my house.

I'm really not heavy. My waist is thirty-four. Of course, that's through the middle.

I'm a light eater. I only eat when it's light!

She just went on a diet. She found out her bathtub was form-fitting!

People who write diet books live on the fat of the land.

I just went on a no-starch diet. But I can eat all the bleach and detergent I want.

Saccharin is the most fattening thing in the world. Every time I look, some fat person is using it.

I started to diet the day I tightened my belt and became three inches taller.

I never eat between meals because, for me, there *is* no between meals!

dinosaurs

Let's imagine that they didn't become extinct. My wife would have wanted one for a pet. What a doggie door we'd have had!

The cavemen were incredible. When they hunted dinosaurs, the decoy weighed two tons!

Two young male dinosaurs happened upon a young female. One of them said, "I'd like to make love to her."
   The other one said, "I don't think so. She's having her century."

"How did dinosaurs make love?"
"Very carefully!"

diplomacy

True diplomacy is when the plumber comes in, finds the lady of the house naked in the tub, and says, "I'll be back later, sir!"

Diplomacy is the art of skating on thin ice without getting into deep water.

A diplomat is a man who can convince his wife she looks bad in mink.

A diplomat thinks twice before shutting up.

A diplomat has to like everybody. One ambassador was asked about Hitler and said, "He was the best at what he did!"

Diplomacy is the art of letting somebody have your way.

Diplomacy is the art of saying "Nice doggie" until you find a rock.

Diplomacy is the art of being able to explain your wife to your secretary.

Diplomacy is knowing how far you can go when you go too far.

Diplomacy is the subtle way of dropping this information at the bar: you drive a Mercedes, your family has money, and you were wounded three times in combat.

Diplomacy is the art of convincing your date that your 1978 Toyota is a loaner!

Your date comes to the door. Her slip is showing, her lipstick is on crooked, and her left shoe has a piece of toilet paper stuck to it. Diplomacy is the art of explaining the surprise recurrence of your malaria a minute ago!

disasters

The house shakes. Everybody quivers. It happens at my house every day until my wife has had her first cup of coffee! When she's in a snit, a 7.3 earthquake could learn from her!

Earthquakes are someting. I have a small piece of oceanfront property in Santa Monica. Three days ago it was in Colorado!

The earth shook so much during the earthquakes that spastics were walking straight lines!

We live on a dangerous fault—my income!

I saw a strange house—a split-level by choice!

It was snowing so much I saw a snowplow hitching a ride south!

We had an early winter in California this year—last Tuesday!

A scuba diver was looking at some coral off the coast of Florida when he received a message: "Surface immediately. The ship is sinking!"

discipline

When I was a kid and said bad words, my mother used to wash my mouth out with soap. One day she found out that I wasn't interested in bad words. I just liked the taste of soap!

I was whipped so often when I was a kid, until I was eleven I thought I was a dog team!

In our neighborhood we have one kid whose parents never hit him except in self-defense!

A teacher wrote home that a young boy was a real discipline problem. It was suggested that the parents give him a good whipping. The parents wrote back, *"You* slug him. We aren't mad at him!"

Little Tina's hands were not exactly clean. Her mother said, "Come upstairs with me and we'll wash your hands."

Tina said, "I don't want to go upstairs."

Grandma said, "Why can't she wash her hands in the kitchen?"

"Because I want her upstairs."

Tina turned to her mother and said, "Don't you ever listen to your mother?"

"Son, this is going to hurt me more than it hurts you."

"Well, make sure you go easy on yourself!"

divorce

It would be impossible without marriage; another good thing to be said about that institution!

My wife won't give me a divorce until she can find a way of doing it without making me happy.

One woman had fourteen kids and finally got a divorce because of compatibility!

Some women believe it's okay for a man to leave them—as long as they leave them enough.

I pay my alimony on the button. I'm afraid that if I don't, my ex-wife will repossess me!

Two women met on a plane flying to Hawaii. Bosom buddies in ten minutes, they started to talk about their families. One woman said, "My daughter just got divorced from a surgeon."

"Maybe it was for the better."

"Before him, she was married to a dentist."

"No kidding."

"She divorced him to marry an attorney. And before the dentist she was married to a CPA."

The other woman said, "Four professionals? Do you know how lucky you are to get such pleasure from one daughter?"

A woman in tears was testifying against her husband in their divorce case. "He was mean," she said. "He was always hitting me. He beat me five times a day."

The husband jumped up and said, "Don't listen to her, Your Honor. She's punch-drunk!"

One marriage out of three ends in divorce. The other two fight it out to the bitter end.

I know a husband and wife who have separate bedrooms, drive different cars, and take separate vacations. They do everything to keep their marriage together!

Two men are talking. One says, "I got married because I was sick and tired of going to the laundromat, eating out, and wearing torn clothes."

The other man said, "Amazing. I got divorced for the same reasons!"

She got divorced because of the housework. She didn't like the way her husband did it.

He wants to divorce himself. He's tired of living together!

If we didn't have divorces, where would we get waitresses?

When he got a divorce, he and his wife split the house. He got the outside.

She gave him a divorce because he was in love with himself and she didn't want to stand in his way.

A country boy went to the local magistrate and asked for a divorce. The judge couldn't understand why this drastic action had to be taken. The young man said, "I was married under false pretenses."

The judge asked, "Isn't your wife all you expected?"

The country boy said, "Yup, but I just found out her pa didn't have a license for that gun!"

An actress asked an attorney how much he'd charge for handling her divorce. The attorney said, "Fifty thousand, or three for a hundred."

Strange world. A few words mumbled by a minister, and people are married. A few words mumbled by a sleeping husband, and people are divorced!

Divorce is the future tense of marriage.

doctors

There's no exhausting this subject. More might show up in "Surgeons" and "Hospitals." It's a fact of comedy life—ten thousand jokes about medicine are born every minute. Once the Chinese start writing them, there won't be room for anything else!

A man sat in a doctor's office and kept up a strange litany: "I hope I'm sick. I hope I'm sick."

Another waiting patient asked, "Why do you want to be sick?"

The man said, "I'd hate to be well and feel like this."

A doctor walked into the sleeping patient's room. The nurse asked, "What are we operating for?"

The doctor said, "Two thousand dollars."

"You don't understand. I mean, what does he have?"

"I told you. Two thousand dollars!"

Dr. Carver still made house calls. This one afternoon he was called to the Tuttle house. Mrs. Tuttle was in terrible pain. The doctor came out of the bedroom a minute after he'd gone in and asked Mr. Tuttle, "Do you have a hammer?"

A puzzled Mr. Tuttle nodded, went to his toolshed, and returned with a hammer. The doctor thanked him and went back into the bedroom. A moment later, he came out and asked, "Do you have a chisel?" Mr. Tuttle complied with the request.

In the next ten minutes, Dr. Carver asked for and received a pair of pliers and a hacksaw. That last request got to Mr. Tuttle. He asked, "What are you doing to my wife?"

"Not a thing," the doctor said. "I can't get my instrument bag open."

Doctors ask you to set an appointment six months in advance. How do you know when you're going to become sick?

Doctors are amazing. They cure poor people faster!

A patient described the pain in his arm. The doctor asked, "Did you ever have this before?"

The man said, "Yes."

The doctor said, "Well, you've got it again!"

An ailing man went to the fanciest doctor he could find. The doctor started off by saying that his first office visit would cost two hundred dollars. The man said, "That's a lot of money. I can't afford that."

The doctor said, "Now that you're here, I'll only charge a hundred."

"Doc, a hundred is too much. I'm taking care of my aged parents."

"Seventy-five, is that all right?"

"With six kids?"

The fee was finally lowered to ten dollars and accepted. The doctor went on, "I'm curious. You know that I'm the most expensive doctor in the city. Why did you come to me?"

The man said, "Where my health is concerned, money is no object!"

The doctor was busy, and it took hours to check all of his patients. Down to Mr. Smith, the doctor apologized to the old man, saying, "I hope you didn't mind waiting so long."

Mr. Smith said, "It's a shame you couldn't see my illness in its early stages."

A doctor called a patient, "Your check came back."

The patient said, "So did my bursitis!"

A doctor examined an airline pilot, asking him, "When was the last time you had sex?"

The pilot answered, "About 1955."

The doctor asked, "So long ago?"

The pilot said, "That wasn't too long ago." He looked at his watch and went on, "It's only 2120!"

Do doctors who treat people for amnesia make them pay in advance?

An old woman went to a gynecologist. When his examination was done, she turned to him and asked, "Doctor, does your mother know how you make your living?"

A man and his wife came into a doctor's office. The man was in bad pain. The doctor examined him quickly and suspected a need for surgery. He said, "You're going right to the hospital in an ambulance. My nurse will make the arrangements, and I'll be there as soon as I take care of my last two patients."

The doctor worked quickly, then sped to the hospital. He arrived at the moment the ambulance pulled up. The door opened and the wife emerged. The doctor said, "This ambulance was for your husband."

Coming up from the outside, the husband heard the last words and explained, "I tried to tell her, but one word led to another and, as usual, I had to take the bus."

In a fancy restaurant, a man started to choke on a bone. A doctor rushed over and gave him the Heimlich Maneuver. The bone popped out. The man was saved. His breath returning, the man asked, "What do I owe you?"

The doctor said, "I'll settle for a third of what you were willing to pay while you were choking."

A doctor said to a patient, "The best thing you can do is to quit smoking. Then you should stop running around with young girls and cut out drinking."

The patient said, "Doctor, I don't deserve the best. What's second best?"

Dr. Carson was brought up on charges at the medical board. He had, it seemed, uttered the vilest profanity to his nurse. He explained, "Let me tell you what happened. My alarm didn't go off, so I woke up late. When I did wake up, I tried to turn on the light in the lamp on my nightstand. The bulb exploded and scared me for a minute, so I pulled the cord out of the wall and the lamp fell over and broke. I was trying to make a little breakfast when a whole army of little Girl Scouts showed up and tried to sell me tons of cookies. I had to buy five boxes to get rid of the kids. By then my coffee was ice cold and my eggs were burned. I gulped down a glass of juice. It turned out to be sour. I started to drive to the office. The car conked out. The alternator was gone. I didn't have my auto club card with me so I had to pay to have the car towed to a service station. I looked at my service book and discovered that the warranty ran out last week. I took a cab to the office, but around Main Street somebody sideswiped us and I hit my head on the door handle. I finally made it into my office when my nurse said, "Doctor, a shipment of thermometers just came in. What shall I do with them?"

"Doctor, you have to help me."
"What's your problem?"
"I have some dimes stuck in my ear."
"How long have they been there?"
"A year."
"Why didn't you come in sooner?"
"I didn't need the money."

A man was in bad shape. He constantly gasped for breath and his eyes bulged. The doctors didn't give him long to live. He decided to live it up. Withdrawing all of his money from the bank, he went on a shopping spree. His last stop was at the most expensive haberdashery in the city. He pointed out a dozen silk shirts. He wore a size fourteen. The clerk said, "Your neck looks bigger than fourteen. You need a sixteen."

The man said, "I know my size. I want them in a fourteen."

The clerk said, "I'll get them for you, but I want to warn you—if you wear a fourteen you'll gasp all day and your eyes will bulge."

A man went to a woman doctor's office. The doctor told him to go into an examining room and take off his clothes. He did so. After a few minutes there was a knock on the door. The doctor entered. She proceeded to examine him completely, looking closely at every part of his body. Then she said, "Do you have any questions?"

The patient said, "I have *one*—why did you knock?"

A woman went to a fertility doctor, who suggested that she and her husband go home and rest up. The next day she was to bring in a sample of her husband's sperm from sex three hours before the appointment. The woman said, "It won't work. My husband couldn't last three hours!"

"Doctor, should I get a second opinion?"
"Why not? Come back tomorrow."

A pretty nudist went to a doctor, who examined her and said, "Young lady, you are pregnant."

The nudist said, "That's not possible. We practice sex only by looking."

The doctor said, "Somebody there must be cockeyed!"

Medicine is a great profession—you get a woman to take of her clothes and then you send her husband the bill.

You can tell when a patient is ready to leave the hospital. He can face the cashier.

"Doctor, there's a ringing in my ears."
"Don't answer it!"

A woman rushes into a doctor's office.

"Doctor," she says, "what should I take when I'm run down?"

The doctor says, "The license number."

Medical science has increased our lifespan, so how come you never meet a woman over forty?

"Doctor, are papayas healthy?"
"I never heard one complain!"

An attractive young lady went to a doctor and told him, "I'm afraid I'm becoming a nymphomaniac."

The doctor said, "Hmm. Why don't you lie down and tell me about it?"

A doctor told a patient of twenty-one, "Go home and tell your husband you're going to have a baby."

She said, "I'm not married."

"Tell your lover."

"I never had a lover."

"Okay, go home and look out of the window. There'll soon be a star in the east!"

The rural doctor came out to the farm to check on the farmer's wife. Upon arriving, the doctor felt thirsty. He walked over to the well to bring up some cool water, but slipped and fell in. The moral is that a doctor should take care of the sick and leave the well alone.

Doctors must wear masks because of their fees!

I told my doctor I couldn't hear. He told me I was better off, the way things are today.

A doctor lost his practice. Desperate, he tried to hold up a bank, but they couldn't read his hold-up note!

A young man resisted going into the examining room and getting undressed. He explained, "I'm built very small and I'm embarrassed. I can't even undress in front of the other guys in school."

The doctor said, "Does it become erect?"

"Oh, that's no problem."

"Okay, would you like to trade it for one that looks good in the locker room?"

A man went to his doctor, who gave him six months to live. The man was unable to pay the bill, so the doctor gave him another six months.

The difference between an itch and allergy is about fifty dollars.

A doctor asked a patient to stand at the window and stick out his tongue. "But I'm here for a foot examination," the patient said.

The doctor said, "I know. But I hate the doctor across the street!"

I have a fancy doctor. You have to make an appointment to make an appointment!

The doctor said, "You ought to quit smoking."

The patient said, "You're right, Doctor. As of this minute I'm through smoking."

The doctor said, "In that case, do you want ten bucks for your lighter?"

My doctor is so fancy he won't even make hospital calls.

A specialist is a doctor with a smaller practice but a bigger home!

Sobbing, a young nun came out of a doctor's office. A priest saw her, asked why she was crying, and, upon learning the reason, stormed into the doctor's office. Furious, the priest said, "How dare you tell that to a nun?"

The doctor said, "Got rid of her hiccups, didn't it?"

I trust my doctor. If he treats you for a broken arm, that's what you die of!

A patient spent three hours in the doctor's office, waiting to be examined. Finally he called it quits and went home to die of natural causes.

A new nurse listened to Dr. Bryce yelling out, "Typhoid! Tetanus! Measles!"

The new nurse asked, "Why is he yelling like that?"

The other nurse said, "He likes to call his shots."

A gynecologist doesn't have it easy. At the end of the day he must be bushed!

A man told his friend, "The doctor told me I'd be dead in a week if I didn't stop chasing women."

"Why would he say that?"

"His wife was one of the women I was chasing!"

One doctor has a wife who's so jealous she listens in on his stethoscope.

dogs

I never had a dog. When I was five, my parents gave me a hairbrush. I tied a string to it and walked it. Then one day my brush got hit by a car. The barber couldn't save it. I'll never forget my hairbrush, Rover. I wanted to call him Spot, but we'd already used that for my brother.

A musician was hired to score a porno movie. A job was a job, so he wrote as good a score as he could. Some months later he passed a porno movie house where the picture was playing. Three steps back and five dollars later he found himself in the dark theater, watching the most explicit sex scenes. The movie had every kind of sex imaginable: lesbian scenes, group sex, sex with animals, sadism and masochism, and even one or two normal sex acts. The nature of the movie was unimportant to the musician. He was entranced by the music. The melodies were beautiful, the musical bridges sweeping in scope. After a while the musician turned to the couple seated nearby and asked, "Isn't that music fabulous?"

The man of the couple answered, "What do we know about music? We came to see our dog!"

They call their dog "Day Worker" because he does odd jobs around the house.

He bought himself a bulldog, and in no time at all he had him eating out of his leg!

There was a dog named Lassie who went to Denmark and came back a cat.

A man walked into a bar with a dog, claimed that the animal could talk, and offered to sell it. The bartender refused to believe the claim and was about to mark it all down to the full moon when the dog said, "Buy me. Somebody please buy me. My owner is mean and vicious. He's always kicking me and hitting me. I happen to be a great dog. I was in the service. I have three medals for bravery. Please buy me."

The bartender asked the owner, "How can you sell such a wonderful dog?"

The man answered, "I'm sick and tired of his lies!"

One dog asks another, "What's your name?"

The other answers, "I'm not sure, but I think it's 'Down, boy.'"

A man recently came up with something that'll make him rich.

It's a dog biscuit that tastes like a mailman's leg!

"I shot my dog last night."

"Was he mad?"

"He wasn't too thrilled about it."

Then there was this Pekingese who married a tomcat. Now they have a Peking tom!

Then there was a man who found his dog eating one of his books. He took the words right out of the dog's mouth!

A woman went into a pet shop looking for a dog. She pestered the owner about every dog he had for sale. Finally she checked out a baby bloodhound. The woman asked, "How do you know it's a bloodhound?"

The owner said to the dog, "Please bleed for the lady!"

One day a group ran to the hounds. By mistake, a bitch in heat was put into the pack. An observer asked, "How's it going?"

Another observer said, "I can't tell for sure, but I think the fox is running fifth!"

Then there's the man who avoided the pooper-scooper laws by dressing his dog in a tree suit.

A few fleas won't bother a dog. Besides, they'll give him something to do so he won't keep thinking about being a dog.

A man bitten by a rabid dog ran home and started to write on the first piece of paper he found. Asked if he was hurrying to get a will down, he said, "Nope. I'm just writing down the names of the people I'm going to bite!"

I sent my dog to obedience school. Now he says grace before he bites somebody.

My dog is like a member of the family—but I'm not sure which one.

My dog's nose is flatter than a pancake. He got it from chasing parked cars.

Looking very sad, a young boy was sitting on his porch. Another boy came along and said, "How come you're crying, Tom?"

Tom said, "My dog Scotty died."

The other boy said, "My grandma died last week but you don't see me crying."

Tom said, "You didn't raise your grandma from a pup!"

A storekeeper went to a dog breeder for a watchdog. The breeder sold him a fierce-looking German shepherd. The dog was placed in the store to guard the goodies. As luck would have it, a burglar appeard at one in the morning. The dog slept through the robbery. The next day the storekeeper went back to the breeder and complained, "Your darn dog slept through all the crashing and banging and dragging. He didn't open an eye."

The breeder said, "What you need now is a small dog to wake him up."

My dog must have been bred by a waiter. He never comes when I call him.

"Why is a dog longer in the morning than in the evening?"

"Because he's let out in the morning and taken in at night!"

A Russian wolfhound and a mixed-breed American dog met one day. The Russian wolfhound described the life he led. "I don't have to work. They feed me three times a day. Somebody brushes my coat every few hours."

The American dog said, "I have to scrounge for food. People shoo me away from their property."

The Russian dog said, "I'd trade with you tomorrow."

"You've got it so good."

"Well, to tell you the truth, I like to bark once in a while."

On a country road, a speeder hit and killed a dog. The dog's owner stood nearby, a gun in his hand.

The speeder said, "Looks as if I killed your dog."

"Sure does."

"I'm sorry. Was it a valuable dog?"

"I wouldn't say that."

"Well, suppose I gave you fifty dollars. Would that be enough?"

"Well, I don't know."

"Seventy-five dollars. That should do it."

"Sounds good."

The speeder reached into his pocket and came up with the money. Pressing it into the man's hand, the speeder said, "I'm sorry I spoiled your plans to go hunting."

"I wasn't going hunting. I was heading out to the woods to shoot the darn dog!"

"**I** want something for fleas."

"Get a dog!"

"**M**y neighbor's dog bit me in the leg today."

"Did you put anything on it?"

"No, he liked it just as it was."

Two dogs were yelping at one another. One said, "You're crazy. You should go see a psychiatrist!"

The other said, "I'd love to, but I'm not allowed on the couch!"

I have an American Legion dog. He stops at every post.

My dog is an Arctic explorer. He goes from pole to pole.

A psychiatrist treated a man who thought he was a dog. After many months of treatment, the patient ran into a friend and told him about the many sessions he'd had on the couch. The friend asked, "How do you feel now?"

The patient said, "Great. Just feel my nose!"

A dog saw somebody putting money into a parking meter and reported to the other dogs, "They're putting in pay toilets!"

A man had three dogs. He named them Whitey, Brownie, and Van Cliburn. Whitey was a white dog, Brownie was a brown dog, and Van Cliburn was the peeinest!

A man tried to board a city bus with a Saint Bernard. The driver refused to allow him entry. The man said, "Buddy, do you know what you can do with your bus?"

The driver said, "If you can do the same thing with your Saint Bernard, you can get on!"

There was once a dogcatcher with a wooden leg. He didn't have to chase the animals. The dogs came to him!

One idiot was elected dogcatcher. He knew that he was supposed to catch dogs—but at what?

Once there was a movie star who followed anyone who whistled at her. Her name was Lassie.

One gent had seventy-two dogs in his house. The doctor told him to stop whistling in his sleep.

He called his dog Seiko. It was a watchdog!

Once there was a neurotic bloodhound. He thought people were following him.

One day a mother dog told her pups about the birds and the fleas.

A dog saw a sign that said WET PAINT, and he did!

A woman explains to her friend that her husband is lazy. The only way she gets him up to work is to throw the cat on the bed. The friend asks, "How does that get him up?"
　　The woman answers, "He sleeps with the dog."

A fire had broken out. The neighborhood kids watched as the fire truck pulled up. High on his usual perch sat the station mascot, a Dalmatian. The youngsters wondered about the dog's function. One said, "He brings the firemen good luck."
　　A second said, "He keeps people away so they can work."
　　A third kid said, "You guys don't know anything. They use the dog to find the fireplug!"

A woman walked into a pet shop, pointed to a puppy in the window, and asked, "What's his pedigree?"
　　The shopkeeper said, "The mother is champion purebred terrier. And the father comes from a very nice neighborhood."

A lot of people have dogs nowadays to protect them from the muggers they wouldn't run into if they didn't have to walk their dogs.

A pair of newcomers to the country life bought a pedigreed bird dog from a farmer. They took the dog out on a brief snipe-hunting expedition. He sat down and slept. One of the newcomers said, "So much for hunting. Now let's throw him into the air. If he doesn't fly, we'll bring him back."

A country gent was exercising his right to tell a fanciful tale. Sitting around the stove in the general store with some friends, old and new, he talked about his old dog. The dog did all the shopping for the family. When supplies got low, he'd go into town and point out whatever was needed from the general store. As soon as the stuff was bagged, he carried it back to the farmhouse. Never once was he short an item. Another old-timer said, "Yup, he was a smart dog, all right, but have you forgotten it was my dog that ran the general store he shopped in?"

A man received word that his mother-in-law was coming to visit. He ran right to the vet and had his dog's tail removed so there wouldn't be the slightest sign of a welcome!

My dog had worms, so the vet told me to feed it lots of garlic. Now its bark is worse than its bite!

A blind man and a wino were standing on a corner. A street dog came along and took a chunk out of the blind man's leg. The blind man reached into his pocket, came up with a piece of candy, and held it for the dog to chew. The wino said, "You're something, man. That dog bit you, and you're gonna give him candy. Why?"

The blind man said, "I want to find out which is his front end, then I'm gonna boot the other end about fifty yards!"

A man was bitten by a dog. The man was taken to the hospital. Some hours later, a man from the pound came to see him and give him the bad news that the dog was mad. The victim said, "How do you like them apples? He bit me and *he's* mad?"

A dog is man's best friend because he wags his tail instead of his tongue.

dreams

I had a terrible dream the other day. This stunning and statuesque movie star with a magnificent bosom was my mother. And I was a bottle baby!

A fisherman was telling a friend about his dream the night before. "I was alone on Lake Tahoe with a gorgeous woman."

His friend asked, "How'd you make out?"

"Great. I caught a six-pound bass!"

A man went to a psychiatrist and told him about the beautiful women he dreamed about every night. The doctor said that a cure was possible. The patient said, "I don't want the cure. Just help me get their phone numbers!"

I had a terrible dream yesterday. I dreamed I was awake all night.

"**H**oney, I had a dream last night in which you bought me a new mink coat."
"In tonight's dream, see if you can come up with the money!"

A football coach was telling a friend about a dream he'd had. "I was in this small town. The waitress at the diner was beautiful, with a stunning body. I ordered coffee and we started to talk. The hours went by and she asked me if I wanted to come over to her house. I couldn't wait."

"Wow, what a dream!" the friend said.

"You haven't heard the good part. She introduced me to her kid brother. He was six-one, had wide shoulders, and could run fifty yards in 4.3 seconds!"

Dreams don't come true until you get up and go to work.

"**M**y wife had a dream in which she was married to a millionaire."
"You're a lucky guy. My wife dreams that in the daytime!"

A man told his friend about a recent dream, "I dreamed that I was gambling at the Lido in Venice. I was breaking the bank."

His friend said, "That's a nice dream. Let me tell you about the one I had last night. I was on the Riviera with three stunning women."

The first man asked, "Why didn't you call me?"

The friend said, "I did. Your answering service said you were in Venice."

drive-in theaters

Where else can you get run over while you're going to the bathroom?

When you go to a drive-in you see raw passion, sex, people linked together panting, and you can also see a movie.

What would they call a drive-in if it didn't have a screen?

A drive-in is a place where you give the kids ten dollars for the snack bar, and you don't see them again until they're thirty.

One night at a drive-in, the projector broke and nobody knew!

How to get from the front seat to the back without spilling the popcorn—that's the real driver's education!

They now practice safe sex in drive-ins—the boy and girl go in separate cars!

A young woman, about to give birth, asked her doctor what the birth position was. The doctor said, "It's just like the position you were in when you conceived."

The young woman said, "With my legs up, in a drive-in?"

driving

People who have driven with me say that I'm the world's worst driver. I hardly come to a stop at a stop sign, I never look to the right or the left; I ride the brakes to death—all techniques I learned from my uncle Charlie, the man who taught me to drive. Uncle Charlie, incidentally, never got a driving license! There may be some truth to the stories about my driving acumen, since my wife asks me where I'll be driving whenever she intends to leave the house. She then makes her plans accordingly.

"My wife drives like lightning."
"She drives fast?"
"No, she hits trees!"

My wife is such a bad driver, she lost control of her car the other day and it went back on the right side of the highway.

She just came up with a new kind of driveway. It's called a lawn.

She must hate the phone company. She keeps knocking down their poles!

He wishes his wife were a backseat driver. He drives a hearse!

I love to take week-long trips by car—two days to travel and five to fold the road maps!

She's getting to be a good driver. Last week she got twenty miles to a fender!

A man is driving with his wife at his side and his mother-in-law in the backseat. The women don't leave him alone. His mother-in-law says, "You're driving too fast!"

His wife says, "Stay more to the left."

After ten mixed orders, the man turns to his wife and asks, "Who's driving this car—you or your mother?"

One day my wife drove up the side of a building and hit another woman driving down!

I have a friend who tells his wife when she goes out driving, "Hurry home so you don't kill anybody!"

"How could you get the car into the living room?"
"I turned left at the kitchen!"

In California, very few people walk. I once saw four cars chasing one pedestrian!

drowning

Not me, don't worry. I do eighty laps a day in my pool. It's a nice pool, almost two feet long! I also have a Mafia hot tub—four feet wide and two thousand feet deep!

A child was playing on the beach when a tidal wave came along and swept him into the water. Ever alert, the lifeguard dove into the water and fought the swells until he reached the child. The lifeguard held the child surely and swam back to shore. The child's mother rushed to them. She kissed her most precious son then turned to the lifeguard and said, "Where's his hat?"

A scuba diver swam slowly from coral reef to coral reef, stopping to admire the multi-colored fish and plant life. His attention was diverted to another diver at the end of a small reef. The other diver was tearing at the coral, huge chunks coming off in his hand. The scuba diver swam over quickly. With a small, jagged rock from the ocean floor he wrote on the side of the coral, "What are you doing?"

The other man picked up a rock and wrote, "Drowning!"

A lifeguard and a beautiful young lady were going at it hot and heavy on the beach. A passerby said to the lifeguard, "You're supposed to give mouth-to-mouth rescuscitation."

The lifeguard said, "Well, that's how this started out!"

A man who'd never been to the ocean before finally went to the beach for the experience. Afraid to go into the water, he asked the lifeguard if he could bring him a bucket of sea water so that he could wet himself a little. Over a period of two hours, the lifeguard brought over a dozen buckets. Grateful, the man gave the lifeguard a ten-dollar tip.

Returning the next day for more sun, the man happened to arrive at low tide. He looked at the lifeguard and said, "You've been doing a lot of business!"

drugs and druggists

Some of us forget that pharmacists are highly trained professionals. You don't learn how to make tuna salad overnight!

"What have you got there?"
"A sleeping pill."
"Well, don't wake it!"

A society matron sent a formal invitation to a well-known physician. She'd love to have him join some other nice people at a dinner. Would he please RSVP?

A few days later she received his reply. His scrawl was impossible to decipher, so she sent her butler to the pharmacy, saying, "Pharmacists can read any kind of handwriting."

The butler handed the note to the pharmacist. In a minute the pharmacist came back with a prescription and a bill for nineteen dollars.

Congress is finally going to take up the marijuana issue. They're planning a joint session.

A man rushes into a drugstore and says, "Do you have a cure for hiccups?"

Without warning, the druggist hits him in the face.

The man says, "What the hell are you doing?"

"You don't have the hiccups now," the druggist says.

"No, but my wife out in the car does!"

A man comes into a drugstore and says, "I want some salicylic phenoepenephritic dichloritate."

The druggist says, "You mean mustard oil."

The man says, "I can never remember that word!"

A gullible man bought and took some pills that were guaranteed to increase his virility. Unfortunately, they backfired and he ended up with piles.

A man walked into a drugstore and asked the female clerk if he could talk to a pharmacist. She said that she was a pharmacist and the only one on duty. Bashfully, the man explained, "I have a terrible condition. I'm always thinking of sex. I'm never satisfied. I can keep having sex twenty hours a day. Can you give me something for that?"

The clerk excused herself and went into the back of the store. She returned a few minutes later and said, "I just talked it over with my sister. The best we can give you is two hundred cash and the store!"

A young lady was suffering from an unfortunate case of crablice. A friend suggested that she get a certain powder.

The girls met two weeks later. The ailing young lady seemed to be completely cured. Her friend said, "Didn't I tell you that powder would kill them?"

The first young lady said, "And a couple of the boys in the mail room too!"

The terrible part of condoms is they have a year's guarantee, but if they break, the guarantee runs out!

A woman rushed into a drugstore and said, "Can I have some tampons, please. And thank God!"

drunks and drinking

I've known a few drunks. I even knew one incredible drinker who received an honorary liquor license!

A policeman stopped a wiped-out drunk and asked, "Where do you think you're going?"

"Home. I just left a New Year's party."

"New Year's was a month ago."

"That's why I figured I'd better head home!"

My wife and I have a rough time. She can't stand me when I'm drunk, and I can't stand her when I'm sober!

A drunk stumbled into a doctor's office and said, "Doctor, please help me to put my penis back."

"Where is it?"

"Right here in my pocket."

"That's a cigar stub."

"My God, I smoked my penis!"

Most of the time, two pints will make a cavort!

A man comes into a café and sits down in a corner. Seated at the long bar is another man who is belting pretty steadily. After the third drink, the belter falls backward and ends up on the floor. The man rushes to him, picks him up, and puts him back on the seat. Two sips later, the man falls again and the Good Samaritan rushes to him again and puts him on the seat. The Good Samaritan does this four times, then says to the man, "You should go home. Tell me where you live and I'll take you."

The barfly mumbles an address, but it's obvious that he's in no condition to walk there. The good soul carries him out to the car, puts him in, and drives him to the house. He rings the bell. The wife opens the door, takes a look, and asks, "Where's his wheelchair?"

Two drunks were walking along the railroad tracks. One said, "I never saw so many damn steps in my life."

"I don't mind the steps," the other said, "but the low railing is killing me!"

The owner of a bar came home and, just as he put up the coffee, heard the phone ring. He answered it to hear a drunken voice at the other end saying, "What time do you plan to open your bar?"

The owner answered sharply, "I just closed. I'll open again at noon tomorrow!"

With that, he hung up. The phone rang again. The same sot was at the other end. "What time did you say you open?"

"Noon, I told you!"

The phone rang again. "This is your old buddy again. What time you open?"

"I told you three times. Noon! Noon! Why are you so anxious to get into my bar?"

The besotted voice said, "In? I just wanna get *out!*"

One guy drank so much he lit the candles on his birthday cake with one breath!

A mountaineer was used to making his own rotgut whiskey. He wasn't in trouble with the law, because he drank his whole supply. After seeing his share of pink elephants, he decided to share his bounty with others. Opening a wooden lean-to on the road, he hung up a sign: ONE HALF-DOLLAR TO SEE THE WILD CRITTERS AND THE PINK ELEPHANTS.

The first morning, business was brisk. A decent number of gentlemen boozers came around for a belt and to see the critters. None of the drinkers had his luck. They never saw the animals and demanded their money back. Fearing bloodshed, the sheriff drove up. As an official part of his investigation, he took a few hefty belts of the whiskey, stomped the ground to cool the burning, yelled, threw his hat in the air, and gave the accused twenty-five dollars for half of the animal exhibit.

Two men staggered into a bar. One said, "Give me a horse's neck."

The other said, "A horse's tail for me. No need to kill two horses."

I have a friend who swears the Bible condones getting plastered: He who sins should be stoned!

Two men met at a hotel bar during a convention. Before the end of the night, they were buddies forever. They promised to meet again at the same bar exactly one year from that day.

A year passed and one of the men rushed into the bar to find his buddy there. He asked, "When did you get here?"

The other man said, "Who left?"

I go in for nutritional drinking. I start each day with the juice from three martinis.

Two drunks found themselves on a roller coaster. One said, "We're making great time, but I'm not sure this is the right bus!

Two men were drinking when one of them fell back from the bar and landed in a dead faint. The other drunk said, "That's one thing about you, Irv. You sure know when to quit!"

One basic difference between a drunk and an alcoholic—the drunk doesn't have to go to meetings!

One barfly told his friend, "Your wife'll hit the ceiling when you get home later."

The other said, "She sure will. She's a lousy shot!"

A cop stopped a staggering drunk at about dawn. The cop asked, "Can you explain why you're out at this hour?"

"If I could," the drunk said, "I'd be home by now!"

Ice is a great healer, especially when used in a glass of vodka!

The drunk staggered into a tavern, put his head on the bar, and said, "Give me a Scotch."

The bartender said, "Man, you can't even raise your head."

The drunk said, "Okay, give me a haircut!"

After a year at sea, a sailor headed for the nearest bar. He pointed at a customer who was lying on the floor feeling no pain, and said, "Give me a shot of that!"

I went into a New York café and asked for a Manhattan. The bartender was an Indian and charged me twenty-four dollars!

A drunk was hanging on to a lamppost for dear life when an old lady walked by and said, "Why don't you take a bus home?"

The drunk said, "My wife would never let me keep it!"

The Baptist minister was asked by a member of the church, "Do you believe that people can walk on water?"

The minister answered, "Much better than they can on whiskey!"

A fireman pulled a drunk out of a burning building and asked, "Do you have any idea how this started?"

The drunk said, "I don't know. It was already on fire when I went in!"

Santa Claus is lucky. He can always come home with a bag on!

A wino cons a dollar out of a man for a shot of booze. The man starts to follow the wino, who asks, "Why are you following me?"

The man answers, "I want to be sure you don't buy food."

A woman decides to frighten her husband out of drinking. She dresses up like the devil and waits for him at the door. When he pours himself in, she says, "Boo!"

The man says, "Who are you?"

The woman says, "I am the devil."

The man says, "Shake hands. I married your sister!"

Two drunks saw a man siphoning gas from a car. One said to the other, "I hope I never get that thirsty!"

Two drunks wandered into the New York subway by mistake. One said to the other, "I don't know who lives here, but I like his train set!"

A nice man passes an apartment building late at night and sees a man leaning against the doorway. "Are you ill or drunk?"

The leaner says, "I'm drunk."

"Well, do you live here?"

"Yup."

"Can I help you up?"

"Sure."

Struggling, the nice man half-carries and half-drags the boozer up to the second floor. He asks, "Is this where you live?"

"Yup."

To avoid being taken for a co-boozer by an irate wife, the nice man opens the first door and gently pushes in his charge.

The nice man is breathing heavily as he walks down the steps. In the vestibule he sees another drunk, this one in terrible condition. "Do you live here?" the nice man asks. At the drunk's assent, the nice man struggles up the steps again, dragging and pulling. On the second floor he opens the first door and again pushes the man in so as not to awaken any wife.

Going downstairs, the nice man makes out a dim figure on the steps. He opens the door and finds an even more bedraggled man. As he is about to repeat his good deed, a policeman comes by. The drunk yells, "Officer, save me from this guy. He keeps throwing me down the elevator shaft!"

He drinks to pass the time. Last night he passed 1995!

Her husband was killed by hard drink. A cake of ice fell on him!

A big drinker was talking about how tough life had been for him. "Things were rough in the old days. There were times I had to live on nothing but food and water!"

An elbow-bender came home to a waiting wife, who put out her hand and said, "All right, hand over your paycheck."

The husband proffered a wad, which she examined. "Where's the other half?" she asked.

"I bought something for the house," he said.

"Oh, that's so nice of you. What was it?"

"A round of drinks!"

A half-dozen gentlemen, feeling no pain, walked down the street at about one in the morning. Laughing and singing, they arrived at an attractive two-story home. One of them managed to get to the door and pound on it. A light came on in a second-story window. The leader of the pack bowed graciously and said, "Is this where Mr. Joseph Smith lives?"

"It is. What do you want?"

"Then, no doubt, I have the honor of speaking to Mrs. Smith. Is that true?"

"I'm Mrs. Smith. What do you want?"

"Could you come down here and pick out Mr. Smith so the rest of us can go home?"

The day after the office party, Andy Parkins came in a little late. His right hand was bandaged. The receptionist asked what had happened. Andy said, "At the office party yesterday, Joe Wilson got drunk and stepped on my hand!"

drunks (insults)

A self-addressed envelope with enough postage on it can get you another pound of these insults. The following hardly scratch the surface. That shows how much the world loves a drunk!

If it wasn't for the olives in his martinis, he'd starve to death!

They called him the town drunk. He lived in New York at the time!

He drinks so much, he's two thousand swallows ahead of Capistrano!

He never drinks when he's driving. He doesn't want to spill any!

Somebody gave him a hotfoot. He burned for three days!

He read about the evils of drinking, so he gave up reading!

He drank so much, one time a doctor took a blood test and offered him a hundred dollars a case!

He couldn't make both ends meet, because he made one end drink!

I never knew he drank till I saw him sober!

He likes to drink because it makes the world go round!

She's an old-fashioned girl. She also likes vodka gimlets and screwdrivers.

He was a born alcoholic. At his birth he was baptized with holy oil and a chaser.

He'd drink spiked heels!

He drinks so much, when he sweats he's a fire hazard!

He spends more time weaving than a loom!

When his spirits get low, he uses a straw!

The way he drinks, solid food makes a splash when he eats it!

One day he saw a sign: "Drink Canada Dry." He went!

He recently had a sobering experience. The bar closed!

He gets up with the lark, then he heads for a swallow!

The other day she saw an unidentified flying object—her husband being thrown out of a saloon.

He would drink a nip in the air!

He must be a baker—he always has a bun on.

His eyes are pretty bloodshot. If he didn't close them, he'd bleed to death.

He ought to go to the blood bank and get his eyes drained!

After the first shot he feels like himself. After the second he feels like a new man. After the third he feels like a baby. He crawls all the way home!

They call him a creep because that's how he gets home at night.

They say he's a hard drinker. Actually, it's the easiest thing he does.

He drinks to calm himself. Last night he got so calm he couldn't move.

He's a real boozer. He thinks any apartment with more than one bath is a distillery!

When somebody asks him if he wants Scotch, gin, or vodka, he says, "Yes!"

He ruined his health by drinking to everyone else's!

Every morning he gets up tight and early!

She spends so much time drinking, her teeth are bottle-capped!

She doesn't wear glasses. She just empties them!

He doesn't drink water because he found out that fish screw in it!

She's so high most of the time, she gets spirit messages.

She drinks so much, when you dance with her, you can hear her slosh!

He's leaned on so many bars, his elbows are padded!

He only drinks at certain times of the day—morning, noon, four, five...

Nobody makes him drink the way he does. He's a volunteer!

They're a nice match—they're always lit!

She never drinks unless she's alone or with somebody!

She must be Mary, Queen of Scotch!

He drinks to forget he drinks!

She can't swim a stroke, but she knows every dive in town.

Twice last week he fell down under his own power!

The other day the cops gave him a balloon test, and it melted!

He proposed to her on hands and knees. She was under the table at the time.

He thinks there's only one thing worse than drinking—thirst!

He felt like a new man. The trouble was that the new man wanted a drink too.

He's a born wino. When he goes into surgery, he demands that they operate at room temperature.

He had a terrible accident. He was driving while drunk, came to two bridges, and took the wrong one!

dullness

This category is a staple of roasts, retirement parties, and general affairs. Audiences love five minutes in which you shred the guest of honor of any semblance of oomph!

She's had a loveseat for six years. Half of it is still new.

One day he was drowning. His entire life passed before him. He wasn't in it!

He could go on color TV and come out in black and white.

He couldn't be the life of the party in a coma ward!

He's so dull, he drinks gray cranberry juice.

He does a lot of charity work for the Home for the Forgotten!

He died at twenty, but was buried at seventy.

He lights up a room by leaving it.

He's so dull he couldn't even entertain a doubt.

He's so dull, one day he was masturbating and his hand fell asleep.

He's so dull he gives half of his money to yawn research.

He never bores anybody by talking a lot. He can do it by talking very little.

There's never a dull moment in his life. Years, yes!

He stays longer in an hour than most people do in a week!

He doesn't shoot the breeze—he kills it!

He wastes his breath . . . breathing!

One day his life flashed in front of his eyes—and he walked out on it.

He's such a dull guy, when he wakes up from a nap, there's a tag on his toe.

He's so dull he could be the poster boy for brown!

He has the same effect on people as a wet holiday.

He's so dull, if he was cloned he'd have two empty suits!

She tried computer dating, and they matched her with mayonnaise!

His neighborhood is the dullest. If it wasn't for mouth-to-mouth resuscitation, there'd be no romance at all!

dumb

It helps if the object of your "dumb" barbs is a little less than bright!

A mind-reader would only charge her half-price.

She was so dumb she couldn't finish a potholder all summer. They had to send her to night camp.

He has a one-track mind, and there's precious little traffic on the track!

If ignorance is bliss, he's Mr. Happy!

If you gave him a penny for his thoughts, you'd have change coming.

He got his varsity letter in college, and then somebody read it to him!

This bank guard wasn't too smart. To make sure the TV camera got results, he asked the holdup gang to stand close together!

She thinks intercourse is the time off between classes!

She's so dumb, she has twins. One is sixteen and the other eighteen.

This girl teller was fired because every time somebody brought in money, she'd ask, "For me?"

He's really dumb. One time he tried to hijack a submarine. He asked for a million in cash and two parachutes.

He lost his job as an elevator operator because he couldn't remember the route!

His brain is always fresh. He's never used it!

He gets up very early, but never bright.

He doesn't act stupid. It's the real thing.

He never gets tired of thinking. He never does any.

He's so full of ignorance it's coming out of his mouth!

The other day an idea went through his head. There was nothing to stop it.

She's so dumb she has to take off her sweater to count to two!

If it was raining soup, he'd be standing there with a fork!

He had a hemorrhoid operation, and at the end of it they found a brain tumor.

He's not too swift. He worked in a bank and they caught him stealing pens.

If you tell him to spell "Mississippi," he asks, "The river or the state?"

He has a point. It's his head!

He has a brain, but it hasn't reached his head yet!

He'll never be too old to learn new ways of being stupid!

He's the flower of youth—a blooming idiot!

They finally told him about the birds and the bees, but it hasn't done him any good. He doesn't know any birds or bees.

Anybody can get lost in a fog. He makes his own!

He's so dumb, he doesn't carry a pocket comb because he has no pockets that need combing!

He was once given the key to the city. He locked himself out.

She has a pretty little head—for a head, it's pretty little!

He changed his mind the other day. The new one doesn't work any better!

The closest he'll come to a brainstorm is a slow drizzle.

He always stops to think. The problem is that he never starts up again.

He has the brain of an idiot. He ought to give it back.

The other day he had a bright idea—beginner's luck!

He says he's got an open mind, but it's really vacant!

He has brain damage. He was hit by a falling napkin.

He's so dumb he could freeze to death in front of a brothel, waiting for the light to change!

Reincarnation must exist. Nobody could become so dumb in one lifetime!

When they were giving out brains, he was in line waiting for a second helping of mouth.

People should be nice to him. He was kicked in the head by a butterfly!

If he was studying to be an idiot, he'd flunk!

He should get a coffin to fit his shoulders. He's dead from there up.

He has a soundproof head!

He'd give you a piece of his mind, but it's not big enough to subdivide.

He ought to send his wits out to be sharpened!

People think he's a wit. They're half right!

He has more brains in his head than he does in his little finger—but not much!

He makes up in stupidity what he lacks in personality.

When he gets an idea in his head, it's a stowaway.

They named a town in Massachusetts after him—Marblehead!

He starts things he can't even begin.

He tried to get a job as an idiot, but he was overqualified.

He tried to sell Father's Day cards at a home for unwed mothers!

He never talks about his IQ. It's beneath him.

She had an open mind, but she had to close it for repairs!

He'd look through a peephole with his glass eye.

When he heard he was going into cardiac arrest, he sent for a bail bondsman!

E

earthquakes

This is a funny subject to anyone who has never been awakened at six in the morning by the sound and sight of another bedroom going by! Actually, my family and I have come up with a course of action for an earthquake. At the first tremor, we get out of bed calmly, stand in a doorway, and start screaming! Maybe you know our system under another name—panic!

A wino was shaken awake by a vigorous earthquake. He turned to a companion, also leaning up against a building, and said, "I don't remember drinking that!"

I knew an earthquake was coming. I saw Richter hand his scale to somebody and leave town.

Two newlyweds were consummating their marriage when an earthquake struck. The bride sighed, lost in love. The groom said, "I have to warn you, honey, it won't always be this good."

I don't know if it was a strong quake, but my Zip Code changed three times!

After an earthquake, a Californian was looking around in Utah. A real-estate agent asked, "Are you house-hunting?"
    The Californian said, "Yup. I wonder if it could have come this far."

The ground was shaking so badly, a rabbi ended up with both sidecurls on one side!

It's a pretty good sign that an earthquake is near if you can go surfing in your bathtub.

It's a quake if you go visiting the people next door without leaving the house.

A crack in the earth said to another, "Don't look at me. It's not my fault!"

Richter quit the earthquake business. He was tired of working for scale.

An earthquake hit the slums the other day and did two million dollars' worth of improvements.

An earthquake hit the local farmlands. The crops went right from seed to tossed salad.

A tremor rumbled through a disco. One dancer called out, "More bass!"

They have an album of earthquake rumblings. You play it on your Cuisinart.

An earthquake hit the zoo. It took six weeks to reassemble the platypus!

Animals can tell when an earthquake's on the way, and they try to get as far as they can from it. Just before the last earthquake we had, I saw a turtle leading a rabbit by two lengths!

eating (insults)

How could I omit those who need two glasses of water when they eat—one to drink, and one to cool down their knife and fork.

She eats like the Russians are at the county line!

She looks sweet enough to eat...and she always does!

She has two heads. When you tell her to stop gorging herself, one head nods in shame, and the other keeps on eating.

She can make sparks come from a knife and fork!

There's a rumor that they feed her oats, but there's not a grain of truth to it.

He eats health foods so he'll be big and strong and won't have to eat health foods.

She suffers from overbite...anything on the table!

The last date she went on, the man had to warn her, "When you get to the white part, that's the tablecloth."

She eats so fast they have to keep throwing water on her silverware so it doesn't overheat.

The last time he started to eat soup in a restaurant, six couples got up to dance!

He quit his job as a food taster. They didn't give him enough time for lunch.

He eats a lot. He has more seconds than a ten-day clock.

She's a light eater. The minute it gets light, she starts!

She eats so much, when she dies she wants to be cremated and her ashes put in a dip.

When he comes into a restaurant, the blue-plate special turns gray.

echoes

There was a short vaudeville bit played in front of an Alpine set. A man would yodel. An echo would repeat the yodel. The man would say, "Helloooo!" The echo would answer, "Helloooo." The man would ask, "How are you?" The echo would respond, "Fine. How are you?" Some version of this bit was used in at least six pictures and always got a laugh. The bit was recently modernized on a TV show. The man yelled out, "Helloooo." The echo answered, "I'm not in right now, but if you leave a message at the tone . . ."

When you're in the Rockies, the echoes keep going for miles. One man was camping. Before he went to sleep he called out, "Time to get up!" Eight hours later the echo came back and got him out of bed.

A woman was being examined by her gynecologist. The doctor finished and said, "Everything looks fine." A moment later, the patient heard the gynecologist's words again. The woman said, "You don't have to repeat yourself."
   The doctor said, "I didn't!"

Standing atop a mountain, surrounded by majestic peaks as can be found in Norway, a Norseman called out, "My name is Petersen!"
   An echo retorted, "*Which* Petersen?"

A woman found herself in a valley surrounded by mountains. She'd say something and it would echo right back. She went crazy trying to get in the last word.

I have so many cavities, the other day I went to a dentist. He capped three teeth and an echo!

economy and economics

My mother was a money magician. She could spread a dollar across the Mississippi. With the twenty dollars we earned the first time we played Albany, New York, she fed the whole family for a week, gave my father an allowance, bought the children underwear, lent my uncle two dollars, and still had enough left over for her Thursday-night poker game. She taught me you can't spend what you don't have—so have!

Mere wealth can't bring us happiness,
Mere wealth can't make us glad,
But we'll always take a chance, I think,
At being rich and sad!

An economist is a man who gets invited to speak at banquets where he tells everybody there's no such thing as a free lunch.

Economy is a way to spend money without enjoying yourself.

An economist's word is never done.

Two businessmen meet. One says, "Did you hear about Baker? He made a killing in Chicago."
   The other businessman responds, "I heard. I heard."
   "And Williams. He made it big in Denver."
   "I heard. I heard. I heard."
   "And Thompson. Destroyed in Memphis."
   "No kidding? Tell me all about it!"

A government economist received a phone call one morning. "I heard your lecture yesterday about runaway prices," the voice on the line said softly, "and I want you to know that my wife and I live comfortably on a quarter a day."

The economist said, "Maybe you know something we don't know. Can you explain how you do it? But please talk louder. I can hardly hear you."

The voice said, "I can't talk louder. I'm a guppy!"

An economist is a guy who'd send you a homing pigeon for your birthday!

An economist is a guy who'd throw you a boomerang for your birthday!

Two businessmen meet in a restaurant for a lunch suggested by one of them. The inviter says, "I have a good deal for you. When I was in Florida, I went to the town where the circus stays during the winter. I happened to pick up an elephant. I could let you have it for a hundred dollars."

The other businessman sipped his martini and said, "What am I going to do with an elephant? I live in a small condo. I don't have room for my furniture. I can't squeeze in an end table. So I'm going to buy an elephant?"

The first businessman said, "I could let you have three of them for two hundred."

"Oh, *now* you're talking!"

Economists believe that when women's skirts get shorter, prices go up. That bears watching!

The best time to buy anything was six months ago.

An economist is a man who knows more about money than people who are loaded with it.

The grownups thought that little Philip was cute but dumb. People would offer him the choice of a nickel or a dime. He always took the nickel. Another kid asked him one day, "Don't you know a dime's worth more than a nickel?"

Phil said, "Yup, but if I took a dime, grownups wouldn't keep making the offer!"

An American went to an idyllic Pacific island and tried to help the natives modernize. He explained to one native, "It's so much better if you get off your back and work."

"Why?" asked the native.

"You can earn a living. You can make money."

"Why do I need money?"

"Well, when you make a lot of money, you can retire. You won't have to work anymore."

"I don't have to work *now!*" said the native.

"See that guy. When he started he had two bare feet. Now he's got millions."

"No kidding. He must be a regular centipede!"

Talk about economy—one gent got married and, starting out for the honeymoon, bought a bag of peanuts to nibble on. After biting into the third one, he told his bride, "It's a big bag. Let's save some for the children!"

Wealth can't buy you happiness. Ask any poor person!

If your money is really yours, how come you can't take it with you?

Noah was a great economist. He floated a

company when the whole world was in liquidation!

A carnival had come to town. Ezra and Billy Bob, two teenagers and good examples of hillbilly upbringing, walked around and checked out all the rides and games. With his only quarter, Ezra splurged on the merry-go-round. It went around and then stopped to let Ezra off exactly where he had started. Ezra told Billy Bob to try the ride. Billy Bob said, "Nope. I watched you get on and get off at the same spot. I've been thinking—you spent all your money, but where you been?"

The teacher asked, "How many make a million?"

Little Pete answered, "Not many!"

The way I figure it is—you work hard and every year you put away ten thousand dollars for a rainy day. But if it doesn't rain, at the end of five years you're stuck with fifty thousand dollars!

I just read about somebody who retired with half a million dollars. He worked hard all his life, skimped, saved, went without, and then an uncle died and left him half a million dollars!

A salary is what's paid to you for what you do. An income is something paid to you for what your father used to do.

Two friends met in the street. One looked forlorn and almost on the verge of tears. The other man said, "Hey, how come you look like the whole world caved in?"

The sad gent said, "Let me tell you. Three weeks ago, an uncle died and left me forty thousand dollars."

"That's not bad."

"Hold on, I'm just getting started. Two weeks ago, a cousin I never knew kicked the bucket and left me eighty-five thousand free and clear."

"I'd like that."

"Last week my grandfather passed away. I inherited almost a quarter of a million."

"How come you look so glum?"

"This week—nothing!"

Talk about luck. I know a man who just bought a seat on the Stock Exchange, and it's behind a post!

education

I went to a school for children in show business. Not overeager to acquire academic skills, I was only a fair student. One day, however, my father solved the problem. He made me sit down to do homework and threw a spotlight on me. From then on I did my homework every day.

Two Phi Beta Kappas opened a business and went broke within a year. The business was taken over by an older man who'd never been to high school. In six months he had made enough money to open a second and a third store. Curious, one of the Phi Beta Kappas asked him, "How did you do it? We applied all the latest business techniques and all the theory we learned in school and we failed. How did you succeed?"

The older man replied, "It's simple. I pay a quarter for something. I sell it for double. One percent profit is all I want!"

An immigrant came to the United States. Unable to speak a word of English, he found it difficult to find a job. The parish priest mercifully let him act as the church beadle. After a while, it was discovered that he was unable to read or write English. He was dismissed and became a helper in a local grocery. He worked hard for years and saved up enough money to open his own grocery store. It was a success, and he soon opened a second. Within ten years he was the owner of a dozen supermarkets. During the holiday season, an official of a large charity group in the city came to him for a donation and showed him the fund-raising brochure. The old man said, "I can't read English. I can't even write it."

The official said, "That's amazing. You became a millionaire without being able to read or write English? Do you have any idea of where you'd be today if you could?"

The old man said, "Sure, I'd be a beadle in the church!"

It takes some girls four years to get a sheepskin. Others go for a mink.

One gambler's child was precocious. By the time he was two, he could count from one to king.

Many a man has acquired a huge vocabulary by marrying it.

"Son, I'm worried about your being at the bottom of the class."
"Pop, they teach the same stuff at both ends!"

"Do you think your son'll forget everything he learned in college?"
"I hope so!"

With a good education, you stand a good chance of getting a job with somebody who didn't get any education.

A school started a sex-education program, and on the first day little Megan came home and told her mother, "We learned how to make babies today."

Stunned at the speed with which the subject was being taught, her mother asked, "All right, tell me how you make babies."

Megan said, "You drop the 'y' and add 'i-e-s'!"

They can't eliminate prayer in the schools. How else could students pass a true-false test?

If they made hookey a major, the dropout rate would go down to zero.

"How many wars has the United States fought in its history?"
"Eight."
"Name them."
"One, two, three, four, five, six, seven, eight!"

Mary, at best a fair student, was asked to add a statement at the end of a final exam. The purpose of the statement was to have the students declare under oath that they had received no help during the test and had given none to others. Mary wrote, "I didn't get any help during this test, and the Lord knows I couldn't give any."

For every student with a spark of brilliance, there are about ten with ignition trouble.

Some schools are going back to the old ways. You have to raise your hand before you can hit a teacher.

I went to parachute-jumping class. The dropout rate was incredible!

Television has even affected spelling. A kid was asked to spell relief. He spelled it "r-e-l-i-e-f" and was marked wrong!

We're pretty lucky. In some South American countries, the kids have to learn the dates of their revolutions!

This is how it is today: The teachers are afraid of the principals. The principals are afraid of the superintendents. The superintendents are afraid of the board of education. The board is afraid of the parents. The parents are afraid of the children. The children are afraid of nothing!

A girl will have a faculty for doing well if she has a student body!

efficiency

I don't like to waste time or energy. I hate duplication. Let me say that again—I hate duplication!

An efficiency expert was about to be buried. As the six pallbearers started to carry the coffin toward the hearse, the lid of the coffin popped open and the efficiency expert sat up and said, "I couldn't just lie there. I had to let you know—if you put this on wheels you could lay off five of the pallbearers."

No man has ever been able to convince his wife that a cute secretary can be as efficient as an ugly one.

An efficiency expert is a man who's smart enough to tell you how to operate your business, and too smart to start one of his own.

An efficiency expert made his rounds. He asked one company employee what he was doing. The employee said, "Not a thing."

The expert went on to a second man and asked the same question. The response was the same as the first: "Not a damn thing."

After talking to a dozen employees, each of whom gave him the same response, the efficiency expert reported to the boss, "I found out what your problem is—too much duplication!"

An efficiency expert is a man who comes into a company in the morning. On his desk is a molehill. He has to make a mountain out of it by five o'clock!

An efficiency expert is a man who, if your wife told you the same thing, would be nagging you.

An efficiency expert told the boss to get rid of the Xerox machine—too much duplication!

An expert started his survey of the company by asking the president, "How many people work in this company?"

The president said, "About half of them."

"Take my efficiency course. I'll teach you how to earn what you deserve."

"The hell with you!"

An efficiency expert is a man, according to a smart country boy, who can explain why "the furtherer you go, the behinder you get!"

An efficiency expert proved that the transport company was wasting money with its scheduling. He showed the head driver how a three-day trek could be cut down to one day. The head driver said, "What are we going to do with the other two days?"

An efficiency expert came back to a company to check up on its progress since he'd implemented a new system. He was proud to see that the company was a beehive of activity and said to the boss, "I'd like to congratulate you on all these new people."

The boss said, "They're the ones I hired to take care of the new system!"

A psychiatrist hired an efficiency expert. A week later there was a sign on the psychiatrist's door: TWO COUCHES, NO WAITING.

egos and egotists

I like egotists. They never get around to talking about other people!

An egotist is a man who tells you lots of stuff about himself that you were going to tell him about yourself!

When success turns your head, you're facing failure!

An egotist is somebody who just happens to be everything you *think* you are.

Put two egotists together and you've got a case of an I for an I.

There's only a little difference between being in a rut and being in the groove.

When you're wrapped up in yourself, you're a pretty small package.

Here's to the man who is wisest and best.
Here's to the man whose judgment is blest.
Here's to the man who's as smart as can be.
Here's to the man who agrees with me!

Some people take ego trips, but they don't have any baggage!

An egotist doesn't necessarily feel that he's God, but he always listens when he spakes unto himself!

ego (insults)

Never leave the house without a few of these in your pocket. Ours is an imperfect world, and you'll always run into some deserving soul on whom you can wreak havoc.

It wouldn't do him any good to see himself as others see him. He wouldn't believe it!

He got himself where he is by the seat of his pants. That's where he shines!

He really believes that if he'd never been born, God would have a lot of explaining to do.

He always walks into a room voice-first.

He made the top of the heap, and that just about covers it.

He'd go broke if he had to pay taxes on what he thinks he's worth.

The only time she doesn't look in a mirror is when she's pulling out of a parking space.

He's carried on a great love affair for years— unassisted!

He's got towels marked "His" and "His"!

He's always me-deep in conversation!

He likes attention. At a funeral, he's sorry he isn't the corpse.

People have to be careful when they talk about him. They're speaking of the man he loves.

If he had his life to live over, he would still fall in love with himself.

She holds her nose so high she has a double chin at the back of her neck!

He's got a terrible inferiority complex. He just met somebody who's as good as he is.

He's going through life with his horn stuck!

elections

Our old precinct in Harlem was politically conscientious. Our ward leader was even able to call in election results six weeks before the election!

It was shortly before the election. Reporters seemed to be having trouble getting one candidate to give straight answers to questions. Finally they cornered him and demanded a straight response to any question, not necessarily even a political question. One reporter asked, "What is your favorite color? You can give us a straight answer to that, can't you?"

The candidate said, "Certainly. My favorite color is plaid!"

I was a little suspicious of last month's election. Amelia Earhart sent in an absentee ballot!

Joe Rizzo owned a small Italian restaurant frequented by local politicians. Because he was popular with his neighbors, Joe decided to run for a minor local office. Jim Mahoney, the local political boss, acted as his mentor. Joe was elected by a landslide.

Several years later, there was an opening for the city council. Mahoney pulled strings, and Joe was elected handily.

Joe moved on to become mayor, a congressman, and finally a senator. Sitting with Mahoney the morning after the election that elevated him to the high office of senator, Joe was not as happy as he could have been. Mahoney asked, "Hey, you're a senator now. That's a big office. What else could you want?"

Joe said, "I was wondering if you could do one more favor for me."

"Sure."

"Could you help me become a citizen?"

I live in an old-fashioned area. Our local congressman wants to be reelected so he can help bring our Minute Men up to strength!

There are two things I don't like about our candidate—his face.

Our candidate for Congress always puts his best foot forward—as soon as he can get it out of his mouth!

Here are a few more late-breaking items—all the campaign promises!

Some candidates aren't dumb. They stand on their records so the voters won't examine them.

I hate political jokes. Too many of them get in!

The most important thing in campaigning is sincerity, whether you mean it or not!

You know election time is getting close when the candidate remembers your name.

I can't understand it—people give thousands of dollars to help elect a two-bit politician.

Our candidate has done the work of two men—Frank and Jesse James!

"Sir, if elected, what will you do about the prostitution bill?"

"I'll pay it!"

You don't have to fool all of the people all of the time. During an election is just about often enough!

In a staunchly Republican community like many that dot the landscape of Vermont, the votes were being counted. "Republican. Republican. Republican. Republican. Democrat. Republican. Republican. Republican. Republican. Republican. Democrat. Re—"

The monitor interrupted, "That man must have voted twice. Let's throw them both out!"

A political machine is a device invented by men who don't like to work!

They elected him to Congress. Anything to get him out of town!

Nowadays a politician is a guy who divides his time between running for office and running for cover.

A lot of politicians were born with silver spoons in their mouths, but the spoons probably had hotel names on them!

Elections consist of two sides and a fence.

In Maine, a candidate was addressing a small group of voters. He seemed to be toying with the truth. One citizen got up and said, "Sir, you and I could go out on the campaign trail, and between the two of us we could out-lie a whole county. And I wouldn't have to say one word!"

A local politician is being investigated because he saved a quarter of a million in ten years. The investigating committee wants to know why it took him so long!

electricity

I make it a point never to hire an electrician with singed eyebrows!

An electrician is a man who wires homes for money.

He's not a genius. When the power went out, he was stuck on the escalator for two hours.

A male firefly flitted around behind a pretty female firefly, waiting to consummate their relationship. The female finally gave in and the male mounted her. Just at that moment, a lightning storm erupted and a powerful zigzag of electricity filled the sky. The female turned and said to the male, "I'm glad I didn't keep you waiting any longer!"

embarrassment

Life is filled with those little moments because of which you'd rather be dead. I compare the feeling of embarrassment to walking up a gangplank, but there's no ship. Questionable grammar and all, that describes the emptiness in the pit of the stomach and the hope that prayer can make a person invisible for a moment!

A young lady came to visit a young man in the hospital. His condition didn't allow too many visitors, but the young lady tried to march right in and was stopped by an older woman exiting. The older woman, who looked like a volunteer "gray lady," said, "There are no outside visitors allowed in this room."

The young lady said, "Oh, that's all right. I'm his sister."

The older woman said, "How nice to meet you. I'm his mother."

A girl was making fun of her boyfriend. She said, "Are you kidding, with that fuzz on your lip? Are you trying to grow a mustache?"

The boy answered, "Why not? You did!"

Two golfers were strolling toward the green when they happened to see two women come up behind them. One said, "Here comes my wife with some old witch she must have found in the clubhouse."

The other golfer said, "Mine too!"

A woman was showing another woman around the house. In the kitchen they found the maid sitting at the table, smoking a cigarette and sipping brandy. Naturally, the woman fired the maid right then and there. Getting up, the maid reached into her pocket and came up with a dog biscuit. Tossing it to the family dog at her feet, she said to the animal, "Thanks for helping me wash the dishes!"

Little Carl, aged ten, was acting up at the dinner table. The dinner guests tried to ignore the goings-on, but before long Mr. Drummond, not generally the dispenser of discipline in the house, had to act. Firmly, he said to little Carl, "Go to your room and don't come out until I tell you to!"

Rising, little Carl said to his mother, "How do you like that, Ma? The pushover is trying to act like you!"

A composer of movie background music was entertaining some guests in his house. After dinner, he sat down at the piano and played his newest score. A guest said, "You play Brahms beautifully. Now play something of yours!"

An older man came into an office and asked the manager, "Can I see Eddie Carson? I'm his grandfather."

The manager said, "He's not here. He's at your funeral!"

A man married his housekeeper of many years. One evening he gave a dinner party. His wife sat at one end of the table, her hands relaxed on the tablecloth. The conversation slowed down and finally stopped altogether. A guest said to the wife, "Awful pause."

The wife said, "Yours wouldn't be in any better shape if you'd done all the cleaning I did!"

A manufacturer retired and moved to the country. He put on denims, boots, and a plaid shirt, and became a country gentleman. An old friend came to visit. The country gentleman showed him around. In the barn, chewing at straw nonchalantly, was the farm's pride and joy—a horse. The host asked, "Wanna go for a buggy ride?"

"I've never been in a buggy," the guest said.

"I go riding just about every day. I hitch up and ride through the woods."

The country gentleman started to harness up the horse, but the animal, happy enough in the barn, resisted having the bit put in his mouth. It was obvious that the new farmer had no idea of how to harness a horse. After the tenth attempt to get the horse to open its mouth so the bit could be slipped in, the guest said, "Why don't you wait until he yawns?"

The nth degree of embarrassment is to look through a keyhole with one eye and see another eye looking back!

Two club members found themselves in the locker room. As they started to undress, one saw that the other was wearing a girdle. Surprised, he asked, "How long have you been wearing a girdle?"

The other club member answered, "Ever

since my wife found it in the glove compartment of my car!"

Embarrassment by the pound: You spend the morning swearing to an IRS auditor that you're steeped in total poverty. An hour later, your brand-new Mercedes sideswipes his ten-year-old Chevy!

emergencies

An emergency is good in that it wipes out, for the moment, all the other problems in your life. Many years ago, I was in love with a girl in San Francisco. Every day I would go to her little house on a hill and warm myself with my love for her. One day she told me that it was all over. She didn't want to see me again. I begged her to reconsider. How could I live without her? I could never forget her. She said that I'd forget. I swore I would never forget. Never! I left her, got into my car, turned on the ignition, started down the hill, put my foot on the brake pedal, and I had no brakes. I forgot about that girl in two seconds!

My wife always drives with her brake on. She wants to be ready in case there's an emergency!

I believe that you should save up for a rainy day. Of course, you're stuck if it doesn't rain!

Although it was winter, the ice on the surface of the pond wasn't yet strong enough to support skaters. Nevertheless, one young man decided to try it. It wasn't long before there were cries for help from the direction of the pond. The farmer, from the farm adjacent to the pond, heard the cries and rushed to the pond.

The young man, his teeth chattering, was shoulder-deep in the water. Putting a board across the ice, the farmer ventured out as far as possible and extended his arm, saying, "Work over to me and grab hold. I'll pull you out."

The young man said, "I can't swim. Just throw me a rope."

"I don't have a rope. Look, you better come toward me. It don't matter if you can't swim. The water only comes to your shoulders."

The young man said, "It's ten feet deep. I'm standing on the fat guy who broke the ice!"

A window washer fell off his scaffold and plunged to earth six stories below. As he lay there, passersby gathered. One of them tried to make the hurt man comfortable and said, to others nearby, "Somebody get him some water. Please get him water. He needs water."

The window washer looked up and asked, "How far do you have to fall for a shot of booze?"

The witness described what had happened: "I was walking down the railroad tracks with Ben. I heard the whistle and got off the track. After the train went by, I looked around but I couldn't see Ben. I did see his hat about fifty feet up the track. I kept walking and then I saw his right arm. Farther up, I saw his left leg. Up a bit farther, his head was in some low branches of a tree. It was then I started to figure that something had happened to Ben!"

A man approached what was certainly a bad car accident. It seemed that a bus had been hit by a truck belonging to a major company. Lying about on the ground were a dozen bus passengers. The man asked one of the passengers, "Has anybody from the insurance company been here yet?" The passenger shook his head from side to side. The man went on, "Good, then you don't mind if I lie down here next to you!"

Tony was small but wiry. He was also persistent, which finally got him a job on the docks. His first assignment was to help unload a steamer bringing in engine parts. Each part came in a box and weighed about three hundred pounds. Tony wasn't fazed. Holding a box under each arm, he started to take off the cargo. As he moved across the gangplank toward the dock, the gangplank gave way and he fell into the water. A stevedore rushed over, only to see Tony's head go under, then come up again. Spitting out water, Tony yelled, "Throw me a rope!"

The stevedore was spellbound and couldn't move. Tony kept yelling for a rope. Finally, Tony said, "If you don't throw me a rope, I may drop one of these damn things!"

A man's pit bull had chewed up half the neighborhood and the neighbors. The court gave the owner two ways of resolving the continued destruction of life and limb. The dog could be put to sleep or, failing that, be castrated. Castration would remove all the anger and venom. The dog would become as docile as a lamb.

Loving the dog very much, the owner chose the surgery. On the day of the appointment at the vet, the owner started to walk the dog to its destiny. A block from the animal hospital, the dog saw an old man walking. Roaring, the dog pulled away from the owner and jumped on the old man. He had just about chewed up the old man when the owner managed to get the leash on again. The owner tied the savage animal to a pole and went to the old man. Helping the old man up, he begged, "Don't make this a police matter, I beg you. I implore you. I'll take care of any costs you may have—medical bills, clothing. I'll get you a new crutch! Whatever you want for your agony. I'll pay anything. And you don't have to worry about my dog. He's on the way to the vet to be castrated. He'll be like a lamb!"

The old man said, "Forget the castration. Better get his teeth pulled out. I knew one second after he came at me that he didn't want to *mate*!"

employers and employment

Many people don't know what good hard work is. I don't know what good it is either!

If work is so terrific, how come they have to pay you to do it?

His employees love work so much they can sit and watch it for hours.

He was a responsible worker. If anything went wrong, they said he was responsible for it!

An employee came home bushed. His wife asked what had happened. The employee said, "Our computer went down and I had to think all day!"

Bosses don't have it easy. They have to get up early to see who comes in to work late!

The employer found it difficult to meet the payroll one week. He went to the First National Bank and asked the loan officer, Perkins, to lend him the needed thousand until the following Friday. Perkins agreed to the loan.

The following week, the employer was unable to come up with the money to repay the loan. He went to Grimes at the Second National Bank and asked for a thousand. Getting it, he went to Perkins and paid his debt.

A week went by and the employer needed to repay Grimes. He went to Perkins and said, "You lent me a thousand and I paid you on the button. I'm a good risk, am I not? I need a thousand again."

The employee used the new thousand to pay back Grimes.

This financial wheeling and dealing went on for a few months. One afternoon the employer happened to see Grimes and Perkins walking together. The employer said, "Look, fellows. Every week you, Grimes, pay Perkins a thousand. The following week, Perkins, you pay Grimes a thousand. You don't need me, so leave me out of it from now on!"

"Please don't tell anybody what I'm paying you on this new job."
"I won't. I'm as ashamed of my salary as you are!"

One employer told a friend, "Jones is a terrible businessman. He's been in business twenty-five years and he breaks even. I've been in business a year and a half, and I already owe eight hundred thousand!"

An employee submitted his expense account. After checking it over, the employer said, "I can't honor this, but I'd like to buy the fiction rights for a movie."

Work is a very unpopular way of making money.

Our latest employee gives the company an honest day's work. Of course, it takes him a week to do it!

I keep asking my brother to learn a trade so he'll know what kind of work he's out of!

One gutsy employee asked for an extra day's vacation to make up for all the coffee breaks she'd missed on vacation.

A young man came in to apply for a job and was asked to fill out a questionnaire. One question asked, "Do you have a prison record?" He answered that he didn't. The next question asked, "Why?" The young man wrote, "Never been caught!"

Owning your own business is like making love—when it's good, it's real good, and when it's bad, it's not bad!

One fellow was fired by the unemployment office, so he stood around and got a check.

A man was fired by his employer. Another employee asked, "When do you plan to fill the vacancy?"
The employer answered, "He didn't leave any!"

Most employers nowadays look for twenty-one-year-old workers with thirty years' experience.

The head of the company called a meeting of all the company brass to discuss firing a female employee. When they were seated, he asked, "How many of you have been dating her?"
Seven of the eight men raised their hands. The boss asked the eighth man, "You've never been out with her once? Not once?"
The eighth man said, "I swear."
The boss said, "Good. *You* fire her!"

An employer took out a classified ad in which he said there was an opening for a young man who would come in late every day, take long coffee breaks, get very little done, and want hourly raises until his salary equaled that of the employer. Asked why he'd placed the ad, the employer said, "Well, since these are the kind of applicants we've been getting with my ad about hard work and long hours, maybe this one'll do better!"

You know your company is in trouble when you have to conduct your inventory in the purchasing agent's garage.

You can cut down on the number of mistakes you make at work by coming in late.

enemies and bad guys

You shouldn't be too mad at your enemies. You're the one who made them!

"You're your own worst enemy!
"Not while I'm around!"

With friends like his, he doesn't need enemies!

It doesn't matter what his politics are. He's got enemies right and left!

There's nothing he wouldn't tell you to your face that he wouldn't tell you to your back!

He has no enemies, but his friends don't like him!

Only your friends can become enemies. Your wife's family is that way from the beginning.!

He's a sweet guy. Once a day he walks his cobra!

He should be an elevator operator. He's always running people down!

If you kicked him in the heart, you'd break your toe!

He'd steal a fly from a blind spider!

He's so vicious, Dial-a-Prayer told him to go to hell.

He picks his friends—to pieces!

He is so hated, he had to be his own buddy at camp.

You can count his enemies on the fingers of the Mormon Tabernacle Choir!

He has knifed more people than a surgeon!

He stabs more people in the back than sciatica!

She has an even disposition—always rotten.

He acts as if the whole world is against him—and it is!

We've all heard the expression, "The worst is yet to come." Well, he just arrived!

His heart is as pure as the driven slush.

He has the personality of a traffic cop with heartburn.

When he was born, something terrible happened—he lived!

He has the disposition of an untipped waiter.

He's got more nerve than a root canal.

He'd love to have the job of delivering bad news for the War Department.

She's a female clone—a clunt!

He'd send boxes of mud to hurricane victims.

She's vicious. When she dies, she wants to be cremated and thrown in somebody's face!

He's followed the Ten Commandments all his life, but he never caught up with them.

He's so low he can read dice from the bottom.

She's a sweet girl. She probably wouldn't hurt a lion.

Does she go to a manicurist or does she do her own claws?

You can't mention his name without a choking sensation—which is what somebody should do to him.

He was born in the hills and hasn't been on the level since.

She ought to take the midnight broom out of town.

He'd give you a penny for your thoughts, and we all know what animal gives a scent!

He brings out a lot in others. He makes them want to throw up!

Why doesn't he go down to the ocean and pull a wave over his head?

He's got the nerve of two porcupines making love.

Why doesn't he leave and let live?

His conscience hurts him when everything else feels good.

He was a member of the human race, but he was dropped.

He steals ashes from funeral homes and sells them to cannibals as instant people.

He has more crust than the Earth!

He wouldn't tell a lie as long as the truth would hurt you.

He avoids the appearance of evil. He sticks to the real thing.

There must be a lot of good left in him, because none ever comes out.

He's low. He threw a canopy over some quicksand and sold funerals.

If he ever needs a friend, he'll have to get a dog.

In this country a man can be anything he wants to be. *He* wanted to be a rat!

Years ago, guys like him weren't invited anywhere. Those were the good old days!

He came from under a rock years ago, and he still hasn't seen the light!

He's so rotten, his cat is willing to settle for eight lives.

He'd make a great death wish!

He used to be decent, but he broke himself of the habit.

He was a rotten kid, too. He used to hide his grandfather's bedpan in the freezer.

He's hostile and nobody knows why. What does a short, ugly, dumb, creepy, poor guy have to be hostile about?

In an emergency, he's always right there when he needs you.

He often contradicts himself—and he's right!

He's the kind of guy who'd get a girl pregnant just to kill a rabbit.

He's such a phony, his birth certificate has an alias.

He would Krazy Glue an octopus together!

energy

In a factory, I once saw a sign that said, SAVE ENERGY! *Under it, an employee had written in pencil, "I do—every minute I work!"*

They have a car that runs on solar energy. It'll kill romance—how can a guy tell his date he ran out of sun?

You can tell your air conditioner is on too high if you have to use an icepick to drink your martini.

The government assures us that there will never be an energy crisis in this country, but I'm not sure about that. I heard that the President has been taking lessons on Skateboard One!

There's a big energy crisis in our company. They're expecting us to show some!

Two less-than-brilliant men were having fun with a flashlight. One turned on the high beam, aimed it at the ceiling, and dared the other one to climb up to the top of the beam. The second brain said, "You can't trick me. As soon as I get to the top, you'll turn it off!"

The funeral of the meanest man in the world was being held. As the coffin was lowered into the grave, a giant flash of lightning zagged across the sky. One of the mourners said, "Well, I guess he got there!"

It was the worst electrical storm any of the bridge players had ever witnessed. Powerful flashes of blue light snaked across the sky. Lightning split the heavens. Seemingly oblivious of the din, Reverend Swanson bid every hand to the hilt. As the Reverend went to slam on an impossibly bad hand, a clap of thunder shook the house. The Reverend said, "Would it be all right if I withdrew my bid?"

engagements

The first time I brought a girl home, my mother said, "Kissing doesn't last. Cooking does!" In that case, the kissing didn't last and the cooking never got started!

Young and attractive Suzanne came home excitedly to tell her mother that she'd just become engaged.

"Who is the young man?" her mother asked.

"He's a musician. Of course, he isn't working right now."

"An unemployed musician? Look, don't tell your grandparents. They wouldn't understand about an unemployed musician. Neither would your father. He hates musicians. Tell him your fiancé sells dope. And don't worry about me. I'm going to the kitchen to put my head in the stove!"

A young man asked his psychiatrist, "Is it possible for a man like me to become engaged to an octopus?"

The psychiatrist said, "You know better than that. It's impossible."

The young man said, "I have another question—do you know anybody who wants to buy eight engagement rings?"

I know a fellow who's been engaged for twenty years. It has one advantage—it shortens the marriage!

Hers had been a typical day. At work, she'd yelled at the receptionist, bawled out her secretary, whipped a kid from the mailroom, thrown out four computer salesmen, threatened her beautician, cursed two drivers in front of her, fired the maid, warned her landlord because of a leak, and at eight-thirty at night, blushed when her boyfriend said, "Marry me and I'll be your protector!"

A young mental patient underwent extensive treatment and was cured of his belief that he was George Washington. He was so relieved he called off his engagement to Martha!

During the Stone Age, a young male dinosaur asked a young female dinosaur to become his betrothed. She said, "I accept on one condition—I want to be married by the Iron Age. I hate long engagements!"

They say that love is blind. If she has the right kind of engagement ring, a girl can show she's not stone-blind!

They say that a diamond is forever. The payments are even longer.

A man never knows what true happiness is until he becomes engaged, and by then it's too late.

It takes two to make an engagement—a girl and her anxious mother.

"Are you still engaged to that ugly Kramer girl?"
"Nope."
"What happened?"
"I married her!"

england and the english

My favorite stoic people. Nothing perturbs the English. I know of one woman who sent her husband out to buy some scones. He didn't return immediately. Eight years later she decided to go to the police because his tea was getting cold!

It was the height of the London blitz. A group of people were in one of those underground public shelters that dotted the city. A warden called down, "Are there any expectant mothers in this shelter?"

One woman answered, "A bit early to tell." We've only been here for a minute or two!

An American met an Englishman in one of those fancy London clubs. The American suggested that they have a drink together. The Englishman said, "No, thanks. I tried it once, but I didn't like it."

A servingman passed by with a tray of delicious-looking hors d'oeuvres. Taking one, the American murmured with pleasure. The Englishman motioned that he'd pass. He explained, "I tried it once, but I didn't like it."

Some minutes passed, and a handsome

young man came into the club. He started to walk toward the pair. Noticing that he looked very much like the Englishman, the American said, "Your son?"

The Englishman said, "Yes. An only child, you know!"

"Miss, would you care for a cigarette?"

"Sorry, but I don't smoke."

"How about a drink?"

"I never drink."

"Dinner?"

"I don't eat dinner."

"You don't drink, smoke, or eat—what do you do about sex?"

"About six I have tea and a scone."

It was the height of the war. The captain of the British ship was searching the North Atlantic for signs of the German navy. Finally, off in the distance, he saw a German cruiser shelling a cargo ship. The first mate said to the captain, "Shall I summon the men to battle stations?"

The captain looked off at the one-sided fray and indicated that nothing be done. He said, "That isn't sporting, but it is war."

The German ship started to spray the ocean with depth charges. Soon, an oil slick showed that a submarine had been hit. Still the captain refused to order battle stations.

As debris from the British submarine floated upward, the German captain raised his hand in victory and spat at the chunks of metal and wood. Seeing this, the British captain turned to his first mate and said, "Battle stations immediately!"

The first mate asked, "Why'd you order that now?"

The captain said, "When he sank a cargo ship, that was the misfortune of war. The destruction of our submarine was unfortunate, but part of the game. However, when he spits in our ocean, it's battle stations!"

An American was walking in the East End of London when an English girl walked by and a breeze from the river wafted her skirt over her head. The American said, "Airy, isn't it?"

The English girl said, "What did you expect—feathers?"

The Duke of Windsor was visiting a small country village. His entourage was greeted by a dozen children waving flags. The Duke thanked the youngsters and the woman who seemed to be their chaperon. He said to the woman, "Lovely youngsters."

The woman said, "They're all mine."

"You have a dozen children?"

"I've got four more at home."

"Sixteen children? Your husband should get a knighthood."

The woman said, "He's got a dozen, but he hates to wear them!"

Two British sports were coming across the ocean on one of those giant ocean liners for which Britain is famous. On the second day out, both of the sports made contact with available ladies. But one of the sports came over to his friend and said, "Could you change, old sport? Because of the fog, I seem to have ended up with an old aunt of mine!"

The Duke of Delling became very ill and it was necessary to feed him rectally. A friend came to visit, and asked the Duke's manservant how the Duke was coming along. The servant said, "He's coming along beautifully. Magnificently. It does my heart so much good to see the Duke's rear end snap at a piece of toast!"

Lady Fothering was lecturing her newly married daughter about the state of matrimony. When the subject turned to sex, Lady

Fothering said, "Try to remember, my dear, that the physical union of man and woman is the most disgusting act in life."

The daughter said, "Mother, you had eight children."

Lady Fothering said, "Only because I closed my eyes and thought of England!"

There may be other cities in England foggier than London, but it's hard to tell which they are, because of the fog.

Prices are very high in London. When I checked into a hotel, I asked for something nice and restful for a hundred dollars. They gave me a sedative!

An Englishman who could have been the model for Colonel Blimp, the starchy British symbol, attempted to use the telephone. Upon getting an operator, he said, "May I have the phone number of Sir Winston Tepping-Grumbly of Marchington Mews."

The operator said, "I didn't quite get that."

"I said I would like the phone number of Sir Winston Tepping-Grumbly of Marchington Mews."

"Sir, could you say that in plain English?"

"Madam, if I could speak more plainly, I wouldn't be British!"

The British never say hello on the telephone. They ask, "Are you there?" If you're not there, there's no reason to go on with the conversation!

An Englishman was showing an American through his trophy room. Stopping at a lion, he said, "That one was from one of Father's safaris. It was stuffed in 1975."

"With what?" asked the American.

"Father!"

A foreigner walked over to an Englishman and asked, "Could you tell me where the British Museum is?"

The Englishman said, "I could."

Then he walked on.

On a train from London to Manchester, an American was telling off the Englishman sitting across from him in the compartment. "You English are too stuffy. You set yourselves apart too much. Look at me—in me, I have Italian blood, French blood, a little Indian blood, and some Swedish blood. What do you say to that?"

The Englishman said, "Very sporting of your mother!"

The Queen and the Prince were giving out medals. They arrived at a ruddy-faced youngster. The Prince said, "It is with a sense of deep and eternal gratitude that I award this medal to you, Lance Corporal Stone."

The soldier said, "Screw you."

Not sure of what he'd heard, the Prince said again, "It is with a sense of deep and eternal gratitude that I award this medal to you, Lance Corporal Stone."

"Screw you."

The Prince turned to the Queen and asked, "What shall I do?"

The Queen said, "Screw him! Let's not give him the medal!"

"Heard you buried your wife, old chap."

"Had to. Dead, you know."

Two Englishmen sat in the sun at Brighton. One said, "Breeding is everything, isn't it?"

The other Englishman said, "No, but it's heaps of fun!"

It was a foggy day, the soup so thick a person couldn't see a hand in front of his face. Nevertheless, a tourist was taking a stroll and, after a few blocks, became anxious. He called out, "Where am I heading?"

A voice answered, "For the river."

"How do you know?"

"Because *I* just came out!"

An Englishwoman had quadruplets one day. Three were born at two in the afternoon. The last one had to wait until teatime was over.

An Englishman was walking along Oxford Street one evening when he was smiled at by a black prostitute. She said, "Would you like to take me home tonight?"

The Englishman said, "What? All the way to Africa?"

The British are extremely shy. I saw a drowning man pulled out of the water. The lifeguard rushed over and gave him handshake-to-handshake rescuscitation!

It was an old scaffold but still in use for capital crimes. The prisoner was brought up, the priest at his side. The prisoner felt the platform creaking under his feet and saw the top swaying in the wind. Turning to the priest, he asked, "Say, old chap, do you think this is safe?"

For years, the British bragged that the sun never set on the British Empire. It was so foggy the sun could never find it!

The British have always been good fighters. After what they do with food, they have to be ready to defend themselves!

A Sunday-school teacher in London was telling her charges about the crowns of glory given in heaven for good deeds. At the end of her lesson, she asked, "Tell me, children—who will get the biggest crown?"

A Cockney youngster said, "'Im what's got the biggest 'ead!"

The air raid had just started and the air-raid warden was trying to get everyone into the shelter. One old woman refused to go, saying, "I'm not going anywhere until I find my teeth."

The air-raid warden said, "What do you think they're dropping, love—sandwiches?"

He who laughs last has to be an Englishman!

An Englishman attended a party in the United States and was impressed by an old toast often given: "Here's to the happiest hours of my life, spent in the arms of another man's wife—my mother!"

When he returned to England he attended a fancy banquet and decided to trot out the toast he'd learned. Standing, he raised his glass and said, "Here's to the happiest hours of my life, spent in the arms of another man's wife—some Yank's mother!"

enthusiasm

Of course, somebody once said, "Let a smile be your umbrella," and ended up with a mouthful of rain!

Enthusiasm is hope with a tin can tied to its tail.

The trouble in being carried away with enthusiasm is that most of the time you have to walk back.

A country boy had proposed to and been accepted by his country sweetheart. At the wedding service in the small church, the prospective groom was rather nervous. Noticing him sweating and licking his dry lips, the minister whispered, "What's the matter, Bobby Joe? Did you lose the ring or something?"

Bobby Joe answered, "I got the ring, but I sure done lost my enthusiasm!"

She's like a woman who's been married eight times on her ninth honeymoon. She knows what she's supposed to do, but she doesn't know how to be enthusiastic about it.

Enthusiasm is a concept created by the young and inexperienced.

His suggestion had all the enthusiasm of Custer asking for more Indians.

A man visited the Grand Canyon for the first time and went on enthusiastically and endlessly about its great beauty. Near him was an older man who didn't seem to be at all excited about the vista. The younger man said, after his fiftieth superlative, "Sir, I can't help but notice that this magnificent view doesn't stir you."

The old man said, "I'm stirring and I'm enthusing. I just ain't *talking!*"

errata

In 1948, I was honored at a fancy dinner. When the speeches were over, the head of the organization honoring me awarded me a beautiful plaque. In the afternoon paper the next day, an article about the affair said, "To repay him for his support, he was given a plague!" Between newspaper reprints and responses to test questions in school, comedy has ample fuel. It's almost impossible to invent funnier statements than those actually made. Have a drawer in which you drop all manner of printed mistakes. Use the same drawer to file jokes and stories you've heard. For some reason, when you write down a joke you're apt to recall it. The act of committing it to paper seems to cement it into memory. There's a parallel with dreams. A dream will be vivid at first. You believe that you'll remember it. A half hour later it's sucked into a black hole and disappears. You can't even remember the general subject matter. However, by writing down several key words you'll be able to bring it back. Trust me!

An abstract noun is one you can't see when you look for it.

Having one wife is called monotony.

A skeleton is what you have left when you take out a person's insides and take off his outsides.

Wind is air in a hurry.

A vacuum is where the Pope lives.

At the end of the stomach you have the bowels. There are five of them—*a, e, i, o, u*—and sometimes *y* and *w.*

In parts of Africa, malaria is popular.

Gender tells you whether a man is masculine, feminine, or neuter.

Artificial perspiration is how you make a person live when he's just dead a minute ago.

When a minister does something wrong, it's a clerical error.

A man called a newspaper and screamed because an item had indicated that he'd died. The man threatened to sue, but the editor promised to make up for the mistake. The next day the man's name was printed in birth announcements.

Then there was the department store advertisement that offered a sale on "the latest things in men's briefs"!

One Midwestern paper told about a Mr. Karns, who "was at death's door until Dr. Brady pulled him through."

ethnic humor

Ethnic jokes should be taken with a grain of salt. When you've made an open wound, rub in the salt! I don't mind tossing a few ethnic jokes about, because I plan to insult every group extant, including about six of which I'm a member in good standing. If you feel that you've been overlooked, please call me. My answering machine is standing by with unkind remarks. It can also insult other answering machines! Most of the ethnic jokes in this book are listed by subject. Those that follow here do double and triple duty!

There was a girl at the United Nations who hated the Swedes and the Norwegians, but she'd do anything for a Finn!

Halfway across the Atlantic, a 747 ran into trouble. To lighten the load and make it possible to reach an airfield, some of the passengers would have to leave the plane. An Englishman said, "God save the Queen!" and jumped. A Frenchman said, *"Vive la France!"* and he too jumped. Then a Texas cowboy stood up, said, "Remember the Alamo!" and pushed off a Mexican!

Who can forget the day that Guatemala and Venezuela went to war. The next morning Italy surrendered.

On a bus one day, an old Jewish man saw a black man reading a Jewish newspaper. A patch over one eye indicated that the black man had limited eyesight. Next to him leaned a crutch. What puzzled the old Jewish man more than anything was the Jewish newspaper. Unable to restrain himself, the old Jew walked over and asked, "Are you Jewish?"

The black looked up and said, "That's all I need."

An American archeological team, working in a South American country run by a general, discovered an ancient tomb in the Andes. In the tomb was a well-preserved skeleton. The members of the team argued about the age of the skeleton and couldn't agree. The local scientist said, "Leave this with my government for a few days. We'll tell you its age."

The team agreed and waited on pins and needles until the government examination was over. The local scientist returned and said, "It is the skeleton of a man exactly one thousand and two years old."

"How did you find that out?" an American asked.

"It was easy. Last night it confessed!"

Max fell in love with Maureen, but the pretty Irish lass wouldn't marry him unless he converted from Judaism to Catholicism. Love being stronger than any other emotion, Max undertook the studies that would make him a good Catholic. Some months later, Maureen ran into her friend Paula, who asked, "When's your wedding?"

Maureen answered, "There'll be no wedding."

"Why not?"

"Max studied so hard he now wants to be a priest!"

"**W**hat do you call a Mexican Jew?"
"Oy of Olé."

There are real differences in the approach toward romance of various ethnic groups. When kissed by her husband, a French woman says sexily, "*Ooh, la la. Je t'adore.*"

An Englishwoman, kissed by her husband, offers, "I'd say you are a jolly good lover, old chap."

The Jewish woman says, "Sam, you know something—the ceiling could use painting!"

A Yank, an Englishman, and an Irishman from Galway had been captured by the enemy and were set to be sent off to their heavenly rewards by firing squad. The captured men discussed various ways of escaping. Finally the Yank came up with a workable idea. He said, "Let's distract them. When they start aiming, yell something. They'll start looking around, and the guy who created the ruckus will be able to get away."

The Yank was put against the wall. As the officer-in-charge started to count, the Yank pointed off and yelled, "Tornado!" The firing squad looked to where he'd pointed. It took a split second for the Yank to disappear into the woods.

The Englishman was set against the wall. As the count started for him, he yelled out, "Flood!" The soldiers looked. In a moment the Englishman was gone.

The Irishman was lined up. The squad started to aim and count off. The Irishman yelled, "Fire!"

A Swede, a Frenchman, and an Italian aboard ship were about to be hung. The noose was placed around the Swede's neck. The noose hadn't been tightened enough, so the Swede slipped out, landed in the water, and swam off.

The Frenchman also found the noose too loose, slipped out, and swam off.

The noose was placed around the Italian's neck. The Italian said, "You better tighten that noose. I can't swim!"

A rich man died and left his estate to an Irishman, an Englishman, and a Scot. There was a catch, however. Each of the lucky heirs had to put five pounds in the coffin to be buried with the deceased. The Irishman duly put in five pounds, as did the Englishman. The Scot put in a check.

A week later, the Scot received his bank statement and saw that the check had been cashed. It seems that the mortician was a Welshman!

"**W**hat do you get when you cross a Pole and an Italian?"
"An offer you can't understand!"

ethnic (do-it-yourself)

Fill in the blanks with the group most likely to get laughs at the moment. Use caution and don't make Italians the brunt of your jokes if you're at a Sons of Italy dance!

The _____ Art Museum was supposed to open, but the opening was delayed. The frame broke.

"**W**hat do you call removing a wart from a _____ 's rump?"
"Brain surgery."

"**W**hy do _____ have pockmarked faces?"
"From learning to use a fork."

One _____ wanted to go into a sport—javelin-catching.

A ____ just opened a string of day-old salad bars.

"**W**hat is a ____ ?"
"A ____ with a job!"

A ____ heard that we only use a quarter of our brain. He wants to know what we do with the other quarter.

"**H**ow do you make ____ chicken soup?"
"You start by stealing two chickens..."

"**W**hy are rectal thermometers banned in ____ ?"
"They cause too much brain damage."

"**H**ow do ____ count money?"
"One, two, another one, another one..."

It was a ____ who invented the toilet seat. Of course, it was a ____ who put a hole in it!

In ____ they stop garbage deliveries if you fall behind in your payments.

"**W**hat do you call a ____ with a war medal?"
"A thief!"

"**H**ow can you tell a ____ funeral?"
"The garbage trucks have their lights on!"

"**H**ow can you tell a ____ used-car lot?"
"They turn back the fuel gauges!"

"**W**hy does the new ____ navy have glass-bottomed boats?"
"So you can see the *old* ____ navy!"

"**W**hy don't ____ have pimples?"
"Because they keep sliding off!"

"**W**hy do ____ have doormats in their houses?"
"So they can clean off their shoes before they go outside!"

"**H**ow can you tell a ____ airliner when it's snowing?"
"It has chains around the propellers!"

"**W**hat is the best thing that ever came over from ____ ?"
"An empty boat!"

"**W**hat do you print on the bottom of ____ shoes?"
"This side up!"

"**H**ow can you tell a ____ bride at the wedding?"
"She's wearing the cleanest T-shirt!"

A ____ heard that most accidents take place within two miles of the home, so he moved.

"**W**hy don't they have ice cubes in ____ ?"
"The recipe got lost!"

"**W**hat does it say at the bottom of a ____ ladder?"
"Stop!"

"**W**hat do you call a cow in ____ ?"
"A date!"

"**W**hat do you call a contaminated landfill?"
"A ____ health spa!"

"**W**hy does a ____ dictionary only cost a few cents?"
"It's not in alphabetical order!"

"**W**hat's the difference between a ____ woman and a bear?"
"Eighty pounds and a fur coat!"

The _____ did a lot for this country—but why in my neighborhood?

_____ aren't allowed to swim in our river. They leave a ring around the shore!

"Why is the average age of a _____ groom sixty-two?"
"Because they get married right out of grammar school!"

A _____ won a great vacation—two days and six nights!

"How many _____ does it take to pave a driveway?"
"About a dozen if you smooth them out!"

Because it rained, last month's _____ yacht race was held indoors.

Did you hear about the _____ jigsaw puzzle? It has one piece.

They held a beauty contest in _____ . The winner came in third.

"How do you sink a _____ submarine?"
"Just knock on the hatch!"

Two _____ got their luggage mixed up at the airport. They both had K mart shopping bags.

"What is dumber than a _____ ?"
"A smart _____ !"

"Do you know how to keep a _____ from drowning?"
"No."
"Good!"

"How does a _____ spell 'farm'?"
"E-I-E-I-O!"

"What takes a _____ wife an hour?"
"Cooking minute rice!"

"How do you break a _____ 's finger?"
"Hit him in the nose!"

etiquette

In my old neighborhood, if somebody said you were born to the purple, it meant that you were black and blue from being beaten up by the other kids!

Soup should be seen and not heard!

I always give my seat to somebody on the bus. I walk to work.

"That child shows evidence of breeding."
"How can you tell?"
"He scratches a lot!"

A coed came home from college very much pregnant. Her mother asked, "Who's the father?"
    The coed said, "I haven't the faintest idea."
    The mother was furious and said, "Your father and I raised you to behave properly. We always insisted on manners. Yet you don't even bother to ask, 'With whom am I having the pleasure?'"

There's no etiquette at an orgy. Somehow, you don't know whom to thank!

A man walked into a plush restaurant, was ushered to a table by a formally dressed headwaiter, and sat down at a table on which were displayed the finest china and crystal. Taking the damask napkin from the solid-silver napkin ring, he unfolded it, put it around his neck, and proceeded to tie a knot in the back. Staring at him, the headwaiter said, between gritted teeth, "Sir, will you have a shave or a haircut?"

His manners are getting better. A girl's purse slipped out of her hand and he drop-kicked it back to her!

A bird in the hand is terrible table manners!

One vain young man bragged about his conquest of Boston, saying, "I've been to every fine home in this city."
   A young Bostonian nearby added, "Once!"

evangelists

In recent years, the poor evangelists have been getting their lumps. Many of their sexual adventures have been page-one stories, giving new meaning to the term "lay preacher"!

The evangelist was haranguing the crowd and carrying on about sin. "The wages of sin are high," he bellowed.
   A young man sitting in back said, "Not if you find somebody who'll do it for free!"

An evangelist was going at it hot and heavy, telling his followers about what lay in store. "God's wrath will devour you," he bellowed. "There will be weeping and wailing and gnashing of teeth!"
   An old man said, "I don't have any teeth."
   The evangelist said, "Teeth will be provided!"

The authorities kept the evangelist from going to the Grand Canyon. They were afraid he'd lay on hands and cure the hole.

One evangelist kept telling his listeners that

there was great comfort in religion. He proved it every time he drove off in his Rolls-Royce.

Nowadays, evangelists never go out on the town and celibate!

The evangelist exhorted the crowd to fill the collection boxes, saying, "You can't take it with you. Give it to me and I'll see that it's sent on ahead!"

One evangelist led a busy life. In the morning he played golf in a charity tournament. At noon he attended a businessman's luncheon. At two o'clock, he played tennis. At four in the afternoon, he went to his television station, spent two hours going over the script of his daily show, rehearsed his songs and jokes, plunked himself down in a chair, where for an hour his makeup man worked on him, then he rushed out to the stage and did his show. The show was over in an hour, and he took off his makeup, dressed up in a tux, and went to a black-tie dinner at a large hotel. He managed to arrive at his home well after midnight. He plopped down on his couch, absolutely bushed. His assistant said, "Why don't you quit this hectic pace?"
   The evangelist said, "Not while I'm doing God's work!"

exaggeration

Show business is built on exaggeration. When actors talk about a play or performance, it is always "the best" or "the worst" or "the greatest show I ever saw" or "the biggest stinker." Now isn't that the greatest statement you ever heard?

Al was a born liar. At lunch with others from the office, he always managed to make up a patently absurd story. His best friend

Lou told him, finally, "Al, you're a great guy, but those stories are bothering everybody."

Al said, "I know. I can't help it. The words pour out."

"You have to do something."

"Tell you what, Lou—maybe you can help me."

"Sure."

"All right. When I start to make up a story, kick me in the leg. Maybe that'll stop me."

"Can't do any harm. We'll try it."

The next day at lunch, all went fine until one of the group at the table mentioned an article in the paper that morning about a huge building to be put up in the city. Al was off and running. "When I was in China a couple of years ago, I saw the most fantastic building. It was four miles long, two miles high, and—"

Lou's foot landed a powerful blow on Al's shin. Taking the cue, but without pausing, Al went on, "One foot wide!"

Uncle David was telling his young nephew about some of his exploits. Uncle David came to his famous "cannibal" story.

"It was a terrible day," he said. "I was surrounded by sixteen cannibals."

The nephew said, "Last time you told me, it was only ten cannibals."

Uncle David said, "Yes, but you were too young then to know the whole horrible truth!"

Jim was on trial for assault and battery. If there was anybody in town who could assault and batter, it was Jim. His shoulders were wide, his muscles bulged, and his hands could crush steel. Put on the stand, Jim admitted that he'd pushed the plaintiff around a little.

Trying to show the jury that Jim was an animal and beyond control, the plaintiff's attorney said, "How little?"

"A smidgin."

"How much is that? Could you demonstrate on me?"

Jim walked over to the attorney, picked him up, slammed him against the table ten times, threw him against the wall, dropkicked him twice, and finally piled him in a heap on the floor. Jim returned to the docket and said, "About a twentieth of that!"

examinations

I think I went into show business so I wouldn't have to sit in classrooms and take tests. I might change my mind nowadays because I often watched my son studying for a big test. His stereo would be blasting, his TV set was on, the telephone was glued to one of his ears, and in front of him there were all kinds of goodies—candy, peanuts, sodas, and, as he grew older, a couple of six-packs. Somewhere in the room was an unopened book. In spite of all these learning aids, his average almost came to a C. It would have, but it stopped at D on the way down. He was a shrewd kid. He once convinced me that F stood for "fine"!

The professor said, admonishing the class for generally low test results, "A fool can ask more questions than a wise man can answer."

A student said, "No wonder so many of us flunked!"

"Children, what comes after O?"
"Yeah!"

My son was studying the Civil War, but he refused to read the end of the book. He didn't want to know how it came out until he saw the movie.

I never knew Twinkies were a studying aid!

One student wanted to make sure he knew the answers, so he wrote them out all over his body. History was on his left leg. Biology was on his right leg. Along his arm he wrote out chemistry formulas. He wrote out so many answers, his skin graduated six months before the rest of him.

One Jewish student was failing his final, so he pledged twelve correct answers!

A writing teacher spent most of the semester explaining that there were four elements in a good short story—brevity, morality, grandeur, and an indication of decency. On the final, the class was given two hours to complete a story. One student finished in five minutes and handed in his test paper. It read, "'My God,' said the Queen. 'Get your hand off my knee!'"

"Sir, I didn't deserve the grade you gave me on this test."
"Do you know a lower one?"

In response to a question, a student wrote, "Even God doesn't know the answer to this question."
When the paper was returned to him, the professor had written, "God and you both flunk!"

A teacher loved to give true-false tests. In one test, made up of a hundred questions, a young student managed to get eighteen correct. The teacher said, "Blind luck would get fifty right."
The student said, "Why don't you give a test where brains count?"

excuses

I don't like to give excuses, but I can't think of other ways out of a tight spot. Of late, however, I've managed to avoid the need for excuses. I get up in the morning and say, "I'm sorry," and that covers me for twenty-four hours!

A man asked his neighbor for the loan of a lawnmower. The neighbor refused, saying, "I need it to wash my car."
The man said, "You don't wash a car with a lawnmower."
The neighbor said, "When you don't want to lend, one reason is as good as another!"

A drunk was staggering down the main street of the city at four in the morning. A policeman stopped him and asked, "Do you have an excuse for this?"
The drunk answered, "If I had an excuse, I'd head home!"

Two boys were late to school, the school bell having chimed through the valley a half hour before. The principal accosted the truants and asked where they'd been. Vinnie said, "I was dreaming that I was going to head for New Orleans on the steamboat. When I heard the school bell, I thought it was the steamship signal and I was too late to make my ride. Figuring that, I thought I'd stay in bed longer."
The principal asked the other boy, "What about you, Edward?"
Edward said, "I was at the dock, waiting to see him off!"

A man who comes up with a lot of excuses is always on his "but."

Then there's the gent who'd been out all night with the fellows. At dawn, he poured himself into the house and said, "Honey, I hope you didn't pay the ransom!"

A gent staggered into the house early in the morning and said, "Honey, I hope you didn't pay the reward."

His wife answered, "You're too late. I gave them a thousand in cash an hour ago!"

The next day she came home with a new coat!

executives

I'd be a good executive. I'd always share the credit with the guy who did the work!

An employee came to the boss and asked for a raise, saying, "I'm doing the work of three men."

The boss, a smart executive, said, "Give me the names of the other two guys. I'll fire them!"

An executive is a man who hires somebody else to do it.

I know an executive who's got a lot of business problems. A big problem came up yesterday, but he can't fit it into his schedule for worrying until next week.

A good executive always wants the lines of communication open with his staff. One executive told his people, "Never be afraid of me. If you have something to complain about, speak up—even if it costs you your job!"

A Hollywood executive once told his assistant, "I'm very worried about this picture. Bite my nails for me!"

I know an executive who doesn't waste any time with female employees. If at first he doesn't succeed, out they go!

The executive was dictating his will. "I want my older son to get a hundred thousand dollars," he started. "Put my younger son down for seventy-five thousand. And my twin daughters should have a quarter of a million each."

His attorney seemed puzzled and asked, "Where is all this money coming from?"

The executive said, "Let them work for it like I did!"

A good executive believes in pluck and more pluck. He also knows whom to pluck.

If you want to make a living, you have to work. To become rich, a good executive knows another way!

"When I started," the executive said, "I didn't have a dime."

"How'd you get off the ground?" a friend asked.

"I wired home for money!"

The owner of a small company was showing a visitor around his plant, which was run by a staff of one. The visitor wondered how the owner made ends meet. "How do you make a go of this place?" he asked.

The owner answered, pointing at the staff, "See my employee—I haven't been able to pay him in six months."

"Close up."

"I don't have to. In another six months he'll get the company. Then I'll go to work for him until I get it back!"

A man came to see a friend, an executive with a large corporation. Pulling out all the stops, the visitor said, "I'm at my wits' end. I'm ready to kill myself. I haven't got money to feed my kids. My wife needs an operation and I haven't a penny for it. The house is about to be taken over. The—"

The executive said, "Stop! I can't stand this." Pushing his intercom button, he said to his secretary, "Jennie, throw this man out. He's breaking my heart!"

exercise

This won't be a long section. I get tired just thinking about exercise. I'm actually not in bad shape. My doctor says that I have the body of a forty-year-old. He even showed me where the corpse was buried!

I can't believe it happened. The other day I jogged backward and put on eight pounds!

My wife has a brand-new exercise. She shops faster!

Last week I was a pallbearer for a friend. I get a lot of exercise being a pallbearer at funerals for friends who exercised!

I went to one funeral where the casket was open. A woman walked by and said, "He looks terrific."
    Another woman said, "Why shouldn't he? He jogs every morning!"

I may not jog or play tennis, but I'm a very brisk eater!

I can do everything today that I could do when I was nineteen. Can you imagine what rotten shape I was in when I was nineteen?

I get a lot of exercise from magazines. I keep picking up all those subscription blanks that keep falling out!

I jog everywhere for my health, but I never find it!

I don't believe in jogging. When I die, I want it to be from an illness!

I hear that exercise kills germs. But how do you get the little buggers to exercise?

I won't say I'm in bad shape, but I have to pause twice when I'm pulling my toothbrush out of the holder!

I woke up this morning with a real desire to exercise. So I stayed in bed till the desire went away!

expenses

Never measure the cost of things. Ask the wino to whom you just gave a quarter!

Two middle-aged men met after not seeing one another for several years. One asked, "How's your daughter?"
    "She's married," said the other.
    "How much did the wedding cost you?"
    "About ten thousand a year!"

It's so easy to meet expenses today. I meet them everywhere I look!

Money doesn't talk nowadays. It goes without saying!

experts

If you want to find some experts, start to do something. In ten minutes, people will come from all around the world to tell you how you're doing it wrong!

A man bought some goldfish and became interested in trying to find out which were the males and which were the females. The petshop sent him to a goldfish expert. The expert explained, "It's very easy. A male goldfish will eat only male brine shrimp, the female goldfish only female brine shrimp."
    The man asked, "How can you tell the male brine shrimp from the female?"

The expert said, "Two blocks down, there's a brine shrimp expert."

An expert is somebody who learns more and more about less and less.

A camel is a horse designed by a committee. A committee is a group of experts, sooner or later!

explorers and exploration

I like men who travel all over the world, go through all kinds of hardships, fight the elements—just so they can have enough slides for a lecture!

An explorer was captured by ferocious natives in the jungles of New Guinea. As they prepared to kill him, he came up with the idea of doing something to impress them. They might think he was some kind of god and let him live. Whipping out his cigarette lighter, he flicked it, and it lit. The natives backed away. A murmur went through their ranks. The chief approached the explorer and said, "That's amazing. We never saw a lighter work the first time!"

I saw a man lecture on Eskimos. He called them "God's Frozen People"!

Two explorers are captured by savage natives. The chief says to one, "You have choice of fate—oompahgalah or mushi-mushi."

The explorer mulls it over and says, "I'll take mushi-mushi."

With that, the natives form a double line. The explorer is forced to run the gamut with each native stabbing at him with a sharp blade or piercing him with long sharp lances.

As he makes it to the end of the line, he keels over and dies.

The chief says to the second explorer, "What do you choose?"

The second explorer says, "I choose oompahgalah."

The chief says, "Fine. Men, he has chosen oompahgalah. But first, mushi-mushi!"

eyes

I was all set to be nice to bad eyes when some more "cross-eyed" jokes showed up. To keep them company, they brought along a few other eye insults and stories!

There must have been something special about her left eye. Her right eye kept looking at it!

Nature is fantastic. A billion years ago she had no idea that we'd wear glasses, yet look where she put our ears!

She was so cross-eyed she could look through a keyhole with both eyes!

He went to a chic eye doctor. He gave him a prescription for wire-rimmed contact lenses.

I was frightened to death recently. I saw this surgeon who was going to operate on me reading a magazine with large type!

He was so cross-eyed he had to head southeast to join the Northwest Mounties!

I never dreamed that my wife was nearsighted, until one day I saw the pill she was taking to keep from getting pregnant—an M&M!

She was so nearsighted she couldn't even see her contact lenses!

Black eyes indicate a strong character and sometimes a very weak defense!

When your eyesight begins to blur, forget glasses, just try weaker drinks.

Here's to the light that lies in a woman's eyes...and lies and lies and lies!

I know this girl who is so fat she has to bat her eyelashes by hand!

faces

My computer can specialize with lines about almost every aspect of the face—wrinkles; warts; beauty marks; noses, big and small, straight and crooked, thick or pointed; earlobes, punctured or otherwise; and any facial feature that can be targeted. Such specialization wouldn't be fair to those of us with a blemish or two. Besides, stomachs, rear ends, and dirty fingernails would demand equal time!

She looks like she had her face lifted and the derrick broke!

She had a well-knit face—with a couple of runs!

This bank robber's wife always listened to her husband. So she put a stocking over her head. Then she realized he never took her on jobs!

To give you an idea of her looks—on her face she had a beauty question mark!

She had a very big dimple, but her face kept falling into it.

She went out for a church production of *Peter Pan*, but she didn't get the part. Her pan petered out!

Her problem was that she was all dressed up and had no face to go!

Her husband looked into the face of death—hers!

Her face was so oily—wildcatters followed her!

Some women have faces that can stop a clock. She could stop Switzerland!

She's had so many facelifts, when she raises her eyebrows she pulls up her stockings!

She was as cute as a button. She had four holes in her face!

She had her face lifted, but it didn't help. There was another one just like it underneath.

His face was so pockmarked he shaved with an ice cream scoop.

Her face was exactly what it was cracked up to be!

She had so many facelifts there was nothing in her shoes!

Everybody knew she would get ahead. The one she had was terrible!

People thought she had bags under her eyes. Actually, she was only wearing her cheeks up that season.

She had her face lifted so many times she finally had "Welcome Home" written under her eyebrows!

She had a little mole on her neck. It was her head!

She had something on her neck that spoiled her looks—her face!

I never forget a face, but in her case I'll make an exception!

"Her lips were like petals."
"Rose petals?"
"No, bicycle pedals!"

Hers was a face, as faces go, and one day it went!

Her face drove some men wild and others out of town!

Men threw themselves at her feet. They couldn't stand her face!

She had so many pimples on her face, you could play connect-the-dots on it.

She was like a great Russian book, but no one could figure out if her face was the crime or the punishment.

People don't know if he's had a facelift. I think he just wears support sideburns!

The last guy who gave her a hickey got fur in his mouth.

She has to go to church every Sunday to confess her face.

She's so ugly her Polaroids wouldn't come out of the camera.

Her neck is so dirty Dracula wouldn't bite it if he was dying of thirst!

She has a face like a bagful of elbows.

When people look at her face, they just think her neck barfed!

Death came for her, took one look at her face, and left.

When they make love, he puts a bag over his head, in case the bag over her head falls off.

She's got a contagious smile—trenchmouth!

She has a face that could wake the dead. But haven't they been punished enough already?

She couldn't get a hickey from a leech!

She goes to a plastic surgeon to have her chins rotated!

She only has three teeth. She looks like the front row at a country-western concert!

She went to the beauty parlor the other day, begging for one last chance.

Her face is so oily she could be one end of a pipeline!

They say love is blind. In her case it would have to be.

She went to a doctor for a vaccination in a spot where it wouldn't show. He vaccinated her face.

His face looks like his hobby is stepping on rakes!

She has a walk-in mouth.

She has the face of a saint—a Saint Bernard!

She's a cover girl—a manhole cover!

facts of life

Schools encourage children to discuss the facts of life with their parents. Otherwise, how would parents learn about these things?

Because Alex was curious by nature, his father decided to tell the ten-year-old the facts of life. The boy listened wide-eyed as his father explained about the birds and the bees. The next day, while walking to school, Alex ran into his friend Timmy and said, "You know what married folks do when they want a kid? My old man told me birds and bees do the same thing!"

The doctor told the husband, "Your wife is pregnant."
     The blasé husband said, "Why shouldn't she be? She's had every chance!"

Youngsters don't know everything yet. My nephew can't understand why a man kisses a girl's neck because she has nice legs!

Eager to involve her eight-year-old in her pregnancy, a mother asked, "Tommy, what would you like—a brother or a sister?"
     Tommy answered, "If it wouldn't get you out of shape too much, I'd like a bike!"

During the mating season, how does a female bird tell her husband that she has a headache?

A man of ninety who'd married a wisp of a girl in her early twenties was concerned about the marriage. His doctor told him, "Be smart. Get a boarder."
     The ninety-year-old man did as the doctor suggested and returned some months later for a meeting. He told the doctor, "My wife is pregnant."
     The doctor said, "Was I wrong in suggesting a boarder?"
     The man said, "No, but she's pregnant too!"

When women start talking about the pitter-patter of tiny feet around the house, many men keep saying it's mice!

One seven-year-old told his friend, "I think my mother's pregnant again."
     "How can you tell?" the friend asked.
     "They're beginning to spell things again!"

I was so shocked when I was born, I didn't say a word for a year and a half!

fairy tales

I've tried a few fairy tales in my life. My wife never believes me! But I love the idea of living happily ever after.

A princess asked her father what "frugal" meant. The king said, "It means 'to save.'"

The next day the princess was swimming in the palace pool when her leg cramped. She called out for help. "Frugal me, somebody!"

A prince came along and frugaled her and they lived happily ever after!

A young lady was walking through the woods when she heard the sound of tiny footsteps behind her. She turned to see behind her a small toad. She started to walk again. The toad followed her. Turning again, the young lady said, "Stop following me."

Suddenly the toad spoke: "I'm following you because you are beautiful and I love you."

"You're a toad."

"No, I'm not. I'm really a prince from another country. I'm under a magic spell. If you took me home with you and held me close to you all night, I'd become a prince again."

The young lady hesitated. Realizing that even though it was a million to one against the toad being a prince, the creature had spoken to her, and there was no reason she shouldn't take the chance. The young lady picked up the toad, carried it home tenderly, gave it some water, and put it into her bed. Later she undressed and joined it, holding it close to her. In the morning, lo and behold—her body was covered with warts!

fame

Famous people all come from crowded neighborhoods. Show me somebody famous, and I'll show you ten thousand people who lived on the same block and went to the same school! I think I have a good fix on fame. I remember asking a famous actor once if he was the most famous graduate of his college class. He told me, "I was until last week." He referred to a classmate of his who'd been murdered the week before by a rejected woman! My mother, an expert on everything, told me when I was a youngster, "Let your fame go to everybody's head but yours!" Then she bit a Broadway columnist because he hadn't mentioned my name in a week!

It makes you humble to attend a dinner where you're the only one you never heard of.

A lot of people think they're famous, when it's actually just been a slow news day for the real stuff.

Fame is the feeling that you're on the mind of everybody who is thinking of everything else.

A few of us wake up and find ourselves famous. Most of us wake up and find we're a half hour late.

Sometimes fame is just a matter of dying at the right time.

At lunch, several businessmen started to discuss fame. One thought that athletes were the most famous people in the country. The second thought fame came from television exposure. The third, Albertson, said, "I'll tell you exactly what fame is. Let's say I were to go to Rome at Easter. Pulling strings, I would get into the Vatican. A million people are gathered in the courtyard. Then there's a roar and people look up at one large window, in front of which is a large banner. Several men appear, among them me. I'm standing right next to the Pope. Now, if somebody points and asks the person next to him, 'Who's that man next to Albertson?'—that's fame!"

family

When all is gone and everybody else has abandoned you, your family is still there. Nobody ever moves out of the house!

A woman, trailed by a dozen kids, was crossing the street against the light. A driver swerved to keep from hitting part of the mob and yelled at the woman, "Hey, don't you know when to stop?"

The woman made a wry face and answered, "They're not all mine!"

Two men were talking about life when the subject started to focus on the family. One man said, "I met my wife at a dance."

The other man said, "That's nice."

The first one said, "I don't know. I thought she was home taking care of the kids!"

"Did I ever tell you about my kid?"
"No, and I appreciate it!"

On a cross-country flight, the plane made a half-dozen stops. At one of them, six-year-old Joey said to his mother, "Mommy, what was the name of the last place we stopped at?"

His mother, busy with a woman's magazine, said, "I'm not sure, dear. Why is it important?"

"Because that's where Daddy got left behind!"

One babysitter quit because the children were too backward and the father was too forward!

"Why do you tell people you married your wife because she's a great cook?"
"I had to give *some* excuse!"

I figured out a great way to solve the problem of visiting relatives. I borrow money from the rich ones, I give it to the poor ones, and none of them ever come back!

My wife didn't come from a fine family. She brought it along!

Mother picks up the kids at school, takes them to Little League and dance lessons, then she takes them for haircuts, and then she takes them home. For most mothers, the real delivery room is the inside of a station wagon!

My wife asked me if I wanted a large family. I told her I did, so she sent for hers!

He's the wage earner, and he's the head of the family to boot!

A family is like a bath. At first it's okay, but then it's not so hot!

The Steiners just received a letter from their son in college. It read, "Dear Folks: Please write to me more often—even if it's only ten or twenty."

An unmarried daughter who's in a family way is often in the family's way!

A large family has its advantages. At least one kid may not turn out like the others.

Leading a half-dozen children, Mrs. Kovin got on the bus. As she headed back, another passenger, a pleasant elderly man, asked, "Are those your children, or is it some kind of picnic?"

Mrs. Kovin answered, "They're mine, and it's no picnic!"

Two women met at a health spa. One

suggested going into the bar for a glass of wine. The other answered, "Thank you, but no."

"Don't you drink?" the first asked.

"Well, not at home, because I don't want to drink in front of the children. And when I'm away from them, I don't have to!"

Two grandmothers, wheeling their grandchildren in fancy carriages, met in the park. One admired the baby in the pink-frilled carriage. Naturally, the other grandmother had to repay the compliment and admired the two in the larger carriage. She asked how old those beautiful babies were. The proud grandmother said, "The doctor is eight months old. The judge is a year and a half!"

The watch I'm wearing has been in my family for years. My grandfather sold it to me on his deathbed.

A family is a unit assembled to spend money the head of the family hasn't earned yet.

I know a man who became a billionaire trying to reach an income his wife and kids couldn't live beyond.

One of my kids ran away from home. It's a good thing, because I was next!

The family that prays together often has to!

I can't understand—my kids are never around, yet they manage to eat me out of house and home!

Tommy's grandmother dropped in for her first visit to town. She said to little Tommy, "I'm your grandmother on your daddy's side."

Tommy said, "Wow, did you pick the wrong side!"

"Is your husband hard to please?"
"I don't know. I never tried!"

A man walked off a train, followed by his fourteen children. A policeman walked over and cuffed him. The man said, "What did I do?"

The policeman said, "I don't know, but as soon as I lock you up, I'll try to find out why the crowd is following you!"

You know you're in for it when your mother-in-law shows up with four valises, a steamer trunk, and a map of the family funeral plot.

Some wives want their husbands to know that a woman's work is never done. Some husbands ask why the women don't start earlier.

famous sayings

A sure-fire way of getting a laugh is to make up a famous saying that could have been uttered by someone but obviously wasn't. What better way to beg off after a speech than to say, "I'd love to go on, but in the immortal words of King Kong—I've got to catch a plane!"

As Caesar said, "Let me mix that salad!"

As Jack the Ripper's mother said to her son, "How come you never go out with the same girl twice?"

As Moses said to God, "Let me see if I have it right—the Arabs get the oil and we get the right to cut off the tips of our *what*?"

As Vincent Van Gogh said after he cut off his ear, "Don't shout!"

As George Washington said when he was crossing the Delaware, "I can't understand it. I paid for a seat!"

As Jesse James said to his brother Frank, "We can't rob that bank. That's where we keep *our* money!"

farmers and farm life

Most of us don't know what it means to rise with the sun, feed the chickens, milk the cows, plow the fields, and then go inside for breakfast! Without the north forty and the barn, however, we'd lose a major source of comedy. In addition, should the laid-back country bumpkin be exiled from our humor, we'd have no one to ask us why we're in such a hurry. City versus country is nothing new. It was the theme of the play Abraham Lincoln was watching that fateful night at Ford's Theater. There is certainly a literature in which the country folk are short on brains, but for each joke in which the urban soul wins, there are ten votes for the gent who chews straw or the lady in gingham. For the raconteur—or the would-be raconteur— "country" jokes are just about failure-proof. Nor will they pain the rustic. The archetypal "country" joke shows how far ahead of us he is: A city gent stops and asks a farmer, "Do you know where Dover is?" The farmer says, "Nope." The city gent asks, "Can you tell me how to get to Haverford?" "Nope," says the farmer. Exasperated, the city gent barks, "Don't you know anything?" The farmer answers, "I ain't lost!"

A farmer hitched his new blue-ribbon-winning Brahma bull to a plow and started to work the north forty. Another farmer happened by and asked, "You got your prize bull attached to a plow?"

"Well," the owner said, "first off, I want to teach him that life ain't all play!"

The college graduate, fresh from the state agricultural school, was checking out the farm on which he was going to do some experimental work. The old-fashioned methods in use made him laugh. Pointing to a fruit tree, he said to the farmer, "With that watering pattern, I can't imagine how you get ten pounds of apples a year from that tree."

The farmer said, "I don't get any. It's a pear tree!"

A farmer was filling out an insurance claim form for a horse that had been killed by a train. The last item was: "Disposition of the carcass." The farmer wrote, "Gentle and friendly."

A farmer wrote one of the giant mail-order companies and asked the price of toilet paper. He received a response that told him to look on page 287 of his catalog. He wrote back, "If I had your catalog, I wouldn't be asking about toilet paper!"

A farmer, on in years, married a lusty young lady. Soon the wife started to grow pale and act fidgety. The marriage seemed to be in danger. The doctor advised the farmer, "Your wife needs much more affection. She needs some more kissing, hugging, and loving. Those young ones want cuddling even during the daytime."

The farmer said, "How can I work that one out? There are times during the day when I'm working land so far off I couldn't see her getting the urge. I can't keep running back every five minutes to check on her, or I'd never get my plowing done."

The doctor pondered the problem and soon came up with a solution. He said, "Carry your shotgun with you. When you feel you can put a smile on her face, pull the trigger, and she'll come running to you."

A month went by. On his way to another patient, the doctor passed the farmer at work and stopped to ask him, "How'd my system work out?"

The farmer said, "It was kind of like a miracle the first week. Then hunting season opened and I haven't seen hide nor hair of her since!"

A congressman, returning to his constituents for the first time since he'd been sent to Washington, was trying to explain a lack of action on his part. His audience, irate farmers who'd been promised much, weren't pleased with his explanations and pressed him. He tried a final explanation: "You men ought to know the facts of life. You can put a bull in the pasture one evening, but you can't expect a herd of newborn calves by morning."

One farmer jumped up and said, "No, but I'd expect to see a heap of smiling from a heap of cows!"

Some Idaho farmers were complaining about the destruction of their crops by a particularly pesky potato bug. One farmer said, "They ate my whole crop in ten days."

A second farmer said, "That was nothing. They chewed up my whole crop in two days and then they set down on the treetops to see if I intended to plant some more spuds."

A third farmer said, "If there was a prize, I'd sure get it. My crop was chewed up in a day, but that's not the worst part. I recognized some of the darn bugs. I'd seen them in the general store that morning, looking at the ledger to see who'd bought seed!"

At the county fair, some farmers were trying to sell a horse to one of the city slickers who put in weekends on the farm. As the city man admired a five-year-old gelding, the owner said, "You don't need a whip to make that horse go."

The next farmer, eager to sell his own horse, said, "That's true. The wind blows the critter along!"

The owner of the car was most concerned. He told the farmer, "I didn't mean to run over your rooster, and more than anything, I'd like to replace him."

The farmer said, "Well, go ahead, then. Introduce yourself to the chickens—they're in back!"

The newscaster for the local country station was interviewing some of the farmers about the state lottery. What would each one of them do if he won ten million dollars in the next drawing? The farmer answered, "I'd dump the farm and head off fishing for the rest of my life."

A second pondered the question and finally came up with his answer, saying, "I figure I'd just keep farming till it was all gone!"

Two farmers, Huckleby and Grimes, had been competing with each other all their lives. Now they were enjoying hand-to-hand warfare on their farms. One morning, Huckleby asked his young son to run over to Grimes's place to borrow a large crosscut saw. "Explain to him," Huckleby said, "that I need it to cut up a pumpkin."

The boy went off but returned without the saw, explaining, "Mr. Grimes said he'll let you have the saw later. Right now he's halfway through one of his radishes."

A Texas Panhandle rancher put a Plexiglas roof on his toolshed. It worked fine until a typical Panhandle twister came along and carried the roof halfway across the county. Since the roof was no longer of use to him, the farmer considered throwing it away. A neighboring rancher intervened, telling him, "There's a GM plant not too far from here. They use Plexiglas parts for things, and might buy this from you."

The rancher thanked the neighbor and sent off the Plexiglas. A week passed, then a letter from the car company arrived. It said, "Sir, we don't have the faintest idea what hit your car, but it'll be fixed by next Monday."

"How's your uncle making out with his farm?"
"Not too well. Eggs are so low it's not worth getting the hens to lay them. Milk prices are worse. It's not worth milking the cows."
"What's he doing about it?"
"He sits up half the night trying to find something else for the hens and cows to do!"

Oil was discovered under what until then were miles of green farmlands. Bulldozers, backhoes, and drill equipment were brought in. Before long, the land looked as if a war had been fought on it. There was no sign of crops or pasture. A reporter, doing an interview on the state of the farm, asked one farmer, "Do you have any oil wells on your property?"
The farmer said, "They just finished putting up about five of them."
"What are you going to do with all the money that's going to pour in?"
"First thing," the farmer said, "I'm going to buy me a darn farm without oil under it!"

A farmer and his wife drove to the market in town the day after a rainstorm. The roads were rutted, with pools of water everywhere. At the outskirts of town, the farmer ran into a neighbor. "How are you getting along?" the neighbor asked.
"Good days and bad days."
"How is your wife?"
Indicating the backseat, the farmer said, "Ask her yourself."
The neighbor said, "She's not with you."
The farmer looked around and said, after a moment's thought, "I reckon that accounts for the splash!"

A rich older farmer had his family over to the house for a fancy Sunday dinner. The farmer looked around and saw his five sons, his two daughters, and the various spouses, but no children of any of these pairings. The farmer said, "I'd love to see some grandchildren sitting at this table. To show you how much I yearn for that, I'm offering fifty thousand dollars to the first one of you who gives me a grandchild. Now let us say grace."
When he looked up again, his wife and he were the only ones left at the table.

A farmer from a remote section of North Dakota visited New York City for a brief vacation and returned home. One day his next door neighbor came by from his own farm twenty miles away. Naturally, the trip came up. The neighbor wanted to know the farmer's impressions of the city. The farmer said, "It's a big place and there's lots to do, but I couldn't get over one thing—it's so darn far from anywhere!"

A farmer bought a mare and soon discovered she was as blind as a stone. Returning to the horse dealer, the farmer said, "That mare is just about blind."
The horse dealer said, "I know she is."
"You never told me word one about it."

"It was a rather delicate matter. The farmer I bought her from didn't say one word to me, so I figured he didn't want it spread around."

Two farmers met and started to converse. One said, "I got a darn mule with the fits. What did you give your mule when it had the fits?"

The other farmer said, "I gave him a mixture of turpentine and kerosene."

The next day the farmers met again. The first one said, "I gave my mule some of that turpentine and kerosene. The mixture killed him."

The other one said, "Killed mine too!"

A city man approached Farmer Van Pelz and asked him what his horse was worth. Van Pelz said, "That depends—are you the county tax assessor or the owner of the car that killed him?"

A Yankee farmer was approached by a city man about the sale of a horse. The Yankee asked, "Where you living?"

The city man said, "Is that important?"

The Yankee said, "Yep. When I sell that horse, I want to be certain I'm through with him and through with all conversation about him!"

A new country bride asked her groom, "When did you first realize you loved me?"

He answered, "When I started getting sore at the guys in the general store when they said you were a horse!"

For a birthday present, a country boy received a wristwatch. It ran for a week and suddenly stopped. He brought it to the general store where it came from. The storekeeper opened the back, looked in, and found a small dead roach. Shrugging his shoulders, the storekeeper said, "We'll have to send it back. The darn engineer is dead!"

farmers' daughters (and sons)

The myth offers the belief that the country girl is young, apple-cheeked, nubile, and willing. The fact is that the city fellow is gullible and will believe anything he's told about the country girl!

A traveler's car broke down. It was too late to call for assistance from a garage, so he walked over to a nearby farmhouse, where, to his surprise, he encountered a farmer's lovely daughter. Hearing his plight, the farmer's daughter offered him a night's lodging. The traveler accepted and was shown to a pleasant bedroom. Later, as he lay thinking of the maiden, there was a knock on the door and the voice of the farmer's daughter asking if he was still awake. The traveler said, "I'm still up. Come in." Wearing the briefest of nighties, the farmer's daughter entered and asked, "Are you lonely?"

The traveler said, "I certainly am."

The farmer's daughter said, "I'm glad, because I've got another traveler outside who needs a room."

The rain poured down. It was impossible to see farther than a foot in front of a car's windshield, so the traveling salesman was forced to stop at a farm and ask for a night's lodging. The farmer was hesitant. The salesman cajoled and finally got the farmer to consider the request. The farmer said, "I don't know, young feller. There's only two beds in this house—mine and my daughter's. Mine's too small for another soul, but I got an idea. You have to promise me that you'll respect my hospitality. I'm going to put a pillow between you and my daughter. You have to promise you won't go over it."

The salesman said, "I swear on my life."

Came ten o'clock in the evening and it was time to go to bed. The salesman took the right side, the farmer's daughter took the left, and between them the farmer put a pillow, reminding the salesman of his oath.

In the morning the salesman was invited to breakfast. A gentleman to the last, he accompanied the farmer's daughter to the henhouse for fresh eggs. As they walked, a gust of wind blew the young lady's bonnet from her head. The bonnet rolled into the pasture. The salesman said, "I'll go over that fence and get your bonnet."

The farmer's daughter said, "What makes you think you can get over the fence? Last night you couldn't get over a pillow!"

A farmer was hesitant about the traveling salesman staying overnight. The young man hadn't stopped looking at the farmer's beautiful daughter since his arrival. The farmer finally said, "I don't think you should stay, sir. You might take advantage of my daughter."

The traveling salesman said, "You don't have anything to worry about. I was in the war, and my romantic equipment was shot off."

The farmer said, "I'm not one to gloat over your miseries. Seeing as how you were a soldier and all shot up, I'll let you stay the night."

The traveling salesman was given a bedroom next to the daughter's. Being human, he managed to open the door that separated them and joined the young lady for some pleasure. At the height of their passion, the farmer came in to check out the situation. Finding the young people coupled, he said, "Shame on you, sir. You said that it had all been shot off."

The traveling salesman said, "It was. But it left a ten-inch stump."

Being rather voluptuous, the farmer's daughter was able to pay off the man who held the first mortgage on the farm. She enjoyed herself no end, and set out, an hour later, to look for the fellow with the second mortgage.

During dinner, the farmer's daughter quietly made arrangements to join the traveling salesman in his makeshift room in the barn later in the evening. Not a trusting soul, her father would lock her in her room. The salesman was to get the ladder from the side of the barn and help her out of her room.

It was about midnight. Quietly, the salesman put the ladder against the farmer's daughter's window. The pretty girl opened the window and was about to start out when she heard the door opening. She whispered, quickly, "My father's coming. You better start painting the house!"

A neighbor came running over to the Peterson farm. Angrily, he asked for Mr. Peterson. Little Amy, the Petersons' ten-year-old daughter, was alone in the house. Coming to the door, she said, "If you come about the bull, my daddy said we charge fifty dollars for his services."

The neighbor said, "I want to see your father."

"He's in town, but if you come about our stallion, I was told to tell everybody we get fifty dollars for him too."

The neighbor was beside himself and bellowed, "I didn't come about your bull or your horse or your rooster. I'm here because your brother Hiram has got my daughter in a family way."

Little Amy said, "In that case, you'll have to come back later. Daddy didn't tell me the fee for Hiram."

The other fellows were proud of Johnny Jim. Of all the farmboys in the county, he alone had seduced Sarah, the pretty salesgirl at the feed store. Puzzled at Johnny Jim's feat, one of the farmboys asked, "How'd you get her?"

Johnny Jim said, "Well, we were out on a date and I couldn't think of anything else to say!"

fashion

I'm not overly concerned with clothes. They've never been too lucky for me. I once bought an expensive Italian silk suit with two pair of pants. I burned a hole in the jacket!

One young lady told a friend, "Whenever I'm down in the dumps I buy myself a dress."

The other one said, "I've always wondered where you got them!"

I've worn one suit so long it's been back in style three times!

He had on a suit with an Italian look—wine stains all over the front of it.

Some girls wouldn't wear jeans if they had some hindsight!

A six-year-old girl became lost in a department store. As they paged her mother, the little girl was asked why she hadn't held on to her mother's skirt. She answered, "I couldn't reach it!"

For some reason, tight clothes don't stop a woman's circulation!

A man wearing purple pants, a maize shirt, and a mauve cap was stopped by a highway patrolman. The man protested that he hadn't been speeding. The patrolman said, "I know. I only wanted to stop you to hear you talk!"

The other day she had a terrible accident. She caught her toe in her neckline!

Men and women are wearing similar clothes today. If a guy was smart, he'd marry a girl his own size!

My wife bought a new bikini the other day. She has a pearl necklace that covers more.

For a while the style for women involved the use of padding in everything. Most women didn't take off their clothes. They unpacked!

fat (weight and tonnage)

I think fat people tend to be jollier because it takes them a long time to get sore through and through!

"See that fat lady over there? That's my Aunt Charlotte."
"You said she was the fattest lady in the world. The woman behind her is fatter."
"She's part of Aunt Charlotte!"

A fat man's tonsils were trying to figure out where they were. Suddenly one said, "I think we're in Capistrano. Here comes another swallow!"

A fat woman got on a drugstore scale. Because it was broken, the scale started to act strangely. The needle went in one direction, then another, and finally spun around, settling on the line indicating ninety pounds.

A kid, walking by, said, "Gee, lady, you're hollow!"

"Your wife looks a little on the heavy side."
"She's heavy on *every* side!"

A man called his stockbroker and said, "What do you think I ought to do about pork bellies?"
   The broker said, "Diet and a little exercise!"

A woman went to a fat farm for a three-week diet and lost twenty-one days!

"My girl just slipped into something comfortable."
"What was that?"
"A telephone booth!"

"She says that her figure is sylphlike."
"I never saw such a big fat sylph!"

"My wife went to a health farm."
"How's she doing?"
"She lost half her weight in two weeks."
"How much longer do you want her to stay there?"
"Two weeks!"

"She's very fat. She ought to diet."
"What color would help?"

A fat lady boarded a bus and asked, "Isn't anybody going to offer me a seat?"
   A small man raised his hand and answered, "I'm willing to make a contribution!"

For Valentine's Day her beau sent her a heart-shaped box of candy. She spent the whole day eating her heart out!

A woman went to an acupuncturist who treated eating disorders with needles. In a week the woman lost ten pounds—through leakage!

A chubbette went around telling her friends that she was on a severe diet. One evening a girlfriend ran into her in a fancy restaurant. In front of the fat girl was a salad dripping with a rich dressing, a two-pound steak, and french fries. The friend said, "I thought you were on a strict diet."
   The chubbette said, "I am, but I need this to give me the strength to go on!"

"What a colorful sofa your uncle has."
"That's not a sofa. It's my aunt!"

fat (insults)

Use the following only sparingly. First read the caveat on insults in the section of this book given over to tricks of the trade. Until you do, it's illegal to throw "fat" jokes in the fire!

She was a little more than plump. She wore her stomach ankle-length!

She's built like a truck. Nobody ever passes her on the right.

She has an unlisted dress size.

The last time he went to New York City, they wanted to make him a borough.

His high school picture in the yearbook was on page 41 and 42—and 43!

Every time he goes through a turnstile, he has to make three trips.

He was such a fat kid, when it started to rain, they made him come into the house so the lawn could get wet!

He looked like a parade standing still!

She was so fat she went on her honeymoon in a U-Haul!

She wasn't baptized. She was launched into the holy water!

She had to bathe in a rubber tub!

When she got on a scale, she got two fortunes.

Her rear end was so big she had to have a girdle for each cheek!

She had an eighteen-inch waist—through the middle!

He was so fat, when he got out of a metal chair he had to fluff it!

At a bar, when he sat down he had a hangover *before* drinking!

He knew he was getting fat when he tried to loosen his belt and he couldn't find it!

She's not exactly fat. She's just a little broad-shouldered around the hips.

Her calves are so fat they moo!

The last time he weighed himself in the bathroom, the needle went around so much it screwed the scale into the floor!

He ran away from home as a kid, and had to take the truck route!

When she passes a drugstore, the scale jumps inside!

The last time he was standing on a corner, a cop told him, "Break it up!"

She was so fat they fed her with a harpoon!

When he gets on an elevator, it better be going down!

She's so fat she has to use stretch soap!

He got on his rowing machine the other night and it sank!

Everything she eats turns to her!

The last time he bought a sports car, they had to let out the doors!

It wasn't that he was fat. He was just short for his weight. He should have been eight-six.

What he lacks in muscle, he more than makes up in flab.

His favorite food is thirds.

He stepped on a dog's tail and it died!

He was so fat he used to go to the desert and sell shade!

In a bus the other day, he got up and gave his seat to four women.

She has so many chins she looks like she's peeking over a stack of wheatcakes!

She entered a Miss America contest—and parts of Canada and Mexico.

He's so fat he could put an apple in his mouth and go anywhere as a luau!

She's so fat, every once in a while she trips over a chin!

When she wears white, she looks like a bandaged whale.

She's so fat, she's having her portrait done by Rand McNally!

There are reasons she's fat. The other day she got an Apple 2 and she ate it!

Somebody ought to give him a fat lip so it would match the rest of him!

She's fat in places where most people don't have places!

She's so fat her husband has been married to her for eight years and hasn't seen all of her yet!

He had a tricycle built for two!

He can't watch what he eats—his eyes aren't fast enough!

She was so fat as a kid—when she got off the merry-go-round her horse limped.

She was so fat she could make a hula hoop cry!

When she sat around the house, she *really* sat around the house!

She never met a meal she didn't like!

In the first place, he's put on about twenty pounds. He also put them on in the second place!

When she sits down, she suctions herself to the seat!

She's so fat, one day she tried to commit suicide by harpooning herself!

fathers

My father was an early "house husband." While my mother was out challenging agents and producers, my father took care of keeping the house in order, feeding and clothing the family, and making sure that the children didn't turn into savages. His voice, when he was stern, packed a wallop like a giant fist. My father was the only person in the world who could temper my mother's whim of iron. When a breathy and pointed "Sarah" exploded from his lips, my mother knew it was time to back off. My father called her Sarah, especially when he was trying to make a point. My mother had several name changes. Born Sarah, she became Sandra when I started to earn well. With my stardom she went on to Sandy. Had she lived to enjoy my success in California, she would have become San!

"What were your father's last words?"
"He had no last words. My mother was with him to the end!"

I figured out why they call our language the mother tongue. Father never gets a chance to use it!

Two kids in a fancy Connecticut bedroom community met on the way to school. One kid said, "My father can lick your father."
    The other said, "Your father *is* my father!"

My son gave me a sweater for my birthday. It has a real turtleneck—green and wrinkled!

A young man called home at two in the morning. His father answered the phone. The young man asked, "Did I wake you, Dad?"
    The father answered, "No, do you want to call back later?"

When you have three young boys, it's hard to know whom to blame if something goes wrong in the house. One father explained to a friend how he solved the problem: "I send all three to bed without letting them watch television. In the morning I go after the one with the black eye!"

I taught my son the value of a dollar. This week he wants his allowance in yen!

It's hard for a five-foot-six father to explain to his six-foot-one son why junk food is bad for you!

A man wanted to have breakfast in bed on Father's Day. His kids put a cot in the kitchen!

A man went from one friend to another, desperately trying to find a summer job for his teenage son, the proud possessor of purple-streaked hair and utter hipness. One friend asked confidentially, "Are you having money troubles?"

"No," the father said. "This has been a great year. But if I don't get that animal a job, we'll have to take him to Europe with us!"

"Son, when I was your age, I used to be thrilled just to get a piece of dry bread for dinner."

"Gee, Dad, you're much better off living with us, aren't you?"

Father's Day is a holiday on which the family takes time out to remember the forgotten man!

A father lectured his son on the real values of life. The father said, "We were put on Earth to help others."

The boy said, "What are the others here for?"

"Son, this is going to hurt me more than it hurts you."
"Then go easy on yourself, Dad!"

The boy of sixteen thinks his father is pretty dumb. When the boy becomes a man of twenty-one, he's surprised at how smart the old man became in five years!

I can always count on getting one thing on Father's Day—all the bills from Mother's Day!

Two fathers met on the street. One said, "What am I going to do? My son doesn't know how to drink. He doesn't know how to play poker. What am I going to do?"

The other father said, "I don't know why you're complaining."

The first father said, "Because he drinks and he plays poker!"

Adam had a lot of trouble buying his father a Father's Day gift. What can you buy somebody who's everything?

The father of our country, George Washington, was first in war and first in peace. How come he married a widow?

If Alexander Graham Bell had had a daughter, he'd never have invented the telephone!

When his mother is out, the easiest way for a kid to get thirsty is to have his father sit down to play poker with the guys!

feet

Without them, you don't have a leg to stand on!

Her feet had immeasurable beauty. After 25EEE you stop counting!

Her feet were so big, her toes had to get their own shoes!

Her feet were so big she was taller lying down than standing up!

Her feet were so big she was often rented by forest-fire fighters for stamping!

This man was obsessed with the notion that he had big feet. He felt that people kept staring at his feet. He was forced to go to a psychiatrist. After ten years and a cost of many thousands, the man was cured. To celebrate, he took some friends to a posh eatery. He asked for the best table in the house. The maitre d' said, "We have a great table. But first you'll have to take off your skis."

The doctor told me that he'd have me on my feet in no time. It was true. I had to sell my car to pay his bill!

fights (and the fight game, revisited)

When I was fourteen, one of the greatest fighters of all time gave me some private boxing lessons. My mother made him stop. She didn't want my beautiful face marred. Kiddingly, I asked the boxer why he'd given in to my mother. She was a small woman with glasses. The boxer said, "Your mother's tongue has the best right hook in show business!"

The boxer struggled to his corner and asked his second, "What round is this?"
The second answered, "As soon as the bell rings, it'll be the first!"

One boxer had a lot of trouble getting to sleep. He'd start to count sheep, but when he got to nine he'd jump up!

He once had a fight with a woman. He would have won if she hadn't hit him back with her crutch!

A fight promoter was trying to talk a third-rate fighter into taking a bout with a fighter who was equally inept. The fighter protested, "A fight like that could ruin my reputation."
The promoter said, "Every little bit helps!"

He was a crossword-puzzle fighter—he came into the ring vertically and left horizontally.

A manager was encouraging his protégé, who was taking a beating in the ring, and said, "You can get to him. Think of it this way—if he was any kind of fighter, would he be in here with you?"

He bled so much, after his fight the Red Cross used to siphon up the canvas!

He never bled after the third round. By that time he was all out of blood.

He has more belts than any other fighter—and all on his chin!

The fighter knew he was in trouble when his second told him, "Knock him out this round. Maybe you'll get a draw!"

figures

When you take a good look at the strange shapes people come in, you have to believe that God made man late in the day!

Her figure was so bad, when she took a physical she kept her clothes on and the doctor got undressed!

They called her "hot potato" because she was built like one!

When a girl has to walk the straight and narrow, she's probably built that way!

She has a Supreme Court figure—no appeal!

She always wore a peek-a-boo outfit—one peek and everybody booed!

Her boobs were so small she had to carry her nipples in her pocket!

She was a perfect "10." Those were her dimensions—10, 10, and 10!

She was so bowlegged they hung her over the door for good luck!

One day she felt a lump in her breast. It was her shoe!

She took off her wig, her false eyelashes, her false teeth, and her falsies, and her date said, "One more false move and I'm getting out of here!"

She had to hold up her bra with suspenders!

She bought a dress for a ridiculous figure—hers!

Even the gardener wouldn't fool around with her, because she'd gone to pot!

She was knock-kneed and he was bow-legged. When they stood together they spelled the word "ox."

She was superstitious. She had a rabbit's foot—and one that was normal!

He was tall and she was fat. When they made love, it looked like an exclamation point in heat.

She was so flat-chested, her hope chest was a training bra!

She looks like a page out of *Vogue*. In fact, nobody is more out of vogue than she is!

She's got an hourglass figure, and all the guys like to play around in the sand.

She's so thin, she got a run in her stocking and fell through it!

She uses her figure as bait. She has breath to match.

She's so thin, it would take three of her to make a topless waitress!

She's so bowlegged she looks like one bite out of a doughnut!

Her dress is so tight, none of the men in her office can breathe!

She would never stoop to anything. She doesn't have to—she's four feet tall!

He looks like an advance man for a famine!

He's so skinny—when he wears trunks he looks like a flag at half-mast!

They took her to a plastic surgeon. He wanted to add a tail!

She must have gone to Notre Dame. She has a large south bend!

She's the only girl in town with a Cross-Your-Navel bra!

She's so fat—if she's not careful, she trips over a chin!

He remembers when a girl with a pair of forty-fours was the real thing—cotton!

She's so fat, it took her three days to pierce her ears!

She put a pencil under her breast and it fell to the floor. So did the pencil.

He's so fat his car has washtub seats!

finance

The bills came today, and so did a few jokes to keep me from crying!

I hate to see my loved ones leave home. I also miss my fives, tens, and twenties.

"Do you save up for a rainy day?"
"I never shop when it rains!"

"There's nothing worse than being old and broke, son."
"Yes there is, Dad—to be young and broke!"

It seems that the only boom you can really have nowadays is the one you fall down and go!

fire

So two businessmen meet. One says, "I'm so sorry about the fire that burned down your plant." The other says, "Shh, it's not until tomorrow!"

I got fire insurance on my car the other day. The agent tried to sell me theft insurance too, but he didn't fool me. Who'd steal a burning car?

Getting old has its advantages. Your friends can come to your birthday party and warm themselves around the cake.

A major brush fire had broken out in a rural area. To help, a city fire unit came in. The sirens screamed as the firemen approached a country lane. A farmer in a small horse and buggy pulled to the side. The fire truck zoomed by. A moment later, a hook-and-ladder came tearing along. As it turned onto the lane, its rear wheel plowed into the farmer's wagon. The hook-and-ladder roared on, leaving the wagon a stack of toothpicks and the farmer a bruised gentleman. A cop car stopped and its two occupants rushed over to help the farmer. He managed to stand, shook his head, and said, "I got out of the way for the fire truck, but where in hell were those painters going?"

Two country souls were in the big city for the first time. They took a room in a hotel and, after seeing all the sights, were tired. Ezra plunked himself down on the bed and soon was asleep. Billy Joe was still excited by the sights he'd seen, and sat down by the window to calm down. As luck would have it, a fire had broken out down the block. In a moment the air was filled with smoke, soot, flames, and the noise of fire engines arriving. Never having seen any fire equipment bigger than the van and buckets used by the volunteers back at home, Billy Joe was impressed, but also puzzled. He called to Ezra to get up. Ezra slept the sleep of the dead. Finally, Billy Joe screamed, "Ezra, you got to see this. They're moving hell, and they took away three loads already!"

fish

Not tonight dear, I have a haddock! Okay, so that one smelt!

It shakes you up a little bit when you open a can of sardines and fifty eyes look up at you!

Fish must be brain food, because they travel in schools!

When I was first married, my wife made salmon three times a week—salmon salad, salmon croquettes, salmon steak, poached salmon. When spring came, I had to resist an urge to go north and spawn!

A teacher was explaining the mating habits of most fish. "The female lays the eggs. The male happens along and fertilizes the egg, and some time later there are little ones."

A cute female student asked, "Well, don't the male and female ever get together?"

"No," the teacher said, "which is why we have the expression 'poor fish'!"

"What fish makes sweet sandwiches?"
"Jellyfish!"

"What fish is a member of a singing group?"
"Bass!"

The waiter served the fish entree. The diner took one bite and asked, "What is this?"

The waiter said, "Filet of sole, sir."

"Well," the diner said, "take it back and see if you can get me a softer part of the shoe!"

A Texan was telling about some of the fish in the pond back home. He'd taken a picture of one of the smaller ones, and the picture weighed five pounds.

One of my goldfish wasn't moving too well, so I called up the local university and asked one of the ichthyologists what the problem was. He said, "It sounds like rheumatism. Keep that fish out of damp places!"

fishing

Men like stories about fishing. Women, not too thrilled with the sport, laugh because the brunt of most fishing jokes is the he-man who is shown up by a six-inch bass. I've been fishing twice in my life. My big adventure was off the coast of Florida, where I fished for giant sailfish. It was a very successful day—I didn't get a bite! The thought of fighting a fish for hours makes me want to take a nap. I don't know why I should fight a fish for hours. I'm not angry with it!

Good fishing is just a matter of timing. You have to get there yesterday.

I fished a lake in Scotland that was so crowded with fish they had to swim standing up!

Kramer was describing the hundred-pound albacore he'd fought for three hours the day before. Young, another fisherman, said, "I saw the Polaroid you took of it. That fish weighed a half-pound."

Kramer said, "A fish can drop a lot of weight in three hours!"

Fishing is a sport with a worm at one end and a dummy at the other!

Fish grow fastest between the time they're caught and the bar in port!

"Are the fish biting today?"
"If they are—only one another!"

A Montana fisherman, proud of his state's rivers, was telling a dude about a fish he'd caught the week before, "It took me an hour to land it. Then I saw it was too small to keep, so me and three other guys threw it back!"

Fishing is a jerk on one end of the line waiting for a jerk at the other!

A Texan was bragging about the fish back home. Sick of listening to him, an Alaskan piped up and said, "I caught a fish last month that was eight inches."

The Texan said, "That's kind of puny."

The Alaskan said, "We measure them between the eyes!"

I once was hurt catching a thresher shark. I dislocated my shoulders trying to describe it!

The Turners were out in a boat at dawn. The air was raw. Bugs were everywhere. Mrs. Turner said, "Tell me again what a good time I'm having. I keep forgetting!"

Two fishermen, Al and Cal, were out on the lake bright and early. They sat silently as they cast for trout. Each one kept still so as not to frighten off any fish. After six hours, Cal shifted his feet. Al said, "What is this with you? Did you come out here to fish or to dance?"

There are more fish taken out of a lake than were ever in it!

A fisherman was describing a fish he'd caught that morning. His hands were outstretched as he said, "So help me, I never saw such a fish."

The fisherman who was listening to him said, "I don't suppose you did!"

There are sport fishermen, and then there are those who catch fish!

A rural sort was sitting on the riverbank fishing, about a month before the season was to start. A game warden sneaked up behind him. Noticing that the law was about to impose a heavy fine, the rural sort started to move the line from side to side and up and down. After a few maneuvers he pulled the line out of the water to reveal a wriggling minnow, and said nonchalantly, "It's darn hard to teach these things how to swim!"

Two men were out on the lake. Tucker wasn't getting bite one. Wilson was pulling them in every minute. Exasperated, Tucker said, "I can't understand it. My equipment is better than yours. I have better bait. I even spray mine with stuff guaranteed to get them to bite. Damn, I haven't had a bite yet."

Wilson said, "Tuck, it's playing hunches that does it."

"What kind of hunches?"

"It's like this—when I get up in the morning, if my wife is lying on her right side, I fish the right side of the boat. If she's on her left side, I fish the left side of the boat."

"What if she's on her back?"

"I don't go fishing!"

A youngster asked his Sunday school teacher, "Do you think Noah did a lot of fishing when he was on the Ark?"

The teacher said, "I imagine he did."

The kid asked, "With only two worms?"

Two men went fishing. For Baxter, the fishing was beyond poor. Gayle had nothing but good luck. Gayle would take some bait out of a brown bag, sniff it, put it on the hook, drop it in the water, and come up with a large trout. Baxter was unable to contain himself. He asked, "What the heck are you fishing with?"

Gayle explained, "I'm fishing with belly-buttons."

"Bellybuttons?"

"Yes, sir. My brother works in a morgue, and he saves me all the bellybuttons from autopsies."

"Why do you keep sniffing them?"

"Well, once in a while he sneaks in a rear end!"

A man from the city was having no luck fishing a small country stream. He was about two casts from retiring when a local appeared. The local asked, "What are you using for bait?"

Mr. Metropolis showed the local his flies. The local reached into his pocket and came up with a small medicine bottle filled with home brew. He poured two drops of the home brew on the worm and said, "Now try it."

The line was thrown in. Two seconds later, there was a tug and the bobber disappeared into the shimmering waters. The city man fought the fish for an hour and eventually brought it in. However, he'd only hooked a tiny perch. But it had a fifteen-pound bass by the throat!

A fisherman returned to shore with a giant marlin that was bigger and heavier than he. On the way to the cleaning shed, the fisherman ran into a second fisherman who had a string of a dozen baby minnows. The second fisherman looked at the marlin, turned to the first fisherman, and asked, "Only caught the one, eh?"

A fisherman raved about his most successful fishing trip, explaining that there were thousands of trout in this one lake. A friend asked, "Do they bite?"

The fisherman answered, "Do they? You have to hide behind a tree to bait your hook!"

"Catching any?"

"About twenty."

"Nice. Do you know who I am?"

"Nope."

"I'm the game warden."

"Know who I am?"

"Nope."

"I'm the biggest liar who ever fished this lake!"

The lady was a novice at fishing, but wanted to show her consort that she was a sport. As they sat in the water, the waves gently lapping the sides of their small rowboat, the lady asked, "How much was that red, white, and green thing?"

The consort said, "The float? It costs about a nickel."

The lady said, "Then I owe you a nickel. My float just sank."

The laziest fisherman in the world was the hillbilly who sat on his porch and watched his line in a small tub of water nearby. A man came along and said, "Hiram, you are a darn fool. You got your line in well water."

"I know. I was just fishing some."

"But you know there aren't fish in that thing."

"Sure I do. But it's darn convenient!"

Dunaway and Shimmick were fishing under the town bridge. Hearing a rumble, they looked up and saw a funeral procession move over the bridge slowly. Dunaway took off his hat and put it over his heart. Shimmick said, "That's nice of you—showing such respect for the deceased."

Dunaway answered, "It's the least I could

do. We would have been married twenty-eight years this week!"

There's nothing a fisherman can do if his worm ain't trying!

An oyster is a fish that's built like a nut!

florida

I like a state where the average age is "deceased"!

It was cold in Florida last winter, but I didn't care. I wanted color and I got it—blue!

The stores in Florida let you know what kind of winter they expect. One store recently featured bikinis with matching gloves and earmuffs!

I'm so happy. They found land on my Florida property!

There's been a longtime land boom in Florida, but one salesman was concerned. He'd sold a man from up North a parcel of fifty acres. The Northerner was coming to town to check out his land and would discover that much of it was underwater. The salesman was at a loss as to what to do, and asked his manager. The manager said, "As soon as he sees his property, try to sell him a boat!"

Florida is tired of receiving sickly people. From now on, anybody not in perfect health coming to Florida will have to use the rear entrance!

It's easy to tell New Yorkers who recently retired to Florida. When it starts to boil, they bang on the air-conditioning vent!

Florida hurricanes aren't all bad. The other day, my car got two hundred miles to the gallon!

I bought a three-story house in Florida—four when the tide's out!

"Look at him in his coffin. He appears so
  healthy."
"Why shouldn't he? He just came back from
  Florida!"

Two women were overheard talking in Yiddish in Florida. Another came by and said, "You're in America now. Do what other Americans do—speak Spanish!"

It's nice to be in Florida during the winter. That's when people dream of a tan Christmas!

flying

A good flying story is a great way to break the ice with an audience. Start by saying you just flew in on such-and-such airline. The airline names are interchangeable, as are the difficulties. Show me an airline that runs smoothly, and I'll show you a bus company!

I generally feel good about flying, but last week I had a few qualms. The plane I was in flew under a ladder!

I remember my first flight. I sat with white knuckles, gripping the sides of my seat, looking out the window, and praying for the engines to keep working. I can recall my last flight too. I sat with white knuckles, gripping the sides of my seat, looking out the window, and praying for the engines to keep working!

I ran into a tough airline on my last flight. They wouldn't seat you after the first ten minutes of the movie!

It was a "white knuckle" flight—the pilot's!

flying saucers

Flying saucers were invented in my kitchen by my wife, during a minor argument. When she's really angry, she throws dinner plates!

Its steering mechanism gone bad, a flying saucer landed deep in the sand trap of the sixth hole of a golf course. The pilot called back to his home planet and asked what he should do. The answer was curt: "Dummy, use your nine-iron!"

There are flying saucers over us all the time. Their occupants want to talk to our responsible leaders, but they're having trouble finding one!

One flying saucer left Earth the day after its arrival. The crew didn't talk to anyone on Earth, but it did pick up all the junk mail sent to "Occupant."

A flying saucer, meant for New York, has circled the Earth for two weeks. It can't find a place to park.

Have you heard of flying saucers? I have a cousin who makes the cups for them.

A flying saucer landed on a nude beach. The pilot emerged to see some magnificent bodies in the sun. Approaching one, the pilot said, "Take me to your leader—later!"

A flying saucer broke when it landed. The woman in the crew started to cry. The commander said, "Don't cry. It's not from our good set."

A woman was all set to be the commander of a flying saucer, but she turned it down. She didn't like the pattern!

food

Food and food jokes are a matter of taste!

I'm a born gourmet. I start out every day with a bowl of Cheerios Rockefeller!

Grapes cost a fortune. One good orgy can put you in hock.

A woman spent months trying to poison her husband. She didn't know that he was immune because he ate in the company cafeteria!

The warden asked the condemned man, "What do you want for your last dinner?"
The condemned man said, "Steak and mushrooms. Until now I've been afraid to eat a mushroom!"

How did the inventor of cottage cheese know when he was finished?

SHE: How do you like the potato salad?
HE: It's great. It tastes almost like you bought it yourself!

BRIDE: The best things I cook are meat loaf and peach cobbler.
GROOM: Which is this?

I hate restaurants where the waiters wear gloves. What's in the food that they're afraid to come into contact with?

I really cut down on my food bill. I find out where there's a Welcome Wagon and I move once a day!

I adore seafood, especially saltwater taffy!

food (insults)

One day my wife said, "I'd like to go someplace I've never been." I said, "Try the kitchen!"

As long as my wife continues to laugh at the terrible beating I give her culinary prowess, I know that democracy is safe. The following can serve anything from a party of four to a huge hall filled with thousands. For those who would chance public speaking, I can honestly say that a funny slap at the chef has never died. Which is more than I can say for some of the food!

Where there's smoke, there she is—cooking!

She's such a bad cook, the family dog barks, "Barf, barf!"

She overcooks everything—she even melts steak!

She's burned so much toast, her toaster has been designated a fire hazard!

She serves him blended coffee—yesterday's and today's!

She feeds him so many TV dinners, he breaks out into test patterns!

Her specialty is in the kitchen. She works for an exterminator.

When she serves him chicken, she brings it in on a wing and a prayer!

Every morning he has his coffee with two lumps—his wife and her mother.

She can't make instant coffee—she lost the recipe.

He found a great way to eat his wife's soup. He pretends it's mud.

She gives him lots of Italian food. After a meal, he goes to the toilet and leaves an oil slick!

His family is made up of big eaters. After each meal they have to count the children!

Her cooking is improving. All her lumps are bite-size!

He bought her a carving set—three chisels and a mallet.

She's such a bad cook, he keeps threatening to go home to her mother!

She punishes the kids by sending them to bed *with* dinner!

She's such a lousy cook, he bought her a range that flushes!

She's such a bad cook, her cat only has four lives left!

She's such a bad cook, she burns a Coke!

She's such a bad cook, we pray *after* we eat!

She's such a bad cook, when she throws away the foil from her TV dinner she's throwing away the best part!

When we have guests, it always presents a problem—what kind of wine goes with heartburn?

When my wife makes a picnic lunch, the forest rangers put flares around her cole slaw.

She got all of her recipes from a magazine—*Soldier of Fortune!*

She always burns the toast so he won't notice the coffee.

She burns everything. I just realized the

other day that there are other flavors besides charcoal.

My wife never throws anything out. The other night she made hamburgers. I couldn't eat mine, so she used it to clean the sink!

The handiest appliance in our kitchen is the fire extinguisher.

She knows nothing about the kitchen. The other day she tried to defrost the stove!

When she gets through with burning a roast, it can only be identified through dental records.

We just celebrated our tin anniversary—fifteen years of eating out of cans.

She makes dehydrated food without adding water. The other day I went out in the rain and gained sixty pounds.

She serves a green with every meal. Most of the time it's the bread!

I once broke a tooth on my wife's coffee!

I once cut my mouth on my wife's soup!

Her biscuits are so hard you have to rivet on the butter!

My wife's cooking can't be matched. Only the army comes close!

She likes to save leftovers. Yesterday we had a twenty-two-pound meat loaf!

She loves to make soup—especially cream of yesterday!

She must be half Italian and half Irish. The other night she made potatoes, but she mashed them with her feet!

She's a mean cook. For punishment she gives seconds!

She made a terrible mistake in the kitchen last night, but I ate it anyway!

football

We didn't have a football team at the special school I attended. Most of the students were dancers, actors, and singers. And lovers. We wouldn't have fit in with bruising contact sports. Yet I watch a football game and I see a lot of hugging and kissing after each play. Maybe we would have fit right in!

Football is a game in which eleven men spend hours trying to move a small object a hundred yards. It's the same as the post office!

One football fan lived and died by his favorite football team in the fall. He had no time for his family or children. He could be found only on the couch, a six-pack or part of one at his side, and his eyes glued to the TV screen. One day his wife marched up in front of the screen, opened her house dress, and said, with finality, "Okay, buster, play me or trade me!"

Football is supposed to build bodies. Baloney! I watched four games this weekend, and look at my flab!

An attractive middle-aged woman, dressed in the team colors and obviously a big fan, was sitting in a two-seat box all alone. The usher approached her and asked, "Why is this seat empty, ma'am?"

The woman said, "It's my huband's seat."

"Where is he?"

"He died."

"Oh, well, couldn't you have given the seat to a friend or somebody in the family?"

The woman shook her head. "Oh no, they're all at his funeral!"

The team had fumbled the ball ten times and dropped a dozen passes. Watching the game, a sub paced the sidelines. Finally he sat down, but he missed the end of the bench and fell to the ground. The coach looked at him and said, "I think you're ready to go in!"

Football is a game in which somebody takes four quarters to finish a fifth!

One professional football player just couldn't get his contract settled. He wanted Sundays off!

A perfumer could make a fortune. All he has to do is come up with a scent that can hold its own against a football double-header.

The violence on the field is nothing compared to what happens when a wife catches her husband drooling over the cheerleaders.

It had rained all day. By nightfall the field was a quagmire. The team captains walked to the center of the field for the traditional toss of the coin. One team called "heads." "Heads" it was, and the captain had his choice of kicking off or receiving. The rain pelting him, he said, "We'll kick off with the tide!"

One professional football player is making so much money, they plan to give him an unlisted number.

One college football star was offered a chance to play in the pros if he'd quit school. He turned down the offer because it would have meant a pay cut!

Most college football players are making straight A's today. Some of them are going on to the B's!

The line for the bowl game was endless. It wound clear around the stadium. A late arrival walked up to the front of the line and tried to push his way in. A burly fan who'd been waiting for the gates to open since ten growled at the late arrival and heaved him fifty feet back into the line.

A second time, the man tried to edge his way into the front. Again, he was tossed back.

After the third time, the late arrival picked himself up and said, "If you don't stop throwing me out of line, nobody's getting in today. I have the key!"

Pro linemen are so big, it only takes three of them to make a dozen!

At some institutions they're trying very hard to come up with a school of which the football team can be proud!

Prospective cheerleaders for one pro football team are given oral quizzes to test their IQs. One girl was asked, "What do you think of the Middle East?"

She answered, "I like Ohio!"

Football confuses me. Each team has a dozen beautiful cheerleaders, but when the team scores, the players hug one another!

Football is a sport in which twenty-two perfect specimens get a three-hour workout while fifty million fans who need the exercise sit back and watch them.

Toward the end of the year, the television screen is filled with one football game after another. One football widow put on a sheer negligee and paraded herself in front of her husband. He looked up from the TV set long enough to say, "Why did you buy a gray negligee?"

The wife answered, "I didn't. It's dust!"

They had a terrible flood one day at a stadium. A hundred thousand fans had been drinking beer for three hours when the cheerleaders got up and said, "Go, go, go!"

It's customary in pro football to greet a new hotshot with some special attention. One new running back was put in the game. On the first play he was knocked down and eleven opposing players plopped down on him with all their weight and more. When they were finally pulled off, the new hotshot shook the cobwebs out of his head, got up, looked around, and said, "How'd all of those eighty thousand folks get back in their seats so fast?"

They have a lot on the ball. Unfortunately, it's never their hands!

france and the french

I honeymooned in Paris. Someday I'd love to see the city!

A Parisian met his ex-wife at a party. One drink led to another and soon he was feeling mellow. He said to his ex-wife, "Why don't we leave and go over to my place for some fun?"

The ex-wife said, "Over my dead body!"

The ex-husband said, "I see you haven't changed one bit!"

Two young French boys happened to peek into an open bedroom where a young couple was locked in love. One youngster said, "Oh, look, they are fighting."

The other, older and wiser, said, "No, they are making love—and rather badly!"

A Frenchman returns home after a brief visit to the United States. Asked by his friends about the United States, he says, "It's an amazing country. You can dine in the best restaurants for free. You can drive a fancy car for free. You can even live in a magnificent apartment for free."

"Did that happen to you?"

"No, but it happened to my sister!"

Carson, seventy-five, ran into his old friend Colmer. Colmer remarked that Carson looked tired. Carson said, "I just got back from Paris."

"Was it nice?"

"Paris was fine. I only wish that I'd been there fifty years ago."

"When Paris was Paris?"

"No, when Carson was Carson!"

A French farmer took his young son to the local fair to buy a sheep. Seeing one that looked promising, the farmer proceeded, as is traditional, to massage the rear end of the sheep with great vigor so that he could gauge the fat content that is important to healthy sheep. The young son asked, "Father, why are you doing that?"

"This is what you do when you buy."

The young boy said, "Really? Monsieur LeBrun was in the house yesterday. I think he wants to buy Mother!"

A Frenchman came home to find his wife entertaining a gentleman. Calmly, the Frenchman shot his wife. The next day his lawyer said, "You would have had every right to kill her lover. Why kill your wife?"

The Frenchman said, "I kill her, it is over. I kill the man, tomorrow I must kill another one!"

Things have certainly changed in France. I just got a postcard from Paris, and it had writing on it!

Two young French ladies were talking. One said, "I am twenty-two and he is sixty-one. Is there too much difference in our ages if he's the president of a bank?"

French kissing is like a toothpick. It works on both ends!

The French have a special way of describing *savoir faire:* If a man comes home and finds a man making love to his wife, that is gauche. If he demands that they continue and the wife's lover *can,* that is *savoir faire!*

friends and friendship

I never try to get even with my enemies. I just treat my friends a little better!

A real friend is a guy who walks in when everybody else walks out!

An old friend was in a financial bind, so I helped him. He told me he'd never forget me. And he didn't. He's in a bind again and he just called me!

A friend in need is a friend you better stay away from.

A friend is anybody who forgives our good points.

Do unto others just what you'd want them to do to you. But do it first!

Last week was Italian-Chinese Friendship week, so I took a Don named Ming Toy to lunch!

You can get more with a kind word and a kick in the rump than you can with only a kind word.

He has no friends . . . to speak of!

A man died and left his best friend the money his best friend owed him!

The trouble with having friends is the up-keep.

He has no friends. He brought a parrot home and it told him to get out!

Heartburn is a sickness brought on by a friend's sudden success.

A cocktail party is a gathering where sandwiches and friends are cut into little pieces.

One woman said to another, "Can you believe that Doris? She has no common sense. She's an ingrate and coldblooded. She has no soul. She's rotten through and through."

The other woman said, "How can you talk that way about her?"

"Why not? I'm her best friend!"

A woman called a friend and asked how she felt. The friend said, "I have a terrible headache, and every bone in my body hurts. I must be getting the flu."

The woman said, "Well, I'll come over. I can cook dinner tonight and help you with the children."

"Oh, that's so beautiful of you."

"I might as well stop off at the market first. What does Jim like to eat?"

"Jim?"

"Your husband."

"My husband's name is Carl."

"Oh my, I must have the wrong number."

"Does that mean you're not coming over?"

The Lone Ranger looked up at the hills to the west and said to Tonto, "There's a big war party of Sioux on the top of that hill."

Tonto said, "We will go to the east."

The Lone Ranger said, "There are Pawnees approaching from the east."

"We will go south, *Kemo Sabe.*"

"Osages."

"North?"

"It looks like a million Blackfeet in the north. Tonto, what if they attack us? What will we do?"

Tonto started to mount up, saying, "What do you mean 'we,' white man?"

A gent who lived by his wits and on the generosity of his friends was given to hanging out in front of a restaurant in which many friends often lunched. Day after day, friends would see him and, on their way into the restaurant, would ask if they could buy him a cup of coffee. Finally the freeloader blew up and asked, "Doesn't anybody eat any meat in there?"

funerals (funeral parlors, plots, and plans)

One thing about this world—you won't get out alive!

Today they hedge on everything. What used to be a cemetery is now a Home for the Terminally Still!

The man at the zoo was crying copious tears. A passerby asked, "Why is he sobbing like that?"

A zookeeper said, "The elephant died this morning."

"He loved the animal that much?"

"That's not it. He's the guy who has to dig the grave!"

The best way to get somebody to live is to lean over and whisper the cost of a funeral in his ear.

With the cost of funerals today, going down is going up.

By the time the minister at a funeral ceremony gets through telling how peaceful and comfortable the deceased is, we all want to join him!

A funeral procession is walking by slowly. Behind the hearse is a man holding two leashed pit bulls. Behind the man is an endless line of men, also walking to the slow, funereal pace. A curious passerby asks the man with the dogs who the deceased was. The man explains that his mother-in-law is on the way to be buried. She'd been set upon and killed by the two pit bulls.

The passerby nodded and asked, "Would you consider lending me the pit bulls for a day or two?"

The man gestured behind him and said, "Get in line!"

A funeral today is where the dearly departed depart dearly!

In California, some cemeteries offer the deceased perpetual care and an answering service!

You can save some money on a funeral if the mortician has a used box!

One smoker was buried in a flip-top coffin!

Mr. Carling was dying. Downstairs in the kitchen, Mrs. Carling was preparing a roast for the wake. The delicious aroma wafted up to the bedroom, Mr. Carling leaned over to his young daughter and said, "I love your mother's roast. Before I die, I would love one thin slice."

The daughter nodded and went down into the kitchen. She returned a moment later, empty-handed, explaining, "Mother says it's for after the funeral!"

"I've always hated you. I'll dance on your grave."
"In that case, I'll be buried at sea."

furniture

All of my family's furniture was antique. Of course, it didn't start out that way. It started out as installment payments!

A woman came into a furniture store and asked for a sexual couch. The clerk said, "You mean a sectional couch."

The woman said, "No, I want an occasional piece in the living room."

My cousin sat in a period piece once—an electric chair! One jolt and—period!

Our living room was done in Early American—we had an Indian in the corner.

A furniture manufacturer went to Paris for a trade show. While there, he happened to walk down a street in Montmartre and was accosted by several ladies of the evening. Being a small-town gentleman and with not even the mastery of one word in French, the manufacturer tried to explain with gestures that he had no idea what was wanted of him. Finally, one prostitute whipped out a piece of paper and a ballpoint pen and drew a bed with two people in it. The manufacturer walked on, puzzled. To this day he can't understand how the prostitute knew he was in the furniture business!

Louis XIV looked around his living room at the Louis XIV couch and the Louis XIV chairs and said, "Get it out of here. I can't stand modern!"

furs

My wife wanted a mink coat. I wanted a new car. We compromised. We bought a fur coat, but we keep it in the garage!

A furrier recently crossed a mink with a gorilla. He got a fur coat, but the sleeves were too long.

A woman gets a mink the same way a mink gets a mink!

His wife wanted a mink set, so he bought her a rifle and a trap.

Two long-legged showgirls were talking. One of the showgirls wore a full-length mink coat and explained that she'd gotten it from a playboy. The other asked, "What did you have to do for it?"

The befurred one said, "Just lengthen the sleeves!"

The mink in the closet is often the reason for the wolf at the door.

future

I look in my crystal ball. I see a tall, dark person coming into your life. Perhaps I see a short, light person coming into your life. I see that you will travel. I see that you will not travel. I see that I have a dirty crystal ball!

"What was Washington's last address?"
"Heaven, I think."

A man was surprised to see his obituary in the newspaper. He called up a friend and asked, "Did you see my obituary in the paper today?"

The friend said, "Yes. Where are you calling from?"

The funeral proceedings were almost over. Standing graveside as the body was being lowered into the new dug hole, the minister said, "Yes, John Malcolm Bronson, you are gone. And we hope that you are where most of us don't think you'll be!"

A college student was bragging about his lack of religious fervor. He kept telling the others having lunch at the same table that he didn't believe in heaven. "There's no such thing as heaven. I'm not going to a dumb place like that. Where is it? Point to it."

Another student looked up from his soft drink and said, "Okay, you can go to hell, but stop making such a fuss about it!"

The séance was in full swing. Suddenly the medium made contact with the businessman in the other world. The air crackled, and just as his widow was about to speak, the businessman put her on hold.

gadgets

How did the race survive before the invention of battery-operated swizzle sticks? Or digital combs? Or—so help me, it's available—a remote-control page turner?

I use an electric toothbrush. It's nice, but twice a year, for a checkup, I have to visit my electrician.

I have an electric toothbrush. Last month I forgot to pay my utility bill, so they came and turned off my teeth.

My wife and I have a waterbed. She calls it the Dead Sea.

I know a real daredevil. He has a waterbed and a passionate girlfriend with long fingernails.

I have a new microwave TV set. I can watch a one-hour show in six minutes!

My wife knows what she wants. If heaven doesn't have a microwave oven, she's not going!

We bought a new stove. It cost a fortune. It was the first time an oven ever cleaned us!

My wife gets mixed up with all the gadgets in the kitchen. Yesterday she tried to defrost the stove.

I just bought something to improve my hearing—a plane ticket out of town for my wife.

I'm not thrilled with all the gadgets in my house. It's scary, having things around that are smarter than I am!

A youngster was watching an astronomer aim a giant telescope at the sky. Suddenly a shooting star zoomed through the sky. The kid said, "Wow, that was a great shot!"

My wife forgot about the speed with which a microwave oven does things. Did you ever have Thanksgiving turkey at seven in the morning?

A man I know joined an electronic dating service. He asked for a small companion who liked the water, dressed up a lot, and didn't talk much. The machine went to work and in two minutes got him a date with a penguin!

I remember the good old days—when radios plugged in and toothbrushes didn't.

My neighbor is a real showoff. He's got a lawnmower with bucket seats.

They've just come up with a new device that is attached to the TV set. It tells what men are listening to. Tested the other day, it showed that eighteen percent were listening to network shows, the other eighty-two percent were listening to the little woman!

They just came up with a robot meter maid. It worked for a while, but then it gave out forty tickets in a drive-in movie!

A super computer-chip company became so successful it started to look for a smaller place!

My wife made me a TV dinner last night. Unfortunately it burned, so she had to call in a repairman.

I have no luck. The other day my waterbed caught fire!

gags

I like to think that a gag is more than a two-cent version of a joke or witty remark. A gag, to me, is a dart, fast and pointed, that hits a target quickly for an automatic response. Its basic strength, beyond its humor, is in the surprise it brings. The best gag is one that starts by leading the ear in one direction and suddenly going off in another. If you tell one, let it sound as if it slipped out. Some people start by indicating that they've heard a funny line and here it is. Wrong! A gag is at its funniest when the teller looks and sounds innocent. The gag is a modern invention. There were laughs in Shakespeare, but almost all were puns or wordplays of some sort. When I started in show business, most comedy performers told stories, some of them lasting fifteen minutes. There were little laughs along the way, of course, but the story aimed for one big punchline. Because the world's pace increased before World War I, it's possible that joke pacing had to speed up. By the time we all started to hum "Over There," stories had been condensed to thirty and forty seconds. The next stop, naturally, was the one-line gag. That enabled some of us to get more laughs. My mother's goal for me was to get eight laughs a minute. By the way, even though I had the reputation of being the Thief of

Badgags, the fact is that I never stole a joke. I merely found it before it was lost!

Last week the beach was really crowded. I had to dive in six times before I hit water!

Christenings are awful. I can't stand watching them hit a little kid over the head with a bottle!

Did you ever stop to think that wrong numbers are never busy?

Our local TV weatherman was fired. He couldn't even predict yesterday's weather!

You know a guy is cheap when he goes around pricing generic funerals!

One movie was so bad, a holdup man went to the box office and said, "Give me everybody's money back!"

Eve must have been Jewish. Who else would have said, "Have a piece of fruit!"

He really comes from an old-fashioned town. The post office has wanted-posters of Robin Hood.

When you're in the bank, be a little wary if the guy ahead of you asks how to spell "Stickup"!

She thought all men were created equal. Then she went to an orgy.

One guy went into the street wearing only his raincoat, and got flashbite.

Miracle drugs are great. They keep you alive until you pay the bill.

I know of this immigrant who came to America a poor boy. Now, forty years later, he's a poor man.

One of my friends just gave up drinking. He was beginning to see the handwriting on the floor.

Nobody likes him. He brought a parrot home and it told him to get out.

My wife isn't talking to me today, and I'm in no mood to interrupt her!

I saved my wife a lot of trouble last Christmas. I gave her an exchange certificate.

A rock-and-roll singer was lost in the Alps, but at the last minute he was saved by a Saint Bernard with a hairbrush around its neck!

I never pay my bills. I have the money, but I'm so lonely I just want somebody to call me.

My son's schoolteacher is Chinese. Every day she gives him homework to take out.

My son took his first bath in a week. When he was through, his toy boat went aground!

I told my wife we were overdrawn at the bank, so she wrote a check to cover it!

They were introduced by a mutual friend— a bellhop!

A guy paid off his creditors at sixty percent on the dollar, and felt forty percent better!

They finally discovered that Brigham Young didn't have forty wives. He had one wife with thirty-nine wigs.

I'll give you an idea of my luck. I once put a seashell to my ear and got a busy signal.

My wife is too neat. I get up at four in the morning for a glass of water—when I come back, the bed is made!

She must be a napkin. She's always in somebody's lap!

A lot of couples break up because it looks like the marriage is going to last forever!

He faced bankruptcy, so he went to the Bible for consolation. He opened it to Chapter 11!

gambling

I watch people in a casino lose fifty or a hundred dollars at games of chance and find it amusing because these people are ignorant of the laws of chance. I go to the tables often and always lose, sometimes a few hundred and sometimes many thousands. The difference is that I know what I'm doing! I know every aspect of the laws of gambling. Ask the two thousand bookmakers whose children I've put through college!

Gambling is a great way of getting nothing for something.

The terrible thing about hitting a jackpot on a slot machine is that it takes a long time to put the money back.

I know a fellow who makes only mental bets. The other day he lost his mind.

I met the ultimate gambler yesterday. I was walking down the street when a manhole cover blew up into the air. A man said to me, "Two to one it's heads."

I know of a man who hijacked a plane and was taken to a gambling resort. He put a dime in a slot machine and three parachutes came up.

I once lost a bet on a wrestling match. My guy was pinned in ten seconds. I couldn't understand it. He'd won the rehearsal!

The casinos wiped him out completely. Except for a single 1975 half-dollar, he was as broke as the day he was born. Walking toward the highway, he kept tossing his coin in the air. His attention was diverted by an approaching car for a brief moment, just long enough for him to let the coin slip through his fingers. It rolled toward a grating in the street. He ran to retrieve it. An oncoming city bus hit him and sent him to the hospital for six months. Rather than risk an expensive court case, the city's insurance company settled for a large amount of money on the poor victim.

Taking the money he'd received, he went through the casinos again. Again he lost every penny. Starting back to the highway, he passed the grating and looked down to see if his coin was still down there. Again he was hit, this time by a taxi. This hospital stay was longer and more painful than the first. But the settlement was also larger.

Once more he tested the gaming tables. Once more he lost. Once more, as he walked to the highway, he looked down for his half-dollar. Once more he was hit by a vehicle.

In the hospital, he lay helpless, every inch of his body in traction. A visitor asked, "How could any man get hit three times in the same place? What made you keep going back to that grating?"

The man answered, "That half-dollar was my good-luck charm. I didn't want to lose it!"

A man won a million in the lottery. His wife, who'd found out about it first, was concerned because he had a heart condition and was scheduled to go to the doctor for an EKG the next day. Coming up with a great idea, the wife called the doctor and asked him to tell her husband about the stroke of luck. If the husband fainted or had any kind of reaction, the doctor would be there to help.

Blissfully unaware, the husband appeared for his examination. The doctor said, at what he felt was the proper moment, "Oh, by the way, Sam, you won a million in the lottery."

The man said, "You're kidding."

"No, it's true. You won a million."

The man said, "Just because you've kept me alive, I'm going to give you half of the money."

The doctor dropped dead.

A man bought a brilliantly colored parrot and took it home. When he put it in a cage, he suddenly heard the parrot singing the Ave Maria. Its version was magnificent and had more shading than its feathers. When Easter came, the man dressed the parrot in a special Easter suit with a pretty bonnet. Arriving at church with the parrot, the man was refused admittance. This, he was told, was a house of worship, not a theater for some side show. The man explained that the bird sang the Ave Maria. Laughing at him, some of the elders were willing to wager a few dollars on the ridiculous claim. The man accepted every challenge. All bets having been placed, the man told the bird to sing. Not one sound did the parrot utter. The man cajoled. Still, not one note came from the bird's throat. The man paid off all the wagers.

A little later, as they walked home, the bird started to hum and then burst into magnificent song, ending, of course, with the beautiful hymn. The man said, "Now you sing? Now? You shamed me before the whole town. Worse still, you cost me a fortune."

The bird said, "Don't take it too hard. Think of the odds we'll get at Christmas!"

A man scrimped and saved for twenty years. He went without lunch and often without breakfast. His dinners were one step above bread and water. He managed to work at three different jobs, giving up his weekends to become a common laborer. His body sweltered in the summer heat, froze in the winter, but he continued his menial work. He gave up the woman he loved so that he'd be spared the expense of a movie or an occasional evening out. He lived in the coldest of cold-water flats.

At the end of the twenty years, he went to the local racetrack with the thousand dollars he'd saved up. He bet the entire amount on a horse in the first race. The horse lost. The man shrugged his shoulders and said, "Easy come, easy go!"

The gambler was being buried. In an impassioned voice, the eulogist said, "I can't believe Ed is gone. No, he's not gone. No! Ed only sleeps. He is not dead!"

Another gambler spoke up: "I got fifty bucks that says he's dead!"

A man approached an acquaintance in a gambling casino and said, "Joe, can you give me a hundred? My wife is dying and needs a medicine that can save her. Without it she'll be dead by morning."

Joe said, "Sid, I'd give you the money right away, but I'm worried that you'll gamble it away."

Sid answered, "No, you don't understand. Gambling money I've got!"

Four men are playing gin rummy. One of them loses a hand that costs his team two thousand dollars. To cap the loss, his head falls to the table. The man is dead. One of the players volunteers to tell the wife of the deceased that her husband won't be home for dinner, or ever again. Going to the house, he knocks on the door. The wife opens the door. The player says, "Your husband lost two thousand at gin."

The wife says, "Let him drop dead!"

The player says, "He did."

Gin players can be sentimental. In a recent game, one player keeled over dead. In deference to him, the rest of the game was played standing up.

We have twelve bingo parlors in our town. All the proceeds go to fight gambling.

Some states have discovered perpetual motion. They give people welfare so that the people can invest the welfare check in the state lottery so the money that comes in can be sent out as welfare.

A man was a gambling degenerate. Every time he came up with a dollar he found a way of losing it. Unable to make him quit, his wife finally drove him to the mint and pointed at the huge building, saying, "You've got to stop. No matter how fast you lose it, they can make it faster."

The man said, "I don't know. I've got them working nights!"

A man played cards with Siamese twins. Somebody asked him, "Did you win?"

The man said, "Yes and no."

gangsters

During Prohibition, a major New York hoodlum fell in love with one of the chorus girls in the show at a notorious speakeasy. To indicate the depth of his passion, the hoodlum sent the chorus girl two dozen long-stemmed roses nightly for a week. With the flowers came a request for a dinner date. The chorus girl turned down the request every night. On the eighth day, when the chorus girl arrived at the club, a small gift was waiting for her—a diamond necklace with some heavyweight stones. Again she turned down the request for a dinner date. At the end of two weeks the chorus girl had amassed, in addition to the flowers and the diamonds, a sable stole, a jeroboam of the most expensive Paris perfume, and a town car. Still the chorus girl was adamant. She refused to go out with the hoodlum. Texas Guinan, a flamboyant blonde who owned the club, asked the girl why she wouldn't go out with the poor man. The chorus girl answered, "I won't go out with him until he asks me in a nice way!"

A part of me salutes the old-time New York gangster. More than any other force, and for reasons of his own, the gangster built the huge nightclubs in which many of us cut our comedy teeth. The gangster, again for private reasons that had nothing to do with the general welfare, backed the shows that lit up Broadway. Needless to say, the illicit presence in our gambling resorts is measurable, but without it, Las Vegas, Atlantic City, and all the other resort cities would be tiny hamlets still. Without these entertainment capitals functioning at high speed, as we are learning, the sources of talent disappear.

Members of the mob like to protect their ladies from the brutal aspects of their profession. One gangster was newly married and had just brought his bride to their new suburban home. As a wedding gift, a rival mobster planted a time bomb in the garage. As set, it went off at about three in the morning. The boom was deafening. The bride jumped up and asked, "What was that?"

The gangster said, matter-of-factly, "Mice!"

The most useless gesture in the world: leaving the porch light on for a mobster who went out for a walk ten years ago!

One mobster wasn't too bright. They asked him to blow up a truck. He burned his lips on the exhaust.

A gangster with connections received some building contracts. His company built the bridge at the edge of town. Another one of his companies put in the river afterward.

Most gangsters have no necks. That's from standing in front of the grand jury, shrugging, and saying, "I don't know anything about it!"

Most gangsters have very good manners. They all talk about time off for good behavior.

Business is bad for the mob. Last month it had to lay off three city councilmen.

Israel has its own mob—the Kosher Nostra!

One young gangster joined the mob. He'd decided to follow in his father's fingerprints.

One mobster was really tough. He never asked you the time, he just took your watch.

New York isn't the safest town for criminals. One guy held up a bank, and on the way to the getaway car he was mugged!

One counterfeiter got caught because he'd been making money too long—about an inch and a half too long.

"How's Marie the waitress?"
"She's dead."
"Dead?"
"She died from herpes."
"You don't die from herpes."
"You do if you give it to big Louie!"

A gangster found a young man he thought might have a future. The gangster decided to turn the young man into a singer. A friend cautioned the gangster, "It'll cost you a fortune. He'll need elocution lessons. He'll need singing lessons, a wardrobe, a publicity man, expensive musical arrangements."

The gangster mulled it over, then said, "You're right. I'll make him a fighter!"

garbage

Lives there a man whose wife hasn't smiled at him sweetly and said, "Take out the garbage!" My wife said that once, and it was three days before I let her brother back into the house!

The garbage on our block hasn't been picked up in so long it's considered a landmark!

Two cockroaches were devouring the garbage in the can. As one of them munched, the other told him about the inside of a house he'd just left. "You'd never believe it," the traveling roach said, "but the kitchen was spotless. Everything—the sink, the utensils, the counters—all were sparkling clean."

The other roach stopped chewing and said, "Do you have to talk like that when I'm eating?"

One garbageman almost died of a broken heart. He came to a house with new trashcans that had been dented at the factory.

I knew a garbageman who couldn't hold a wife. He kept bringing his work home.

Two alien life-forms landed in a large city. Famished after the long trip from their galaxy, they spied a trashcan. Without pausing for a moment, they jumped on it and started to eat it. By the time they'd worked their way half down, one said, "The crust is nice and crunchy, but the filling is so soft!"

In my neighborhood, the garbage truck comes twice a week—to make deliveries!

A woman rushed after the garbage truck and asked, "Am I too late for the garbage?"
  The collector said, "No, jump in!"

A woman slipped on a throw rug, fell out of a window, and landed in a trashcan. A Frenchman was passing by and walked over. He shook his head sadly and said, "These Americans are so extravagant. She was good for another year!"

The best way to get rid of garbage is to gift-wrap it and leave it near an open window when you park your car at a mall!

Two flies watched the garbage disposal swallow and grind down all the leftovers from dinner. One fly said to another, "And I thought *I* had an appetite!"

gardening

We have a Japanese gardener. For fifty-one weeks a year he can't speak a word of English. Asking him to perform a special chore like pruning a certain tree is like talking to the tree. Our gardener bows and smiles a lot, then goes into a torrent of Japanese. The week before Christmas, however, he becomes a Rhodes scholar. Is there anything Madame would like? Shall I feed the begonias? Naturally, he gets a handsome gift. Two days later, it's back to Pearl Harbor again! I've tried to take over some of the flower gardening, but I don't seem to have the thumb. I once killed ceramic tulips!

I don't have the knack for growing houseplants. I bought a hanging fern and the rope died.

My wife must be lending our power mower to the neighbors. There's strange blood on it.

I think I'm overfeeding my lawn. I have the only fat grass on the block.

I have a Peter Pan garden. It never grew up.

My potato crop turned out great. Some are as big as a kid's marbles, some are as big as peas, and then there are a few *small* ones!

When a man is described as having a green thumb, it doesn't necessarily mean he's a great gardener. It could also mean he's a rotten painter!

I can't get anything to grow in my vegetable garden. I bought the best seed. I planted peas and tomatoes, and I paid thirty cents a can for them!

The first time I saw pictures of the surface of the moon, I thought they had the same gardener we did!

May is the time you realize your fall bulbs didn't come up.

If you cross a rambling rose with a pansy, you get a rose that still rambles, but it also skips!

Last month I put in a rock garden. Two of them were dead in the morning!

A garment manufacturer made a fortune and retired. Taking up gardening, he soon had a garden that was a riot of color and blossom. Proud of his ability, the manufacturer invited another garment manufacturer to see the gardener. The second manufacturer was more than impressed. His eyes opened wider and wider with each kind of rare flower. The men came to a small area that was covered with bright red flowers. The second manufacturer asked, "What kind of flowers are those?"

The first manufacturer answered, "How should I know? Am I in the millinery business?"

My lawn is perfect. Each blade of grass is three feet high!

I don't exactly have a green thumb. I once killed a flagpole!

My lawn was covered with dandelions. I tried every kind of agent to kill them off, but had no luck. I went to a neighbor who was great in the garden. I explained my plight. He mentioned a dozen liquids that were supposed to kill dandelions. I explained that I'd tried all of the liquids. The neighbor considered the matter and finally said, "I have a great idea—learn to love dandelions!"

If flowers don't talk back to you, are they mums?

I'm a terrible gardener. Last month my artificial lawn died.

He must be a good gardener. He and his plants are both potted!

Something weird happened on my lawn. I planted some weeds and the grass took over.

Recent pictures of other planets show vast stretches of arid land. If there is life on those planets, they must be gardeners!

I subscribe to a science-fiction magazine— *Better Homes and Gardens!*

Gardening is only a man's effort to improve his lot.

I always keep the empty seed packages. They're great for keeping the whole crop in!

We called in a tree doctor, but he fell out of his patient!

We had to get a new tree doctor. He was becoming emotionally involved with his patient!

I know a man who flunked tree-doctor school. He fainted at the sight of sap!

garments and the garment district

When you say "a man of the cloth" nowadays, it's probably polyester. Having gone on record in another category about my feelings for the gangster, I must acknowledge appreciation to the denizens of the garment center, especially in New York. Without them, there'd probably be no Broadway. Their expense accounts poured more money into plays than the backers. Buyers came to the city from department stores and specialty shops all over the country. They saw the fashions and were treated to at least three plays. Beyond that, garment-center men, eager to rub shoulders, elbows, and other parts of their anatomies with the famous, backed many shows.

Many of them lost their money. Unfazed, they went back to their lofts, cut velvet, saved up another batch of greenbacks, and angeled another show. One shirt manufacturer put money into one of my shows. Although the show had a decent run, there wasn't enough money to pay off his investment. At the closing-night party, he gave the cast and crew an assortment of short-sleeved shirts, explaining, "Another two months, we could have had long sleeves!"

Stein had worked hard all of his life. His business at a peak, he decided to enjoy himself for the first time in his life. He called in a kid from the shipping room and said, "I want you to get me some cocaine, then get me some marijuana, and three beautiful girls, six-foot-six with long black hair."

The youngster left, returning a few hours later with a report. "I got the cocaine," he said. "I got the marijuana. But I can't find three six-foot-six hookers with long black hair."

Stein said, "All right, so cancel the order and get me a diet cola and a pretzel!"

A nouveau-riche garment manufacturer went to his first fancy party. Seeing the canapés, he said, "How do you like this? They're serving dinner swatches!"

A garment manufacturer had a disastrous season. Suicide was his only out. He went to the roof of the building, kissed the city goodbye, and jumped off. Passing the eighth floor, on which a successful manufacturer had his plant, he looked in and saw what the cutters were working on for the next season. His body hurtled downward, but as he passed the fifth floor where his company was, he yelled to his partner, "Cut suede!"

Two garment-center manufacturers, Carter and Lusk, were on the verge of bankruptcy.

All that could save them and their lives was a loan from the bank. They filled out the proper papers, which were forwarded to the main office. Their loan officer said, "This looks pretty good. If you don't hear from me by the end of the week, it means you're in."

Carter and Lusk didn't sleep a wink for the next few days. They had no appetites and spent their time chain-smoking and praying. The last day came. As the hours ticked by, the loan seemed to look good. With one hour left, the minutes went by as if they were glued to the clock. Exactly at one minute to the hour of closing at the bank, a knock on the door startled the men. Each was afraid to go to the door. Finally, Lusk walked toward the door. Each step was like the last step of the last mile. Opening the door, he saw a messenger with a wire. Tears filled Lusk's eyes. His hands shook as he opened the telegram. Then a huge smile broke out on his face and he yelled to Carter, "Good news. Your brother died!"

"I lost ten thousand two months ago. Last
  month I lost fifteen thousand."
"Why don't you close up your shop?"
"How would I make a living?"

A garment-center manufacturer accosted his partner. "You rat! I just learned you've been sleeping with my wife."

The partner said, "I swear—not a wink!"

Two garment-center manufacturers decided that their names mitigated against business. One felt that a mainstream name would be helpful. He changed his name to Thompson. Won over, the partner also changed his name. As soon as it was official, the receptionist started answering the phone with, "Thompson and Thompson." If it was for one of the bosses, she'd add, "Which

Thompson do you want to talk to—Abramowitz or Karelsky?"

A man called the coat firm of Krupnik, Krupnik, Krupnik, and Krupnik. He asked for Mr. Krupnik. The voice at the receiving end said, "He's not in."

"All right, let me talk to Mr. Krupnik."

"He's not in."

"I'll talk to Mr. Krupnik, then."

"He's not here."

"How about Mr. Krupnik?"

"Speaking!"

A garment-center manufacturer berated his partner, "You're so crooked—the wool you're trying to pull over my eyes is half polyester!"

Two garment-center manufacturers shared the favors of an attractive female employee. Fate intervened and impregnated the young lady. One of the partners, at the hospital when she gave birth, called his partner. "She had twins. Mine died!"

Two manufacturers were lunching and bemoaning business. One said, "Come into my showroom. It's like a haunted house."

The other said, "You're lucky. At least you have ghosts!"

A teacher asked the class, "What are the seasons?"

The son of a garment manufacturer answered, "Slack and busy!"

Two garment-center men, living in the same neighborhood, shared a taxi home. For fifteen minutes, each sat back silently as he thought of his business. Finally, one sighed. The other said, "You're telling me!"

It was unseasonably warm, and a coat manufacturer said to a friend, "My coats are better than money. Money you can get rid of!"

One garment manufacturer fired his secretary because of a lack of experience. All she knew was shorthand, typing, and filing!

The garment-center partners were at the track when one of them remembered something he'd forgotten to do earlier. Worried, he said to his partner, "I left the safe open."

The partner said, "What's the problem? We're both here."

A garment manufacturer told his shipping clerk, "You've been like a son to me—loud, insolent, disrespectful!"

The annual synagogue fund drive was under way. Various members of the congregation made contributions from a few dollars to many hundreds. Finally, Sauber, the garment-center tycoon, rose and said, "I, Alex J. Sauber of Princess Frocks, the frock with the royal look, located at 315 East 36th Street, phone number 555-2718, pledge ten thousand dollars—anonymous!"

gays

I, for one, am glad that "gay" jokes are finally out of the closet. They are too rich a source of humor to be kept in limited circulation!

At the evening mass, a transvestite happened into a church. Seeing one of the richly clad priests walking down the aisle, an incense burner swinging its pleasant aroma among the parishioners, the transvestite called out,

"That outfit is a stunner, sugar, but you better be careful—your purse is on fire!"

Two gays were standing on a corner when a beautiful young lady with an incredible figure passed by. One of the gays said, "It's times like this that make you wish you were straight!"

A man was recently accosted by a group of gay muggers. They threw him to the ground and for three hours they did his hair!

They have a new gay church. Its ritual is different—only every other person kneels!

Father Donald was a fine priest, but unfortunately had a tic that made it seem as if he were always winking. One day, Father Donald went to a brothel in an attempt to preach the staff into less evil ways. "Ma'am," he said to the madam, "I would like to talk to one of your girls."

His wink confused the madam, who said, "I understand. I have one girl who'll knock your socks off."

The priest said, "Oh no. I'm not here for that. I don't do things with girls."

He winked again. The madam nodded. "I get it." Then she called out, "Get the handyman!"

A man found himself shipwrecked on an island with six lovely women as his only companions. Since they were all young and lusty, the man felt it only fair that he divide his time and energies equally. He arranged for the entertainment of one woman each day.

After several weeks of this most delightful hobby, the man found himself a little jaded. He was tired of the sameness of the routine. He wanted, more than anything else, to have a male companion with whom he could talk sports or politics. Luck seemed to be

with him. One morning a sail appeared on the horizon. It grew larger as what was obviously a raft approached. It arrived at the sandy white beach. Its crew of one was a young man. The island dweller ran to him and welcomed him with open arms.

The new arrival said, with a pronounced lisp and feminine undertones, "I'm so glad I made it." He waved his hands in obvious joy. "This is such a cute place."

The island dweller shrugged and said, "Oh well, there goes Sunday!"

Graffiti in a men's room said, "My mother made me a homosexual."

Under it, somebody had written, "If I gave her the wool, would she make me one too?"

He isn't exactly gay—you'd just call him a near miss!

He once entered a hundred-yard dash and was disqualified for skipping. He thought it was a drag race.

His father wanted a boy and his mother wanted a girl. They were both satisfied.

"What do you call a gay dentist?"
"A tooth fairy!"

Two motherly types met in the park. One said, "How's your son doing?"

The second mother said, "He's a doctor in Manhattan and he makes half a million dollars a year. How's your son getting along?"

The first mother said, "He's never worked a day in his life. He's just a homosexual, that's all."

The second mother said, "Oh, that's terrible."

The first mother said, "It's not so bad.

You see, he knows this doctor in Manhattan who makes half a million a year!"

He's so gay, when he gets stopped by the cops they ask him to fly a straight line!

On their wedding day they tossed a coin to see which one would wear the gown!

He opened a gay bathhouse because he found a lot of backers!

They came into their honeymoon suite. He took off his clothes. She took of her clothes. He put on her clothes and she hasn't seen him since!

One day he went to San Francisco and turned prematurely gay.

A myth is an effeminate moth.

One gay was so ugly he had to date girls!

"What do you get when you cross an Italian and a gay?"
"A Sissylian!"

A gay is a man who believes in vice versa.

gentlemen

Gentility comes either from years of breeding or from one stock that splits and quadruples in price. A gentleman has to be careful because he's a tenth of an inch from being a snob. Like the time I went to a fancy men's club in Boston. Introducing myself to an old codger, I said, "My name's Berle." He looked at me and said, "Mine isn't!" A smidgin past gentleman!

In England, a guy who doesn't do anything is called a gentleman. Here we call him a bum.

The gentleman's paramour told him she was pregnant, and said, "If you don't marry me, I'll kill myself."
    The gentleman answered, "That's rather nice of you!"

A gent is a man who steps out of the shower to tinkle.

A gentleman is a wolf with a little patience.

A gentleman always opens the door for his wife when her arms are filled with groceries.

He comes from a moneyed family. His brother is worth fifty thousand, dead or alive!

He won't tell his girl he's too good for her. He wants it to come as a surprise!

Men like him are very rare. They should be well-done!

He doesn't even walk in his sleep. He has a stretch libido!

When there are ladies around, no gentleman ever swears at his wife.

germany and germans

A student of the German psyche, in part because my family came from the land of the Rhine, I believe that Germans have been much maligned. They are not militaristic, like a nation of first sergeants. The Germans are soft and friendly. When they talk to you, their tones are musical, pleasant, soft, and you will listen!

A member of the Czechoslovakian underground was taken prisoner just before the sowing season. Fearful for his life, he was even more concerned that his wife wouldn't be able to seed the fields. He came up with an idea. A letter was smuggled out to her in which he told her not to touch the fields because guns for the underground were buried there. He managed to alert the Germans, who intercepted the letter. By the end of the week, all of the fields were plowed up as the Germans worked overtime to find the weapons. The next morning, the wife seeded the fields!

The Nazi party was at the height of its power. Several Germans were lunching. One shook his head sadly, a second let out a long sigh, and a third uttered a deep groan. A fourth German stood. Starting away, he said, "I'm going to my own table. You men ought to know better than to talk politics in public!"

Early in the rise of Hitler's Germany, a Nazi boy was asked by the Jewish kid on the block if he wanted to play. The Nazi kid said, "I can't play with you because you're Jewish."

The Jewish kid said, "That's all right. We won't play for money!"

"What do you call removing a splinter from a Nazi's rear end?"
"Brain surgery!"

Herr Schmidt was a machinist in a refrigerator plant. Tired of their old icebox, his wife implored him to steal a brand-new refrigerator for their home. Herr Schmidt protested that he'd be caught. His wife said, "Bring it home piece by piece and you'll put it together on your day off."

Herr Schmidt started to bring home pieces. Finally he had all the parts he needed. On his first day off he started to assemble them. Hour after hour went by and he wasn't making any progress. His wife came to him in the backyard and asked what the problem was. Herr Schmidt said, "I've tried four different ways. It always keeps coming out a cannon!"

A schoolteacher in Berlin asked her class, "What is the size of the National Socialist Party?"

One seven-year-old stood up and said, "It's about two meters."

"How did you come up with that?"

The boy said, "My father is a head over two meters. Whenever he hears somebody talk about the Nazis, he puts his hand on his throat and says, 'I've had them up to here!'"

There was only one thing that kept Hitler from being a barefaced liar!

I once had a meal in a German-Chinese restaurant. The food was delicious, but an hour later I was hungry for power!

It was a gala festival, with music and champagne flowing like water. One Prussian officer found himself seated next to a stunning redheaded woman with amazing curves. As the salad was being served, the Prussian officer decided to take some liberties. Putting his hand on the woman's thigh, he started to move his fingers along. The redheaded woman leaned over and said, "I suggest you don't go too far. My name is Max and I'm a secret agent!"

Germans have sharp minds. One read that cigarettes caused cancer in mice, so he put his packs on a higher shelf!

One day a Greek insulted a Spaniard. The next morning, the Germans declared war!

A German soldier attacked a French peasant

girl. Proud of himself, the German soldier said, "In nine months from now you will have a little boy. Call him Hans."

The French peasant girl said, "In about nine days from now you'll have a little rash. You can call it hives!"

Hitler went to an astrologer and asked if the stars could tell the day he'd die. The seer said, "You will die on a Jewish holiday."

Hitler said, "What day is that?"

The seer said, "Any day you die will be a Jewish holiday!"

ghosts

I don't believe in ghosts. I can see right through them!

A young boy was spending the night in a haunted room. At midnight there was an eerie scratching sound and a voice said, "There's only you and me, there's only you and me."

The boy jumped up. "Let me get my pants. There'll soon be only you!"

Then there was the ghost who was a bed wetter. He went around in a rubber sheet!

Two ghosts were arguing. One wanted to do something difficult. The other ghost said, "You don't stand a man of a chance!"

A Klansman died on the way to a gathering. His body drifted up to the entrance of heaven reserved for ghosts. The angel at the desk said to another angel nearby, "We're getting them already dressed now!"

A ghost was assigned to a new territory. After a few days he asked the boss ghost, "Can I go back to my old haunts?"

gifts

I knew a chorus girl who used to say, "It takes all the fun out of a diamond bracelet if you have to buy it yourself!"

A man, in to have a watch repaired, saw a friend buying a fancy pearl necklace. The man asked, "An anniversary gift?"

The friend said, sighing, "No—a fight!"

I give people fruit liquors. They seem to like the fruit and the spirit in which it's given!

They say it's better to give than to receive. I say it depends on the gift!

'Twas the month after Christmas and Santa had flit.
A letter came for Pop that said, "Please remit!"

FIRST KID: Thanks very much for the gift you gave me for my birthday.
SECOND KID: It was nothing.
FIRST KID: That's what I thought, but Mom said I had to thank you anyway!

It's the kind of gift you take out of the box while you're looking for the present!

I gave her a gift that keeps on giving—a pregnant cat!

When it comes to giving, some people stop at nothing.

The trouble with some folks who give until it hurts is that they are sensitive to pain!

Miss Emily was everybody's favorite spinster. Every year, for her birthday, she received dozens of little gifts from friends and family. Year after year the knickknacks were added to, and soon filled every corner of the house. On her hundredth birthday, her niece asked what she wanted this year. Miss Emily said, "I'll take a kiss. Anything I don't have to dust!"

A man walked into a stationery store and asked for a nice pen. The clerk said, "A surprise?"

The man said, "It will be. My daughter's expecting a car!"

I know the perfect gift for the man who has everything—a burglar alarm!

"What do you give a man who has everything?"
"The latest antibiotic!"

When I was a kid, they bought me a bat. I took it out in the street to play with it, and it flew away!

girls

Until I was nine, I thought girls were just soft boys!

Girls are dynamite. If you don't believe that, try dropping one.

One sixteen-year-old had received a friendship ring from her beau. None of the girls in her class seemed to notice it. Finally she sighed and said, "It's so warm in here. I think I'll take off my ring."

She's like a photograph of her father and a phonograph of her mother!

Two young boys were talking about girls, One said, "I like that Alice Brown. Every day last week I walked her to school. I carried her books, too. I did her homework. And yesterday I bought her a soda. What do you think—should I kiss her?"

The other boy said, "I don't think so. You've done too much for her already!"

Girls who look good in the best places get taken there a lot!

She was wild when I met her, but now I've got her eating out of my pocket!

She knew her oats. That's what they fed her!

"She's a knockout."
"That pretty?"
"No, she's just a good boxer!"

She's one of those unemployed schoolteachers—no class and no principles!

Never marry a girl who can open envelopes with her breath!

I wouldn't marry a girl I'd met at a police lineup!

Never marry a girl who uses Raid as a deodorant!

I'd stay away from women who bathe only in months without an *R!*

"My girl has the face of an eighteen-year-old."
"Tell her to give it back. She's getting it wrinkled!"

She was a cover girl. When a guy met her, he ran for cover!

Her boyfriend adored her. He even bought her a diamond for her leash!

"**M**y boyfriend has dandruff."
"Give him Head and Shoulders."
"Really? How do you give shoulders?"

"**I** got my girl something she can't get into."
"Get her another dress."
"What dress. It's a VW!"

A woman walked into her nineteen-year-old daughter's room. She was aghast to find her daughter in bed, but lying next to her was a handsome young man with the face and figure of an Adonis. The mother asked what was going on.

The daughter explained, "I was walking through the woods on my way home last night. I heard a plaintive croaking coming from the pond. I saw this tiny frog who seemed to be talking. He told me that he was really a prince and had been put under a spell. If I brought him home and slept with him, he'd become a prince again. You can see that it worked. The spell is broken."

The mother said, "I wouldn't believe that story if he wasn't green!"

"**I**t's my birthday."
"Many happy returns. How old aren't you?"

A young lady was rather discouraged at her lack of a boyfriend. Her friend told her, "There's a man for every woman and a woman for every man. You can't change that."

The young lady said, "I don't want to change it. I just want to get in on it!"

She refused to go to bed with him because they weren't married. He married her. He carried her across the threshold. She took off her lashes, her makeup, her padded bra, and her girdle. When she was through, he re-spected her. He didn't recognize her, but he respected her!

She said, "If I stay with you all night, I'll hate myself in the morning."

He said, "Sleep late!"

She named her baby Diploma because she brought it home from college!

She must have been descended from Egyptian queens. Every time he made a wrong move, she said, "Tut, tut!"

One father said to another, "I noticed that your daughter didn't come in until three in the morning. Mine was in by one."

The other father said, "I know, but my daughter *walked* home!"

girls (insults)

Would you believe I have over eight hundred "girl" insults in my files? However, I'll never use one if it can really hurt. I do suggest, however, that ugly people stay home more!

Men should have a little respect for her, and most men do!

She always walks the straight and narrow, because that's the way she's built!

She caught her boyfriend making love. That's as good a way as any!

She swore she was a virgin when they met. She also swore because!

She doesn't care whom she makes love to. She's an equal-opportunity enjoyer!

She's so unpopular, she used to go to Lover's Lane and try to pick up a cop!

She must be very capable. She's worked under a lot of men!

She wanted to see something in fur, so her boyfriend took her to the zoo.

She must be a taxidermist. She'll mount anything!

All her jobs are temporary. As soon as the boss's wife sees her, she's gone!

She made Phi Beta Kappa—one by one!

She has a million-dollar figure, but the top half is counterfeit.

She looks like a million dollars—all green and crumply.

She hates sex in the movies. She tried it once and the seat folded up!

She uses so much perfume, when she stands still she makes a puddle!

She's Miss Frigid. She could be a test pilot for chastity belts!

The other night she was in bed with a man and didn't say one word. She never talks to strangers!

Men fall for her so hard they even lose their balance in the bank!

She recently ran into somebody she knew when they were the same age.

She's been crazy about boys ever since she found out she wasn't one.

She found a way of getting rid of temptation. She yields to it!

She couldn't get jumped if she was playing checkers!

She talks so much she's listed in *The Guinness Book of Broken Records!*

She never makes the same mistake twice. She always finds new ones!

She could turn a date into an allergy!

She's the last of the lukewarm mamas!

By comparison, she loses!

She'd love mud-wrestling if it wasn't for the bath afterward!

She'd never hurt a fly. She eats them whole!

god

There are no atheists in foxholes or onstage!

Most people pray collect!

Two guppies were flitting about in a tank when one of them announced that he no longer believed in God. The other guppy was aghast and said, "All right, don't believe in God, but then you tell me who changes the water!"

God isn't dead. He's just getting a second opinion!

"He's changing his religion."
"You mean he no longer believes he's God?"

A great epitaph for a waiter: "God finally caught his eye!"

A youngster, trying to help his impoverished parents, sent a letter to God. In it there was a request for twenty dollars. The letter arrived at the main post office in Washington, where it was read by the postmaster. Feeling sorry for the youngster, the postmaster sent a return letter in which he included a ten-dollar bill.

A few weeks later, a letter came back from the boy. It said, "God, thanks so much, but the next time you send me money, don't let it come from Washington. They keep half!"

God took six days to complete the world. But that was in the days before building permits.

Her looks were made in heaven, which may be why God took a day off.

I don't like to be interrupted while I'm saying a prayer. There's something about putting God on hold . . .

What if God takes the Earth back to the shop?

I think one of these days God will ask to have his name removed from our money. He doesn't want to go into Chapter Eleven.

gold diggers

I knew a few of them. They all used the males to defraud! Some of them even loved a man for all he was worth! But after all, a person has a right to pick her friends, and a gold digger picks them clean!

She's not dumb. She knows a good thing when she sues it.

You know what they say—a man and his money are some party!

He's got what it takes, and she's taking what he's got.

They met in an interesting way—he opened his wallet and there she was!

A great way for a girl to get a mink is to find a wolf and skin him.

One day I told her about my rich uncle. Now she's my rich aunt.

Half of the women in the country are working women. The other half are working men!

Mary was miserable because her ninety-year-old grandfather had married his twenty-year-old nurse. Discussing the event with her husband, Al, she said, "I can grasp what December sees in June, but what can June see in December?"

Al answered, "Christmas!"

A chorus girl asked another if she'd marry a rich old man. The second chorus girl said, "Honey, if somebody offered you a check for a million dollars, would you stop to look at the date?"

One gold digger told another, "He's old enough to be my father, but he's rich enough to be my husband!"

The easier she is on the eye, the harder she is on the pocketbook!

"Your heart is harder than steel. Nothing can soften it."
"Try diamonds!"

One thing about a gold digger—she's as strong as her weakest wink!

She drives a conversible. Everybody's talking about how she got it!

She likes to wear black garters in memory of those who have passed beyond.

golf

This used to be my game until one day I took a swing off the tee and a man watching asked, "Does your husband play too?"

Golf has let the cows out to pasture and let the bull in!

Sunday is the day when most of us bow our heads. Some of us are praying and the rest are playing golf.

As the pro told him, he kept his head down. While his head was down, somebody stole his golf cart!

Golf is *flog* spelled backward!

I like to play golf. I get to hit the ball more often than anybody!

You can tell a boss and the employee. The employee is the one who makes a hole in one and says, "Oops!"

Two ants sat on the grass watching a duffer dig up the course. One said to the other, "Let's get on the ball before he kills us!"

What a game. You can spend your whole day with hookers and your wife doesn't care!

Two can live as cheaply as one can play golf.

This morning I missed a hole in one by eight strokes!

I played golf during a hurricane. I got a hole in none!

Gold isn't too expensive for me. I can't hit the balls far enough to lose them!

The prospective bride rushed up to the prospective groom on the first tee. The groom looked at her in her bridal finery and said, "I told you—only if it rained!"

You can always tell the golfers in church. When they put their hands together to pray, they use an interlocking grip.

"What do you think I ought to leave for the caddy?"
"Your clubs!"

A behavioral scientist taught an ape to play golf. One day he tested his work on a real golf course. The ape teed off and hit the ball four hundred yards on the fly. The ball landed two feet from the cup. The ape studied his position, then took another swing and hit the ball another four hundred yards.

My doctor told me to play thirty-six holes a day, so I went out and bought a harmonica.

Two men are playing. One of them is bubbling over with enthusiasm, having taken some lessons earlier. Looking toward the next hole, a dogleg about two hundred yards away, he says, "I'm going to sink this mother in two strokes."
Teeing up, he swings and sends the ball about ten feet from the tee. Still not fazed, he says, "Now for one hell of a putt!"

Last week I played with my boss. On the first tee, he topped the ball and it landed fifty feet away from the tee and three hundred from the green. I conceded the putt.

A man was waiting on the green of the hole his group was playing. A ball zoomed out of the sky and hit him in the head. The hitter came running over and the victim said, "I'm going to sue for five thousand dollars."

The hitter said, "I said 'fore.'"

The victim said, "I'll take it!"

As a group of men were preparing to leave the green for the next hole, a ball rolled up from another player on the fairway. A gleam filled their eyes and one of them nudged the ball into the cup. A minute later, a heavyset player came up to them. "Did you men see a ball around here anywhere?"

One of the foursome said, "It went into the cup."

The heavyset player was surprised beyond belief at his good fortune. Retrieving the ball, he yelled back to his own companions, "Fellers, I got a twelve!"

Last year the Russians invented a game that resembles golf. I think I've been playing it for years!

"You're so involved with golf, you don't even remember the day we got married."

"Sure I do. It was the afternoon after I sank a forty-foot putt."

You can always tell when the boss has retired. More members of the staff start to beat him.

After a round of a hundred and forty-two, the golfer said to his caddy, "Am I the worst golfer you ever caddied for?"

The caddy said, "I'm not about to say that, but I've been in spots today I never knew were on the property."

You should worry about playing with a guy who writes down his score and then wipes his fingerprints from the pencil.

The duffer swung, saying, "I'd move heaven and earth to break a hundred and twenty."

His companion said, "Work on heaven. You've moved enough earth already!"

With the price of golf gear today, it's not only the clubs that can get the shaft!

Two chubby duffers, ordered to play golf by their physicians, managed to get to the first tee. One duffer said, "I don't have the energy to play too long."

The other one said, "Okay. We'll quit as soon as either one of us gets a hole in one!"

The minister was out on the course with one of his flock. The man was given to quick bursts of temper and well-chosen cusswords when the ball didn't bounce well for him. Unable to stand the profanity, the minister said, "I've played golf with some of the finest players in the country. Last week I played with a man who went six under par for this course. I didn't hear one word of profanity from him."

The player said, "What the hell did he have to curse about?"

The club pro walked over to a duo of ladies and asked, "Do either of you want to learn how to play good golf?"

One of the women answered, "Maybe my friend would. I learned yesterday!"

The game of the century was about to be played by two women who'd each taken one lesson. The first lady approached the tee, set herself, pulled back the club, and hit the ball with all her power. The ball hooked off to the left at a ninety-degree angle, hit the roof of the pro shop, ricocheted to a tall tree, bounced between the trunk of the tree and the trunks of a grouping of three others, was whipped forward by a snapping tree limb, bounded off, hit a large rock, rolled forward, and slowly rolled into the cup for a hole in one.

The second woman frowned and said, "Why didn't you tell me you've been practicing?"

I have a friend who needs psychological help. He treats golf as if it were a game!

Two men were playing golf together for the first time. The first player teed off and hit the ball into a clump of trees. Finally on the fairway, he swung again and sliced a new ball into a deep water hazard. A third swing resulted in a new ball flying over the fence onto a busy street. The second player said, "You should use an old ball."

The first player said, "I never *had* an old ball!"

Sitting at the bar after a game, Joe said to a club member, "I'm not about to play golf with Jim Walsh anymore."

"Why not?"

"Well, he found his lost ball two feet from the green."

"That's possible."

"Not when I had the ball in my pocket!"

After a rough eighteen holes, the neophyte asked the club regular with whom he'd played, "What do you think of my game?"

The regular said, "It's okay, but I'd rather play golf!"

The golf pro started his lesson by telling the duffer, "Go through the motion of the swing without driving the ball."

The duffer said, "That's the problem I'm taking lessons for!"

I got a hole in one the other day, but I'm going crazy trying to figure out how to mount it!

A golfer rushed into the locker room and said to his anxious cohorts, "I almost didn't make it. A lot of work showed up at the office and it was a toss-up whether I'd stay there or join. On the fifteenth toss, you won!"

A golfer had had a little too much at the club bar before going out to play. Through a combination of training and skill he reached the first green in twelve strokes. After the fourth putt he was still forty feet from the cup. Looking up as his next shot crossed the green and went into the distant trap, he said, "I wish you'd stop interfering with my game. Tilt the green once more and I quit!"

Two men reached the ninth hole of a difficult course. The hazard on the hole was a ravine about as deep as the Grand Canyon. One player managed to get his ball on the green. The other watched his ball disappear into the darkness of the ravine. Rather than take the penalty, the player went down to play out his ball. As the sun sank in the west, the ball finally bobbed out onto the green. A moment later, the player appeared and said, "Not bad for three strokes."

His partner said, "I heard at least six strokes."

The player said, "Three of them were echoes."

The duffer had been out for three hours

and was still on the first nine. As he planned his next missed shot, his caddy lay down on the grass nearby. The duffer said, "You must be pooped from carrying my clubs so long."

The caddy said, "I'm not tired of carrying, but I'm sure tired of counting!"

A member of the foursome dropped dead on the fifth hole. One of the other players returned home later and was asked by his wife if he'd had a nice day. He answered, "It was terrible. We played, then we had to drag him. Then we played and dragged, played and dragged . . ."

A minister went out to play one afternoon. On the fifth hole he missed a putt by a tenth of an inch. He shook his head and said, "Drat."

His caddy said, "Padre, cursing like that, you'll never break par!"

I bought a dozen golf balls the other day. The clerk asked, "Shall I wrap them up?"

I said, "No, I'll drive them home."

Then there's the Scotchman who gave up golf after twenty years. He lost his ball.

I've got more ways to slice than a delicatessen counterman!

It's a wise golf course that knows its own par.

An irate golfer threw away his last club. The caddy watched, then said, "How about your sweater? Will you be wanting that?"

"Isn't Joe out of the bunker yet? How many strokes has he had?"
"Fifteen club and one apoplectic!"

The duffer reacted as the caddy laughed, saying, "If you laugh again, I'll knock your block off."

The caddy laughed, the duffer came at him with a club, and missed!

good times

When you're down in the mouth, just think of Jonah. He came out all right!

The world is in some shape. Pessimists never had it so good!

Things are getting better. I only need one more raise so my take-home pay can equal the deductions.

Half the battle is looking prosperous. The other half is trying to get credit on how you look.

They said things wouldn't get better until we worked harder. So we worked harder, and they were right—things didn't get better!

gossip

Over the years, people have said about me that I'm an egomaniac, power-mad, and vicious. Then there are others who lie about me! I don't mind gossip. I subscribe to the show-business axiom, "I don't care what they say, as long as they talk about me." I recall that some time back I hired a press agent who was supposed to plant items in all the newspapers. A month went by and my name wasn't mentioned once. Accosting him, I asked, "Where are the plugs?"

He said, "They're all talking about you."

Another month. Not one mention in a newspaper or magazine. I asked what was going on. He said, "They're all talking about you."

A third month passed and again he said, "They're all talking about you."

I said, "What are they saying?"

He said, "'Whatever happened to Milton Berle?'"

It's terrible when people talk about you. It's almost as bad as when they *don't* talk about you.

A gossip is somebody who syndicates her [or his] conversation.

Wind a gossip up and she'll run somebody down.

Gossips are the spies of life.

"Dad, Mom says that half the world doesn't know how the other half lives."
"Son, she shouldn't blame herself. It's not her fault!"

You can't believe everything you hear, but you can repeat it.

"Did you tell everybody?"
"No, I didn't know it was supposed to be a secret!"

The best thing about a gossip is that she [or he] usually is talking about somebody who's more interesting than she [or he] is.

The town gossip managed to find Reverend Brown walking quietly of an evening. Unable to resist practicing her hobby, she joined the minister in his walk and, for two hours, told him every bit of idle rumor in the town. Finishing, she said, "Reverend Brown, when I met you before I had a bad migraine. Just talking to you made it disappear. It's gone."

The minister said, "Of course it is. I have it!"

gossip (insults)

Have no mercy with these!

She gossips so much her ear has a fence attached to it!

She hates for people to talk when they only have something to say!

She has a lot of friends—to speak of.

After all is said and done, he never is.

She's like an old shoe. Everything's worn out but the tongue.

She's an amazon—big at the mouth!

Gold is the only thing she hasn't panned.

She doesn't like to repeat gossip, but what else is there to do with it?

She's got a keen sense of rumor.

His mouth is so big he can whisper in his own ear!

gourmets and gourmands

My wife made one thing that enabled me to enjoy food—reservations at a good restaurant! Actually, I have a trained palate and eat well. I feel that I deserve it after years of eating on the road. I used to think that heartburn was a way of life. I'll give you the best idea—I used to check into hospitals for the food!

Everybody is a gourmet today. The other

day I heard a man specify the vintage when he ordered club soda.

"The food in this restaurant is garbage."
"I know, and such small portions!"

"Does Jimmy eat between meals?"
"Jimmy has no between meals!"

There was a young lady of York
Whose dad made a fortune in cork.
He bought for his daughter
A tutor who taught her
To balance petit pois *on her fork!*

I tried to order from a menu in French and ended up with an order of well-done "Watch your hat and coat!"

A man orders a lobster in a restaurant. The waiter returns with his order, but the crustacean has a broken claw. The man asks what happened. The waiter says, "He was in a fight."
    The man says, "Go back and get me the winner!"

A man sits down at a table in Scandia, the fanciest Swedish restaurant in the city. At the waiter's inquiry, the man says, "I'll have the endive salad with your wine vinegar dressing, a tart, and coffee."
    The waiter says, "Take the herring appetizer too."
    The man says, "I don't want the herring appetizer."
    The waiter says, "It's a part of the luncheon."
    "All right, bring it."
    The waiter returns with a long, thin Icelandic herring. The man looks at it and sees the herring's eyes staring at him. The man is unable to eat.
    The next day he comes back for lunch and orders creamed onion soup with croutons, chocolate mousse, and a glass of red wine.
    The waiter says, "Will you have the herring appetizer?"
    "I don't want it."
    "It's part of the luncheon."
    "All right, bring it."
    A few moments later the man finds himself staring down at a herring that is staring back at him. The man is unable to eat.
    The next day, the man goes to another Swedish restaurant and orders another meal. The new waiter asks about the herring appetizer. Rather than battle again, the man accepts it. He looks down at the herring, which looks up at him and says, "Don't tell me you've given up on Scandia!"

"What do you call a Pole who chases a garbage truck?"
"A galloping gourmet!"

government

Where else but in the government could you find the following: A clerk is told to destroy a whole series of documents because there isn't enough space to store them. But, the order goes on: he is to make a copy first!

Try explaining to the kids why a government that just spent sixty million on nuclear bombs is trying to outlaw firecrackers.

In communism, everybody shares equally in getting the short end of the stick from the government. Capitalism makes longer sticks.

To err is human. To shrug is civil service.

Government regulations are like salad dressing—you get too much or too little!

Some cutbacks are ridiculous—coin-operated guns?

The government just put a wonderful machine in all of its buildings. It does the work of six people. Of course, it takes twelve to operate it.

The head of a government office retired recently. His staff threw a party for him, gave him a watch, and also told him what his job had been!

A contractor wanted to grease the wheels for a deal by offering the government agent a small token of appreciation. The contractor asked if the agent would mind having a nice foreign sports car. The agent was indignant.
"I can't accept a gift like that. It's a bribe!"
The contractor said, "Would it be all right if I *sold* you the sports car?"
"For how much?"
"Ten dollars."
"In that case, I'll take two!"

I think I could take care of my government obligations, but I'm rather sneaky. I'm keeping a family on the side!

I appreciate the way the government spends billions on weapons, bombs, chemical warfare, and anti-missile missiles. I know that the government would use these things in a constructive way!

I found a great way to show that crime doesn't pay—let the government run it!

Some government officials are so economy-minded. They manage to save a million dollars a year on a salary of thirty thousand!

A government worker is an ass upon which everyone has sat except a man!

"Do you know anybody who favors government ownership of the railroads?"
"One guy—he's a conductor, his son's a train engineer, and he's got two grandsons who want to be brakemen."

The nearest thing to immortality is a government bureau.

A Vietnamese applied for citizenship. He was asked, "Who is the President?"
The Vietnamese answered quickly.
"Could you become the President?"
"No."
"Why not?"
"I very busy in restaurant!"

graduation

I cried at my son's graduation. My accountant just sat back and grinned!

A graduation is where a commencement speaker tells five hundred graduates all dressed the same that individuality is what makes the world tick!

Nowadays, when a speaker tells the graduates that the future is theirs—is that a promise or a threat?

Graduates are told that the future is theirs. Then they go look for work and find that the present isn't!

Graduation is when the real world beckons to the students, but not necessarily with the right finger.

My son graduated six months ago, but he's still not ready to look for a job. He doesn't realize that *commencement* means "to begin"!

School really readies a student for life. My nephew bought a tie last week and wondered if it came with instructions!

When she posed for her graduation album, she didn't have to pose with the rest of the class for a group picture. She was a group picture!

She was so ugly she was barred from her graduation yearbook!

A grandfather is a man who can't understand how his idiot son has such brilliant children!

A grandmother was educating her granddaughter. "My dear," she said, "there are several words in your vocabulary that aren't ladylike. One is 'good' and the other is 'lousy.'"

The granddaughter said, "Tell me what they are. I won't use them anymore!"

I don't mind being a grandfather, except that it means I have to sleep with a grandmother!

grandparents

My grandchildren swear by me. They think I'm funny. I send them gifts. I'm patient. I send them gifts. I'm helpful. I send them gifts! Somehow, I have the feeling that if a grandfather became an astronaut, on his return, the grandchildren would ask, "What did you bring us?"

"Did I ever tell you about my grandchildren?"
"No, and I appreciate it very much!"

A grandmother proudly wheeled her grandchild into the park. An acquaintance came by, peeked into the carriage, and said, "My, what a gorgeous child."

The grandmother said, "Wait till you see her pictures!"

A grandmother is a woman who's thrilled because her grandchild can recite the Gettysburg Address at eight when Lincoln didn't do it until he was much older!

He told her that he wanted some old-fashioned loving, so she introduced him to her grandmother!

groceries

One supermarket has just come out with a brilliant new invention—a shopping cart that goes in the same direction as the customer! I also have learned how to cut down on the cost of food. I fill a basket, get in the express checkout, and keep eating until I'm down to eight items!

A woman asked a grocer, "Are these eggs fresh?"

Walking toward the display, the grocer said, "Let me feel them to see if they're cool enough to sell!"

Most of us must be getting stronger. Last year I couldn't carry twenty dollars' worth of groceries. This year it's easy!

"How much are the apples?"
"Ten cents each, ma'am."
"I'll take one."
"Oh, you must be throwing a party!"

One supermarket chain has lost so many shopping carts, it's started to print their pictures on milk cartons!

When my wife goes into a supermarket, she tastes everything. She nibbles at cookies, loose candy, produce, anything that isn't sealed in steel. Last month she put on eight pounds and never got a receipt!

I'm always careful when I go through market doors. What if the electric eye is near-sighted?

I waited until the new checker finished ringing up my grocery purchases, then I said, "Miss, you don't know me, but could you bag my groceries in a special way? Break four of the eggs in the carton and then put the carton on the bottom of the bag so the yellows will leak out. Then tear the bread wrapper so the bread gets all clammy from the wet lettuce you're going to put next to it. Then put the cans on top so the cans squoosh the tomatoes. And make sure the bag is torn."

The checker said, "I can't do that, sir."

I said, "Why not? The regular checker does!"

gypsies (crystal balls and séances)

Years ago, there was a headlining act that consisted of gypsy violinists. The conductor swore that he was a real gypsy. Another conductor laughed at him and refused to believe that he had gypsy blood coursing through his veins. The first leader said, "All right, I'll show you. I'll go to a store and steal something!" Another time, a member of the ensemble was late for work. Asked why, he explained, "My wife went to a baby shower and I was waiting for the earrings!"

A man goes to a gypsy fortune-teller who says, "For twenty dollars, I'll read your future and you can ask three questions."

"About what?"

"About anything."

"Isn't twenty a lot of money?"

"Not too much. Now, what is your last question?"

I know a man who made a fortune opening a string of empty stores for gypsies!

A woman paid a fortune to a medium, hoping that she'd be able to contact her ex-husband, a waiter. A séance was set up. A group of people gathered at the medium's table. Eerie music filled the dark room. Suddenly a tapping was heard. The medium said, "I'm in contact with your husband."

The woman said, "Let me talk to him."

The medium concentrated for a moment, then said, "I'm afraid he can't talk to you. This isn't his table."

Then there was the dumb gypsy who was told to read palms. She couldn't figure out how to climb them.

Then there was the gin rummy seance. The departed knocked, but one of the people at the table undercut him.

One gypsy discovered that she could increase her business by reading instant tea.

H

habits

During the run of a show I was in, one of the other stars, an older actor who played "grandfather" roles, used to bite his nails. We tried not to watch him, but our eyes were always drawn to the total dedication with which he chomped down to the cuticles. One afternoon his wife came in with a smile on her face. She told us that he hadn't bitten his nails all day. Asked how that had happened, she said, "I hid his teeth!" Many comedians have a habit or two that serve them well and may even have become gimmicks or trademarks. A habit-gimmick can help you punctuate your comedy. If you tell an audience verbally that a funny line is on the way, it will generally punish you with silence or at best a titter. Scratching an eyelid, puffing on a cigar, rolling your finger on your lip—visual hints— let the audience know in an acceptable way that you're preparing a whopper. The audience feels that you may be unaware of the move and then laugh because you think the joke is funny. Then, of course, there's the bad habit of overanalyzing comedy!

Every once in a while a guy without a single bad habit gets caught!

An army colonel retired and took along the orderly who'd worked for him over twenty years. The colonel told the orderly that his job would be the same one he'd had in the army. The first morning after being hired, the orderly came into the colonel's room and woke him. Then the orderly slapped the colonel's sleeping wife and said, "Okay, honey, it's back to camp for you!"

A man tells a co-worker, "I can't break my wife of the habit of staying up till five in the morning."

"What is she doing?" the co-worker asks.

"Waiting for me to get home!"

From the first day of his marriage, Tom had spent every Tuesday evening with the guys. One Tuesday, however, he left the house and didn't return. Ten years later he walked into the house. His wife was thrilled to see him and said, "I'm so glad you're home. Let me make a special dinner tonight. We'll have champagne and wine and candlelight."

Tom said, "Don't you know this is Tuesday?"

Joe, a new man, asked Phil at the next desk for a cigarette. Phil obliged. A moment later, Joe asked for a match. Phil again obliged. Then Joe asked, "Do you have an ashtray?"

Phil said, "Pal, you've got nothing but the habit, have you?"

The cost of living is the difference between your net income and your gross habits!

Tommy had worked in a grocery store before he became a hotel desk clerk. When a man walked over to the desk and asked, "Is a Mr. Walter Barnes staying here?" Tommy looked at the register and answered, "No, but we have something even better!"

He was a theater critic. The victim of a

terminal disease, he was bedridden. The end was in sight, so he got up and left five minutes before!

A man bragged, "For ten years my habits were like clockwork. I got up at six, had breakfast at seven, and at seven-fifteen I was at work."

Another man nearby said, "No kidding? What were you in for?"

A boss tried to help one of his employees improve his ways by telling him, "You have one bad habit. You never listen when people are talking to you. You get a faraway look and your mind wanders off. Promise me you'll work on that."

The employee responded, "What was that you were saying?"

One bank robber got into trouble when he tried to rob a local branch. The teller wouldn't accept his holdup note without identification!

I just can't break some habits. I worked my way through college. Now I'm working my son's way through!

hair and hairiness

I never thought about hair much, but a few weeks ago I went to my barber and he suggested Astroturf!

There was so much hair on her face she had handlebar eyebrows!

A woman came into the den with her hair topheavy with curlers and clamps. Her husband looked at her, puzzled. The woman said, "I just set my hair."

The husband said, "What time does it go off?"

Two old women met on the street. One said, "What did you do to your hair? Good heavens, it looks like a wig."

The other woman said, "It *is* a wig."

The first one said, "Really? I could never tell!"

Once there was a teenager who spent a whole year trying to find himself. He got his hair cut and there he was.

She dyed her hair so often she slept in a vat!

She had something that men want—a mustache!

She has so much hair on her face—when she shaves, streetlights dim!

Nothing makes gray hair more attractive than baldness!

She parted her hair sideways. Her dates went crazy, whispering in her nose!

How do you explain it to children that Dad gets grayer and Mom gets blonder?

She didn't shave her legs much. Most of the time she just put them up in curlers!

She has a lot of long hair under her arms—one day she sneezed and almost whipped herself to death!

She has so much hair on her face, her electric razor has three speeds—slow, fast, and "Timber!"

A barber looked at a young man's head of greasy hair and asked whether he wanted a cut or just an oil change.

He was so hairy he didn't have to wear clothes. When he was planning to go out, he just buttoned up his body!

She used to pluck her eyebrows—if the lawnmower wasn't available!

A Hollywood actor went to a stylist and asked for a great haircut. The actor was going to London for a command performance and would be meeting the Queen. The stylist did his best. A few weeks later the actor returned. Back in the stylist's chair, he described his trip. The flight over to England was magnificent. In London, he'd had three gorgeous days. The command performance had gone splendidly. After the show, he'd been granted a private audience with the Queen. The stylist said, "Tell me what happened, tell me!"

The actor said, "She leaned over and said, 'Who gave you that lousy haircut?'"

She had bobbed hair—under her chin!

She was so hairy she didn't need a fur coat—she *was* a fur coat!

She's so hairy her knees have bangs!

She not only has pigtails—she oinks!

She's so hairy she has to shave twice and then dynamite the stumps!

Her legs belong to a religious group—the Hairy Krishnas!

Her legs are so hairy she has to shampoo her knees!

He's got so much hair on his chest, he could hide guerrillas!

When she shaves under her arms, she starts at her ankles!

She used to sit and play with his hair. Then one day she got his scalp.

His hair is so long, other men won't undress in front of him!

Fleas love her hair. They leave their babies there.

He has no hair, but he still has dandruff.

He's got so much dandruff, snowplows follow him!

My son has so much hair we had to let out his beanie twice!

halloween

On Halloween, I really knew how to scare people. I rang their bell and did my act!

She was so ugly, Frankenstein came to the Halloween party as *her!*

She looked as if she'd gone to a Halloween party and forgotten to come back!

Last Halloween I opened my door and there were my three kids, dressed up as the scariest things I could imagine—my three kids!

Last Halloween I really scared my brother. I went over to his house dressed as a job!

You know you're not much on looks when you can go trick-or-treating dressed as is!

On Halloween, a little boy knocked on my door. He took a look at my wife in her mudpack and gave *her* candy!

Years ago, kids used chalk on Halloween. They'd mark up a man's pants if he didn't pay off. One kid liked it so much he grew up and became a tailor.

On Halloween, little girls get to dress up in Mommy's old clothes. Boys can't wear Daddy's old clothes, because Daddy's still wearing them!

happiness

John Barrymore told me this a long time ago: Happiness always sneaks in through a door you didn't know was open! That's good enough for me!

Money doesn't make you happy. Is a man with eight million happier than a man with seven?

Happiness is coming home and finding your girl in a two-piece outfit—a left and right slipper!

A man doesn't know what true happiness is until he gets married. Then it's too late.

Money can't buy happiness. It just helps you look for it in more places.

When happiness shows up, give it a comfortable seat.

A widow went to a seance in hopes of contacting her recently departed husband. The spirits were willing, and she soon heard his voice: "Honey, is that really you?"
   "Yes, my dear."
   "Are you happy?"
   "I'm happy."
   "Happier than you were with me?"
   "Yes, my dear."
   "Oh, heaven must be a wonderful place."
   "What makes you think I'm in heaven?"

One hour in paradise isn't bad either!

hash

In theatrical boardinghouses, hash was generally the main dish at dinner. Anybody who could identify any of the ingredients got seconds!

"What's the connecting link between the animal and vegetable kingdoms?"
"I think it's hash!"

"Do you believe in reincarnation?"
"I eat it every day. It's called hash!"

You don't make hash—it accumulates!

Hash, like life, is what you make it.

Hash is what you get when a cook puts all she has into her cooking!

Hash in a restaurant makes me shaky because I don't know what they put in it. Of course, I'm also shaky at home because I *know* what's put into it!

hawaii

The most famous personality in Hawaii is the singer Don Ho. When I go to Hawaii I always stay in his house—the Ho house!

The hotels in Hawaii are classy. I stayed in one that had an air-conditioned steam room!

Two Hawaiians were doing the hula. As one made some moves with her arms, the other said, "Stop talking dirty!"

She was only a girl from Hawaii, but oh, what a lei!

At a Hawaiian luau they eat with their fingers. I have a family at home like that!

They still have a lot of hippies in Hawaii. One day my wife put on a grass skirt and two of them tried to smoke it.

In Hawaii, some of the girls do everything under the sun!

After all, a hula is only a shake in the grass!

Hawaiians are taciturn. One Hawaiian worked in the pineapple fields hour after hour without exchanging a word with the man in the next row. After about ten hours, the Hawaiian finally spoke, saying, "Damp, no?"

The next day and the next, and for months afterward, the Hawaiian continued to work in the fields. Toward the end of the season, six months from the start, the Hawaiian spoke again to the man in the next row. "Damp, no?"

The man in the next row answered, "Complain, complain, complain, that's all some of you guys do!"

Hawaiians are proud of their heritage of mixed blood. In fact, recently they had a race riot in Honolulu, and the crowd couldn't figure out whom to scream at.

Some of the Hawaiian estates are huge. One rancher was bragging to a mainlander, "Do you know how big my place is? Why, I can get in my car, drive for ten hours, and still be on my property."

The mainlander said, "Back home we have cars like that too!"

health

I never complain. I merely think of the lifetime guarantees I've outlived! To keep me from appearing on other networks, NBC gave me a lifetime contract. I can't figure out why it ran out ten years ago!

People are healthier than ever. In a San Diego retirement home I saw a ten-speed wheelchair.

I've got bad arthritis, but I can't kick.

Poverty is helpful in medicine. If you have it, the doctor cures you faster.

The trouble with people is that they'll do anything in the world to feel better but give up what's hurting them.

You can tell if a man is healthy by what he takes two at a time—stairs or pills.

When Jewish people drink to your health, they say "L'chaim." I have an uncle doing L'chaim right now.

My teeth lack calcium. The other day I broke a tooth on Jell-O.

Tranquilizers let you go around with your head held . . . high.

I ruined my health by drinking to other people's.

I'm as sound as a dollar, but I'll get better.

I get winded winding up a conversation.

A patient said, "I'd like a second opinion."

The doctor said, "All right, I'll tell you again!"

I get out of breath winding up a digital watch.

I found a great way of keeping a head cold from my chest—I tie a knot in my throat.

I've had a lot of antibiotics lately. When I sneeze, I cure somebody!

At my age, my memory isn't too good. I went to a doctor for it, and he made me pay in advance!

I tried acupuncture a while back. Not feeling too good one evening, I called my acupuncturist. He told me, "Take one safety pin and call me tomorrow morning!"

I'm in such rotten shape, my health club makes me come in the rear entrance!

health foods

I haven't touched health foods since the day I ate some sunflower seeds, went out in the rain, and sprouted!

I've been drinking lots of carrot juice because it's good for my eyes. But I'm wondering if I'm not overdoing it. When I try to sleep, I can see through my eyelids!

Food addicts say that onions are a secret health food. But how do you keep them secret?

I stopped buying natural foods when I found out that eighty percent of people die from natural causes.

I won't eat organic foods. I need all the preservatives I can get.

One thing bothers me—how come the clerks in health-food stores look like death warmed over?

According to dieticians, there are four basic food groups—fresh, frozen, fast, and junk!

Health foods killed my uncle. They were in the truck that ran over him.

heaven

Lately, I've been thinking a lot about harps. I keep wondering what heaven'll be like with all those harps playing. On every cloud a harp. Nothing but harps. I may spend my time in heaven praying for just one accordion!

A shipment of husbands had just arrived. Saint Peter thought he'd speed up the processing, so he said, "I want all the husbands who acted like mice on Earth to form a line on the right. Those of you who were truly kings in your own castle, step to the left."

The men rushed to take their places. The line of henpecked husbands stretched beyond the horizon. One man stood in the other line. Saint Peter asked, "Are you sure you belong on the macho line?"

The man answered, "I don't know, but this is where my wife told me to stand!"

A man arrived at the processing station for heaven and was interrogated by the angel at the desk. The man allowed that he'd lived a good life. "However," he said, "I think I have one mark against me. When I was a young man, I played baseball for St. Petersburg. In a game against St. Paul I tried to score from second base on a single to the infield. I was called safe, but the fact is that I never touched the base. I never admitted that."

The angel said, "I'm aware of that incident."

The man said, "Oh, you are Saint Peter himself."

"No," the angel said, "I'm Saint Paul!"

Saint Peter and Saint Francis were playing

golf. At the end of six holes, each had six holes in one. Finally, Saint Peter said, "Look, let's forget about miracles and just play golf!"

A man arrived at the Pearly Gates. Saint Peter greeted him and started to ask the usual questions. On Earth, had he blasphemed, drank, smoked, caroused with women other than his wife, lied, cheated, or stolen?

The man said, "I was never guilty of one of those sins."

Saint Peter said, "What kept you so long?"

A woman arrived in heaven and asked that she be allowed to talk to the Virgin Mary. Finding nothing in the rulebooks against such a request, Saint Peter sent for the Virgin Mary. The woman kissed the Virgin Mother's hem and expressed incredible joy at being allowed to meet the object of her many prayers on Earth. Finally the woman said, "You must be so proud. Your son is worshipped on Earth. How does it feel to be the mother of a Savior?"

The Virgin Mary said, "To tell you the truth, we were hoping he'd be an accountant!"

Reverend Endicott died and went to heaven. Strolling through the clouds on his first day, he went hours without seeing another soul. At the end of the day he'd found only three other men. They didn't seem to be too happy. One explained that his afterlife was dull. He read all day, he napped, and once in a while he exercised. Puzzled, the reverend asked Saint Peter if a scouting trip to hell was possible. Saint Peter waved an okay.

The reverend found himself in a fiery region, but as he walked on, he heard music coming from the distance. He walked faster, almost breaking into a run, and soon arrived at a strange scene. He seemed to be in some kind of cabaret. People sat at the tables drinking and carousing. On the huge dance floor, thousands, perhaps millions, of people danced to a rock-and-roll ensemble with twenty guitarists, a dozen men at synthesizers, and drummers too numerous to count.

Now even more puzzled, the reverend asked to be returned to heaven. He asked Saint Peter, "How come Hell is dancing and music, and up here things are so quiet?"

Saint Peter answered, "Do you think we'd hire a band for just three people?"

A black man arrived at the Pearly Gates, only to be stopped by Saint Peter. The angel was apologetic but explained, "We're a little crowded right now. We can only take heroes."

The black man said, "I'm a hero."

"What did you do that was heroic?"

"I happened to marry a beautiful white girl on the steps of the county building in Manassas, Virginia, at high noon."

"And when did this happen?"

"About forty seconds ago."

The Sunday school teacher asked, "How many of you want to go to heaven?"

Every hand went up but Jeff's. The teacher asked, "Don't you want to go to heaven?"

Jeff said, "Not with this bunch going!"

Three astronauts showed up at the gates of Heaven. Saint Peter greeted them and asked if they wanted to come in. One astronaut said, "No, we'd just like our capsule back!"

A cardinal and a U. S. senator arrived in heaven at the same time. The cardinal was given the key to a small room, while the senator got the key to a huge penthouse. The cardinal asked, "Why do I get a tiny room and how come he gets special treatment?"

Saint Peter said, "Well, we've got lots of cardinals up here, but he's the first senator we ever saw!"

Tired of asking the same old questions of the day's arrivals, Saint Peter decided to ask about their automobiles. When asked what kind of car he'd driven, one said, "A Toyota." Saint Peter pushed a button and the applicant fell through a hole into the fiery depths below. A second drove a Mercedes. He too went down through the hole. A third said, "I drove a Chevy." Saint Peter opened the gates wide. "Come on in," he said. "You've been through hell already!"

It was anniversary time, a zillion years since heaven had been placed in the sky. To celebrate, Saint Peter wanted to have a big party, with the honored guests being Adam and Eve. Unfortunately, because of the heavy traffic over the eons, Saint Peter had lost track of Adam and Eve. One angel volunteered to find them. He returned in two minutes with Eden's former residents. Saint Peter asked, "How did you find them?"

The angel said, "I looked for a couple without bellybuttons!"

Saint Peter looked at a new arrival, checked in the book, and said, "You're not supposed to be here for five years. Who was your doctor?"

A woman checked in and asked to join her former husband, Walter Smith. Saint Peter said, "We have five million Walter Smiths. Give us a little clue."

The woman said, "My Walter is bald and

has blue eyes, and he said that if I ever slept with another man he'd turn over in his grave."

Saint Peter motioned an angel forward. "Take her to Whirling Walter!"

A famous man, known for everything but heart, arrived in heaven. Saint Peter asked, "What did you ever do on Earth that would qualify you for heaven?" The man thought and thought. Finally his face brightened. He said, "Forty years ago I gave a blind man a quarter."

Saint Peter turned to another angel and said, "Give him back his quarter and let him go to hell."

An oil wildcatter comes to the Pearly Gates but is told that the wildcatter limit in heaven has been reached. He can't gain entry unless another wildcatter is made to leave. The wildcatter thinks it over and comes up with a great idea. If Saint Peter will let him in for ten minutes, he'll start a rumor about an oil discovery in limbo. One or two of the wildcatters should bite. Saint Peter isn't averse to some fun, so he lets the wildcatter come in and play his prank. A minute after the rumor is spread, there is a stampede of wildcatters heading back into limbo. A few steps behind the last emigrant is the new wildcatter. Saint Peter asks, "Where are you going?"

The wildcatter says, "There could be something to that rumor!"

A nun dies, but her accommodations in heaven aren't ready. Saint Peter says, "Go back to Earth and call me in two weeks."

The following week, the nun calls, "Saint Peter, this is Sister Penelope. I'm in California. Everything is fine except that I had a drink the other day."

Saint Peter says, "That's no big deal. But

your room isn't ready. Call me next week."

The call comes the following week. "Saint Peter, this is Sister Penelope. I wish you'd hurry. But last night I went discoing."

"Discoing isn't so terrible. Call me again Tuesday."

Tuesday, another call is made. "Pete, this is Penny. Forget it!"

A Pope dies and enters heaven. He is given a personal tour by Saint Peter, who shows him all the accommodations and tells him, "You can see that all the accommodations are the same. Everybody is equal in heaven."

The Pope says, "Just as I expected."

They walk on and they come to a movie house. A man in a white coat with a stethoscope around his neck arrives, but instead of taking his place in line, he marches right to the front of the line, and enters the theater. The Pope says, "I thought everybody was equal here."

Saint Peter explains, "Oh, that's God. Once in a while he likes to play doctor!"

Saint Peter explains that in heaven the good are rewarded, the bad punished. Pointing out a man walking with an attractive woman, he says, "That man was almost a saint on earth. He gave a great deal of money and time to charity, so you can see he was rewarded."

They walk on and see another couple, an elderly man with a stunning young woman. Saint Peter says, "This man was a poet on Earth. He gave us lovely poems. You can see his reward."

They walk on and come to a third couple. The man is rotund, ugly, and talking boorishly. The woman, however, is much prettier than the first two. The newcomer says, "I recognize that man. He was a baseball umpire. Everybody hated him. How come he received such a reward?"

Peter said, "You got it a little wrong. He's her punishment!"

Two saintly men arrive in heaven. A mixup has resulted in their paperwork not being ready, so Saint Peter says, "You can go back to Earth for a while. To make up for the inconvenience, you can go back as anything you want to be. One man says, "I'd like to be a giant condor floating over the Rocky Mountains." The other says, "If you'll indulge me, I'd like to be a stud."

"Both wishes granted," says Saint Peter.

The next morning, because the new computer has speeded up processing, the paperwork arrives. Saint Peter tells an angel to go to Earth and fetch the two men.

The angel asks, "How will I find them?"

Saint Peter says, "One will be easy. He's in Colorado flying over the Rockies. You'll have to go to Montana for the other. He's somewhere in a snow tire!"

Saint Peter greets a Pennsylvania farmer, but announces that due to crowding he'll have to show that he merits a home in the clouds. He asks the farmer to tell him the story of the crucifixion.

The farmer tells the story beautifully and in complete detail. Saint Peter says, "That was a magnificent rendition of the first part of the story. What happened after the crucifixion?"

The farmer said, "There's a cave and they bury him in it. The stone rolls away from the entrance on the third day. He rises out of his tomb, comes outside, and if he sees his shadow that means we'll have a cold winter!"

heckle lines

Committed to memory, these lines will protect you against those who think they're funnier than you are, and who try to prove it except when it's their turn to speak! I think heckle is related to the word hackle, the long-toothed comb used to get knots out of certain fibers. Heckle lines can be used to comb loudmouths out of your hair!

Come over to my pool. I'll give you drowning lessons!

You're a man of the first water—a drip!

Why don't you freeze your teeth and give your tongue a sleigh ride?

You could give failure a bad name!

You have the makings of a perfect stranger!

If they ever put a price on your head, take it!

You have some great thoughts. Let them work their way up to your mouth!

You have a lot of get-up-and-go. Please do!

No wonder you were stood up at the father-daughter dance!

Try a mind reader. You can get in for half-price!

When you were born, your parents hit the jerk-pot!

Some guys are jerks, but you're making a career of it!

You've been compared to many people, and quite unfavorably too!

No wonder the FBI put you on the un-wanted list!

I could make a monkey out of you, but why should *I* take all the credit!

I like you. You've got the kind of face I'd like to shake hands with!

Youth will be served—and then carried out!

If he disappeared suddenly, it couldn't happen to a nicer guy!

I'd like to break you in half, but who wants two of you around?

You could be a distant relative . . . the farther the better!

Don't fall on your head. It'll knock you conscious!

It's lucky for you I'm a gentleman—and a coward!

When you get up in the morning, who puts you together?

Why make a monkey out of me? You already have a mate!

Miss, you're annoying the man I love!

Why don't you leave and let live?

I have no idea what makes you tick, but I hope it's a time bomb!

Why don't you go down to the shore and pull a wave over your head?

You have a ready wit. Let me know when it's ready!

He just made a big list—America's Ten Leading Nobodies!

If you want a battle of wits, I'll check mine and we'll start even!

Next time you give your old clothes away, stay in them!

Let's play Library. You be the "silence" sign.

You go too far, but you don't stay there!

If you ever need a friend, buy a dog!

Read a blank book and improve your mind!

Please throw your hat away, but leave your head in it!

I can see you believe in reincarnation. You came back as a wet blanket!

I've listened to your humble opinion—and it has every right to be!

I believe in human rights. You *are* human, right?

One of these days, you'll find yourself. You're in for some disappointment!

And a Happy Halloween to you, honey!

Don't you ever get tired of having yourself around?

Please try to act decent—or don't you do imitations?

I don't need your criticism. At home I have a wife and a teenage daughter!

If you have your life to live over, don't bother!

Can I see your X rays? I'd like to find out what your date sees in you!

Lady, you're a great argument for twin beds!

You have a fat chance to succeed, and a head to match!

If I've said something to insult you, I meant it!

Brains aren't everything. In your case they're nothing!

You're not yourself today, and I've noticed the improvement!

Go away. I'd like to forget you just the way you are!

He's not all here, and we're grateful!

Your doctor just called. Your spare mouth is ready!

heirs and heirlooms

There were no heirlooms in my family. Whenever we got something, we only held it long enough for the pawn shop to open!

A woman showed off her jewelry, and another woman asked, "Are those heirlooms?"

The other said, "Are they? Why, this necklace goes all the way back to Alfred, but the earrings are newer. They only date from the conquest!

Then there was the eighty-year-old man who was heir-minded but he just wasn't heir-conditioned!

Heirlooms are all the things your grandmother wanted more than money!

People always admire his family jewels—he wears earrings!

heroes and heroism

Cowards die many times. Heroes die only once. Those who look away and say they didn't see a thing live a long time!

Joe the gangster was found with thirty bullets in his back. The papers reported that he'd died from something that disagreed with him.

When I was in the army, I saved a hundred men. I killed the cook.

It's easy to be a hero from a safe distance.

He held off forty of the enemy with one bullet. If they'd had more ammo, it wouldn't have been so easy.

Nowadays the real hero in a movie is the one who sits through it.

He kept yelling, "Advance! Advance!" But his boss wouldn't give him one.

highbrows

I've tried the rarified air of culture, but I don't seem to fit. My wife told me that we were going to Swan Lake, *so I packed my* fishing *gear!*

I've been going to opera ever since I could walk. I knew Madame Butterfly when she was a cocoon.

I drink tea with my pinky out. Every time I take a sip, I blind the guy on my right.

Then there was the surgeon who loved culture. He went to every opening.

He's a real highbrow. He listens to classical music even when he isn't put on hold.

He wouldn't stay in a hotel unless the desk had an unlisted number.

He wouldn't stay in a hotel unless it had wall-to-wall carpeting—on the ceiling.

I've slept through more books than Rip Van Winkle.

hillbillies and hicks

Although most of us have never seen a hillbilly, we still make fun of them. Hillbilly jokes always seem to work. Hillbillies laugh louder than anybody when they hear a joke about rustics. They don't know who we're talking about. They're smarter than we are. I remember driving to Florida from New York. On a detour road in southern Georgia, I drove into a pothole that was deeper than the Grand Canyon. It was filled with water that sloshed through my engine and killed it dead. It cost me a hundred dollars to have the car towed into town and another seventy-five to get the engine repaired. I asked the hick who was working on the car, "Why don't you fill in that rut?" He said, "It's hard to do in the daytime—too much traffic." I asked, "Why don't you fix it at night?" He said, "That's when we fill it with water!" I confess—it's only a joke. But it might have a speck of truth to it!

A country girl who'd gone off to the big city returned and ran into Andrew, her old beau. Wanting to show off when he came over, she said, "I didn't get your name."

The hillbilly said, "You sure tried hard enough!"

A hillbilly who'd been married only a few days dropped in at the general store in town. The owner asked how married life was. The hillbilly said, "'Tain't half bad, except when my twelve-year-old wife tries to give orders to the thirteen-year-old I had with my first wife!"

Esmeralda had never been married, but she explained it: "I got a dog that growls, a chimney that smokes, and a cat that stays out half the night. Would a husband do more'n that?"

Zeke's wife was taken to the hospital. The staff tried to find blood to match hers, but couldn't. Zeke said to the doctor, "Have you tried a panther's?"

A hillbilly goes to a movie for the first time. He watches a love scene in which the hero kisses the girl on the forehead, then on the eyes, the cheeks, the nose, and then to the neck and the shoulders. The hillbilly says to the man next to him, "That feller sure don't know where to kiss a girl, does he?"

Hillbillies get married young. Weddings aren't consummated until after the bride is burped!

A hillbilly was dying. He called for his only son and said, "Child, I'm about to tell a secret I couldn't take with me to heaven. I thought you'd like to know that wine can also be made from grapes!"

Elmer decided to take up law. He left town and returned a week later. His father asked, "How do you like the law?"

Elmer said, "Don't like it much. I'm sorry now I learnt it!"

A Kentucky hillbilly drank a jug of moonshine every day of his life until he died at ninety-six. When he was cremated, it took a week to put out the fire!

After dinner, Jethro liked to light up a home-rolled cigar. One night his wife was clearing the table when she sniffed. Something was burning. Looking at her husband, she gasped and said, "You've set your whiskers on fire."

Jethro said, "I know it. Can't you see I'm praying for rain?"

A hillbilly went to a doctor for a checkup. The doctor asked, "How do you sleep?"

The hillbilly said, "I sleep good at night and I sleep good in the morning, but comes the afternoon I gets restless!"

"Slattery's run off a new batch of moonshine."
"How can you tell?"
"This morning his mice kicked the tarnation out of my dogs!"

A forty-year-old hillbilly carried a younger hillbilly into the doctor's office, deposited him on the examining table, and said, "See if you can patch him up soon. I shot up his rear end like it was a tail on a possum. Don't hurt him none, 'cause he's my son-in-law."

The doctor said, "Why would you shoot your son-in-law?"

The hillbilly said, "He warn't my son-in-law when I shot him!"

A hillbilly went to the justice of the peace in the small town a few miles from his farm. The hillbilly said, "I'm thinking of marrying up with Hesperia Parker next Sunday morning. Would you be able to say the word we'd need?"

The justice of the peace said, "I'd be proud to, my boy."

Three days later the hillbilly returned and said, "I think I got confused. I don't plan to marry Hesperia Parker after all. I think I'll marry me Nettie Jo Graham."

The justice of the peace said, "I made out the papers already. If you want me to change them, it'll cost you a quarter."

The hillbilly mulled it over, then said, "Leave it be. There ain't a quarter's difference between them."

A hillbilly woman was asked by the town banker to open a bank account. She declined, saying, "I keep my money safe to the house."

The banker said, "You've got four strapping sons. Don't they try to get at your bankroll once in a while?"

The hillbilly woman said, "I keep it where they won't find it."

"Where would that be?"

"Under the soap!"

A hillbilly went to town and bought himself a new outfit so he'd surprise his wife. Coming to the creek a stone's throw from the house, he stopped his wagon, got out, took off his old clothes, burned them, bathed, and then went back to get his new clothes. They'd been stolen. Getting back into the wagon, he said to his horse, "Giddyup, Hortense, we'll surprise her anyway!"

hippies

Gone are those days when curls came halfway down the back, when pink and chartreuse were the colors of clothes, and they had flowers in their hair. And the girls looked nice too!

A hippie walked down the street wearing one shoe. A passerby asked, "Did you lose a shoe?"

The hippie answered, "Nope, I found one!"

One hippie went home. To make him feel loved, his parents bombed his room.

Two hippies were married. Both the bride and the groom had long hair. After pronouncing them man and wife, the minister said, "Will one of you please kiss the bride?"

A man came into a bar, ordered a drink, and happened to see a younger man sitting nearby. The younger man had long, stringy hair that hadn't been washed in years. The man continued to look. Finally the hippie walked up and said, "Man, what the heck are you staring at?"

The man said, "Well, about twenty years ago I made love to a buffalo, and I was wondering if you were my kid!"

A hippie moved into an apartment. It took him six months to learn that it didn't have water.

There was a hippie who went to the barber once a week—to have his hair matted.

They even had a Hippie Ku Klux Klan outfit. They burned driftwood crosses.

Hippies used to cut up vegetables and then put in a dash of marijuana so the salad would toss itself!

One hippie came home and gave the dog fleas!

history

I used to love history in school, but I gave up on it. They were making it faster than I could learn it!

Primitive people didn't have it good. They had to do the washing down by the river with a rock. It abused the clothes. Can you imagine what it did to dishes?

I know why they were called Minutemen. They were lousy lovers!

An out-of-stater was visiting the Alamo. A local waxed eloquent about how a small band of man had fought off the entire Mexican army. The out-of-stater said, "Back home we had patriots too. Didn't you ever hear of Paul Revere?"

The local said, "Paul Revere? Wasn't he the guy who went for help?"

The Civil War broke out. A slave was asked to fight, first by his master and then by an agent sent in by the Yankees. The slave said, "Thank you, but no thanks. You've seen two dogs fight over a bone, but have you ever seen the bone get up and fight?"

My son is following in the footsteps of great men. He just went down in history!

History is an account of something that never happened, written by someone who wasn't there.

Are you sure Lincoln was one of the common men? You can't find a picture of him taking out the garbage.

The trouble with history is that every time it repeats itself, the cost goes up.

History is an agreement on a group of lies.

"Son, when I was your age, history was my best subject."
"When you were my age, what had happened?"

A historical novel is a book with a wench on the jacket, and inside, no jacket on the wench!

Do you want to feel shaky about history? Just listen to two men describe what happened at the accident they both saw!

Can you imagine what would have happened if Columbus had a wife? All he had to do was come home and tell her that Queen Isabella had given him three ships for nothing!

Lincoln traveled twenty miles to borrow a book, so why do they close the libraries on his birthday?

If Washington was first in war, first in peace, and first in the hearts of his countrymen, how come he married a widow?

hockey

I live in California, where there are thousands of Canadians. All of them came here for the sun and because they hate hockey! In fact, not long ago the man who brought professional hockey to the West Coast met a friend and asked, "Would you like to get screwed?" The friend said yes, so he sold him the team!

Our local team wasn't doing too well. During one game, none of the players had even taken a shot at the goal. Finally, one of them got the puck and a voice from the stands yelled, "Shoot it! The wind's with you!"

A Canadian youngster missed Sunday church. Running into him later, the minister started to let him have what-for, telling him he would be damned for going off to play hockey with his friends. The boy said, "I wasn't playing hockey. Come over to my house and you'll see the fish I caught!"

I once went to a fight, and a hockey game broke out!

A young man was bragging about his prowess in hockey. He said, "Do you remember last year's Yale-Brown game. I helped to win it for Yale."

Another young man said, "Which team were you on?"

Our team lives hockey. It dreams hockey. It eats hockey. Now if it could only *play* hockey!

A hockey coach fell on bad times. Swallowing his pride, he went to the present coach of the local team and begged for any kind of work. He said, "I'll take anything. I'll sweep up after the game."

The other coach said, "My contract is up in two months. That's the job I was planning for myself!"

holidays

Most people celebrate a holiday by not going to work. In my family, we celebrate when my brother does! It's not that he's lazy. He likes to take a few days off for Christmas. He starts on January 6! In addition to all the major American holidays, my brother also celebrates Tuesday, Thursday, Guy Fawkes Day, and the day the couch was invented!

The post office closes on New Year's Day and not one letter or package moves. The clerks practice all year for that!

For next Thanksgiving they've just come up with a cross between a turkey and a porcupine. It's delicious and you can pick your teeth at the same time!

The beaches are jammed on holidays. Last Easter, in Malibu they didn't have one drowning. Just eight crushings!

Do you realize there are millions of Indians who wish Columbus had been on standby?

I had a busy Labor Day holiday with my family. First I had to explain what a holiday

was to my wife. Then I had to explain labor to the kids!

With the price of Valentine candy, it's cheaper to have lust in our hearts than chocolate!

My wife likes to give sensible gifts at Christmas—like handkerchiefs and mink coats.

September 8 is a holiday in Beverly Hills. That's the day the new Mercedes comes out.

My brother drinks a toast on holidays: "Here's to our holidays, all 365 of them!"

A woman complained that her husband never bought her anything. For Valentine's Day this year she wanted something to protect her and something she could drive. So he bought her a hammer and a nail!

hollywood

It has been said that Hollywood is a phony, backstabbing, pretentious, money-grubbing place. That's only a rumor started by people who've been there!

A big Hollywood producer bought a massive ranch in Santa Barbara. He stocked it with a hundred Guernseys. A friend visiting him said, "Do the cows give milk?"

The producer said, "In my bracket, they don't have to!"

A famous actor grew a beard for a part in a biblical extravaganza. During a lull in the shooting, he ran off and started to play a round of golf. On the third hole he managed to put himself in a deep sand trap. As he started to play out of it, another actor came up and gaped. "My God," the second actor said, "how long have you been in this trap?"

I was invited to a Hollywood wedding. Traffic was heavy, so I got there late—just in time for the divorce.

One female star gives full credit to her wardrobe. She says, "My clothes are always magnificent. I've been a hit with them, on and off, for twenty years!"

The hardest thing in Hollywood is to keep the marriage a secret until the divorce leaks out.

"This picture came clean from Hollywood." "Is that possible?"

In Hollywood they get married early in the morning. If it doesn't work out, you haven't wasted a whole day!

One Hollywood mogul has a dozen yes-men around him at all times to do whatever he bids. Once he was overheard to say to a sycophant nearby, "I'm nervous. Bite your nails for me!"

An actor put a move on an actress who had a minor part in his movie. The actress rebuffed him, saying, "It's nothing personal, but I'm a lesbian. Do you see that pretty extra down there? I'd like to rush over to her, throw my arms around her, crush her to me, and kiss her everywhere."

The actor started to cry. The actress asked, "Why are you crying?"

Looking at the extra, the actor said, "I think I'm a lesbian too!"

Hollywood's a town where they shoot too many movies and not enough actors!

Then there's the Hollywood producer who got married and sent out tickets for the opening night!

He's an associate producer. He's the only one who'll associate with the producer!

A producer was telling a friend about how liberal the head of the studio was. Genius that he was, the mogul didn't want people around him to agree with everything he said. He wanted them to give their points of view, no matter how far off they were from his. The friend asked the producer, "What happens if you disagree with him?"

The producer said, "Not much. He goes off on his yacht and you take the bus home!"

The actor was beyond despair. He hadn't worked in two years. His creditors were hounding him day and night. He decided to end it all. Walking to a downtown bridge, he was about to leap off when he heard a voice, "Don't do that, handsome."

He looked and saw a witch emerging from the mist. She was as ugly as sin. Her nose was long, crooked, and covered with warts. Her hair was matted, her dark clothes filthy.

The witch went on, "At this very moment your agent is closing a deal for the biggest role of your life. *Shazzaaam!* On the way to your house, by messenger, is the script. It is the best script this town has ever read. *Shazaaam!*"

The actor said, "Is this really true?"

The witch said, "Not yet. But it could be if you did one thing."

"What's that?"

"You must take me to a motel and spend the night making love to me."

The actor hesitated. He looked at the witch's misshapen discolored teeth and the sores on her lip. Mulling over the choice, he decided that fame was better than a funeral. The actor and the witch went to a nearby motel, where they spent the night in one embrace after the other.

In the morning, the actor showered and started to get dressed. From the bed, the witch purred, "How old are you, handsome?"

The actor said, "Thirty-four."

The witch said, "Aren't you a little too old to believe in witches?"

The movie starlet was examining a coat she wanted to wear to a premiere. Not sure of whether she could dry-clean it or merely have it pressed, she said, "I wonder what I should do for this coat."

Her roommate said, "Honey, haven't you done it yet?"

A starlet was auditioning for a part. An awful actress, she destroyed the scene. Then she asked, "What shall I do next?"

The director said, "Get married if you can!"

Everybody in Hollywood is a big baby. There, the flavor of the month is "thumb"!

An actress was complaining, "Two years of studying and whom has it gotten me?"

One actress was sentimental. She always got divorced in the dress her mother was married in.

One Hollywood kid asked for a bigger report card. He wanted all of his parents to sign it.

A man driving across the country saw a pretty young lady getting ready to board a bus for Hollywood. Smiling his best, he said, "I'm going West."

The pretty girl said, "Good. Bring me back an orange!"

They have a new game in Hollywood called Sex Roulette. You have your choice of six starlets. They're all beautiful, but one of them is writing a book and will sue!

Then there was the starlet who walked out on the director who was keeping her because she found a better-paying position!

One starlet was just thrown out of the apartment her producer boyfriend was paying for. It seems that the louse had expired!

A Hollywood bride looked around as the groom put her down after carrying her across the threshold. Puzzled, the Hollywood bride said, "This place looks familiar. Have we been married before?"

One Hollywood actor lives in a giant mansion. The kitchen has twelve rooms!

Hollywood is a rich town. Where else but in Hollywood can you look in the collection plate on Sunday and find credit cards?

A lot of movie stars don't get a reputation until they've lost one!

A casting director said, "Miss, I'm afraid you won't do."

The actress answered, "Did I say I wouldn't?"

Then there's the Hollywood producer who was always trying to make a little extra.

I made a picture once that was so bad even the popcorn was panned!

Hollywood pictures cost a fortune. They just finished one—the intermission cost twelve million!

The town hero was back from Hollywood, where he'd made it big. His buddies were glad to see him, and pumped him about Hollywood. Was Hollywood that wild and crazy? Were the stories printed in the newspaper true?

The town hero answered, "Hollywood is just like any other town. We all live normal lives. An actor is just like a guy who works in a factory. He gets up early, works hard, and he's in bed by no later than ten-thirty. In fact, the other day I was telling my wife, "Bruce . . ."

One Hollywood actress ran out of men to marry, and had to start marrying those she'd been married to before.

One Hollywood kid is very proud. At the last PTA meeting he won the prize for having the most parents there.

A producer prepared a giant movie on the Bible. In his version, Adam refused to eat the apple proffered to him by Eve. Another producer told the first, "You can't do that. That's not what happened."

The first producer said, "So I changed the story a little. Who'll know?"

An actor came home to his beach cottage in Malibu to find another actor in bed with his wife. The actor said, "My God! What are you doing?"

The second actor said, "Well, next week I'm doing a soap opera. Then I have a picture. Then . . ."

homes

It wasn't comfortable. Five of us slept in a bed. Then one of my brothers got married and we slept six to a bed. Actually, it wasn't that bad. We lived in a railroad flat. That's an apartment made of a foyer. There was one bathroom at the end of the hall on each floor. We weren't lucky. There was another tenant on the floor who was a long reader! I promised myself that I'd grow up and become rich. I'd build a house with twenty rooms. Each room would have its own bathroom. I grew up. I built a house with twenty rooms. Each room had a bathroom. Now I can't go! All right, I exaggerate some. But no subject hits home more than the home!

Where else but in America can somebody borrow a few thousand for a down payment payment, get a first mortgage, a second, and then call himself a homeowner?

One guy got in trouble for deducting money because he had water in his basement. The government found out he lived on a houseboat.

Home is a place where, when you go to it, they have to take you in.

She's a housekeeper. Every time she gets divorced, she keeps the house.

Nothing bugs a woman more than when friends drop in and see the house as it generally is.

I found a sure-fire way of making my house look better. I go out and price new ones!

Home is where you don't have to make reservations in advance.

I love it at home. I come home and stand with my back to a roaring wife.

I found out my pipes were frozen the hard way. I looked in the washing machine and watched my socks hit an iceberg!

A man was complaining that his wife was always painting the house. A friend said, "How many times could she have painted? Twice? Three times?"

The complainer said, "I don't know, but when we moved in, the bedroom was ten by eighteen. It's now six by eight!"

Home is where you wait until your son brings home the car!

I know a ninety-year-old man who married a twenty-year-old girl. Everybody made fun of him until he told them, "Just because there's snow on the roof doesn't mean there's no fire in the house!"

Home is where you scratch wherever it itches!

There's no place like home—once in a while!

I bought a bungalow. The builder bungled it and I still owe!

In the moving business, "fragile" could mean "slam dunk"!

I have poor insulation in my house. We have the only vacuum cleaner with snow tires.

I think our builder made a mistake. I even said that to my wife this morning when I was walking downstairs to the attic.

My house is cold. You know the candy that doesn't melt in your hand? In my house, ice cubes don't!

It's very drafty in my house. This evening my wife tossed a salad and it landed in the den!

I'll give you an idea of the shape my house is in. My electrician has no eyebrows!

My house could never blow away. No hurricane could lift my mortgage!

My house is a split-level. Of course, it didn't start out that way!

One fellow in California put in a pool but filled it with seltzer water. It's awful. You swim one stroke forward, burp, and go back two!

I have a mobile home. Of course it wasn't until last week's hurricane!

The only thing that hasn't sunk in my house is the "for sale" sign!

I have a sunken living room and a feeling to match!

A man's home is his castle. It looks like a home, but it costs like a castle.

There was an old lady who lived in a shoe. And she could hardly make the payments on *that!*

hometowns

I wish I came from a small town. I'd have a lot of good material. If you come from a pint-sized place, you can get mileage out of it.

She came from a hometown where all the women were ugly. They once had a beauty contest and nobody came in first, second, or third!

In his hometown they had a "beautiful body" contest and a phone booth won.

His hometown doesn't have a town idiot. The people take turns.

His hometown was so dull, the drugstore sold picture postcards of other towns.

The town was so small there was no place to go that you shouldn't!

His hometown is real dull. A train used to come through and blow its horn at eight in the evening. They made it stop because it woke everybody up.

If you went out for a night on the town in his hometown, it took eighteen minutes.

They didn't have a sanitation department in his hometown; they had a cleaning woman come in once a week.

The classified phone book in his hometown has one yellow page.

In his hometown, there's nothing doing every minute!

His hometown is wild. They just changed the name of Lover's Lane to Sex Drive!

His hometown has one street, and it's a one-way street. If you want to turn, you have to go all around the world.

His hometown is so small the gay is straight!

The only way to have fun in his hometown is to move away!

His hometown is so small the sheriff's posse has to ride out six to a badge!

He comes from a poor town. The doctor's stethoscope is on a party line!

honesty

Honesty has one great advantage. You never have to remember anything!

An honest politician is any public servant who'll stay bought when you buy him.

Will the person who lost a hundred-dollar bill ten minutes ago form a double line at the cashier's desk?

Honesty pays, but some people aren't sure it's enough.

The boss was explaining the facts of business life to a new employee. "If you want to succeed in business, you need two things—honesty and smarts."
    "What's honesty?"
    "The truth. Keep your word when you've given it."
    "What are smarts?"
    "Never give your word!"

Be on the level and you won't go downhill.

Honesty comes from training, background, and fear of getting caught.

Honesty is the best policy because it has so little competition!

honeymoons

I like honeymoons. A honeymoon is something that only takes place every couple of years!

The cab arrived at the hotel. Getting out, the new bride asked her husband, "What can we do to hide the fact that we've just been married?"

The groom said, "You carry the luggage!"

The newlyweds were taking the train to Florida. Cuddling together in an upper booth, they had a merry old time. After the third marital joining, the bride said, "Darling, I just can't convince myself that we're really married."

From a berth halfway down the train, a deep voice bellowed, "Convince her! I'd like to get some sleep!"

Finished with canvassing all the stores in a town, a traveling salesman checked out of a hotel. On the way to the airport, he realized he'd left his hairbrush behind. He returned to the room, but it had just been given to a honeymoon couple. As he was about to knock, he heard, from inside, a nervous bridal voice say, "And whose pretty nosey-wosey is that?

The groom said, "Yours, dear."

"And whose big wide shouldy-wouldies are those?"

"Yours, dear."

"And whose chesty-westy is it?"

"Yours, dear."

Unable to wait any longer, the salesman yelled through the door, "When you get to the crushy-brushy, that's mine!"

A young couple from the country honeymooned at a fancy resort. As they were checking out, the clerk told the new husband, "That'll be thirty dollars apiece."

The new husband put down three hundred dollars.

The newlyweds could hardly wait to get to their room. Both tore off their clothes. The groom puffed out his chest and said, "A hundred eighty pounds of dynamite."

The bride said, "It's the fuse that worries me!"

As they prepared to face their first morning after the honeymoon night and were sipping coffee, the bride said, "I never mentioned this to you because I didn't think it was terribly important—I suffer from asthma."

The groom said, "Thank God. Last night I thought you were hissing my performance!"

The new bride was shy. Before they checked into the honeymoon hotel, she told the groom not to tell anyone they were newlyweds. The next morning she came down to the lobby and all the other guests stared at her. At the breakfast table, she said to her new husband, "I asked you not to tell anyone we were newlyweds."

The groom said, "I didn't. I told them we were just good friends!"

A secretary had just returned from her honeymoon. The secretary at the next desk asked, "How did you and your husband register at the hotel?"

The first secretary said, "Great. Just great!"

The Cabots and the Lodges, two old and respected families, finally joined hands in the marriage of Hortense Cabot and Carter Lodge. Because the families were important in the area, the fathers arranged for security at the honeymoon hotel. The private detective hired for the evening stood guard all night in front of the door to the suite.

The next day the detective reported back to the fathers, who asked, "What happened last night?"

The detective said, "Well, when the groom carried the bride into the room, she told him, 'I offer you my honor.' He answered, 'I honor your offer.' And that's how it went all night long—honor, offer, honor, offer . . ."

After the fourth day of a nonstop honeymoon, the newlyweds walked into the hotel restaurant. The waiter came over and asked for their orders. The bride purred to her husband, "You know what I like, sweetheart."

The groom said, "Sure, but we have to eat something one of these days!"

A couple checked into a honeymoon hotel. As the bride prepared herself, the groom went down to the lobby to get some cigarettes. Returning, he found his bride in bed with four bellhops, each of whom was having some sexual pleasure with her. The groom said, "What's going on here?"

The bride said, "You know I've always been something of a flirt!"

The honeymoon's over when you're no longer drinking to one another, but because of!

A honeymoon needs a short period of adjustment. Marriage is a long one!

The groom stared down at the bride's first attempt at breakfast. What she had done to dry cereal, toast, and coffee was criminal. The groom shook his head sadly and said, "I can't believe this. You can't *cook* either!"

The honeymoon's over when the groom stops helping the wife do dishes—and starts doing them himself!

They made a rather strange couple. He was seventy-five if a day. She was at most twenty-one. However, on the fourth day of the honeymoon, it was the bride who was

begging for mercy. The new groom hadn't left her alone for five minutes. While he was shaving and getting ready to pounce upon his new wife again, the bride managed to get out of the suite and into the hotel coffee shop. The waitress who'd seen them upon their arrival said, "What's going on? You're young and you look like hell."

The bride said, "The old geezer double-crossed me. When he told me he'd been saving up for fifty years, I thought he meant money!"

A hillbilly reported on his bride during the honeymoon, "That up-and-down motion was natural, but that round-and-round motion was learned!"

You know the honeymoon's over when the husband calls home to say that he'll be late for dinner and the answering machine explains that it's in the refrigerator!

Then there was the cheapest honeymoon of all time. Instead of Niagara Falls, they drove through a car wash slowly!

A young man married a famous opera star. She was incredibly homely, but when she sang, listeners forgot about her looks. The morning after the honeymoon night, the young man looked at his bride on the other side of the bed. Without makeup, she looked uglier than usual. Grabbing her, he started to wake her and bellowed, "Sing something!"

horniness

In Hollywood the women have nothing but sex on their minds. Sex! Sex! Sex! I'm not complaining—I just want to get in on it! Even at eighty I felt like a twenty-year-old. But there never was one around!

She's so oversexed her thighs have an answering service!

They call her Rumor. She goes from mouth to mouth!

Her rape whistle takes requests!

She loves orgies. Her diaphragm has service for eight!

She's one for the books, and she's in everybody's!

She's made love to so many sailors, her IUD goes in and out with the tide!

She doesn't care if her boyfriends kiss and tell. She needs the publicity!

He tried to become a sex fiend, but couldn't pass the physical!

He keeps touching the top of her head because everybody says she's horny!

In school, she was chosen as the girl most likely to!

She must be with the Secret Service. She's always under cover!

She's a homebody. Anybody's home!

He's got a one-track mind. But what scenery along the track!

She's so oversexed, her knees haven't met in years!

He comes from a sexy family. His grandfather died at a hundred and two. He was shot by a jealous husband!

When you go out with her, it's cafeteria-style. You help yourself!

She fools around so much, each knee thinks it's the only one!

She's so horny she has landing lights on her stomach!

The only way she could keep out of trouble would be if they glued her pants on!

Why do people say she's a wild girl? Anybody can pet her!

She's so oversexed, her rape whistle plays Cole Porter ballads!

She believes that to err is human, but it feels divine!

He wants to make it easy on his wife. He's willing to do the cheating for both of them.

She has forty towels in her hope chest—each one from a different hotel!

She's like a flower. She grows wild in the woods!

She was a telephone operator for a while and had three close calls!

She knows where bad little girls go—everywhere!

She's the kind of girl half the men in town want to marry. The other half already have!

In school she made the band. She also made the football team, the basketball team, and anybody else who went by!

She's a great secretary—types fasts and runs slow.

The only time he likes to see a girl stick to

her knitting is when she's in a wet bathing suit!

The poor guy can't keep his wife in clothes. He got her a house, and he can't keep her in that, either.

He'd be in great shape if his blood had as much circulation as his wife!

He wears a girdle—ever since his wife found it in the glove compartment of his car.

It's not easy to become her beau. First of all, you have to be listed in the phone book.

He often accuses her of infidelity, but she swears she's been faithful to him many times!

She never tells him when she's having a climax. He's never around!

He doesn't know where his wife keeps her dimes and pennies, but he sure knows where the maid's quarters are!

The only thing she ever gives is in!

horse racing

My two accountants swear that I've lost fifteen million dollars betting on the horses. My accountants don't understand that I love horses, so I give all my money to the improvement of the breed. I've also managed to make my betting deductible. I have a bookie who changed his name to Red Cross! I'm not the worst track degenerate in the world. I know stars who go to the track every day. I at least only go when it's open!

Vito looked over the form and picked out the longest longshot in the history of the track. With five minutes to post, not one penny had been bet on it. Vito didn't care. Disregarding the advice of his companions, he bet his last two dollars on the horse. The horse won and paid two hundred thousand for a dollar. Vito collected at the window, looked at the huge stack of bills in his hand, and said to his pals, "I have no luck. I hit a two-hundred-thousand-to-one shot, and I only have two dollars on it!"

A boy told his mother that his father had taken him to the zoo. The mother couldn't believe it. She said, "Your father would never take you to the zoo in his whole life."

The boy said, "He did. And one of the animals paid thirty dollars!"

A horse is an animal that can take thousands of people for a ride!

An eight-year-old horse was dropped into a claiming race at a big track. He'd never raced before, and went off at a hundred to one. He won by a dozen lengths, beating the track record for the distance. Wary, the track stewards called in the owner and asked, "This horse is eight years old. Why haven't you raced him before?" The owner said, "We couldn't catch him till last Monday!"

My horse would have won the race, but he kept looking back for his plow!

I finally found a way to beat the first six races. I show up for the seventh!

A highway patrolman stopped a car and asked the driver why he was going so fast. The driver said, "I'm very sick."

Spying the racing form in the empty seat next to the driver, the highway patrolman said, "It looks as if you're going to the track."

The man said, "That's not a sickness?"

He was so slow his jockey died of malnutrition!

He was so slow the jockey's wife won a divorce for desertion!

I like to bet on jockeys with bad breath. The horses win just trying to get away from them!

A horse showed up at a ballpark. He headed for the manager and said, much to the manager's surprise, "I'd like to try out for the team."

The manager eventually recovered from hearing a horse talk, and said, "Really? Let me see you catch a few."

The horse walked to third base and caught every ball hit to him. The manager asked him to throw. The horse whistled the ball toward the first basemen with unerring accuracy and speed. Picking up a heavy bat a few minutes later, the horse proceeded to hit a dozen balls over the centerfield fence. The manager said, "Not bad at all. Now let me see you run."

The horse said, "If I could run, I'd be at the track!"

He's a perfect mudder. That's what he eats!

My horse was so slow he won the next race!

A prospective buyer looked over Tomboy and could find nothing wrong with the horse. He asked the owner, "How come you want to sell him so cheap?"

The owner said, "I'm bored with him. He's a showoff. He's an actor. When they take his picture after a win, he turns his profile. When they play a fanfare, he starts to dance. He even whinnies to music."

The prospective buyer said, "Those antics could be cute. I'll buy him."

The owner said, "Okay, Tomboy, get up and do your 'lame' impression!"

When he came back into the stable, my horse tiptoed so he wouldn't wake the other horses!

My horse was so slow, it ran faster when it became glue!

I like to follow horses—which follow other horses!

My horse was so slow I think they made him mascot for the post office!

My horse said to his jockey, "Why are you hitting me? There's nobody behind us!"

Some people play horses to win. I play them to live!

A pessimist is an optimist on the way home from the track!

Walking toward the betting window, a man mumbled that he didn't know which horse to bet in the next race. He knew only that he wasn't going to bet on Majestic. Hearing him murmur, a man walking next to him said, "Why are you mumbling that you don't like Majestic? He looks like a good horse."

The first man said, "I own him, and I know he's not going to win."

The other man said, "I own the other four horses. This is going to be a real slow race!"

An owner was tired of his horse losing races. Just before sending the horse out for one final try, the owner said to him, "You better win today. If you don't win, at five o'clock in the morning I'm going to take you to the glue factory."

The race began and the horse started to

fall back. The jockey kept whipping him. Finally the horse turned to the jockey and said, "Why are you hitting me? Don't you know I have to get up at five o'clock in the morning?"

horses

The last time I sat on a horse, I was three. In those days, a photographer with a large box camera on a tripod came around to take pictures of children posed on a bedraggled Shetland pony. Seated on the pony, I dreamed of becoming a cowboy, maybe even the fastest Pony Express rider in the world. The horse took one step, an inch at most, and I tumbled off. At that moment, a song-and-dance man was born!

A country gentleman decided to buy a horse from a minister who was leaving for an assignment as a missionary in a place where horses weren't of much use. The minister said, "This horse has spent his life among religious people. He won't respond to 'giddy-up.' You must say 'Praise the Lord' if you want him to go. To make him stop, just say, 'Amen.'"

The deal was consummated. The new owner rode off on his horse. Some miles down the road, a noise startled the horse and he took off into the woods, heading straight for a deep canyon beyond. The new owner tried to rein in the horse, yelling, "Whoa! Whoa! Whoa!" Remembering suddenly, he said, "Amen." The horse stopped two feet from the edge of the canyon. The new owner wiped the sweat from his face, looked down at the gaping canyon, and said, "Praise the Lord!"

A man was trying to break in a spirited horse. The horse started to kick and finally got a hoof caught in the stirrup. Starting to dismount, the man said, "All right, if you're planning to get on, I'll get off!"

It was a most rustic town. At the train station there were no taxis to bring any of the tourists to the nearby resorts. Instead, farmers waited with horses and wagons. A newly arrived tourist hired Mr. Vandermeer. The luggage was loaded onto the cart and the slow procession to the resort began. Every few seconds the horse stopped and turned around. The tourist asked why so much stopping was necessary. Farmer Vandermeer explained, "He's deaf and he's so afraid of not hearing me say 'whoa,' he stops every once in a while to check!"

Two Yankees were horse-trading. Ebenezer said, "This here roan'll cost you five hundred dollars."

Zev said, "I was only planning to spend fifty."

Ebenezer said, "Sold."

Zev asked, "How come you run it down so fast?"

Ebenezer said, "You're my friend. I thought it would be nice if you owned yourself a five-hundred-dollar horse!"

"Marge won't talk to me since I took her horseback riding."

"She could be sore about something!"

I used to have a riding academy, but business kept falling off!

A circuit preacher was uncertain about the way to a town. At a crossroads he stopped to ask for directions from a boy of twelve who was fishing in the pond at the foot of an embankment. The boy said nothing. He merely stared at the circuit rider's sorry-looking horse. Swaybacked, it looked as if its next step would be its last. The circuit rider asked for directions again. "Which fork do I take to get to Coreyville?"

The boy asked, "Who are you, mister?"

The preacher said, "I follow the Lord."

The boy said, "Don't matter much which road you take. On that nag, you'll never catch up with him!"

hospitality

I never try to make guests feel at home. If they wanted to feel at home, they should have stayed there!

The relatives were visiting for the first time. "You've got a nice place," said Aunt Bea.

Uncle Bart said, "But it looks sort of bare yet."

Cousin Jed, the host, said, "That's because we just put in the trees. I hope they'll be grown much bigger before you come here again!"

The hostess was eager to please her guests. When one woman arrived, the hostess said, "I won't offer you any alcohol. I heard that you were the head of the Temperance League."

The woman said, "I'm head of the Anti-Vice League."

The hostess tried to smile and said, "I knew there was *something* I wasn't supposed to offer you!"

hospitals

I have an endless store of "hospital" jokes. I could destroy just about every hospital, but to tell you the truth, I don't feel too good!

In a hospital today there's lots of TLC—Take Lotsa Cash!

Hospitals are so crowded nowadays. They used to have semiprivate rooms. Today they have semiprivate beds!

The guy in the bed next to mine was bandaged from head to toe. I asked, "What do you do for a living?"

He said, "I wash windows."

I said, "When did you quit?"

He said, "Halfway down!"

The candy striper smoothed the blankets to make the patient more comfortable and said, "Mr. Kemp, see if you can smile and look happy for the doctor when he comes in."

The patient said, "I'm not going to smile. I feel miserable."

The candy striper said, "Couldn't you manage a little smile for the doctor's benefit? He's so worried about your case!"

A man visited his sick wife at the local hospital and asked the doctor about her condition. The doctor said she was improving. Because he had to work the next day, the man had to call to inquire about her condition. Again he was told that she was improving. Each day she seemed to be improving more and more. Then one morning he called and asked how his wife was. The nurse said that she was dead.

The man ran out of his house to head for the hospital. A neighbor stopped him and asked how his wife was. The man said that she was dead.

"I'm so sorry," the neighbor said. "What did she die of?"

The man answered, "Improvements!"

A male patient told the nurse, "I'm so in love with you, I hate to get well."

The pretty nurse answered, "Don't worry. The ward doctor loves me too, and saw you trying to grab a feel before!"

If you don't believe there's something called women's lib, try getting a back rub from a nurse's aide!

I love those hospital gowns. The front is rated "G" and the back is rated "X"!

This hospital had a new recovery room built five years ago. It's never been used!

After surgery, they put me in the expensive care unit!

It was a wonderful hospital—Our Lady of Malpractice!

My surgeon sent me a get-well card, and in it was a bill for ten thousand dollars!

At the clinic, business was brisk as usual. Mrs. Malcolm was present for her daily visit. A woman well up in years, she had few friends. She enjoyed talking to the doctor and the nurses. They in turn looked forward to her visits and treated her complaints with seeming concern.

On this day, her first visit in a week, the doctor said, "How come you haven't been in the hospital all week?"

Mrs. Malcolm said, "I was sick!"

A visitor in Houston asked, "What's the fastest way to the hospital?"

A local said, "Say something bad about Texas!"

In the emergency room, I told them I had shingles. One of the doctors tried to trade for aluminum siding!

The nurse picked up the phone to hear that somebody wanted to know about Mr. Selwin's condition. The nurse answered, "Mr. Selwin is doing fine. He'll be going home in two days. Who shall I say called?"

The voice at the other end of the line said, "This is Selwin. My doctor won't tell me a damn thing!"

On my last stay in the hospital I was examined by a man in a white coat—a Good Humor man on his lunch break! I didn't mind because I was glad to see anybody!

An unattractive nurse was telling another nurse, much better looking, about a patient. "That handsome man in Room 716 has the most fantastic tattoo. On his you-know-what he has the word 'Swan.' Puzzled, the handsome nurse went into Room 716 to check. Returning, she said to the other nurse, "It doesn't say 'Swan.' It says 'Saskatchewan'!"

I wouldn't allow my surgeon to use a local anesthetic. I can afford something foreign!

Hospitals are weird. They put you in a private room and then give you a public gown!

A visitor left the patient, walked over to the pretty nurse, and asked, "Is he making any progress?"

The nurse answered, "Not in the least. He's not my type!"

This surgeon told his patient, "I have bad news and good news for you. The bad news is—I cut off the wrong leg. The good news is—your bad leg is getting better!"

A surgeon told a patient, "I have bad news and good news for you. The bad news is—I slipped during your prostate operation and cut off your testicles by mistake. The good news is—they weren't malignant!"

Visitors, it seems to me, spend most of their time talking to cute nurses and patients in other rooms. I was home three days from my last surgery before my wife found out!

The food was so bad I begged them to put me back on intravenous feeding!

The surgeon was studying the patient's chart. The patient asked, "Will my operation be dangerous?"

The surgeon answered, "No. You can't get a dangerous operation for six hundred dollars!"

The nurse smiled and asked me, "How do we feel today?"

I took a cue from her and touched our knee. So she slapped our face!

A patient was being fed intravenously. When the doctor was making rounds, the patient said, "Doc, could I have an extra bottle today?"

"Why?"

"I'd like to invite somebody to lunch!"

hotels

On the road for years in vaudeville, I've spent most of my life in strange rooms. When I first went on the road, my mother and I shared a room for a dollar and a half. We paid in advance. My mother gave me the bed and slept on what was an excuse for a couch. We ate breakfast in the room, splitting an orange and, as times improved, a roll and butter. Folks in show business had a diet that worked better than all the fancy protein diets today. The show business diet had one simple rule: You only ate during weeks you had money!

My room wasn't bugged, but the bed was!

An older man is taking a nap when there's a knock on the door of his hotel room. Calling out, he asks the party outside to enter. A beautiful young girl appears in the doorway and says, "Oh, I must be in the wrong room."

The older man says, "This is the right room, but you're forty years too late!"

Bellhops love to gather tips. I once ordered a deck of cards, and the bellhop made fifty-two trips!

Some of the new hotels are gigantic, more like cities than hotels. I checked into one of the largest in Hawaii. Before I got to my room I owed three days' rent!

A man checked into a hotel. As he was signing the register, he stopped and threw down the pen. The desk clerk asked, "What's wrong?"

The man said, "I've seen roaches on the floor. I've seen roaches on the wall. I've seen roaches in the bed. But never before have I seen a roach looking at the register to find out my room number!"

A man checks into a hotel. Feeling lonely, he arranges for the bell captain to send a lady of the evening up to his room for a brief visit. As the man and woman start to cavort in the bed, a fire breaks out in the hall. The smoke alarms sound off. Nude, both the man and the woman rush out of the hotel and into the street. The woman runs off, as does the man, each going off in a different direction.

A few moments later the fire has been put out. The man starts back toward his room. Seeing another man in the nude, he says, "Buddy, if you see a naked woman walking around in the hall, you can make love to her. She's paid for!"

My room was so small the refrigerator door opened *in!*

A man checks into a hotel with a young

lady of questionable maturity, and they go up to a room. A few minutes later, concerned about the reputation of the hotel, the house detective rushes up to the room and breaks in. He finds the young lady in a sheer negligee. She lies seductively on the bed, looking as tempting as Eve in Eden. The man, however, sits fully clothed on the couch and reads a magazine. The house detective says, "Is she eighteen?"

Licking his chops, the man looks at his watch and slowly says, "In seven and a half minutes!"

I called room service and said, "Is this room service?"

"Yes."

"Good, send me up a room!"

The closet in my room was so small I had a hunchbacked hanger!

"Would you like a room with a tub or a shower?"

"What's the difference?"

"Well, with a tub you sit down!"

Hotel walls are so thin when you want to sleep, but so thick when you want to eavesdrop!

There wasn't a single roach in the hotel room—just married couples with large families!

It was a suspicious hotel. The Gideon Bible was on a chain!

Service was the slowest in this hotel. If you ordered room service, you had to leave a forwarding address!

The walls were so thin I got sunburned without leaving the room!

A man checks into a hotel. The clerk says, "Sir, I want you to know that this is a respectable hotel. We tolerate no fooling around."

The man goes to his room, puts away his clothes, then hears a noise in the hall. Opening the door, he looks into the hall. A man is chasing a nude woman. Upset, the new arrival goes to the phone and calls the clerk. "You told me that this was a respectable hotel. I just opened the door and saw a man chasing a nude woman."

The clerk said, "Did he catch her?"

"No."

"Then it's still a respectable hotel!"

A man comes down to the hotel desk to pay his bill. One item shows that he was charged for room service. He says to the clerk, "I didn't use it."

The clerk said, "It was there for you to use."

Taking the bill, the man wrote in some fancy figures that brought his bill down to almost nothing. The clerk said, "Sir, you've deducted a hundred dollars for your wife?"

The man said, "Well, she was there for you to use!"

The train was getting near Corryville. A traveling salesman, new on the route, asked another salesman, "Which is the best hotel in Corryville?"

The other salesman said, "The Green Lion."

"Do you stay there?"

"No, but I've stayed in all the others!"

A man said to the cabbie, "Take me to the best hotel in town."

The cabbie said, "Sorry, I won't do that."

The man said, "Why not?"

The cabbie said, "Because you'll think I'm one hell of a liar!"

In Hawaii, on a hotel door you can find a placard that asks, "Have you left anything?" It should ask if you have anything left!

A hotel is a place where you give good bucks for poor quarters.

A hotel guest is somebody who leaves his room because he can't get it in his valise!

I like the registers in hotels. You can always make a name for yourself!

hunting

Personally, I could never shoot Bambi's mommy!

Two hunters came across some lion tracks. One, the smarter no doubt, said, "Follow the tracks and see where he went. I'll go back and see where he came from!"

"Any luck shooting?"
"I shot fifteen ducks."
"Were they wild?"
"No, but the farmer who owned them was!"

An English hunter fought his way through thick and ungiving underbrush. Finally he came to a lake. Her long hair sparkling in the sunlight, a young woman, completely nude, was cavorting in the water. The hunter said, "Please forgive me, but I'm looking for game."
The young woman said, "I'm game."
So he shot her!

The wolves of the West are notoriously vicious. One hunter, eager to collect large bounties on wolf pelts, loosed his dog into the wilderness, anticipating that the dog would flush out all the wolves. A few minutes later, the man heard the howling of a wolf and the barking of his dog. The man

waited for wolves to emerge from the woods. Time went by, and no animals came out. A little worried, the man started to track his dog. He finally reached a farmhouse where a farmer sat, smoking a pipe and rocking on the porch. "Did you see a wolf and a hound dog?" the man asked.
The farmer said, "Yup."
"What was happening?"
The farmer said, "It was nip and tuck, but I suspect the dog was about a length ahead!"

One day, Little Algy went out hunting for bear. Algy met a bear. The bear became bulgy. The bulge was Algy!

An amateur huntsman came back to the hunting lodge and said, "I shot an elk."
Another guest said, "How'd you know it was an elk?"
The amateur hunter said, "By his membership card!"

When I go out into the woods hunting, I'm fully equipped. I take a half-dozen bottles of bourbon for snakebite. I also take two snakes!

A small country boy was standing with his father's shotgun as a dude came by and asked, "What are you shooting?"
The boy said, "Don't know. Ain't seen it yet!"

He saw a sign that said "Bear Left," so he went home!

A man flew to Australia and went on a kangaroo hunt. Standing in the back of a jeep, he looked around for some prey. He finally sighted a kangaroo and pointed it out to the driver, who took off like the proverbial bat. Over hill and dale, through brush and dry country, going at breakneck speed, the jeep was unable to catch up with the kangaroo. The man tapped the driver on the shoulder and said, "Let's forget it. We'll never catch that thing. We're hitting seventy and he aint' even put down his front feet yet!"

I'm a born hunter. Last week I went after ducks, and the *decoy* got away!

Two men are bird hunting. One takes aim and shoots. He starts to jump up and down, saying, "I got me a pheasant. I got me a pheasant."

The other bird hunter said, "That's an owl."

The first one said, "Don't matter. I eat the meat, don't care about the voice!"

A group of duck hunters were trying to smoke out some mallards. They had no luck until one fat duck popped down out of the sky and started to hover three feet from the head of one of the hunters. Excited, the hunter shot away at the mallard and missed. Not a feather was ruffled. As if in disdain, the bird flew off. Afraid that the other hunters would make fun of the bad shooting, the hunter who'd missed called after the mallard, "And don't you ever come back again!"

A young guide took a man hunting. The man got a good share of ground squirrels but, unhappy with the lack of real sport, said, "Young feller, take me where there's some action. There's some danger in going after cougar or puma or bear."

The young man said, "If you're looking for danger, you ought to go out with my dad. Last week he shot my uncle!"

The last time I went hunting, I was confronted by a grizzly. I jumped up to catch a limb ten feet over my head. I missed, but luckily I caught it on the way down!

A hunter came up with a brilliant idea. He sat in a tree so that other hunters wouldn't take him for a deer. His strategy worked. He was shot for a bear!

A big-game hunter went on safari with his wife and mother-in-law. One evening a week later, while they were still deep in the jungle, the wife woke to find her mother gone. Rushing over to her husband, she insisted that he try to find her mother.

The husband picked up his rifle, took a swig of whiskey, and started to look for his mother-in-law. In a clearing not far from camp, he and his wife came on a chilling sight. The mother-in-law was backed up against thick, impenetrable brush. A large male lion stood facing her.

The wife said, "What are we going to do?"

The husband said, "Nothing. The lion got himself into this mess. Let him get out of it!"

Pointing to the bear rug on his den floor, a hunter told a friend, "I got this one in Canada. It was either him or me."

The friend said, "Well, he makes a better rug!"

A hunter, proud of his ability, had never hunted moose. He went to Canada and checked into a hunting lodge. A guide offered to take him to moose country. Moreover, the guide promised, he would make sure that there was a buck moose to shoot at. The guide explained, "We will take along my brother Pierre. He makes the sound of a female moose in heat. It is a perfect rendition. Males would come from fifty miles away for that sound. But you must promise me one thing—when that male crashes through the woods, you must get him with your first shot."

The hunter said, "Why the first shot?"

The guide said, "Because if you don't, that moose will make love to my brother Pierre!"

I'm worried about my wife. She just bought me a deerskin coat for a hunting trip!

husbands

Over a twelve-month period, the average man hears one thousand seven hundred and eighty-two jokes about married life. In self-defense, he forgets most of them. If you plan to evoke a few laughs along the way to senility, either as a speaker or merely across a drink and chaser, start saving "domestic" jokes. But a cheap tape recorder, the mini-size is perfect, and talk the day's haul into it. I know some professionals, physicians and attorneys, who keep extensive joke files. I suppose an evoked chuckle buffers the bill for professional services, but, even more, it's friendly. In seventy-five and more years, I've never heard bigger laughs than those about domestic life. Put those you hear on tape. You can also write them on a small pad that fits easily into a hand. That's ammo, public or personal.

He's a model husband, but not a working model!

A husband bragged, "I talk. She listens. She talks, I listen. We both talk. The neighbors listen!"

He married late so that Medicare would pick up eighty percent of the honeymoon!

A husband is what is left after the nerve has been extracted!

He stopped calling her "the little woman" when she started to call him "the big mistake."

Many husbands make themselves scarce because they know they're not wanted. Others do because they know they *are!*

As a husband, he's a cross between nothing!

The quickest way for a man to dry his wife's tears is to throw in the sponge.

He's going through a midlife crisis. He has no life in his mid!

I'd admit my biggest mistakes, but between my wife, her mother, and my kid, it's too close to call!

A husband is a man who lost his liberty in the pursuit of happiness.

A caring husband is a man who is so interested in his wife's happiness that he'll hire a detective to find out who's responsible for it.

I take my wife out every night. But she keeps coming back!

We share household chores. I dry the dishes. My wife sweeps them up!

This husband had everything a man could want—wealth, a beautiful condo, a gorgeous woman—but one day his wife walked in!

Many a husband keeps reading his wedding license, looking for a loophole!

Some men lead a dog's life. They come home with muddy feet, make themselves comfortable, sit back, and wait to be fed!

He's lucky. He has a VCR, a remote control, and a wife—and they're all working!

During the hippie days, a young man carried a sign that said "Make Love, Not War." A man, passing by, said, "I'm married. I do both!"

A salesman asked, "Are you the head of the household, sir?"

The husband answered, "I certainly am. My wife's out shopping!"

A man worked out his budget and told his wife, "One of us will have to go!"

You can tell when a husband isn't handy when he asks the man next door how to get blood off a saw.

A husband is a guy who'd like to do all the things his wife thinks he does.

He told her that a husband was like a fine wine, so she locked him in the cellar!

Married men don't live longer than single men. It only seems like it!

He's not a yes-man. When his wife says no, *he* says no!

He's had a lot of children because he's trying to lose his wife in a crowd.

When an application asks him for "marital status," he writes, "Below wife!"

When he said, "I do," his mother-in-law said, "You'd better!"

He keeps wishing his wife was his mother, so he could run away from home!

If he didn't toss and turn in his sleep, they wouldn't have had any children!

He doesn't want to set the world on fire—just his wife!

He gets up early so he'll have more time to hate his wife!

He was a different man when he met her. He used a phony name!

Many men don't have wives who worship and adore them. Neither does he!

hypocrisy

Tell the truth. If somebody raps you in the mouth, the next time you'll shut up!

He can't be two-faced, or he'd be wearing the other one!

A network executive asked an agent what he thought of a certain comedian. The agent said, "He's the worst performer I ever saw. He loses an audience and never gets it back!"

The network executive asked about another comedian. The agent replied, "He has no sense of humor. What's worse, he badgers the audience."

The network executive said, "I asked you because I just hired both of them for a show."

The agent said, "Now why did you trick me into saying things about two of the best comedians in the business?"

Hypocrisy is okay if you can pass it off as politeness.

The ideal hypocrite is a youngster smiling on the way to school.

A hypocrite is somebody who sets a good example when there's an audience around.

An executive looked at a new product being worked on by his company, and told the designer, "In part, this is not totally without merit!"

I

icebergs

In the 1930s I took several trips to Europe on luxury liners. On the northern run, icebergs could be seen off in the distance. Some of them were huge. All were beautiful, giant ice castles set against a bleak sky. After running out of Titanic jokes, I amused myself with some ice fantasies. One was about a drinker ordering some beverages from the purser. Waiting for the drinks, he looked out of the porthole and saw a giant ice floe. Puzzled, he said, "I know I ordered ice, but this is ridiculous!"

A parrot worked aboard ship with a magician. In one illusion, the magician would cover the parrot with a cloth, make several things disappear, and then take off the cloth to reveal that the parrot, too, was gone. In the middle of an Atlantic journey, the magician went into his customary spiel of bad jokes and covered the parrot. At that moment the ship hit an iceberg and sank quickly. As the cloth floated off, the parrot was amazed at what he saw. The boat was gone. The parrot said to the magician, who was holding on to some debris, "Hey, you're getting better. But you can tell *me*—what did you do with the boat?"

A ship hits an iceberg and starts to sink. A passenger, rushing off to the lifeboats, is stopped by another passenger, who says, "What about the women?"

The first passenger says, "Screw them!"

The second passenger asks, "Do you think we'll have time?"

Two icebergs got married. A year later they had a baby daughter. They named her "Floe"!

Due to a bad break, an Eskimo family ended up on an iceberg. With no boat, and unable to swim in the icy waters, the father and mother Eskimos raised their small son on the iceberg. The boy grew to manhood. On the eve of his eighteenth birthday, his parents asked, "What would you like for a birthday gift?"

The young man answered, "Anything but another darn icepick!"

ignorance

Ignorance is when you don't know something and you're afraid somebody will find out!

Contrary to rumor, ignorance is not a required course in college today.

He was told to take up nude painting. The next day he got pneumonia.

Even insects can be ignorant. One mosquito was so dumb it bit a Las Vegas showgirl on the arm.

A woman was berating her husband. "You are an ignorant man. Ignorant! Ignorant! If they had a contest for ignorance, you'd come in second."

The husband said, "Why would I come in second?"

The wife said, "Because you're an ignorant man!"

They say that ignorance is no excuse. In his case it must be. Nothing else can explain him.

With him, ignorance is a religion.

illness

Show people are extremely sensitive to illness. Many of us are third-degree hypochondriacs. I had a writer who considered it an insult to his libido and id if he didn't come down with the disease of the day. When my television show rehearsed in a ballroom on the top floor of a leading hotel in New York, my writer came in ecstatic. He swore that he'd blacked out twice in the elevator. This was possible, as ours were the fastest elevators in the East. One afternoon the power was cut down by Con Edison and it took hours for the elevator to creep up to our floor. Another of my writers said to the first one, "There was no chance of blacking out today." Mr. Dying pointed to his stomach and said, "Bends!"

A man felt poorly. A bit of a hypochondriac, he decided to go to a famous medical clinic three thousand miles from home. Plane connections were difficult, but he managed to arrive at his destination two days later. He was given a battery of tests, the total cost of which was in the thousands. Twelve specialists conferred on his case and finally agreed on a diagnosis. The man was told that he was in excellent health but his blood pressure was too high.

The man flew back to his home city and hailed a cab to take him to his house. As they rode, the man said to the driver that he'd just completed a physical. Before he could explain the results, the cabdriver said,

"You look to be in excellent health. Except maybe your blood pressure is too high!"

We have to be on the lookout for an outbreak of the Chinese flu. It has only one symptom—you get up at four in the morning and have an urge to iron a shirt!

A medical lecturer was explaining the difference between arthritis, rheumatism, and the gout. He offered, "Put your finger in a vise. Turn the vise until a pain shoots up your arm. That's arthritis. Turn the vise tighter. The pain that radiates out is rheumatism. Now turn the vise twelve more times. That's gout!"

I just got a brand-new pill from my doctor. It has nothing but side effects!

I know a girl who just had artificial insemination. She went to bed with a robot!

Two women met in an elevator. One said, "I'm going to see my doctor. And do I have a symptom to throw at him today!"

The doctor tried to reassure the patient. Not impressed, the patient said, "Doctor, if you pull me through this, I'll contribute a million for your new hospital."

Time went by and the patient recovered. One afternoon the doctor ran into him and said, "I've been thinking about calling you— you know, the million for my hospital."

The patient said, "What million?"

"You promised a million if you recovered."

"I promised? That'll give you an idea of how ill I was!"

I have a doctor who gives shots for everything. You know him immediately because if you go by his office you see the patients backing in!

DOCTOR: Do you feel dull and listless?

PATIENT: If I felt that good, I wouldn't be here!

Something has to be wrong—we spend sixty million a year on medical research and two billion on get-well cards!

You have two chances—you either get the bug or you don't. If you get the bug you have two chances—you get the sickness or you don't. If you get the sickness, you have two chances—you live or you die. If you die, you still have two chances!

A doctor examined a woman and told her husband, "I'm not too thrilled with your wife's looks."

The husband said, "That makes two of us!"

PATIENT: I want a second opinion.

DOCTOR: All right, I'll tell you again!

I don't feel so great. I swallowed a doorknob, and it keeps turning my stomach!

"I just came back from my doctor."

"Which doctor?"

"He's been called worse!"

immigrants

The immigrant brought his theater with him, especially the comedy. Sixty seconds after the arrival of a shipload of immigrants from anywhere, a stage was built and people jammed into the theater to laugh. The immigrant laughed mostly at himself. It's a shame that there are so few records of the great immigrant performers. Today we're lucky. The whole world has a minicam on its shoulder and records everything. It's a huge loss not to have film of a comedian like one I still recall vividly. He had a long, flowing, Sicilian mustache. Appearing in a scene, he seemed to ignore the story and concentrate on his mustache. He pretended that it was alive, an animal attacking the rest of him. How he fought it off! It also got fresh with the pretty but hefty heroine of the play onstage at the time. Like some giant, furry antenna, one side managed to search out her cleavage and take refuge in it innocently. All gone now!

Pierre announced his intention to emigrate to the United States. A gray-haired lady from the next street told Pierre that she had a son in America who hadn't written a letter to her in ten years. Giving Pierre the address, she begged him to tell her son to write.

Pierre arrived in America, rode a bus for six hours to a large city, walked eight blocks from the bus stop, and finally came to the right house. He then walked up five flights of steps, knocked on the door of an apartment, and, when the door was opened, asked, "Are you François LeBrun?"

The man who opened the door said, "Yes."

Pierre said, "Why don't you write your mother?"

Toddy Sullivan had just arrived in the United States from Dublin. He soon found a pub in Manhattan where there were other Irishmen. Toddy offered to buy a round for the boys to celebrate his having gotten a job.

"What kind of work are you doing?" asked Feeney.

Toddy said, "That's the great part of America. I'm only a laborer, but I'm getting paid to help tear down a Protestant church!"

income tax and the irs

It's been said that only two things are inevitable—death and taxes. In the last few years, much work has been done on making people live longer. Eternal life may be just around the corner. I don't look forward to that. All those taxes we'll have to pay!

No wonder the government never has money. It's all being sent in by mail!

It's a privilege to be able to pay taxes. If they keep going up, I may have to give up the privilege!

It's easy to find out who is going to become a tax collector. In the nursery, give all the kids lemons. The one who squeezes it dry is going to work for the IRS.

The new tax form just came in the mail. Who says blanks can't hurt you!

The IRS is like a bad laundry. You keep losing your shirt!

A businessman was audited and brought along his various ledger books. All the ledger books were filled with scrawls and strange symbols. The businessman explained that the scrawls and strange symbols was a language he used to write down financial dealings. The auditor said, "Well, you'll have to tell us what your company earned that year."

The businessman said, "Never! I didn't even tell that to my partner!"

The new IRS office is fully equipped. It even has a recovery room.

The IRS is to the people what pantyhose are to quick sex.

My kid is as good as gold, especially on my taxes.

Birth-control pills are deductible, but only if they don't work.

Every year, millions of tax returns are filed. On some of them there's also a little chiseling.

On April 15, I get a chill thinking back to the time when our country was founded so we wouldn't have to pay taxes!

On the President's desk in Washington is a sign saying "The buck stops here." Not mine. They go as far as the IRS and that's it!

I like to count my blessings. After taxes, what else is left to count?

Next year the IRS is going to start selling gift certificates!

I have only one question: If the government isn't a dependent, what is it?

America is a land of untold wealth. Most of it is untold on the tax forms!

A businessman told me that he had wanted his children to share in his business, but the government beat them to it.

I told the IRS to have a heart. They said they'd take it!

At tax time, it's better to give than to receive. Safer, too!

If I'd invested in taxes twenty years ago, today I'd be a rich man!

Tax loopholes are just like parking spaces. As soon as you get there, they aren't there anymore.

I hate IRS audits. They make a federal case of everything!

The trouble is that when you don't pay your taxes in due time, you may do time!

The IRS checked up on a large religious donation made by a Mr. Thompson. The investigator asked the minister of the church about the contribution: "Did Mr. Thompson give a gift of ten thousand last year?"

The minister answered, "He certainly will!"

The IRS has finally put poverty within our reach!

A man was audited, and came in with six hundred notebooks all filled with expenses. The auditor asked, "What do you do for a living?"

The man said, "I sell notebooks!"

Don't put off until tomorrow what you can do today. There may be a tax on it by then!

There's a new drink you can give a date. It's called the tax cocktail. If she drinks two, she withholds nothing!

I feel great. I just paid my taxes, and I'm even for 1952!

india

Honest to God, one of the first jokes I wrote was about India: "My uncle lives in New Delhi. He runs the New Delhi-catessen there!" It received the same groan in the old days too!

My son spent twelve hundred dollars for a plane ticket to India, checked into a hotel at two hundred a day, hired a cab to take him a hundred and twenty miles at a cost of three hundred dollars to an ashram, and then he meditated on the simple life!

Then there was the midget Indian fakir who did the string trick!

The India rubber man met an India rubber woman and they had a stretched-out affair!

In India there are more children born each day than in Turkey, which means that more people talk turkey in India than in Turkey.

An Indian woman who had reached the age of one hundred was interviewed by a reporter. The reporter asked, "Have you ever been bedridden?"

The Indian woman said, "Many times. And once on the back of an elephant!"

The fakir lay on a bed of nails. As still as a dead man, he was obviously asleep. A woman tourist said to her companion, "Just look at him. He doesn't even move."

Her companion said, "It's a good thing. On a bed of nails you don't want to toss and turn!"

Then there was the mischievous Hindu teenager who used to short-sheet his father's wardrobe!

During the days of the British Raj, a missionary went among the Indians and tried to convert them to Christianity. He explained how heaven would belong to the faithful. One Indian said, "Your heaven can't be too good."

The missionary said, "It is wonderful."

The Indian said, "Then why haven't the English taken it over?"

indians

Nobody tells Indian jokes anymore. Today's climate is such that after one syllable, a protest line would appear and circle the joke-teller. I like Indian jokes. I also like Indians. I even met an Indian girl once and took a chance on an Indian blanket!

Four Indian chiefs went into a restaurant for a bite. The maître d' asked, "Do you have a reservation?"

One Indian chief answered, "Certainly. In Arizona!"

The Indians recently opened a bar in New York. You pay twenty-four dollars for a Manhattan!

A movie company went on location in southern Utah. Because the weather in that part of the country changes every ten seconds, a local shaman was hired to tell the producer what the weather would be the next day. The shaman did well for a week. On the eighth day he was unable to come up with a weather report. The producer asked, "What happened to your magical powers?"

The shaman answered, "My radio broke!"

One Indian smoke-signaler became health-conscious. He switched to filtered smoke signals!

One Indian girl did a naked rain dance and made the Creeks rise!

He was a Swede and she was a Sioux. When they had a kid, they named her Swede Sioux!

They just made a new movie about Indians. In it, the medicine man went to Johns Hopkins!

There was an Indian chief named Running Water. He had two sons named Hot and Cold. He also had a nephew named Luke!

We wouldn't be having trouble with the Indians today if we'd had stricter immigration laws!

An Indian donated blood. Giving him some orange juice, an attendant asked, "Are you a full-blooded Indian?"

The Indian said, "Not anymore. Now I'm a pint short!"

I come from a family of old Indian fighters. The young ones fight back!

The Indian chief addressed his braves, saying, "On this journey of many moons that we are about to take, you must have the strength of a bear, the pride of an eagle, the heart of a cougar, the eye of a crow, and it wouldn't hurt to stop at a Motel 6 either!"

The chief had two sons—Pointed Arrow and Falling Rocks. Unable to decide who would take his place, the chief sent both sons out into the forest. Without weapons or food, they were to test their hearts and nature. The first one back with a brown bear would be the new chief. Seven moons later, Pointed Arrow returned, on his back a huge brown bear. Falling Rocks didn't return. To this day they are looking for him. Everywhere you will see this sign: "Watch Out for Falling Rocks"!

Walking with his squaw, an Indian saw billows of smoke rising from a giant forest fire in the distance. The Indian said, "Boy, I wish I'd said that!"

A tourist stopped off at a small railroad

station where, sitting by the side of the tracks, there were Indians selling their wares. The tourist saw a blanket he liked very much, and was told that the price was a hundred dollars. The tourist offered fifty. The Indian said, "Price is one hundred. Bargains like Manhattan you no get anymore!"

My son must be Indian. Whenever I ask him to do something he says, "How?"

We claim that this country was founded in 1776. The Indians want to know when it was losted!

The Indians are puzzled. Unlike everybody else, they were conquered by the U.S. and still didn't come out ahead!

A man sees an Indian on the side of the road. The Indian has his ear pressed to the ground and seems to be listening intently. The Indian says to him, "Small car, Toyota, black, redheaded woman driving, large dog on other seat. Car license CRD-287."

The man says,"Incredible! By putting your ear to the road you can tell all that?"

The Indian says, "What ear? Car run over me ten minutes ago!"

A man, driving through rural Oklahoma, hears Indian tomtoms. The drummer is a weatherbeaten Indian. The man asks, "Are those war drums?"

The Indian says, "No, we need water."

The man says, "Then you're playing a rain dance."

"No," the Indian says, "sending for plumber!"

An Indian stops on the mesa, puts his head to the ground, and says, "Buffalo pass here hour ago."

The paleface with him asked, "You can hear them in the distance?"

The Indian answered, "No. Ground still wet!"

It is at the peaceful bend of the Little Bighorn. From across the river can be heard the constant beat of Indian drums. General Custer says to an aide, "I don't like the sound of those drums."

From the Indian side of the river, an Indian yells, "He's not our regular drummer!"

An Indian had a nightmare. He dreamed that we gave him back the country!

inflation

When it comes to inflation, we're all in the same boat—the Titanic! *But then, money isn't everything. In fact, nowadays it's nothing!*

Nowadays, when you order a twenty-dollar meal, you really get a mouthful!

Prices must be going up. This morning I saw a gum-ball machine that takes bills.

My take-home pay can hardly survive the trip!

I joined an organization that fights inflation. An hour after I joined, they raised the dues.

I don't feel bad about inflation. Why should I? The money I don't have isn't worth as much as it used to be.

Inflation is being broke with money in your pocket!

At today's prices, you're lucky if you can make *one* end meet!

I have a twenty-thousand-dollar car. Four years ago I bought a ten-thousand-dollar car on time.

I figured out a way to slow down inflation. Let's turn it over to a government worker!

We have the highest standard of living in the world. Now if we could only afford it!

A man walks out of a building, slips, and lands on his head. He goes into a coma. The coma lasts thirty years. He wakes up well into the twenty-first century and calls his stockbroker, who tells him, "Your General Electric stock split again. Your original shares are now worth thirty-five million dollars."

The man is thrilled. Just then the operator cuts in and says, "Your three minutes are up. Please deposit eight million dollars."

My son must know the value of a dollar. He keeps asking for ten!

I have to spend a lot of money on food. My family won't eat anything else.

Inflation has really hit. I asked for two dollars' worth of Swiss cheese. The clerk wrapped up six holes!

You know that inflation is rampant when you're afraid to ask anybody, "What's up?"

They've just come out with a new change-maker. It takes fifties.

We couldn't lick inflation if they made it an ice cream flavor!

insanity

There are no firm rules as to who is sane and who isn't. The definition is made by the people with the key! I'm reminded of the man who thought he was George Washington. He was treated for years and finally went back to being himself. He told his doctors that he was unhappy, saying, "I used to be somebody! Now I'm nobody!" There's a litmus test for stories about crazy people. They work if the joke is on the supposedly sane. If the butt is an insane person, the storyteller is kicking somebody when he's down. Try to remember that he may have the key tomorrow!

"They call him 'Peanut Brittle.'"
"Why?"
"Because he's half nuts!"

They call her Venus de Milo because she's not all there!

"What's the matter with your brother?"
"He lost his wife and he's going crazy."
"Is he going to get married again?"
"No, he's not that crazy!"

He's the flower of manhood—a blooming idiot!

He just got a job in a small town. He's the village idiot!

Then there was the cuckoo bird who went into a clothing store to buy a straitjacket with two pairs of pants!

"My sister is a waitress in a crazy house."
"What does she do?"
"She serves soup to nuts!"

"Does he suffer from insanity?"
"No, he enjoys every minute of it!"

I spent two years in an asylum. I was crazy about the place!

An inmate was telling the gardener about a way he had of killing bugs. The inmate explained, "I catch them and put them in a jar. Then I let them out and hit them on the head with a hammer."

The gardener said, "I just swat them."

The inmate said, "That's a good way too!"

An inmate watched a gardener tend to the strawberries and asked what was happening. The gardener said, "I'm putting fertilizer on the strawberries."

The inmate said, "And they think *I'm* crazy!"

insects

With all the scientific research going on, I'd like to find one scientist who can tell us when mosquitoes sleep!

A fly landed on somebody's nose in Warsaw. Then it leaped onto another nose. It was the longest flight in history. The fly went from Pole to Pole in one jump!

"What's the difference between a grasshopper and a grass widow?"
"There's no difference. They both jump at the first chance!"

A silkworm makes silk. A moth makes holes. I crossed the two of them, and now have a bug that makes lace!

"What's the best thing for fleas?"
"Get them a nice dog!"

Then there's the moth who almost starved. He spent the winter in a bikini bottom!

In my closet I have a golf moth. It makes eighteen holes in one day!

How do moths survive if they only eat holes?

A garment-center salesman retires. He takes up the common hobbies like gardening and collecting stamps, but isn't satisfied. He wants something unique. Learning about butterfly collecting, he decides that this is the hobby for him.

In a matter of months he collects every butterfly in the area. Once again he has too much time on his hands, but he hears about the huge number of butterflies and bugs in Africa. He can't wait to go on an insect safari. Disregarding the cost, he flies to Africa, hires a guide, and starts off on his butterfly safari.

Walking through the jungle, his net at the ready, he runs into another salesman from the garment center. They exchange greetings and start to bring one another up to date. It seems that the second salesman is in Africa for the same reason. He too is a bug collector. He takes several bugs from his pocket. "Do you have these?" he asks.

The first salesman studies the tiny creatures and shakes his head. "These," he says, "are ordinary."

The second salesman reaches into his hair and comes up with another bug. The first salesman says, "This isn't a bad bug. But its leg is broken, so it's valueless to a collector."

The second salesman shows his friend two dozen bugs. Some are too ordinary. Others are flawed. Finally the second salesman collects his bugs and says, "Give me back my samples and I'll see you next season!"

insomnia

Performers don't seem to sleep much. Most of them don't go to sleep until dawn. Then they go to bed and have daymares! Because comedy gets a grip on your sleep buds, I suggest that if you plan to give a speech, prepare during the day. Trying to edit or memorize at night is guaranteed sleeplessness. You can try counting sheep, but they'll all keep saying "Baa" at your jokes!

Counting sheep is not a guarantee against insomnia, because babies can't count!

I have a brother who suffers from insomnia. He wakes up every few days!

"Honey, I have terrible insomnia."
"If you go to sleep it won't bother you!"

"What can I do for insomnia?"
"Pretend you're a night watchman!"

I finally got a night's sleep last night, but it didn't do me a bit of good. I dreamed I was awake all night!

Insomnia is what you have when you lie awake all night for ten minutes!

A patient called his doctor and complained of not sleeping. The doctor told him, "Eat a big meal and then lie down."
The patient said, "Last week you told me not to eat before going to bed."
The doctor said, "There's new scientific research every day!"

Insomnia is the triumph of mind over mattress!

I know a man who has insomnia so bad he can't even go to sleep when it's time to get up!

I know somebody who had a job testing sleeping pills. They fired him because he fell awake on the job!

insults

We were discussing being insulted by audiences. One comedian took umbrage at the thought. He told us, "I've been spat at. I've had vegetables thrown at me. I've had pitchers of water tossed at me. But insulted—never!" Here's a treasure trove of insults I've found successful over the years. Use them sparingly!

He's got a hole in his head, but that's beside the point!

There's nothing wrong with him that reincarnation won't cure!

He should go home. His cage is clean!

People would like to break him in half, but who wants two of him?

He should have his ears cleaned out—with a .38!

How can people miss him if he won't go away?

He ought to play clarinet for a deaf cobra!

He's not a complete loss. He could always be a horrible example!

His soul should find peace—and the sooner the better!

He ought to break out into little dice and crap all over himself!

He sure is a card—the lowest in the deck!

People like to hate him in installments so it'll last longer!

If he could train a donkey to talk, there'd be two smartasses in his family!

He needs only one thing to make a fool out of himself—a chance!

He leaves a bad taste in people's eyes!

He's all right in his place, but they haven't dug it yet!

I understand that you are kind to inferiors. Where do you find them?

If this guy had greatness thrust upon him, he'd ask if it came with directions!

One habit gives her away. She likes to nip a stranger's heels!

When you get home later, throw your mother a bone, will you!

You have Van Gogh's ear for comedy!

I won't say she's rotten, but when you're with her you get the sinking feeling that Eva Braun didn't die in that bunker!

Every time she wants to express herself, people suggest UPS!

He lives on the wrong side of a one-track mind!

He never did a thing in his life, and he didn't do that well!

He'd give away the shirt on his back. The Board of Health would insist on it!

He's so miserable without her, it's almost like having her with him!

His clothes are so threadbare, all that's holding them together are the fleas!

He's a man who started at the bottom and sank!

To him, bubble-gum cards are part of the Great Books series!

His suit is very nice. It cost him two installments and a change of address!

He's the type who never exaggerates his accomplishments, but he tries his best!

His suit can really hold a crease. In fact, it can hold thousands of them!

Her mouth is big enough to sing duets!

She's the kind of woman who bolsters her husband's feelings of self-doubt!

The other night he was down in the dumps. That's where he lives!

He's learned from his mistakes, but he should have studied more for the test!

He's filled with the juices of life—mostly prune!

He wants only one thing in a woman—a rich father!

He can't see a belt without hitting below it!

He just came up with a hundred new ways of becoming a burden to his family!

He's so vain he would take his own hand in marriage!

She comes from a real wild family. Her family Bible has only six commandments, and two of those are just requests!

He's really moving, but that's because he's going downhill!

He's going through a nonentity crisis!

If she wanted to let it all hang out, it would have to take two trips!

He wears his socks so long he has to blot them off!

She didn't have to be elected the girl most likely to. She volunteered!

She's the kind who would go to Overeaters Anonymous and overeat!

They have a society that freezes bodies. She must be a charter member!

His name must be Theory, because he never works!

He wouldn't have any milk of human kindness if he drank a cow!

The secret of his success still is!

They once caught him skinny-dipping in the pool—the secretarial pool!

If he worked on a suicide-prevention hot line, he'd take the phone off the hook!

She was pregnant for eleven months. She always carries things too far!

She's a nature girl. She likes to go all the way in the woods!

She inherited her beauty. Her father left her the drugstore!

One thing about her past bothers men—its length!

The way she finds fault, you'd think there was a reward!

He's so narrow-minded, he sees through a keyhole with both eyes!

He's not a bookworm, just an ordinary worm!

People should be glad they don't have his nerve in a tooth!

Everybody loves him, and so does he!

He'd buy Toulouse-Lautrec a gift certificate to a tall men's shop!

He went to school for twelve years and still couldn't make illiterate!

He used to be a go-getter, but now he has to make two trips!

She has a great set of values, but she never uses them. She doesn't want to break up the set!

He has no hangups. Everything he owns is on the floor!

She always gets nostalgic for the fifties—and the twenties and the tens!

He must be an old bed. People keep turning him down!

She tried to practice being a nice girl, but she wasn't very good at it!

If his IQ were any lower, he'd trip over it!

She has a walk-in mouth!

Whenever he walks into a room, people give him a cringing ovation!

He gives dullness a bad name!

He once thought about getting a job, but that was the coward's way out!

When he crosses his heart, he uses an O!

She must be a pianist. She has long white fingers with black nails!

He smokes three packs of cigarettes a day because it give his hands something to do—shake!

He's got as much heart as a doughnut!

Anybody can be in a fog, but she makes her own!

He has all the charm of a dirty Christmas card!

There must be a lot of good in him, because none of it ever came out!

He'll never get dizzy from doing a good turn!

He wants to divorce himself. He's tired of living together!

He's got as much future as a cake of ice!

He has a lot of class—steerage!

She must be older than she says she is. She has a recipe for curds and whey!

She could make crows return last year's corn!

He's got more attachments on him than an Apple computer!

By comparison, she loses!

He'd salt his rump and hang over a bear!

insurance

Joke insurance would be nice!

An adjuster came to a home where there'd been a robbery the day before. The lady of the house explained, "When I came home, all the drawers were pulled out. Everything was on the floor."

The adjuster said, "Why didn't you report it then?"

The lady of the house said, "I thought at first it was my husband looking for a clean shirt!"

The other day a cat burglar broke into an insurance company and had amazing luck—he got away without buying anything.

A man had no life insurance, but he did have fire insurance. So his wife had him cremated.

Since I got a big insurance policy, when I leave the house my wife keeps saying, "Take chances!"

One insurance agent didn't last too long with his company. He kept insuring people over ninety because the tables showed that few people over ninety died!

Applying for a position, a man asked about some of the benefits. The personnel manager mentioned medical insurance, explaining that the premium would be deducted monthly from the paycheck. The applicant said, "In my last company, they paid the medical." He went on to explain that a large life insurance policy was part of the package, as well as months of sick leave, a full year's severance pay, bonuses several times a year, two-hour lunches, and unlimited coffee breaks.

The personnel manager asked, "Why did you leave the job?"

The applicant said, "The company folded."

An insurance agent was trying to sell a policy to a potential client who was rather hesitant and wanted to know if the company paid promptly. The insurance agent explained, "I had a client the other day who took out an accident policy. When I was leaving, he slipped and fell out of the window. As he passed the third floor, on which our company office is located, a clerk handed him a check!"

An insurance agent told a newlywed man, "Now that you're married, you should take out some insurance."

The man said, "Nah, I don't think my wife will be dangerous!"

An insurance agent suggested that a client who had fire insurance take out cyclone insurance on his business. The client asked, "How do you start a cyclone?"

Life insurance payments keep me broke, but there's a silver lining in that cloud—when I die I'll be rich!

Life insurance is weird. The company bets that you'll live; you bet you won't, invest a fortune, and hope they win!

I just signed for group insurance. If I die in a group, I get a hundred thousand!

I tried to get a life insurance policy, but after a physical examination they offered me fire and theft!

I never worry about insurance companies paying off. It's good to know that after I'm gone they'll still be here!

An insurance salesman sold me a great retirement policy. I gave him the first payment and he retired!

inventions

An inventor showed me this writing utensil that worked on an entirely new principle. For twenty-five hundred dollars and the promise that I'd promote the invention, I could have a third of the company. I laughed and told the inventor that I saw dozens of gizmos every week. I passed on the ballpoint pen. Another time, a clubmate showed me a device to be used in television. It did away with the need for bulky cue cards and would enable people on television to read without seeming to be reading. I turned down the Teleprompter! It's a good thing I never knew Alexander Graham Bell or Thomas Alva Edison. Actually, I did meet Edison. Being six years old at the time, I wasn't inpressed. Edison didn't sing, dance, or tell jokes!

A man comes home to his wife and says, "I saw the most amazing thing this afternoon—something that sews on buttons."

His wife said, "What is it?"

The man says, "A needle and thread!"

They've just come up with a new radio for drunk drivers. It's so loud you don't hear the crash.

Thank the Lord for TV. I'd hate to sit down and have a frozen radio dinner.

A company has just come up with a great new car. It has no motor, wheels, or brakes. One little problem—they can't drive it out of the factory!

They have a new device for keeping the inside of your car quiet. It fits right over her mouth.

I just bought an electric shoe horn. It's great, but it sets my socks on fire.

I just bought a state-of-the-art washer-dryer. It talks. This morning it told me what it did with the other sock!

They've come up with a new soap with fluoride in it. You wash your clothes once and never get a hole in them.

They just came out with a new kind of smoke detector. It has a snooze alarm.

The thermos is a great invention. How does it know when to keep things hot and when to keep them cold?

One monk said to another, "They've changed to all-digit dialing. If you want information, you have to dial IV-I-I."

Up at my winter cabin I have a woodburning blanket!

They just invented a holder for bad batteries. It's called a bathroom scale!

Farmer Johnson bought a state-of-the-art chain saw that was guaranteed to cut down five trees an hour. The next day, Farmer Johnson was back in the store and explained that he'd only been able to cut down five trees the whole day. The salesman took the saw and pulled the starter cord. The resul-

tant buzz was deafening. The farmer said, "What's that noise?"

How about a frozen bandage for cold cuts?

It took Alexander Graham Bell twenty years to invent the phone. It only took my wife three minutes to invent the busy signal!

The idea may have been great, but there isn't much of a market for chastity suspenders!

We've just come up with a new anti-anti-anti-anti-missile. It has one drawback—it keeps shooting itself down!

Two cavemen huddled together near a fire as, above them, lightning flashed and thunder roared. One caveman said, "You know, we didn't have weather like this before they invented the bow and arrow!"

"**T**he wheel was invented in Egypt. But unfortunately it was square. The slaves had one heck of a time pulling those carts. So the inventors sat down and finally came up with something."
"I know. They invented the round wheel."
"No. They came up with the whip. You should have seen those carts move!"

If necessity is the mother of invention, how come so much unnecessary stuff is invented?

I have a friend who invented a brand-new type of burglar alarm. Unfortunately, somebody stole it.

Somebody just came up with a great idea for married people at breakfast. It's a cellophane newspaper!

My brother just invented something that can take a car apart in ten seconds—a locomotive!

This man spent years perfecting a musical instrument. He fashioned it by hand, adjusted and readjusted its parts, put it to his lips, and blew. No sound came out. He blew again. No sound came out. He went back to the drawing board and worked for many more years. He put the instrument to his lips, but still no sound came out. The frustration killed him. When he died, they buried him in a place of honor, and right next to his body they placed his violin.

A man wrapped spaghetti strands around a meatball and invented a hot yo-yo!

investing and investments

The astuteness of my business advisers can be summed up in one investment. They told me about a geothermal company in Utah whose stock was underpriced at a dollar. I bought ten thousand shares. The stock went up fifty cents. I bought twenty thousand shares. At three dollars, I bought fifty thousand shares. I kept buying. When it got to ten dollars, I suggested to my advisers that we sell. They said, "To whom?"

Many people who bought "securities" are wondering whether they understand English!

A man walked into the office of one of these fly-by-night investment firms. He asked for change of ten. They made him a partner!

A tycoon was interviewed by some students and asked about his origins. He told them, "I came to this city fifty years ago. All I had were the clothes on my back and a plain white handkerchief folded in my pocket."
One student asked, "What did you have in the folded handerchief?"
The tycoon answered, "As I remember it,

I had four hundred thousand in cash and a quarter of a million in negotiable bonds!"

The way it's been going, the future tense of "invest" is "investigation"!

A man, eager to make an investment, went to his bank and asked for a big loan. The banker said, "Can you give us a statement?"
The man said, "I'm optimistic!"

A huge shipment of sardines came in from Spain and was warehoused. Because the warehouse bill wasn't paid, the owner of the warehouse sold the sardines to a friend. As word came out that the price of fish was about to skyrocket, the owner of the warehouse bought back the sardines at a higher price. This began an endless round of buying and selling, with the price going higher and higher. After the tenth transaction between the two men, the friend thought it would be a good idea to sample the merchandise and see what they had.
A can was opened. The sardines were dreadful—bony, skimpy, and drenched in an acrid oil. The friend told the warehouse owner, who said, "Look, these sardines aren't for eating. They're for buying and selling!"

ireland and the irish

There was an act called Ryan and Duffy. Ryan was really Al Schwartz. Duffy was born Isadore Shapiro. The Irish name for the act was due to a passing fad for Hibernian performers. Ryan/Schwartz died of food poisoning. Duffy/Shapiro teamed up with a real Irishman named Rourke. Rourke became Ryan. Duffy/Shapiro died. Rourke/Ryan teamed up with another real Irishman, Lenahy. Lenahy became Duffy. A true Irish act had evolved. But show business is quirky and, because of the success of Sarah Bernhardt, French acts became popular. "Ryan and Duffy" became "Marcel and DuPont." Not for long, however. Marcel and DuPont were killed in a train accident on the way to the premiere performance. No one stepped forward to claim the bodies. Because their luggage still had the original names of Schwartz and Shapiro, both men were buried in a Jewish cemetery!

The Irish are always talking about the wee people. Could it be that they have a kidney problem?

The church was jammed. Father O'Malley was beside himself. When Patrick McVey came for confession, the priest said, "Look, you're always here. You're not a big problem unless you've committed murder since the last time. You haven't, have you?"

McVey shook his head and started out. At the door he met Dennis McNulty and said, "You might as well go home. He's only hearing murder cases today!"

Two IRA vets were having a pint and listening to the news when an account of an outbreak of hostilities up north was announced. One said, "'Tis a terrible war."

The other said, "'Tis. But it's better than no war at all!"

Dennis was a typical Irish farmer in a section of Ireland where electricity was still a rumor. One day his pregnant wife, feeling the pains, knew her time was near, so the doctor was sent for. The doctor asked Dennis to bring him a kerosene lamp so the delivery could be performed. The doctor asked Dennis to hold the light up close. The doctor worked for a while, and then the sound of a crying baby was heard. The doctor said, "You've got another son."

Dennis said, "That deserves a bit of a drink, doesn't it?"

The doctor indicated that there was more work to do. Soon another baby emerged, and the doctor reported, "That's two boys."

"I think I'll open the good whiskey," Pat said.

The doctor said, "Hold the light closer." In several minutes he came up with a little girl. He displayed her for the stunned father, who said, "Do you think the light's attracting them?"

There's a difference between an Irishman going off to meet his Maker and anybody else. When another person dies, he's as dead as a doorknob. When an Irishman dies, they have to watch him for three days and nights!

Two Irishmen chipped in for an animal to work the land. Mike said that the animal was a donkey. Eamon insisted that it was a mule. Rather than fight, they consulted Father O'Malley, the local priest. Father O'Malley said, "The Bible says that this animal is an ass."

The men returned to their farms. As luck would have it, the animal died. As they were digging the grave, the priest passed by and asked, "What are you doing this fine morning? Are you digging a posthole?"

Together Mike and Eamon answered, "Not according to the Bible!"

As they worked on the frame of a skyscraper, Pat and Mike were having their usual difference of opinion when Pat said, "You half-pint! I bet I can carry you up to the top of the building in my hod."

Mike said, "You haven't got the nerve to make it up the bare planking. It's a hundred-foot drop."

Pat said, "I'll bet you a dollar I can."

"It's a bet!"

As soon as Mike was comfortable in the carrier, Pat started up the planks. When he got to the tenth floor, his foot slipped and the carrier almost tipped over. Another inch and Mike would have plunged to the ground. Pat managed to regain his footing and made it to the top. "I won," he said.

Mike said, "You did that, but I had high hopes when your foot slipped!"

The sermon, as usual, was about drink. "Drink," Father McNerney said, "makes you spat with your neighbors. It makes you force them into a fight. It makes you put up your dukes. And it makes you miss!"

An Irishman dropped dead in the pub. One of the regulars offered to tell the widow about the bad stroke of fate. When she opened the front door, the regular said, "Your husband dropped dead an hour ago."

The widow said, "No!"

The regular said, "Well, wait till you see who they're dragging in through the back door!"

A priest and a rabbi were making plans for a lunch to be shared by members of both religious groups. The priest said, "We'll serve some nice ham sandwiches."

The rabbi said, "Good. And we'll hold it on a Friday!"

A beggar approached a couple on a large street in Dublin and said, "May the blessings of the Lord follow you."

The couple walked on without giving him a penny. The beggar went on, "And never overtake you!"

A bum approached Hogan and asked for a handout. Hogan said, "You'll only waste the money."

The bum said, "No, I need it for food. I don't drink, I don't smoke, and I don't gamble."

Hogan said, "No? Tell you what—come over to my house and I'll give you a dollar."

They arrived at Hogan's house. Mrs. Hogan opened the door and looked at both men sternly. "What's this about?" she asked.

Hogan said, "I just wanted to show you somebody who doesn't drink, smoke, or gamble!"

israel

I have a forest of ten thousand trees in Israel, and once a month I have to send my gardener!

An Israeli scout is sent out to find a way across a river. Returning, he says, "To the right of the bridge there are about a hundred tanks, mortars, and two regiments of soldiers. To the left are five hundred missiles, three hundred antitank guns, and three regiments of soldiers. We'll have to cross on either the right or the left."

The commandant says, "How about going over the bridge?"

The soldier says, "Impossible. They have a big brown dog at the other end!

An Israeli soldier takes over the post at a chasm that seems to be as deep as the Grand Canyon. Facing him, farther along on the same side of the chasm, is an Arab soldier. The newly arrived Israeli looks over the cliff and counts, "Fifteen, sixteen, seventeen."

The Arabian says, "What are you counting?"

The Israeli says, "Come over here and look."

As the Arab arrives and looks down, the Israeli gives him a slight push into the chasm and goes on, "Eighteen, nineteen, twenty..."

Israel had just become independent and was short of all military supplies. One American tried to enlist, but was turned down. They had no uniform for him. Trying the air force, he was again turned down. The air force had no planes. The American tried to join the Israeli navy. The recruiting sergeant asked, "Do you swim?"

The American said, "Don't you have any ships either?"

Very few people read murder mysteries in Israel. You know the ending on the first page.

They have a new show in Israel. It's on from nine-thirty to nine o' clock!

An Israeli sharpshooter was bothering the Arab regiment as it tried to take the hill. Angry, the Arab commanding officer ordered all of his men, five hundred in number, to wipe out the sharpshooter. The troops took off. An hour later they returned, no mark on any of them. The sharpshooter was still at work. The Arab officer asked why the whole detachment had returned. The noncom in charge said, "We turned back. There were two Israelis!"

An Israeli executive has three trays on his desk—In, Out, and Don't Ask!

In Israel they give you the hourly news with, "When you hear the tone it will be exactly 6:00 P.M.—or a few minutes later."

An Israeli recruit asked his commanding officer for a weekend pass. The commanding officer said, "How could you ask for a pass? You've only just arrived. I can't give you a pass unless you were to do something heroic, something magnificent."

The recruit got into his tank and took off, but returned a half hour later in an Arab tank. This seemed to be an incredible feat. The recruit was given a pass. On the way to

town, another soldier asked him how he'd managed to get an Arab tank. The recruit explained, "When I got to the front lines, I saw an Arab soldier. I asked him if he wanted a weekend pass. He said he did. So we exchanged tanks!"

Israeli diplomats are always on the way to or from another country. One diplomat died and went to heaven. As Saint Peter greeted him, he said, "I can only stay a few days!"

In a small town in Israel they have a statue dedicated to the Unknown Soldier. At the base of the sign is a legend that says, "Here lies Seymour Stein, accountant."

A visitor asked a local, "How could the unknown soldier have a name?"

The local answered, "As a soldier, Seymour was unknown, but as an accountant he was famous!"

Tne new cantor had just sung beautifully at the Wailing Wall. A member of the congregation said to another, "Doesn't he have a magnificent voice?"

The other member said, "If I had a voice like his, I could sing just as well!"

Then there was the Israeli pilot who shot down eighteen enemy planes—six with his cannon and twelve in pledges!

Israel is now making tires. They not only stop on a dime, they pick it up!

An Israeli sea captain is called a Yom Skipper!

They have no golf courses in Israel. One good drive could mean war!

They just opened the first Mexican restaurant in Israel. It's called the Casa Hadassah!

italy and italians

On every vaudeville bill could be found one Italian singer. Although most of them, male or female, had never been within ten feet of a plate of pasta, they sang light Italian arias and Neapolitan love songs. A famous newspaperman consulted an abacus, the calculator still being a thing of the future, and concluded that of a population of sixteen million Italians, thirty-one million were tenors and six million divas! For those who want to tell Italian stories in dialect, a caution—the accent is deceptive. It seems to be easier than it actually is. It helps if you use your hands a lot and look at them while talking. I have no idea why this last item works, but it does. It may have something to do with the movement of the hands conducting the voice. Oddly, a French accent doesn't work well if you look at your hands while speaking. No ovation is necessary, but you've just picked up ten thousand dollars' worth of acting lessons!

A sociologist from an American university went to Italy to study the longevity of the Italian lover. As he was en route to a large city, he passed a field where a man in black pants and a plain white shirt was working in a vineyard. Since this was an opportunity to survey the people of the countryside, the sociologist stopped and asked the man about his sexual activities.

The man said, in broken English, "I have sex maybe fifteen times every year."

The sociologist said, "That's not too much."

The man said, "That's not bad for a priest without a car!"

I had a great vacation in Italy. Rome took my breath away. Venice was grand. And Florence—oh, Florence—she took me for five hundred dollars' worth of traveler's checks!

I have a Mafia car—there's a hood under the hood.

You can always tell a prude at a Roman orgy. She's the one washing the grapes.

I met a dumb tourist in Italy. He thought Vat 69 was the Pope's phone number.

A plane sputtered over the Neapolitan coast. The pilot went on the intercom and said, "Ladies and gentlemen, you have all heard the expression 'See Naples and die.' I would suggest you look out the window!"

I have an Italian friend whose grandfather came to America as a young man without a penny to his name. Yet, by the time he got deported . . .

Italian women wear very tight skirts. I tried to pinch one and broke two fingers.

A bigamist could be an Italian fog.

J

jail

I did a benefit show at Sing Sing once. It was a great audience, and I said, "You guys are terrific. After the show, let's go somewhere!"

The warden gave the burglar his best good-bye speech, as the burglar's sentence was up. The warden pointed out how it would be necessary for the burglar to change his ways completely. When the warden was finished, the burglar continued to stand before the desk. The warden said, "What are you waiting for?"

The burglar said, "My tools!"

The condemned prisoner sat in his cell. Coming to him, the warden asked what he wanted for his last meal. The prisoner asked for watermelon. The warden said, "There won't be any watermelon until next year."

The prisoner said, "I'll wait!"

A prisoner was in jail for breaking into a dress shop three times. His cellmate asked, "Why did you go back to the same shop three times?"

The prisoner said, "It was my wife's fault. She kept changing her mind!"

A convict explained to his pals, "I'd love to escape with you, but I can't. My wife's out there!"

A prisoner is offered the famous last meal on the eve of his execution. He orders a salad with mushrooms, mushroom soup, and a steak smothered in mushrooms. Asked why all the mushrooms, he answers, "I was always afraid to eat them!"

The prisoner's wife was visiting him and giving him what-for. "Look at you—attempted robbery, attempted burglary, and last month, attempted murder. Why are you such a failure?"

A mountain man found himself in jail for using his still to make gasohol. Another inmate asked how good the stuff was. The mountain man said, "Well, I got me a year to the gallon!"

A prisoner escaped on visiting day. When caught, he explained, "I thought it was Open House!"

Two new prisoners are put into a cell. One prisoner asks, "How long are you in for?"

The second prisoner says, "A hundred and twenty years."

The first prisoner says, "I'm serving a hundred and fifty. You take the bed nearer the door because you're getting out first!"

One prisoner spent many hours each day in the library. He was always reading escape literature.

It was the annual baseball game between the townspeople and the prisoners. When his turn at bat came up, the leading hitter of the prison team took a vicious swing and sent the ball zooming into the far reaches of the outfield. He rounded first. He rounded second. He rounded third. He headed for home. They finally caught him between third base and the Mexican border.

Two prisoners in jail had a big fight. One called the other a dirty number!

A prisoner was gifted by his wife with a cake, in the middle of which was a saw. He had to ask for another saw to get into the cake!

There was a real epidemic in the local prison. Six prisoners broke out with hacksaws!

Then there was the convict who was a disgrace to his uniform!

A prisoner was released. Outside, waiting for him, was his wife, with her sixteen-year-old son next to her. The wife explained, "This is your son. He was born nine months after you went to prison fifteen years ago."

Some of the new jails have all kinds of comforts. There's one that's so up to date you have to have references to get in!

A prisoner was visited by an old woman from a charity. The woman asked, "How long are you in for?"
   The prisoner said, "Eighty years."
   The woman said, "Well, there's another day nearly gone!"

My cousin spent two years on an island in the Pacific—Alcatraz!

A felon explained his being in jail by telling a friend, "I've always wanted to be a warden, so I thought I'd start from the bottom!"

Then there was a chap who was in jail because of jealousy. He was trying to make the same kind of money as the government.

Stone walls do not a prison make, nor iron bars a cage. But they sure do help!

A guard tells a prisoner, "The sooner you finish all your cereal, the sooner you get out on the rockpile with everybody else!"

A felon was convicted and sent away to a large penitentiary. His wife came to see him. As they talked, the wife remembered something and said, "Oh, honey, I just had to tell you—I'm not frigid anymore!"

One thing about jail—You're here today and you're here tomorrow!

japan and the japanese

Once upon a time, things made in Japan were good only for a laugh. Objects broke one minute after being bought. Now Americans buy Japanese cars, TV sets, computers, and almost everything else because of the care with which they are made. It's gotten so that a young couple I know wanted a baby. They were afraid of our quality, so they made it in Japan!

I have no business sense. I just opened a tall men's shop in Tokyo!

It's great when you marry a Japanese girl. She's petite, she's warm, she waits on you hand and foot, and your mother-in-law is in Yokohama.

I finally found out why the Japanese bow so low. Under their kimonos they have tight suspenders!

Japanese pitchers are among the best in the world. That's because if they get knocked out of the game, they have to go to the shower—with a sword!

A Japanese girl went with an American named Harry. He promised to return after wrapping up some business back in the United States. One day he received a wire from the young lady. It said, "You late. Me late. Will it be Harry or hara-kiri?"

jealousy

My wife didn't have a jealous bone in her body. I have a private secretary and my wife didn't care in the slightest about looks as long as he could type!

Jealousy is when you have poison envy!

The stunning blonde displayed her curves and sold a soft drink in a TV commercial. A wife looked at her stunning figure and said, "What do people see in her?"
The husband said, "I have no idea. Let me take a closer look!"

A married couple were strolling down the avenue when a well-endowed young lady, passing in the other direction, purred a hello at the husband. The wife asked, "Where did you meet her?"
The husband said, "Business."
The wife said, "Hers or yours?"

A businessman hired an attractive secretary. Seeing her for the first time, the man's wife suggested that there was no reason to spend money on a secretary. She, the wife, could do all the necessary work and thus save the business a lot of money. In no time at all, they could have money to buy a house at the beach.

The secretary was fired. Sure enough, the money piled up and the businessman bought a cozy cottage at the beach—for the ex-secretary!

Jealousy is hard to explain. Why would a man who hasn't gone within a mile of his wife for a year hit a man who does?

Jealousy is always pictured as being green. I can see why when I watch other people count their money!

Jealousy is one woman's friendship for another.

A woman sent her husband to the bakery for a loaf of bread. Two years passed and the husband didn't return home. The wife went out looking for him. After searching everywhere, she finally tracked him down in another city. Without waiting for her knock at the door to be answered, she burst into the apartment and found her husband in bed with another woman. The wife said jealously, "How did this start?"
The husband said, "Well, they were out of bread!"

jewelry

Many women live for diamonds. Not my wife. She also took gold, silver, platinum, and negotiable bonds! I remember when I first saw her engagement ring in the jewelry store. Something told me I was going to buy it for her—her mother!

The only things harder than a diamond are the payments!

A man sitting at a bar was approached by another man who whispered, "Would you like to buy a gold watch?"

The man asked, "Where is it?"

The second man said, "Shhh. The guy next to you is wearing it!"

A man admired the fine gems in the top jewelry store in town. Shaking his head sadly, he said, "I'd love to smother my wife in those."

The salesman said, "There must be a cheaper way!"

This girl got one of those new artificial diamonds from a gent she dated. Both the stone and the girl were man-made!

jewish-american princesses

As with most ethnic jokes, the brunts are interchangeable. A "Jewish-American princess" joke in the United States is a "commissar's wife" joke in Moscow. If we find a female Martian with long red fingernails, the form will go to outer space and get big laughs from Venusians, Neptunians, and Plutonians!

A Jewish-American princess always closes her eyes when making love. She doesn't want to see her husband having a good time!

A Jewish-American princess was arrested for raping a man. Fortunately, it wasn't a moving violation.

A Jewish-American princess makes something great for dinner—reservations!

A Jewish-American princess has sex every six weeks so she won't be considered a nymphomaniac.

There's a wonderful way of stopping a Jewish-American princess from being oversexed. Marry her!

Some Jewish-American princesses have been known to drop their nail-polish remover during an orgasm!

It takes three Jewish-American princesses to change a light bulb—one calls an interior decorator and the other two decide what to wear!

jews

If proof were needed that humor can insulate a people against everything that history can throw at it, look no farther than the Jews. At no time in the last two thousand years has there been a time when the Jews were allowed to practice their religion without some oppression somewhere. It's no surprise that many of the writers in early radio and television were the Jewish sons of immigrants. Most of my writers grew up in the ghettos of large cities. Humor protected them. With a little success, they moved west, put on cowboy boots, bought ranch homes, and named their children Trevor and Megan!

Sam Goldstein, a Jewish businessman who had been known for his religious tendencies, retired and decided to live it up. He went to a plastic surgeon who gave him a cute button nose. A hair stylist worked his graying hair over and made him a dark blonde. Throwing out all of his old clothes, he bought a dozen Italian silk suits and started to wear the latest fashions. Out in the marina on his new yacht, with a captain's cap and blazer, he hit a large rock, capsized the boat, and started to drown. As he struggled in the water, he called out, "God, I've always been such a good man. How could you do this to me?"

The Lord answered, "To tell you the truth, I didn't recognize you!"

Show me a Jewish boy who didn't become a doctor, and I'll show you a lawyer!

A Jewish woman had plastic surgery the other day. Her husband cut up her credit cards!

Abe was walking down the street with his arm crooked and his hand on his hip. A friend said, "What's with that walk?"

Abe looked down and said, "Oh God, I lost my rye bread!"

Abe and his wife had just gone to bed when Ruth, the wife, said, "Close the window. It's cold outside."

Abe pretended to be asleep. Ruth said, "Close the window. It's cold outside."

Abe tried snoring, but Ruth persisted, "Close the window. It's cold outside."

Getting out of bed, Abe slammed down the window and said, "I closed the window. Now it's warm outside?"

An elderly Jewish lady went to her dentist and said, "The new teeth don't fit."

The dentist examined her mouth, studied the bite, and said, "The teeth fit perfectly."

The elderly woman said, "Not in my mouth! In the glass!"

Two Jewish businessmen met at a resort. One who had recently retired was describing his life, "I get up late in the morning. I have a fantastic breakfast and then I lie down on my veranda and relax. I go inside for lunch, have great salads, the best coffee, and I go out and lie on my veranda again. When it gets dark I have a great dinner with the finest wines. I smoke a Havana cigar. Then I go out and lie on my veranda again."

The other Jewish gentleman acknowledged that this was a life to be envied. Later he reported the conversation to his wife. She asked, "What's his wife's name?"

Her husband said, "I'm not sure, but I think it's Veranda!"

"When does a Jewish fetus become a person?"
"When it graduates from medical school!"

A Jewish woman hired a private detective to follow her husband and find out what his mistress saw in him!

Jesus must have been Jewish. He went into his father's business!

jobs

Work is a very unpopular way of making money. I'm grateful to be in a line of work that results in a bow. I've often wondered what would happen if I had to take a regular job. I know that I'd get fired a lot! My three brothers never had that problem. They never got fired from a job. They never had a job! My brother Frank actually went to school to learn a trade so he'd know what kind of work he was out of! Brother Jack did learn a trade, but there are very few openings for harpooners nowadays! My brother Phil was the real prize. They used to send him unemployment checks in advance!

I go out on a lot of job interviews. My resumé is in its fourth printing!

I hate to come in early. The boss always asks if I'm having trouble at home!

I drink so much coffee, I toss and turn at my desk all day!

I just had surgery. I had a water cooler removed from my side!

I'm worried about my job. I tried to use the intercom before, and it was disconnected!

I used to sell doorbells door to door. But when I rang, people who needed my product didn't know I was there!

I worked at a fire-hydrant plant for six months, but I quit. I could never park near the place!

A recent job applicant wrote: "I graduated first in my class at Harvard. Last year I refused to accept a vice-presidency at GM. I don't care what salary I'm offered because money has no meaning to me. I never look at the clock and will work eighty hours a week if I have to."

After examining the application, the personnel manager said, "Don't you have even one weak spot?"

The applicant said, "They say I fib a little."

A young man applied for a position as a personal pilot for a rich man. The nabob told him, among other things, "I hope you've got both feet on the ground. My last pilot took the most incredible chances. I need a conservative pilot who'll play it safe."

The pilot said, "You're looking at the right man. Can I have my first check in advance?"

My brother fainted the other day—from underwork!

Two comedians met. One complained that he hadn't had a job in six years. The other said, "I haven't had an offer in eight years."

The first comedian said, "If I were you, I'd get out of the business!"

A comedian tried to make his mark in personal appearances. The jobs became fewer and fewer. Eventually he joined a circus. His sole job was to follow the elephants and remove all signs of their having made a no-no. Another comedian saw him one day and said, "This is demeaning. Why don't you quit?"

The first comedian said, "And get out of show business?"

A young lady applied for a job and was asked, "What was your last position?"

She answered, "Missionary!"

An entertainer returns home to find his wife bruised and battered. In tears, the wife says, "Your agent came by two hours ago. He was an animal. He threw me on the couch and attacked me."

The entertainer said, "Did he leave a message for me?"

The boss called in a young employee and said, "I'm going to mix business with pleasure. You're fired!"

He works as a salesman for a company that makes superchips. They just gave him a new territory—Japan!

Two business partners are about to hire a new receptionist. Choosing a pretty young lady, amply endowed, one partner says, "Look, first off, we have to teach her what's right and what's wrong."

The other partner says, "Agreed. You teach her what's right!"

My brother is a steady worker. He hasn't missed a coffee break in twelve years.

A boss walked over to his beautiful receptionist and said, "I have to tell you this. I just got a call from my accountant. I'm broke. I don't have a penny in the world."

The receptionist said, "Don't fret. I'll always love you, even if I never see you again!"

My cousin just got a job replacing a machine that found the work too dull!

I know the latest dope on Wall Street. He's my wife's cousin.

jobs (insults)

With these you can take on every enemy at the office party. You can also make a few more!

There was a blessed event in his house—his wife got a job.

He's fired with enthusiasm—every time!

She went to work for her new boss and said she'd take any position. They're up to the fortieth.

He heard there was plenty of room at the top, so he wanted to start there.

He hates any kind of work. He once found himself unemployed and quit.

He's looking for a job. His kids found out other kids eat three times a day.

When she applies for a job, under "Sex" she writes, "Try me."

He got fired from a job at the bank. He tried to take home his work.

Hard work never killed anybody. He doesn't want to take a chance on being the first victim.

He's so underpaid he could cash his check on the bus!

Years ago he used to dream about the salary he's starving on now.

He found the perfect job for him. The mandatory retirement age is six weeks.

He recently was given a little job to tackle—his!

He's got a problem at work. He doesn't do anything, so he doesn't know when he's finished.

He's a plant manager. All day long he waters them!

She doesn't take shorthand, but she's great at taking hints!

There's no excuse for sloppy work, but she keeps trying to think of one.

She thinks that getting to work on time makes the day seem longer!

He likes to kill time, but he doesn't like to work it to death!

She must be in great demand. She's had four jobs in one month.

He doesn't mind working. It's just that he has an inordinate fear of getting tired.

He thought about getting a job, but that was the coward's way out!

He belongs to five unions, so he's always on strike!

He's not afraid of work. He's been fighting it for years!

He works eight hours a day and sleeps eight hours a day—the same eight hours!

jogging

It was the fashion of the day to get up bright and early, put on running shoes, and go jogging. I got up bright and early. Donning an outfit that cost a month's salary, I headed for the small park near my home. I jogged between five and ten feet, felt eighty-two muscles and tendons tear, fought back the pain, and gave up health forever. My jogging outfit went at a celebrity garage sale. My big exercise now is crying when I hear about somebody who had a heart attack while jogging!

I know the exact day I gave up jogging. It's on my birth certificate!

If all the joggers were laid end to end, it would be easier to drive to work in the morning!

If all the joggers were laid end to end—and they soon will be...

I jog very slowly. In fact, the other day I was jogging and got arrested for loitering!

Everybody in my neighborhood runs. In my neighborhood, that's how you survive!

I like jogging, except for the part after you put on your sneakers!

joke fads

I suppose it starts out with one joke on the subject. By nightfall there are a hundred. Most often, youngsters or college students are in at the beginning.

"Waiter, there's a fly in my soup."
"Hold on, I'll get a spider."

"Waiter, what's this fly doing in my soup?"
"Looks like the backstroke."

"Waiter, there's a fly in my soup."
"Go ahead and eat it. There's more where that came from."

"Waiter, there's a fly in my soup."
"All right, I'll bring you a fork."

"Knock knock."
"Who's there?"
"Darwin."
"Darwin who?"
"Darwin young man on the flying trapeze!"

"Knock knock."
"Who's there?"
"Hair comb."
"Hair comb who?"
"Hair comb the bride!"

"Knock knock."
"Who's there?"
"Lipset."
"Lipset who?"
"Lipset touch liquor shall never touch mine!"

"Knock knock."
"Who's there?"
"O.A."
"O.A. who?"
"O.A. down south in Dixie!"

"What kind of girl does a hamburger go for?"
"Any girl named Patty."

"**W**hat opera is about hamburgers?"
"*The Barbecue of Seville.*"

"**W**hat dance does a hamburger love?"
"The char-char."

"**W**hat is a hamburger's favorite story?"
"'Hansel and Gristle.'"

"**W**hy are hamburgers better than hot dogs?"
"Because hot dogs are the wurst."

"**W**hat burger can tell your fortune?"
"A medium."

There are also "elephant" jokes:

"**H**ow do you make an elephant fly?"
"First, you take a zipper about three feet long..."

"**H**ow do you know an elephant just went to the bathroom?"
"You can't get the seat down."

"**W**hat comes in quarts?"
"An elephant."

"Color" jokes are in good supply:

"**W**hat's black and white, black and white, black and white?"
"A nun tumbling down a hill!"

"Pun" jokes:

"**W**hat smells like hell, has four wheels, and flies?"
"A garbage truck!"

A popular fad came from a radio show some years ago. It helps youngsters learn a little geography:

"**W**hat's the cheapest state?"
"Pennsylvania."

"**W**ho do you go to when you're Chicago, Ill.?"
"A Baltimore, M.D."

"**J**uneau if she's going with us?"
"Alaska!"

And of course, "light bulb" jokes:

"**H**ow many car mechanics does it take to change a light bulb?"
"Six. One to try to hammer it in, and the other five to go out and buy parts."

"**H**ow many Washington clerks does it take to change a light bulb?"
"One to find it, his immediate supervisor to authorize a requisition to be made, the head of the department to initial the requisition, a mailroom boy to bring twelve copies to the filing room, six filing clerks to file eleven copies, another mailroom boy to pass the twelfth copy on to the requisition department, a secretary to put the form on the section head's desk, the section head to sign it, another mailroom boy to take it to the purchasing department, a purchasing agent, a receiving clerk, another mailroom boy to..."

"**H**ow many Californians does it take to change a light bulb?"
"Three. One to screw it in and the other two to share the experience."

"**H**ow many gays does it take to change a light bulb?"
"Two. One to screw it in and the other to say, 'Couldn't you just die?'"

"**H**ow many loggers does it take to change a light bulb?"
"One, but he uses a chain saw."

"How many New Yorkers does it take to change a light bulb?"

"Go to hell!"

"How many White House staffers does it take to change a light bulb?"

"Twelve, but only if they can write a book about it."

"How many Zen Buddhists?"

"Two. One to screw it in and one not to screw it in."

jokes

I know six million jokes. I suppose I have to have that kind of inventory, as my work depends on it. I'm sure that I've been told more than six million jokes. People always stop and ask if I've heard this one or that one. No matter my response, they go into an act. Some even carry a piano player and a drummer with them. I don't complain about being overwhelmed with lines. Ten times a day I'll hear a good joke. I may borrow it. For those who plan to make a fortune or fame as speakers, I suggest that you start a file. When you hear a joke that makes you laugh, get it down on paper or tape. Sooner or later, you'll use it. Being a kind soul, I'll help you start your collection with some non sequiturs.

I saw a man lying in the gutter and asked him, "Are you hurt or something?"

He said, "I'm fine. I just found a parking place and sent my wife out to buy a car!"

A man went to a doctor who told him, "I've got bad news for you. You could go anytime."

The man said, "Great. I haven't gone for five days!"

My dentist just put in a tooth to match my other teeth. It has three cavities!

A hunter asked an old guide, "Have you ever been lost in the woods?"

The old guide said, "No, sir, but one time I was bewildered for a week and a half!"

A Jew and a Christian were debating their respective heritages. The Jew said, "Listen, when your ancestors were living on roots, mine already had diabetes!"

Joe Slocum was already the father of nine children and had just made the pilgrimage to the maternity ward, where his wife presented him with a tenth. He kissed his wife sweetly on the forehead. Purring, the half-awake woman said, "Joe, are you starting in again?"

Once there was a man who took a vacation to forget everything. In his hotel room he opened his luggage and found out that he'd forgotten everything!

Business has to be bad. Some friends of mine went in and asked for the businessman's lunch, and they made them pay in advance!

Things must be awful. The other day a going-out-of-business store did!

A young man said to his girl friend's obstetrician, "Tell me the truth, Doctor. How long do I have to leave town?"

A wife nagged her husband, "All month long I've been telling you not to get me anything for my birthday, and you still didn't buy me anything!"

A lawyer was walking down the street and

saw two cars smash into one another. Rushing over, he said, "I saw everything and I'll take either side!"

A great Hollywood director died and went to heaven. He was greeted at the gate by Saint Peter, who said, "Listen, we want you to direct a picture for us. The budget is eighty million. The script is by Shakespeare. If you want Edison on the camera and Michelangelo for the set designer, just say so."

The director said, "Who's the star?"

Saint Peter said, "Well, you see, God has this little girl . . ."

judges

Poke fun at authority and you're way ahead. Unless, of course, it gets to you first!

JUDGE: Have you anything to offer this court before I pass sentence?
DEFENDANT: Nope. My lawyer took every last penny.

One small-town judge gave a hillbilly a divorce from his fourteen-year-old bride because she'd acted like a kid!

The judge cautioned the jury, "When you go in to deliberate, for those of you who watch law shows on television, let me remind you that once in a while the district attorney wins!"

Then there was the judge who had a mirror in his chambers. Every time he passed it, he asked, "Who's the fairest of them all?"

Three cross-eyed prisoners faced the cross-eyed judge. The judge said to the first prisoner, "What's your name?"

The second prisoner said, "Tom Jackson."

The third prisoner said, "I didn't say anything!"

JUDGE: If you don't stop drinking, you'll end up in the gutter.
DEFENDANT: I just came from there, Your Honor!

JUDGE: Why do you drink?
DEFENDANT: I often wonder!

JUDGE: You robbed a quarter of a million from a bank?
DEFENDANT: It was out of desperation, Your Honor. I was hungry!

JUDGE: Where were you between five and six?
DEFENDANT: In kindergarten!

JUDGE: Do you ever listen to your conscience?
DEFENDANT: Yes, but I get very poor reception!

The defendant looked out of place in court. Scholarly looking, gray at the temples, and dressed nicely, he hardly seemed the type to be a Peeping Tom. Yet the policeman who had arrested him had caught him red-handed at his window, staring at a girl across the street through a pair of strong binoculars. The defendant said, "I'm not guilty."

The judge said, "You were caught."

The defendant said, "It's my hobby. I'm a birdwatcher."

"Sure," the judge said, "and you were just testing your binoculars and happened to look into a window where a girl was undressing."

The defendant said, "The girl was a girl, but, Your Honor, you should have seen her parrot!"

"Your Honor, I wasn't going seventy miles an hour."

"Sixty is still too fast in that zone."

"I wasn't going sixty. Or fifty. Or forty."

"Okay, thirty dollars for illegal parking!"

"Just for that, the court will give your wife eighty a week."

"Thanks, Judge. And to show you I'm a nice guy, I'll throw in ten myself!"

Judges don't always seem to make sense. A man found himself in front of a judge on two matters. In the first, the man's wife was trying to get a divorce because he was impotent. In the second, his secretary wanted child support. The man lost both cases!

The judge called the prisoner into his chambers and said sadly, "I'm afraid clemency is impossible in your case. The governor just got indicted!"

juries

There's more humor in a courthouse than one category can hold. This batch shows how deep the streak runneth!

A jury is a group of twelve who decide which side has the better lawyer.

A jury returned to the courtroom after a whole week of intensive deliberation. The judge asked if it had reached a verdict. The foreman said, "Yes, Your Honor. We have."

"What is your verdict?" the judge asked.

The foreman said, "We, the jury, find that we don't want to become involved!"

The attorney was questioning the witness, who was responding directly to the attorney. The attorney said, "Please speak to the jury."

The witness smiled at the jury and said, "Hi there!"

She was on trial for having shot her husband. She'd been found with the smoking gun in her hand. But the jury let her go because she was a widow!

It was in the days when scarlet women were branded. One young lady who was rather free with her favors was put on trial. The prosecutor explained in detail how often and in which ways she had committed adultery. The jury came in with a verdict. She was to be branded with an *A*. The judge asked, "Why an *A*?"

The jury foreman said, "That's the highest grade we give!"

Then there was the nymphomaniac who got herself arrested so she could be tried by the jury!

A jury heard a case and brought in a verdict of not guilty, explaining, "It was an act of God under very suspicious circumstances!"

A lawyer was doing his best with the jury, telling the twelve men who sat in judgment, "Shall we find this lovely, long-legged blonde guilty and keep her from returning to her lovely condo, telephone number 555-3267?"

It takes a thief to catch a thief. The trouble is—the jury lets him go!

justices of the peace

I knew a justice of the peace in Connecticut. He found out one day that his license had lapsed some time back and that the last several hundred people he'd married weren't legally wed. He wrote each couple and said that he'd perform a second ceremony to make the marriage binding. Eight husbands told him to forget the second ceremony. They'd pay him well if he'd send them copies of the lapsed license!

A couple, eager to be united in matrimony, went to a justice of the peace. The justice explained, "In this state you have to take a blood test, make out some forms, and wait forty-eight hours."

The bride-to-be looked at him helplessly and asked, "Can you say a few words that'll tide us over for the weekend?"

A man complained that justices of the peace were misnamed. He'd been married by one and hadn't had any peace since!

juvenile delinquency

We were good kids. Not one kid on my block went to the electric chair. None of them lived that long! The truth is that we were slightly more respectful. If I got out of line, my father would haul off and kick me halfway across the room. He'd stomp on me and spank my bottom until it was bright red. I wouldn't be allowed food or drink for the whole day. Then at night my mother would come home and really punish me! When you tell jokes about juvenile delinquents, never tell them about your own children. They become a neighbor's kids or some distant relatives. For some reason, people laugh more if the delinquents are far enough away not to make the audience uncomfortable. As it is, half the audience will have an anxiety attack merely walking back to the car and passing four teenagers dressed in leather!

He's really tough. He went to a reform school on a dean's scholarship!

If he ever lives to be an adult, it'll be a testament to his teachers' patience and his parents' self-control!

Our country will never be invaded. Our juvenile delinquents are too well armed!

He has a birth certificate with the Surgeon General's warning on it!

He's too young to drive, so he steals only cars with chauffeurs!

He's a delinquent masochist. He slashes his own tires!

He was part of the bathroom gang. In fact, he was the ring leader.

A class of juvenile delinquents was asked who had killed Lincoln. Three of them took the fifth!

A father said to a juvenile delinquent, "How can you disobey your mother? Do you think you're any better than I am?"

A teacher was telling a friend about one of her students. "He cheats, he lies, he steals, he hits, and to make it even worse, he's the only kid in the class with a perfect attendance record!"

A juvenile delinquent received a razor for his sixteenth birthday. He didn't know what to do first—shave or slash tires!

He was a tough baby. His father had to play strip poker with him to get him to go to bed!

A juvenile delinquent bragged to the judge that he'd shot another kid for a quarter. The judge said, "How can you shoot somebody for a quarter?"

The delinquent said, "You know how it is, Judge. Two bits here, two bits there—it adds up!"

He can't help being a juvenile delinquent. Where he comes from, *both* sides of the tracks are the wrong side!

The mother of a delinquent was telling another woman, "My son was sent up for ten years, but he got off for good behavior."

The other woman said, "It must feel good to know you have such a fine son!"

A delinquent snatched a woman's purse. He got six dollars and a hernia!

A juvenile hurt himself accidentally. He was cleaning his slingshot and it went off!

He was a born delinquent. When he was four years old, he was already the head repaint man for a hot tricycle ring.

He was such a delinquent, his folks left home when he was seven!

Today's delinquents are the same as those fifty and sixty years ago. Only the weapons have improved.

It was a juvenile delinquent band. The leader played a switchblade guitar.

One teacher had a class filled with delinquents. One time a spitball was thrown at him. The doctor gave him a fifty-fifty chance to live!

His was the typical story. He went from day school to night court.

He got thirty days so often they named a month after him!

A delinquent bragged about his brother, "The judge just gave him two years for forgery."

His delinquent friend said, "Your brother's pretty smart. He ought to pick it up in that amount of time!"

He was the only kid in the neighborhood without a gun. He bought a gun. Two weeks later he was the only kid in the neighborhood!

He went to a very exclusive school. You had to be sent there by a judge!

He had to be a tough kid. In his neighborhood, on the police emergency number there was a three-year waiting list!

kangaroos

Not far from where we lived when I was about ten was a world-famous zoo. It was a treat for me to go there and forget everything else. One of my earliest conclusions after intensive study was that the kangaroo and the elephant should change tails! I don't know many kangaroo jokes, but in Australia they once published a whole book of jokes about this strange animal. One joke asked, "What does a kangaroo eat for breakfast?"

The answer is a classic: "Pouched eggs!" (A semi-classic?)

A mother kangaroo complained to a friend, "I hate it when it's raining and the children have to play inside!"

Kangaroos never win. They're always left holding the bag.

In Australia, a kangaroo was hit by a car and rushed to a hospital. The next morning the ward doctor made his rounds and asked, "Was he brought here to die?"
    The nurse answered, "No, he was brought here yesterdie!"

A kangaroo kept getting out of his enclosure at the zoo. Knowing that he could hop high, the zoo officials put up a ten-foot fence. He was out the next morning, just sauntering around the zoo. A twenty-foot fence was put up. Again he got out. When the fence was forty feet high, a camel in the next enclosure asked the kangaroo, "How high do you think they'll go?"
    The kangaroo said, "About a thousand feet, unless somebody locks the gate at night!"

karate

I believe that we should be nice to those who practice the martial arts. If they're happy, there's no kick coming. I practice an ancient martial art called Choo Dai Yuk. When I'm attacked by an enemy, I scream. If that doesn't scare him off, I go into my battle stance, kick out with my feet, slash at him with my hands, and butt him with my head. If that doesn't stop him, I go back to screaming.

Then there's the poor black-belt karate

champ who broke his hand trying to cut a Christmas fruitcake in half!

I have a black belt in karate. It's not that I'm good. It's just that I never wash it!

Karate makes sense. If you practice breaking boards in half, you'll be able to protect yourself the next time a board attacks you!

After four karate lessons, I can now break a two-inch board with my cast!

A karate expert in a small car put out his hand to make a left turn and made a traffic cop Jewish.

kids

There's already a "Children" category. Since I assembled it, the population of the world has probably doubled. They say a woman has a baby every thousandth of a second. We must find this lady and stop her!

"Hey, Ma, is that dinner I smell?"
"It is, and you do!"

His sister and her beau started a petting session, which was a signal for little Barry to come into the darkened living room. He watched them go at it hot and heavy until out of the corner of her eye his sister spotted him. Afraid that he'd report the proceedings to the folks, she said, cajolingly, "Barry, what do you want for Christmas?"
    Barry said, "I wanna watch."
    So they let him.

A woman said to her husband, "We ought to buy Junior a bike."
    The father said, "Will that make him behave better?"

The woman said, "I don't think so, but it'll spread his rotten behavior over a bigger area!"

A father tried to reason with his kid. "If you behave, you can grow up and be just like Lincoln."

The kid said, "Who the hell wants to be a tunnel?"

A young boy is given to profanity. His mother threatens him, "If I hear one more ugly word out of you, you can pack up and get out of this house."

The kid sneaks in a good four-letter word in the next minute. His mother forces him to pack and throw him out of the house. The hours go by. A little concerned when it becomes dark, the mother decides to go look for her son. As she opens the door, she finds him sitting outside. The mother says, "You thought it over and decided to change your ways? So you've come home."

The kid says, "Where the hell could I go?"

A kid who doesn't believe Santa can get a million things in one bag ought to look inside his mother's purse!

A small girl was at her play table, drawing with crayons. Her mother asked, "What are you drawing?"

The small girl said, "God."

The mother said, "How can you draw God? Nobody has ever seen him. Nobody knows what he looks like."

The small girl said, "They'll all know when I finish this!"

A kid asked his father, "Who brought me that moped for Christmas?"

His father said, "Santa, of course."

The kid said, "Well, Santa was here an hour ago for last month's payment!"

A kid was telling his friend about the changes in his home life. "You see, we have this new scale in the bathroom. On the bottom, it has a dial. I keep turning it, and you can't imagine how much nicer my mother is!"

Four sets of twins, accompanied by their mother, boarded a bus. The driver asked for the fares. The mother said, "Oh, these two are six and a half, so they don't have to pay anything. These are only five and they get on for free. These two will be eight in four months, so they still don't pay. And these two are only four."

The driver asked, "Do you always get two at a time?"

The woman said, "Oh, no. Sometimes we don't get any!"

A father caught his son at a prank and asked, "Don't you know the difference between right and wrong?"

The boy said, "Of course I do."

The father said, "Yet you always do wrong."

The kid said, "That shows you it's not guesswork!"

A few months ago I told my son that he should be smart enough to know there are things he cannot change. So he started—with his socks!

Oh, for the good old days when tires weren't belted and kids were!

Realizing that she's been too permissive with her three youngsters, a mother decides to take them in hand by starting with their tendency to curse. On the next school morning, as the three wild ones sit at the breakfast table, the mother asks Teddy, "What do you want for breakfast?"

Teddy says, "I'll have some of that god-damn dry cereal."

At the epithet, the mother sees red. Haul-ing off, she slaps Teddy halfway across the room. She asks her second, Freddy, what he wanted. Freddy says, "I'll have some of that goddamn dry cereal." Once again the mother lets go. This time the victim bounces off one wall and into another. The mother turns to Eddie, her third son. "What do you want for breakfast?"

Eddie said, "You can bet your ass it won't be that goddamn dry cereal!"

Two tykes were playing together when a cute, curly-haired girl walked by. One tyke said, "You know something? When I stop hating girls, I think I'll stop hating that one first!"

"How old are you, little girl?"
"When I'm home I'm eight, but when I'm on the bus I'm five!"

If you see a kid with a lump on his head, you can bet a dollar that the night before his father helped with arithmetic homework!

She was so ugly as a child that one day she left the house and her parents couldn't find her. They never looked for her!

He was a weird child. At the age of six he was abandoned by an orphanage and raised by wolves.

Two kids were trying to figure out what game to play. One said, "Let's play doctor."

The other kid said, "Okay. You operate and I'll sue!"

My son is shrewd. When he got D's and F's on his report card, he swore they were vitamin deficiencies.

Little Carl was having dinner at Steven's house. Trying to help their guest, Steven's mother asked, "Are you sure you can cut the meat by yourself?"

Carl answered, "Sure. We have it this tough at home, too!"

My son was a smart youngster. One time he brought home his report card and said, "Dad, here's my report card, and here's one of yours I happened to find in the attic!"

Kids will never understand why parents make them go to bed when they're wide awake and then make them get up when they're sleepy!

An eight-year-old hadn't said one word in his entire life. One day, however, as the family sat down to have breakfast, the boy asked, "Do we have any jam?"

The family was stunned. When they'd recovered, his father said, "How come you never said one word before?"

The boy said, "Well, up until now, every-thing's been okay!"

Alex had hurt his finger while working on his model airplane. He ran to his mother, who kissed the wound and made it better. On the way to the store a little later, Alex fell off his bike and scraped his knee. He ran to his mother, who kissed it and made it better. Returning from the store, Alex ran into the town bully, who kicked him in a very pri-vate part of his anatomy. Alex rushed home. His mother said, "Son, you're getting more like your father every day!"

A little boy walked into a drugstore and asked for a bottle of liniment and some epoxy glue. The clerk asked, "Are they for one person, or should I wrap them sepa-rately?"

The little boy said, "I don't know. Mommy broke her fancy serving platter, so she wants the glue. And Dad's what she broke the platter on!"

A young boy came home from school and told his mother, "I had a big fight with Sidney. He called me a sissy."

"What did you do?" the mother asked.

"I hit him with my purse!"

A young boy asked his father, "Dad, what's a sweater girl?"

A little baffled, the father hemmed and hawed and finally said, "A sweater girl is a girl who works in a place where sweaters are made." Pausing in relief, he went on, "Where'd you get a question like that?"

The kid said, "Forget the question. Where did you get the answer?"

Jenny watched her mother put cream on her face and asked, "What's that cream for?"

The mother said, "It's facial cream to make me look gorgeous."

A few minutes later, the mother removed the cream. Jenny stared and then said, "Didn't work, did it?"

He was an unwanted child. They taught him to look in both directions before crossing the street—up and down!

Kids today don't appreciate conveniences like air-conditioning. It doesn't sound right if you say, "Somewhere in Africa, children are sweating."

The new baby was bawling in his crib as his five-year-old brother stood by. The five-year-old asked his mother as she started to attend the infant, "Where'd we get him?"

The mother said, "He came from heaven."

The baby screamed again and the five-year-old said, "I can see why they threw him out!"

A little boy told his friend, "We're going to get a new mini-car."

The friend asked, "How do you know?"

"Dad has the spare tire already. I saw it in his wallet!"

He was always a loner. They had to put a pork chop around his neck so that the dog would play with him!

A small boy confided to a friend, "I know all about the facts of life, but I don't know if they're true!"

He was an insecure kid. When he was four, he was kidnapped, and the ransom note only asked for expenses!

Kids have saved many a marriage. Neither side wanted them!

A Beverly Hills father complained to his son, "When I was a kid, I had to walk a block to the school bus every day!"

A mother took her son to a psychologist and wanted him treated for insecurity. The psychologist asked, "Is he terribly insecure?"

The mother said, "He isn't, but the whole neighborhood is!"

My son doesn't have to learn how to speak. He gets everything he wants by screaming!

kindergarten

God invented kindergarten because in one more day Mother would have gone off her rocker! Of course, nowadays we have preschool and pre-preschool. The other day, a doctor delivered a baby and slapped it several times. The baby said, "Hurry up, Doc, I'll be late for my bus!"

The teacher told the class, "All right, now pick out a friend to sit next to."

Little Annie stood motionless.

The teacher said, "Annie, don't you have a friend?"

Annie said, "Karen's my friend, but I hate her!"

Grace, a five-year-old, returned from her first day in kindergarten. She waxed eloquent about her teacher. Grace's mother asked, "How old is your teacher?"

Grace said, "I'm not sure. She's either an early lady or a late teenager!"

A kindergarten teacher asked, "What is the shape of the Earth?"

Little Arvin said, "Terrible!"

Just before the Thanksgiving holiday, the teacher asked her kindergarten class, "What do you have to be thankful for?"

One youngster said, "I'm thankful I'm not a turkey!"

One kindergarten was very progressive. The children were given computers. An official from the state was horrified to find that young children were being subjected to such advanced learning. He ordered that the children be given Erector sets. The first day, two of the children built a computer!

kissing

Women remember the first kiss they ever got long after a man has forgotten the last! I'm sentimental about kissing. I'm good at it too,

and it must show. When I walk by, people say, "Wow, what a kisser!"

When some women get kissed, they have a quickening of the impulse!

I once got beaten up for kissing the bride after the ceremony. It was three years after the ceremony!

*The shades of night were falling fast
When for a kiss he asked her.
She must have said yes, because
The shades came down much faster!*

A young woman was talking about men to a new roommate and explaining her philosophy of life and love. The roommate said, "What about kissing?"

The young woman said, "I just kiss the men I know and those I like."

"That's just about everybody. Is there a difference?"

The young woman said, "Well, those I like, I help out!"

A man was on trial for stealing a young lady's purse in a movie theater. Put on the stand, the young lady explained what happened. "Just before the picture started, he came in and sat next to me. Before I knew it, he was sort of rubbing his hand against mine. When the picture began, he came closer and kissed me on the cheek. Soon he was kissing me on the lips. The next thing I knew, he was gone. My purse was gone too."

The judge said, "While he was doing all that kissing, why didn't you call for the manager?"

The young lady said, "I didn't know he wanted my purse!"

A kiss is a strange thing. A small boy gets it

for nothing. A young man has to steal it. And an old man has to pay for it!

They say that Eskimos kiss with their noses. How do you get a nose to pucker up?

There was a young lady named Florence
Who for kissing professed great abhorrence;
But when she'd been kissed,
And found out what she'd missed,
She cried till the tears came in torrents!

A man was having a passionate affair with his best friend's wife. As they made love, the wife said, "Kiss me. Kiss me."
  The man said, "Kiss you? I shouldn't even be doing *this!*"

He kissed her with avail. Then he tried kissing her without a veil!

There once was a maiden of Siam
Who said to her lover, young Kiam,
"If you kiss me, of course,
You'll have to use force,
But Lord knows you're stronger than I am!"

A lot of women fight back when you try to give them a kiss, but most of them just take it lying down!

A secretary was transferred from one branch of a company to another. When she reported for work, her new boss told her, "Do exactly what you did in the last office."
  She started to take off her lipstick!

A man sent his wife a letter, which ended with a check for a thousand kisses. The next day, the mailman cashed it!

ku klux klan

The last person in a white sheet I liked was Gandhi. We should dedicate ourselves to taking on hate groups. I know what hate can do. After playing a theater in Indiana a long time ago, where I'd made fun of the Klan meeting the night before, I was told by the redneck sheriff to get out of town quickly. The only one who packed faster was my drummer! Humor is the best weapon against hate groups. You know you're a hit if they don't hang you!

I know a Ku Klux Klan member whose wife just divorced him. He came home one night wearing a different sheet!

I know some youngsters who burn Jewish stars on Ku Klux Klan lawns!

Klan meetings are popular with the wives. Imagine fifty-three women wearing the same outfit you have on!

Two Klansmen met. One said, "You know that I just became the Imperial High Executive Regal Potentate of the Klan?"
  The other Klansman said, "When did you join the Klan?"
  The first Klansman said, "Yesterday afternoon!"

knock-knees

In a search for humor, no stone should be left unturned and no knee unknocked!

She was so knock-kneed her legs walked in single file!

Nowadays, with the new wardrobes, you can tell right off if a girl is knock-kneed. In the old days you had to listen!

She was so knock-kneed she had to wear her pantyhose sidesaddle!

She was so knock-kneed she had to play the cello sideways!

She knocked everything but her knees. There nature had beat her to it!

When she walks past a closed door, somebody always says, "Come in!"

When she sits down, you have to pry open her legs to make a lap!

Her knees haven't been separated since her honeymoon!

knowledge

Knowledge is wealth, except in my bank. I can recite the capitals of all the states, and the bank won't lend me a quarter. On the other hand, an errand boy became a vice-president because of knowledge—he knew who the boss was fooling around with and he knew the address of the apartment the boss had on the side!

A repairman came in to fix the new giant computer. Studying it for a moment, he took out a screwdriver and turned a small screw an eighth of an inch to the right. The computer started to hum. The repairman filled out a bill for three hundred dollars and handed it to the company accountant. The accountant demanded that the bill be itemized. Three hundred dollars was a bit much for such a simple repair. Taking another piece of paper, the repairman wrote out: "Turning screw eighth of inch to right—$.50. Knowing where to turn—$299.50."

The building elevator was being repaired. Unknown to Joe Thomas, the cables had been disconnected while repairmen worked on it. Late as usual, Joe rushed out of his apartment, pushed the elevator button, and, when the doors opened, stepped in, only to plunge down five stories. There goes the theory that what you don't know won't hurt you!

Why study? The more we know, the more we forget. The more we forget, the less we know. The less we know, the less we forget. The less we forget, the more we know. Why study?

Knowledge is what's left after we smarten up!

A tourist happened onto a country road. Stopping for directions, he saw a farmer playing with his dog. The dog did a dozen amazing tricks. The tourist asked, "How did you teach your dog all those tricks? I can't get mine to sit or fetch."

The farmer said, "Well, you have to know more than the dog in the first place!"

A young pupil asked the teacher, "What did I learn today?"

The teacher said, "That's an odd question."

The young pupil said, "Yup, but they'll ask me when I get home!"

A man priced a plant in a nursery and whistled at the high cost. He said to the nurseryman, "That's exorbitant."

The nurseryman said, "Mister, it's this way—when somebody knows the Latin name of the plant he's growing, the zoological name of the bug that eats it, and the chemical name of what kills the darn insect, somebody has to pay for it!"

Colleges are a storehouse of knowledge, but that's because the students take so little of it out!

L

lady drivers

Lady drivers may not be worse than male drivers, but in comedy they have to be. A survey by statisticians at Stanford University showed that women have one-third fewer accidents than men. The survey also proves that Stanford isn't a funny university!

One lady driver said it all. "The thing I hate most about parking is that noisy crash!"

My wife is a careful driver. She always looks both ways before hitting somebody.

My wife is getting to be such a good driver, she now opens her eyes in a passing lane!

A highway patrolman stopped a woman for speeding. She explained that she was only going 70 in compliance with the signs. The officer said, "That's the number of the highway."

The woman said, "It is? I'm glad you didn't stop me on Route 148!"

A lady driver was breaking just about every rule of the road, and made a turn from the wrong lane into the wrong street. A policeman whistled at her. She refused to stop. The policeman finally caught up with her and asked, "Didn't you hear me whistle?"

The lady driver said, "When I'm driving, I don't flirt!"

My wife never really parks her car. She abandons it!

I have a queasy feeling. My wife just flunked her driver's test for the twelfth time. I think she's carrying on with the tester.

A lady driver explained to her friend about parallel parking. "You back up until you hit the car behind you. Then you go forward until you hit the car in front."

My wife is such a bad driver, her driver's license has a picture of Saint Christopher on it!

My wife has a Saint Christopher medal hanging from the rearview mirror. It's the first time I ever saw a saint with a crash helmet on!

A lady driver was distraught. She said to her friend, "I don't know where we can park. I don't see an empty block!"

A lady driver was stopped by a motorcycle cop and said to him bitterly, "If I was speeding, so were you!"

The clerk at the motor vehicle bureau asked the lady applicant, "Have you ever driven before?"

The lady said, "Fifty thousand miles, but not from the front seat!"

The way I see it is—if you don't like the way women drive, stay off the sidewalk!

My wife is such a bad driver—instead of a mirror, she has a rearview scorecard!

My wife's car is insured with Lloyd's of Oops!

landlords

Mr. Hecksher was the landlord of our house in Manhattan. A rotund man with a thick German accent, he came around for the rent on the first of each month between noon and three in the afternoon. A sentimental sort, he knew that the children would be in school during those hours and wouldn't see how their parents were thrown out on the street for nonpayment. Mr. Hecksher blamed all evictions on his wife. If it was up to him, he swore, people wouldn't have to pay rent at all. One day, Mrs. Hecksher died. Blame was transferred to Mr. Hecksher's mother. She'd been dead twenty years, but that didn't bother Mr. Hecksher. Sunday morning, he'd visit the cemetery in New Jersey and, from beyond the grave, his mother would give him the list of who was to be thrown out that week. When Mr. Hecksher died in 1913, he was interred between his wife and mother. It served him right!

A landlord took his own time showing up when a tenant complained of a bad water leak. Arriving, the landlord saw the foot-high pool and started to cry crocodile tears. He was so sorry. He was miserable. He was ready to kill himself. The tenant said, "It wasn't all bad. While you were taking your time coming here, I taught my kids to swim!"

My landlord gave me three days to pay my rent. I picked Easter, Thanksgiving, and New Year's Eve of 1996!

I don't know what makes my landlord so obnoxious, but whatever it is, it works!

Nowadays if you give a man an inch, he'll rent it out.

My landlord has a heart of ice. He has to start his pacemaker with antifreeze!

If my landlord ate his heart out, he'd break two teeth.

I told the apartment manager we had roaches. He tried to raise my rent for keeping pets.

My landlord would steal the teeth out of your mouth and then feed you hard food!

My landlord is rough. When he gets a blood transfusion, it has to be nailed on.

My landlord never acts like a human being. He can't do imitations.

He's a beauty. He could be the first landlord who was ever impeached.

language and languages

At a dinner in Palm Springs sponsored by a large industrial firm, I was hired to perform for a Japanese audience. With an interpreter at my side, I went on and fought for my life. The result wasn't the best show I ever did. Afterward, the vice-president of the company thanked me and asked if I would work for them again at Christmas. I didn't understand. I hadn't been a smash. The vice-president explained, "The audience thought you were very funny. It didn't like the interpreter." During the Christmas season, this time in San Francisco, I did a repeat performance. The results were much better. This time the audience liked the interpreter!

A young man bought an expensive parrot as

a pet for his mother. When he visited her the following week, she invited him to dinner. Lo and behold, on the table she put the parrot, roasted to perfection. The man jumped up. "Ma," he said, not believing his eyes, "that parrot cost a fortune. It spoke seven languages. How could you roast it?"

His mother answered indignantly, "If it spoke seven languages, why didn't it say something?"

Two Iranians met in California. One started to greet the other in the language of their mother country. The other Iranian motioned for him to stop and said, "We're in America now. Speak Spanish!"

A man went in for an eye examination. The ophthalmologist pointed to his chart and asked the man to read the third row from the bottom—XDRGHFUFQ. "Read that," he said.

The man gulped and said, "Can you give me a clue? What language is it in?"

Returning from a trip overseas on a giant ocean liner, Markowitz was placed at a table with another man. The man, a Frenchman, nodded and said, *"Bon appetit."*

Markowitz nodded back and said, "Markowitz."

For several days the ritual was repeated. One afternoon, Markowitz mentioned it to another passenger. The other passenger said, "It's not what you think. *'Bon appetit'* is the French way of telling you to enjoy your meal."

At dinner that evening, Markowitz came in, nodded, and said, *"Bon appetit."*

The Frenchman rose and answered, "Markowitz!"

Shakespeare used only twenty thousand words. It takes more than that to start my car in the winter!

Tom, the teenage son, came in from the fields and said, "I've got to get this damn manure off me."

The assembled ladies of the bridge club were aghast. When the teenager left the room, one said to his mother, "He shouldn't say 'manure' in the company of ladies."

Tom's mother said, "We should count our blessings. You don't know how long it took me to get him to say 'manure'!"

las vegas

When it started, Las Vegas was a stopping point for those who wanted to get fresh mounts for their trip farther west. Everywhere people looked, they'd see only horse stables. That'll give you an idea of what Las Vegas is built on!

A Martian landed in a Las Vegas casino just as a slot machine paid off its grand jackpot. As the money poured out, the Martian said to the slot machine, "You ought to take something for that cold."

I go to Las Vegas twice a year just to visit my money!

He made a seven the hard way—two dice and a sleeve.

If you want to be happy in Las Vegas, do what the poet says: Get a jug of wine, a loaf of bread, and thou. Then get a marker for another thou . . .

It gets hot in Las Vegas. The other day I even saw a *winner* sweating.

Famous last words in Las Vegas—Give me the money I told you not to give me!

Not far from Las Vegas is the big, beautiful Boulder Dam. While there, a tourist saw a lever and pulled it. In two seconds he hit for ten million gallons of water.

I went to Las Vegas last week for laughs. In one day I laughed away my car!

In Las Vegas they give you odds you'll never get even!

I walked past a funeral parlor in Las Vegas. Four coffins were laid out at the entrance, ready for the cemetery. I smiled at the mortician and said, "Business must be good."

The mortician said, "Business is terrible. They're all shills!

The poker hand was winding down. The two players, cowboys to the core, bet the limit. One said, "I have five aces."

The other player said, "I have five aces."

The first player said, "Who wins?"

The dealer said, "The one who draws first."

It was so crowded in Las Vegas last weekend, I had to go to a psychiatrist to find a place to lie down.

lateness

I have the feeling there's a correlation between getting up in the morning and getting up in the world.

A man walked into the railroad station of a small town and asked what time the train arrived. The agent said, "It comes in at eight P.M. and leaves at eight-fifteen."

Because it was only six o'clock, the man started to walk into town for a cup of coffee. When he was two blocks away from the station, he heard the whistle of an approaching train. He rushed back just as the train arrived and said angrily to the agent, "You told me the train came at eight. I could have missed it."

The agent said, "Keep your shirt on, buster. This is yesterday's train!"

After a youngster left the supermarket with an order for his mother, he ran into a friend and started to talk. Twenty minutes later, the store manager went outside and saw the youngster still around. The store manager said, "You'll be late for dinner."

The youngster said, "I can't be. I got the food!"

At five every morning he opens his bedroom window wide and climbs in.

Punctuality is the ability to guess how late the other couple is going to be.

On my watch I have a setting that tells me the time in the next time zone and when my wife'll be ready!

My wife was an hour late for the honeymoon. I had to start by myself.

Then there was the boss who gave his secretary a big raise because she was late—two months late!

laundry

At night, in the privacy of our hotel room, my mother washed and ironed my outfit so I'd have something fresh to wear onstage. No one ever found out that, at the time, it was the only stage outfit I had. After I made a little bit of a name and some money, I didn't let my mother wash that one outfit anymore. I bought another outfit so she'd have two!

I brought my laundry home this morning. They refused it!

A man placed some red candy drops in his shirt pocket. Because of the unseasonable heat, the candy melted, creating a round red stain on the pocket. His wife brought it to the laundry. The laundryman nodded, impressed, as he looked at it and said, "Good shot!"

My son came home from camp with a valise filled with clothes that didn't belong to him. My wife sent everything to the laundry. Three days later, we had our son's own clothes back!

I like old-fashioned laundries where they tear off the buttons by hand!

My son isn't neat. We have to wash his clothes at home so we can send them out to be laundered.

In the old days, they did laundry by going down to the river and beating each piece of the laundry with a rock. It was easy to tell who had the cleanest laundry—it was the stuff with the most holes.

My shirt must be made of an Indian fabric. To clean it you have to beat it against a rock.

Laundries aren't what they used to be. I sent four shirts out last week and they lost the buttonholes!

I don't believe Jack the Ripper ever died. I think you'll find him in the laundry, doing my shirts!

To make things easier for our housekeeper, we bought a washer-dryer that breaks down in Spanish.

We send our stuff to a hand laundry. The stuff comes back dirty, but the laundryman's hands are nice and clean!

You can always tell my son's dirty clothes. His is the stuff that's eating the hamper.

I like to wear cufflinks, but I don't have any shirts with French cuffs. So the other day I had my wrists pierced!

lawns

I planted Bermuda grass this summer. I had the gardener throw out some seed and I went to Bermuda!

With all the throwaways, my lawn could win a prize for newspaper coverage!

Dew is a big problem on my lawn. Every morning ten dogs dew on it!

I just got my water bill for last month. That's all I needed—two trees and a lawn with a drinking problem!

Why is crabgrass so crabby? It's winning!

With my new power mower, I've tried all kinds of mulch—grass shavings, leaves, toes . . .

I'm not too good with a lawn. I put in new grass, and four sprinklers died!

I didn't work on my lawn this year. I went straight from winter to back X rays!

lawyers

You can always work a lawyer joke into the conversation or a routine. The difference between lawyer jokes and attorney jokes is about fifty dollars an hour, with the latter on top. I've found that professionals—doctors, lawyers, psychologists—enjoy jokes about themselves. At stag roasts, the more vicious the attack, the greater the laughter. However, it's more than possible that these professionals get the last laugh anyway, when they send us a bill!

Two lawyers were going at one another as the trial started. One lawyer said to the other, "You are a complete and total fraud."

The other lawyer retorted, "You're a penny-stealing ambulance chaser."

The judge cut in, saying, "Now that you've identified one another, shall we go on with the case?"

This lawyer helped a woman lose a hundred eighty pounds of fat. He got her a divorce.

Two very rich people got divorced, and their lawyers lived happily ever after.

A felon on trial is concerned about his chances. His lawyer tells him, "Be calm. I'm a terrific lawyer. I'll prove to the jury that you were in Hong Kong when the crime was committed. I'll put on two doctors who'll prove that you were temporarily insane. I'll pay off two of their witnesses. I have two school buddies on the jury, and my wife's uncle is the judge. Meanwhile, try to escape!"

A lawyer is a man who prevents somebody else from getting your money.

A client asked his lawyer how to plead. The lawyer said, "On your knees!"

Hell hath no fury like the lawyer of a woman scorned.

An attorney asked for a continuance because he was feeling poorly and needed minor surgery. The judge said, "Look, your client was caught red-handed and confessed everything. What new things can you add in his favor?"

The client jumped up and said, "I'm curious about that too, Your Honor!"

A lawyer's wife was unhappy with the state of their home. The furniture was old and dirty, the drapes torn, and the carpet half eaten away. She demanded a complete redoing. The attorney said, "Look, sweetheart. I just got a new divorce case today. As soon as I break up their home, we'll start fixing up ours!"

A lawyer called an electrician to do some home repairs. The electrician charged eighty-five dollars an hour. The lawyer said, "Eighty-five dollars? I don't make that as a lawyer."

The electrician said, "Neither did I, when I was a lawyer!"

A lawyer was cross-examining a famous pathologist and asked, "When did you conduct the autopsy?"

The pathologist said, "Eleven P.M. on the fourth."

"And he was dead at the time?"

"No," the doctor said patiently. "He was just lying around on the table, wondering why I was performing an autopsy on him!"

A man calls a law firm. The voice answers, "Stein, Stein, Stein, and Stein."

The man says, "May I speak to Mr. Stein?"

"He's not in."

"All right. Let me talk to Mr. Stein."

"He's away."

"Then let me to talk to Mr. Stein."

"He's out of the office."
"How about Mr. Stein?"
"Speaking!"

A bartender tried to give his lawyer a retainer of some whiskey. The lawyer counted the bottles and said, "There's only seven bottles. I can't make a case out of that!"

Clothes don't necessarily make the man, but a good suit makes a lawyer.

Appearing for a conference with a prospective attorney, a client tells the details of his case. The attorney mulls it over for a moment and says, "This is a pretty strong case."
　　The client says, "I'd better not sue. I told you the other guy's side of it!"

A lawyer was questioning one of the witnesses. "Are you sure my client shot him at close range?"
　　The witness said, "Very close range."
　　"Were there powder marks on him?"
　　"Yup. Why do you think she shot him?"

His mother is Catholic. His father is Jewish. When he goes to confession, he brings along his lawyer!

laziness

I can't understand lazy people. I would tell you exactly what my opinion of them is, but I think I have to lie down...

He goes through revolving doors on other people's pushes!

Then there's the lazy stickup man. He makes carbon copies of his holdup notes!

He could fall asleep in the middle of a nap!

When he plays golf, he falls asleep on his own backswing!

He's got a great way of starting a day. He goes back to bed!

His feet fall asleep when he's running for a bus!

He doesn't walk in his sleep. He hitchhikes!

A hobo complained about a city, "The folks in this town are really lazy. Everywhere you go, somebody offers you work!"

Lazy? If opportunity knocked, he'd sit back and complain about the noise!

The government was building a road. One morning the foreman learned that they had run out of shovels. He called his office for instructions and was told, "There are no more shovels. Tell the men to lean on one another!"

Jones was a truly lazy man. His friend Brown came to him one day and said, "I just heard of a new gold field in Australia. The gold is strewn all over the ground. You just have to bend down and pick it up."
　　Jones said, "You say you have to bend down and pick it up?"

He's so lazy, he's got an itch and he's six months behind in his scratching!

He's so lazy he won't even exercise discretion!

He puts popcorn in his pancake mix so they'll turn over by themselves!

He's taking a vacation from a job he doesn't even have!

He could sleep twenty-four hours a day. The trouble is, he sleeps thirty hours a day.

People shouldn't say he's lazy. He's always carrying a load!

He discovered a new antiperspirant—unemployment!

He's so lazy he lets his fingers do the walking—which accounts for the corns on his thumbs!

He's so lazy he could become a landmark!

He missed his nap today. He slept right through it!

The laziest man in the county was sitting on his porch, waiting for a wind to come along and start his rocker. His wife saw a fantastic display of natural fireworks in the sky as meteors showered down, planets zoomed by, and galaxies came apart. The wife said, "I've never seen anything so beautiful in my life. There must be a million meteors showering down."
    The man said, "Shame I'm facing the other way!"

He doesn't know how long he's been out of work. He can't remember his birthday.

She's so lazy a rapist tried to attack her and fell asleep!

He's so lazy, he died at twenty-six and nobody found out until he was fifty!

legs

Sitting at lunch together, we were discussing our lower limbs. I said, "I have great legs. I have the legs of a sixteen-year-old." From the right, a joker said, "Give them back. "You're ruining them!" I wasn't upset. I do have great legs. I also have a fantastic elbow!

"What has a hundred legs and lives on yogurt?"
"An aerobic class!"

She was so bowlegged she looked like two giraffes kissing!

She was so bowlegged she had to get out of bed at night to turn over!

She had such varicose veins, her legs looked like long road maps!

She's so bowlegged you could hang her over the front door for luck!

She has the skinniest legs. One day there was a tear in her pantyhose and she fell out!

A woman with a wooden leg started to dance with a man at the Saturday-night town party. As they moved along the dance floor, the man noticed that the woman was getting taller and taller. Finally he asked what was happening. The woman explained, "Well, you see, I have a wooden leg. You're turning me the wrong way!"

lesbians

Once taboo in polite company, jokes about lesbians have joined the jokes about gays and condoms as viable material. I remember an occasion when there was a tumult at my network because the word "pregnant" was found in a script. I like the new candor. I worry only that it may overcompensate for the old prudishness by demanding the elimination of all jokes that don't contain at least two "dirty" words. If you intend to tell jokes, especially at an affair, try to feel comfortable with the new freedoms in both subject matter and language. Test a line or story on yourself. Your comfort or lack of it will tell you whether it should be used. At no time, however, even with a measure of comfort in you, tell jokes about transvestites and chickens to the Library Club!

A lesbian was haranguing a crowd of demonstrators. From the crowd, a man called out, "Don't you wish you were a man?"
The lesbian said, "Don't you?"

A young woman comes home to her mother. The young woman is in tears. "Mother," she says, "I think I'm a lesbian."
The mother says, "That's nonsense. Now go up and shave!"

There was one lesbian who was still unsure of her rights. When having orgasm with a man, she would call out her own name!

A woman is writing a book about her lesbian daughter. It'll be called, *My Daughter the Son*.

Many lesbians pray to God. They know she'll listen!

"I'm a lesbian."
"No kidding? How are things in Beirut?"

liars

Theatrical agents are notorious tamperers with the truth. I had an agent just before World War II who had a master's degree in lying. He was once called to testify in court. The clerk asked him if he promised to tell the truth, the whole truth, and nothing but the truth. My agent asked, "For how long?" My head writer some years later was a dedicated liar-hater. Retreating from a brief encounter with Arnie, a masterful liar, my head writer told me, "I think I just caught Arnie in the truth."

You can tell when he's lying. His lips are moving!

He can lie without moving his lips!

With her, truth is like a girdle—she stretches it!

She doesn't exaggerate. She just remembers big!

The way he handles the truth, he could work for the weather bureau!

Truth may not be stranger than fiction, but in his mouth it's much scarcer!

If he asks you to guess what he makes a week, you couldn't go wrong if you said, "Half!"

The only thing that lies more than he does are falsies!

He's been chasing the truth for years. He's never caught up with it.

His lips lie so much, he had to go to a plastic surgeon to get an oath!

She found the secret of youth. She lies about her age.

Half the lies they tell about me aren't true.

Love lies in a woman's eyes, and lies, and lies!

If George Washington never told a lie, how did he become President?

I wouldn't believe him if he swore he was lying!

One country gent is such a liar—when it comes time for the hogs to eat, he has to get somebody else to call them!

For a man, a lie is a last resort. For women, it's first aid!

A notorious liar died. As his acquaintances passed by the open casket, one said to another, "I still don't believe him!"

A member of the parish helped himself to a Bible just about every Sunday, taking it home after the service. The minister didn't mind because the parishioner was a liar, and the minister hoped that some of the truth of the Bible would rub off on him. Costs started to mount, so after a service one Sunday, the minister asked the parishioner if he'd taken a Bible. The parishioner denied doing so. Weeks went by and more Bibles were missing. The minister went to the parishioner and asked point-blank, "Have you been taking the Good Book from us?"

The parishioner said, "No, Reverend. I'll swear to that on a stack of Bibles!"

libraries

By the time I was ten, I'd worn out our branch library. I'd read every play and comedy book. I even stole a book by Elbert Hubbard, a funny writer. A lifetime later, I ran into Mrs. Devlin, the librarian. She asked, "Do you plan to return the Hubbard book?" She'd known about the theft all along. I still have the book. By now, I must owe two hundred thousand dollars

in late payments. Whether there are sanctions or not, I don't suggest the taking of books!

I met a librarian the other day who carries a card in his wallet that reads, IN CASE OF EMERGENCY, SHHHHH!

It was suggested that a young man improve his mind by reading. In the library he asked for a good book to read. The librarian asked if he wanted something light or heavy. The young man answered, "It doesn't matter. I've got my car with me."

A young boy returned a book that had seen better days. It was worn, with a cover that barely held the pages together. Examining the volume while the youngster watched, the librarian said, "This is pretty technical, isn't it?"

The youngster said, "It was that way when I got it!"

A borrower called the branch library and asked, "Do you ever mail books to people?"

The librarian said, "Can't you come in?"

The borrower said, "I can't find parking!"

life

Life is very simple. The first thing you should remember about life is: Don't worry about it. Actually, there are only two things to worry about—either you're a success or you're not. If you're successful, you have nothing to worry about. If you're not, there are two things to worry about—either you're healthy or you're not. If you're healthy, what's to worry about? If you're not healthy, there are two things to worry about—you'll live or you'll die. If you die, there are still two things to worry about. Will your destination be heaven or hell? If it's heaven, you're cool. If you go to hell, you'll be so busy greeting all your old friends you won't have time to worry! Let's face it—life is great and you can never get out alive!

I get the feeling that I'm cutting the lawn of life with cuticle scissors!

The only thing I regret about my past is its length. If I had my life to live over, I'd make the same mistakes, but a lot sooner.

One way to live longer is to cut out the things that you want to live longer for.

It's not surprising that women live longer than men. Look how long they're girls!

It's rough to go through life with your contents looking as if they settled during shipping!

An elderly gentleman was given a complete physical. Afterward, the doctor said, "You'll live to be ninety."

The man said, "I *am* ninety."

The doctor said, "See, what did I tell you?"

I feel like a tap dancer in the canoe of life!

Now that I've learned to live life, most of it is gone!

She married him for life, but until now he hasn't showed any!

May you live as long as you like, and have what you like as long as you live!

The Hebrew toast is "L'Chaim." It means "Life!" I know a fellow who's doing L'Chaim at Sing Sing!

A young man wanted to know the meaning of life. Learning that a swami in Nepal knew the answer, the young man sold off all of his property and went off to Nepal. He traveled through the harshest land, eating the most basic foods and sleeping on the bare ground. He arrived at the foot of the high mountain atop which the swami lived. The young man climbed the mountain. His feet were blistered and bloody, but he kept going. He reached the top and approached the swami. He asked, "Swami, what is the meaning of life?"

The swami said, "Life is a bowl of fruit."

"And?"

"No 'and,' my son. Life is a bowl of fruit."

The young man said, "Swami, I sold my worldly possessions, I traveled through all kinds of terrain, I suffered, and all you can say is, 'Life is a bowl of fruit'?"

The swami said, "All right. Life is not a bowl of fruit!"

The seven stages of man are:

First stage: He sees the earth.

Second stage: He wants the earth.

Third stage: He hustles to get it.

Fourth stage: He decides that half will be enough.

Fifth stage: He becomes even less demanding.

Sixth stage: He'd be thrilled to get a six-by-two strip of it.

Seventh stage: He gets the strip!

Considering the alternative, life isn't such a bad deal!

Life isn't a dress rehearsal!

limericks

Jokes seem to be funnier when colored with tricks of language. Rhymes are one of the best aids. Since you get a lot of rhymes in a limerick, the punch line concentrates them and the laugh is bigger. The limerick isn't the easiest form to master, but once you get the idea of lines flowing into one another freely, you can come up with a good poem. George M. Cohan once told me that a limerick was an Irish jig made of words.

A valiant young sportsman named Fisher
Once fished from the edge of a fissure.
A fish with a grin
Pulled the fisherman in;
Now they're fishing the fissure for Fisher!

A maiden who walked on the Corso
Displayed a great deal of her torso.
A crowd soon collected
But no one objected
And some were in favor of more so!

There was a young lady named Clair
Who had a magnificent pair.
Or that's what we thought
Till we saw one get caught
On a thorn and begin losing air!

There once was a man not unique
Who imagined himself quite a shique,
But the pickings were dim
For a fellow like him,
Who only made sixty a week!

There once was a charmer from Exeter
Who made all the men crane their nexeter,
And some who were brave
Would take out and wave
The distinguishing marks of their sexeter!

There was a young lady from Penn
Who said, "Let us do it again—
And again and again
And again and again
And again and again and again!"

God's plan had a hopeful beginning,
But man spoiled it all just by sinning.
We trust that this story
Will bring back God's glory,
But at the moment, the other side's winning!

While trying to live like a Bedouin,
A daring young fellow named Edouin
Attempted to sneak
A cute slave from a sheik
But in a moment or two he was a dedouin!

A senile, decrepit crustacean,
His mind on a mild molestation,
Attempted to grab
A luscious young crab
But experienced only frustration!

An ambitious young amateur sleuth
Behaved in a manner uncouth,
In pursuing a victim,
He floored him and kicked him
And fractured his features forsooth!

One night an amorous young Sioux
Had a date with a maiden be knioux,
The coroner found
The couple had drowned
Making love in a leaky canoe!

lions

The king of beasts deserves a few pages of his own!

Rogers and Brown went on a safari. The first night out, they bet a hundred dollars on who would bag the first lion. In the morning, both went their separate ways. An hour later, a lion approached the jeep in which Brown sat, watching the vista. The lion asked, "Do you know a guy named Rogers?"

Brown said, "Yes, I do."

The lion said, "Well, he owes you a hundred dollars!"

A lion complained to another animal, "I must be going crazy. Every time I roar, I have to sit through a movie!"

A woman went to an agency and hired a maid without explaining that the household was unique. The woman and the maid walked into the house, where they were greeted by a large male lion, obviously the family pet. The maid turned to the woman and said, "I think I'll have to quit. I don't work in any house where there's a big lion running around. I know I should have told you at the office, but I didn't think it would come up!"

A lion and a rabbit walked into a restaurant. The rabbit ordered a nice salad. The lion shook his head. He didn't want anything. The rabbit explained to the waiter, "Look, if he was hungry, do you think I'd be sitting here?"

A lion escaped from the zoo. The head zookeeper went over to a new man and suggested that he chase the lion down. The new man wasn't keen on going. The head zookeeper said, "Take a good shot of booze first."

The new man said, "No, thank you. Whiskey gives me too much courage!"

I was surrounded by a bull and a lion. I shot the lion first, because I could always shoot the bull!

A lion and an elephant were talking. The elephant said, "I fill my whole trunk with peanuts."

The lion said, "No kidding? Where do you keep your clothes?"

A hunter visited another hunter and was given a tour of the house. In the den was a stuffed lion. The hunter asked, "When did you bag him?"

The host said, "Three years ago, when I went hunting with my wife."

"What's he stuffed with?"

"My wife!"

A hunter on safari in Africa had made life miserable for his guide. The hunter would insist that they go in one direction, then another, and still another. By now, the hunter had no idea where they were. He yelled at his guide, "You said you were the best guide in all of Kenya."

The guide said, "The trouble is we're in Nigeria!"

The lion tamer had lost his pet lion. Rather than close down the act, the lion tamer decided to hire a man to put on a lion's skin and pretend to be a lion. Needing a job desperately, a man took the job. Came eight-thirty at night, the crowds filled the large tent. The band played a fanfare and the lion tamer made his entrance. Into the cage he went. After taking a dozen bows, he snapped his whip. The lion to the right of the false one bellowed at being hit. The false lion backed off and was ready to end his short career in the circus. The other lion leaned over and whispered, "Take it easy. You weren't the only guy who needed a job!"

logic

Logic is what's left after all the excuses have been given. Among the most common expressions around my house: "Let's be logical!" It comes into play when I want to go to a ball game, play poker, or express a desire not to have cousins come over for the evening. "That's not logical" surfaces after I suggest that the house-keeper be fired for blowing up the washer-dryer and half of the kitchen. "Use your head for once" is the third of my wife's debate-stiflers. It could have stopped Hitler in Czechoslovakia!

A young Marine recruit was called into the office and told that he'd failed to show up for camouflage class. The young marine asked, "How did you know?"

Unhappy at the state of Junior's room, his mother came up with a new rule. Each time she had to pick something up off the floor of his room, Junior would have to pay her a dime. At the end of the week, she added up the chores and demanded ninety cents. Junior paid her and said, "Thanks, Ma. Keep up the good work!"

A man went to visit a friend and was surprised that the friend kept bees. The man asked, "Where's your hive?"
  The friend said, "Oh, I keep them in a sealed glass jar."
  "Don't they suffocate?"
  "Sure, but they're only bees!"

Worn out from carrying the luggage and running for the train, the husband said, "If you'd moved a little faster, we would have caught that train."
  The wife said, "If you hadn't rushed, we wouldn't have had to wait so long for the next one!"

The party that picked up the phone after I dialed told me that I had the wrong number.
  I asked, "Are you sure?"
  The party said, "Did I ever lie to you before?"

While hunting, a woman said to her husband, "Of course I heard it moo. Why shouldn't a moose moo?"

I know a man who didn't have a penny to his name. So he changed his name!

A man riding an Amtrak train went around saying, "I'm George Washington. I'm George Washington."
  The conductor called out, "Valley Forge," and the man got off!

A woman who finds she's able to ward men off should go out with stronger men!

Money can't buy happiness, but it makes misery more comfortable!

You can teach your dog to play fetch by tying your cat to a boomerang!

loneliness

Show people can define loneliness better than just about everybody else. Out on the road, with the best restaurant in town closing at nine and the movie house just outfitted for talkies, an actor can tell the weight of loneliness. Unless, of course, you can become friendly with a bear or a moose. You may not know this, but a female bear can be a good dancer. They like to dip! Jokes about loneliness hit harder than "lazy" or "skinny" or "short" jokes. I'd never use jokes on the subject against the truly lonely.

She was so lonely she used to walk her wig!

A man was very lonely. One day he met an ugly woman, courted her, and soon they were married. One morning when the man awoke he saw the mess lying next to him, her eyes crossed, her mouth drooling, blemishes all over her, and said out loud, "God, nobody can be that lonely!"

She's so lonely, when somebody calls her, her phone applauds!

Her answering machine died of rust!

He's grateful he's a schizophrenic. It gives him somebody to talk to.

She's so lonely her echo never comes back!

She sent her picture to a lonely hearts club. They sent the picture back and said, "We're not that lonely!"

Every time she tries to get a computer date, the machine tilts!

los angeles

This splendid city is one of the great comedy targets. Just indicate that you've been there recently for a visit, or that you live there, or that you have friends and family there—any book will do—and you can lambast the size of the city, the laid-back attitude, and, of course, its great air. Sex jokes work better with Hollywood, as there is something lascivious about the notion of moviemaking and stars. Angelenos laugh at the barbs being thrown at their home sweet home. They know the rest of the world would give its eyeteeth to emigrate to the city of sunshine, cool, and annual record automobile accidents. One year, L.A. wasn't leading the nation in fatalities. A wag said, upon hearing the news, "Come on, folks, we're not doing our part!" The key to L.A. is in its manic urge to be the first in everything—the best or the worst. It usually wins!

Los Angeles has hosted many political conventions because it makes work easier. If you want a smoke-filled room, you just open a window!

Some men don't understand L.A. One visitor took a cab from the airport. The lady cabdriver asked, "How far do you want to go?"

His case comes up Thursday!

In an L.A. haberdashery, a customer looked at the suit he was trying on and said, "Do you mind if I go outside and see how the fabric looks in the smog?"

In L.A. there are many restaurants with outdoor patios. But you have to eat fast before your soup gets dirty!

What they need around L.A. is a good detour!

My uncle was the town drunk—but Los Angeles?

There's no place I want to get to as fast as the L.A. freeways can take me!

L.A. is different. Where else can you find unemployment offices with valet parking?

L.A. lives for speed. Last night I saw two hearses drag racing!

A crook robbed a bank in L.A. the other day and vanished into thick air!

If you see a bluebird in L.A., it could be a sparrow holding its breath!

Los Angeles is the home of the three little white lies: "The Ferrari is paid for," "The mortgage is assumable," and "It's just a cold sore!"

You have to be brave to cross a street in L.A. It's the only town where the front bumpers know karate!

In L.A. the girls are easy on the eyes. Now if only the air was too!

In L.A., if you shoot an arrow into the air—it stays there!

You know you're in L.A. when you put air in your tires and they cough!

Where else but in L.A. can you be awakened in the morning by birds coughing?

In L.A. you can't breathe until you put the air through a blender!

The people of L.A. are cool. I saw a manhole cover shoot fifty feet into the air. A passerby said, "Heads!"

Older people come to L.A. to retire. I know one neighborhood where the average age is "deceased"!

love

It depends on the audience. Younger marrieds seem to resist a tear or two in the fabric of romance. I guess, after a few years, you become numb. Older people, except for nine people in South Dakota, scream at love ridiculed. College audiences don't relate to the subject unless it's salted with sex.

Love is when a man takes out the garbage and his wife goes with him!

I've been in love with the same woman for thirty years. If my wife ever finds out, she'll kill me!

A man in his eighties kept giving in to his amorous urges. Attractive to women, young and old, he put a notch in his cane for each conquest. A month later he died. He made the mistake of leaning on his cane!

A young man and woman had a most pleasant date. Taking the young lady home, the young man hinted that he'd like to come in and really fulfill the evening. The young woman said, "My roommate's home."

The young man said, "What about this mat that says 'Welcome'?"

The young woman said, "I don't think there's enough room for us on that!"

Two older men sat on a bench in the park. One said, "I hear that eating raw oysters puts lead in your pencil."

The other man said, "I don't like raw oysters, and to tell you the truth, I don't have any women to write to!"

She said, "All right, I'll make love to you, but only if I can hear bells ringing and see lights flashing."

He made love to her on a pinball machine!

Love is the oldest story in the world: He falls, she falls, and Nigara Falls!

Then there's the girl who fell in love with a one-legged detective. But she ended the affair because she wanted the sleuth, the whole sleuth, and nothing but the sleuth.

It is better to have loved and lost. Much better!

Love makes a man think almost as much of a woman as he does of himself.

I'll tell you how much in love I am. When my girl and I were necking, her dog took a chunk out of my leg and I didn't notice it until I got home!

A man returned from his honeymoon. A

friend asked, "Well, how's marriage?"

The man said, "Not bad. It's almost like being in love!"

A husband and wife were making love, but the act seemed without any passion. After a while the husband asked, "What's the matter? Can't you think of anybody either?"

A husband and wife were making love when the husband asked, "Did I hurt you?"

The wife said, "No, not at all. Why?"

The husband said, "I thought I felt you move!"

A salesman stayed overnight at a farmhouse. In the shank of the evening, the farmer's daughter appeared and asked if he wanted anything. The salesman reached over and attempted to embrace the girl. She said, "Stop, or I'll tell my father."

The salesman then attempted to kiss the girl. She repeated, "Stop, or I'll tell my father."

On his third attempt, the salesman was successful and the young lady joined him for some entertainment. After a pleasant love bout, the young lady asked if they could do it again. The salesman obliged. A third time, the young lady asked for some food for her passion. The salesman obliged again. At the fourth request, the salesman sat up and said, "Stop, or I'll tell your father!"

Many women are music lovers. Some can make love without it!

A couple made love and the young woman said, "My mother always told me to be good in bed. Was I?"

luck (good and bad)

Ordinarily I wouldn't believe in luck, but how else can I explain other people doing well?

I'll show you a lucky man—his secretary's lipstick is the same color as his wife's!

One chap was unlucky from the day of his birth. Nothing good had ever happened to him. To help him out, some of his friends got together and decided to give him some money. Knowing that he wouldn't take it as charity, they arranged a drawing in which all the numbers put into the hat would be the same as his. The evening of the drawing came. The man put his hand into the hat to draw the winning number. He pulled out a number—7¼!

My luck is always bad when thirteen people are sitting at a bar and I'm picking up the check!

I have no luck. A girl stopped me once and asked me if I wanted to have some fun. I told her I did. So she sold me a joke book!

Two men met on a street. One had an empty sleeve where his right arm had been until recently. Over his right eye was a dark patch. The other man was a living mummy. His head was covered with a thick bandage. His left leg had a cast on it. He walked slowly because of his crutches. Around his neck he wore a whiplash collar. As they passed one another, the first man said, "Hi. How are you doing, Lucky?"

I have no luck. I had a ten-dollar check, and the only one who could cash it was a guy I owed nine dollars to!

I'm very lucky. I've been to Europe almost as often as my luggage!

I have no luck. I once went to the Grand Canyon and it was closed!

I'm the kind of guy who gets paper cuts from get-well cards!

I once yodeled from a mountaintop in Switzerland. An answering service yodeled back!

I bought an anti-magnetic, anti-gravity, waterproof watch. I lost it!

If I didn't have bad luck once in a while, I wouldn't have any luck at all!

Since the day I got married, I keep looking for the mirror I must have broken!

I'll show you bad luck. I saw a guy hit a truck that was delivering mirrors!

I knew somebody who really had bad luck. He was a total zero—poor, sickly, and unhappily married. He believed in reincarnation, so he put a gun to his head and pulled the trigger. He came back as himself!

Luck always seems to favor the guy who doesn't need it!

maids

I have to be careful with what I say about maids. Mine checks the pages I write. If I cast aspersions on her, even indirectly, she won't dust. The last time, we had to beg her to take up the broom and the vacuum cleaner. She finally dusted and we found Lawrence of Arabia! When our maid feels put upon, she gets a look on her face that can only be erased by a raise. Of course, she's tired of raises now. She just wants property! Almost every Wednesday she comes to me, sobbing. Her sister is in the hospital and she has to go see her. I can see why there is a shortage of hospital beds in our city. My maid has sisters in most of those we do have!

The lady of the house scolded the maid, saying, "There's a month's dust on the furniture."

The maid said, "Can't be my fault. I've only been here two weeks."

The lady of the house said to her maid, "I'd be so lonely if you left me."

The maid said, "Don't worry. I won't leave you until you have a house full of company!"

The maid was called by her best friend. What were they going to do on the weekend?

The maid said, "To tell you the truth, I'm afraid to leave the baby with its mother!"

"That Mrs. Baker is a fine lady to work for."

"I like her."

"You can't do too much for her."

"I don't intend to!"

A maid was telling another maid about a party at the house. "You never saw such pretty ladies," she said. "All dressed up, with jewels dripping to the floor."

The other maid asked, "What did they talk about?"

The first maid said, "Us!"

Two maids were discussing their week's work. One said, "All day long it's 'Yes, ma'am,' 'Yes, ma'am,' 'Yes, ma'am.'"

The other one said, "My trouble comes at night. 'No, sir,' 'No, sir,' 'No, sir'!"

My maid quit the other day. We treated her like one of the family!

Since we got our new maid, we can't get *Good Housekeeping* delivered to our house!

Our maid just started her spring cleaning. She's already picked up most of the tinsel.

We had to fire our maid because she spilled things. She told the other maids what went on in our house!

Our maid can't stand dirty words—like "dust," "wash," "cook" . . .

I think our maid is getting lazy. The other day I found her washing the dishes in bed!

mail (and the post office)

Long castigated, berated, spat upon, and humilitated, the post office deserves more. It deserves reprobation, odium, denunciation, and a tad of vituperation. Actually, I'm one of the few who salute the men and women who cannot be slowed down by snow, sleet, or hail. It's nice weather that slows them down!

Columbus took the wrong direction from Spain when he went looking for India. He landed in the West Indies and decided that he'd reached America. Not bad for a guy who never worked for the post office!

Stamps are so expensive, college kids are screaming that they can't afford to write home for money!

The other day at the post office, I gave the clerk a word of thanks. He dropped it!

I wrote a letter to the Postmaster General, telling him how to improve the mail service. It got lost!

When you write "fragile" on a package, it helps the clerks at the post office. When they hear the sound of glass breaking, they know which package it came from.

Some people complain about how slow the mails are, but I got a letter from New York that was sent to me in California in one day. Of course, it was supposed to go to Montana.

One thing about the post office—it's two hundred years old, and yet it's never been hindered by progress!

Most of the time people get what's coming to them—unless it's mailed!

The post office is two hundred years old. If I were that old, I'd move slowly too!

My mail is a little slow. Last month my flower seeds came as a bouquet!

The post office workers started a slow-pitch league last year. The first game lasted all season.

They just came out with the perfect stamp. It's got a picture of people waiting on line for stamps.

I just got my new driver's license in the mail. It expired last month!

If the world is getting smaller, why do they keep charging more for letters?

Last year they had a three-week strike at the post office. Nobody knew!

Bad news doesn't travel fast, not if you mail it!

Spring is a little late this year. It must have come by mail!

The mail clerks in my post office are considerate. All packages marked "fragile" are thrown underhand!

I sent a package the other day. On it I wrote: PICTURES—DO NOT BEND. Two days later they arrived with a note that said, "They certainly do!"

A woman mailed an old family Bible. When it arrived a week later, six of the Commandments were broken!

manners (good and bad)

I believe that in order to amount to anything today, a person must have impeccable manners. You just can't make it if you have peccable manners!

A country gent, not used to the fancy ways of the big city, went to a fancy cocktail party. He kept putting his fingers in the dip. Seeing him, one of the other guests walked over and said, "Don't put your fingers in the dip. That's what the crackers are for."

The country gent spent the rest of the party putting his fingers in the crackers!

I have manners. I believe you should knock on an oyster shell before you open it.

A photographer had taken some pictures of a society matron. Looking at the one he liked most, the matron said angrily, "That's a terrible picture. Does that look at all like me?"

The photographer said politely, "Mrs. Chappell, the answer is in the negative!"

A man with manners will always put his ashes in an ashtray if there's no carpeting around!

He had the manners of a gentleman. I just knew they couldn't belong to him!

One midtown cop with manners is terrible at giving directions. He won't point!

One day he drank some furniture polish by mistake. He had a fine finish!

If it weren't for toothpicks, some people wouldn't have anything to do after dinner!

"How do you grow old so gracefully?"
"I give all of my time to it!"

He's living proof that stuffed shirts come in all sizes!

He may be in *Who's Who*, but he doesn't know what's what!

marijuana

Don't look at me. If I could handle pot, I'd have become a musician!

He smokes so much grass—once a month he has to mow his stomach!

I remember the days when a cool smoke was menthol!

You know he smokes a lot of marijuana. His couch has seatbelts!

I know a considerate pusher. He sells candy reefers to kids who are too young to smoke!

They now have a marijuana-flavored toothpaste. You still get cavities, but you don't care!

You can always tell a marijuana grower. On his lawn he has a sign—KEEP ON THE GRASS.

I remember when roll-your-own meant a hoop!

marriage

"Marriage is a great institution, but who wants to live in an institution?" The first marriage joke I ever told on the floor. I was about twelve. Nobody laughed. I learned a great comedy truth: Know what you're talking about! Half of the jokes in the history of the world have been about married people. One of fifty is for it. I subscribe to an affection for the little woman. In fact, I've been in love with the same woman for thirty-eight years. If my wife ever finds out, she'll kill me! That's the second joke anybody ever tells about marriage. It still works. You can't go wrong with a "wife" or "husband" routine. Co-misery must breed an intense desire to laugh!

Anybody who claims that marriage is a fifty-fifty proposition doesn't know the first thing about women or fractions!

My wife and I have been happily married for thirty-five years because of our compatibility—we both love to fight!

The psychiatrist had a tremor in his voice as he told Mr. Cooper, "I regret that I have to tell you this—your wife's mind is gone."

Mr. Cooper said, "I'm not surprised. She's been giving me a piece of it every day for twenty years!"

My brother is an inconsiderate husband. He won a trip for two to Paris. He went twice!

He hung the embroidered sign in the kitchen. It read BLESS OUR HAPPY HOME. His wife took a look and said, "It goes on the other wall, dummy!"

One fellow felt that his marriage was secure. But a month after he moved from New York to Kansas City, he discovered that he still had the same mailman.

The boss was sympathetic when Otto asked for the day off to attend his wife's funeral. He granted permission quickly. A week later Otto came in and said, "I need another day off."

The boss asked, "Why?"

Otto said, "I'm getting married."

The boss said, "Your wife has only been dead a week."

Otto said, "I don't hold a grudge long!"

My niece is so happily married. She's got a husband who's scared to death of her.

I told my wife that a husband is like a fine wine—he gets better with age. The next day she locked me in the cellar.

My wife and I never go to bed mad. We stay up until the problem is resolved. Last year we didn't get to sleep until March!

They have something now called Marriage Anonymous. When you feel like getting married, you call somebody and he sends over a woman with curlers, cream on her face, and a torn housecoat!

The maid showed up at work with a black eye. The mistress of the house said sympathetically, "That looks awful."

The maid said, "It could be worse. I might not be married at all!"

My wife and I have a perfect understanding. I don't try to run her life and I don't try to run mine!

A man bought his wife a burial plot. The following year he didn't buy her anything and she complained. He answered, "You didn't use the present I bought you last year!"

I saw a tombstone that said, HE HAD BEEN MARRIED FOR THIRTY YEARS AND WAS PREPARED TO DIE.

I married her for her looks, but not the ones she's been giving me lately!

The cooing stops with the honeymoon; the billing goes on forever!

"How'd you get along after I left you last night?"
"A cop hauled me to the police station. I spent the whole night there."
"You lucky dog. I made it home."

The typical marriage story: They started out to be good friends, but later they changed their minds!

A husband was telling a friend, "If my wife really loved me, she would have married somebody else!"

"Will you love me when I'm old and bald?"
"It's tough enough now, when you're young and hairy!"

Father Tomlin had just finished a sermon on the pleasures of married life. On the way out of the church, Eamon said to Pat, "I wish I knew as little about the subject as he does!"

Single people die earlier. Marriage is healthier. If you're looking for a long life and a slow death, get married!

My uncle believes that marriage and a career don't mix, so when he got married he stopped working!

The judge said, "I understand that you and your wife had some words."
The defendant said, "I had some, but I didn't get a chance to use them!"

My son was about seven when he looked into our wedding album and said, "Pop, are these pictures of the day Mom came to work for us?"

Marriage is a good way for a woman to keep active until the right man comes along!

The wife said, "If it weren't for my money, this TV set wouldn't be here. If it weren't for my money, the chair you're sitting on wouldn't be here."
The husband said, "If it weren't for your money, *I* wouldn't be here!

I'm so henpecked I cackle in my sleep!

One of those afternoon TV talk-show hosts interviewed an old couple. The TV host asked, "How old is your wife?"

The husband said, "She's ninety-two, and may she live to be a hundred and ten."

"How old are you?"

"I'm also ninety-two."

"How long would you want to live?"

"Till I'm a hundred and eleven."

"Why would you want your wife to live to a hundred and ten and you to a hundred eleven?"

"To tell you the truth," the husband said, "I'd like one year of peace!"

Jed was eating his dinner outside, leaning against the barn. Henry, a neighbor, came up and asked, "How come you're eating outside like this?"

Jed said, "My chimney's smoking."

Figuring that he'd be a good soul, Henry started toward the house to see if he could repair the chimney. As he opened the door, Jed's wife came at him with a broom, stopping only when she saw it wasn't her husband.

Henry retreated and sat down next to Jed, saying, "Don't worry, Jed. Sometimes my chimney smokes too!"

"**I** haven't seen my wife in a month."

"Do you miss her?"

"Not yet!"

A jealous husband hires a private detective to check on the movements of his wife. The husband wants more than a written report; he wants movies of his wife's activities. A week later, the detective returns with a reel of film. The man and the detective sit down in the living room to watch. Although the quality is less than professional, the man sees his wife metting another man. He sees the two of them laughing in the park. He sees them enjoying themselves at an outdoor café. He sees them dancing in a dimly lit nightclub. He sees a dozen activities shared by both the man and woman with utter glee. The husband says, "I just can't believe this."

The detective says, "It's up there on the screen. What can't you believe?"

The husband says, "That my wife could be such fun!"

I met my wife at a dance. It was so embarrassing. I thought she was home with the kids!

"**Y**ou don't deserve a wife like me."

"I've got arthritis, and I don't deserve *that!*"

Marriage is one of the few institutions that allow a man to do as his wife pleases.

A husband said to his wife, "I've really taken you over all the bumps of life, haven't I?"

The wife said, "That's true. I don't believe you missed any of them!"

She's been married so many times she has rice marks on her face!

All marriages are happy. It's the living together afterward that's rough!

"**I**s it true married men live longer than single men?"

"No. It only *seems* longer!"

My wife and I were introduced by a mutual friend—a bellhop!

A husband stormed out of the house and rushed off to the nearest saloon. At two in the morning he called his wife and told her, "I'm coming home."

The wife said, "Well, you've finally decided that home is best after all."

The husband said, "Not necessarily, but it's the only place open at this hour!"

It's bad luck to see the bride before the wedding—and sometimes for the next ten years!

The man who married her got a prize. He should have gotten a reward!

A wife said to her husband, "Let's not stay home all the time. Let's go out three times a week."

The husband said, "Good idea. You go out Monday, Wednesday, and Friday!"

A young woman confided to a friend, "For ages I couldn't figure out where my husband was spending his evenings."

"You should have hired a private detective."

"I didn't have to. I went home early one night, and there he was!"

I knew a couple who tried an open marriage, but one day the husband forgot the wife's address.

A fellow sitting at a bar struck up a conversation with another man. As they became friendlier, the fellow said, "Pal, I didn't want to say anything, but you've got your wedding ring on the wrong finger."

The other man said, "Yup. I married the wrong woman!"

When I was first married, I felt that I had to let my wife know who was the boss. Right off, about five minutes after the ceremony, I looked her right in the eye and said, "You're the boss."

My wife has been having morning sickness lately. She's not pregnant. She's just sick of mornings!

A young wife and her husband were sitting with her gynecologist. The wife told the doctor that she was pregnant. The doctor asked, "How many times have you missed?"

The husband said, "Not one night, so far!"

Marriage is like a violin. After the music is over, you still have the strings.

My wife keeps telling me that she gave me the best years of her life. If those were the best, now I have to worry about what we've got coming up!

We've been happily married for ten years. Ten out of thirty isn't bad!

The wife sat beside her ailing husband in the hospital. As she held his fever-warm hand, the husband said, "You know something, dear? You've been with me through a million bad times. You were at my side when I went into the army. You become a nurse. When I was hit by a bullet, you were at my side to nurse me. After the war, when my business failed, you were there to give me support. When we lost the house, when my health failed, when I almost died of pneumonia, you were at my side. To tell you the truth, I've been thinking—you're bad luck!"

Marriages may be made in heaven, but most of the details are worked out on earth!

A real fairytale ending: "And they lived happily even after!"

martians

Years ago, there was a magician who billed his act "Magic from Mars." Wearing a metallic outfit with a weird hat, he kept up a strange clicking gibberish as he did his act. He never even spoke offstage, only that clicking noise. We used to think he was a fruitcake. But what if he was the real thing? What if he'd traveled millions of miles to break into show business? It may be more than conjecture, because one day he disappeared while playing Detroit. He was never seen again!

A Martian walked by a piano store and said to the baby grand in the window, "Stop laughing!"

Not long ago there was a news bulletin: "We have good news and bad news for the people of America. The bad news is that we have been invaded by thousands of Martians. The good news is that they eat politicians and pee gasoline!"

A Martian landed on a nude beach. Looking at the curvaceous young ladies, he said, "Take me to your tailor!"

A flying saucer landed in Manhattan. It was soon surrounded by gaping onlookers. After a moment, the hatch atop the saucer opened, and a Martian emerged. His skin was green. Six arms wiggled from his triangular upper torso. The crowd drew back, but a brave policeman motioned that he'd try to make contact. He walked up to the Martian and said, "Hello."

In perfect English, the Martian said, "Hello."

The policeman said, "Are all of you green?"

"Yes."

"Do you all have so many arms?"

"Yes."

"Do you all have such bulging eyes?"

"Yes."

"And do all of you have those pimples on your face?"

"Only the teenagers!"

A Martian walked into a Las Vegas casino. Strolling over to the slots, he started to pull down the arm that triggered the whirling wheels. After a while, he said to the one-armed bandit, "I'll keep on shaking hands as long as you want, but smile once in a while!"

A Martian was telling his friend about his new passion: "She's smart and she's gorgeous. You should see her. Skin like aluminum siding!

A Martian returned to his planet and was debriefed. The debriefing officer asked, "Is there any life on Earth?"

The Martian said, "A little on Saturday night!"

A team of Martian explorers, each of whom had the usual twelve arms for which the people of the Red Planet are famous, went off to explore Venus. Venusians have sixteen arms. The Martian explorers returned after their expedition and were debriefed. They were asked to tell what they had done. The Martian leader said, "Well, for the first year we shook hands!"

maternity

It's a good thing men don't have to go through childbirth. Otherwise, Cain and Abel would have been just about it!

When Marge discovered she was pregnant, she told her husband. Ecstatic, her husband said he'd buy her a brand-new car when the baby was born. For nine months, Marge went through morning sickness, discomfort, feelings of ugliness, and eventually a difficult labor and delivery. Lying in the recovery room, she said to another new mother, "This is a hell of a way to get a new station wagon!"

A nurse brought a beautiful brown-skinned baby into the waiting room and asked the only man pacing, "Is this yours?"

The man said, "It must be. My wife burns everything!"

The doctor explained that a baby wasn't really much trouble, saying, "Just remember to keep one end empty and the other end full!"

Maternity is a fact. Paternity can be a matter of opinion!

I have a friend who just started a new business. He manufactures maternity bridal gowns!

The labor pains had arrived. The father-to-be called the doctor and nervously said that the time had come. The doctor asked, "How far apart are the pains?"

The father-to-be said, "I'm not sure, but I think they're all in the same place!"

The baby, a girl, was born two days later than expected. Holding her, her father said, "Two minutes old and she's already kept a man waiting!"

medicine

Are you like me? If I visit my doctor and he doesn't give me medicine, I feel cheated. I must have a pill! Society is just about the biggest pusher, isn't it?

My doctor just gave me something he says is good for migraine. I wish he'd give me something that's *bad* for migraine!

My doctor gave me a strong laxative. Now I'm sitting pretty!

My wife has stopped taking tranquilizers. She was starting to be nice to people she didn't even want to talk to!

Medicare is great for some people. They get so many tranquilizers they don't care what shape the country is in!

Chicken soup is a traditional remedy for many people. One woman had two chickens. One became ill. She killed the second one to make chicken soup for the sick one!

We really live in a world of medical specialists. Today, four out of five doctors recommend another doctor.

A ninety-year-old doctor just came up with a pill that can make a woman pregnant. He's ninety, what does he care?

Amnesia is nature's way of saying "Forget it!"

Al was fining it difficult to sleep at night. He begged the doctor to give him a strong sedative. The doctor obliged, but told him to take only half of the prescribed pill. To make sure he slept, Al took a whole pill and went to sleep.

As dawn came up, Al awoke. He felt refreshed. Cheerful, he went to work. As he walked into the office, he saw the boss and said, "I'm ready. I slept like a log. I jumped out of bed like a kid this morning."

The boss said, "Nice. But where were you yesterday?"

If you think McDonald's has the golden arches, try going to a podiatrist!

Socialized medicine would be nice. Unless, of course, the nurse is ugly!

I called my acupuncturist last night and told him I was in pain. He told me to take two safety pins and call him in the morning!

The nurse told the doctor, "Better take a tranquilizer. 40–25–38 is here for a physical!"

A doctor had worked out the vacation plans for the half-dozen people he had working in his office. As they looked at the schedule, the doctor said, "All in favor, stick out your tongue and say, 'Ah.'"

A patient went to his doctor because he had walking pneumonia. The doctor gave him a prescription and said, "Take one every few miles!"

memory

It was once said of me that I could remember things in advance. A good memory isn't a bad trait for a comedian, or even for a would-be part-time comedian. The ability to remember isn't necessarily innate. It can be learned through practice. I recommend memory schools highly. Although they teach tricks, the practice lets you bone your memory cells. However, don't be like my brother. He thinks he went to a memory school, but he can't remember!

An old black man told everybody who would listen that he'd seen Abraham Lincoln in the flesh. One day he got religion and stopped bragging. A stranger asked, "Did you or didn't you see Lincoln?"

The old black man answered, "I used to remember seeing him, but since I joined the church, I forgot!"

I have a bad memory. So far this month, I forgot my wife's birthday, our wedding anniversary, and who's the boss!

A man in his seventies was telling some of his cronies about a problem with his memory. "Last night," he said, "I went to bed and about two in the morning I woke up. I felt very sexy, so I asked my wife if she wanted to have some fun. She told me that we'd already had fun twice between midnight and two. It's pretty sad when a man can't remember things like that!"

Two men meet at an airport. One says, "Hey, if it isn't Tom Clark of 4206 Maple Street, the guy I met six years ago last Thursday at about seven on that rainy night outside the Clover Club."
    The other man says, "What can I do for you?"
    The first man says, "Nothing. I sell memory courses!"

They say that too much sex can cause memory loss. Now, what was I about to say?

I have a photographic memory, but once in a while I forget to take off the lens cap!

men

We are Creation's masterpiece, but don't bet any money on it!

For every woman who makes a fool out of a man, there is another woman who makes a fool out of a man!

Many a man has lost his best friend by marrying her!

The ideal man is about as numerous as there are women to describe him.

A grammar-school girl wrote, "Men are what women marry. They drink and swear, but they never go to church. They are more logical than women, but are afraid to feel something. Both men and women sprang from monkeys, but women sprang a little farther!"

At *ten, a child; at twenty, wild;*
At thirty, tame, if ever.
At forty, smart; at fifty, rich;
At sixty, good, or never!

To a smart girl, men are no problem. To a smart girl, a man is the answer!

When God made man, he didn't make the spine so that man could pat himself on the back!

There's one thing that makes man different from all the other animals, but I'll be darned if I know what it is!

All men put their pants on one leg at a time. Of course, some men take them off more often!

men (insults)

Go to it, ladies. These are all custom-made!

He's a fugitive from the law of averages!

Is he a self-made man, or does somebody else have to take the rap?

He gives failure a bad name!

He's a self-made mouse!

He made a fool of himself. You can tell he's a perfect craftsman!

He's got a terrible inferiority complex, and he's right!

He loves three things—women, money, and both!

It wouldn't do him any good to see himself as others see him. He wouldn't believe it!

He got his stooped posture from living up to his ideals!

He's on his back so much, he hasn't seen his shadow in years!

He comes from an alert family. His father was the lookout at Pearl Harbor!

He puts off until tomorrow everything he's put off until today!

If he had his life to live over, he shouldn't!

He never opens his mouth unless he has nothing to say!

He's had it rough lately. His organ grinder died!

He doesn't have any enemies, but his friends won't be seen with him!

He once got a job as a pharmacist, but he was fired. He always broke the bottles in the typewriter!

He has a soundproof head!

When he gets an idea in his head, it's a stowaway!

When he cleans his nails, he loses twenty pounds!

He has black hair, and nails to match!

He wears turtleneck sweaters to cover his flea collar!

He's like French bread—lots of crust!

He has knifed more people than a surgeon!

He's so mean he'd steal the suckle from a piglet!

He's wrapped up in himself, and he makes a very untidy package!

He was determined to climb the ladder of success. He's not a success, but can he climb ladders!

He broke his nose the other day. His boss stopped short!

If he wasn't crazy, he'd go nuts!

He was a precocious child. When he was four months old he was already eating solids—pencils, crayons, paper...

He was an unwanted child. When they gave him a rattle, it was still attached to the snake!

He was always running into things—like debts!

He doesn't need X rays. Everybody can see through him!

He would make a perfect stranger!

He's so negative he won't even eat food that agrees with him!

He's not a good artist, but he draws flies!

He always sees germs in the milk of human kindness!

His way of being right is to be wrong at the top of his voice!

He's such a louse. When he went on jury duty they found him guilty!

He's upstanding. They just took away his furniture!

He's addicted to snooze!

People like to help him out . . . as soon as he comes in!

When his mind goes blank, he often forgets to turn off the sound!

He's so mean he went deaf and won't tell his barber!

He started at the bottom and lost ground!

He's so conceited, he calls Dial-a-Prayer and asks for his messages!

He never repeats himself. He gets it trite the first time!

He quit smoking cold turkey. The feathers made him gag!

He's nobody's fool. He free-lances!

When he was a kid he swallowed a spoon. He hasn't stirred since!

He was on the tug-of-war team in college. He was the third jerk from the left!

mental institutions

I feel a pang when I tell a joke about somebody who's going through life without his porch light on. Yet I sometimes have the feeling that he may be smarter than I am. In a Broadway play of some years ago, there was a so-called madwoman who read only one issue of the newspaper because it reported on a day when everything went well with the world. Is she the mad one? I know that I can't start the day without six murders, a famine, a flood, a fire, and a new disease that threatens to wipe out all of Savannah, Georgia. That's just page one!

A patient who believed himself to be Abraham Lincoln said to the staff psychiatrist, "My wife is trying to get rid of me."

The psychiatrist said, "How do you know?"

The patient said, "She keeps wanting me to go to the theater!"

A patient at a mental institution was sitting at the edge of the water fountain at the entrance to the main building. In his hand he held a fishing pole, the end of which dangled in the fountain. A visitor, passing by, asked, "Catch anything?"

The patient said, "You must be nuts. This is a fountain!"

In Dallas there was a young man who had himself committed. He was a Texan and ashamed of it!

A visiting psychiatrist was invited to address the inmates of an institution. He started by asking, "Do any of you know why you're here?"

One inmate answered, "Yup, 'cause we're all not there!"

A doctor met a patient in the hall. Wanting to know if the patient was on the way to therapy, the doctor asked, "Are you coming or going?"

The patient said, "If I knew that, I wouldn't be here!"

Escorted by a doctor, a man was visiting an institution. The man saw a male patient sitting in a corner, playing with a doll. The doctor explained, "He went crazy because he lost the girl he loved to another man."

They walked on. Suddenly, another patient ran up the hall. His violent nature was obvious, and he looked as if he was ready to explode. The doctor explained, "He's the man who got that girl!"

A patient walked into the doctor's office and complained about his roommate, saying, "Herbie keeps elephants in the room. It smells awful."

The doctor said, "Why not open the windows?"

The patient said, "And let my eagles out?"

It was another typical visiting day. A patient said to his wife, "I'd like a watch that tells time."

The wife said, "Don't you have a watch that tells time?"

"No. You have to look at it!"

A patient was hammering a nail, but was attempting to do so by hammering the pointed end with the flat end against the wall. Another patient said, "You're doing it wrong. That nail is for the other wall!"

Stinson put on his Napoleon coat and walked into the office of the head of the asylum. "Doctor," he said, "you may think I have everything in the world—armies, fame, greatness. But I have a big problem."

"Tell me about your problem."

"It concerns my wife. She thinks she's a Mrs. Stinson!"

A patient at the asylum said to another patient, "I'm not feeling myself today."

The other patient said, "That makes four of us!"

A patient, his ear against the wall, listened for hours. Seeing him, an orderly put his ear against the wall and also listened. After a moment the orderly said, "I don't hear a thing."

The patient said, "It's been that way for two days!"

mexico and mexicans

While some laugh at Latin ways, the Latins, most of them Mexicans, have given us many of our foods, styles, customs, and about ninety percent of the outfielders in major-league baseball. I tell very few Mexican jokes. I almost never use an accent. Few Anglos should, because we don't have good ones. Spanish is pure music. We sing flat!

Jim, a young sailor, crossed the border into Mexico. After viewing the sights, he went into a small bar. Seeing a beautiful, raven-haired señorita, he walked over and sat down next to her. He smiled and said, "Do you speak English?"

The señorita said, "A little."

Jim said, "A little? How much?"

"Fifty dollars!"

A Mexican hated to see his wife on her hands and knees, scrubbing the floor. On her birthday he had the floor removed!

A young Mexican was telling a friend that he was now in the army. The friend asked, "Did you get a commission?"

The young Mexican answered, "No, only my salary!"

"What is matched Mexican luggage?"

"Shopping bags from the same supermarket!"

There was a terrible accident in this Mexican apartment. Nine people got hurt. The bed broke!

The idea of daylight savings time must have come from the Mexican who cut off half of his blanket and sewed it to the other end to make it longer!

Tourists to Mexico come home bragging about a new Mexican invention—the waterless shower!

A cowboy signed on as a ranch hand in southern Texas. He asked some of the other ranch hands what they did for fun. One said, "Well, on Saturday night, we take our Mexican cook and dress him up like a señorita. Then we take him dancing in town."

The new man said, "Is that fun?"

The ranch hand said, "Not for the Mexican cook. That's why it takes six of us!"

A clothing store in the barrio made a fortune when it put in a line of maternity gowns in the colors of the local high school!

A tourist traveling off the beaten track in Mexico saw a man who had the look of an American cowboy. Wearing a cowboy outfit, the man had red hair and freckles. He was riding a magnificent gray stallion. On its hind quarter was burned the brand, Bar Double A.

The tourist said, "That's as beautiful a horse as I ever saw. If you could take off that brand, I'd pay you ten thousand for the animal."

The cowboy said, "If I could get that brand off, I'd still be in Oklahoma!"

In Mexico you can get a fifty-pound sack of sugar, two bushels of corn, a pint of booze, and a wife for about twenty dollars. Trouble is, the booze is awful!

miami

The last time I was in Miami, I saw a man walking with his widow. What a town for jokes and laughter!

Where else but in Miami can you see people dreaming of a tan Christmas?

A man checked into a Miami hotel and said, "Please wake me at seven."

The clerk said, "The receptionist doesn't get in until eight. Maybe you could wake her!"

At the height of a convention that had filled every hotel room in Miami, a young lady found herself in the city with no place to stay. Going from hotel to hotel, she begged and cajoled, but no rooms were available. At the last hotel in the city, she was about to walk out when a man in his eighties said, "Look, I have a room. Take my room."

The young lady said, "I couldn't do that, but I'd be thrilled to sleep on your couch if you have one. I realize that I don't know you and you don't know me, but I'm willing."

The man said, "I happen to have a couch."

Upstairs, the young lady thanked the old man and tried to sleep on the couch. Unable to, she walked over to the old man in bed and said, "Look, I don't know you and you don't know me, but maybe I could lie down on top of your blanket."

The old man agreed.

Still not comfortable, the girl said, "Look, I don't know you and you don't know me, but maybe I could get under the covers with you."

A moment later she was under the covers. After a moment, she leaned over to the old man and said, "Let's have a party."

The old man said, "Look, I don't know you and you don't know me—who are we going to invite to the party?"

A man saw a retirement hotel in Miami on fire. He rushed in and became a hero. In ten minutes he rescued six mink coats and eighteen canes!

A middle-aged woman, vacationing in Florida, disregarded warnings and found herself going down for the third time in the undertow of Miami's waters. A bellhop from a nearby hotel saw her, whipped off his shoes and coat, and dove into the water. A minute later he had the lady safely back on the glistening beach. The woman turned to another vacationer and said, "What do you tip for this?"

An elderly couple decided to see some sights around their hotel. The woman said, "Alex, let's take a walk to the corner."

Alex said, "While we're at the corner, we'll go into the drugstore and buy some suntan lotion for Evelyn."

The woman said, "Listen, why should we do everything in one day?"

I had some great news from Miami the other day. They found land on my property!

Alvin Cooper flew to Florida to see his father in the retirement home. Going to the desk, Alvin asked for Joe Cooper. The practical nurse motioned that Joe Cooper was coming down the hall. Alvin looked. A wrinkled man who could hardly move was speeding along at about a foot an hour. Alvin said, "That's not my father."

The practical nurse said, "Oh, you must mean the *old* man! Room 119!"

Alex, a widower, went to a senior citizen's dance. There he met Ruth, a woman also advanced in years. Alex and Ruth danced every dance. Afterward, they went out for coffee. As they walked home, Ruth said, "You remind me of my fourth husband."

Alex said, "How many times have you been married?"

Ruth said, "Three!"

Phil and Sonia met at a senior citizens' dance. Sonia asked about Phil's background. He explained, "I just got out of jail. I was there for fifty-one years."

Sonia asked, "What was your crime?"

Phil said, "I killed my wife. She made me so angry that one day I went after her with a knife and carved her up."

Sonia said, "Oh, then you're single!"

Looking for a human-interest story, a reporter for a Miami paper approached three mature gentlemen sitting on a bench. The reporter asked, "What do you do all day?"

The first mature gentleman said, "I don't do anything."

The second mature gentleman said, "Neither do I."

The third mature gentleman said, "What a question! Look at this beautiful place. Look at the cloudless sky, the shining sun, the warm air, and nature giving us every bounty."

The reporter said, "But what do you do all day?"

The third mature gentleman said, "I help them!"

middle age

I'm not there yet!

You know you've reached middle age when your wife tells you to pull in your stomach, and you just did!

Forget exercising and dieting—let somebody come up with younger mirrors!

I don't have wrinkles. Those are laugh lines. I guess I do a lot of laughing.

Fifty-five on the calendar is just like fifty-five on the road. Everybody seems to pass you!

I'm not sure I'm getting wrinkles. It's possible that my skin is turning to corduroy!

Middle age is that time of life when you can afford to lose a golf ball, but you can't hit it that far.

Middle age is when it takes longer to rest than to get tired.

You know you're slipping when you have to put tenderizer on puffed rice!

Two boys were talking. One said, "My father gets up at seven every morning to jog five miles."

The other boy asked, "What does he do in the afternoon?"

The first boy said, "The end of the first mile!"

You know a woman is getting on in years if you find her reading *The Joy of Sex* and knitting a whip!

The terrible thing about middle age is that you'll outgrow it!

I know some women who even lie about their dog's age!

A man is as old as the woman he feels!

Everything's just starting to click for me— my elbows, my neck, my knees!

Middle age is when you're faced with all kinds of temptations and you pick the one that gets you home by nine!

Middle age is when work is a lot less fun and fun is a lot more work!

A woman is middle-aged when her girdle pinches and the men in the office don't!

Middle age is when you don't need a roomful of antiques to sit down something fifty years old!

Middle age—when you turn from stud to dud!

Middle age is that terrible feeling that comes over you when you're talking to your son and he says, "What's a running board?"

Middle age is when you're at the beach and you've got a great color—blue, from holding in your gut!

A man read that middle age is when you pull back from physical activity. If he shovels snow, a middle-aged man can easily have a heart attack. It snowed a few weeks ago. My neighbor asked his son to shovel the snow in front of the house. "If I shovel," my neighbor explained, "I could keel over from a heart attack."

His son said, "Sure, Dad. I'll do it."

The neighbor keeled over from a heart attack!

Middle age is when you can't turn your TV set off or your wife on!

Show me a man with his head held high, and I'll show you a guy having trouble with bifocals!

You've reached middle age when you know your way around, but you'd rather not go!

middle east

The Middle East, the President of Israel once hinted to me, was designed by the same entity that designed the camel. Somewhere along the line, the blueprints were lost and a lot of ad-libbing followed. There's hope because the Middle East is finally entering the twentieth century. One of the Arab countries just put up a fifty-story tent!

Some of the Arab countries complained about the previous wars in the area. One leader said, "It's unfair. Israel has three million Jews. We don't have one!"

Where else can you get "Love Thy Neighbor" samplers with bullet holes in them?

I heard of an Arab soldier who deserted his outfit and stood his ground!

Then there was the Egyptian girl who forgot to take the Pill and became a mummy!

There'd be no trouble in the Middle East if the Arabs and the Jews would start acting like good Christians!

mistakes

To err is human. To sue for malpractice is more human!

A doctor operated on a man for kidney problems. Unfortunately, the patient's problem was in his leg. After the patient's death, the county medical committee warned the doctor, "No more mistakes. If you operate on kidneys, make sure the patient dies of kidney trouble!"

To err is human. To admit it isn't!

My secretary is great. She erases eighty words a minute!

I'll tell you a real mistake—joining an all-girl band as an accordion player!

A mistake is a lesson on its way to be learned!

You can always learn from the mistakes of others. The trouble is—I'm always the others!

A mistake is what a lawyer gets paid for and a doctor buries!

You only learn from your mistakes. That's why I don't do anything right!

mistresses

Now it's getting interesting!

A mistress is better than a wife. You don't have to do the dishes!

The difference between a wife and a mistress is like day and night!

A young woman was active in a charity group. One day after the monthly meeting, the young lady called over one of the older women and said confidentially, "Look, I don't know who else to ask. Tell me, how do you start an affair?"
    The other woman said, "First you sing 'The Star-Spangled Banner,' then the invocation . . ."

Two women met. One said, "Did you hear? Joe Baker is having an affair."
    The other woman said, "Really? Who's the caterer?"

She's been kept so often she was recently declared a national playground area!

models

Not far from where I live is the Hollywood office of one of the leading model agencies. Every morning you see young women with portfolios and makeup kits walking into the building. The ladies are eighteen or nineteen. Each is more beautiful than the one before. Outside, you can see the dirty old men like me, crying! I watch commercials on television and can't understand where all these gorgeous faces come from. It wasn't like that in my old neighborhood. If you found one girl with a face, you made a holiday! But, as I told my wife the morning I went off to the set to do a picture with Marilyn Monroe, "Looks aren't everything!"

Two dress models were putting on outfits for the fashion show. One said, "I can't get into my shoes."
    The other said, "No kidding. Your *feet* swelled too?"

I know a model who wanted larger breasts. She couldn't get silicone, so they put in Silly Putty!

She's also a bit of a call girl. She lives in the finest hotels—an hour at a time!

The artist finished painting his nude model, walked over to her, and started to kiss her. Not fighting him off too fiercely, the model said, "Do you do this to all your models?"

The artist said, "No. You're the first one I ever tried to go to bed with."

The model said, "How many models have you had before me?"

The artist replied, "Three—an apple and two bananas!"

A model didn't want to pose this one day. She just wasn't in the nude for work!

A pickpocket was in night court, awaiting arraignment. He faced jail time of at least a year. Ahead of him were some ladies of the evening. The judge asked the first one what she did for a living. She said, "Your Honor, I'm a model."

The judge sentenced her to sixty days in the county jail. Going on to the next, he asked about her story. She too said that she was a model. The judge gave her sixty days.

A third "model" appeared before the judge and was given the same sentence.

The fourth lady of the evening said openly, "I'm a prostitute."

The judge said, "Your honesty is refreshing. I'm giving you a ten-day suspended sentence."

The pickpocket was up next. The judge said, "Tell me your story."

The pickpocket said, "Well, I started out as a model. Then I became a prostitute!"

Men have their price. A model has her figure!

A famous photographer fell head over heels in love with a new model. After a day's shooting, he said to her, "You can really go far if you're nice to somebody like me."

The model understood. The next day she brought him a box of candy!

money

Money isn't everything, but it sure keeps you in touch with your kids!

Rappaport hit it big in the import business. After buying out every fancy shop, jewelry store, and boutique, he and his wife got into their brand-new, hundred-thousand-dollar car and headed for the fanciest restaurant in town. As two headwaiters hovered over them, Mrs. Rappaport said, "Order the most expensive thing you can think of, but say it out loud so everyone'll hear how rich we are."

Rappaport took a sip of water and yelled to the headwaiters, "BRING ME EIGHTY DOLLARS' WORTH OF LOX AND ONIONS!"

With today's inflation, there's no money in money!

I can't save up for a rainy day. One good drizzle would wipe me out!

The trouble is—you may not have time to count it on Judgment Day!

I try to save my money. Who knows, maybe one day it'll become valuable again!

Money can't buy you love, but it puts you in a great bargaining position!

I have what no millionaire has—no money!

If you're rich, you can get a room. If you're filthy rich, you can get a room with a bath!

My wife and I are having money troubles. The only time we make both ends meet is in bed!

My brother has a great way of saving his money. He uses mine!

I lived within my income last year. It was easy—I just borrowed some money!

I'm not crazy about money, but it quiets my nerves!

Money must be the root of all evil. Look how it's going into the ground!

A two-dollar bill is supposed to be bad luck. Tell that to the guy with twenty thousand of them!

Remember when people had get-up-and-go, and your money didn't?

The life of a twenty-dollar bill is six months. How come none of them ever die in my hands?

I'm a quarter.
I'm not on speaking terms with the butcher.
I'm too small to buy a pint of ice cream.
I'm not big enough to buy candy in the movies.
I can't buy a gallon of gas.
I'm hardly big enough as a tip.
But on Sunday, in the collection box, I'm considered a big deal!

Making money isn't a problem. The problem is trying to pass it!

I've got enough money for the rest of my life—unless I want to buy something!

You know a guy is rich when he has bills so big we don't have Presidents for them!

He has no folding money. His wad is so big he can't bend it!

I went on a vacation. I left all the lights on to discourage burglars from taking my cash and valuables. Nothing was lost, but my electric bill was eight hundred dollars!

A man lost a wallet with a thousand dollars in it. Using the public-address system in the restaurant where he'd lost it, he announced, "I'll give a hundred dollars to anyone who returns my wallet and money."
    A man dining at a nearby table said, "I'll give two hundred and a free dinner!"

A kid went into the bank and withdrew fifty cents from his savings account. The teller asked him why. The kid explained, "I want to have a little cash on weekends!"

I've never had money problems. *Lack* of money problems, yes!

Money won't buy you happiness. Money won't buy you love. Money won't buy you health. But the way I see it is—give me the money and I'll rent them!

You know you've got money when you get a calendar from the World Bank!

It's amazing how fast later comes when you buy now!

There are more important things in life than a little money—a lot of money!

Money really isn't that important. Is a guy with fifty million dollars happier than a guy with forty-eight million dollars?

If bills are rectangular, how come they keep rolling in?

He saves money by visiting people. In the summer he keeps cool by sponging!

A little girl walked into the local drugstore, held out a dime, and asked for an ice cream cone. The clerk said, "An ice cream cone is a quarter."
    "How about a Coke?"
    "That's also a quarter."
    "A pack of gum?"
    "Thirty-five cents."
    The girl sighed, put the dime on the counter, and started to walk out. The clerk said, "Honey, you've forgotten your dime."
    The girl said, "What good is it? It doesn't buy anything!"

mormons

I love Mormon country. I spent a year there one night! But how can you say anything against a group of people who voluntarily settled in a place where it gets to be a hundred and twenty in the shade!

A Mormon wedding was in full swing. The minister started the part where each bride or groom is asked if he or she accepts the other's hand in marriage. His voice was so low, one of the brides said, "Please talk louder. Those of us in back can't hear when to say 'I do'!"

And in the immortal words of Brigham Young, "I don't care how you bring 'em, bring 'em young!"

Mormon marriage is fun, but think of all those stockings drying in the bathroom at the same time!

It took the Mormons six months to come west. That's what happens when you let the women read the road maps!

Mormons are so moral, one house of ill repute had to take out a second mortgage.

How can the Mormons justify more than one wife? Doesn't the Bible say a man shouldn't serve two masters!

One Mormon threw out his mothers-in-law and emptied the city!

A visitor jumped into Great Salt Lake, sipped, and said, "It needs water!"

The Mormons were coming west. An advance scout rode back and reported, "There's a wonderful land ahead. It has a giant lake. That is where we should stop our wanderings. In this Promised Land we will spend our time fishing and making love." Sticking his head out of his tent, Brigham Young said, "Salt the lake!"

A cloud as dark as night, hundreds of millions of locusts chewed every living green thing in a feeding frenzy. A man watching them turned, walked over to Brigham Young's house, and said, "I'm the gardener. I quit!"

morticians and mortuaries

I've always wanted to go to a crematorium and ask, "What's cooking?"

One mortician I know got a little mixed up.

On his honeymoon, he saw his bride lying still and he crossed her arms!

The young mortician was having trouble with Mrs. Garber. She couldn't make up her mind about her deceased husband's casket, the time of the funeral, or even the kind of funeral she wanted. Finally, she chose. Preparations were made. To check, Mrs. Garber came in and was aghast. "My husband is in a brown suit. He looks terrible in brown. Change that."

The time for the funeral came, and there lay Mr. Garber, radiant in a blue suit. Another mortician who worked at the same mortuary asked the new mortician, "How'd you manage to get that done so fast?"

The young mortician said, "There was another client in a blue suit."

"Yes, but it takes time to change the clothes."

The young mortician said, "I just changed the heads!"

The service for Joe Henderson wasn't going too well. A monster in life, Joe was the most disliked man in the county. When the minister asked somebody in the hall to say a kind word about Joe, there was an awkward silence. It seemed to go on and on. Finally, Bill Jacobs, the town barber, got up and said, "Well, he wasn't a hard man to shave!"

mother

My mother came to all my performances. She'd lead the laughter and applause. If anybody spoke too loudly or coughed, my mother shushed them with an iron stare. While I was onstage at the Loew's State in New York, a man sat down next to my mother and started to get fresh. Holding him off gently, she made no attempt to call the manager or even alert an usher. I was onstage; I wasn't to be interrupted. As soon as I went off, my mother pummeled the man with her purse, kicked him, and bit him once. Then she called the manager and had the man ejected.

Mother is the name of God on the lips of children!

"What's the difference between an Italian mother and a Jewish mother?"
"The Italian mother says, 'If you don't eat what's on that plate, I'll kill you.' The Jewish mother says, 'Eat everything or I'll kill myself!'"

A gangster walked out of a restaurant and was machine-gunned by two men in a passing car. His blood seeping out of a dozen wounds, the gangster crawled to the corner. Almost unable to breathe, he pushed his way through the door of the first tenement. Slowly, ever so slowly, he crawled up the steps to the apartment where his little old Sicilian mother lived. He managed to knock on the door weakly. His mother opened the door and gasped as she saw her son. In the quietest of whispers, the gangster said, "Mama, Mama."

His mother said, dragging him in, "First you eat, then we'll talk!"

If evolution really works, how come mothers only have two hands?

One woman is so proud of her son. He goes to a psychiatrist every day and spends the whole hour just talking about her!

"How many Jewish mothers does it take to screw in a light bulb?"
"None. They'll just sit back and say, 'It's all right. I'll just sit here in the dark!'"

A teenager was greeted by his mother when

he returned home one evening. The mother said, "Son, let's have a heart-to-heart talk."

The son said, "Fine."

The mother said, "Why don't you run away from home?"

mother's day

My mother was adamant about Mother's Day gifts. She said she'd refuse them and did. She wanted me to save up the gifts for when she really craved something. I sent her flowers. She was angry. I stopped sending flowers, gifts, and cards. When I was in California for a movie in the fifties, Mama and I were walking in Beverly Hills. She stopped at a famous fur salon. In the window was a magnificent sable coat. Mama said, "It's Mother's Day!" Laughing, I said, "You could buy this with your own money." She said, "What kind of card could I send me?"

He's so sentimental. For Mother's Day he sends his laundry home in a heart-shaped box!

Kids, give your mother something she'll always be grateful for—move out!

Mother's Day flowers cost a fortune. The flowers are cut, but you're clipped!

On Mother's Day, all the kids come over to her house. They get together to make a great meal. After the meal, they go into the kitchen, wash the dishes, and put everything away. A little later, they leave. As soon as she's sure they're gone, Mama washes all the dishes again!

mothers-in-law

An endangered species, mothers-in-law.

I bought my mother-in-law a nice new chair, but she won't let me plug it in!

Adam wanted to buy his mother-in-law a gift, but what can you buy a rib?

I sent my mother-in-law to the country. They refused her!

The home for the aged came for a contribution. He gave them his mother-in-law.

Some airlines have a mother-in-law flight. It's nonstop!

To some men, the mother-in-law is the bark from the family tree.

Behind every successful man stands an amazed mother-in-law.

My mother-in-law is very well informed. She can complain on any subject!

I never met a mother-in-law who was outspoken.

I sent my mother-in-law to the Thousand Islands and suggested she spend a week on each!

A man received a wire from a mortician in another town. The man's mother-in-law had died. The mortician wanted instructions on whether he should bury, embalm, or cremate the old woman. The man said, "All three. Let's not take any chances!"

Standing at the edge of the lake, a man saw a woman flailing about in the deep water. Unable to swim, the man started to scream for help. A trout fisherman ran up. The man said, "My wife is drowning and I can't swim. Please save her. I'll give you a hundred dollars."

The fisherman dove into the water. In ten powerful strokes, he reached the woman, put his arm around her, and swam back to shore. Depositing her at the feet of the man, the fisherman said, "Okay, where's my hundred?"

The man said, "Look, when I saw her going down for the third time, I thought it was my wife. But this is my mother-in-law."

The fisherman reached into his pocket and said, "Just my luck. How much do I owe you?"

My mother-in-law has a new exercise. It's called aerobic nagging!

With some men, you can't tell whether they want to succeed to please their wives or spite their mothers-in-law!

My mother-in-law is very neat. She puts paper under the cuckoo clock!

My mother-in-law may live with us forever. I don't mind. It's her place!

I have a real problem—last month my wife left me for good, but my mother-in-law didn't!

My mother-in-law left me for good. It's only been two days, but already it's an improvement!

My mother-in-law speaks 110 words a minute, with gusts up to 150!

I know a man who kept his mother-in-law from visiting by selling every room in his house but one!

mouth

Here are a few insults that might shut up a few people.

Her mouth was so big she could play the tuba from both ends!

She has a voice that's hard to extinguish!

She never shuts her mouth. The other day she came home from the beach with a sunburned tongue!

His mouth is so big he can whisper in his own ear!

They ought to call her "Amazon." She's big at the mouth!

He's not stubborn. He approaches every subject with an open mouth!

He thinks a pause is a disease!

You couldn't get a word in with him if you folded it in half!

movies

I made my first movie when I was a baby. They padded my part. That was a good thing for the leading lady who was holding me at the time!

In the old days, performers used to play parts. Now they reveal them!

A couple who'd been married a long time went to a romantic movie. On the way out, the wife asked, "Why don't you make passionate love to me, like he did on the screen?"

The husband said, "Are you kidding? Do you know how much he gets paid for that?"

When they said they shot the picture, they should have meant it!

An actor died and went to heaven. He was greeted by Saint Peter, who asked what his profession was. Learning that the man was an actor, Saint Peter gulped and said, "You can't stay here." He indicated down below.

The actor reported to hell, where the devil asked, "What did you do for a living?"

"I was an actor."

The devil started to shake. "You can't stay here!"

The actor said, "Does this mean I have to go back to MGM?"

I can always tell when a sexy scene in a movie is coming up. My wife fogs up my glasses!

A producer came to the head of the studio and said he wanted to do a movie about a man who thought he was a horse. The head of the studio didn't exactly cotton to the idea, saying, "If you think I'm about to put ten million in a picture about a man who thinks he's a horse, you're crazier than he is!"

The producer said, "What if we give it a happy ending and have him win the Kentucky Derby?"

This Hollywood yes-man swore that he was a stooge for no man. He free-lanced!

The waitress stared at the actor. Finally she asked, "Have I ever seen you before?"

The actor said, "You might have seen me in the movies."

The waitress said, "It's possible. Where do you like to sit?"

A producer wanted to have a sneak preview for his picture, but had to call it off. He couldn't find enough sneaks!

It was a super movie. It looked like it was made by a super!

The movie had a real happy ending. The audience was thrilled that it was over!

A couple was in a drive-in theater. When the show was over, the manager came over and said, "Listen, we're putting in a new picture tomorrow, but we'd like to hold *you* over!"

They're making incredible movies today. They're not only bigger than life, they're dirtier than life!

They just finished a new horror movie. It's so bloody, it'll be rated Type A!

One new picture is so sick they gave it a rating of Rx!

In one new movie, the star was so bad, they left in her voice, but dubbed in her acting!

A screenwriter brought in his latest work. The head of the studio was aghast. "You're mad," the head of the studio said. "You killed off your co-star in the middle of the movie. You can't do that. Every great writer had his co-stars live until near the end. Look at Shakespeare."

The screenwriter said, "Shakespeare had his technique. I have mine!"

A drive-in played an X-rated movie. In order to get in to see it, your car had to be twenty-one!

muggers

When I lived in New York, muggers didn't bother me. They actually made life interesting.

I'd take the subway, get off at my station, and walk the block and a half to my house. When I got inside my brownstone, I was excited and thrilled. I'd made it home again alive!

I saw some gay muggers go after a department store floorwalker. They were after his carnation!

Muggers are tough on the police. The other day I saw half a cop!

Muggers are tough. Nowadays you can find an unmarked police car, but you can't find an unmarked policeman!

Thank God for the muggers in Manhattan. Without them, there'd be no human contact at all!

It was so slow in my neighborhood the other night, two muggers had to mug one another!

One mugger I heard of won't work after dusk. He's afraid to walk around with all that money at night!

"Do you know where Eighth Avenue is?"
"No."
"All right, I'll mug you here!"

A mugger stuck a knife into a man's ribs and said, "Give me all your money."
   The intended victim said, "What's wrong with you—holding me up with a knife?"
   "I'm trying to save enough money to buy a gun."

There are so many muggers around today, you can walk twenty blocks without leaving the scene of a crime!

I know somebody who got mugged at an anti-mugging rally!

music

My violin lessons with Mr. Sklar, a neighbor, cost twenty-five cents an hour. One day, the other neighbors offered me thirty-five cents an hour to give it up. One neighbor offered me ten dollars in cash if I'd burn my violin. It was Mr. Sklar!

A famous rock star was asked if he could read music. He answered, "Yeah, but not enough to hurt my singing!"

A violinist told a young man that he was going to play on a two-hundred-year-old violin. The young man said, "That's cool. Nobody'll know!"

A great pianist was playing for a small group of people at a private home. For an opening number, he played an étude that had many rests in it. When he was finished, the hostess leaned over and whispered to him, "Play something you know!"

The local music society was giving its usual Saturday-evening concert. As usual, the clarinetist was having trouble. After his tenth clinker, a man in the audience yelled out that he was a bum. The conductor stopped the music and asked, "Who called our clarinetist a bum?"
   The voice from the audience said, "Who called that bum a clarinetist?"

The conductor offered the musician a good deal, saying, "I'll break my leg if you'll break your violin!"

I'm a fairly good songwriter. I do great with the verses, but the choruses are a problem. I can't get them to go out with me!

She wouldn't be on key if she sat on a Yale lock!

My trombone looks better in my derby than I do!

A music student asked her teacher, "Do you think I'll ever be able to use my voice?"

The teacher said, "Only in case of fire!"

Did you ever see some of those marching bands? The way they play, it's a good thing they keep marching!

When I hear some of those rock groups, I clap—both of my hands over my ears!

You've heard of the lost chord? The way some of the kids play, the chord isn't lost. It's hiding!

He played in Key West. It was the first time he knew what key he was in.

At a fancy garden party, the hostess obliged nobody in particular by singing "April in Paris." Tears gushed from the eyes of one of the guests. Another guest leaned over to the weeper and asked, "Are you Parisian?"

The weeping guest said, "No. I'm a musician!"

music (insults)

If they can't sing or play, and hold you hostage while they do, show no mercy!

What did you folks think of her execution? *I'm* in favor of it!

He's one of the finest musicians of the day. Of course, when night comes, something seems to leave him!

He's a true musician. When he hears a girl singing in the bathtub, he puts his ear to the keyhole!

She had everything a singer should have, and a good voice too!

She has high notes that could make a cow take back milk!

She has high notes that could make a train back off the track!

She sings for charity. She needs it!

Millions couldn't buy a performance like hers. And I'm one of the millions!

He has a great voice. Unfortunately, it's in somebody else's throat.

When he was a kid, he was a basso. Everywhere he went, people said, "There goes that little basso!"

The other day he hit a high C. But how often do you back into a spear?

She sings Southern songs so naturally, people put cotton in their ears!

N

names

He who steals my name has nothing. He who steals my credit cards with my name on them, now he's got something!

I saw a sign that said CASEY'S TOOL WORKS. Mine does also, but I don't brag about it!

A dowager went into a pet shop to buy a dog. Seeing one she liked, she asked the price. The storekeeper said, "That bitch'll cost you two hundred dollars."

The dowager almost fainted. The storekeeper went on, asking, "Didn't you ever hear that word before?"

The dowager said, "Yes, but this is the first time I heard it used for dogs!"

A small-town policeman stopped a speeding car and asked the name of the driver. The driver said, "My name is Ladislav Zybkcicraznovskaya."

The policeman said, "Well, don't let me catch you speeding again!"

I can recite ten pages of the phone book by heart—Smith, Smith, Smith, Smith . . .

When a woman says, "I don't want to mention any names," it's no longer necessary!

It was the first day of school. The teacher pointed to the first row and asked each student to identify himself. The first boy said, "My name is Juley."

The teacher said, "You should use your formal name in class. Your name is Julius." She pointed to the next boy and said, "What is your name?"

The second boy said, "Bilious!"

A bellhop walked through the hotel lobby, paging a Mrs. Zamradoskiovich. Calling him over to where she was sitting on a club chair, a woman asked, "What's the first initial?"

An illiterate went to court and asked if he could change his name from X to O!

The son came home from his first day in school with tears in his eyes. The other children had made fun of his first name. His father dried his tears and said softly, "Son, you should be proud of the name 'Ming Toy.'"

The boy said, "They like 'Ming Toy.' It's 'Goldstein' they make fun of!"

A young writer brought a manuscript into a publisher. The publisher said, "We only publish books by authors with well-known names."

The writer said, "Terrific! My name's Jones!"

The old black man was greeted at the door by the swami's assistant. The assistant asked, "Do you wish to have words with the High Potentate Serene Swami?"

The old black man said, "Yup. Tell him his pa from back in Alabama is here to see him!"

The coach asked his assistant, "What's that new fullback's name?"

The assistant said, "He's from Thailand. His name is Bandanakadriyariki."

The coach said, "I hope he's good. That'll get me even with the newspapers!"

The doorbell rang and the little girl ran to open the door. In the doorway stood a man with a clipboard. He explained he was from the Census Bureau and wanted to know how many were in the family. Coming over, drying her hands on her apron, the mother said, "Let's see. There's me and my husband, my children Tracy, Katherine, Amanda, Alfred, Benjamin—"

The census taker interrupted, saying, "I'm not interested in the names. The numbers will be enough."

The little girl pitched in, "We don't use numbers. We haven't run out of names yet!"

At the baptism of the baby, the minister said, "His name?"

The father said proudly, "Walter Steven Alfred Nathan Thomas Parker."

The minister turned to his aide and said, "A little more water, please!"

The passenger noticed the placard in the cab that gave the driver's name. Making conversation, he said, "I see your name's Winston Churchill."

"That's my moniker."

"That's a pretty famous name."

"Darn right. I've been driving a cab here for thirty years!"

Mulcahy was feeling no pain as the policeman who'd arrested him held him up at his arraignment.

"Your name?" the judge asked.

"Mulcahy, Your Honor."

"I want your full name."

"Full or empty, it's Mulcahy!"

nationalities

It would be unfair to allow some ethnic groups to get away unscathed because they don't come to mind as easily as others. Iceland would feel unhappy about the neglect. I've been to Iceland, and it has a lot to be unhappy about. Actually, it's not a bad place if you're a dried fish!

Then there was the girl who worked at the United Nations. She didn't like the Swedes or the Norse, but she was ready to do anything for a Finn!

A Norwegian went ice-fishing. He came back with seventy pounds of ice!

The Viking longboat glided through the water. The first three rows of oarsmen were erect. Their oars were powerful in the water. The oarsmen of the second three rows were also energetic and disciplined as their oars worked the waves smartly. The last three rows of oarsmen seemed to be cut of a different fabric. These men looked worn out, more dead than alive, and totally listless. As land was sighted, the chief gave orders for the beaching, saying, "Yonder is an English village. You men in the first three rows will pillage it. You in the middle will burn and stamp it out."

Before the chief could go on, one of the men in the third segment said to the man next to him, "Don't tell me we have the rape detail again!"

"How can you spot an Icelandic plane in a snowstorm?"

"It has chains on its engines!"

In Brazil, the workers don't get five-minute coffee breaks. It takes too long to retrain them!

A Burmese went on an elephant hunt and got a rupture from carrying the decoys.

A group of Bolivians were hired to put up telephone poles. An executive of the phone company came around in the afternoon and discovered that the work gang had only put up two poles. Upset, he said, "That's ridiculous. Look down the road. The work gang yesterday put up thirty poles."

One of the workers said, "Sure. But look how far out of the ground they left them!"

The big problem with some African presidents is that they expire before their terms do!

A man born in Poland is a Pole. Does that mean a man born in Holland is a Hole?

I just spent some time in the Sahara. I can't see it for dust!

The Swiss have a special thing for lost movie actors. They send out a Saint Bernard with a hairbrush!

I spent five months in Alaska recently. Actually, I was planning to stay all night!

My girl speaks Danish like a sweet roll!

I went to a Greek dance the other night. It was great, but the *girls* kept cutting in!

I'd like to be with our embassy in a Latin country. I keep reading that every day they get stoned!

They have a temple in Thailand that's still standing after two thousand years. It would be different if they let my wife drive there!

Many of the world's greatest runners come from Kenya because they have a unique training program there—it's called a lion!

Bolivia is an old-fashioned country. The other day they had to shut down the airline because they ran out of coal!

A Syrian general had to go to a psychiatrist to be treated for delusions of grandeur. He thought he was an Israeli corporal!

A citizen was talking to the representative of the oppressive government in a Latin capital. The citizen asked, "What are you going to do when the people rebel?"

The representative said, "I'll put on my sombrero and get out of town."

The citizen said, "What are you going to put your sombrero on?"

The cable car taking the tourists to the top of the Swiss mountain was filled with tourists. To keep them calm, the Swiss conductor explained, "This is the safest transportation you will ever use. Our cable is thicker than a man's arm. It can take the weight of ten cars. Should it accidentally snap, which is highly unlikely, there is another cable under it that is even thicker. It is made of the strongest steel and can hold any weight put on it."

A tourist said, "What happens if the electrical power goes out?"

"Impossible! There are three power sources. Each one can take over for the others, should there be a need. Of course there will be no need."

Another tourist said, "It can happen, and then we'd slide down this cable and smash into the mountain at a hundred miles an hour."

The conductor said, "Ah, not so, sir. Do you see that thick piece of metal behind the car? That is the braking mechanism. Should the electricity fail, almost an impossibility, the brakes go on automatically and hold the car in position."

"Brakes have been known to fail," the first tourist said.

"Not these, sir. But, for argument's sake, let's say they do fail. Under this car is a second brake. It locks the car in position immediately."

The second tourist said, "What if they both fail?"

The conductors laughed and said, "Over this car there is a giant set of tungsten steel claws that will shut tight and grip the car, holding it steady until the passengers are rescued."

The first tourist said, "And if the claws don't grip, you can kiss the conductor's rear end."

A third tourist said, "I was ready to kiss it after the second brake failed!"

natives

It must be a terrible life, living on a tropical island with fish in the lagoon waiting to be caught and cooked, sweet succulent fruit everywhere on the green trees, and no traffic, no taxes, no business problems. Day after day, primitive people go along not knowing what they're missing!

A famous anthropologist visited a verdant island where a so-called primitive tribe lived. Worried that they were missing out on so many things, as they walked toward the tribal compound, the anthropologist addressed the men who had greeted his boat. "I come from a land where there is great peace."

In unison, the natives said, *"Wonabaka!"*

The anthropologist went on, "Each man is treated equally."

"Wonabaka!"

"I have come here to show you our ways so you can become truly happy."

Again, the natives roared, *"Wonabaka!"*

Some of the tribe's cattle appeared on a grassy knoll. The anthropologist stopped to admire them. "May I go over and touch them?" he asked.

The head native said, "Yes, friend. But don't step in the *wonabaka!"*

I was on a laid-back Pacific Island. It was easy living, but on weekends there was nothing to do. The chief had the shoes!

In Polynesia the women, wearing reed skirts, undulate vigorously when they dance. I saw one who had to quit. It was the last straw!

The tribal chiefs met in conclave to formulate laws for the entire country. The subject of eating human flesh came up. A vote was taken. Twelve chiefs said that eating human flesh was evil. Eighteen chiefs voted "Delicious."

Hour after hour, the natives pounded their feet into the flat earth, their movements as one with the incessant beat of the drums. Hour after hour, without stopping to rest, they let themselves go in a frenzy of movement. As the drums slowed down, signifying the end of the ritual, one of the natives said to another, "Let's go to town tonight."

The second native said, "That's fine with me."

"What do you want to do?"

"I'll go anywhere. But no dancing!"

The natives were decked out in their ultimate finery. Each wore pelts of animals he'd killed—lion, leopard, gazelle, fox. The drums started to pound. Slowly, each native rose from his seat around the midday fire and let himself melt into the rhythm. As the beat quickened, the dancing grew more vigorous. Before long, the natives were flinging themselves around in a frenzy never before seen. One tourist said to another, "Isn't this something?"

The other tourist said, "Of course you'd like it. You're a furrier!"

nature

Nature is fantastic. What else could come up with a flyswatter at the end of a cow's tail?

Nature made one goof. Mornings are too early!

The electric eel at the aquarium was unhappy. The head ichthyologist came to the conclusion that the poor fish needed a mate. A nearby bay was raided and a female electric eel was caught and placed in the tank with the male.

The ichthyologist rushed to the tank the next morning in hopes of finding a delighted male electric eel. Instead, he found the poor fish sadder than before. As the ichthyologist looked on, puzzled, the male electric eel pointed to the female and said, "DC!"

A virgin forest is one that can run faster than a nonvirgin forest!

A worm has some things going for it. For instance—it can't fall down!

navy

I'd look good in an ensign's uniform. I'll never know why I opted for a Wren's. During World War II, I christened a supply ship at the Brooklyn Navy Yard. For some reason, the rope

holding the champagne bottle was too taut. Twice I tossed the bottle toward the prow, and twice it missed. One of the officers shook his head in awe and said, "Maybe you could hold the bottle still, and we'll aim the ship at it!"

A naval officer, the image of a movie star in his dress uniform, died and went to heaven. When he reached the gates, from inside, Saint Peter asked him to identify himself. He did. Saint Peter said, "Wait out there for a minute."

Finally, Saint Peter opened the gate. As he walked in, the naval officer asked, "Why did I have to wait outside?"

Saint Peter said, "We had to lock up the women!"

At the ship's sailing party, the naval version of the office party, a young one-striper had a little too much to drink. As he downed his sixth, he found himself standing next to the ship's captain. Looking at the endless rows of gold service stripes on the captain's blazer, the one-striper said, "Wow, you're in this pretty deep, aren't you?"

I feel sorry for the young man who joined the navy to see the world, and spent the next three years in a submarine!

"What shall we do, sir? The enemy are as thick as peas."
"Shell them, of course!"

The teacher asked the young students, "Was George Washington a soldier or a sailor?"

One smart kid said, "He couldn't have been a sailor. He wouldn't have stood up in the boat!"

"Have you swabbed the decks and polished the brass?"

"Yes, sir. And when nobody was looking, I took out my binoculars and swept the horizon!"

Two young sailors from the Midwest were traveling aboard ship for the first time. As they left port, one motioned to the wide expanse of ocean and said, "Did you ever see so much water in your life?"

The other sailor said, "Nope. And we're only looking at the top of it!"

The navy psychiatrist was interviewing a potential sailor. To check on the young man's response to trouble, the psychiatrist asked, "What would you do if you looked out of that window right now and saw a battleship coming down the street?"

The baby sailor said, "I'd grab a torpedo and sink it."

"Where would you get the torpedo?"

"The same place you got your battleship!"

The captain had executed a few maneuvers that had never been taught at the Naval Academy. Angrily, the admiral in charge of the fleet flashed a quick message to the captain, saying, "You are the dumbest, most ignorant, absolutely idiotic sailor ever put on God's blue ocean!"

When it was delivered, the captain told the radioman to read it to him. The radioman hesitated. The captain insisted. The radioman coughed and read the degrading message in front of a whole bridgeful of officers. Without skipping a beat, the captain covered for himself, saying, "Take that below and have it decoded!"

The fog was pea-soup thick. The captain ordered the ship's engines to stop. The ship was going to lay to. A young sailor said, "Sir, the sky is clear. I can see the heavens."

The captain said, "Well, until the engines burst, we aren't going that way!"

The poor sailor was beyond seasick. A corpsman asked, "Can I bring you something?"

The sailor said, "How about an island?"

Feeling the helplessness that comes with seasickness, the young sailor told another new sailor, "I knew I was a landlubber, but until now I didn't know how much I lubbed it!"

A sailor was on a convoy through enemy waters. Because the seas were rough, his stomach felt as if a herd of elephants were dancing around in it. The captain passed by and saw the young man in the throes of the mal de mer, crying for help. The captain said, "Don't worry, young fellow. A torpedo from a U-boat just hit us amidships. We'll sink in ten minutes."

The sailor said, "Why does it have to take that long?"

"**W**hy does the new Italian navy have glass-bottom boats?"

"So it can see the *old* Italian navy!"

nazis

Jokes about Nazis reflect a truth about most good comedy: humor is based on serious matter. We laugh at "smog" jokes because the truth is that smog can kill. I like to keep "Nazi" jokes alive because they remind us of a deadly philosophy that was and can still be as fatal as poisoned air. To be aware is to be on guard against it. Through laughter, the processs of remembering is less painful. Also, the study of "Nazi" jokes and "smog" jokes teaches that, when we are creating humor, we should know what our jokes are against. The first question to ask is, simply, "Is the adversary deserving of attack?" In a world where nothing is wrong, there is little humor!

A GI, now being held prisoner, was aggravating his Nazi captors. All day long he shouted, "Hitler smells! Goering smells! Goebbels smells!"

He was brought before the commandant, but kept up the litany. The commandant said, "You keep saying that Hitler smells and Goering smells and Goebbels smells. Let me tell you something, American dog—Clark Gable smells!"

Two Nazi soldiers were sitting in a foxhole. As enemy artillery shells burst about them, one said, "I just came up with something that could end the war in ten minutes."

"What's that?"

"A rifle with a white flag on top of it!"

As the war started to wind down, a German soldier wrote home that the army was out of ammunition. His letter was intercepted by the censor. To stifle defeatist talk, the high command put the soldier on trial, found him guilty, and ordered a death sentence. As the soldier was being marched back to his cell to await execution, he asked his guard, "How will I die?"

The guard said, "You will be hanged."

"See," the soldier said, "we're out of ammunition!"

The Nazi officer sat down on a bench not far from where Epstein, a Jewish prisoner, was gardening. Not a bad sort, the Nazi officer offered Epstein a part of his ham sandwich. Epstein declined the offer, saying, "I'm not supposed to eat ham."

The Nazi officer said, "All right, then have a swig of my Moselle wine."

"I don't drink wine."

"Drink! If you don't take a swig, I'll put a bullet through your head!"

Epstein took the proffered bottle, drank, and said, "In that case, could you pass me that half of the ham sandwich?"

Hitler was taking a stroll at his mountaintop retreat. Losing his footing, he fell into the deep lake next to the path. As Hitler fought to keep from drowning, a Jewish prisoner at work nearby jumped into the icy waters and saved the German leader.

Recovering his breath, Hitler said, "I'll give you anything you want. Just name it. You saved my life."

The Jewish prisoner said, "I have only one request—don't tell my father!"

The Nazi leaders were playing bridge. One of them said, "I open with a diamond."

The next one said, "Two spades."

The third said, "Five diamonds."

Then Hitler said, "One club."

Everybody passed!

Toward the end of the Second World War, when the fate of the Nazis was just about sealed, it became difficult to get new members into the Party. A system of rewards was announced: anybody who brought in a new member would be allowed to resign. Two new members would bring a certificate denying that the person had ever been a member of the Nazi party. If a man brought in three new members, he would be allowed to wear the Star of David!

neatness

I like it when things are neat and orderly. Everything in my personal office has a place. The only problem is that the rest of the house is messy. I can't find the entrance to my office. My wife has a plan for the house. It's called neglect!

Kids today walk taller. That's because everything they own is on the floor.

It's easy to keep a desk neat. You just need patience, a system, and about thirty drawers.

She's so neat, when her husband makes love to her, she complains that he's messing up the bed!

She's so neat, when her husband gets up at three in the morning to go to the bathroom, he returns and finds that the bed is made!

She's so neat, she has a hand vacuum that works on voice command!

People won't believe me when I tell them my house is only ten years old. They look at my son's room and can't believe that happened in only ten years!

My wife doesn't have to worry about neatness. She redecorates every two weeks.

My wife has plastic slipcovers for everything in the house. I can understand the couch and the club chairs, but the refrigerator?

My wife is so neat she irons spaghetti!

I knew a woman who was so neat she divorced her husband because he had one little hair out of place. It was blond and on his jacket!

My wife is very neat. Even when we went to a nudist colony, she hung everything up.

I believe in things being in their proper order. I have only one book in my library, but it's in alphabetical order!

My wife really is neat. In a Chinese restaurant, she won't mix things like everybody else. She picks things up with her chopsticks and knits a meal.

There's one good thing about being bald. It's neat!

neighborhoods

A man should never forget the old neighborhood. I know a man who came from the slums and eventually made ten million dollars. He still goes to the old neighborhood once a month—to visit his parents! As a joke source, the old neighborhood or hometown is a gold mine. Oddly, people toss off lines about their roots even when they're not trying to be funny. A ballplayer from West Virginia was talking about the depressed situation back home and he said, again not trying to be funny, "In my hometown, you have to get in line to rob the bank!" Although West Virginia is a border state floating in space between the North and the South, its mentality, like the ballplayer's, is basically Southern. Southern is a special way of thinking. Southern is one of the last American refuges for fresh language and images. Figures of speech, some of them very funny, still pour out of Southern. Anybody who is lucky enough to pal around or work with Southerners should kiss his grits gratefully. I note down every Southern expression I hear. How much more nervous can a person be than a cat with a long tail in a room full of rocking chairs? Or is there a better description of a leech than, "He was standing there with a handful of 'gimme' and a mouthful of 'much obliged'!" As this is being written, a local election is taking place. One of the candidates for a major office has a dubious past. A musician I work with, an Alabaman by birth, described him earlier today: "He's so crooked, it would take a month of hiccups to straighten him out!" Nestle up next to a Southerner, write down what he or she says, and you'll be a hit at the next party. However, don't feign a Southern accent. If it isn't real, it'll probably come out wrong—unless, of course, you've spent a lot of time in a neighborhood that was so far south the town bird was a boll weevil! Or it was so far south they haven't heard of grits yet!

I came from a tough neighborhood. Any cat with a tail was a tourist!

In my neighborhood, everybody had mad money. If you carried any, you were mad!

In my old neighborhood, a good day was when you got home with thirty-two teeth—ten in your mouth and the rest in your pocket!

In my neighborhood, when you make out your weekly budget, you put in a few cents for mugging!

In my neighborhood, they take out rental ads that read, "Only a short run to the subway!"

In my neighborhood there wasn't one bank. The loan sharks gave out calendars!

I know somebody who was born in a real small town, but as soon as he found out about it he left!

In his hometown the judge was a doctor of laws, and he got rich doctoring the laws!

His hometown was so small the Howard Johnson's had only one flavor!

In his hometown there wasn't a town prostitute. They took volunteers!

Somebody moved into my neighborhood the other day and was fired on by the Welcome Wagon!

His hometown was so dull, one day the tide went out and didn't come back!

In my old neighborhood, if you paid the rent on time they arrested you for robbery!

It was an outlying community. The people could outlie anybody!

It was the only town in the world with dead-end one-way streets!

One couple was married three times. The town was so small they kept getting introduced!

In his hometown they won't buy a traffic light. They can't agree on the colors!

His hometown is so old-fashioned you can't buy a bra without a prescription!

When he left the old neighborhood he took the bus—the driver chased him for two miles!

He lives in a neighborhood where nobody is allowed to build a house they can afford!

The Boy Scouts in her hometown made her an honorary Scout, but she wouldn't go along with the good deed for the day!

In his hometown, people are so poor, the kids can only get rickets in one leg!

His hometown is so dull, if an atom bomb landed on it, it would just lie there and grow.

The town was so poor, the doctor couldn't afford to sterilize his tools. In the morning he took them to the YMCA steam room!

They recently improved my old neighborhood. They tore it down and put up a slum.

A storm just hit my hometown. It did ten million dollars' worth of improvements.

My neighborhood was such a slum, they had to rebuild it before they could condemn it.

In my old neighborhood, women took in laundry and kept it!

In my old neighborhood, the most common form of transportation was the stretcher!

In my old neighborhood, men used to go around with chewed-off shotguns!

He came from a dry town in Arizona. The fish there are still learning how to swim.

The death rate in his hometown is very low. Nobody wants to be caught dead there!

His hometown is so small, the barbershop quartet has only two members!

His hometown is so small, the road map is actual size!

His hometown is so dull, the TV newscast goes on a week in advance!

His hometown is so dull, the all-night 7–Eleven closes at six P.M.!

His hometown is so small, the last one to go to bed at night has to turn out the light!

In his hometown the art museum is a painted turtle!

His hometown is so small, they had to shoot somebody to get a cemetery started!

neighbors

I don't know the people who live in the house to the right of me. We've never spoken to each other. During the last earthquake, when their den fell in my pool, we almost spoke, but fortunately, sanity prevailed!

Nothing needs changing more than your neighbor's habits!

My life was perfect until a new neighbor with a green thumb moved in!

The developer who put up the houses in our neighborhood was a genius. He bulldozed all the trees, then named the streets after them!

We have such generous neighbors. It's great how they're always willing to share their appetites with our barbecues!

A man approached his neighbor. "Joe," he asked, "will you need your golf clubs Sunday?"
Joe said, "I'm playing golf all day."
"Good. Then you won't need your lawnmower!"

I just made a great deal with my neighbor. I'll stop trying to keep up with him if he stops trying to keep up with me!

My wife always says to me, "Why can't you come home exhausted like the man next door?"

A neighbor is a guy who has nothing to say and keeps saying it!

I never cash a neighbor's check on Friday. It gives me two days to sweat about it!

My wife is just like the girl next door, which is another reason I don't come home much!

I often go over to my neighbor and borrow a leg of lamb, a ten-pound sack of lawn seed, five pounds of flour—things like that. My neighbor comes over to me and borrows a stamp, an egg, a bar of soap—things like that. He's a great neighbor. He knows a lot about friendliness. He doesn't know a thing about borrowing, but he does know friendliness!

newlyweds

This is how it begins. The honeymoon is the start of the process by which love blossoms into the need for revenge! Women love "honeymoon" jokes. Strangely, many men are unable to tell jokes about romantic interludes. They often inhale the punch line. A joke won't work if the teller is tentative about the punch line. Once committed to the telling of a joke, you must become proud of the punch line. Don't be a boor, just be decently proud. A joke is your baby. If you're ashamed of its looks, don't show anybody the picture in your wallet!

It was the morning after the start of the honeymoon. The young groom ran down to the hotel coffee shop for some orange juice and strength. Returning to the third floor, he saw that the rooms weren't numbered. He started to walk from one to the next, knocking and calling, "Honey. Honey. Honey. I'm here."

At the fifth door, a brusque male voice called out from beyond the thick door, "Go to hell, honey. This isn't a beehive!"

"Am I the first girl you ever made love to?"
"It's possible. Were you in Pittsburgh in June of 1980?"

One hotel coffee shop in Niagara Falls has the perfect salad for newlyweds—just lettuce alone!

"Sweetheart, I wish you'd learn to make the bread my mother makes."
"Sure, if you learn to make the dough my father makes!"

It was the morning after the consummation of their marriage. The new bride awoke, purring. Hearing her husband running water in the bathroom, she said. "Did you just brush your teeth?"

The husband answered, "Yes, dear. And while I was at it, I brushed yours too."

The newlyweds returned home from a short honeymoon and found a pair of tickets to a big Broadway play. With the tickets was a card that read, "Guess who sent these?"

The couple went to the theater on the designated night. Returning home afterward, they walked into an apartment that had been sacked. Every piece of furniture, every gadget, everything had been cleaned out. On the kitchen counter was another note. It said, "Now you know."

My niece just got married. I was worried at first, but this afternoon she proved that she had the homemaker's instinct. She asked my wife to give her the recipe for dry cereal!

One outfit got raided the other day. They had a come-as-you-are party and invited only honeymooners!

He looked at his plain bride and didn't feel bad at all. In twenty years she'd be as pretty as ever!

The justice of the peace handed the new groom the license and wished the young couple well. The young couple left for the motor lodge a mile away that the justice of the peace had suggested.

Going over his papers a little later, the

justice of the peace discoverd to his horror that he'd given the couple a fishing license by mistake. He rushed over to the lodge and yelled in, "If you ain't gotten to it yet, don't do it. You don't have the license for it!"

The first anniversary of marriage is paper. Wouldn't iron be more like it?

The first anniversary is paper. That's because the husband is beaten to a pulp by then!

Unlike most newlyweds, she could boil water, but the groom got tired of having it seven days a week!

She was a sleepy bride. She couldn't wake up for a second!

The bride started to cry as soon as she saw the twin beds in the hotel room. The groom asked her why she was crying. She said, "I thought we were going to get a room for ourselves!"

news

I have a giant respect for newspeople. When my adoration falters, I think of this old story told to me by a columnist: It is Christmas Eve. The city editor tells one of his reporters, "Get down to the mission and do a story about the turkey dinner for the homeless. Then go to the senior citizens' home and write up their turkey dinner. Pop into the county jail. They're having a big turkey dinner. And on the way back, pick me up a hamburger and coffee."

A small-town newspaper came out with a headline that said NEXT WEEK WE'LL BRING YOU UP TO DATE ON ALL THE DIRT DUG UP IN TOWN. The issue was sold out before it was printed. The following week the paper's headline said FARMER SMITH FINISHES PLOW-ING.

A small-town editor ran a contest for the biggest potato in the county. It was a lot of bother, but at the end of the week he had enough potatoes to last him the year!

I used to be an old newspaperman, but there's no money in old newspapers!

I get so upset when I see the obituary page. If you go by the photos, they all look so healthy!

In a special column on the first page, a small-town paper explained why the issue was two days late. The column said, "The trouble started when some corn was planted last spring. It grew in the sun and rain, fermented, aged, was put into a jug, and just last weekend it got to our printer."

Competition for the market is keen among the New York newspapers. Not long ago, a famous actress was hospitalized. Looking for a scoop, the *Post* sent a lady reporter out to get the story. She was to dress up as a nurse, sneak into the hospital, and interview the actress.

The next day the reporter returned to the office. Her editor asked, "Did you get the story?"

The lady reporter said, "No. I got thrown out by the doctor from the *Daily News!*"

A newsboy was standing on the corner with a stack of papers, yelling, "Read all about it. Fifty people swindled! Fifty people swindled!"

Curious, a man walked over, bought a paper, and checked the front page. Finding nothing, the man said, "There's nothing in here about fifty people being swindled."

The newsboy ignored him and went on,

calling out, "Read all about it. Fifty-one people swindled!"

A reporter summed up an accident at the circus succinctly: "The lion tamer needed a tamer lion!"

I get the papers every other day. That way I don't have to read the denials!

A high-tension wire had fallen across the main street of the town. The local editor sent two cub reporters on the story, saying, "One of you picks up the wire. If it's live, the other one writes the story!"

A young reporter asked the city editor, "Should I put more fire into my articles?"
    The city editor answered, "Vice versa would be nice!"

A reporter for an Israeli newspaper landed a big scoop. Rushing to the phone, he called the editor and said, "Hold the back page!"

A young reporter showed his article to an old pro and asked his opinion. The old pro said, "It isn't worth two cents."
    The young reporter said, "I know, but give it to me anyway!"

At the end of a long work week, the editor of a small-town newspaper left his errand boy in charge, telling him, "If nothing important happens, sit back and relax, but if a real big story breaks, get an edition out on the streets in a half hour."
    At about ten in the evening, the errand boy happened to look out the window and saw a dog nip at a passing stranger. In ten minutes the youngster had the presses rolling. Relaxing at home, the editor's attention was caught by a sound from outside. He walked outside and saw one of the paper's newsboys holding a stack of papers and

yelling, "Extra! Extra!" The editor grabbed a paper, read the story about the dog bite, and hurried to the office. The errand boy sat there, a grin on his face. "What do you think, sir?" he asked.
    The editor said, "It's a good story, but to tell you the truth, I was saving that size type for the Second Coming!"

A reporter covering a Washington scandal called his paper and said, "I'm having a big problem. My exaggerations can't keep up with the facts!"

A little drunk, the reporter called the paper. A voice answered, "City desk."
    The reporter said, "Which drawer?"

new year's and new year's eve

I'll never know why people celebrate the ending of a year. It only means that your car depreciated again! Last year, I had a big fight with my wife on New Year's Eve. She accused me of being an awful procrastinator, so I stopped carving the Thanksgiving turkey and walked out of the house!

Last year, we toasted the New Year at home. My wife had rye and I had whole wheat.

I have a lot of problems at New Year's. I often misplace things—like New Year's Day!

I don't like eggnog. It's like drinking milk from a smashed cow!

Last year the auto club was way off on New Year's accidents. My wife didn't take out her car!

I pray for one thing at New Year's—I want

my troubles to last as long as my resolutions.

New Year's must be coming. My liver is beginning to cringe!

There's only one thing more depressing than staying home on New Year's Eve. That's going out on New Year's Eve!

My wife got sore at me because I came home late from a New Year's party at the office—June!

I take New Year's with a grain of salt—and three aspirin!

New Year's Eve—that's when your guests pass out at about the same time as the old year!

Last New Year's Eve, I was out with the biggest spender in town—my wife!

On New Year's Eve, I go crazy. Last year, just at the stroke of midnight, I grabbed the person next to me and kept kissing until "Auld Lang Syne" was finished. I'll never forget that night. I don't think that busboy will either!

There's a new thing that sobers people up after a lot of New Year's drinking. It's called the check!

I know that the New Year's party is over when I can lie on the floor without holding on!

new york

The Big Apple is special. It has accents, attitudes, and a unique way of looking at life. Only in New York can one find taxi drivers who interview potential riders. Unless the rider has a college degree, is a citizen, openly embraces the Ten Commandments, and hates firearms, he will not be given a ride. I often sit in my comfortable California home and dream of New York. I recall it during an oppressive summer heat wave, with garbage and transportation strikes going full blast while the power had decided to go out. Then I also think of a bad day in New York!

A visitor was telling a Mormon in Salt Lake City about coming from New York. The Mormon said, "I've heard of New York. I believe we have a missionary there."

An Indian came to New York for the first time and checked into a hotel. Tired from a long bus ride, he went right to his room. On the bed was a blanket. The Indian picked it up and walked down to the lobby. Putting the blanket on the check-in counter, he told the clerk, "Last man in room leave overcoat!"

New York City streets are safe. It's the *people* who have to watch out!

In New York's zoos, animals are kept behind bars—for their own safety!

I asked a subway guard, "What's the best way to get to Queens?"
    He called me a cab!

I went to an outdoor café in New York. A busboy mugged me!

New York is unique. Where else can you buy mutual funds with your welfare check?

A country lad went to New York for a visit. Returning home, he was asked about the metropolis. He said, "Tell you the truth, there was so much going on at the depot, I never did get to town!"

You can tell a summer is hot in New York when you pass Grant's Tomb and the window's open!

The population of New York keeps going up. There are so many toll booths on roads leading out of the city, nobody can afford to leave!

I have a great solution for the traffic problem in New York—I encourage car thefts!

In New York they don't give you the key to the city. They send a guy over who tells you how to pick the lock!

Most people in New York got there by selling the farm. Now they're working to make enough money to buy back the farm!

Draped in a high-style mink coat, a woman walked into an exclusive New York restaurant. Looking over the menu, she said, "I'd like some caviar, but please see that it's imported because I don't know the difference!"

A New Yorker finds himself dying in London. He cries out, "Please bury me in Yonkers."

An Englishman nearby says, "What are yonkers?"

There were six million fewer passengers in the New York subway last year. Nobody noticed!

A guide said, "That is a skyscraper."

A little old English lady tourist said, "Oh, my. I'd love to see it work!"

A man was mugged on a dark Manhattan street. He had no money with him, which caused the mugger great chagrin. Afraid that the mugger would hurt him, the man said, "Can I give you a check?"

The mugger said, "Do I look stupid? I wouldn't take your check. I don't even know you!"

You know it's hot in New York when you find out that Grant went to the mountains!

It was an outdoor production of *Julius Caesar*. The people in Central Park were enthralled, but when Caesar was stabbed, about half the audience left. They didn't want to get involved!

A man with a package arrived at a Manhattan tenement. He rang the bell for the Margolins. In a minute, a woman's head appeared from a fourth-story window. The woman said, "What do you want?"

"I have a package for Margolin."

"Where is it from?"

"Pittsburgh."

"Who sent it?"

"Bronson."

"Is it heavy?"

"About two pounds."

"Does it make a noise when you shake it?"

"No."

"Good."

"What apartment are you in, Mrs. Margolin?"

"I'm not Mrs. Margolin. She'll be back Tuesday!"

nightclubs

Nightclubs are history. At the dawn of civilization, I recall there have been eight important nightclubs on one block in New York City. I miss the nightclubs, but not nearly as much as the paying customers should miss them. Where else could you have a Saturday night on the town, a show with flash and fun, watery drinks, and a steak no cow ever saw, all for less than a hundred thousand dollars?

I worked in a nightclub that had midget waiters—to make the drinks look bigger!

One night I walked out on the floor and there was one customer. The club made money. It held him for ransom!

I worked in a nightclub where there were no set show times. Somebody would call and ask, "What time is the next show?"

The boss would answer, "When can you get here?"

The show was so bad at the nightclub, the critics panned the waiters!

The drinks in that nightclub were so watered the cops used it for a drunk tank!

I won't say they spare the alcohol in this club, but you get a martini on a stick!

It's a shame the tables are reserved but the customers aren't!

They really water the drinks here. If you ask for a chaser, they give you a double!

It's awful to come back from spending a hundred at a nightclub and find out the baby-sitter has had a better time than you had!

I don't know why they call them singles bars when a Coke costs five!

noise

A man worked in a boiler factory. All day the hammers clanged against the thick curves of steel as they were fashioned into giant receptacles. All day long, the sound of rivets plunging into the seams echoed in the large factory.

After work, the man drove his diesel truck home. The grinding of the gears was deafening.

Arriving home, a small house next to a laboratory where rocket engines were checked, the man sat down to dinner. Nearby were his two children, watching and listening to a blaring television set.

The man went to bed at ten o'clock, which was the hour that the dozen city helicopters checked in, their landing paths passing right over his bedroom.

One night, however, the man went to sleep. Suddenly, the rocket testing stopped. There were no choppers overhead. The children and wife were away, the television set was off. As the last sound disappeared, the man sat up suddenly and said, "What was that?"

A country lad was riding his mule home when a vicious rainstorm began. Claps of thunder echoed around him. In the distance, bolts of lightning lit up the sky. The farmer was unable to see his way. Looking skyward, he said, "Lord, the noise is fine, but could you give me a little more of that light?"

A man who'd had a snootful the night before came down to breakfast with a powerful headache. His wife asked, "Do you want some aspirins? I just bought some yesterday."

The man said, "I think two might help. But go easy when you pull the cotton out."

You can't catch a mouse by banging on a kettle.

Two men were riveting sheets of steel onto the side of a new ship. They'd been at work for months. But on this day, one of the men threw up his hands in disgust and went over to the foreman and said, "I'm telling you for the last time. I'm going to quit if he don't stop that humming!"

"You can't say I made any noise when I came in last night."
"You were quiet. But the men who carried you in were noisy!"

"Daughter, your boyfriend stayed very late last night."
"Did the noise bother you, Dad?"
"No, but the long periods of silence did!"

The best way to get rid of the noise in the back of your car is to leave her home!

A Cockney wife heard an eerie sound outside and said to her husband, "What's that?"
The Cockney husband said, "That's an owl."
The wife said, "I know it's an 'owl, but who's 'owling?"

nonsense

After preaching for years that good comedy has a basis in reality, I find that humor can exist in a special vacuum too. Some jokes are funny simply because they are funny. They can't be explained. Freud didn't understand two things— one was women. He didn't know what women wanted. He died still ignorant of what made the ladies tick. The other chink in the Freud armor concerned humor. He didn't know what humor was. After several monographs on the subject, he was still at the starting point. He did concede that humor could be destroyed by explanation. Thus, an explanation of the jokes that follow would bring tears to our eyes!

"Will you join me in a bowl of soup?"
"Is there enough room for the both of us?"

A driver saw a sign at a large iron gate that barred entry to a large mansion beyond. The sign read, RING FOR CARETAKER. Stopping his car, the man rang the bell and waited. Five minutes later, a jeep pulled up and a man, obviously the caretaker, got out. The driver asked, "Why can't you ring for yourself?"

A panhandler walked over to a man and asked for money. The man said, "I'm broke. Maybe I can give you some tomorrow."
The panhandler said, "Do you have any idea how much I lose giving credit?"

Rushing toward the bus, a man kept yelling, "Hold that bus for me. Hold that bus for me!"
The bus took off just as he arrived. Shrugging his shoulders, the station dispatcher said, "It slipped out of my hands!"

Did you hear about the gypsy fortune-teller who took a speed-reading course and started to read instant tea?

If at first you don't succeed, I suggest you don't play Russian roulette!

A man praised a certain doctor, saying, "Last week, he operated on my deaf ear and it worked. Yesterday I heard from a cousin in Cleveland!"

"Is your name Pierre Gedempoterahnick?"
"No."
"Aren't you glad?"

The Mafia funeral procession wended its way to the grave site. Looking in back of the hearse, a mourner saw no corpse and said to the mourner next to him, "There's no body."
The other mourner whispered, "He's in the trunk!"

A man lay spread out over three seats in the second row of a movie theater. As he lay there breathing heavily, an usher came over and said, "That's very rude of you, sir, taking up three seats. Didn't you learn any manners? Where did you come from?"

The man looked up helplessly and said, "The balcony!"

A man walked into a hardware store and said that he wanted to see some wallpaper. After the clerk showed him several patterns, the man asked, "Can I put this on myself?"

The clerk said, "Yes, but it might look better on a wall!"

I've been reading this book by a stripteaser, but the cover keeps coming off!

A man showed up late for work. His boss said, "What happened?"

The man said, "The clock woke everybody but me."

"How could that happen?"

"Well, it was set for seven, and there are eight of us in the house!"

noses

I wonder what happened to my old one. As a kid I had a real honker. I could make a fair livelihood selling shade in the summertime! The first time he saw me, the plastic surgeon suggested that I forget about a nose job. "Just learn to eat ants," he said.

She went around with a permanent wave—her nose!

His nose was so big he could smoke a cigar in the shower!

Her nose was so big, one time it got caught in her ear, she sneezed, and blew her brains out!

Her nose isn't much trouble. She just has to lift it a little to eat!

She had a nose operation. It was put between her eyes!

His nose was so big it had its own Zip Code!

His nose was so big it had its own heart and lungs!

At a bus stop he could shelter six people from rain!

She parted her hair sideways. Dates went crazy whispering in her nose!

She was so stuck up, when it rained she almost drowned!

Her nose was so big she had to use a tissue for each nostril!

Her nose was so big it could have used a wheel!

Her nose is so big, when she uses nose spray it's by plane!

Her nose is so big she inhales with an echo!

He got some of his features from his parents, but that nose had to be his own idea!

He has a Roman nose—all over his face!

On his face he has the map of Italy. His nose is the boot!

He has a fairly good nose, as noses run!

nuclear energy

I'm not up on scientific advances. In fact, I think it was a cousin of mine who changed the fuse at Chernobyl! I also worry about the atomic future. While playing Las Vegas, I ran into some atomic scientists who were there for a convention. I watched one of them going wild at the dice table. I said to one scientist, "He's playing like he knows something." The scientist said, "Maybe he knows something!"

I don't mind a little radiation. I won't have to buy batteries. My pocket calculator can run on *me!*

You never have to worry about waking up and finding out that nuclear war has broken out. If you wake up, it hasn't!

I don't care about all the great advances in nuclear medicine unless they come up with something better than chicken soup to cure a cold!

In his lab, working away, George Washington Carver took a minute out for prayer. "Lord," he said, "teach me the mysteries of the universe."

   The Lord pointed to the peanut and said, "This is more your size!"

The way they keep coming up with nuclear weapons, harp-playing may soon become a college course!

We've come a long way from that first mushroom-shaped atomic explosion. They now come in carrot, zucchini, and celery!

I have a friend who lived near an atomic laboratory. One day there was a slight explosion. He's now a streetlight in Tulsa!

The world is destroyed by a nuclear explosion. The only ones left alive are two monkeys in Africa. One turns to the other and asks, "Shall we start all over again?"

Scientists have come up with a mixture of atoms they call nuclear soup. Other scientists are now in the lab trying to invent the nuclear spoon!

nudity

It takes a lot of practice to learn how to walk around in the nude. I started slowly—I wore a hospital gown! Jokes about nudity are fail-safe. The subject helps the neophyte joke-teller because it is already funny. For those who don't chuckle at the human form, I suggest standing au naturel in front of a mirror for ten seconds. The male form, especially, is a ha-ha. It looks as if it was invented by somebody who got fired that morning!

My wife won't go to a nudist colony. She'd hate any place where all the women are wearing the same thing!

The cops raided a live sex show. They gave it one year to get out of town.

If you believe that all men are created equal, try going to a nudist colony.

With the way women dress today, there's no longer such a thing as a blind date.

I went to a wedding at a nudist colony. It was easy to see who was the best man!

A man told another man that he was a nudist. The other man asked, "How many kids do you have?"

   The first man said, "Eight."

The second man said, "You're no nudist. You just never had time to get dressed."

I'd hate to be a psychiatrist at a nudist colony. He has to *listen!*

How does a nude show have a dress rehearsal?

I like nudism, but then I've always liked one-button suits!

Nudists are selfish. They're only wrapped up in themselves!

"I was at a place where you could walk miles without seeing a human face."
"Where were you?"
"A nudist colony!"

The marriage ceremony was being held at the nudist colony. The minister asked the bride, "Do you take this man?"
The bride-to-be said, "Well, if I had a choice, there's a guy in the second row..."

A man at the nudist camp saw a nude woman and said, "My wife has the same outfit!"

"What do you think of my birthday suit?"
"It needs ironing!"

Two visitors were being shown around the nudist camp. A man with a long beard appeared. One of the visitors said to their guide, "Why does he have that long beard?"
The guide answered, "Somebody has to go out for coffee!"

Then there was the girl nudist who wanted to be vaccinated where it wouldn't show, so the doctor put it on her face!

It's easy to see the Peeping Toms at a nudist colony. They're always looking at the girls outside!

Can't you just see life in Eden? Adam comes home and sees Eve walking around naked and says, "Is this the way you run around the house?"

My girl wants to be a nudist, but she has a problem—her birthday suit has too much material!

I went to a nudist colony. The door was opened by the butler. I'm sure it was the butler. It couldn't have been the maid!

A girl with a tan all over may have done everything under the sun!

They have a big problem at nudist weddings—where do you keep the ring?

When you see a sign at a nudist colony, PUT BUTTS HERE, it could mean a bench!

I must have a low sexual threshold. I saw some topless dancers picketing, and I read their signs!

It was getting to be a wild party. One of the guests, a minister, thought it would be wise of him to withdraw to a quiet room. He walked up the steps and into a small den, where he sat down to watch the night. A moment later, a nude, well-endowed lady came in. "Did you want me?" the minister asked.
"No. I drew you!"

If you need a lesson in being careful, watch a nude man climb a barbed-wire fence!

I like initiation time at my nudist club. All you have to do is examine new members!

nurses

During my last stay in the hospital, the nurse who took care of me most of the time was about thirteen feet tall, weighed two hundred, and could easily have bench-pressed the entire floor. She was all work. I tried to clown with her, but she wasn't interested. She also insisted that I follow the hospital regimen to the letter. The chart said, "Walk for ten minutes." I had to walk for ten minutes. I even ate my dinners, a hard thing to do for anybody who has ever seen gray broccoli and bearded ground meat. I joked about the food. Madame DeFarge was having none of it. On the fourth or fifth day, my doctor came for his daily visit. I whispered that I didn't need a nurse anymore. "Tell her I don't need her tomorrow," I said. The doctor said, "You tell her. You're already in the hospital!" What bothered me most about my keeper was the fact that my picture of a nurse was tinged with romance. Nurses were petite, warm, and cuddly. My inner turmoil was short-lived. One morning, getting out of bed, I slipped. I was about to clobber myself on the steel bed frame when my nurse caught me with one little finger. I was saved some pain and a lot of embarrassment. Then, for the first time, she smiled. She said, "Don't make any more jokes!" Her smile became a full-fledged and hearty laugh. I never saw her after that day. How could she show her face again, after that smile?

"I was out with a nurse last night."
"Well, if you behave, maybe they'll let you go out without one!"

The young male patient couldn't hold back anymore. He told the nurse, "I love you. Without you I'll die."
The nurse said, "That's possible. Your doctor loves me too!"

I know a nurse who is so efficient she can make the patient without disturbing the bed!

A nurse was showing some visitors through the hospital. Pointing to a special section of a ward, a group of young men, she said, "This is the most hazardous place for a nurse. These men are almost well!"

A practical nurse is one who marries a wealthy patient.

They nicknamed one nurse "Appendix" because every doctor wanted to take her out!

A less-than-brilliant student nurse was taking her driving test. Coming to an intersection, she went right through a red light. The instructor said, "Do you know what a red light is for?"
The student nurse said, "Certainly—a bedpan!"

A man complained to a friend about his recent stay in the hospital, saying, "The worst thing was that the nurses were so possessive. It was 'How are we today?' and 'How do we feel?'"
The friend said, "That doesn't sound terrible."
The man said, "Well, one morning, I put my hand on her knee and she slapped our face."

One nurse knows her work. When she takes a patient's temperature, she deducts twenty points for cleavage.

When I was in the hospital, I had a day nurse and a night nurse. In the afternoon I rested.

The man who created those "slow" signs for hospitals must have gotten the idea when he rang for a nurse!

O

obedience

In my house, my word goes. If I don't like it, I have to go too! Around the house I say fewer words than the canary!

My wife lets me wear the pants in the family—right under my apron!

Most men are spousebroken!

I can make my wife do anything she wants to do.

A man was telling of his power at home, saying, "I'm the boss at home. Just this morning there was no hot water. I blew up. I demanded hot water and got hot water. I can't wash dishes in cold water!"

Armed by a pep talk from someone he'd met at a bar, a man went home and bellowed to his wife, "From now on, I'm the king of this castle. My word is law. When I want to eat, you'll run in and cook. When I want my bath, you start the water. We can start right. Lay out my tuxedo because I'm going out. Alone! And do you know who's going to tie my black tie?"

His wife said softly, "The undertaker!"

A New Yorker had an important meeting scheduled in Cleveland. A very hard sleeper, he was concerned about waking up in time to get off at the right stop. To protect himself, he told the porter, "I want you to be sure I get off in Cleveland. When this train stops, get me off this train. I'm an animal when I'm awakened, so you may have some trouble. I'll yell and scream, but make certain I get off. I'll scratch, I'll hit, I'll bite—but get me off!"

Came morning, the man woke up to find that he was in Chicago. Fuming, he ran to the porter and berated him, using every curse word known to man. The porter said, "Mister, you have some temper. But nothing like that guy I threw off in Cleveland!"

An important executive said to his gathered minions at a board meeting, "I want some real discussion from this group. I'm sick of your taking every word I say for gospel. You must have an opinion of your own. That's it—I don't want any of you to say yes before I'm finished!"

A storm was coming up. A man who demanded total and immediate obedience from his children told his son, "The wind swirls down from the attic. Check the attic door. Make sure it's shut tight."

The boy said, "Wait a minute, Dad."

"I want the attic door shut tight!"

"Dad—"

"Don't 'Dad' me. This isn't a debate. I want the door shut immediately!"

An hour later, the man went into the kitchen but couldn't find his wife. He asked his son, "Where's your mother?"

The boy said, "In the attic!"

Most wives lead double lives—their husbands' and their own.

obesity

Obesity is one step beyond fat and two milli-
meters short of "tent"!

A mother had great difficulty with her son's eating habits. The child refused to take so much as a bite of food. The mother told her sad story to another woman in the super-market. The woman said, "I have an answer for you."

"I'd love to have an answer."

"It's not that complicated. Your son is what—four? Five?"

"Five."

"Figures. Look, he doesn't eat because food has no fun for him. Tell him a story during meals. He'll eat."

The mother went home. She sat her son down at the table and started to tell him a story. "Once upon a time . . . drink your juice."

The boy drank his juice.

"Once upon a time there was a boy named Jack . . . take a spoonful of your dry cereal."

The boy ate his dry cereal.

"Now Jack lived with his mother . . . eat your toast and eggs."

The boy ate his toast and eggs.

"Jack was a good boy . . . jam on the toast."

The boy is now seven years old. He's never heard the end of the story, but he weighs two hundred and twenty pounds!

You can always depend on obese people—they won't stoop to anything!

You can tell when obese people get married. The guests throw puffed rice at them!

A rather obese lady was walking in the park. Suddenly she detected a presence near. She turned and saw a man following closely behind her. She walked on. The man still followed her. Finally she stopped and said, "If you don't stop following me, I'll call a policeman."

The man said, "Don't do that, lady. You're the only shade in the park!"

A scale is something that, when you stand on it, you start to curse!

A rather obese lady licked up the last drop of a sundae and walked over to the drugstore scale. Putting in a penny, she was aghast at the reading. She took off her coat, put another penny in the scale, and weighed herself again. Not too happy, she removed her hat and shoes. She put in another penny and still received no reading that pleased her. A young boy who'd been watching her said, "Don't stop now. I got a pocketful of pennies!"

She came within two feet of being a beauty queen—one on each hip!

She's so obese, she's been married ten years and her husband hasn't seen all of her!

If she puts on another pound, they're going to have to let out their den!

A very obese woman got on a scale. Because the machine was broken, the hand on the dial only went up to 110. Seeing this, a little boy whistled and said, "Gee, lady, you're hollow!"

Then there was the obese lady who went to a masquerade party as a party!

A woman should suspect something when

she has to put on a girdle to be able to get into a muumuu!

obscenity

A famous Supreme Court justice said that he couldn't define obscenity, but he knew it when he saw it. One of his law clerks asked to see the evidence because he was good with definitions! I personally have no great qualms about obscenity. After all, when stripped naked, what is it?

I get so much unsolicited, sexually oriented mail, my mailman wears a plain brown paper uniform!

The height of gall is somebody who makes an obscene phone call collect.

I got a magazine the other day that was so dirty the mailman had to be accompanied by a parent!

A censor is a man who can find a third meaning where there were only two!

The way a censor interprets clean lines is a dirty shame!

Some of the newer comedians use a lot of four-letter words, but it doesn't bother me if they're in good taste!

A show had to be closed recently because of the four-letter words. They came from the critics!

Last season there was a nude version of Shakespeare. It was the first time the show was clean and the cast was blue!

A censor is a man who checks upon what can be done with raw material!

Children should be seen and not *ob!*

obsolescence

How do appliances know that they have to break down an hour after the warranty is up?

A group of women met at a restaurant. One said, "Jane, you have beautiful diamonds."
Jane answered sadly, "Last year's!"

I look at those plastic Christmas trees that break if you breathe on them, and think back to the good old days when trees were the real thing—aluminum!

I got a terrific present the other day—a ballpoint pen that is guaranteed to last longer than a lifetime. If you die, it'll write six feet underground!

One car company is carrying planned obsolescence too far. It just started to manufacture secondhand cars.

The company engineers worked for months on the computers, trying to work out a design that would make the new product obsolete in a year. They had to stop. The computer became obsolete!

They designed it with curves and sharp angles. Working parts were made of cardboard. It was covered with a layer of paint that chipped in both the light and the dark, cold days and warm. They unveiled it. The salesmen gasped in amazement. One salesman said, "What is it?"
The engineers said, "We don't know, but in six months they'll have to buy a new one!"

A man rushed into an appliance store.

Angrily, he said to the salesman, "You sold me a refrigerator last week. It was guaranteed for life but now it doesn't work."

The salesman said, "Well, when you bought it, you didn't look too good!"

occupations

"Job," "trade," "profession," and "occupation" all have different meanings, except, of course, to my brother-in-law. He's still at "resting up"!

A man applied for a position with a large food chain. Asked for his experience, he replied, "I eat every day!"

I have a friend who's never out of work. He's a picket!

I'm going to maître d' school. I've already learned "Palm."

Then there was the guy who was shot out of a cannon in the circus. He got a nice salary and mileage.

My brother went broke at his last occupation. He had the hatcheck concession at a synagogue.

He used to be a tree surgeon, but one day he fell out of a patient!

A janitor is a man who'd rather sleep than heat.

A little old man and his wife came into a department store and asked for the owner. They were interested in buying the store. By some odd circumstance, the owner happened to be there, showing some foreign investors around. Thinking he'd have a little fun, the owner had the old couple brought to him. After a quick introduction, they asked him how much he wanted for the store. The owner said, "I think thirty million would be a fair price."

The old man and woman mulled it over, then the wife said, "We want to look around a little more."

The old couple excused themselves and walked around for an hour. Finally they returned to the owner and said, "I'm afraid it's not what we're looking for. It doesn't even have a place in back to sleep!"

An old couple came into a giant department store and asked the price. Laughing, the president of the store quoted a price of forty-five million dollars. The man said to his wife, "All right, give me that paper bag you took from under the bed."

The wife handed him the paper sack she was carrying. Dumping the contents on a table, he started to count the bills. Finally it was all counted. It came to forty-one million dollars. The old man sighed and said to his wife, "You brought the wrong paper bag!"

Two store owners met at lunch. One said, "Did you hear about Barton the printer? His place burned down."

The other store owner said, "He's a nice man. He deserved it!"

Then there was the man who supplied the Mafia with its cement. Business was very slow. The customers were staying away in mobs!

A new elevator was installed in the penitentiary. Learning that one of the inmates had run an elevator in a department store, the warden put him in charge of the new one. The operator used to stop at a floor and say,

"Laundry, rock detail, sewing, license plates . . ."

For a while he was a night watchman, but he was fired—somebody stole three nights!

She's so ugly, three days a week she rents herself out to car dealers as a guard dog!

He knows his job backwards. That may be the problem!

A patient was about to be released from a mental institution. The last hurdle was an interview with the staff psychologist. In reply to the psychologist's question about what prospects were available after the patient's release, the patient said, "I have a degree in social work. Combined with my firsthand experiences here, that would enable me to take up the cause of those who indulge in behavior inimical to the patterns of society."

The psychologist said, "That's a worthy goal, but what if there are difficulties with licensing?"

"I also have a law degree. I could venture to practice law as it affects the civil rights of the mentally handicapped, the retarded, and those who find themselves victims of psychotic lapses."

"Licensing may be a problem there too."

"Well, if that one fails, I have another option—I could become a microwave oven!"

A man was arrested for being a camera fiend. He never took a picture, but he did take a lot of cameras!

A boy of six, visiting the country for the first time, came running to his mother. Bubbling over with excitement, he said, "I just saw a man who makes horses."

"Are you certain?"

"Yup. The horse was almost done; the man was just nailing on his back feet!"

He was a Southern planter—an undertaker in Atlanta!

Where he worked, he had four hundred people under him. He was a guard in a cemetery.

offices

The idea of an office is great. It gives a person a place to escape from the miseries of home. Any and all offices are funny offices. Any ten office jokes, chosen at random, exist in living color in every real office. It's as if offices were designed by a sketch writer. I'm not sure I'd want to do business with an office that didn't have a clown and/or a receptionist who wore sweaters to keep the rest of the staff warm.

The boss was yelling at the new errand boy who had come in late. "Don't you know what time we start to work here?" the boss asked.

The errand boy answered, "Nope. I've been here three days, and every time I showed up, everybody was working already!"

The boss caught the female filing clerk and the stockboy in the back of the supply closet during a coffee break. Angrily, the boss said, "Explain this."

The filing clerk said, "Well, neither of us likes coffee!"

We have a typist who is 44-24-36. She's an expert at touch typing. She has to be. She can't see the keys!

If you work eight hours a day faithfully, you

can become the boss and work sixteen hours a day!

The office manager happened by the stockroom and saw a number of the office help playing dice. Wheeling, he marched back to his office, called in his assistant, and said, "Get in there and break up that dice game!"

The office manager turned to his day's work. The crap game slipped his mind until he saw some of the help returning to their jobs. Glancing at his watch, he saw that an hour had passed. He called in his assistant and said, "I thought I told you to break up the dice game."

The assistant said, "I tried to, but I only had two dollars to start with!"

You can always tell a good office manager. He's got that worried look on his assistant's face!

The boss said, "What's this I hear about your going to church and praying for a raise? Don't ever go over my head again!"

The new office manager was a health hazard. He was bowlegged, and the secretaries kept falling through his lap!

We just bought a new conference table that sleeps sixteen.

She quit because her boss drummed his fingers. It made runs in her pantyhose!

Two partners took out an ad for a receptionist. They interviewed a well-endowed young lady at length. When she left, one of the partners said, "She's not for us. She's too big in the first place."

The other partner said, "In the second place too!"

I won't say my office is small, but my chair has to swivel up and down!

I had a chance of coming out ahead on my paycheck last week, but one of the girls in the office is getting married, so that dollar went for a gift!

The only man who ever got his work done by Friday was Robinson Crusoe!

The errand boy said to his boss, "Can I have tomorrow off so I can go to the ball game? My grandmother's playing center field!"

The office computer system was down. After working on it for hours, the repairman came up with the answer: the big computer was shoving all the work off on the little computer!

A young man applied for an office job. The manager said, "We pay sixty-five a week."

The young man said, "That's an insult."

The manager said, "We pay once a month. That way you don't get insulted as often!"

officers

Officers were invented so that soldiers could have something to gripe about. After all, army food is good—no complaints there. Army facilities are great. The work is easy and there's lots of free time. Actually, I salute the officer corps. I think back to World War II, when I was entertaining at military posts. At one air base where most of the officers were airmen, I noticed that some of the majors and colonels looked to be too young to be in the service. The colonel in charge of the base looked sixteen but was really twenty-two. He was the oldest fighter pilot in the group. I asked him, "How do you get to be a colonel at your age?" He answered, "You just have to live!"

Some enlisted men were having trouble getting past the guard at the train station. He said that he couldn't allow anyone through without a ticket. Anyone! An officer came along. The guard explained, "Look, I like GIs. I mean, they're protecting us, but I have orders. They're trying to get on without a ticket."

The officer said, "Let me take care of this." Turning to the men, he barked, "Attention! Now forward march!"

Smartly, past a stunned guard, the men marched through the gate and onto the train. Once aboard, they relaxed and patted the officer on the back, saying, "You're terrific, sir. You're a great guy."

The officer said, "That's all right. I didn't have a ticket either!"

At the edge of a forest, a patrol was taking a beating from enemy small-arms fire. A reporter joined them and asked, "Why don't you hide behind the trees?"

One of the soldiers said, "We're enlisted men. They don't even have enough trees for the officers!"

The officer of the day, a lieutenant, told the guard at the entrance to the post, "Look smart. Any minute now, a five-star general will be coming through."

The guard marched up and down for an hour. The lieutenant returned and asked, "Did General Starkey show up yet?"

"No, sir."

The lieutenant went away and came back another hour later. "Any sight of the general?"

"No, sir."

Finally, at about midnight, in rode General Starkey. The guard stopped the command car and asked, "Who goes there?"

"General Starkey."

The guard saluted smartly and said, "You're late, General. Are you going to get it from the lieutenant!"

The enlisted men were having a beer at a café off post. When the topic got off girls, they started to talk about soldiering. Most of them were bitter about being drafted. One said, "Sure, you know who didn't have to get into uniform—the sons of the big shots! They used pull!"

From the next table, a voice said, "Men, you have it all wrong. I've been in two months and I can tell you that all kinds of men get taken into the army. My dad's a senator and I'm here!"

The other soldiers nodded and said, "Well, maybe you're right, Major Brown!"

old age

As honorary chairman of the American Longevity Association, I have fought and still do battle with the stereotypes of old age as a terrible illness. I'll kid around about getting on in years, and hope the audience will be able to discern that a man in his eighties is up on the stage or at a dais telling the jokes.

There's only one thing wrong with going through second childhood. You can't blame your parents!

My wife never lies about her age. She just tells people she's as old as I am. Then she lies about *my* age!

I know a man who's really going through a second childhood. He went to a dentist and had braces put on his dentures!

I'm growing old by myself. My wife hasn't had a birthday in ten years!

I know an old man who goes horseback riding every day of the year except for the month of June. That's when the man who puts him on the horse goes on vacation!

As far as I'm concerned, old age is fifteen years from now!

At eighty, there are six women for every man. What a time to get odds like that!

The best time for men to have babies is when they're eighty. That's when they have to get up ten times a night anyway!

Old age is when a woman buys a sheer nightie and doesn't know anyone who can see through it!

old age (insults)

A little ammunition for the one time in a thousand that the oldies turn on you!

He's so old his mind has gone from passion to pension!

She doesn't show her age, but if you look under her makeup it's there.

People who knew her thirty years ago say she still looks like she looked then—old!

His wife powders, and he puffs!

She doesn't make up her face—she assembles it!

She was born in the Year of Our Lord only knows!

He dines with the upper set. He should use his lowers too!

His plan for getting ahead is to stay even!

He's gone from "Why not?" to "Why bother?"

Instead of a daily dozen, he's got a daily doesn't!

All women look alike to him!

She was named after Betsy Ross, but not long after!

The ancient Greeks had a word for it, and she was there to hear it!

She's been pressing sixty so long it's pleated!

He keeps her picture on his desk, but doesn't remember why!

He looks like he gave his pallbearers the slip!

He's so old he has a digital sundial!

Old age is creaking up on her!

He's so old his typewriter runs on wood!

old maids

My second cousin Libby was twenty-four and had no husband. There were no prospects on the horizon. Nobody in the family mentioned Libby's name. Her parents were ostracized. The year was 1915. Much of a century has gone by. I now have another second cousin in Baltimore. At the age of thirty-five she came to her mother and said that she was getting married. Her mother said, "Why are you rushing?"

An old maid with a farm found herself the hostess of two salesmen who needed a night's lodging. One of the salesmen was put off by the old maid's looks and wouldn't have anything to do with her. Figuring that any port in a storm is still a port, the other salesman availed himself of what the old maid considered her charms.

Six months later, a lawyer came to the firm where both salesmen worked. He asked the more discriminating salesman if he was the one who had made love to the old maid. The salesman shook his head and pointed to his colleague. The lawyer said to the other one, "Did you fool around with the old maid that night you needed lodging?"

The salesman hesitated, then nodded.

The lawyer said, "Good. Just sign this paper. She died last week and left you twenty thousand and her farm!"

Two old maids were walking down a country road when they heard some noise. Looking, they saw a hen running away from a rooster. As the rooster got closer, the hen cackled defiantly and rushed into the road. A passing car ran over her. One of the old maids said, with pride in her voice, "Did you see that? She'd rather die!"

An old maid is a woman who knows all the answers, but nobody asks her the questions!

An old maid is somebody who's been good for nothing!

A man ran into an old maid in the drugstore and said, "Emily, I hear you're getting married."

The old maid said, "It's not true, but thank God for the rumor!"

Two old maids were reading the paper when one of them spied an article of special interest. In the obituary column was a notice that a woman's third husband had died and would be cremated in the morning. One of the old maids said, "It's not fair. We can't get one, and some women have husbands to burn!"

Two old maids, inmates of a mental institution, were sitting on the lawn. One of them said, "I'd love to have a man throw his arms around me right now and hug me and kiss me and make love to me."

The other old maid said, "You'll be out of here soon!"

An old maid is a woman who has been made a long time!

There were two old-maid sisters. One was trying to diet. The other was dying to try it!

An old maid was complaining to the police about an obscene phone call. "For an hour and a half," she said, "he kept saying the filthiest things he wanted to do with me!"

An old maid found a burglar under her bed. Calling the police, she insisted that they send somebody over in the morning!

A man saw two old maids sitting on the porch of their home. Tipping his hat, the man asked, "Would either of you ladies like to have a little sex?"

The old maids bristled.

The man shrugged his shoulders and said, "Well, some do and some don't!"

Klein had a truly ugly fifty-year-old daughter. He was visited by a marriage broker who said, "Your daughter should get a man."

"I think so."

"Al Baker is available."

"I wouldn't let him near my house."

"Joe Gold?"

"He's an animal. Worse than Baker."

"Phil Stein?"

"Forget it. I'll dig somebody up for her."

The marriage broker said, "That's your only hope!"

She was once a mere slip of a girl, but she's slipped a lot since then!

She was rejected so often, her hope chest developed a cough!

An old maid heard that burglars sometimes hide under the bed, so she got twin beds and doubled her odds!

The old maid expired, saying with her last breath, "Who says you can't take it with you?"

old men and women

This category is like "Old Age" but with a little more bite. It's a way of getting even for arthritis!

The old man growled, "Where the heck are my glasses?"

"On your nose," his wife said.

"Be more specific!"

A con man was selling a magic elixir guaranteed to make people live forever. "Take a good look at me," the con man said to the crowd of older people gathered outside of the supermarket. "Feast your eyes on a man who is two hundred and fifty years old."

An old man asked the con man's young assistant, "Is he really that old?"

The assistant said, "I don't know. I've only been working for him for seventy-five years!"

A man visited a part of the country where people one hundred years old aren't uncommon. Seeing an old man walking by, he asked a local, "How old is that man?"

The local said, "About a hundred and five."

"He must be special to you people."

"Heck, no. Do you know how long it took him?"

Mr. Stone was ninety. Walking at his usual pace of a mile a month, he reached his friend Larson, who was sitting on the park bench, waiting for the usual checker game. Stone said, "I'm getting married. I've been alone too long."

Larson said, "Who are you going to marry?"

"Jenny, the checker in the supermarket."

"Jenny is nineteen years old. Ninety and nineteen are going to get married?"

"Why not? She's exactly the age of my first wife when I married *her!*"

My uncle died the other day at 106. He was shot by a jealous husband!

My aunt died at 102. Thank God they saved the baby!

An old man has an affair every six months with a widow in town. After their January tryst, he says to her, "I'll see you in July."

She says, "Don't you ever think of anything but sex?"

opera

I go to the opera whether I need the sleep or not!

I took my son to the opera when he was a kid. He sat through a half hour of *Aïda* and asked me, "Why is somebody hitting that fat lady?"

I said, "Nobody's hitting her."

He said, "Why is she screaming?"

Opera would be great if it weren't for all that singing.

The way I see it is that no matter when you get to an opera, you've gotten there on time!

Most of the songs in the opera aren't as bad as they sound.

"Have you seen *Lohengrin?*"

"No, but I've seen Minnehaha!"

A burglar broke into the home of a voice coach. Before he could make his getaway, the heavyset coach came into the room and gave one of her students a voice lesson. After an hour of listening to the powerful high notes, the burglar stepped forward from where he was hiding behind the drapes, put up his hands, and said, "I demand that you call the police!"

"What did you hear at the opera yesterday?"

"Lots of stuff. The Browns are getting divorced. Joanne's pregnant . . ."

Tanata, the opera tenor, was irate because the newspapers indicated that he was conceited. "Me, conceited?" he said. "Me—the Great Tanata!"

I found out why they call it grand opera—that's what you'd give not to go!

opportunity

I know all about opportunity. It knocked on my door once. I wasn't home, so it stole my TV set and VCR!

Joe was trying to lead a horse in the street, but was having much trouble. A passerby stopped and asked if he could help. Joe was grateful. After much pushing and shoving, they finally got the horse to the front door of Joe's apartment. Joe indicated that the horse was to go through the door. More pushing and shoving. Once inside, Joe and the passerby managed to work the horse up the steps and into Joe's apartment on the third floor, then through the living room and into the bathroom, where the horse was deposited in the bathtub. Wiping the sweat from his brow, the good Samaritan said, "I don't want to be nosy, but this is most unusual."

Joe said, "When my wife comes home, she'll look in the bathroom and say, 'There's a horse in there.' How many times in my life will I get the chance to say, 'I know! I know!'"

A sewer worker came home for dinner. His wife yelled, "What a life—I sweat and slave in this hot kitchen all day. And you—you get to hang around in a cool sewer all day!"

The case was about to begin. The judge asked, "Where is the defendant?"

One of the jurors stood up. "I'm the defendant."

"What are you doing in the jury box?"

"They brought me in with the rest of them."

"You can't be the defendant and on the jury too."

The defendant smiled and said, "I figured I was a little too lucky!"

Seeking to make his fortune, a young man left for California, the land of opportunity.

In a few weeks he wrote to his father, "Dear Dad, I just got a nice job in a bank. That should be a feather in my cap."

The father read the letter with a growl. He hadn't wanted his son to go west. But the letter indicated something good.

The father received another letter two months after the first. It read, "Bought a restaurant. It's doing well. That's another feather in my cap."

A third letter said, "Bought farm upstate to grow my own vegetables. That's another feather in my cap."

The fourth letter came a week later. "Lost everything. Send money for plane ticket home."

The father wrote back, "Glue those feathers to your rear end and fly home by yourself!"

At a church picnic, Luke met Emily, the girl of his dreams. They spent the entire day together. As they walked home down the country road from the park, Luke thought he'd take a chance and kiss Emily. There was one problem: Luke was about five feet tall; Emily was six-one in her bare feet. Luke was unable to reach her ruby lips. Luke's heart was breaking until he saw a tree stump ahead. Pulling the heavy stump out of the ground, he pushed it over to Emily, stood on it, and gave her a long, wet kiss. They then walked on toward Emily's home. Arriving there a half hour later, Luke said, "Can I kiss you again?"

Emily said, "Well, I don't know. I mean—"

Luke said, "If I don't have a chance, tell me. I'm tired of carrying this here stump!"

optimism

I like optimists. They show me how I'd feel if I wasn't a pessimist!

An optimist is a guy who looks forward to the great scenery on a detour!

An optimist looks forward to marriage. A pessimist is a married optimist.

An optimist is a ninety-year-old man who gets married and looks for a house near a school!

I was an optimist when I installed the VCR by myself. Now I get movies on my electric can opener!

An optimist is a guy who, when a girl serves him with papers, thinks she wants to continue the relationship!

Two pals—one an optimist, the other a pessimist—get into an accident. While waiting for the ambulance, the pessimist says, "I think all my bones are broken."

The optimist says, "You're lucky you're not a herring!"

An optimist is a guy who comes down with pneumonia and thinks it'll get better if he meets a girl with a high fever!

An optimist is a guy who does his laundry in the laundromat, folds a sock, and thinks he's found an extra one!

An optimist is a man who only sees the down payment!

"Terrible weather, isn't it?"
"Better than no weather at all!"

An optimist is somebody who always sees the bright side of your problem!

An optimist is somebody who gets treed by a bear and enjoys the view!

outdoors

There's nothing like being in the great outdoors, with the sun beating on your face, the wind rushing through your hair, the trees creaking, and the birds singing without a stop. There's nothing like it. That's why I stay indoors a lot!

Two friends met. One said, "I just got back from Yellowstone Park."

The other said, "How was Old Faithful?"

"Not too good, but I had to take her with me!"

A group of men got together and decided that they'd relive the trek west made by the Conestoga wagons. After traveling all day from their starting point at the base of the Rockies, they made camp. One rugged individual got under a wagon and went to sleep. In the middle of the night the temperature went way down. One of the other men suggested that the man under the wagon come inside one of the tents. The rugged individual indicated that he was fine. "But," he said, "if you're really worried about me, throw on another wagon!"

People appreciate getting out into the great outdoors. So do the mosquitoes!

I love the open road. But I can't cheer for open plumbing!

I love to get out in the desert, where there's nothing doing every minute!

ozarks

There are hillbillies and there are those who live in the Ozarks!

A census taker asked an Ozarkian, "What's your birthday?"

The Ozarkian said, "February 8."

"Which year?"

"Every year!"

Ozark sportsmen never enter big races like the Kentucky Derby. They can't get their racing mules to run that far!

A neighbor happened by when Ezra was wrestling with a big bear. Off to one side was Ellie, Ezra's wife, leaning on her rifle and watching. The neighbor said to Ellie, "What are you waiting for? Shoot the beast."

Ellie said, "I was hoping that the bear would finish him off for me!"

An Ozark lady yelled at her husband, "You get your ass across this divide!"

He said, "How'd you know?"

"What's smarter than two Ozark hillbillies?"

"*One* Ozark hillbilly!"

A hillbilly walked into a hotel lobby. The doorman said, "You'll have to wipe off your shoes."

The hillbilly said, "I ain't going home to fetch them just for that!"

P

parents

My mother used to say to me, "I want you to have kids just like you." I'll never forgive her!

There is only one beautiful child in the world, and every parent has it!

Mrs. Tuttle deposited the baby in its daddy's lap, saying, "I have some work in the kitchen. Please mind the baby."

Mr. Tuttle grunted an agreement of sorts, put the baby down on the floor to let it crawl around, and became involved in the sports section of the newspaper.

Eager to discover the world, the baby crawled out of the room, into the hall, to the steps leading to the ground floor, and managed to tumble down, head over heels. It was more frightened than hurt, but the resultant cry could be heard all over town. The husband rushed downstairs and, covering as best as he could, said to his wife, who was rushing in, "Look, dear. The baby just took his first twelve steps!"

"Dad, where are the Himalayas?"
"Ask your mother. She puts everything away!"

Parents spend the first few years of a child's life trying to get him to talk. They spend the rest trying to get the kid to shut up!

Every father was a kid once. Every mother is trying to convince the neighbors she still is one!

The baby-sitter didn't voice an objection because the parents were so late, saying, "Don't apologize. I wouldn't be in a hurry to come home either!"

There were twelve kids in our family. My parents didn't buy us any toys. They made us play with the stork!

The psychiatrist examined ten-year-old Willie and told his mother, "Mrs. Bronson, you need some help too. You're too concerned and nervous about your son. I'll give you some tranquilizers that you'll take regularly until I see you next week."

The following week, the Bronsons returned. The psychiatrist asked, "How's Willie?"

Mrs. Bronson said, "Who cares?"

A father doted on his nineteen-year-old daughter. Forced to make a long trip, he asked a dear friend to take care of the innocent child. After the father was gone, the guardian made plans for the few days. Since he had no space, he put an extra bed in his twenty-year-old son's bedroom. Between the two beds he put a screen.

The days passed. The doting father returned. Hearing about the sleeping arrangements, he became irate. "How could you do this?" he asked. "You've been my friend for thirty years."

The guardian said, "Nothing could happen. There was a screen between them. My son couldn't go through the screen."

"What if he walked around it?"

The guardian thought it over, then said, "In that case, something could happen!"

The youngsters arrived in camp. The head counselor started to inspect the gear of each of the campers. Inside little Herbie's bedroll, he found a rolled-up umbrella. Sheepishly, little Herbie said, "Did you ever have parents?"

At the last meeting of the Planned Parenthood Association, they announced some of the wonderful things they won't be doing in the near future!

He was the father of twenty and never left the city. In fact, he never left home!

Parents like to spoil their children nowadays. I bought my son an expensive space suit. But he won't go!

It's possible his parents didn't want him. For his birthday, they put a live teddy bear in his crib!

One day he ran away from home. His parents never found him. They never looked for him!

A parent is the price a minor pays for being here.

His parents loved children. They would have given everything if he had been one!

parking

I solved the parking problem a long time ago. I bought a parked car! A sure way to get an audience on your side is to tell them about the trouble you had parking your car. It equals in comedy value the sharing of troubles brought on by your flight to town. The audience becomes one large sympathetic ear and, in feeling sorry for you, will try to be nice by laughing. You can give yourself a boost by making an announcement. Ask how many gave their car keys to the young man who parked their cars. Then announce that the hotel or auditorium has no valet parking!

I remember the good old days when it cost more to run a car than to park it!

I know of a young man who couldn't qualify as a parking-lot attendant. By mistake, he passed his driver's test!

I just bought a raffle ticket. The second prize is a car. The first prize is a parking space!

An old woman is having one heck of a time with a parking place. A good Samaritan stops and starts to tell her which way to turn. This way, that way, more that way, this way. Finally the old woman's car is safely nestled between two others. The good Samaritan nods, but before he can leave, the old lady says, "Thank you, but I was trying to get out!"

I heard of a parking-lot attendant who got fired for dereliction of duty—he never parked over eighty!

I'm constantly amazed—you give your car to a sixteen-year-old attendant, and yet you sweat if your son asks for the car!

A parking-lot attendant had to go into the kitchen to help out. In ten minutes he dented six salads!

Parking meters were installed on the avenue. Passing by the first night, a cocker spaniel said to a German shepherd, "How do you like this—they've put in pay toilets!"

I saw a parking lot the other day just filled with compacts. Of course, they weren't like that when they came in!

At many restaurants it costs a fortune for valet parking. One owner was making so much money on parking, he tore down the restaurant because he needed more parking spaces!

parrots

We can learn a lot from our gaily colored birds. Or at least be forewarned—the parrot is the biggest talker and the worst flyer!

A man who had never seen a parrot before was visiting another man who had an all-time raunchy parrot. Allowed the freedom of the house, the parrot kept saying, "Papa! Papa! Polly wants a cracker."

The visitor couldn't help staring at the bird. Finally he asked, "Was your daughter born like that, with all those feathers?"

A man brought his parrot to the office of a late-night talk show. Knowing that the show was always looking for offbeat guests, the man told the talent coordinator, "If you pull his left leg, he'll sing 'The Camptown Races.' Pull his right leg, he'll sing 'Swanee River.'"

The coordinator said, "What if you pull both legs?"

The parrot said, "I fall off the darn perch, dummy!"

A woman told a neighbor, "I'm going to give my parrot away."

The neighbor said, "Why?"

"I just found out that when I'm not around, he's been giving *me* away!"

Parrots like short words, not polly-syllables!

A farmer has an order for three dozen chickens. Coming up with only thirty-five, he adds an old parrot to the last portable coop, puts all the fowl on the back of his wagon, and takes off. About a mile down the road, he turns to check on his poultry and finds that all the chickens are walking behind the wagon. The parrot, riding the tailgate, is saying, "If any of you girls change your mind, let me know, and you can ride!"

A young woman wakes up, has a cup of coffee, and goes into her den. As she takes the cover from her parrot's cage, the phone rings. Her boyfriend wants to come over for an early visit. Agreeing to a frolic, the young woman puts the cover back over the parrot. The muffled voice of the parrot is heard as he says, "Wow, what a short day that was!"

A man buys a parrot and brings it home. For weeks the man tries to teach the parrot to speak but the parrot says nothing. The man continues to try. A few weeks go by, and the man is becoming more and more upset. He grabs the parrot and starts to walk back toward the pet shop. A block from the pet shop, a car zooms down the street. The parrot yells, "Watch out!"

Too involved with himself, the man doesn't hear and is run over by the car. Looking down at him as it flutters in the air, the parrot says, "He spends months trying to teach me to speak. I finally say something, and he doesn't listen!"

A fellow becomes concerned about his depressed parrot, and takes the sad bird to a veterinarian. After examining the parrot, the vet says, "No wonder he's depressed. He needs romance."

The fellow buys a pretty female parrot for fifty dollars, brings her home, and deposits her in the cage. Humming a romantic song, he goes into another room. Suddenly he hears a terrible racket. He rushes back to the cage, where he sees his male bird clawing at the female and ripping off her feathers. The man says, "What on earth are you doing?"

The male parrot says, "For fifty dollars I want her naked!"

A parrot is given to much profanity. Exasperated, his owner warns him, "One more word of profanity and you go into the refrigerator."

The parrot says, "Damn!"

With that, the owner grabs the bird and tosses him into the refrigerator. Getting used to the darkness after a while, the parrot sees a dressed chicken and says, "All I said was 'damn.' What the hell did *you* say?"

My new parrot must have been raised in a tough neighborhood. He won't talk without an attorney!

A priest has two male parrots. Doting on them, he makes small sets of rosary beads for them to hold. At the same time, he teaches him to say the rosary. After a few months, the priest meets a nun with a female parrot. The nun is concerned because the female parrot seems to be wild. The priest suggests, "Why don't you put her in with my parrots? Their piety may get to her."

Agreeing that the priest may have a point, the nun brings over the bird and duly deposits the little lady in the cage. One of the male parrots says to the other, "Let's throw away these darn beads. Our prayers have been answered!"

A man in Texas has a parrot that weighs three hundred pounds. It keeps saying, "Polly wants a cracker NOW!"

In a pet store to shop for fish food, a man's attention is diverted to a parrot in a nearby cage. In addition to being handsome, the parrot is singing "Easter Parade." The man buys the bird, takes it home, and dotes on it.

At Easter, the man has some visitors. Offhandedly, he remarks that he has a bird that is able to sing "Easter Parade." His friends laugh at him. He's willing to bet money. His friends put up fifty dollars against his fifty. Taking the bird out of the cage, he pets it gently and says, "Sing." The bird doesn't open its beak. He asks it to sing again. Not one note. He demands that the bird sing. Not one note. No matter what he does, the bird won't sing. The man pays off on his bet.

When the friends leave, the man grabs the bird and says, "I may cook you tonight. Why didn't you sing?"

The bird says, "Take it easy. Just think of the odds we'll get this winter with 'White Christmas'!"

partners

I was briefly a silent partner in a company that manufactured window shades. In fact, I was the most silent partner in history. When it came to splitting up the profits, my name was never mentioned!

The three partners of a firm went to a convention out of town. As the plane carried them to their destination, one of the partners gulped and told the second partner, "I forgot to lock the safe."

The third partner said, "There's nothing to worry about. All three of us are here!"

After doing business with a concern for years, a man joined the enterprise as a partner. His new partner told him, "Be careful. Don't let anybody screw you like I've been doing all these years!"

The company was doing badly. It was one order away from going under. Nevertheless, young Al felt he was underpaid. He did all of the work in the mailroom and didn't earn enough to pay his bills. He walked into the office of the boss and demanded a raise.

Five minutes later, Al walked out, pale and visibly shaken. A secretary asked, "Did you get fired?"

Young Al said, "Worse! They made me a partner!"

patriotism

I know all the choruses of "The Star-Spangled Banner," so I guess I qualify as one of the good guys.

A soldier slogged back to camp from a firefight. Covered with mud, dead tired, his eyes red from having been awake for two days, he told another soldier, "I believe in my country. I'll fight for my country. I'll starve for my country. I'd die for my country. But after this war, I'm never going to *love* another country!"

After the morning playground recess, the teacher asked, "Who discovered America?"

The question being aimed at him, little Dave said, "Teacher, could you ask me another question?"

"Why?"

"Because during recess, the same question came up. O'Rourke said it was some Irish saint. Svenson said it was a Viking. Parolli said it was an Eye-talian named Columbus. And if you'd seen what happened, you wouldn't ask a runt like me!"

Patriotism, for some, is the willingness to make any sacrifice as long as it doesn't hurt business.

paychecks and payday

Most people have to take their paychecks to the bank. The darn things are so small they can't go themselves!

Some women get a man's paycheck. Mine does, every Friday night!

The pay clerk dropped Aggie's check on the floor by mistake and said, "I hope you're not afraid of germs."

Aggie said, "I'm not worried. No germ could live on what I make!"

Every week, this man gave his wife his pay envelope. At the end of the year she'd saved up fifty-two envelopes!

Business must be good. On my last check, the government gave itself a raise!

My wife wanted to see my paycheck go farther, so she took it to Paris!

peace

We all root for peace. We'll keep fighting until we get it!

O'Malley was hauled into court for disturbing the peace. He insisted that he loved peace. He adored peace and quiet.

The judge said, "Then why did you hit Murphy with a two-by-four?"

"Well, Your Honor, after I connected, you never saw such a peace-loving man as Murphy."

A man walked into a big-city bar and looked around admiringly, saying, "This is a cute place. And I like the sawdust on the floor."

The bartender said, "That's not sawdust. It's last night's furniture!"

The best way to put an end to war is not to start one.

Lots of peace has been made, so why is it always in short supply?

I met the world's oldest peacenik. He wants us to take our troops out of Valley Forge!

pedestrians (and jaywalkers)

I got my first ticket in Hollywood on the second day I was in town. Without thinking, as I was chatting with a local show-business character, I crossed the street against the light. Sure enough, a cop stopped me and wrote out a ticket. The show-business character asked the policeman, "How fast were we going?" The policeman didn't crack a smile. Then I said, "You could have fired a warning shot first." The policeman didn't laugh. I thought about getting on the next train out of California!

The pedestrian started to brush himself off. A man came running over to him and asked, "Have an accident?"

The pedestrian said, "No, thanks. Just had one!"

A pedestrian is an object in the street that's invisible to drivers!

A pedestrian knows what a motorist is driving at!

A pedestrian is a man who thought his wife gassed up the car!

Somehow, in a race across the street, a car and a pedestrian always tie!

I changed my car license from 1988 to 1989. She just hit another pedestrian!

My wife is a great backseat driver. She can hit a pedestrian from there!

A pedestrian is a man who walks on the suicide of the street!

The other day I stopped on a dime. Unfortunately, it was in a pedestrian's pocket!

I have the feeling that the kangaroo was nature's attempt to make a pedestrian with a chance!

The worst thing about hitting a pedestrian is having to fill out the report!

There's not much traffic in my neighborhood. This morning I saw four cars chasing the same pedestrian!

Pedestrians don't understand that they come first. They have the right-of-way in the ambulance!

A pedestrian is the last step before angel!

pessimism

If optimists have their day in the sun, so should pessimists. Of course, pessimists would worry about sunburn!

A pessimist is always building dungeons in the air!

If you have to get some money, borrow from a pessimist. He doesn't expect to get it back!

A pessimist is a man who gets a clean bill of health from his doctor, then goes to get a second opinion!

A pessimist's views are often caused by an intimate knowledge of himself!

A pessimist is somebody who's afraid that somewhere, somehow, someone's having a good time!

A pessimist is anybody who knows what's going on.

A pessimist is an optimist on the way back.

When a pessimist looks up and says, "It's a bird! It's a plane!" it's always a bird! A pigeon!

A pessimist has the feeling he isn't going anywhere and he's already arrived!

It's always good when the TV weatherman is pessimistic about the weather. People feel so good when he's wrong!

pets

Take a good look at the shape of your carpet. Look at the legs of your favorite chair, the wooden frame half eaten away, and then try to remember that a dog is man's best friend!

A man was feeling poorly. Having taught his dog how to bring in the morning paper, he thought that he could improve on that by letting the dog go to the store for him. Stuffing a five-dollar bill and a shopping list under the dog's collar, he sent his pet off. An hour went by. There was no sign of the dog. Two hours went by. Frantic, the man dressed and started toward the store. Passing an alley, he heard a familiar bark. He looked and saw his dog nuzzling up to a female dog.

The man ran to the dog and said, "I can't believe this. You've never behaved like this before."

The dog said, "I never had the money before!"

A small boy brought a dog home and said to his annoyed mother, "Mommy, it only cost me a nickel, and for that we got a dog who's going to have puppies!"

My wife is a real killjoy. She just had my male guppy fixed!

Two dogs are walking in the park. One says to the other, "What happened to me this afternoon shouldn't happen to a man!"

We had an awful tragedy in the house. My son had a gerbil. One afternoon I sat down in my favorite chair without realizing it was the same color!

We have a neurotic canary. He hangs by his feet all day and thinks he's a bat!

A mother cat yelled at one of her kittens for coming home late. The kitten said, "Can't I lead one of my own lives?"

Two horses are talking in the corral. One says, "What kind of saddle do they put on you?"

The other says, "I don't know. What kinds are there?"

"There's English and there's Western."

"Is there a difference?"

"The Western doesn't have a horn."

"I guess that must be the one, because I never go out in traffic!"

In my old neighborhood, when the cats got hungry they hijacked a cow!

I gave her something that keeps on giving—a pregnant cat!

philanthropy

A wise man once said, "Feel for others—in your pocket!"

A beggar stands outside a fancy restaurant. Seeing him in the cold, a good soul gives him a twenty-dollar bill. Five minutes later the beggar is in the restaurant, with an order of caviar before him. Seeing him, the man who'd given him the twenty dollars walks over and says, "You shouldn't be eating caviar."

The beggar says, "When I have no money, I can't eat caviar. When I have money, I can't eat caviar. When can I eat caviar?"

A philanthropist is a man who gives away publicly the fortune he stole privately.

Mr. Klein stands up in the temple and announces, "I, Sam Klein, of J&W Fabrics, 199 West Thirty-eighth Street, purveyors of the finest natural wool fabrics, give one hundred dollars—anonymous!"

One philanthropist had a daughter who kept giving it away!

One comedian wanted to run a telethon for a disease, but he had a problem—all the good sicknesses were taken!

A philanthropist is a guy who gives away what he should give back!

philosophy and philosophers

My father didn't mind philosophers and philosophy, but preferred immediate action. More than once he said, "If you keep looking past the stars, you may walk into a puddle!" Yet, when the rest of us would overreact, my father would motion for us to slow down. It was time to think things out. After a rough day, my mother said, "Moses, you want us to do. When we want to do, you tell us to think it over. How can you accomplish both?" My father said, "That's a good one to start thinking about!"

Two old friends were sitting on a park bench looking at the beautiful trees. One man said, "You know, Joe, life is like a tree."

The other said, "Why is life like a tree?"

"How should I know? I'm not a philosopher!"

There's only one way to handle a woman, but nobody knows what it is!

It'll be a sad day for the smart ones when there are no dummies!

The best way out of a difficulty is through it!

Life may not be all you want, but it's all you have.

People who think they know it all always bug people who do!

One day the worm will turn—but it's the same on both sides!

Everything is relative. In a hamburger, a quarter-pounder is great. If you're buying a bra, it's not too good!

I like to count my blessings, but I wish I was better at fractions!

Arrogance is the humility of the uncertain!

Just when you start winning the rat race, you run into faster rats!

One thing about stupidity is that you can be pretty certain it's real!

Motivation is when your dreams put on work clothes!

If it really was a dog-eat-dog world, they wouldn't sell so much kibble!

Telling a bride today what she should do on her honeymoon is like telling a fish how to swim!

Hope must spring eternal, or old men wouldn't order oysters!

Abstinence isn't bad if practiced in moderation!

Fame is only a tail wind!

It's better to sleep on what you intend to do than stay awake all night over what you did!

When all you have is a hammer, all problems become nails!

Philosophy is finding out how many things there are in the world that you can't have if you want them, and don't want if you can have them!

Philosophy is slow sweat!

pills

Society has become the ultimate drug pusher, so I poke fun at pills as often as I can.

Two men were discussing the vitamins they were taking. One said, "I get a special vitamin. It's fifty times stronger than a normal vitamin."

"I wouldn't take that. It could affect you badly."

"Not in the slightest. I take twenty a day and they don't bother me one bit. I do notice one little thing—when I take a pill and go outside, I'll be walking down the street and somebody will hit me in the back of the head with a sledgehammer, and when I turn around I don't see anybody!"

"You'll sleep," the doctor said. "This green pill will make you think of a beautiful native girl in Tahiti. With the white pill you'll dream of a fiery, dark-haired Italian girl in Venice. And with the yellow pill you'll dream of a voluptuous señorita in Rio."

The patient went home and told his wife, "I have to take three pills. Don't wake me!"

The other day I went in to get a refill of a prescription for some pills. The pharmacist almost threw me out. "I sell stamps, stationery, greeting cards, perfumes, toothpaste, T-shirts, bric-a-brac, radios, TVs, magazines, books, and candy. Don't ask me to take time off for your lousy pills!"

At a health show I saw a ninety-year-old man who looked like a teenager. He stood around in his booth, happy as a lark. I asked him how he kept his health. He said, "Pills. Pills. More pills."

I said, "What kind do you take?"

He said, "I don't take them, I sell them!"

A woman well into her eighties begged her doctor for birth-control pills so she could sleep better. The doctor refused her request, but she kept begging. Finally he gave in. A month later the woman returned and asked for more pills. The doctor said, "Do they really help you sleep better? There's not one word in the literature about the sedative effect of this pill. How does it work for you?"

The old woman said, "In the morning I put one in my granddaughter's juice. I sleep like a log!"

"**W**hat's that you're taking, Marge—the Pill?"

"No, it's a tranquilizer. I forgot to take the Pill!"

One woman I know got hooked on the Pill. She popped them like candy. One day she sneezed and sterilized all the girls in her bridge club!

There's a new birth-control pill. It's just sugar mixed with cocaine. You fly so high, your husband can't get near you!

This hypochondriac spent his living taking pills—iron pills, calcium pills, potassium pills—all the pills. When he died, his family had a big fight over mineral rights to his body!

When a woman talks about the Pill today, she could also be referring to her husband!

They now have a brand-new contraceptive. It's a pill a foot across and it weighs fifteen pounds. By the time a woman finishes taking it, her husband has to get up to go to work!

Seeing a grape for the first time, a drunk said, "How do you like that—they're making wine in pills now!"

A doctor gave a patient a pill that would help him become sexually excited, saying, "Put one of these in your soup at night."

The patient called the doctor the next day and said excitedly, "Doc, I got a problem. I can't get the noodles to lie down!"

A young lady married a man of seventy-five. Concerned about his lovemaking potential, she got some special youth pills from her doctor. At breakfast the first morning, she put two of the pills in her husband's coffee. When he snacked just before noon, she added two more pills to his food. At lunch and then later, at dinner, she added three pills. At bedtime the husband got into bed. As his bride reached for him, he fell asleep and slept through the night.

Early in the morning, the old man got out of bed and started to get dressed. His young wife purred and said, "Lie down next to me for a few minutes."

The old man said, "I can't. I'll be late for school!"

plants

I used to talk to my plants, but it's no fun. They think they knew everything!

Remember the immortal words of Eve, who said, "Don't forget—I wear the plants in this family!"

I saw something strange on one of my houseplants—a leaf!

I have a potted palm in the living room. I also have a potted brother-in-law!

My wife didn't like my playing around with one of our ferns. Fern was the maid!

The biggest plant we have in our house is an onion my wife forgot to throw out!

We have a wonderful window box. It stores about eight windows!

I'll give you an idea of how bad I am with plants. I fed a plant the other day and it threw up!

Do you want to know how long it's been since I watered my houseplants? Well, the other night Lawrence of Arabia knocked on the door!

My wife spends hours training the roses, but it's a waste of time. They don't do one trick yet!

I know a guy who went crazy trying to teach his dogwood to fetch!

playboys and playgirls

I've been a faithful husband for over thirty-five years. It has to do with morality and a lot of fear! However, I do have a standing offer—I'll give ten dollars to the first woman who helps me cheat!

He has a good head on his shoulders—a different one each night.

He's a fast worker. When he hits a new town, he just walks over to the first girl and says, "Can you direct me to your house?"

It's hard for a girl to say no to him. He keeps holding her for futher questioning.

He's the outdoor type. He loves to go into the bushes!

She's crossed more state lines than an eighteen-wheeler!

A playgirl is out for pin money, but she doesn't sew!

She wouldn't marry a go-getter. She wants somebody who already has it!

She won't play ball unless the man furnishes the diamond!

She was in bad company. That's why she was having a good time!

He's a born playboy. If he was the sheik of a harem, he'd still have a girl on the side!

She talked him into a new outfit. He talked her out of it!

She knows half of the house detectives in this town by their first knock!

A columnist wrote that a certain movie star was engaged to her costar. The actress was furious and said, "Can't I sleep with somebody without the rumor starting that we're engaged?"

When the wages of sin are paid, she'll get time and a half for overtime!

She's put more men in the driver's seat than a car-rental outfit!

He's like a good dry cleaner. He works fast and doesn't leave a ring.

He loves his neighborhood—he starts with the wives!

She must have married him for his money. The wedding ceremony was conducted by an accountant.

She doesn't mind if a man doesn't fit the bill, as long as he foots it.

He collects Old Masters and young mistresses!

One playboy got himself in trouble calling a girl his sugar. He ended up paying a lump sum.

He's every pinch a gentleman!

She goes for the strong, solvent type!

He took a girl to Florida to Tampa with her!

He believes in love at first sight. It saves time!

He's a guy with no wife expectancy!

He's a man of few words: Let's! My place! Now!

She won't go anywhere without her mother, and her mother will go anywhere!

She's a regular Cinderella—you have to slipper ten, you have to slipper twenty...

She's a popular girl. She knows how to play tennis, golf, and dumb!

He's not choosy. He likes her for what she is—rich!

plumbers

I don't know much about plumbers. The ones in Beverly Hills wear white gloves and tails. And they don't make house calls. If a pipe bursts in your house, you wait until it's flooded. With any luck, you'll float past the plumber's shop!

A schoolboy returned home in the afternoon. "Ma," he called out, "where did that statue under the sink come from?"

His mother said, "Shhh. That's the plumber!"

A plumber knocked on the door. The lady of the house opened it and looked at him, puzzled. The plumber said, "I came to fix the kitchen leak."

The lady said, "What kitchen leak?"

"Aren't you Mrs. Thomas?"

"No. This is the Collins home. We've been living here for a year."

"How do you like that? They call up with an emergency, and then they move!"

The plumber came up from examining the damage and said, "Your basement has a bad leak. Should I fix it, or do you want to pretend you live in Venice?"

The plumber asked the lady of the house, "Where's the drip?"

She answered, "He's in the basement, trying to fix the leak!"

poland and the polish

Poland and the Poles are a prolific playground for pungently perverse punnery with potent potential. But that's opening another can of P's!

There's a new Polish parachute. It opens on impact.

Two Poles froze to death in a drive-in movie theater. They went to see "Closed for the Winter."

A man walked into a car showroom in Poland and started to study the cars on display. A salesman walked over and said, "Did you ever see such a good-looking car? It'll last forever, too. But then, what else can you expect from Soviet technical brilliance?"

The man said, "This car was made in America. You should know that."

The salesman said, "I know that. It's *you* I don't know."

A Pole read that nicotine causes cancer in mice, so he hid his cigarettes on the top shelf, where the mice couldn't get to them!

Only a Pole could get up on the wrong side of a Pullman berth!

The Poles just came out with a dictionary that doesn't cost much. It's not in alphabetical order.

Once there was a set of Polish twins—one was eighteen and the other was twenty-two!

The Poles are upset about the jokes being made about them. They're marching on Washington to protest. Some of them have already reached Seattle!

"What do you call a pretty girl in Poland?"
"A tourist!"

The Pole heard that whiskey kills more people than bullets, so he went out and drank a fifth of bullets!

"What happens when you cross a Jew with a Pole?"
"You get a janitor who owns the building!"

"When do you stop calling a Pole a Pole and start calling him an American?"
"When he marries your daughter!"

A cop stopped a Polish woman and said, "You don't have a red light on your car."

The Polish woman said indignantly, "It's not that kind of car!"

Only a Pole rents flashbulbs!

The Polish football player told his teammates, "We shouldn't feel down. We can still go to a bowl game if we win ten out of the last five games!"

One day a Pole gave blood to the blood bank and demanded a toaster!

Santa Claus must be Polish. Who else would wear a red suit?

"Why don't they have ice cubes in Poland?"
"The lady who knew the recipe died!"

A Pole was stabbed thirty times the other day. He was learning to eat with a fork!

A Pole entered the Indy 500. He made ninety pit stops—three for gas and the other eighty-seven to ask directions!

police

As an honorary policeman in twenty-two cities across the United States, I have many badges. I never really knew what to do with them. One day, however, I was heading for northern California. My mind was elsewhere, so I started to speed. A cop stopped me. As I went for my license, I happened to flash one of my badges. After the cop got through telling me what I could with the badge, I finally knew what I could do with all of them!

This town has really been cleaned up. I met a dope dealer who had to lay off three cops!

The new street patrol has really worked. Not one street has been stolen!

A policeman stopped a lady for speeding. The lady said, "I wasn't doing ninety."

The policeman said, "I'm going to give you a ticket for trying!"

A mild-mannered man walked over to a patrolman and said, "Officer, I've been waiting for my wife for two hours. Please tell me to move on."

The officer reported to the watch commander about having no luck with the witness. "Did you browbeat him, yell at him, and ask him every question you could come up with?" asked the watch commander.

"We certainly did."

"And?"

"And he said, 'Yes, dear, you're right,' and dozed off!"

The computer sent six different photographs of a wanted man all around the country. The next day, the eager police chief of a small town called and said, "I got five of them. The sixth is under observation and we'll pull him in later!"

A cop called in, "Somebody was robbed on Fifth Street, and I got one of them."

"Which one?"

"The man who was robbed!"

A tourist stopped in a small Pennsylvania town. Seeing the town cop, he asked, "What's the speed limit here?"

The cop said, "Don't matter much. Just try to get out of town without being arrested!"

The town elected a new police chief. His first job was to arrest the *old* police chief.

A sergeant bawled out a rookie. "Did you watch all the exits like I told you to?"

"Yup," the rookie answered. "I think he must have left by one of the entrances!"

A man walked into a police station and asked to see the man who'd been arrested for robbing his house the night before. The desk sergeant said, "This is unusual. Can you give me a reason?"

The man said, "I want to find out how he got into my house without waking my wife. I've been trying to do that for twenty-five years!"

The police lieutenant asked the eyewitness, "How far were you from the deceased when he was shot?"

The eyewitness said, "Thirty-two feet, seven and a half inches."

"How can you be that exact?"

"I figured some idiot might ask me, so I measured it!"

A cop spotted a woman driving and knitting at the same time. Coming up beside her, he said, "Pull over!"

"No," she replied, "a pair of socks!"

The cops in downtown L.A. work on the buddy system. One says, "Let's check this dark alley."

The other one says, "Not me, buddy!"

A Scottish cop was asked how he'd break up a crowd. He answered, "I'd take up a collection!"

politeness

Politeness was drummed into me from the first day I could talk. I was taught to thank people and ask them to excuse me if I infringed on their space. That chivalry lasted until I was about three years old and learned that the kid with the longest reach gets the chicken leg! Actually, I am gentle and not pushy. I still say "Excuse me" to anybody six foot six or over! If anybody six foot six or over asks me to sing "Zippety Doo Da," I'll do that too!

When a man opens the door of a car for his wife, one of them is bound to be new!

Miniskirts give men manners. I never saw a man get on a bus in front of one!

A thin man started down the escalator in a shopping mall. Behind him was a rather plump lady. The plump lady lost her footing and crashed into the man, dragging him down the escalator with her. At the bottom, the man brushed himself off and said, "Thank you, but this is as far as I go!"

Politeness today has come to mean offering your seat to a lady as you get off the bus!

A Yankee boarded a bus in the South. A Southerner got up to give his seat to a lady. The Yankee beat her to it. The funeral is next Monday!

He's short on horsepower and long on exhaust!

A cop walked over to a man in a stalled car and said, "What's the matter with you?"

The man said, "Nothing. I had a cold last week, but now I'm fine."

Success hasn't gone to his head—just his mouth!

In the days of the shtetl, the Eastern European villages in which Jews lived in the early part of this century and for centuries past, it was customary for a well-to-do member of the community to provide lodging for a young male student so that upon graduation the young male would marry the daughter of the well-to-do man. Because of this custom, a certain young man from Warsaw was invited to live with the family of Fein, the leather merchant.

At the first dinner, the soup was brought in. Sipping it, the young man belched. Mr. Fein said, "Blessings to the Lord." When the meat dish was served, the young man belched again. Mr. Fein repeated, "Blessings to the Lord." Through the dessert course, the cake and tea, and the final sips of local brandy, the young man belched and Mr. Fein thanked his divinity.

Unable to understand the custom, the young man said, "Mr. Fein, please explain. I keep belching and each time you give thanks to God. Why?"

Mr. Fein said, "I thank God that you don't go to the toilet on the table!"

He has the manners of a gentleman. Obviously they don't belong to him!

He eats with his fingers and talks with his fork!

He was so polite, his tombstone reads, "Pardon me for not standing"!

politics and politicians

Bless election years! We get a chance to go at the scoundrels and scalawags. Smart would-be speakers and toastmasters schedule their appearances to come around election time. The latest political jokes can warm up any audience. Oddly, year after year, decade after decade, the same jokes work with a minimum of switching. The trouble is that those who live by the joke aren't nearly as funny as the clowns we put in office!

A candidate was telling the farm community, "Yes, we must grow more wheat."

A heckler yelled out, "What about hay?"

The candidate said, "We'll get to your specialty in a few minutes!"

A man ran for dogcatcher eight times and lost each time. His chances for election the ninth time were good, but somebody ran over the dog.

How can you call the mayor a cheap politician? He's cost the town a fortune!

The last mayor was all for improvements. The first thing he did was have a nice paved road put in. It ran the whole length of his property!

Politics is like sex. You don't have to be good at it to enjoy it!

Most politicians can't stand on their records until they get their feet out of their mouths.

I know a politician who left public life the hard way—he didn't write a book!

A traitor is a man who quits your party to join the other one. A man who quits the other party to join yours is a convert!

A candidate tried to get a man to vote for him. The man said, "I gave the other candidate my promise."

"Well," the candidate said, "there's a difference between promising and delivering."

"In that case, I promise to vote for you!"

You have to hand it to a politician. He's going to get it anyway!

One candidate was so dull, there was a rumor he'd had a charisma bypass!

Concerned about his son's future, a man decided to test the youngster. He put the lad in a room with only a Bible, an apple, and a five-dollar gold piece. If the boy sat down and read the Bible, a career in the ministry would be indicated. The boy would become a farmer if he ate the apple. A banking career would be suggested if the boy toyed with the money.

The boy was brought in. Sitting on the Bible, he chewed on the apple. After mulling it over, he put the coin in his pocket.

The man smiled. His son would be a politician!

Politicians have three hats: one they wear, one they toss in the ring, and one they talk through!

Tepper, a businessman, was having nothing but trouble trying to figure out some of the regulations about his workforce. His lawyer admitted defeat; the working of the rules was beyond even his Harvard mind.

Tepper flew to Washington. He told his lawyer to wait at the entrance while he went in and had it out with the Secretary of Labor.

Stopping at the information desk, he stated his purpose. "I want to see the Secretary of Labor."

The receptionist said, "Down the hall. At the end, turn left, and go to the last door on the right."

Tepper did as directed. In the room at the end, he saw a man sitting. "You wish to see the Secretary of Labor?"

Tepper nodded. "No other."

The man said, "Go out through this other door, zig right, zag left, up the little flight of stairs, and keep going until you get to room 17."

Tepper zigged and zagged as suggested and arrived at room 17, where another man sat. "The Secretary of Labor? Head downstairs and go left until you come to a door marked 'Private.'"

Tepper marched on. He went through the door marked "Private" and found himself in the street where his attorney waited. The attorney asked, "Did you see the Secretary of Labor?"

Tepper said, "No, but let me tell you something—they have some system down here!"

The teacher was telling the class how great our political process was, saying, "This is the best country. Anybody in this room could grow up and become President of the United States. You all have a chance."

Little Teddy, a black boy, said, "I'll sell you mine for a quarter!"

People who don't know why America is the Land of Promise should be here during an election campaign.

When I hear a politician say he's a self-made man, I'm thrilled that he took the responsibility off the rest of us.

A man ran for office, was elected, got hold of the town treasury, and ran again—for the border!

Politicians like to stand on their records. That way, nobody can see them!

A politician is a man who approaches every question with an open mouth!

I hate political jokes. They always get elected!

Our last mayor did the work of two men— the James brothers!

Many a politician starts to behave, not because he saw the light, but because he was starting to feel the heat!

In some cities they close the bars on election day. In one town, four candidates got locked in!

A congressman just became the subject of an investigation. He saved up two million in five years. Congress wants to know why it took so long!

Most politicians don't believe a word of what they say. They're surprised that *we* do!

I'd like to run for President. It's inside work, and you don't have to do any heavy lifting.

A public official is very often a man who has risen from obscurity to something worse.

I don't vote for the better candidate. I vote for the one who'll do the least harm!

I went to hear a candidate the other night, but I was a little late and had to wait outside. Nobody was seated during the first three campaign promises!

He won't admit that honesty is the best policy. First he wants to try the other one!

A bribe is a gift with which the giver says, "Thanks," and the receiver says, "Don't mention it!"

A politician was speaking to a large gathering. Concluding, he said, "My opponent has been stealing you blind for eight years. Give me a chance!"

What would happen if everybody believed what the candidates said about one another and nobody won?

I've decided to stop voting. It'll be great not to feel that I'm responsible for what goes on in Washington!

A good politician fulfills his campaign promises, no matter how crooked he has to be to do it!

I'm wondering about whether or not a certain politician is on the take. He's learned how to say "For me?" in sixteen languages!

He's just the man to get our town moving. If he wins, I'm moving!

Politics consists of two sides and a fence!

pollution

They are actually selling canned air in some gift shops. It's supposed to be a gag gift. They don't seem to realize the regular air makes you gag too!

I have a lot of windows in my apartment. That way I get cross-pollution.

Hollywood gets in your blood . . . and in your hair . . . and on your shirts . . .

Smog is bad for people like me. I'm a chain breather.

Pigeons spoil the downtown area. We can get rid of them if each of us has one for lunch!

Pollution is so bad, the other day I saw a seeing-eye mugger!

The air is so bad, I sat outside in the sun for a half hour and instead of a tan I got a beautiful stain!

The smog is real bad. This morning I saw a robin breathing through a worm.

The rivers are so polluted, fish have to wear spurs!

The smog was so bad it caused one TV weatherman to get fired. It was so thick he was unable to predict yesterday's weather!

Our waters are in trouble. The other day a dam gave way, but the lake didn't!

I never believed I'd see the day when indirect lighting meant the sun!

We went to the beach last Sunday. We walked up and down for hours collecting drift garbage!

A stranger was being shown the lake that was the pride and joy of the town. Unfortunately, it hadn't rained in almost a year. The proud citizen told him that the lake was kept clean. The stranger said, "I wouldn't clean the darn thing. I'd just mow it!"

The other day they filled the Goodyear blimp with air, and it died!

I try to clean up the air—I inhale!

A crook recently got himself into trouble. After rifling a home, he waved good-bye to it and left his fingerprints in the air!

There's so much pollution off the Atlantic coast, you have to oil the tides to get them in!

popularity (and unpopularity)

Will Rogers once said, "I never met a man I didn't like." I know a man with a wife like that!

I was an unpopular child. I once threw a boomerang and it never came back.

She's not popular. One day somebody took her out and left her there.

She couldn't get a date on her tombstone!

She had to go to the senior prom with a security guard!

When men look at her, it rings a bell—an alarm bell!

People keep telling him to let himself go. They don't want him around!

She would make a great distant relative!

People like to help him out—as soon as he comes in!

She's been on more manhunts than the FBI!

His hosts like to see him to the door—as soon as possible!

She has a lot of friends, to speak of!

He didn't even go to his own wedding. Nobody invited him!

They told me I could charm the birds off the trees. I went outside and got attacked by a flock of blue jays!

pornography

The word obscenity *is less common than* pornography. *That may be the reason nobody ever goes to see an "obsco" movie!*

I know a porno actress who quit. She didn't like the parts she was given to play with!

A man and his wife went to see a porno movie. During a wild scene, the wife said, "Well, I never!"
In the movie, they were!

One town banned *Flash Gordon*. It didn't like what he was flashing.

In a G-rated movie, the boy gets the girl. In an R-rated movie, the bad guy gets the girl. In X-rated pictures, *everybody* gets the girl.

A pornographer who sold explicit pictures of sex was hauled before a judge. The defendant said, "Your Honor, these pictures aren't dirty. Didn't you ever see eight people in love before?"

I like X-rated films. It's nice to see somebody making out!

An X-rated picture is one in which the plot is underdeveloped but the cast isn't.

I saw a movie that was so dirty, people in the balcony stopped to look.

I know a porno star who got his start by going around and showing his résumé and baby pictures.

A transvestite was supposed to star in a porno movie, but illness prevented it. He just didn't feel like herself.

She's been in a zillion pictures. One of them was a movie.

poverty

One of my favorite toasts came from an Irish vaudevillian. I can just see him, sipping from a flask being passed around backstage and saying, "May poverty always be a day's march behind you!"

A traveler stopped off at an Oklahoma farm during the days of the dust storms and the drought. Seeing a young boy scratch at the barren ground for ten minutes and come up with two scrawny turnips, the man said, "Sure is a hard life you lead."

The young boy said, "Don't need your pity, mister."

"I was only commenting about your poverty."

The young boy said, "I ain't as poor as you think, mister. I only *work* here!"

My home state is very poor. Our electric chair is wind-up!

I was so poor, my folks used to buy bread in the day-old bakery. Until I was sixteen I thought whole wheat was green!

I was a poor kid—if they took away my poverty, I wouldn't have had anything!

We were so poor my father would give me a dime to pretend I'd had dinner. When things got good, he gave me a quarter!

When I was a kid we had nothing to eat in the house. But I was grateful because I had a good appetite!

When I was a kid, I thought a spoon was jewelry!

I knew a guy who was so poor he got married just for the rice!

I like to think of poverty as bad luck. The bad part is that most people consider it a crime!

I know somebody who never had one penny to his name, so he changed his name!

Not long ago we had a war against poverty. I know two people who wanted to know where to go to surrender!

I finally found out why we have such a hard time keeping up with the Joneses. They're on welfare!

prayer

There are no atheists in foxholes—or onstage!

The tailor prayed to the Lord, "Please explain something to me. I'm devout, I pray to you ten times a day, and yet I have nothing but misery and pain. My family is always ill. My children have no future. Next door there's the butcher. He has a thriving business, two cars, a beautiful home, his children are doing well, and his family has never been sick one day. Why is a devout man like me always in great difficulty while he's always sitting on top of the world?"

The Lord said, "Because he isn't always bugging me, that's why!"

They say a prayer just before every session of Congress. I think it begins with "Now I lay me down to sleep..."

Grandpa had a fast ten-speed bike. His little grandson came over and asked if he could have it. Grandpa said, "When I want something, I pray for it. That's how I got this bike."

The little grandson said, "Well, give this one to me and pray yourself up another one!"

preachers

A preacher is really a rabbi without the cutting remarks!

A preacher spends most of his time talking about hell, but that's the last place he wants to go.

David said he wanted to be a housekeeper in the house of the Lord so he'd be near the door when the preaching started.

A preacher always got into his sermon about noon. At that time, the train would go through the town and blow its whistle. Several members of the congregation went to the train company and begged them to change the schedule. The darn whistle was waking everybody up!

After his inspiring sermon, the preacher passed around his hat. The hat came back without a single penny in it. The preacher whispered to the organist to start a lively hymn. At the end of it, the preacher wanted to thank his flock. The organist said, "They didn't give you a penny. What have you got to be thankful about?"

The minister said, "I got my hat back!"

Mrs. Culpepper was snoring away as the minister started into the last lap of his sermon. Because the rest of the congregation was annoyed at the sawing of wood, the minister whispered to a young boy, "Wake her up."

The boy said, "Why don't you? You put her to sleep!"

A nervous young minister, new to the church, told the flock, "For my text today, I will take the words, 'And they fed five men with five thousand loaves of bread and two thousand fishes.'"

A member of the flock raised his hand and said, "That's not much of a trick. I could do that."

The minister didn't respond. However, the next Sunday he decided to repeat the text. This time he did it properly: "And they fed five thousand men on five loaves of bread and two fishes." Smiling, the minister said to the noisy gent, "Could you do that, Mr. Perkins?"

The member of the flock said, "I sure could."

"How would you do it?"

"With all the food I had left over from last Sunday!"

He was a terrific preacher. At the end of his sermon there was a terrific awakening!

precision

Anybody who has ever worked with me knows that I'm a terror when it comes to things being exactly as I want them to be. I check the lighting, the sound, the music, the sets, the wardrobe, and sometimes even the tissues in the dressing rooms.

On one of my television shows, a stage actress who was notorious for being slovenly was rehearsing a sketch with me. I kept insisting on things being precise. This bell didn't ring loudly enough. That door didn't close fast enough. I was a demon. After the tenth time I ordered a halt to the proceedings, she said, "I quit." I said, "Really?" She said, "Precisely!"

Jim Alberts believed in precision. Everything in his life had to be exact. After dating a young lady for a month, he called her one night, and said, "Gloria, I adore you. I don't mean I like you, I'm fond of you, or I love you. I mean *adore*. I'm coming over tonight. I don't mean tomorrow, the day after tomorrow, I mean tonight. I'll be at your house at eight. Not seven fifty-six, seven fifty-eight. Not five after eight."

At the exact tick of eight he was at Gloria's house. He said, "I'm wearing my fancy watch with the sweep hand, so I will give you exactly thirty minutes to tell me whether you will marry me or not. I don't mean twenty-nine minutes, thirty-two minutes. One half hour exactly."

The hands of the watch moved on and on. At the half hour, he said, "Will you be my wife?"

Gloria said, "Yes."

Jim said, "You've made me the happiest man on Madison Avenue between Twenty-fifth and Twenty-sixth streets!"

You can always tell the new members. They get to the committee meeting on time!

The minister told his housekeeper, "The Powells should be here for dinner at seven, but knowing them, I think I'll give them a half hour of grace."

The housekeeper said, "That'll teach them to be on time!"

The customer was driving the butcher crazy. She wanted a piece cut off the fourth slab in the display. Was it fresh? Was the meat local? What had the cow been fed? Motioning to her, the butcher said, "I know exactly what you want." He started for his meat locker. At the door he stopped and turned. "The cow's name was Mildred, is that okay?"

pregnancy

Pregnancy is an example of a woman's ability to take physical pain. No man could go through it. When a man cuts his finger trying to peel an apple, he has to lie down for ten days. No man could stand morning sickness. After the first urge to retch, he'd say to himself, "If that woman tries to kitchy-koo again, I'll kill her!"

A marriage broker was trying to interest a client in a bride. After a glowing description of the girl's appearance, the marriage broker said, "She also has several hundred thousand dollars and a good business."

The client said, "You say she's gorgeous. She's rich. There must be a problem somewhere."

The marriage broker said, "Well, to tell you the truth, she's a little bit pregnant!"

A woman was sitting in the doctor's office near another woman who had a cute little four-year-old girl with her. The woman said, "I wish I had a little girl like you."

The little girl said, "Why don't you become pregnant?"

Millie was sixteen and very pregnant. She remembered when she had conceived. It was at home, while her parents were away at the movies.

The doctor said, "Why didn't you go to the movies that night?"

Millie said, "It was for adults only!"

The doctor said, "Mrs. Brown, I have good news for you."

The patient said, "It's *Miss* Brown."

The doctor said, "Well, Miss Brown . . ."

A couple hailed a cab and said, "City Hall. Then Doctor's Hospital. And go like mad!"

presidents

To hunt, fish, drive, or own a dog, you need a license. But anybody who wants to can run for President!

The President is doing the best he can. That should scare you!

George Washington wore high-heeled boots, tight satin pants, a ruffled silk shirt, and a curly wig. He ran for President in the thirteen colonies and won. In Waco, Texas, he'd have to run for his life!

A recent President said each incoming President should have three envelopes. During the first year, when the going is always rough, he should open the first envelope. The message inside reads, "Blame the guy who was in the office before you!"

If things are still less than smooth at the end of the second year, he should open and read the second letter: "Blame Congress!"

At the end of the next year, when he's battered and bloody, he should open the third envelope and read its message: "Prepare three envelopes!"

One President was supposed to take a trip on Air Force One, but he couldn't remember the number of the flight!

prices

They say that what goes up must come down. Would you like to bet on it?

We have an understanding butcher. He gives us easy terms on a steak!

There are a lot of things your money can't buy—like what it bought two weeks ago.

I spend all of my money for food. My wife won't eat anything else!

A lawyer said to one of his clients, "When I was a kid, I wanted to be a pirate!"

The client said, "Congratulations!"

Anybody with a hundred thousand can always find a bargain!

A sailor, arriving at a foreign port, availed himself of the services of a young lady. Satisfied, and knowing that the young lady could use money, he reached into his pocket and discovered a dime. He offered it to her. She smiled at him and said, "I don't have any change!"

Not long ago, I was rear-ended. I didn't get whiplash until I saw my attorney's share of the settlement!

A certain store advertises that it doesn't want a penny down. When you go in, they want about five hundred dollars down!

Do you know how much it costs to take a bus today? It's gotten so the cheapskates take cabs!

The prices of cars are incredible. I never knew you could pay so much for something that didn't come with a lawn!

profanity

When I was a kid, they'd wash my mouth out with soap if I said a dirty word. They never found out I don't like dirty words. I love the taste of soap!

Two deaf mutes were talking about a third. One said, "He threw a real tantrum. Every other word was a cussword."

"It couldn't have been that bad."

"No," the first one said. "He cussed so much he blistered his fingers!"

A man was helping his wife hang pictures. As was and is customary during such a chore, he landed a blow on his thumb with a hammer. He started to curse. His wife said, "Don't curse like that."

Hitting his thumb again, the husband said, "If you know a better way to curse, let me know now!"

A skywriter made an error while in the air. Upset with himself, he flew behind a cloud and wrote a dirty word!

property

We don't really own anything. If we did, we could take it with us when we go! There is a new theory that we may be able to transport our assets into another life. I'm not eager to test that theory!

He's got property in Atlantic City. A hotel has two of his bags.

Wives can't lose. Most of them operate under the belief that what's yours is theirs and what's theirs is theirs.

The Bible says that the meek shall inherit the earth. I'm glad, because I have my eye on a piece of property in Malibu.

He didn't marry her because her father left her a hundred thousand acres of prime land. He would have married her no matter who had left her the land.

An Englishman was being given a tour of a large Texas ranch. "I'll give you an idea of the size of the place," the owner bragged. "You could board a train at one end of my property and still not be at the other end in twenty-four hours."

The Englishman said, "We have trains like that too!"

In America we believe that a person's property is his own—except when he goes to summer camp for two weeks!

prostitution

The mayor of our city is very eager to get the prostitutes out of our city. Just the other night I saw him driving two of them.

Why do people keep hammering on prostitution? It's the only industry that isn't leaving the city.

A doctor told a prostitute, "Take these pills, eat a bland diet, and in three days I'll have you back in bed."

A prostitute met a ninety-year-old man at a bar. He asked if she wanted to have some fun. She said, "You've had it."

The old man said, "How much do I owe you?"

An out-of-towner went into a bar. As he ordered a beer, a young lady of questionable virtue sidled up and asked if he wanted to have some fun. The man said, "There are three reasons I wouldn't become involved with you. First of all, I have no money. The sec—"

The young lady cut him off, saying, "Let me tell you what you can do with the other two reasons!"

She's worked the streets so long they made her an honorary lamppost!

A prostitute took a client to a motel. Before she was willing to submit to him, she demanded a hundred dollars cash. The customer handed her a crisp one-hundred-dollar bill. As soon as they were undressed, the customer started to spank the prostitute. It was starting to hurt, so she asked, "How long are you going to do this?"

The customer said, "Until I get my money back!"

A well-endowed prostitute was being questioned during her trial for soliciting. The city attorney said, "Have you anything to offer the jury on your behalf?"

The well-endowed prostitute said, "No thank you, but that's why I'm in here!"

She's walked the streets so long her panty hose have curb feelers!

A man from out of town picked up a prostitute at the hotel bar. After a drink or two, he brought her up to his room and they had some fun. The next day, the man, his business finished, went to the desk to settle his bill. The clerk said, "Shall I put your wife on this bill?"

Rather than make a big deal out of it, the man agreed. The hotel couldn't charge too much for his "wife."

When the bill was handed to him, he almost fainted. It was for three thousand dollars. Angrily, he pushed the bill back at the clerk. "This is all wrong. I was only here two days."

The clerk said, "Yes. But your wife has been here ten weeks."

proverbs

When you talk about big things coming in small packages, you're talking proverbs. They're close to adages, but I think they pack a bigger punch! You can make a quip funnier if you dress it up like a proverb and ascribe it to some ancient sage—as the great Persian philosopher Herbie said. Start off as if a profound thought were about to be offered: "A horse that eats an oat..." "When the sun shines over a mulberry tree..." My favorite has always been, "A wet bird never flies."

A pig bought on credit is forever grunting.

The greatest king is put in his grave with a shovel.

What is the world to a man, when his wife is a widow?

The measure of a man's character is what he would be if he knew he would never be found out.

Few people blame themselves until they have exhausted all other possibilities.

It's a bad cook who can't lick her own fingers.

You always get the last word if you argue alone.

Think of the tragedy of not teaching children to doubt.

It is no advantage to a man with fever to change his bed.

When we are flat on our backs, there is no way to look but up.

Words, once spoken, can never be recalled.

Only the wise can be perplexed.

To the wise, life is a problem. To the fool, a solution.

The borrower is servant to the lender.

The fear of death is the greatest compliment we pay to life.

A crowd is not company.

If you want him to mourn, leave him nothing.

Love comes unseen; we only see it go.

psychiatry

On a late-night show, years ago in Chicago, the host and I told "psychiatrist" jokes for a half hour. After that, the audience called in with its own "psychiatrist" jokes. With all those jokes, however, we didn't mine out one good vein in the mother lode. After the show went off the air, a hundred other jokes surfaced. In a testimonial, if you're called on to speak, personalize some psychiatrist, making the guest of honor the brunt, and you'll be the hit of the event. Anybody who doesn't know any psychiatric jokes should be on the couch!

A man goes to a psychiatrist. Lying on the couch, the man says, "I'm dead."

The psychiatrist says, "You're not dead."

"I'm dead."

"You're not dead." Stabbing the patient with a pin so that blood trickles out, the psychiatrist goes on, "Dead men don't bleed."

The patient looks down, sees the slight trickle of blood, and says, "How do you like that? Dead men bleed!"

The new patient said, "I feel like a new man."

The psychiatrist said, "Can this new guy afford me?"

Bothered by his patient's attitude, the psychiatrist said, "Do you have any faith in me?"

"Sure," the patient answered, "but I still have that screw in my navel."

"No, you don't."

"I do. It's a little round screw."

"If you had faith in me, you'd believe me. You have no screw."

"Doc, I can feel it."

"All right, let's do this—have a screwdriver handy when you go to sleep tonight, and when you're about to fall asleep, unscrew the screw. In the morning it'll be gone forever."

The patient returned the next day, more disconsolate than ever.

The psychiatrist asked, "Did you do as I said?"

"Yup."

"You unscrewed the screw?"

"Yup."

"What happened?"

"My rear end fell off!"

A man took his wife to a psychiatrist and said, "What's-her-name here complains that I don't give her enough attention!"

A car mechanic went to a psychiatrist, who said to him, "Get under the couch."

The man on the couch said, "I see my brother Alex. He's blindfolded and two men are leading him down a corridor, up a dozen steps, and through a small door. What do you think, doctor?"

The doctor said, "If they're not playing blindman's buff, your brother is in real trouble."

A psychiatrist took his patient over to the window and said, "Stick out your tongue."

The patient said, "Why?"

"I don't like the psychiatrist across the street."

My psychiatrist cured me of a ringing in my ears. Now I have an unlisted head.

The psychiatrist waited until the patient became comfortable on the couch, then said, "Why don't you start at the beginning?"

The patient said, "Okay. In the beginning I created the heavens and the earth . . ."

Four out of five people are mentally ill. Take a good look at your four closest friends!

"Doctor, I just can't stop believing I'm a dog."

"How long has this been going on?"

"Since I was a puppy!"

I stopped going to the psychiatrist because he kept asking me the same question my wife asks: "Who do you think you are?"

Then there are some who say that a psychiatrist is a Jewish doctor who hates the sight of blood!

The patient pulled out a gun and told the doctor, "You're a great doctor and you helped me a lot, but now you know too much!"

One psychiatrist had two baskets on the top of his desk. One was marked OUTGOING; the other was marked INHIBITED.

A patient walked into a psychiatrist's office and said, "I'm a schizophrenic."

The doctor said, "Don't worry, the four of us can handle it."

"How many psychiatrists does it take to change a light bulb?"

"One. But the light bulb has to *want* to change."

A neurotic builds castles in the air. A psychotic lives in the castle. The psychiatrist collects rent from both of them!

The patient said to the psychiatrist, "I'm so unhappy. Nobody takes me seriously."

The psychiatrist said, "No kidding?"

One psychiatrist specializes in teenage girls. Instead of a couch, he uses a backseat.

A young man took therapy for ten years. At the end of that time, the doctor told him, "You're finished. You don't need me anymore."

The young man left, but phoned a week later, saying, "Doctor, I can't be out there alone. You're a mother to me."

"I'm not your mother."

"I depend on you for everything."

"You'll do fine. You don't need me to mother you. Where are you now?"

"I'm having breakfast."

"What kind of breakfast?"

"Black coffee, that's all."

"Do you call that a breakfast?"

My psychiatrist just went broke. People kept giving him a penny for his thoughts.

One psychiatrist loves to work in the great outdoors. Instead of a couch, he uses a sleeping bag.

A woman explained to a psychiatrist that her husband thought he was the Lone Ranger. The psychiatrist asked, "How long has this been going on?"

"About twenty years."

"Bring him in. I'll cure him."

The woman nodded and said, "I guess it's the right thing to do. But Tonto is so good with the children!"

A patient goes to a psychiatrist for the first time and is given some tests. The psychiatrist draws a circle and says, "What does this make you think of?"

"Sex."

The psychiatrist draws a tree and repeats his question.

"Sex," the patient answers again.

The psychiatrist proceeds to draw simple figures of all sorts—a house, a car, an apple, and so on—each time getting the same response. Sex, sex, and sex. Finally, the psychiatrist says, "You have an obsession with sex."

The patient says, "Me? You're the one who's drawing all those dirty pictures!"

A patient says, "I think I'm an umbrella."

The psychiatrist says, "A cure is possible if you'll open up."

The patient says, "Why? Is it raining?"

A psychiatrist is a man you go to see when you're going crazy, and he helps you!

A man went to a psychiatrist and told his sad story. "I'm insecure about my height," he said. "I'm so short I want to kill myself."

The psychiatrist said, "Size doesn't matter. Giant oaks from little acorns grow. A little acorn, no bigger than the nail of your thumb, can become a hundred-foot oak."

The patient was relieved and left. He decided to take a shortcut home through the park. A squirrel ate him!

One psychiatrist had to cure a man who had a split personality. When the man ate at a restaurant alone, he'd ask for separate checks!

The woman said, "When I came into the bedroom, there was my son. He was in high heels, putting on a bra, a dress, pearls, and earrings."

"That's not too good," the psychiatrist said.

"I know. I've told him a hundred times—stay away from your father's things!"

The psychiatrist said to the patient, "You have to give up smoking. You must give up smoking. I insist. No more smoking!"

The patient said, "Is it that bad for me?"

"No, but you're burning holes in my couch!"

Two psychiatrists were at a convention. As they conversed over a drink, one asked, "What was your most difficult case?"

The other replied, "I had a patient who lived in a pure fantasy world. He believed that an uncle in South America was going to die and leave him a fortune. All day long he waited for a letter to arrive from an attorney. He never went out, he never did anything, he merely sat around and waited for this fantasy letter from this fantasy uncle. I worked with this man eight years."

"What was the result?"

"It was an eight-year struggle. Every day for eight years, but I finally cured him. And then that stupid letter arrived!"

"Doctor, is it okay to marry an octopus?"
"Of course not."
"Tell me one more thing—what do I do with eight engagement rings?"

"Mr. Gerber," the psychiatrist said. "You're all better now. Your treatment is over."
Mr. Gerber said, "Oh, Doctor, I can't believe it. Is there something I can do for you in return for all these years?"
"You've paid your bill, and that's all I require."
"But, Doctor, that isn't enough. You're incredible. I could hug you and kiss you."
"Please don't do that. Actually, we shouldn't even be lying here on the couch together."

Dr. Paulson was out for a spin in his new sports car. At an intersection, another car disregarded the stop sign and rammed into him. Jumping out of his new car, Dr. Paulson was ready to kill. "Idiot! Moron! Imbecile!" Then, remembering his background, he went on, "Why do you hate your mother?"

When you go to a psychiatrist, why do they call it *free* association?

One psychiatrist decorated his office with furniture made of overwrought iron.

A man with a split personality went to a psychiatrist who was nice enough to give him a group rate.

putdowns

Putdowns are a smidgin stronger than heckler ripostes. Putdowns are only used to get even. Like heckler lines, putdowns must be used sparingly. To spray them relentlessly is to invite sympathy for the other side. We don't want an audience feeling bad for a loudmouth!

You have a wonderful head on your shoulders. Whose is it?

Why don't you leave and let live?

I never knew what real happiness was until you got here. Now it's too late!

I may not agree with what you say, but I'll defend to the death your right to shut up!

I was at her wedding. Nobody wanted to give her away. They finally held an auction!

Somebody get a plumber. There's a drip in here!

You're the salt of the earth. People should try to shake you!

You're as useful as a glass eye at a keyhole!

He looks like he finished last in the human race!

Her face is her fortune. She should keep it in a vault!

He's a man of exact words. When he sees a sign that says "wet paint," he does!

We ought to throw him a dinner—and hope it hits him!

He gives people warmth. Of course, you can get the same feeling from a rectal suppository!

I won't say he's got a big head, but Sears wouldn't paint it for $99.95!

Try going for a long walk on a short pier!

We'll make him eat those words—as soon as he gets teeth!

What can you say about him that hasn't already been said about warts!

He's not a bore—he's just a carrier!

If they put a price on your head—take it!

This guy has taken a lot of abuse—and rightly so!

Someday you'll find yourself—and will you be disappointed!

Read a blank book and improve your mind!

He doesn't know himself, which makes him pretty lucky!

Every time she tries to be nice, it makes her irritable!

She stays longer in an hour than most people stay in a week!

She has everything. She should be quarantined!

quakers

We have some fine Quaker furniture in our kitchen. During an earthquake, we also have a lot in the other rooms!

A man from another state was traveling through the farm country of Pennsylvania. Stopping in a Quaker town, he asked a boy to explain Quaker ways. The boy said, "Quakers never have disagreements. They never fight. They never become angry."

The man said, "Do you come from a Quaker family?"

The boy said, "My pa is a Quaker, but I don't think my ma is one!"

Simon woke with a start. Certain that he'd heard a noise downstairs, he got out of bed and tiptoed down the steps. A burglar was searching through the drawers of the credenza. Raising his gun, Simon said to the burglar, "Sir, thee are standing exactly where I plan to shoot!"

A man was complaining about the many Quakers in the area, saying to the counterman at the diner outside of town, "I wish I could go where there weren't so many darn Quakers."

A Quaker sitting next to him said, "Thee can go to Hades, sir. Thee won't find any!"

Quakers believe that each man is a minister. After a Sunday meeting, Isaac went home and sat down to a sumptuous meal. His friend Judah dropped in for a visit and saw the table laid out with many fine dishes—a roast, sausages, broiled lobster, and a sea of steamed vegetables. Judah said, "Thee are eating muchly, Isaac."

Isaac said, "The minister deserves a special meal once in a while!"

A stranger went to a typical Quaker service and wondered about its simplicity. He told one of the Quakers, "In my church we have great costumes and all kinds of fancy rituals."

The Quaker said, "We all worship the Lord differently. Thee in your own way and I in His!"

Many Quakers shake as they worship. An earthquake hit one of their conclaves and one Quaker said to another, "Are thee praying without me?"

A Pennsylvania rabbi said to an associate, "We'll have to do something. Many of the younger people are converting to the Quaker faith."

The associate said, "You've noticed that too? In my temple, some of my best Jews are Friends!"

Hiram came into the kitchen for a cup of coffee. As he sat down to sip the delicious hot brew, his wife, Rebecca, came in. In one of her rare moods, Rebecca went at her husband with a vengeance. He was lazy and inconsiderate. He was stupid. He was neglecting the farm. There was no food for the chickens and not enough hay for the horses.

When she stopped to take a breath, Hiram said softly, "May I have some more coffee?"

Rebecca said, "Now comes the crowning insult—thee are having a temper tantrum!"

A typical Quaker, lusty even in his forty-fifth year, Aaron had suddenly started to feel pain in his groin. After examining him, the doctor said, "How often do you make love?"

Aaron said, "Three or four times a day with my wife, Hannah. Maybe three times a day with Greta, our serving girl."

The doctor said, "You'll have to slow down. Cut out the serving girl."

Aaron said, "I can't do that. She'll want wages!"

qualifications

A famous comedian, known for his biting wit, was accepted into a select club. He refused to accept membership because he said he wouldn't belong to an organization that would have him for a member! I applied to join a very special club and was blackballed four times by one man. Explaining his four negative votes, he said, "I can't vote for a guy who's been turned down three times!"

I tried to become a sex fiend, but I couldn't pass the physical!

The prospective boss asked, "Can you write shorthand?"

The pretty applicant said, "Sure, but it takes me longer!"

A man had a head that came to a sharp point, two sets of lips, three eyes, one of them under his right ear, and bright blue skin. He walked into the office of the "Believe It or Not" people and said he'd like to talk to the man in charge. The receptionist said, "About what?"

Some ladies were being interviewed as to their qualifications for the position of live-in maid. One of the ladies was a bubbly, eager twenty-year-old from Egypt. Asked if she had any special qualifications, she said, "I can milk a camel!"

A rich young lady fell madly in love with a bum who'd shown up at her mansion to ask for a few cents. The passion was instantaneous and so overwhelming that the rich young lady asked the bum to become her husband.

"I have to have a special kind of woman," the bum said.

"I'll do anything you want," the rich young lady said. "Just tell me what you want."

The bum said, "Will you travel all over the country with me?"

"I'll go anywhere."

"Will you beg the way I do? If you love me, you'll show it by begging."

"To share your love, I will travel and beg and grovel in the gravel. That's how much I love you."

After a quick, private marriage conducted by a nearby justice of the peace, the rich young lady and her husband started their travels. For six months they went up and down the coast, stopping at each door to beg for a handout. At the end of that time, the bum said, "You've proved that you truly care. Let's quit begging, go home to your mansion, and live in plenty."

The rich young lady said, "Okay, but first let's finish up this last block of houses!"

A country fellow was explaining about his applying for a job in town at Mrs. Fielding's grocery store, saying, "I came in all spiffed up and she liked that. She wanted to know if I had the muscles to lift up heavy boxes. I showed her my arm. She liked that. Then she asked me if I could raise those boxes up to the highest shelf. I showed her my strong back. She liked that. Then she asked me to show her my testimonials. I guess that's when I lost the job!"

A Broadway producer was putting together a moral musical, almost religious in theme, and asked that all the chorus girls be virgins. One attractive young dancer went to her doctor and got a note attesting to her purity.

The next day she showed up at the tryouts with the note, which she handed to the producer. He looked at it and said, "What good is this? It's dated yesterday!"

An eighty-year-old man was accused by his ex-nurse of being the father of her baby. The old man's family tried to get the charge dropped, but the old man refused to let them. His middle-aged daughter said, "Dad, you know you couldn't have fathered her child."

The eighty-year-old man said, "Of course not, but I'll be so proud when I plead guilty!"

The personnel manager asked, "Are you good at filing?"

The pretty applicant said, "On my last job I filed seven hours a day. If you don't believe me, look at my nails!"

quarrels

My wife and I made a rule: if we quarreled, the one who was wrong would walk around the block. My wife hasn't been out of the house since 1981! Actually, we are inseparable. Last night it took three people to separate us!

A wife was berating her husband. He motioned for her to slow down, saying, "Don't unleash the beast in me."

The wife said, "I'm not afraid of a mouse!"

The wife was a little more furious than

usual, and said, "I should have listened to my mother twenty years ago."

The husband said, "Go ahead. She's still talking."

They had a good battle. The minute he walked in, she started to shoot from the lip!

"I heard you had words with your wife."
"We had no words."
"Nothing passed between you?"
"Only a plate and a platter!"

The husband poured himself into the house at about two in the morning. His wife wrung her hands and said, "If you don't stop this kind of behavior, I'll kill myself."

The husband sneered and said, "Promises. All I get is promises!"

One kid told another, "My mother has never said a hasty word to my father. She stutters!"

A woman was letting her husband have it with just a soupçon more venom than usual, saying, "You're an idiot. You always were an idiot. You'll always be an idiot. If they had an idiot contest, you'd come in second."

"Why would I come in second?"
"Because you're an idiot!"

Last night, some hot words flew between them. She heaved some alphabet soup in his face!

In the midst of their worst quarrel of the day, the husband decided to take a walk. After an hour he was calmer and called the house. "Honey, what are you making for dinner?" he asked pleasantly.

His wife answered, "Poison!"

"Make only enough for one. I'm eating out!"

My wife was in a snit today. Something she agreed with was eating her!

The wife topped her tirade by saying, "I should have listened to my dear mother. She begged me not to marry you."

The husband said, "That's terrible—all these years I've hated her!"

If you have right on your side in a quarrel, that's important. If you have a two-by-four with a nail in it, that's not bad either!

They're always holding hands. If they let go, they'd kill one another!

You can't hear an angry word from them. Their apartment is soundproof.

My father never raised a hand to me. He didn't want to break the cobweb under his arm!

Last night, words passed between us. She hit me with a book!

Many people patch up their old quarrels so that they look as good as new ones!

A quarrel is ended as soon as one party deserts the battlefront.

In a quarrel, he gives in a lot. What's his word against thousands of hers?

A man was hauled in front of a judge for shooting out the windows of his house. The man explained, "I'd had a few belts and I was a little ornery when I came home."

The judge said, "That's the curse of drink."

The man went on, "One word led to another and I got sore. I took out my gun and shot at her."

"That's the curse of drink. But you missed?"

"Yup. That's the curse of drink!"

The deaf man and his wife were having a fight, but he couldn't get a finger in edgewise!

Angry at being tossed out of the house, the husband yelled up at his wife inside, "I had you before we were married!"

From inside, an answer floated out, "And so did all of your friends!"

A husband said to his wife, "Honey, I've been thinking it over since this quarrel started, and I have to say that you were right. Everything you said was right."

The wife said, "It's too late. I changed my mind!"

A woman walked into a gun store and said, "I'd like a nice gun for my husband."

The clerk said, "Did he tell you what kind of gun he wanted?"

The woman said, "Of course not. He doesn't know I'm going to shoot him yet!"

Two women met while shopping. When they started to discuss their home lives, one of them said, "I've been fighting day and night with my husband. It's so aggravating, I've lost twenty pounds."

The other woman said, "Stop arguing."

The first woman said, "Not yet. I want to lose another twenty!"

questions

I'm the president of the Society for the Prevention of Foolish Questions. We're only a small group at present, but give us time and we'll put an end to your getting a phone call at three in the morning and the voice at the other end asking, "Did I wake you?" No, you moron! I had to get up to answer the phone. When you bring a young lady some flowers and candy, she asks, "For me?" No, for your dog! Then there's the beauty where you're walking across the street, get dusted by a car, fall to the ground in a heap, and the driver calls back, "Did I hurt you?" Of course not! I always bleed when I walk! The foolish questions asked by various people where a would-be speaker works provide great sport for part of a humorous speech. You can get big laughs by mentioning by name any dummy who always walks over to a secretary typing away with ninety fingers and asks, "Are you through yet?" My internist had a receptionist who always asked, "Are you here to see the doctor?" No, I want to fool around with a nurse! In roasting someone, especially at a "clean" roast, the roastee can always be accused of asking ridiculous questions. He may not do so in real life, but the audience will believe he does if you say so. Audiences will believe anything that has a basis in what sounds like the truth. If you tell an audience that the guest of honor was once a drunk, it will want to believe you. Any questions?

The new secretary had just gone to work for the ASPCA. Mr. Crain, the executive director, said to her, "If you have any questions, please ask me. Don't be afraid."

An hour later, the secretary called him on the intercom and asked nervously, "Is it all right if I swat a fly?"

A great actor was asked for the ten thousandth time, "How'd you get to be a star?"

He answered, "I started out as a gaseous cloud. Then I cooled."

A couple went to buy tickets for a top Broadway show. The woman in the ticket booth told them, "We're sold out, but we do have some standing-room-only spots."

The husband asked, "Are they together?"

One youngster got kicked in the rear for one question. He went into a funeral parlor and asked, "Do you have any used boxes?"

A man saw a one-armed man come into a café and saunter over to the bar. The man asked, "Did you lose an arm?"

The one-armed man looked at his side and said, "Hey, you're right!"

They had just consummated their marriage. The new husband asked, "Darling, was I the first?"

The bride said, "Why does everybody ask me that question?"

quips

Related by marriage to putdowns, quips have immediate bite, but leave no lasting marks. They taunt, repay, and deflate. They live not through the damage inflicted, but by the reportage made by eye- and earwitnesses. Because they are off the cuff, quips tend to sound brighter than they really are. It's difficult to prepare remarks that will sound like ad-lib responses because there's no way of knowing what the other player in the dialogue will come up with. At a party in Malibu some time ago, a less-than-appreciative guest said to me, not aware that the host was nearby, "For a nickel, I'd leave this party." The host said, "Let me give you a quarter. You can stay away from my next four!" My wife is a brilliant quipper. At a charity event to which she had donated thousands of hours and much of her energy, a boorish guest complained about the seating arrangements. He had passed boorishness and rudeness, and was well on the way to miserable, when my wife faced him down and said, "Let's you and I go outside and settle this man-to-man!" During a highly dramatic play, a woman sitting in front of us kept chattering away to her companion. After a few minutes, my wife tapped the woman on the shoulder and asked, "Is our silence bothering you?" I hope someday to write a book about my wife's life among the famous and infamous, and how she survived through some cogent remarks. Rather than follow this introduction with quips often quoted in books, I offer some my wife quipped. She is, after all, the handsome lady who listened to a guest at dinner try to get my brother to repeat a quip I'd made at the other end of the table, and who finally said to the guest, "Leave him alone. He's not his brother's quipper!"

We were at an art gallery where an artist with a one-track mind was showing. All of his paintings were depictions of plates of food. We approached one oil showing a huge bowl of soup. A viewer already at the painting, obviously a fan, said, "Isn't that magnificent?"

My wife said, "Needs salt!"

At a fund-raiser for a political candidate, my wife was in agony because the candidate waffled on every issue. He was devoid of backbone. When one of his backers asked my wife for a contribution, she said, "I'd give ten thousand if I knew it was going toward starch!"

We took our seats in the movie theater, sat back, and waited for the picture to begin. However, fate was against us. A couple sat down in the seats directly in front of us. Both were tall, but the man was immense. His shoulders blocked out completely my wife's view of the screen. After straining to find a view to the left or the right, my wife tapped the lady in front and said, "Could you bend him in half?"

We lost the first six races and were studying how to lose the seventh. A horse owner, filled with giggles and giggle water, came over to our box and asked if we'd join him for a drink. We declined. More obnoxious than ever, he insisted we join him. My wife said, finally, "All right, we'll join you."

The horse owner said, "When?"

My wife said, "Will the year be close enough?"

A dress salesgirl was pushing too hard. Studying my wife in a certain dress, the salesgirl said, "That dress is you."

My wife said, "Too bad. I have such terrible taste!"

It was the social event of the season. The wife of a well-known producer went all out. Her incredibly expensive gown was covered with sequins, pieces of fur, and anything else that could be sewed to cloth. There was obviously nothing left in the family jewelry safe, as she wore every diamond ever mined by man and gold in the form of chains, strands, and chunks. Modeling for my wife, she asked, "What do you think?"

My wife said, "Pearls would be nice if you had the room!"

quiz and game shows

If you watch any of the game shows or quizzes on television, you can understand why somebody once called television the thinking man's medium. That somebody now resides in a room with soft walls and is only allowed to write with crayons. Some years ago, I was offered the chance to become the master of ceremonies of a show in which, by answering tough questions like "Who was the first President?" contestants could win as much as a quarter of a million dollars. I told my agent to forget about the offer and to see if he could get me on the show as a contestant!

I'm in favor of the daytime game shows. If it weren't for them, millions of women would be out driving cars!

The quizmaster asked the contestant, "What's the first thing you'll do with this ten thousand?"

The contestant said, "Count it!"

They now have a Polish quiz. The first contestant to answer the question right gets a prize. In twelve weeks they haven't had a winner yet!

They say that game shows are aimed at a twelve-year-old. A twelve-year-old *what?*

quotations

They are now called "sound bites." Once clues to greatness, quotations have fallen into disfavor. You still can't go wrong, however, if you dredge up a good quote or two. The audience will be glad to know that Aristotle and Shakespeare helped you with your routine!

A married philosopher belongs to comedy. —Friedrich Nietzsche

Advertise, or there's a good chance the sheriff will do it for you.—P. T. Barnum

These really are good times, but only a few know about it.—Henry Ford

Anybody can win, unless there's a second entry.—George Ade

A yawn is a silent shout.—G. K. Chesterton

He's so crooked, he'd steal two left shoes!— Wilson Mizner

When women kiss, it reminds me of two boxers shaking hands.—H. L. Mencken

A fanatic is a man who can't change his mind and won't change the subject.—Winston Churchill

God will pardon me. It's his business.—Heinrich Heine

All husbands are alike. They have different faces so they can be told apart.—Anonymous

None preaches better than the ant, and she says nothing.—Benjamin Franklin

The best way to fight a woman is with your hat—grab it and run!—John Barrymore

There's some folks standing behind the President that ought to get around where we can watch 'em!—Frank Hubbard

R

rabbis

The stereotype of the typical rabbi is 180 degrees off. The long beard, the black coat, the skull cap or hat aside, the rabbi was and is often painted as a somber fuddy-duddy, second in grimness only to a parish priest. The fact is that I've found clergymen to be spunky and humorous. They're much quicker with a joke or story than my liquor dealer. They laugh with as much vigor as the rest of us. Their laughter may even be heartier, because they recognize our fallibility and the silly games we play to hide it. Also, the literature of humor is thick with material on men and women of the cloth. There are more "nun" jokes than we can commit to memory. In the shtetls, the small towns of Eastern Europe where a rich rabbinical tradition existed for so long, there are countless jokes about the rabbi's wife, the poor rabbinical students, and the revered head rabbis of the provinces. I believe this is because laughter is the first step to wisdom. Wisdom is the narrow path to faith. Strangely, I become serious when I talk about faith. I suppose I'm not sure of my eventual direction, and I'm covering my rear end! In telling jokes about rabbis and ministers, try to avoid accents. Few have mastered a solid Yiddish, Irish, or Italian accent. More important, the joke should be able to stand on its own if told well.

Anguished, the rabbi went on a ten-day fast. He spent his days in total prayer. After a week, the Lord spoke to him. "My friend," the Lord said, "why are you so troubled?"

The rabbi said, "My son is about to become a Christian."

The Lord said, "*Your* son!"

A rabbi and a minister were at the neighborhood picnic. As they rode in one of the boats on the lake, the rabbi stood up, stepped out of the boat, and walked over the water to the nearest stretch of land. Astonished, the minister decided to see if he could duplicate this miraculous feat. He stepped out of the boat and sank. But he managed to swim ashore. As he started to dry himself off, the rabbi walked over and said, "If you're a nice guy, next time I'll show you where the rocks are!"

A boy of twelve returned from studying at the synagogue and was asked by his father what lesson was taught that day. The boy said, "We learned the prayer for the dead. That's what you say when your father dies."

The father ran to the temple, accosted the rabbi, and said, "How dare you teach my son the prayer for the dead. I'm a young man. I'm in good health. I feel great!"

The rabbi said, "Don't panic. Just live as long as it takes your son to learn it!"

It was near the end of the Yom Kippur services, when the ram's horn is blown to signify the arrival of a new year. Ethel, a spinster, was mad about the young cantor. She devoured him with her eyes. She bathed in the air he breathed. Her obsession was overwhelming.

When the services ended, the cantor divested himself of his silken prayer shawl. When he turned away, Ethel grabbed the shawl and hid it under her dress. As she started to walk out, the rabbi came over and said, "Give back the prayer shawl."

"What prayer shawl?"

"Ethel, I saw you take it. It's under your dress. Put it back."

Caught red-handed, Ethel raised her dress to get out the shawl she'd tucked into her panties. Because she was nervous, she was unable to control herself and let out a little flatulence. The rabbi said, "And while you're at it, give us back the ram's horn too!"

One temple was so reformed, its rabbi was a Baptist!

One rabbi opened a discount temple—all you can pray for a dollar!

A brisket is a rabbi's toolbox!

The man implored the rabbi, "Please help me. I have fifteen children I can't feed. What shall I do?"

The rabbi said, "Haven't you done enough?"

A Canadian rabbi bragged to one from the United States, "We have over a hundred thousand Jews in Montreal, and not one is in jail."

The American rabbi said, "It must be restricted!"

Priests know more than rabbis, because the parishioners tell them everything!

railroads (and amtrak)

I remember trains with wide shoulders. Some were as sleek as racehorses. Others were dark, with the gray smell of burning wood or coal. I remember the scent of, first, the straw seats, and, later, rich, lustrous fabrics. I remember the best ham and eggs in the whole world, served on sparkling plates as white as the tablecloths and napkins, with cutlery strong enough to take into battle as weapons. I remember waiters and porters as erect as guards at Buckingham Palace, and conductors who looked like Santa Claus on his day off. I even remember arriving on time!

Acting out some fantasy, two men kidnapped another and asked his family for a large ransom. There was no response. The two men tied their victim to the railroad tracks. The poor victim starved to death before the next train came!

I think traveling by train is safer than flying. You don't have to worry about the conductor sitting on the engineer's lap!

Amtrak is very precise. If you call up and ask what time the noon train gets to California, the agent will tell you, "Eight P.M.—give or take a few days!"

A conductor went down the aisle, calling, "Change for Marietta. Change for Marietta."

A country boy, a first-time passenger said, "I don't know who that gal is, but I'll throw in a quarter!"

They have a train now that goes 130 miles an hour through Nevada. That's not a bad way to go through Nevada!

A young man arrived in the United States unable to speak one word of English. In a half hour he got a job at the depot—as a train announcer!

The railroads will do anything to attract riders. I was telling a friend that I'd just seen a train with a sauna and a pool.

My friend said, "There are a lot of trains with saunas and pools."

I said, "*Freight* trains?"

A Long Island Rail Road train was moving along at its usual five-mile-an-hour clip when it stopped suddenly. A passenger ran into the opening between his car and the next and said to the conductor, "Why are we stopped?"

The conductor said, "There's a big turtle on the track."

The passenger said, "We stopped for a turtle ten minutes ago."

The conductor said, "I know, but we caught up with it again!"

Then there was the conductor who got the wrong wife. He married beneath his station!

The train was about to pull out of the station. Swinging a large valise, a young man managed to reach the train, throw his valise onto the rear observation car, and climb aboard, gasping for air. Looking at him, another rider said, "Young man, you should be in better shape. At your age, I could catch the train by a gnat's whisker and still be fresh. Look at you, panting away."

The young man took a deep breath and said, "Pop, I missed this train at the *last* station."

A handsome young man met an attractive young lady as they both boarded in San Diego. By the time the train stopped in Los Angeles to pick up travelers heading farther north, they were close friends. They started to kiss. After a long, deep kiss, the girl started to cry and said, "I'm married to the most wonderful man in the world, and here I am—necking with a man I hardly know."

The train started up and continued northward. Still talking about her husband, the young woman affected her new gentleman friend so much that he started to cry too.

The train arrived in Seattle. Both left the train and went off in their separate directions. Met in the main hall of the depot by his brother, the young man related the incredible experience of the past hours. The brother asked, "What happened?"

The young man said, "Nothing. Hour after hour, it was just necking and crying, necking and crying, that's all!"

The conductor glanced at the ticket belonging to the well-dressed lady. Shaking his head sadly, the conductor said, "I don't know how to tell you this, but at the last water stop, I learned that your station had burned down this morning."

The woman said, "I'm not worried. By the time this train gets there, they'll have a new one built!"

"**A**mtrak is mentioned in the Bible."
"Where?"
"Where it says, 'The Lord made all creeping things.'"

A man said to the ticket agent, "I'd better take the Amtrak to Cleveland."

The ticket agent said, "I wish you would. We're sick of it here!"

A railroad magnate took a dollar-a-year job as the head of a government committee to oversee train safety. He attached his private car to the end of a line in the Northwest that was noted for its disregard of speed regulations.

In the middle of the night, the railroad magnate was awakened by the motion of his speeding car. He rushed forward to the first car and said to the engineer, "How fast were you going ten minutes ago?"

The engineer said, "Forty-five, like it says in the regs."

The railroad magnate said, "The private indicator in my car said that you were going seventy."

The engineer said, "No kidding? I never saw you pass me!"

I got off the train at Grand Central Station. I put down my bags and said, "New York, New York." I looked down. No bags. Then I knew I was in New York, New York!

"**G**ive me a round-trip ticket."
"Where to?"
"Back here, dummy!"

A woman boarded a train and asked the

conductor, "Does this train stop in Los Angeles?"

The conductor said, "If it doesn't, there's gonna be some splash!"

rain

If not in the first five jokes I told, surely the following was in the first ten: It's raining cats and dogs. I know because I just stepped in a poodle! Among the first twenty: It's terrible weather for rats and mice, because it's raining cats and dogs! In the old days I knew no shame! Audiences go for weather jokes even today. A famous television talk-show host can't wait for the raindrops to start falling on his head so he can warm up the audience with a clone of "It's so wet outside, an hour ago I saw a robin putting sandbags around its nest!"

It was so rainy, statues were soaked to the skin!

I never carry an umbrella in the rain. It looks as if I can't afford to be rained on!

It was raining so hard I got seasick walking home!

It's grim in the Texas Panhandle. The other day it rained and a farmer fainted. To revive him, they threw a pail of sand in his face!

It had rained incessantly for two weeks. Although the roads were rivers of mud, a farmer decided to venture into town and get some supplies. Donning his oldest clothes and a pair of hip boots, he aimed for town. He hadn't done a quarter of a mile when he hit an old pothole and started to sink. Soon the mud was clear up to his neck. Another farmer with a big wagon came by and saw him. "Let me help you out."

The muddied farmer said, "No, thank you. I'm not ready to let go of my horse yet."

Rain makes the flowers grow. It also makes cabs disappear!

A Kansas farmer had the ear of a traveler and was telling him how little it rained in that part of the state. He swore that he had a son who'd never seen a cloud. The traveler said, "You must get some rain once in a while."

The Kansas farmer said, "We do. Remember that flood Noah built his boat for? Well, when it was raining forty days and nights where he was, we got almost a half-inch in this part of Kansas!"

Seattle gets more than its share of rain. If two days pass by without rain, a city holiday is called and a giant celebration held. One day a Hopi Indian from sun-drenched Arizona came to town for a business meeting. Signing in at the hotel, he left to go to his room. The next man in line said to the desk clerk, "I can see he's Indian, but what tribe?"

The desk clerk said, "He's a Hopi. They worship the sun."

The man said, "I'll bet he's just passing through!"

At the Sunday service, the minister decided to lead the congregation in a prayer for much-needed rain. Farmer Olson didn't join in. Asked by another farmer why he'd refrained, he said, "I've been noticing—praying don't do much good without a wind from the southwest!"

reading

On the shelves of my den I have the complete works of Dickens, Victor Hugo, Herman Melville, Balzac, and almost all the other great writers. On one shelf, I also have some books to read!

"That book has a great ending."
"How about the beginning?"
"I didn't get to that yet!"

I just finished my first book. Next week I may read another one!

An Eskimo was reading to his son: "'Little Jack Horner sat in a corner.'"

The son interrupted, "Daddy, what's a corner?"

Keep your eyes glued to this book. That way you'll know where they are!

real estate

I have invested in property twice in my life. Tempted by a glowing description from a glib real-estate agent, I bought desert property. Somehow, the housing developments she foresaw didn't develop. She insisted that I buy more. "All that's needed," she insisted, "is water." Water never showed up. I finally sold out to a jackrabbit and a cactus. After my stirring triumph in western land, I went into property in western Florida. It was all swamp, but that was no problem to the real-estate agent. This one, a man, said, "All it needs is dry land!" I sit home now and wait for the urge to take my third real-estate plunge.

Interested in buying a summer place, a man asked a farmer, "How does the land lie around here?"

The farmer said, "The land don't lie. It's the real-estate people that lie!"

It was a two-story house—the real-estate agent told him one story before he bought, and another one afterward!

"What's that new building?"

"If I can sell it, it's a bungalow. If I can't, it's a barn!"

Two boys of six were discussing fibbing. One said, "A fib is just a story, and a story is a lie."

"It is not."

"It is too. My father told me, and he's a teacher."

"My father is a real-estate salesman. He knows more about lying than your father!"

The owner of a home berated the real-estate agent from whom he'd bought it, saying, "When you snookered me into buying this house last year, you said I wouldn't give it up for a hundred thousand."

The real-estate agent said, "You haven't, have you?"

A movie mogul whose last three pictures had made him a cool—or warm—half-billion dollars asked a real-estate agent to find him a house with about ten rooms. The real-estate agent said, "You need a large house. How are you going to impress anybody with a small house?"

The movie mogul said, "Who do I have to impress?"

A real-estate agent bought a sports car and had the engine reworked so that it would go even faster. Asked why he needed to go a hundred fifty miles an hour, he answered, "I advertise this one house as being five minutes from shopping, and I don't want to lie!

If you want something that'll last forever, take out a mortgage!

I finally figured out what they meant by the high-rent district. It's land!

Columbus planted the flag and said, "I claim this island for the Queen of Spain." It surprised most of the Indians, because they didn't know the place was listed!

When they say that the house is maintenance-free, they could mean—so far!

Robin Hood had a lot of trouble getting rid of Sherwood Forest. It only had a Little John!

references

A lady whose name turned out to be Pincus accosted me in a hotel elevator one evening and said, "My three sons should write for you. They are the funniest writers you'll ever have." I said, "I don't know if I'm hiring writers now." She said, "These three you'll hire. They have a great sense of humor. Their names are Elwood, Charlemagne, and Horatio." I said, "Elwood, Charlemagne, and Horatio Pincus? Who gave them those names?" She said, "I did." I said, "How would you like a job writing for me?" It was on her recommendation that I did interview her sons. Although the names had to be changed slightly, and only slightly, due to pressure from the publisher's attorneys, the anecdeote is true. All three young men became top-flight comedy writers. The mother didn't. She went back to the Bronx and housework.

"You say you have references?"

"Ma'am, I have a hundred good references."

"How long have you been a maid?"

"Almost three months!"

A young man applying for a position refused to show his references to the personnel manager. "Why not?" asked the personnel manager.

The young man said, "They don't do me justice!"

A young man applied for a job, bringing with him glowing references from his minister and a dozen elders in the church. The prospective employer nodded with pleasure at the written statements, but said, "These are very nice. Could you get one from somebody who knows you on weekdays?"

reincarnation

I'm not sure about reincarnation, but if it exists, I'd like to come back as a bull in Montana!

There has to be something to reincarnation. I couldn't have gotten this far behind in just one lifetime!

Two women were discussing reincarnation. One asked the other if her husband believed in it. The second woman said, "Does my husband believe in life after death?" My husband doesn't even believe in life after dinner!"

The best thing about reincarnation is that everybody used to be somebody famous!

Reincarnation is a letdown. Just think—150 years ago I was Lincoln!

rejection

I think I know what rejection is. When I was a kid going to school, my folks used to wrap my lunch in a road map! Not true. My folks loved me. When they moved, most of the time they left a forwarding address for me!

The kids used to play house with me. I was the door and they slammed me!

For a moment they didn't recognize him. They never spent a more delightful moment!

She has the looks that turn heads—and stomachs too!

He has a lot of distant relatives, including a father and a mother!

She's been turned down so often she has hospital corners!

He wrote to her, asking for her hand in marriage. She rejected him. He wrote again. Again she rejected him. He wrote a hundred times and was rejected a hundred times. He finally stopped writing to her and married the girl who sold him stationery!

A young lady found herself in a delicate condition. Going to the gent who'd impregnated her, she said, "If you don't marry me, I'll kill myself."
    The gent said, "That's very nice of you!"

A man found himself on a deserted island with a strange dog. After several days, a female porpoise swam into the lagoon around which the island was curled. As if she were a female of the human persuasion, the dolphin flickered her eyes and moaned soft sounds. The man became fascinated with the dolphin. Deciding that he had to embrace her, he started into the water. The dog jumped between him and the dolphin. Barking ferociously, the dog bared its sharp teeth. Day after day, at all hours, the man tried to go to his lady dolphin, only to be met by teeth glistening and ready to tear him to shreds.
    The months passed. One morning a beau-

iful young woman washed ashore. Her lovely body was framed by what was left of her dress. Thrilled at the sight of a male, she purred, "I'm the answer to your prayers. I'll do anything for you."

The man said, "Great! Will you hold this damn dog!"

relatives

Relatives have always gotten a bum rap. I, for one, am glad because they've given me precious subject matter. Everybody loves in-law jokes and "my brother" jokes. Grandparents and mothers are the only dangerous areas for comedy. The image of a grandparent is Rockwellian—gray hair, rockers, and knitting or whittling. Mother is soft and sweet, an angel. How can anyone lay a humorous finger on such saints? For a few years, Mother was an acceptable target. During the twenties and thirties, the mother was usually the authority figure at home. Many of our humorists and comedy writers were formed during these years. They took on Mother with a vengeance. They made fun of the guilt she handed out like cookies. Yet this was the time of the birth of reality comedy. It became possible to talk about the real, non-gag moments in life. I remember a comedian-storyteller who got five minutes of laughs out of a description of the way his mother bundled him up in the winter when he was a boy.

My wife's family is coming to visit us, and I'm getting ready for them. All week long I've been erasing letters from the welcome mat!

Many women come from a fine family. My wife brought hers with her!

I have a relative who came to the United States penniless and without understanding one word of our language. He managed to make a fortune by mastering only three words: "Stick 'em up!"

My great-aunt was unhappy because my great-uncle wasn't paying any attention to her. To get him interested again, she ran past him in the nude as he watched television. Returning a few minutes later, dressed again, my great-aunt asked, "Did you see something go by?"

My great-uncle said, "Yeah, and whatever it was, it needed ironing!"

We have so many relatives dropping in on us, I had to hire a hockey goalie to guard the icebox!

My brother-in-law borrows so much money from me—at night my wife goes through *his* pockets!

I hate my relatives' guts. They're full of my food!

religion

It must have been when I was about ten. One of my brothers came home with a very fat lip and explained that it was the result of his having made a crack about the Pope to Jimmy McCoy. My other brother said, "Didn't you know that Jimmy was Catholic?" The fat lip said, "Yeah, but I didn't know the Pope was!"

A man goes to heaven. Escorted by an angel, he walks around. As they pass different areas, the angel points out the Catholics, the Jews, the Seventh-Day Adventists, and many other groups. They reach a high wall. The angel responds to the man's inquiring look, saying, "The Protestants are on the other side. They think they're the only ones up here!"

Priests should be allowed to marry. That way they'll know what hell is really like!

"About what should I preach?" the new minister asked.
"About heaven and fifteen minutes!"

Priests have a very low divorce rate!

Once there was a bishop who labeled his files "Sacred" and "Top Sacred"!

One young girl had to quit the Salvation Army. Her mother found out she was hanging around streetcorners!

The trouble with religion today is that a lot of people practice it but not too many are good at it!

The sexton ran into the rabbi's apartment near the temple and said excitedly, "Rabbi, somebody broke into the synagogue office yesterday and stole eight thousand dollars in pledges!"

It must be wonderful to be a religious leader like the Pope. You could call up Dial-a-Prayer and ask, "Any messages?"

Four men of the cloth were chatting. The rabbi confessed, "I like ham once in a while." The Baptist minister said, "I take a few belts of Scotch every day." "Me," the priest said, "I have a girlfriend." Reverend Swanson of the Lutheran church said, "I love to gossip!"

A Jew told a Christian, "We gave you the Ten Commandments."
    The Christian said, "You can't say we kept them!"

Moses' parents did okay. They not only had fun in bed, but they made a small prophet!

Some people don't realize that the Ten Commandments aren't multiple-choice!

It shakes you up today to hear kids praying, "Our Father who art in 7-Eleven..."

For Jews, eating pork is like the sin of adultery. I have friends who've tried both, and can't see the comparison!

Somebody found out I was an agnostic, so he burned a question mark on my lawn!

The dead mule lay in front of the church for two days. Finally, the minister called the Department of Health. A smark aleck answered his ring, listened for a moment, then said, "Don't you take care of the dead?"
    The minister said, "Of course, but first we get in touch with their relatives!"

An Irish cop stopped a speeding car. The driver was a priest. Putting away his citation book, the cop said, "Father, I just stopped you to tell you there's a Protestant cop at the next light!"

It's hard for religious Catholics to get fire insurance. Too many candles in the house!

Father O'Hara was having dinner with his good friend Rabbi Melnick. Teasing, Father O'Hara said, "When are you going to break down and taste some pork?"
    Rabbi Melnick said, "At your wedding!"

The sermon was endless. Getting to another point, the minister said, "What else can I say?"
    A member of the congregation yelled out, "Amen!"

In a small community there were four churches. A newcomer went to one for Sunday services and saw that the congregation wasn't too supportive. After the services, the newcomer said to the minister, "Your church isn't doing too well, is it?"

The minister answered, "Not too well, but, thank God, the other three are also in trouble!"

Put two Jews on a deserted island. In two weeks there would be three temples!

In a small town in the South, the two dozen Jews have three synagogues—a reform synagogue, a conservative synagogue, and a synagogue neither element would be caught dead in!

I mix religion with science. I count my blessings on a computer!

The minister asked, "What must we do before we can expect forgiveness of sin?"

A teenager in the front row said, "Sin!"

I heard a faith healer the other day. He was so great, the audience gave him a kneeling ovation!

An honorable man lay on his deathbed. His minister sat down, patted him on his feverish hand, and said, "Have you made your peace with God?"

The honorable man said, "We have never had a fight!"

The Protestant Reformation was when they split from the Catholic Church and began to forgive their own sins!

It was during the gold rush in the Yukon Territory. Joe Alexander packed a bag, grabbed his Bible, and started out of the tent he shared with Guy Thomas. Guy asked, "Where are you going?"

"I'm heading into Fort Dawson. I hear it's the wildest town anybody's ever seen. There's booze you could take a bath in, gambling, and women who'll drive you crazy with their favors."

"Why are you taking your Bible?"

"Well, if it's as good as they say, I'm planning to stay over Sunday!"

One synagogue decided not to charge for the High Holidays. The rabbi didn't want people staying away at such a high cost!

Some kids have no religious training at all anymore. I heard one little boy, as he and his parents passed a church, ask, "Why do all the churches have plus signs on top?"

My church welcomes all denominations— tens, twenties, fifties . . .

A minister was called to a meeting of the elders and told that his contract wouldn't be renewed. Surprised almost beyond belief, the minister asked, "Didn't I speechify? Didn't I glorify? Didn't I magnify?"

The elder said, "You didn't 'wherein.' We need a minister who can 'wherein'!"

A priest had the weight of the world on him and was showing the effects. The church sent him to a psychiatrist, who ordered him to take a week off. The priest went to the largest city in the area. After about a dozen belts of neat whiskey, he found himself in one of the city's clip joints. A waitress in a flimsy, low-cut uniform came over and asked, "What'll it be, Father?"

The priest felt to see if he was still wearing his collar by mistake, but he had none on. "How did you know I'm a priest?" he asked.

The waitress said, "I'm Sister Mary Margaret. I go to the same psychiatrist!"

A young Jewish lad entered Notre Dame to play football. At the end of the season, he returned home. As luck would have it, he ran into his rabbi at the airport. The rabbi asked, "Are they trying to convert you at South Bend?"

The youngster said, "Of course not, Father!"

When I hear the Christmas story of Jesus being born in a manger, I have the feeling that Mary and Joseph had the same maternity benefits I do!

En route to Los Angeles, a plane started to shake. Somebody said, "Do something religious."

A priest in the third row took up a collection!

The first thing the meek will do when they inherit the earth is hire some strong guys to protect them from losing it!

In one monastery, the monks spent most of the day flagellating themselves and praying. When Easter approached, one of the young monks said to another, "You'll never guess what I'm going to give up for Lent!"

Most of my friends belong to a new church. They're Seventh-Day Absentists!

It was Monday night at the fights. Rabbi Schwartz and Father Devlin walked in and sat down in the first row. New to the experience of watching men walking into a ring to knock each other senseless, Rabbi Schwartz saw one of the fighters genuflect and cross himself. The rabbi asked, "Will that help him?"

Father Devlin said, "Only if he can punch!"

At a nondenominational party given in a fancy home, by mistake the caterer put a few bottles of vodka in what should have been a grape punch. However, none of the ministers spoke up. All merely sauntered over to the fruit bowl on the buffet table and started to fight each other for the grape seeds!

A minister was preparing a sermon on sex. His wife said, "Dear, I'm not sure you should discuss that subject. Speak about something else. Sex is so private."

"You're probably right, dear. I think I'll talk about sailing."

That night the minister's wife became ill. She was still in bed that Sunday morning. Her absence freed him to discuss sex. After church was out, two of the women of the congregation visited the wife. They waxed eloquent about the minister's sermon. He had spoken with such gusto and vigor. The minister's wife said, "How could he sound so smart? He only did it twice—once in the harbor and once just past the breakwater. And both times he threw up!"

"Why do Baptists object to fornication?"
"I don't know. Why do they?"
"They're afraid it might lead to dancing!"

The town madam wanted to make a big contribution to the local church. The debate as to whether or not to accept the money was hot and furious. Finally, one of the elders said, "Let's take the money. It's ours anyway!"

remedies

Our family elixir was the most potent known to man. One sip brought on the Chicago fire, the San Francisco earthquake, floods, and an internal hurricane. However, it was effective. Stom-

achaches, colds, pains—all symptoms disappeared never to show up again. If they did, it would mean another spoonful of the elixir. I was once cured of pneumonia in six seconds. On the way to Poughkeepsie, New York, one summer day, my mother and I sat across from a traveling minister with a bad cough. After he'd coughed up half of his guts, my mother made him take a sip of the elixir. Sipping, he turned twenty shades of burning red. He asked my mother if he could get some of the elixir. My mother said, "It's a family secret." The minister said, "Too bad. I preach hellfire, and I thought it would be good if I had some samples!" Our family elixir is no longer in use. It was replaced by penicillin, antibiotics, and caplets of something or other. They're probably more effective. But they're not nearly as romantic!

Harvey listened intently as his teacher in medical school spoke. "I don't want you to forget," the professor said, "that you have an obligation to medical science. When you start to practice, keep a complete diary of your work—the things you read, the materials you use, the patients—everything. Your observations could help medicine."

Harvey graduated, met a girl whose father set him up in a practice, and opened his notebook to start taking notes.

His first patient was a cabdriver with a high fever. Harvey told him, "You have a terrible strep infection. You could die in two days."

Harvey made a note in his book: Cabbie. Strep. Dead in two days.

Three days later, the cabdriver was back, feeling like a million dollars. Surprised, Harvey asked, "What happened to you?"

"It's like this, Doctor—when you told me I'd be dead in two days, I decided to go out with a blast. I love Chinese food, so for two days I ate nothing but Chinese food. I feel sensational."

Harvey made another note in his book: Cabbie. Strep. Chinese food, great.

A bus driver came in to see him. He was burning hot. His throat was killing him. Checking him out, Harvey told him that he had a bad strep throat. An orgy of Chinese food was in order.

The next afternoon, Harvey called to check on the patient's well-being. The patient, the wife told him, had dropped dead in a Chinese restaurant.

Harvey wrote, "In case of strep throat, Chinese food works on cabbies but not on bus drivers!"

Feeling edgy, a man took a hot bath. Just as he'd become comfortable, the front doorbell rang. The man got out of the tub, put on terrycloth slippers and a large towel, wrapped his head in a smaller towel, and went to the door. A salesman wanted to know if he needed any brushes. Slamming the door, the man returned to the bath.

The doorbell rang again. On went the slippers and towels, and the man started for the door again. He took one step, slipped on a wet spot, fell, and hit his back against the hard porcelain of the tub.

The man struggled into his street clothes and, with every move a stab of pain, drove to the doctor. After examining him, the doctor said, "Nothing's broken. But you need to relax. Why don't you go home and take a hot bath?"

A patient came into the doctor with walking pneumonia. The doctor billed him by the mile!

"**D**octor, my arm got broken in two places."
"Don't go back to either of them!"

republicans

For a long stretch of time, Republicans didn't fare too well in national politics. Attending a big dinner one night during that period, I sat next to a high official. After the salad, I said, "I hear there are some Republicans here tonight." The official said, "I know. One of them waited on me!"

They should call the Republican Party the New Left, it's so far from being right!

"I was born a Republican," he said. "I live as a Republican and I'm going to die a Republican."
A listener called out, "So much for your ambition!"

Standing in front of a fancy supermarket, a young boy tried to give away some newborn kittens. He had no takers, even though he pushed the little bundles of fur as good Republican kittens.
Some days later, the youngster was back with his kittens, calling out to all who passed by, "Get your Democratic kittens."
A shopper said, "When you were here a few days ago, they were Republican kittens, weren't they?"
The young boy said, "Yup. But since then their eyes have opened!"

Politics makes strange bedfellows, but they soon get used to the bunk!

"Dear, what makes you think the baby's going to be a Republican?"
"He says so many things that sound great and mean nothing!"

Republicans seem to spend their time passing laws and then helping their cohorts evade them!

A New Hampshire farmer had fifteen children. When they grew up, all voted Republican except Sam. The local political leader asked the father to come up with some explanation for this aberrant behavior. The father said, "I taught them about being Republican from the day they could walk, and they became good, decent Republicans. But Sam got to reading..."

Republicans are always trying to shed the image of wealth and high-class origins. Finding out that his Democratic opponent was bragging about being born in a log cabin, the Republican went him one better and said that he was born in a manger!

Republicans have just added an eleventh Commandment: Thou shalt not commit thyself!

Taking a brisk morning constitutional on a typical December morning in Chicago, O'Malley saw some little boys throwing snowballs at a man. O'Malley asked, "Why are you hitting that man?"
One of the kids said, "He's a Republican."
"That's no reason. Republicans are people just like us. They breathe, they sleep, they eat, they feel pain just like us. They're good citizens. They love America. Don't throw snowballs at him because he's a Republican."
Another kid said, "I bet you're a Republican yourself!"
Grabbing the boy and getting ready to spank him, O'Malley said, "That I won't stand for!"

Many people today are Republicans because their fathers were Republicans. Many people are Democrats today because their fathers were Republicans!

A doctor told an expectant heart-transplant

patient, "I have good news and bad news. The good news is that we have a heart for you. The bad news is that it came from a Republican!"

"**R**epublicans can't get life insurance."
"Why is that?"
"Nobody knows their policy!"

"**W**hat's a Republican turkey?"
"One with two right wings!"

A Republican was convicted of murder. A reporter said, "Do you have anything to say?"
The Republican said, "Not at this time!"

respect

I want to get respect. I also give respect. Of course, giving is beating getting by about twenty lengths!

When I was young, there was no respect for youth. Now there's no respect for the old. I missed it both times!

People have always thought so little of me. When I was a kid I went to see Santa. He gave me a loaded gun!

Nobody respected me, even as a child. One day they told me to go out and look for my brother. They gave me a piece of his clothing to smell!

I belong to a yacht club, but I'm the only member who has to swim in!

restaurants

My wife used to make the best things for dinner—reservations! The joke aside, we did eat

out a lot. I've eaten in one restaurant so many times I finally got my own coat back! Jokes about restaurants are generally winners for the after-dinner speaker or would-be comedian. We all identify with the misery and pain. How many times have you made the mistake of telling the waiter that you're in a burry? He puts down the menu and you don't see him again until the following Tuesday. Waitresses are the same. As soon as you're seated, they go off to hide behind the butter dishes and the coffee urns. When one of them really makes me wait forever, I always give her a wide smile on her return and ask her, "Did the girl who was waiting on me before leave a next of kin?"

The customer said, "I want some oysters, but they mustn't be too big or too tough or too old, and they should be sweet and I want them right away."
The waiter said, "Would you like them with or without pearls?"

You know it's a cheap restaurant if you ask for a menu and the waiter tells you somebody else is using it!

I ordered a whole meal in French the other night, and the waiter was surprised. It was a Chinese restaurant!

Checking the menu, a restaurant customer ordered a bowl of vegetable soup. After a couple of spoonsful, he saw a circle of wetness right under the bowl on the tablecloth. He called the waitress over and said, "It's all wet down here. The bowl must be cracked."
The waitress said, "You ordered vegetable soup, didn't you?"
"Yes."
"Maybe it has a leek in it!"

A man walked into a restaurant and said, "I'd like a plate of stew and a kind word."

The waitress brought his stew in a moment. As she put it down, the man whispered, "How about the kind word?"

The waitress said, "Don't eat the stew!"

I won't say it's a bad restaurant, but yesterday the catch of the day was fish sticks!

A cheapskate said to his companion in the restaurant, "Look, you paid the last six times we ate lunch. Let's toss for this one!"

A man went into the greasy spoon next to where he worked. He ordered a tuna on whole wheat. The waitress said, "We don't have whole wheat today. You'll have to take white."

The next afternoon, the man again ordered tuna on whole wheat. There was no whole wheat bread. For a week, he asked for whole wheat, only to be told that there was none. At the next lunch, he decided to end the charade and said, "Give me tuna on white."

The waitress said, "Aren't you the man who usually orders whole wheat?"

Two travelers stopped off at a roadside diner. When the waitress came over, one man said, "I'd like some coffee with milk and sugar."

The second man said, "I'd like the same, but could you make sure the cup is clean?"

The waitress returned a few minutes later with their orders and asked, "All right, which one of you gets the clean cup?"

The fresh guy sat down at the counter and said to the waitress, "Hi, there. Where have you been all of my life?"

The waitress answered, "Out of it, thank the Good Lord!

I go to a restaurant not far from where I live that has the worst service. Sometimes I have to wait an hour to be served. I don't mind. The food is awful!

Hotel coffee shops charge according to the Bible. If you look at the prices, you're reminded of the quotation, "I was a stranger and ye took me in."

This restaurant is consistent. It serves steak, coffee, and ice cream—all at the same temperature!

"Waiter, what was my offense? I've been on bread and water for three hours!"

I went into a restaurant that advertised, "All you can eat for $3.98." I loaded up my plate, finished, and returned for seconds. The manager stopped me and said, "That's all you can eat for $3.98!"

I went to a salad bar in Detroit. They change the oil every six months!

A black man sat down at the finely set table of a fashionable restaurant and asked for a plate of grits. The waiter said, "We don't have grits."

"Can I get some ham hocks and red-eye gravy?"

"I'm sorry."

"How about turnip greens and catfish?"

"We don't have those."

The black man stood up, smiled at the waiter, and said, "This restaurant isn't ready for integration!"

An inspector walks into a restaurant and says to the boss, "You have too many roaches in here."

The owner says, "How many am I allowed?"

I know a restaurant with real bad food. The only card they take is Blue Cross!

I went to a real bad restaurant the other night. I took a doggy bag, and on the way out I was arrested for cruelty to animals!

Two men finished a meal and looked at the check put down by the waiter. One man said, "Let's split the check. You wash, I'll dry!"

The food in that restaurant is so bad you don't get a check. The waiter hands you a citation!

I went to a restaurant where you can have all you can eat for ninety-nine cents. I took one bite. That was all I could eat!

"What's wrong with this chicken? It's all bruised."
"It was in a fight."
"Well, take it back and bring me the winner!"

"Do you serve milk-fed veal?"
"We certainly do."
"Good. Squeeze some out and bring me a glass of milk!"

A customer said, "I'd like some very soft-boiled eggs."
  The waiter said, "Is it all right if I just carry them through a hot kitchen?"

"I'm so hungry I could eat a horse."
"You've come to the right place!"

"Waiter, there's a fly in my soup."
"That's possible. The chef used to be a tailor!"

"This sauerkraut isn't sour enough."
"It's not sauerkraut. It's noodles."
"For noodles it's sour enough!"

riches

A country wit who played all around the Midwest was at the same theater I was playing in Ohio. The headlines that day concerned one of the wealthiest men in the world. He'd just been operated on for a stomach condition that kept him from eating solid food. Backstage, while waiting to go on, the Irish tenor said that he envied the rich man all of his millions. The country wit said, "He wouldn't be so rich he could eat!"

He's so rich he eats in Pheasant Delight!

A girl can always live on love—if he's rich!

He was so rich, if you asked for a salad in his house, they served you shredded money!

He's so rich he has catered icebox raids!

He's so rich, when he flies, his wallet is considered carry-on luggage!

I think I know why Robin Hood robbed the rich. The poor didn't have a quarter!

Our next-door neighbors just put a bird feeder in their backyard. It has a salad bar!

Wealth can be a curse—if your neighbors have it!

He's so rich, when he buys a suit the tailor has to let out the pockets!

Mere wealth can't bring us happiness,
Mere wealth can't make us glad.
But we'll always take a shot, I guess,
At being rich and sad!

"Was your house ever robbed?"
"Probably, but we wouldn't notice!"

I don't knock the rich. I never got a job from a poor person!

It's easy for a stingy guy to get rich, but what's the use?

If you want to make a living, you have to work for it. If you want to become rich, you have to find another way!

It is better to live rich than to die rich!

It doesn't matter if you are born poor and die poor, as long as you're rich in between!

You probably won't have time to count it on Judgment Day!

He made his money the old-fashioned way—he inherited it!

riddles

A riddle gets about as much respect as a pun. I find that a riddle or two placed in the middle of a monologue or comedy spot about someone being roasted is a welcome change of pace from the right-on joke and story. Extra laughs can be garnered by reacting to the guest of honor's inability to give an answer. As with a pun, the greater the groan, the funnier the riddle. I write down riddles asked of me. I find, too, that if I ask a riddle three times, it's imprinted on my mind. The writing down and the few repetitions are good memory aids. It's a shame that I can't share some of my meatier riddles, those I use at stag roasts. We'll have fun with those if you come to my house. We pull down the shades and riddle away!

"What game do judges play?"
"Tennis, because it's played in courts!"

"What acts like a male rock star, looks like a male rock star, and talks like a male rock star?"
"A female rock star!"

"What's at the bottom of the sea and shakes?"
"A nervous wreck!"

"Three men get under a small umbrella. Why don't they get wet?"
"It's not raining!"

"What stays hot even if you put it in the freezer?"
"Pepper!"

ritzy people

Ritzy people are beyond snobs. They are not, however, beyond being laughed at. I remember once accusing my wife of being a little too ritzy. She looked at me and said, "Moi?"

She's so ritzy, the bags under her eyes are Gucci!

Lettered on a sign in the window of a small jewelry shop was the name Carlington. A ritzy lady, passing by, wondered if the people who owned the store were in any way related to the Carlingtons who were the fanciest people in her hometown. Going on, she asked, "Are you the Westport Carlingtons?"
    The owners said, "No. The Westport Carlingtons are Kleins. We're the Shapiros."

A ritzy lady was showing a friend the lovely doghouse she had put up for her purebred terrier, saying, "The best part is, a French poodle comes in twice a week."

Mrs. Dell was bragging about her recent

trip. "Money was no object with us, you can see. We went to Italy for a month."

Mrs. Rivetti said, "So? I was born there!"

A woman whose husband had recently made a fortune bought him a huge yacht. Writing out a check for the amount, she told the salesman, "Make sure you wrap it good so he won't be able to guess what it is!"

She's become so fancy, she now has Perrier on the knee!

Inspired by the rabbi's sermon on the worth of man, a member of the congregation, Joe Lapidus, jumped and said, "I was a poor boy. Today I have ten million dollars. But when I hear your words I am nothing."

Phil Presser, a second member, stood up and said, "I was born in poverty. Today I have twenty million dollars. But when I hear your words I'm nothing."

Up jumped Simon Margolis. "I am a tailor," he said. "I make a hundred dollars a week. But when I hear your words I'm nothing."

Lapidus turned to Presser and said, "Look who wants to be a nothing!"

She won't eat ladyfingers unless they're manicured!

robbery

I've covered this category earlier and will go at it again under "Theft," but these two jokes sneaked out of my files when I wasn't looking!

A neighbor called me one day and asked, "Are you watching your TV?"

I said, "No."

The neighbor said, "I wouldn't be surprised. A guy just came out of your kitchen window carrying it!"

A young lady went to the shop where her aunt worked and picked up her aunt's pay. On the way home she was robbed, so she called the police and said, "I just lost my aunt's pay."

The desk sergeant said, "Unnyfay. Unnyfay!"

romance

Don't ask me about love and passion. When I was a kid, I carved a girl's name on a tree. The tree fell on me!

It was the night of the prom. They were on the way home. He asked her if she wanted to stop for a while in Lover's Lane. She was willing. On the way, he said, "You're really beautiful."

She said, "Thank you."

"I never saw such pretty hair."

"Thank you."

"Your eyes are like deep blue lagoons."

"Thank you."

"Your lips are as red as berries, and your teeth glisten like the sun."

"Thank you. But tell me one thing."

"Yes, my angel?"

"Can you drive with one hand?"

"Hmmm. Sure I can."

"Good. Wipe your nose—it's running!"

The young man said, "We're going to have a great time tonight. I have three theater tickets."

The young girl said, "Why do we need three tickets?"

"They're for your father, mother, and kid sister!"

The bride said, "My little plum."

The groom said, "My little peach."

The minister said, "I now pronounce you fruit salad!"

A showgirl broke off with her newest fiancé, explaining to the other girls in the dressing room, "I saw him in a bathing suit this afternoon, and he looked so different without his wallet!"

Years ago, young people believed in long engagements. Today they don't even believe in a long introduction!

One girl complained about her previous date, "He not only ran out of gas, but he had a trailer with him!"

A twenty-year-old beauty examined her curves in the mirror and sighed, "Look at this body, and who has got me?"

Then there was the young Chinese girl who was asked, "How do you want your rice—fried or steamed?"

The young Chinese girl answered, "How about thrown?"

She sighed, "You used to kiss me."

He kissed her.

"You used to hold my hand."

He held her hand.

"You used to bite me on the back of my neck."

"Hold on."

"Where are you going?"

"To get my teeth!"

A prisoner fell in love with the warden's daughter and married her. The warden was miserable. It seems that they eloped!

A woman worked in her tiny flower garden in front of the house as her nineteen-year-old daughter, obviously pregnant, sat on the porch knitting tiny garments. A newcomer to town happened by and was impressed by the sight, saying to the mother, "This is like a painting. Especially the way your daughter sits back, so relaxed and domestic."

The mother said, "It is nice. I'm so thrilled she's taking an interest in something besides running around with boys!"

A woman might as well propose. Her husband will claim that she did!

The woman complained, "Four years of college, and who has it got me?"

Just give me my golf, my great outdoors, and a gorgeous girl. And you can keep my golf and the great outdoors!

"When is your sister thinking of getting married?"

"All the time!"

A mother asked her daughter, "How come I don't see that boy around anymore?"

"Which one?" the daughter asked.

"You know—the one you couldn't live without!"

Romancing girls is like opening a jar of olives. If you can get one out, the rest come easy!

The candles flickered and the music was low and bluesy. Popping open the champagne, he said, "Say when."

She said, "Right after the first drink!"

rottenness

Ammunition for roasts. These jokes can really help cook somebody!

He's the kind of guy who would throw mud to a drowning man!

Success hasn't changed him. He's still the same rotten bastard he always was!

He's so rotten, even Helen Keller wouldn't have a feeling for him!

People should be glad they don't have his nerve in their tooth!

He's the poster boy for snakebite!

The AMA just named a fungus after him!

He's a man of letters—N.G.!

He takes in stray dogs and feeds them to stray mountain lions!

He can't see a belt without hitting below it!

He's such a miserable bastard—he calls Dial-a-Curse!

He got a hernia once during a consciousness-raising session!

He's got as much heart as a doughnut!

His mind is so filthy, if it were a building it would be condemned!

He's so rotten, instant coffee makes him wait!

He's so rotten, in Israel people uproot trees in his name!

For him, Hallmark put out a "get sick" card!

He's so rotten he'd steal meat tenderizer from cannibals!

He'd moon a widow at the funeral!

He never hits a man when he's down. He kicks him!

All his life he's followed the path of least assistance!

His family used to hang around a lot, especially from trees!

Some people say she's a pain in the back. Others have a much lower opinion of her!

She's a female clone—a clunt!

He'd make an obscene phone call to a telethon!

His idea of fun is to call in phony reprieves to death row!

He's the kind of guy who'd epoxy a worm to the ground so the early bird would get a hernia!

He could be the only civilian who was ever impeached!

He could be a great acupuncturist. He's been sticking it to people for years!

He makes women shorter. They shrink from his touch!

She has everything. She should be quarantined!

She looks like she's smelling something bad, and he looks like what she's smelling!

She'll never get dizzy from doing a good turn!

He'd make dice out of his mother's knuckle-bones!

He's a boss spelled backwards—Double ess, oh, bee!

He stood on the edge of his roof and called the suicide hotline. They told him to call Dial-a-Shove!

He would Krazy Glue an octopus together!

He's been called mean, vicious, and rotten, but that's only his family's opinion!

He has more crust than a pie factory!

russia and russians

Perestroika and glasnost *aside, the Russians are always good for a few laughs. "Perestroika and* glasnost" *sounds like a Russian law firm anyway!*

For many years, the border between Poland and Russia was volatile. Poles were Poles one day and Russians the next, or vice versa. Due to a political shift, a farmer found that he was no longer a Russian. He'd become a Pole. Thrilled, he told his wife, "Thank God! No more of those freezing Russian winters!"

A Russian athlete won an Olympic medal for throwing the hammer. A television announcer told him, "That's an amazing feat. No one has ever thrown the hammer that far."

The Russian athlete said, "Get me the sickle, I'll throw it farther!"

A Russian walked into a department store, marched to the shoe section, and asked for a pair of shoes.

"What size?" the clerk asked.

The Russian said, "I wear a forty-one, but give me a thirty-six."

"Why?"

"Well, when I take them off, it'll be the most pleasure I've had all day!"

His tooth throbbing with incessant pain, an American tourist dragged himself to a Moscow dentist. The tourist learned that the fee for extracting the tooth would be five hundred dollars. The American said, "Ridiculous! Where I come from, it costs twenty dollars to pull a tooth!"

The Russian dentist said, "We have to pull it through your ear. You can't open your mouth in Russia!"

An important political figure went to a Moscow brothel. After being taken care of, he sat down for a glass of tea with the prostitute. Upon learning that she wasn't a member of the Communist Party, he urged her to join.

The prostitute said, "I don't think so. My mother hardly let me join this brothel!"

A young woman in Moscow asked her supervisor, Madame Sonya, "May I take off early to go to the opera?"

The supervisor said, "Don't call me 'madame.' We're equals. What opera are you going to see?"

The young woman said, *"Comrade Butterfly."*

A Communist is somebody who has nothing and wants to share it with you!

If I have to go to hell, I want to go to the Russian section. That way I'll know for sure the heating won't work!

Russian roulette isn't a bad game, but not enough Russians are playing it!

I can understand why the Russians are getting ahead of us. They don't spend half their time fighting communism!

A woman managed to board the bus just as

it started from the station. Breathing heavily, the woman said, "Thank the good Lord."

The driver said, "You don't say 'Thank the good Lord.' You should thank the Communist Party."

"What happens if the Communist Party disappears?"

"Then you can say, 'Thank the good Lord'!"

When the Russians send track teams over here, the biggest problem is not keeping the men and women apart. It's trying to *tell* them apart!

Two rabbits met in Siberia. One said, "We have to get out of here. They're going to castrate us."

The other rabbit said, "They're only castrating camels."

The first rabbit said, "After they castrate you, try proving you're not a camel!

In Russia, a man can *really* talk his head off!

It's finally happened. Russia has just run out of shortages!

"Why do Russian police walk in threes?"
"Why?"
"One can read, a second can write, and the third one is there to guard these two members of the intelligentsia!"

A Russian magazine ran a contest for the funniest antigovernment joke. The first prize was twenty years!

They have the secret ballot in Russia now for those who want it. You step into the booth, pull the curtain, and vote. When you open the curtain, you're in Siberia!

Comrade Popov got up at the meeting and asked, "Why do we have so many shortages? Why do all our products break down? Why is everything so expensive?"

The council chairman said, "I'll answer your questions at the next meeting."

At the next meeting, Comrade Bulgov got up and said, "I only have one question—whatever happened to Comrade Popov?"

The Russians have really come up with unique ways to farm. They plant wheat all over Russia, and at the end of the growing season they harvest it in Kansas!

Two Russians met on the street. One spat. The other said, "Comrade, let's not talk politics!"

To repay Russia for its many shipments of food and arms, the Egyptians sent a mummy to Moscow. The Egyptian scientist said he was sorry that he didn't know how old the mummy was. The Russians said they'd find out.

A week later, a Russian scientist called the Egyptian and said, "We know the exact age of the mummy."

"How did you find that out?"

"The mummy confessed!"

S

sales (salesmen and salesgirls)

At a department store perfume counter, a salesgirl was trying to interest my wife in one of those perfumes that sell for two hundred dollars a drop. The salesgirl said, "This is the best perfume we've ever had. It's irresistible." My wife said, "If it's so irresistible, how come you're still working here?"

"What is your pleasure, sir?"
"My pleasure is making love, but I came in for a tie!"

A government investigator said to an insurance agent, "You can't sell insurance without a license."

The agent said, "I knew I wasn't selling any, but I never knew the reason!"

Henry and Alex, two traveling salesmen, met at the bar of their hotel. Henry moaned about how bad business was. He hadn't made a sale all day.

Alex said, "The President says that business is terrific."

Henry said, "Maybe he's got a better territory!"

A salesman walked into an office and said, "I'd like to talk to somebody with a little authority."

An office boy said, "I'm your man. I have as little authority as anybody!"

A man walked into a clothing store and was immediately swallowed up by a salesman who aimed him at a rack of ugly sportcoats that the store was trying to get rid of. The salesman sized up the customer, nodded to himself, then put a yellowish coat on the man, saying, "This is you." The salesman turned the man to the right and then to the left, adding, "It's perfect."

The customer said, "Can I try on something else from over there?"

"You don't have to. Let me see it from the back." He turned the customer around. "Nice, let's see how it looks from the side."

Seeing the salesman working so hard, the owner of the shop came over and smiled at the way the coat fit the customer. "It was made for you," the owner said, taking over the selling job.

The customer said, "I'll take it."

When the customer was gone, the owner said to the salesman, "Do you see how fast a sale can be made?"

The salesman said, "Yeah, but who got him dizzy?"

The sales manager called all the salesmen into the conference room and told them, "I'd like to announce that we're going to have a sales contest. The man who wins gets to keep his job!"

A man applied for a job and was asked to tell about his work experience. He said, "From time to time I was a door-to-door salesman selling wall-to-wall carpeting on a day-to-day basis with a fifty-fifty commission in Walla Walla."

"How was business?" the interviewer asked.

"So-so."

A youngster deposited fifty dollars in the bank. Handing him his receipt, the teller asked, "How'd you get so much money?"

"I sold greeting cards."

"You must have sold them to a million people."

"I sold them all to one family—after their dog bit me!"

In a fairly remote section of Appalachia still served by the itinerant peddler, one knocked on a farmhouse door. Seeing him, the farmer's wife said, "I don't need anything."

"How about an aluminum pan?"

"No. Please go away. I don't want a thing."

"A battery-operated clothes brush?"

"No."

"Notions? Thread?"

"If you don't leave, I'll whistle for the men in the fields!"

"Do you want to buy a whistle?"

A salesman approached a home on a nice quiet street and said to the young boy playing on the sidewalk, "Is your mother home?"

The young boy said, "Yup."

The salesman knocked on the door a dozen times without evoking a response. Turning to the boy, he said, "I thought your mother was home."

The young boy said, "She is. I live down the block!"

"I had a fabulous day. I made a lot of friends for the outfit."

"I didn't sell anything either!"

A salesman was on the road for an extensive

swing through a dozen states. After each state, he submitted an expense account. One frequent item covered the salesman's involvement with young ladies of the evening. It stated, "Man is not made of wood—$50.00." After the next state and the next, the same item: "Man is not made of wood—$50.00."

A month into the trip, the company president wrote back, saying, "Expense account denied. Man isn't made of iron either!"

I'd like to say that our sales department has had the best year in its history. Wow, would I like to say that!

"What can you suggest for a man of fifty?"
"A girl of twenty!"

A man walked into a general store and asked the shapely clerk, "Do you keep stationery?"

The shapely clerk answered, "Until the last few seconds, then I go crazy!"

A shoe salesman said to a customer who'd gotten him to pull out every box on the shelves, "Mind if I rest a minute? Your feet are killing me!"

A salesman met a young lady at a bar. Smiling at him, she said, "Are you buying? I'm selling."

The salesman bought, then forgot about the matter until a week later, when he discovered that he had contracted a rather private disease. With a dozen penicillin shots and care, the condition cleared up.

The salesman found himself in the bar again, and once again the lovely damsel said, "Are you buying? I'm selling."

The salesman said, "What are you selling this week—cancer?"

My brother was put on a starting salary

recently. Unfortunately, the salary started but he didn't!

A good salesman can convince his wife that polyester is the generic name for mink!

A department store salesman lived for his work. One night a burglar broke into his house and the salesman said, "Silverware, step this way!"

The saddest thing in the world is a salesman with an unlimited expense account and an ulcer!

A man came back to the used-car dealer who'd sold him the car allegedly driven only by a little old lady. The salesman was concerned and asked, "Is there anything wrong?"

The customer said, "No, I just want to return some of the things the little old lady left under the seat—this chewing tobacco and a fifth of whiskey!"

The salesman showed the young couple around the showroom. They stopped at one car, asked the price, and almost fainted when he told them the cost. The young man said, "That's almost what you'd have to pay for a big car."

The salesman said, "That's the way it is today—if you want economy you have to pay for it!"

A salesman dies on the road. The hotel manager wires his company, "What shall I do?"

The company wires back, "Search the body for orders and send the samples home by freight."

The traveling salesman is told that space on the farm is limited. He'll have to choose between sleeping in the barn and sleeping with the baby of the family. He chooses the barn.

The next morning, bright and early, he comes into the kitchen and sees a beautiful young lady preparing breakfast. He asks, "Who are you?"

She answers, "I'm the baby!"

A salesman's wife gets a report that her husband is carousing on the road. She wires him, "Come home. Why waste your money on what you can get at home for nothing?"

The salesman wires back, "To hell with you and your bargains!"

Because of a snowstorm, a salesman found himself stranded in a small town. He called the home office and asked for instructions.

The boss replied, "That's up to you. Your summer vacation started today."

The salesman pointed out the benefits of his company's life insurance policy. Spicing it with a little emotional blackmail, he asked, "How would your wife carry on after you're gone?"

The potential customer said, "That's her business, as long as she behaves while I'm still around!"

Everybody's favorite clerk died and went to heaven. He pointed to a special cloud and asked if that could be his. Saint Peter said, "Sorry, that one is sold, but we have one just as good!"

He's a great salesman. During the war he sold pension plans to kamikaze pilots!

One salesman said that he'd gotten three orders that week—get out, stay out, and don't come back!

We just got a painting of our sales department. It's a still life!

My brother is an independent salesman. He takes orders from no one!

She was only a salesman's daughter, but she gave away lots of samples!

school

One of my early report cards indicates that I was absent a great deal, paid no attention to my studies in class, brought in no homework, and talked at every opportunity. However, my teacher concluded, forced to find something nice to say, that my handwriting was good. So there went my medical career!

Nowadays there are two important days in the life of a student: the day he starts school and the day he's booted out!

A teacher asked, "What did Paul Revere say at the end of his famous ride?"
A student answered, "Whoa!"

An eight-year-old was giving his kid brother some advice as the younger one was about to enter the halls of academe. "Don't learn how to spell 'cat,' because if you do, after that the words just get harder and harder!"

It was a tough school. The kids on the debating team took steroids!

One kid was so bad in school, his parents went to PTA meetings under an assumed name!

A mother walked into her son's room and said cheerfully, "Up. Up. It's time to go to school."

The son said, "I don't want to go to school."
"You have to go."
"I hate that school. The kids are mean and rotten."
"You still have to go."
"It's like a jungle. One fight after another. They threaten me a hundred times a day."
"You must go."
"Why must I go?"
"Because you're the principal!"

A little boy in kindergarten raised his hand because he had to go to the washroom. Given permission to go, he left but returned a few minutes later, saying, "I couldn't find it."
The teacher stopped an older boy in the hall and asked him to lead the youngster to the proper room. He did so.
The kindergarten boy returned a little later, relieved, and said, "We finally found it. I had my pants on backwards!"

My brother was kept back a dozen times. When he graduated, instead of a diploma, they gave him a dinner and a watch!

Kids hate it when teachers strike. They have nobody to hit!

Schoolbuses have a right to be yellow. Did you ever see what they have to carry?

"I'm ashamed of you. When I was your age, I could name all the Presidents in order."
"Teach, there were only two of them then!"

A teacher took a class of first-grade students to a racetrack on a field trip. Seeing one tiny person squirming, she led him into the bathroom and started to help unzip his pants.
Astonished at what she saw when the job was done, she asked, "Are you in the first?"

The tiny person answered, "No, I'm riding Black Bart in the fifth!"

science

We need science to help us solve all the problems we wouldn't have if there were no science!

The personnel manager was impressing the applicant with the prospective job. "We make parts for microscopes. You'll be required to work with lenses that are ten-thousandths of an inch thick."

"I can handle it," the applicant said. "I used to slice meat in a delicatessen."

Somebody asked a professor how science helped the business world. The professor replied, "What would the belt business be without the law of gravity?"

Scientists have learned that germs always work in large groups. This may explain why we never saw a measle running around on its own!

A geneticist was intent on developing bigger drumsticks for the turkey served during holidays. Failure after failure occurred. Finally he crossed a turkey with an ostrich. It was his worst failure. He ended up with a scrawny-looking bird that kept burying its head in the yams!

Concluding his lecture on space, the scientist said, "All the data points to one fact: other planets are not able to support life."

A man in the audience yelled out, "It's not so easy on this one either!"

A scientist, showing slides of the Grand Canyon, explained, "It took two hundred million years to make this."

A man in the audience said, "Was it a government project?"

Scientists have just laid out the flight schedule of our newest space probe. Of course, it starts out the usual way—an hour layover in Atlanta!

"If there are people on other planets, why don't they contact us?"
"Would you?"

Scientists finally found out the truth when they discovered the North Pole—there's nobody sitting on top of the world!

I know a girl who thinks she's a robot because she was made by a scientist!

The reason that lightning never hits the same place twice, scientists have discovered, is that after it hits the first time, the same place isn't there anymore!

The convention of scientists was being held in Las Vegas. At the dice table, Dr. Prather, an astronomer, was throwing his money around. A cohort whispered to another, "Prather is gambling as if there were no tomorrow."

The second cohort said, "Maybe he knows something!"

A scientist is working on a project that will enable him to heat a giant apartment building with one lump of coal. If he's smart, he'll consult my landlord, who's been doing that for years!

Scientists have just discovered that there is life on Venus. One of their satellites sent up a message and they got a busy signal!

They've just come up with a pen that writes

for ten years. The problem is that your hand falls off!

scotland and the scots

There are only about a hundred ethnic groups that play it close to the vest. Bavarians, according to Germans from the north, are tight-fisted, as are the Swiss. Basques can squeeze a coin so hard it'll end up with only one side, say some Frenchmen. All over Malaysia there's a strong rumor that the Chinese don't spend. A hundred and one ethnic groups are noted for their ability to down a wee dram of the good stuff. Only the Scots alone have become world-famous for combining these characteristics and adding a kilt!

"**D**o you know why the Scots are so brave in battle?"
"Why?"
"They play the bagpipes going into battle, and would rather die than have to listen to them!"

A Scotsman's ideal vacation is to stay home and let his mind wander!

A Scotsman had a great time in the big city. Every time he went out to eat, he found some money under his plate!

Mrs. MacTavish was very sick. The only light in the room, coming from a tiny candle, showed the pallor of her complexion. "I don't think I'll make it through the night."

"I got to go back to my chores," Mr. MacTavish said. "But if you feel yourself slipping, be sure to blow out the candle!"

Then there was the Scotsman who needed money so badly he took some out of the bank!

A Scot stopped a New York cabbie and asked how much it would cost to go to a destination. The cabbie gave him a price. The Scot said, "Tell you what, lad. We'll toss a coin and it'll be double or nothing."

"Fine."

The Scot tossed a coin, the cabbie guessed heads, and heads it was. The Scot said, "Too bad. Now I'll have to walk!"

One Scotsman slept with his mother-in-law to save the wear and tear on his bride!

A Scot was describing a frightful moment he'd had, saying, "There I was in the water. I was going down for the second time. The current kept pulling me down, and I went down for the third time. Just then, my whole life flashed in front of me. It was one picture after another."

His listener said, "Did one of them happen to show you borrowing a fiver from me ten years ago?"

A Scottish minister, walking down a country road, saw one of his flock lying in the road and feeling no pain. The minister said, "Where you been, Jock?"

Jock said, "Either a wedding or a funeral. I don't know which, but it was a howling success!"

A Scot saw a friend coming down the path toward the Scot's house. The Scot said, "Everybody grab a toothpick and go out on the porch!"

In a train station, a Scot meets another Scot and explains that he's going to Glasgow on his honeymoon. The other Scot asks, "Where's your wife?"

The first Scot says, "She's been to Glasgow!"

The stingiest man in Scotland was the man who gave his daughter a dime not to eat dinner, stole it from her when she was asleep, and then refused to give her breakfast the next morning because she'd lost the money!

A Scotsman's last daughter married, and it thrilled the old man no end. The confetti was getting dirty!

A man returned to his native town in northern Scotland after having been away twenty years. He was greeted at the airport by his brother, who had a beard down to his knees. The returning man asked, "What are you doing with a beard?"

The bearded brother said, "When you left, you took the razor with you!"

A Scotsman put a penny in the Sunday collection box. Months went by and he contributed nothing. After the services, the minister came over and said. "Your penny ran out today!"

Paddy's wife was about to have her fifteenth baby. As she waited for the pains, she told Paddy, "Let's get a new crib. I've used the one we've got for fourteen children."

Paddy said, "It looks sturdy enough."

Paddy's wife said, "Darling, it's coming apart. The wheels are all worn. We should have a new one."

Paddy said, "All right, I'll pick one up later. But this time I want one that'll last!"

A Scot took his girl out on the town. After they'd seen a movie he took her to a fish-and-chips shop for a bite and said, "Don't go hog-wild, because it isn't costing you anything!"

The handyman had just returned from a backbreaking job removing rocks in one of the fields. To thank him, the farmer's wife, Mrs. MacDougal, handed him a drink of Scotch, saying, "This is good stuff. It's twenty-five years old."

The handyman studied the glass and looked at the tiny amount of whiskey in it and said, "One thing's for certain—it's small for its age!"

It's a sure sign of summer when a Scotsman throws away his Christmast tree!

Two Scots were walking down the street when one of them found a ten-dollar bill. The other borrowed it from him to buy glasses!

A Scots golf pro, after ten years of retirement, went back to the game. He found his ball!

The Scots have a new use for old razor blades—they shave with them!

During the battle, a Highlander was unlucky enough to get his head blown off. The word was communicated to his closest friend, who asked, "Do you know where his head is? He was wearing my tam!"

The Scot told his wife, "Make sure you take off your new glasses when you're not looking at anything!"

The jet plane started to rattle. Quickly, the pilot turned northward. As soon as he crossed the border into Scotland, everything tightened up!

There was a collection going on. As the band played hymns, young lassies went about collecting money. One came to a Scot and asked, "Could you give a penny for the Lord?"

The Scot said, "How old are you, lassie?"

"Sixteen."

"I'm eighty. I'll be seeing him first, so I'll hand it to him myself!"

A Scot had to send a wire home to the effect that Uncle Paddy had died. The cheapest price would be three dollars for ten words. The Scot wired, "Uncle Paddy died yesterday. No pain. Seven, eight, nine, ten."

MacTavish walked into the drugstore and asked for a baby bottle. The druggist was taken aback and said, "You're being a little extravagant, aren't you, lad?"

MacTavish said, "It's the wife's fault. She had triplets yesterday."

An Englishman became angry when the conversation consisted of nothing but jokes about the Scots, saying, "You'd think the Scots were the only race on Earth! Why don't you tell a joke about an Englishman?"

Sandy said, "Tell you why, lad. It's hard enough being an Englishman without making a joke about it!"

MacDougal was going over the weekly accounts with his wife. Finishing one difficult page, he said, "What's this first item for?"

His wife said, "I had to get plasters for my corns."

"And the next item?"

"Medicine for my bad tooth."

"Don't tell me the next one is for medicine too."

"Aye. It was for my ulcer."

The Scot slammed the account book shut and said, "Dear, you're going to have to stop spending so much for your own personal pleasure!"

Winters are fierce in northern Scotland, so the owner of the estate felt he was doing a good deed when he bought earmuffs for his foreman. Noticing, however, that the foreman wasn't wearing the earmuffs even on the bitterest day, the landlord asked, "Didn't you like the muffs?"

The foreman said, "They're a thing of beauty."

"Why don't you wear them?"

The foreman explained, "I was wearing them the first day, but somebody offered to buy me a drink and I didn't hear him!"

It was a great party. The Italian brought wine. The Englishman brought a roast beef. The Frenchman brought pâté. The Scot brought his brother!

seasickness

I had mal de mer once, aboard a private yacht. If somebody had killed me, I would have made him my sole heir!

Aboard the luxury cruiser, the wife yelled to her husband, "Look, we're passing a ship."

The husband said, "Don't call me unless we're passing a tree!"

There was a young man from Ostend
Who vowed he'd hold out till the end.
But when halfway over
From Calais to Dover,
He did what he didn't intend!

The husband was feeling worse than he'd ever felt in his life. He motioned for his wife to sit with him in his stateroom and started to clean up his affairs. "There's a will in the top drawer of my desk. There should be no problems, but if something turns up, call my attorney. And if I die before we get to Europe, promise me one thing. Bury me there. I could never stand the trip back!"

You get on the cruise ship and it's gorgeous. Then you go out into the ocean and it becomes dis-gorgeous!

secretaries

A secretary becomes indispensable about an hour after a temp takes her place!

A woman marched into her husband's office unannounced and found a pretty secretary on his lap. The man tried, "Don't get into a snit. I didn't want to let you know that business is so bad I'm studying how to be a ventriloquist!"

I know a boss who's so dedicated he keeps his secretary at his bedside all night in case he wants to send a letter!

I asked my secretary to take a letter. She picked "N"!

The boss was glowing at his new secretary's work. Calling her over, he said, "I've never seen such an improvement in typing. Look, only nine mistakes."

"I'm glad you're pleased, Mr. Stone."

"Now let's go on to the *second* line!"

A secretary said to a co-worker, "I finally got my boss to laugh out loud."

"Did you tell him a joke?"

"No, I asked for a raise!"

Some secretaries think their bosses are bigoted. "Imagine," one said, "mine thinks there's only one way to spell a word!"

A well-known businessman committed suicide by jumping out of his office window. His secretary, a lovely redhead, was ques-

tioned and said, "I've only been working here three weeks."

"Were you and the boss friendly?" the detective asked.

"Well, we did have a little fun every day. In fact, after our first affair, he bought me a lovely gold bracelet. The second time, he bought me a mink. Last week he bought me a car."

"What about today?"

"All I know is that he said he hadn't bought me a gift. He asked me how much money I'd take to make love to him. I told him that he could have it for five dollars, even though I charge all the other men in the company ten. That's when he jumped out of the window."

My secretary saves me money. She orders correction fluid by the six-pack!

One secretary told her boyfriend, "Stop and/or I'll slap you!"

My secretary is brilliant. She can make five carbons without an original!

The secretary was angry at the way the boss criticized her. She looked at him and said, "How do you spell 'quit'?"

My secretary just discovered something that has given her a new lease on life. She found out that the dictionary was alphabetical. It once took her nine days to look up "zoo"!

My secretary is great in math. She added up a column of a dozen numbers ten times and showed me all ten answers!

A secretary was complaining to another, "My boss yelled at me because I asked him if he wanted the carbons double-spaced too!"

The boss said, "You must answer the phone when it rings."

The secretary said, "Most of the time it's for you!"

My secretary is honest. Yesterday she didn't come to work. She called in lazy!

My new secretary isn't too bright. This morning she asked me how to dial the pencil sharpener!

My secretary can type ten words a minute, but only if the wind is with her!

We sped up work in our typing department. We just got an electric eraser!

My secretary has a perfect attendance record. She hasn't missed a coffee break in three years!

"Does your boss pace when he gives dictation?"
"If he did, I'd fall off his lap!"

secrets

I'm for secrets. Otherwise, I wouldn't let the world in on my secret file. I have an even more secret file. It's so secret I don't know where it is!

A husband said to his wife, "Did you tell your sister what I said was in the strictest confidence?"

The wife said, "No. I didn't want her to think it was important enough to repeat!"

What with bikinis and miniskirts, it would be hard for a woman to keep a secret today, even if she wanted to!

My wife is great at keeping a secret. She knew four weeks ago that we were going to buy a car and never told me!

The man of the house was angry with the maid because she'd told his wife what time he'd poured himself into the house. The maid denied the charge, saying, "I didn't tell her what time you came in. I just said I was too busy getting breakfast ready to notice!"

servants

I saw a great science fiction movie recently. The first act takes place in a fancy home. The second act takes place a week later and they still have the same maid!

The maid liked to sleep late and thus wasn't available to make breakfast for the children. Forced to get up and do so, the lady of the house told the maid, "From now on, each time you miss breakfast you have to give me a quarter."

Came the next morning and no maid. When she deigned to come into the kitchen at about nine o'clock, the lady of the house greeted her with an icy look and demanded a quarter. The maid paid.

Week after week went by and the maid still didn't get out of bed in time. Having had enough, the lady of the house said, "I'm getting a little angry. I've been making breakfast every morning."

The maid said, "Why should you be sore? You're getting paid for it!"

The maid said that she was quitting. The lady of the house said, "How can you leave us after all these years? I've treated you just like one of the family."

The maid said, "Oh, now you admit it!"

Old Mr. Collins staggered into the house

and told his young wife, "I'm going to fire that chauffeur. He almost killed me a dozen times."

The wife said, "Dear, let's not be hasty. Give him one more chance!"

The burglars had ransacked half the mansion. Finally hearing the noise they were making, the butler put on his robe and came into the den they were now cleaning out. Seeing him, the burglars took off, heading out of the window they'd jimmied open. True to his training, the butler said, "Who shall I say called?"

We had a great dinner today. Our cook made a delicious salad and a soup. Then the girl we hired after her made the roast!

I have a great stereo system, a perfect color TV set, terrific furniture, and my own bathroom—I just moved into the maid's room!

Many a maid is a jewel, but she always leaves for a better setting!

The neighbor, always eager to cause trouble, told Jones, "It's none of my business, but this afternoon I saw your wife in back kissing this tall man."

Jones said, "Did he have glasses?"

"I think so."

"Red hair?"

"Seems to me he did."

"That was our gardener. He'll kiss anybody!"

sex

This category needs no explanation. As my wife said, "Cover me up when you're through!"

A pregnant woman goes to the doctor and asks what position she should be in when she gives birth. The doctor says, "The same position you were in when you began it."

The woman said, "Do you mean I have to go up to Lover's Lane and dangle my feet out the car window for an hour?"

A phone solicitor asked a man, "Will you contribute to the Sexual Advancement League?"

The man said, "I gave at home last night!"

An innocent couple, one of the few in the world today, came to the doctor for sexual advice. The doctor had the woman undress, lie down on the table, and then allow him to demonstrate the sex act. When it was over, the doctor said, "That was the sex act. Do you understand?"

The man said, "Sure. How often do I have to bring her in?"

An older man went to a doctor for some potency shots. When the doctor's bill came, the older man wrote out an amount much larger than was requested. Getting the check, the doctor's nurse called up to see why the amount was higher than had been charged. The older man said, "The extra ten dollars is from my wife!"

There are things that are better than sex. There are things worse than sex. It's impossible to find anything just like it!

The minister nodded, pronounced the young couple man and wife, and said, "You may kiss the bride." Lifting the bride's veil, the groom kissed his new wife.

In the back of the room, a small boy whispered to his mother, "Is this where he sprinkles pollen on her?"

"I can't believe we're really married. I can't
    believe it. I can't believe we're really mar-
    ried."
"Let me get this shoelace untied, you'll
    believe it!"

A sex lecturer was talking to a large gathering at a men's club. Wishing to check some
data against that of this group, he asked,
"How many of you have sex every night?"
    A number of hands were raised.
    "How many have sex twice a week?"
More hands. "Once a month?" Still more
hands. "How many of you have sex once a
year?"
    An old man in the back row jumped up
and said, "Me. Yippeee!"
    The lecturer said, "Why are you so cheer-
ful?"
    The old man said, "Because tonight's the
night!"

I wonder about China. Any country with a
billion people that says Ping-Pong is its favorite sport will fib about all kinds of things!

An older man complained to his doctor,
"Do something for me. The man next door
is a year younger than I am, and he says he
makes love to his wife twice a night."
    The doctor said, "Say the same thing!"

Sex is overrated, but can you imagine where
everything else stands?

Sex before marriage isn't bad unless it inter-
feres with the ceremony!

A man told his wife, "In Turkey, women
pay men fifty dollars when they have sex
with them. I think I'll go to Turkey."
    His wife said, "I'll go with you."
    "Why?"
    "I want to see how you can live on fifty
dollars a year!"

It's a shame. Now that the sexual revolution
is on, I'm out of ammunition!

Not long ago they had a conference on
premature ejaculation. It was set for eight in
the evening. One visitor arrived at five to
eight, but the conference was over.

A senator and his wife were lying in bed.
His wife said, "Stop talking politics. Can't
you talk about anything else?"
    "Sure."
    "Good. Let's talk about sex."
    The senator said, "Fine. How many times
a week do you think the President has
intercourse?"

Sex with somebody you love is great. Sex
without love isn't terrible either!

Last night I gave the performance of my life
in bed. Too bad my wife wasn't awake!

My trouble with sex is that I keep trying to
prove I'm as good as I never was!

A famous expert on sex was introduced to
the audience. He stood up and said, "It gives
me great pleasure!"
    He sat down!

"How do most college men propose?"
"You're gonna have a what?"

"Does your wife smoke after sex?"
"No, but she sizzles a little!"

I know a woman who wants her sex in the
back of her car. But she wants her husband
to drive!

My psychiatrist told me and my wife we
should have sex every night. Now we'll
never see one another!

My girl speaks eight languages, and can't say no in any of them!

"**I**'d like to get something off my chest."
"What's that?"
"Your eyes!"

God told man, "I'm going to give you ten years of a normal sex life."

Man said, "That's not enough. The way I feel, I need much more."

God said, "If I give you something, don't complain."

Man said, "But sex isn't just something."

God said, "Look, I'm busy. We'll talk again."

God called the King of the Beasts to him and said, "Lion, you've got twenty years of sex life."

The lion said, "Ten will be enough."

Man said, "Let me have the extra ten."

God nodded and said, "You've got it."

God gave the monkey twenty years. The monkey said that ten would be enough.

Man raised his hand. God nodded and gave him the extra ten. Before the day was over, God had given man ten years the donkey didn't want and a final ten that parrots couldn't use.

That may explain why men have ten normal years of sex, ten years of lion about it, ten years of monkeying around with it, ten years of being an ass about it, and ten years of talking about it!

Two people met in Laguna Niguel, a retirement community in California. Both were ninety years old. Since love knows no years, one look was enough for them to know this was it. They were married a week after they met.

On the first night of the honeymoon, they got into bed, held hands, and squeezed them.

On the second night, they squeezed hands again.

On the third night, the husband pressed his wife's hand. She said, "Not tonight. I have a headache!"

We have a great birth-control device—a good fight!

Mrs. Abercrombie was unhappy with the way Elena the maid cleaned. Finding a layer of dust on the dining room table, she started to chew out the maid. Elena said, "I'm a better cook than you. I clean house better than you."

"Who told you that?"

"Mr. Abercrombie. I'm better in bed than you, too."

Mrs. Abercrombie sneered and said, "I suppose my husband told you that too."

"No. The gardener!"

He has a one-track mind—a dirty track!

She named her first baby after the father—Army!

She never tells him when she's reaching a climax. He's never around!

I could have a very healthy normal sex life if it wasn't for my wife!

I have twenty-twenty eyesight. Every woman I meet is forty!

A Frenchman and an Italian were in the woods. Suddenly, a beautiful nude girl ran by. The Frenchman said, "I'd love some of that."

So the Italian shot her!

It's easy to tell the bright ones from the dumb ones in sex education. The dumb ones are pregnant from homework!

"Do you know how to keep a sex maniac in suspense for twenty-four hours?"

"No. How?"

"I'll tell you tomorrow!"

Two married women were talking about a neighbor. One said, "He dresses so well."

The other woman said, "And so quickly, too!"

In college she was voted the most likely to succeed—with almost anybody!

I had a sheltered youth. I was twenty before I was allowed to have a full-length mirror!

It's amazing that King Solomon fell asleep with a thousand things on his mind!

Even in school she was something. She once went to the principal's office and stayed four weeks!

She's been boarded more times than Amtrak!

I know a girl whose boyfriend doesn't smoke, drink, gamble, or run around. He also makes his own dresses!

shaggy-dog stories

Illogic is the root of shaggy-dog stories. When heard, the shaggy-dog story demands a reaction only a step short of hanging. Yet time gives the shaggy-dog story a sense of reality. Suddenly, a good argument can be put up for the illogic. The quintessential shaggy-dog story is about the worker in a plant who sits down to have lunch at the scheduled time. Taking a sandwich from his lunchbox, he makes a face and says, "Darn it, tuna!" The next day at lunch he opens his lunchbox, takes out a sandwich, and complains again, "Darn it, tuna!" Every day for a month he has the same complaint. His buddy says, "Why don't you have your wife make you another kind of sandwich? The man says, "Oh, I make them myself!" Explaining the joke won't help. If nothing else, however, it gave me a chance to write "quintessential"!

A man saw a pig with a wooden leg hobbling in a farmyard. More than a little curious, the man went over to the farmer, who was whittling away as he sat on the porch. The man asked the farmer to explain the pig's wooden leg.

The farmer said, "That pig is something special. About three weeks ago, I was out in the fields working with my big reaper. The darn thing hit a rock and tumbled over with me under it. That pig saw what had happened and he ran back to the house, fetched my wife and son, and saved my life. A week or so past, my wife slipped and fell into the well. That pig dragged me out of the barn and pushed me at the well. I saved my wife just before she was going down for the third time. Just the other day, the house caught on fire. That pig dragged the baby out and saved her."

"But why does he have one wooden leg?"

"Sir, you don't eat a pig like that all at once!"

A man walked into a doctor's office with a duck on his head. The doctor said, "What's your problem?"

The duck said, "I want you to get this man off my rear end!"

Leaving for a vacation in Alaska, a man promised to mail his friend a piece of glacier. The friend said, "By the time it gets here, it'll be gone."

The man said, "You're crazy. Who'd want to steal a piece of glacier from an envelope?"

Two men went to a convent and asked if there were any midget nuns around. There happened to be one, the only one in any order within a thousand miles of the city. One of the men asked her, "Sister, were you out on the town last night?"

The nun said, "I should say not. I was here praying all evening."

The man thanked her, then he and his friend left. Getting into his car, the man said, "I can't believe it. I spent the whole night dancing with a penguin!"

A man was playing chess with his dog. The man mated the dog in three moves and started to gloat. The dog said, "Let's find a hydrant and play *my* game!"

The minister was ill. Unable to find a last-minute replacement, the minister asked his dog to deliver the sermon. The dog spent all of his time with the minister and knew his mind as well as anybody.

Sunday, the dog delivered the sermon and took up the collection. Returning to the house with the collection plate, the dog emptied the contents on the table. The take was the largest in the history of the church. The minister asked, "How did you accomplish this?"

The dog said, "I told them to come across or I'd bite them!"

shapes

It's worth repeating because I gave birth to it: I called her my melancholy baby. She had a shape like a melon and a face like a collie!

One day she sent a picture of her body through the mail. They put it in the dead-letter office!

They call her the Dragon Lady. Half her body is always draggin'!

Her rear end is so big it has its own heart and lungs!

If it wasn't for her Adam's apple, she'd have no shape at all!

I've seen better bodies than his on a used-car lot!

All a sweater does for her is make her itch!

She was cute from her head to her feet, but what a mess in between!

She sat on a piece of broken glass and cut a fancy figure!

She must like plants. Her figure's gone to pot!

She has a great job—she stands in front of a drugstore making people ill!

She's in great shape for the shape she's in!

When a doctor examines her, he has her open her mouth and say "Moo!"

She has a wonderful way of protecting herself from a Peeping Tom. She keeps her shades up!

A pregnant woman tried to involve her small son in the birth process. At breakfast one morning, she asked, "What would you rather have—a brother or a sister?"

The small son said, "If it won't get you out of shape too much, how about a pony?"

sheriffs

All sheriffs and deputies are named Bubba. They are a mean-looking lot, and when they tell you to sing "Zippety Doo Dah," you'd better sing it!

The town bank had been robbed. To catch up with the culprit, the sheriff appointed a deputy who also happened to be his son. After a week, the sheriff asked the deputy, "How you comin' with that bank robbery case?"

The deputy said, "We're moving like lightning. Just this morning we got a full description of the bank!"

The election was over. When the votes were counted, the results showed that Sheriff Brown had received three votes to the six hundred for his opponent. True to the tradition of the town, Sheriff Brown resigned, but the morning after the votes were tabulated, he appeared in the street with sixguns on his hips and carrying a shotgun. A citizen said, "You're not the sheriff anymore. You shouldn't be carrying those guns."

The sheriff said, "Anybody who's as unpopular as I am had better be ready to defend himself!"

Sheriff Bailey was a smart one. Because the jail was overcrowded, the food bill was up too high. The sheriff decided to visit the jailhouse and see whom he could release. As he started to walk down the cell block, prisoners started to clamor for mercy and understanding. No one was guilty of any crime. All were victims of mistaken identity or bad luck. Arriving at the last cell, the sheriff saw one man sitting back on his cot. The sheriff said, "What's your story?"

The prisoner said, "I tried to rob a store and I was caught red-handed."

The sheriff turned to his deputy and said,

"Release this man. He's a bad apple, and we wouldn't want him to contaminate all those good guys back there!"

One sheriff got caught in the transition from old to new. He tried to saddle up his pursuit car.

A sheriff ended up in the hospital with every bone broken and not an inch of his skin without a black-and-blue mark. Asked what had happened, he explained, "I was riding along in my chase car when this other car came barreling down the road at ninety. I started to chase him. He kept getting farther and farther ahead. I figured that my engine had stalled, so I got out to take a look!"

shopping

One of several sports in which my wife had a black belt!

A woman goes into a fish market and says, "I don't like the looks of that halibut."

The storekeeper says, "For looks you buy goldfish!

A wife walks in and explains the many packages in her arms: "I read about all that crime in the streets, so I didn't want to carry a lot of cash with me!"

My wife has a ready answer: "All right, so I spend a lot of money. Name another extravagance I have!"

A woman in a supermarket picked up a tomato, squeezed it ten different ways, then asked the produce man, "How much do you want for this rotten tomato?"

"What do you need with six new dresses?"
"Six hew hats!"

A sign in the window of a hardware store bragged, EIGHT LANGUAGES SPOKEN HERE. A Korean customer walked in but couldn't make himself understood. He pointed to the sign in the window. The clerk said, "I speak one language. My customers speak eight languages!"

Asked by a salesgirl for his wife's size, a man said, "Big and fat is the closest I can come to it!"

A woman was giving the butcher a bad time. One piece of beef was too lean, another too fat. Too tall, too short, too round ...Finally the butcher said, "Why don't I wrap up a whole cow for you?"
The woman said, "Let me see it first!"

A woman asked for a Long Island duckling. Brought to her by the butcher, the duckling looked attractively fresh. Shaking her head, the woman said, "I'm not sure this is a Long Island duckling."
"It's a Long Island duckling."
With that, the woman picked up the bird, held it up to the light, looked through the carcass, thrust a finger inside through the rump, and started to feel around. "This duckling," the woman said, after a complete examination, "isn't from Long Island. Are you trying to pull a fast one on me? Where are you from?"
The butcher turned his back to her, bent over, and said, "Suppose you tell me!"

Grapes are so expensive. One good orgy can break you!

It's sad to realize that coffee is worth more a pound than I am!

If supermarket clients are so smart, why do they have to wear their names on their shirts?

I bought some oysters the other day. I found a pearl, so I broke even!

shortness

Shortness gets more laughs than tallness, so pray for an audience of midgets!

He's so short, when it rains he's the last to know!

When she wore a miniskirt, the hem got dirty from dragging on the floor.

She's so short, when she sits she's taller!

He's so short he can milk a cow standing up!

He's so short he can read dice from underneath!

When he sits down and stands, he's the same size!

He's so short he has a lap when he's standing!

He's real short. When he goes horseback riding, he has to stand on a stool to reach the stirrups.

He's so short his belt is a halo!

He's so short, he once put on a pair of pants and fell in the cuffs!

He's so short he's a waste of skin!

He's so short, the world smells different to him in a crowded elevator!

show-offs

Joe Margo was our block show-off. For an ounce of adulation, he'd jump out of a third-story window and hope to land on the back of the ragman's wagon. Joe had to be the best, and to outdo everybody. At the end of World War I, there was an outbreak of influenza. My fever went up to 105, about average. Joe Margo insisted on going higher. He died in the hospital.

Kibbee loved to show off in front of his friend Callino. Having just redone his home, Kibbee therefore invited Callino to see it. Callino drooled at every object in the house. Each item was costly.

Leaving, Callino ran into Kibbee's next-door neighbor. The neighbor told him that everything in Kibbee's house had been bought on time. Eager to get even with his friend, Callino went back to Kibbee and said, "You're a fake. Everything you bought is on time."

Kibbee said, "Of course. It's more expensive that way!"

A lady tried to show off with a smattering of French. Hearing her, another woman said, "How gauche."

The lady said, "Fine. How gauche with you?"

A writer bragged about his brilliance, saying, "I believe I'm a writer for the ages."

Another writer nearby said, "Yes. Ages six to ten!"

The show-off was bragging about how far he'd gotten, saying, "I'm worth two million now. And I started out on a farm in Wisconsin."

A man near him said, "It's amazing what they can do with fertilizers today!"

Every time he opens his mouth, he puts his feats in it.

He married a girl who could take a joke—him!

He has a great reputation as the death of the party!

He's short on horsepower but long on exhaust!

She was told to be herself. That's terrible advice!

He's always starting out on a boast-to-boast tour!

shyness

Don't pummel shy people. The step after shyness is a tear in the eye.

She's so shy, when she hears the word "intersection" she blushes!

She's so shy she's afraid to watch a TV show with a studio audience!

He's so shy he won't read a book with an "f" in it!

A shy woman went to a doctor for a physical examination. She insisted that he turn out the lights before they proceed. A little later, she asked, "Where are my clothes?"

The doctor said, "On the table—right next to mine!"

She has to blindfold herself when she takes a bath!

She blushes when she hears a minister say, "Dearly beloved..."

A shy young man went to a bookstore to buy a book on the most effective way to find and romance a woman. The store clerk was a woman, so the shy young man couldn't bring himself to ask her for help. Searching every shelf, he finally came up with a book titled *Ways to Woo.* He brought it to the counter. The woman clerk said, "Are you sure you want volume twelve of the encyclopedia?"

He was shy from birth. When the doctor slapped him right after he came out, he thought the doctor was angry because he'd been up there in the first place!

siamese twins

I like the way Siamese twins get along. They're so attached to each other!

Somebody asked Siamese twins if they'd had a pleasant date that evening. The twins said, "Yes and no."

A Siamese twin got married and, all packed for his honeymoon, said to his brother. "Want to tag along?"

One Siamese twin consummated his marriage. The next morning he said to his brother, "We're not identical anymore!"

Then there were the Polish Siamese twins. They weren't joined.

It was so windy the other day, I saw a Siamese twin looking for the other one!

Siamese twins don't have money troubles. They can always make both ends meet.

A pair of Siamese twins bragged that they knew many famous people. One said,

"We've spent a lot of time with the President."

People had no cause to doubt them until the President came to town for a political rally. Being members of the same party, the Siamese twins were present. When the speech was over, the President shook hands with many of the people in the crowd. Coming to the Siamese twins, he acted as if he didn't know them and moved on.

Later, friends said to the Siamese twins, "You were supposed to be so chummy with the President. He walked right by."

One of the twins said, "Maybe he didn't recognize us!"

A Siamese twin became very angry with his brother. It seems that his brother had forgotten his birthday.

The girl Siamese twins were approached by two young men when the band started to play jitterbug music. The young men asked for a dance. One of the twins said, "Sure. But none of that over-the-head stuff!"

The Siamese twin sisters did a song-and-dance act. At one show, a young man seemed to fancy one of the girls. After several winks passed between him and the girl, he could hardly wait for the show to end. After the finale, he went backstage and found both girls lying in a special double cot. The twin he liked said, "Sit down next to me."

"Do you think I should?"

"Sure."

A few minutes later, the man started to feel romantic. His twin said, "Lie down next to me and we can cuddle."

"But what about your sister?"

"Oh, she'll read a book. Come on, we can have fun."

The young man accepted the invitation and a good time was had by all.

Six months later, the sisters were back in town. The young man was again in the audience. Dancing by him, the one he'd spent time with said, "Remember me?"

silence

Somebody once told me that silence was the college yell of the school of experience.

A good way to save face is to keep the lower half shut.

Silence is a long conversation with an Englishman.

A priest was playing golf with several laymen. On the eighteenth hole, the priest was two feet from the cup. A tap would make him winner for the day. He stepped to the ball, studied it, then putted. The ball ringed the cup and jumped out. The priest stared for a full minute, his lips forming some famous four-letter words. One of the laymen said, "That was the dirtiest silence I ever heard!"

Silence is good, because you never have to explain something you didn't say.

sins and sinners

Jokes about sin are sure-fire and accepted with gusto by all audiences, especially the nice old ladies with blue hair. Nice old men with blue hair can't always remember what sin is. Some of them don't know whether they've had lunch yet, either! For those who want to be risqué, be warned that a little titillation goes a long way.

A minister just came up with 812 ways of sinning. I wish he'd make a list so I'd know what I was missing out on!

An old spinster was having dinner with the minister. When the subject turned to sin, the minister said, "My dear, the greater the sin, the greater the sinner."

The spinster said, "Why didn't you tell me that when I was young!"

Today the sins of the children are visited on the father!

After the Sunday services were done, the minister stood outside and said good-bye to the people of the congregation. A spinster shook his hand and said, "Thank you so much, Reverend. I didn't know what sin was until you got here!"

Sin is making for the hay while the sun shines.

A sinner is a man who barks up the wrong "she."

Do you think there would have been sin if Adam had given Eve back the apple afterward?

Men fought for her honor. Too bad she didn't!

Sin is skating on thin ice and ending up in hot water.

She was just a local girl who everybody made good!

She says she has a clear conscience. Actually, it's just a bad memory.

She sowed her wild oats and then prayed for a crop failure!

Her boyfriend's car stalled, but she didn't!

small towns

Some towns are so small they deserve a special category.

My hometown was so small the clinic was called Joe's Hospital and Grill!

My hometown was so small, when they had a boxing match both men had to sit in the same corner!

My hometown was so small you couldn't buy a house there unless you had exact change!

I tried to call my hometown the other day, but the area code was busy!

My hometown was so small it didn't even have a porno movie house. Once a week somebody left the shades up!

I come from a very small town. I called my sister the other day and the operator told me, "I don't think they're home. The car is gone!"

My hometown is real small. When they wanted to paint a white line down the middle, they had to widen the street!

My hometown is real small. The town hooker stands under a flashlight!

In my hometown the Howard Johnson's has only one flavor—Guess!

My hometown is so small the town square is a dot!

My hometown is so small the Ramada Inn sleeps four!

My hometown is so small you have to make a reservation if you want to use the parking meter!

My hometown was so small the picture postcards were blank!

My hometown is so small we bought our fire engine from Water Pik!

I'll tell you about a small hometown. Where I come from we have a big car race every year. They say, "Start engines." And that's it!

smog

L.A. has the best smog in the United States. Where else can you wake up in the morning to hear clouds coughing!

It gets real smoggy in Los Angeles. The other day I got mugged by two guys, and all they took was my cough drops.

It was so smoggy the Coast Guard pulled up and boarded it!

You just know there's a smog alert when you go to a funeral and hear coughing from inside the coffin!

Where I live, you have to put the air in a blender before you can breathe it!

I shot an arrow into the air. It stayed there!

The other day the smog was so thick my lungs had to chew the air!

In L.A. the smog is so thick, some people think it's hillside property!

All cars in California must have a smog

device. It must work great, because we have so much smog!

The other day a man fell out of a plane at twelve thousand feet. He didn't get hurt. He landed on the smog!

I won't say that Los Angeles has a lot of smog, but the town motto is Latin for "emphysema."

smoking

A good cigar is my only vice. I guess lying is another! After a good meal there's nothing like a good cigar. Now if my wife would only make me a good meal!

A woman was visiting another woman and saw a small vase on the mantelpiece. She said, "This is a lovely vase."

The other woman said, "Those are my husband's ashes."

"I didn't know he was dead."

"He isn't. He smokes and can never find an ashtray."

They say that smokers are in trouble. When they get to heaven, Saint Peter shouldn't smell the smoke on their breaths. I solved this problem. When I go, I'm going to leave my breath behind.

This anticigarette campaign is hurting some people. I know one fellow who tried to kill himself. He doesn't smoke. He makes ashtrays!

One poor soul drowned from smoking. He burned a hole in his waterbed and fell in!

It's easy to stop smoking. All you need is a reason, determination, and a pack of wet matches!

"How many cigars do you smoke a day?"

"A dozen."

"What do they cost?"

"A dollar each."

"That comes to twelve dollars a day, eighty-four dollars a week, over four thousand a year. Now tell me, how long have you been smoking?"

"Fifty years."

"That adds up to a lot of money."

"It certainly does."

"Do you see the big building across the street?"

"It's nice."

"If you didn't smoke, you probably could own that building."

"Have you ever smoked?"

"Never."

"Do you own that building?"

"No."

"Well, I do!"

An international effort to study space was made. Three astronauts from different countries were chosen to lift off together. Because of limited space, each astronaut was allowed to take along 100 pounds or so. The American took along his wife, who weighed 105 pounds. The Japanese astronaut took along 125 pounds of technical books. The Russian took along 125 pounds of the best Havana cigars.

Thirty-six months later, they returned. The American and his wife stepped out of the capsule with a baby. The Japanese carried a thick notebook with amazing new scientific formulas. The Russian stepped out of the capsule and screamed, "Does anybody have a match?"

I know somebody who went to the stockholders' meeting of a tobacco company and wanted to sit in the no-smoking section!

I spent hours trying to get the fellow next to

me in the office to stop smoking. I said, "Look how yellow your hands are."

He said, "What do you want from me? I'm Chinese!"

The first time my wife saw me bite off the end of a cigar, she said to me, "Why don't you buy one the right size right off?"

You can always tell an ex-smoker. When he finishes eating a candy bar, he always grinds the paper out with his foot!

snakes

I've never gone near a snake. I think we both like that!

A city visitor saw a farmer dropping dead snakes onto his land and then mixing them with the soil. The city slicker asked the reason and the farmer said, "Snakes make good fertilizer for the corn. Corn grows high and I can make a heap of whiskey. I drink the whiskey and there's more snakes. Best kind of crop rotation I ever saw!"

Some large snakes can travel as fast as people. I'd like to bet on that!

Several snakes were wrapped around the high branches of a tree, basking in the warm sunlight. One of the snakes slithered over to another limb, from which hung some ripe fruit. He tasted one. As he crushed it between his lips, a sweet, syrupy taste filled his mouth. He licked his chops. Another snake, seeing the obvious enjoyment, said, "Why don't you bring this fruit to human beings?"

The first snake thought the suggestion a good one. He gathered up several of the fruits, placed them gently in his mouth, and slithered off to town. On the way, he saw a woman scattering food to her chickens.

Sidling up to her, the snake dropped the fruit at her feet. Looking down, the woman, whose name happened to be Eve—Eve O'Malley—stepped back. Grabbing a shovel, she started to hit the snake. He took a brutal pummeling before he managed to get away. Arriving back with his pals, he said, "Wow, does she hold a grudge!"

A city man asked a moonshiner as the good old boy worked his still, "Is there a better cure for snakebite than moonshine?"

The moonshiner said, "Never asked!"

speed

We had a cameraman who could tell you what speed wasn't. He did everything at a snail's pace. His favorite statement was, "The faster I go, the behinder I get!" Well, the opposite of that is speed!

The soldier was being interrogated by an officer, who asked, "Did you hear the bullet whiz by you?"

The soldier said, "Twice."

"How could that be?"

"I heard it when it passed me, and I heard it again when I passed it!"

A young man ran into a group of tough bikers, who, having nothing better to do, decided to tear up the town. Later the sheriff asked the young man, "Did you run like the wind?"

The young man said, "Nope. But I passed three other guys who were running like the wind!"

The witness said he'd heard two shots. The attorney asked him how far apart the shots had been. The witness slapped his hands together twice to indicate an interval of a tenth of a second. The attorney asked, "Where were you when you heard the first shot?"

The witness said, "I was in my hotel room next door."

"Where were you when the second shot was fired?"

"At the airport, buying a ticket!"

A hillbilly was driving his wagon to town for the first time. Seeing a sign that said, SPEED LIMIT 35, he started to whip his mule, saying, "Come on, fella, I think we can make it!"

The fastest man I know could turn off the light switch on the wall and be back in bed before the light went out.

"This plane goes to Los Angeles in ten minutes."

"That's moving!"

I've been learning speed reading. Yesterday I read the complete works of Dickens. But then I had nothing to do for the rest of the evening.

I've never been pinched for going too fast, but I've been slapped!

I don't know how fast we were going, but the needle kept pointing toward my beneficiary!

spelling

Long my forte, spelling, as far as I'm concerned, is what separates the men from the boyes!

My kid has such bad handwriting his teachers can't tell if he can spell or not!

"How do you spell 'weather'?"
"W-e-t-h-a-r."

"That's the worst spell of weather I've ever heard!"

A man walked into a Western Union office and said, "I want to send a wire to Atchafalaya."

The clerk said, "How do you spell that?"
"If I could spell it, I'd write a letter!"

They have a little book that contains the hundred words most often misspelled. It works beautifully. My secretary now misspells every one of those words!

If you ask my brother how to spell Mississippi, he'll want to know if you mean the river or the state!

spinsters

A spinster is an old maid with cobwebs!

Here lies Annie Cooper.
For her, death has no terrors.
Born a virgin, died a virgin;
No hits, no runs, no errors!

A spinster hired a young lawyer to assist her in the drawing up of a will. The stipulations were simple: Of the million-dollar estate, a quarter of a million would go to the local classical orchestra, a quarter to the zoo, a quarter to an orphanage, and all but ten thousand dollars of the last quarter million to the Sierra Club.

"What happens to the ten thousand?" the lawyer asked.

The spinster said, "I plan to give that to the man who will help me experience love and passion before I die. If you want to, you can be that man."

Not the richest man in town, the lawyer

went home and discussed the offer with his wife. After all, he indicated, he'd only have to hold the woman's hand and say nice things to her. The wife agreed.

Several hours after the husband returned to the spinster's house, the wife became nervous. She phoned her husband and wanted to know what was going on.

The attorney said, "She's already agreed to forget about the orchestra and the zoo. Give me another hour and I think I can get her away from the orphanage and the Sierra Club."

She didn't look like an old maid. She looked more like an *un*made!

She applied for rape insurance, but the company wouldn't send anybody!

Carrying a package, a spinster walked into a taxidermist's shop. Uncovering the package and revealing two dead cats, she said, "These were my dearest friends. Can you do what it is that you do?"

The taxidermist said, "Would you like them mounted?"

The spinster said, "Oh no, just shaking hands. They were only good friends!"

A spinster finally met the right man. Although she was getting on in years, marriage agreed with her. One day she ran into another spinster, an old friend, and told her, "My honeymoon was like a cruise on a painted ocean. It was glorious."

Hearing this, the other spinster went to work and managed to find herself a husband. On the honeymoon night, they disrobed and got into bed. As the husband started to whisper strange things in her ear, the spinster shrugged. This wasn't what she'd thought it would be. As her husband bit her ear and started to shiver with expectation, she said,

"I don't understand. This isn't like a cruise on a painted ocean."

The groom said, "Bon voyage, my dear. I'm sailing without you!"

There once was a lonesome old spinster
And luck had always been much ag'inst her.
When a man came to burgle,
She yelled, with a gurgle,
"Stop, thief, while I call in a min'ster!"

The burglar said, "Don't scream. I just want your money."

The spinster said, "You're just like all the other men!"

"Did you see the new altar in our church?"
"No, lead me to it!"

He looked at her, and it was love at first sight. But it was the second sight that ruined everything!

Men always wanted her hand in marriage, but the problem was that they had to take the rest of her too!

stocks and bonds

Another one of my early jokes: I was in stocks and bonds. I worked in the stockroom in Bond's!

Two stockbrokers met in a café. Ordering drinks, one said, "Let's not talk shop tonight. Let's talk about women."

The other stockbroker said, "Fine. Common or preferred?"

"I used to be bullish, then I was bearish. Now I'm brokish!"

Yesterday the market went down so fast, three blue-chip stocks turned white!

A stockbroker called a client and said, "Procter & Gamble split today."

The client said, "It's a shame. They've been together so long!"

I don't understand the market. How can you lose your life savings on something called securities?

The market really turned around today. I saw a broker jump out the window, see the computer through another window as he fell, and make a U-turn!

If money is the root of all evil, then the stock market must be the Roto-Rooter!

It makes me shudder. Lots of people drive to their brokers' offices in Rolls-Royces to get financial advice from somebody who came to work in a bus.

When there's a news item about the stock market breaking two thousand, I'm one of them.

I know what it is. In the middle of the night, Dracula comes in and bites my stocks in the neck.

I have a lot of "sweet chariot" stocks. The minute I buy them, they swing low!

stupidity

If "dumb" doesn't cover it, here are some that might!

He's so dumb he put beer in his waterbed so he'd have a foam mattress!

She's so stupid she thinks a boycott is a male bed!

There's a good reason he has a stupid look on his face—he's stupid!

He's so stupid he wants a hernia transplant!

She's so dumb she thinks a mushroom is a place for necking!

He's not bright. He just bought a bicycle with an air conditioner!

Brains aren't everything. In his case they're nothing!

He'll never be too old to learn new ways of being stupid!

He'd have to dip his finger in a glass to see if he had a soft drink!

She has a forty-inch bust and an IQ to match!

He doesn't buy toothpaste because his teeth aren't loose!

He's got more brains in his whole head than most of us have in a little finger!

When he got out of kindergarten he was so excited he could hardly shave!

She has ivory skin and a head to match!

stuttering

Stutterers may be a little sensitive, so I take it easy on them. I give them a little love kick once in a while. Most stutterers have fun with the problem. A friend of mine, a great country singer, can't wait to go on a talk show. Of course, by the time he says hello, the show is over!

A man rushed into the airport and asked, "Where's the plane to San Francisco?"

The man he'd asked said, "It's ggggate nnnni—. Ifff you hadn't asked me, you cccould have been on it!"

A man signed up for sky-diving classes. He learned how to fold a chute, which cords were to be pulled at what time, and all about the vagaries of the wind. Then he asked for a lesson on the exact procedure. The instructor pointed to the ripcord and said, "You count to ten and then you pull this red lever."

The man said, "Wwwwhat wwwwwas ttthat nnnummmbber agggain?"

The instructor said, "Two!"

A man rushed into a sandwich shop and said, "We've got a big meeting going on. Let me have six tuna sandwiches, four ham and cheese, a hamburger, two bacon and tomato, four Cokes, three black coffees, a diet cola, and a tea. I'll be back in ten minutes."

He rushed out.

The counterman said, "Hhhhhello..."

A stammerer sat in the theater watching a hit musical and commenting to a friend about the performances. Finally the man in front of them turned and said, "Sir, I wish you'd keep your comments to yourself. Please stop that hissing!"

The stammerer said, "Who's hisssssinggg? I've been tttttelllinggg my ffffriend how sssensatttional the sssssinging is."

A man stopped another man on the street and asked for directions on how to get downtown. The second man said, "Bbb-buddddy, there are ttttten thoussssand ppp-people in this ttttown who ccccan't talk. Why ddddid you pick on mmme?"

Joe Cohen applied for a job as a radio announcer. He started to read some test copy: "Gggggoooddd mmmorning lllladdies anddd gggentlemmen."

After wincing as he went on, the station manager told Cohen that he wouldn't do.

Cohen became indignant and said, "Tttthey ttttold mmme you wwwouldn't hhhire a JJew."

I know a man who married a girl with a bad stutter so he could get a word in edgewise!

A stutterer is somebody who sssttammmers!

suburbia

We spend our lives saving up money to buy a house in the suburbs. By the time we make it, the suburbs have suburbs. All the houses in the suburbs look alike. I know a man who came home to the wrong house and stayed there three weeks. He got more respect there! He went home when he got an ultimatum to clean out the garage!

A suburban housewife came home from her bridge game to find her husband in bed with a voluptuous lady. The wife bellowed, "What's going on here?"

The husband said, "Don't get excited. This girl was on the road, trying to get a ride. I offered her a ride. She hadn't had anything to eat all day, so I brought her home to feed her. I happened to notice that her clothes were torn, so I gave her that old pair of jeans you don't wear. Her blouse was in bad shape, so I gave her that tailored shirt you haven't worn in five years. She was barefooted, so I gave her those white sandals. You'll never wear them. And then she asked me, "Is there anything else your wife doesn't use anymore?"

The suburbs are a section of town where the houses are farther apart and the payments closer!

When you live in the suburbs, you don't

have to keep hunting for things to do. Just look in any direction.

One suburban housewife was afraid she'd burn the meat, so she put suntan oil on it!

A suburban home is where heat comes out of a vent, water comes out of plastic pipes, and nobody comes out of the bathroom!

Suburbs are where you consolidate all your little bills into one large, impossible one!

The hottest thing in the suburbs is an after-shave lotion that smells like chlorine. It makes the guys in the office think you have a pool!

The suburbs would be great except for one thing—everybody who wanted to get away from it all got away at the same time!

In the suburbs you start out by playing cards, and then you go on to shuffling husbands!

My wife wanted beautiful roses like those next door, so I waited until it got dark...

I live so far out of town, the mailman has to mail me my letters.

I live twenty minutes from the heart of town—by phone!

We don't bother our next-door neighbors in the suburbs. There's a couple next door. They just sit around hugging and kissing and cooing all day long. Two of the nicest guys I've ever met!

They don't have much wife-swapping in our neighborhood. Too many of the guys end up with their own!

There's a lot of sexual hanky-panky going on in the suburbs. I know one area where mouth-to-mouth resuscitation is a second language!

I used to be down in the dumps. Now they're suburbs!

success

Success is two things—luck and pluck. You need luck to find somebody to pluck!

I'd rather be a Could-Be
If I cannot be an Are;
Because a Could-Be is a May-Be
Who might be reaching for a star.
I'd rather be a Has-Been
Than a Might-Have-Been by far,
For a Might-Have-Been has never been
But a Has was once an Are!

For years he looked for the secret of his success, then he finally found the answer—he was not a success!

I borrowed ten thousand from my father-in-law to open a law office, and in no time at all I had a case—my father-in-law sued me for ten thousand!

A lot of people who itch for success never want to scratch for it!

He stays awake nights, trying to figure out how to become successful. Now if he'd only stay awake days!

You can't become a success if you drop the ball and then complain about how the ball bounces!

We might all be able to learn a lesson from the chameleon. Put on a red cloth, he turned red. A blue cloth made him turn blue. On yellow he turned yellow. But one day he put on a plaid cloth and went crazy trying to make good!

Success is relative. The more success, the more relatives!

If at first you do succeed, it's got to be your father's business!

You've got it made when your name is in everything but the phone book!

He worked his fingers to the bone for years. At the end of that time he had very bony fingers!

When opportunity knocks on his front door, he's out in back looking for four-leaf clovers!

suicide

The grimmer the subject, the funnier it can be, I always say. I believe that. People like to laugh at fates worse than their own.

A woman decided to end it all. Borrowing her husband's gun, she shot herself in the breast and blew off her kneecap!

A man goes to a doctor, who examines him and says, "Your drinking days are over. One more shot of whiskey is suicide. You're a dead man."

"But what do I do when I'm edgy?"

"Eat something."

The man renounces drink and is doing well until he's walking home one evening and, glancing into an open window, sees a man hanging himself. The ex-drunk starts to quiver, turns, and runs into the cafeteria on the corner. "Quick," he yells, "give me a tuna sandwich!"

A man checked into an Atlanta hotel. Going straight to his room, he forced open the window, got out on the ledge, and prepared to jump. A policeman rushed up and started to calm him. The policeman said, "Don't jump."

The man said, "I have nothing to live for."

"What about your family? For your family's sake, don't jump."

"I have no family."

"Think of your friends. Don't jump."

"I have no friends."

"Then for the honor of the South and the spirit of Jefferson Davis, don't jump!"

"Who's Jefferson Davis?"

"Jump, Yankee!"

Through an open ground-floor window, a policeman saw a man acting strangely. "What are you doing?" the policeman asked.

"I'm committing suicide."

"Why do you have the rope around your waist?"

"When I put it around my neck, I can't breathe!"

One man I know tried to commit suicide a half-dozen times, but he gave up trying. It was ruining his health!

The cheapest man I knew was the guy who grabbed his shotgun on Christmas Eve, went into another room, pulled the trigger, came running back, and told his kids, "Santa Claus just committed suicide!"

One rich man tried to commit suicide. He jumped off his wallet!

Suicide is the last thing a person should do!

superman

I did a Superman sketch on my television show. To make up for a shortage of muscles on what I foolishly call my body, a whole set of muscles was sewed into my costume. When I came into my dressing room to put the costume on, I couldn't find it hanging in my closet. After searching all over, I finally found it in the back alley, hand-wrestling with a Tarzan costume!

Superman's been wearing that one outfit for fifty years. He's strong—and a little gamy, I think!

As mild-mannered Clark Kent, Superman is afraid of girls. He's worried that he'll run into the one he stole the red-and-blue outfit from!

Superman's strength was beyond measurement. It could only be lost, little by little, if he made love to a mortal woman. Catching him when he'd had a little too much *vino*, Lois Lane took him to her apartment and made love to him. With each expression of love, Superman lost some of his power.

In the morning, Superman woke, got out of bed, walked to the window, lifted the shade, and went up with it!

Now I know why Superman left Krypton. Earth was the only place he could get steroids!

Because of his powerful vision, Superman is unable to pass an eye test. When he looks at an eye chart, he sees through to a billboard in the next county!

Lois Lane is crazy about Superman. On Valentine's Day she sends a card to the phone company!

Superman climbed the Empire State Building and challenged King Kong to a fight. King Kong said, "I don't have time. I have to catch a plane!"

After seeing a Superman movie, a hippie on LSD said to his friend, "That Superman's not so hot. I can fly around a building too." Climbing to the top of a high-rise building on the next block, the hippie got on the ledge of the roof and dove off. He plummeted straight down and luckily landed on the canvas top of a truck, breaking his fall. His friend helped him down to the ground. The first hippie said, "Man, you know I could have been killed. Why didn't you stop me?"

The second hippie said, "Man, I thought you could make it!"

Superman can fly across the country in ten minutes. A little longer if he's on standby!

Superman used to fly across the country much faster. Now he has to go by way of Atlanta!

Flying over the beach at Malibu, Superman looks down and sees Wonder Woman lying on her back in the nude on the white sands. He zooms down and covers her with his body. Wonder Woman opens her eyes and Superman says, "I'll bet you're surprised."

Wonder Woman says, "Not as much as the Invisible Man!"

surgeons

I finally figured out why surgeons wear masks over their faces. If something goes wrong, you don't know whom to blame!

I met a naval surgeon the other day. They really specialize nowadays, don't they?

On one of those magazine TV shows a surgeon operated on a patient, with cameras showing each move on the air. Unfortunately, the patient didn't make it. The surgeon went over to the widow and said, "I'm truly sorry."

The widow said, "Well, that's show business!"

A young surgeon was feeling rather inadequate. Having just lost a patient, he told another surgeon, "I don't know if I was cut out to be a surgeon."

"You're a fine surgeon."

"I'm not even going to send them a bill."

"Maybe you *weren't* cut out to be a surgeon!"

A surgeon liked to have his patients up and about as fast as possible. On the eve of a surgery, he told one patient, "Ten minutes after the operation, I'll put you on your feet. Twenty minutes after the surgery, you'll walk around the room. In a half hour, you'll walk around the entire floor."

The patient said, "Doctor, is it okay if I lie down for the operation?"

The surgeon asked the new nurse, "Are my instruments boiled?"

The nurse said, "How can I tell?"

The surgeon said, "Stick a fork in them!"

A man went to a surgeon for a penile transplant. Some time later, he told the friend who'd recommended the surgery that the new part wasn't doing him any good. The friend said, "They must have given you my old one!"

A college coed asked her surgeon, "How soon will I know anything when I come out of a recovery room?"

The surgeon said, "You're expecting a lot from a recovery room!"

The surgeon made a slight mistake and cut off Kemp's leg, the wrong one. When Kemp awoke, the surgeon said, "I have bad news for you—we took off the wrong leg. But I also have good news—the other leg is getting better!"

Surgeons can perform wonders. One operated on a tone-deaf man and had him playing a harp in two days!

The surgeon was apologetic. "We amputated your good leg by mistake. So we had to remove your infected leg too. But there's some good news also. The orderly wants to buy your shoes!"

I got a little shaky at my last surgery. Before the anesthesia worked on me, I could hear the surgeon singing, "De knee bone connected to the thigh bone. De thigh bone connected..."

I like to go to East Side General, because that's where all the truck drivers get operated on!

suspicion

I'm a very trusting man, but I do become a little suspicious when I walk into a bank and everybody inside is doing business lying down!

I'm suspicious when my next-door neighbor tells me that the men in the moving van said, "Thanks!"

The holy day of Yom Kippur is a day of fasting. Abramowitz suspected that his friend Schwartz wasn't fasting, even though Schwartz bragged about his ability to do without food. After four hours of solid prayer, Schwartz sidled out of the synagogue. His suspicious friend followed him. Sure enough, Schwartz headed for a restaurant around the block. Abramowitz hid behind a large potted palm. When the waiter arrived, Schwartz ordered a dozen oysters. As soon as they were brought, Abramowitz jumped from behind the potted palm and said, "Is this how you fast? To even make matters worse, look at what you've ordered—oysters!"

Schwartz said, "What's the matter? Yom Kippur has an *r* in it!"

I'm suspicious when a three-hundred-pound man knocks on my door and says he's the Fuller fat man!

I'm suspicious if a man wakes me up in the middle of the night and says he can guess my weight!

I'm suspicious if there's a SWAT team at my house and a real-estate agent is showing people around!

I'm suspicious when I come home and find my guppy gagged and bound!

A garment manufacturer took out fire insurance on a Monday. The same day, his factory burned down. A little suspicious, the insurance agent said, "You took out insurance at ten this morning. The fire was at noon. Can you explain the delay?"

swimming

I think I was an unloved child. They gave me drowning lessons!

Somebody I know just married a great swimmer. She should be—for years she was a streetwalker in Venice!

There's nothing like running to the beach, jumping into the water, and letting the waves brush over you. There's nothing like it. So why do it?

I know one stroke. If I go in over my head, I get one!

A man recently swam the English Channel. Asked to explain his secret, he said, "Every time I got tired, they threw water in my face!"

Surfing must be a religion to some kids. They do it kneeling!

I'm a little wary of people who use my pool. When I filled it, I put in ten thousand gallons. Later in the year I emptied it and took out eleven thousand!

A small child slipped and fell overboard. A body hurtled over the rail of the liner and saved the child. Coming back on board, the man who'd swum to the child was cheered by the other passengers. The captain said, "What can we do for you?"

The man said, "Tell me who pushed me!"

A Southern lady called the army post and said, "It's very warm. I wouldn't mind if you sent over a half-dozen young soldiers to swim in my pool. However, I wouldn't want any young men of the Hebrew faith."

An hour later, six black GIs appeared at the front door. The Southern lady said, "There must be some mistake."

One of the black GIs said, "No, ma'am. Captain Goldstein doesn't make mistakes!"

sympathy

A sympathizer, I've discovered, is a guy who's all for you as long as it doesn't cost anything!

A man who'd obviously had more than one or two got on a subway car. People started to suggest that he be put off at the next station. One man stopped the vigilantes and said, "Let him sit down."

The drunk nodded to him and, sitting down, said, "I can tell you're a man who knows what it means to be smashed!"

"**D**addy, what's sympathy?"
"That's what you give someone when you
   don't want to lend him money!"

A man was invited to a wake for somebody whom he hardly knew except for a few words at work. The man put on his dark suit and headed for the home of the deceased. By mistake, he went to the same house number, but on the wrong side of town. 116 *West Nineteenth Street*, where he ended up, was a brothel. The man asked the madam where he should go. She told him to go upstairs. Upstairs, he was greeted by a lovely young lady. Taking off her clothes, she proceeded to make love to him. When they were through, the man went downstairs. The madam asked him to make a contribution, like all the visitors. The man gave her the requested money, then shook her hand and said, "I hope we meet again under happier circumstances!"

synagogues

For some reason, average audiences don't go to pieces for "synagogue" or "rabbi" jokes. I suspect that a Jewish audience perks up its ears and becomes suspicious. Gentile audiences don't seem to know much about the Jewish faith. However, with an ethnic crowd, one good story about the synagogue works well. Three or more cause those ears to shoot up!

Jewish temples earn money for salaries and upkeep by selling tickets to the special prayers said as Jews welcome in their New Year. A man is stationed at the door of the temple to check for tickets.

This one season, a man came to the door and asked to be allowed in. The guard said, "Where's your ticket?"

The man said, "I don't have a ticket, but I must talk to my brother."

"You must have a ticket."

"It's very important for me to talk to my brother."

The guard relented. "All right, go in and find him, but don't let me catch you praying!"

During the holiest day of the year, a businessman went to the synagogue. During a special prayer in which communion with the Lord is supposed to be closest, the businessman prayed, "Lord, please make my two hundred thousand shares of stock in the phone company go up. See if you can double the price of my four hundred thousand shares of airline stock. I own this company in Alabama. Could you arrange a buy-out of my six million shares?

Going on to ask for changes that would make him a millionaire many times over, his status at the moment being that of a millionaire only a few times over, the businessman offered great sums to the temple.

On the way out, after the end of the ceremony, the businessman's attention was diverted to a man still at prayer. "Lord," the man said, "help this poor sinner. Let me make enough of a living to feed my family. Just enough for a new suit, shoes, maybe a shirt."

The businessman reached into his pocket, took out a wad of bills, peeled off several of them, and tossed them at the praying man, saying, "Don't bother God with that little stuff!"

T

tackiness

I admire people with couth. I admire people who know what couth is so that they're aware when they're being un!

He's so tacky they won't sell him a first-class plane ticket!

The only uplifted thing about her is her bust!

He's so tacky he can pin himself to the wall!

A woman went to a garage sale. Picking up a broken knife, she asked the price. The owner said brusquely, "That'll be a penny!"

The woman retorted, "Just for that, I won't even make you an offer!"

Tackiness is buying a large car when you can finally afford to buy a small one!

Tackiness is serving your guests a lot of beer and putting an "out of order" sign on the bathroom door!

Tackiness is throwing cigarette butts in a urinal. It makes them so hard to light!

Tackiness is hand-washing used Kleenex!

Tackiness is calling the ruler of a foreign country "Queenie," especially if you don't know him!

tact

Tact is simply being able to explain why you're wearing brown shoes and a tux at the wedding!

A lieutenant was brilliant in military matters, but lacked a few social graces. One day he called a soldier into the office and said, "Kramer, your grandmother died."

The soldier fell apart. After he left, the colonel told the lieutenant, "You could have been a little more tactful. I have some books home that could help you."

The lieutenant read the half-dozen books lent him by the colonel and was ready for the next crisis. Private Taylor's grandfather had passed away. The next morning, at reveille, the lieutenant said, "Men, how many of you have a grandfather still living? Not so fast, Private Taylor!"

The young man put the engagement ring on his fiancée's finger. Studying it, the fiancée said, "I feel sorry for all my girlfriends who don't have twenty-twenty eyesight!"

A customer said to a topless waitress, "I'd like a dozen oysters, but can you bring them one at a time?"

It was definitely late. The host and hostess would have given anything to be rid of their last two guests. The hostess came up with a good hint. Looking at her watch, she said,

"Who cares about time when good friends are together. Why, it's only two twenty-seven and nineteen seconds!"

The other day my car was banged up while it was in a parking lot, but the perpetrator was pretty tactful. I couldn't get sore when I read his note: "I banged up the back of your car. I'll never do it again!"

It hadn't been the best of evenings. As they were leaving, the visitors said, "Shall we get together again soon?"

The host said, "Sure, we must get together soon. Have a nice summer!"

Two mercenaries were about to be shot. One said, "I think I'll ask for a blindfold."

The other said, "Don't make trouble!"

A florist finished making deliveries and stopped off in a coffee shop. As he sat there, three bikers right out of a biker movie came in. Garbed in black leather, with tattoos running the length of their arms, the bikers looked at the mild-mannered florist and tried to get him riled. They made fun of his pink shirt. They threatened him in a dozen ways. He smiled at them, finished his coffee and pie, and started out. The bikers followed him out. In the parking area, they again tried to get him to put up his fists. He walked away. Laughing at him, the bikers strode back into the coffee shop.

A few minutes later, a man who'd witnessed the taunting outside came into the diner and said, "That guy wasn't much of a fighter. I'll tell you something else, too. He isn't much of a driver either. He just ran his van over three bikes!"

A young man went off on vacation, leaving his dog with a brother who still lived at home with his mother. Lonely for his dog, the young man called from another country and asked about his dog. The brother said, "He keeled over and died."

The young man was distraught. "How could you say it so coldly? I'm your brother. We're close. Instead of blurting it out, you should have prepared me. You should have said, 'Your dog was taking a walk on the roof. A wind came up and blew him off the roof.' I mean, you could have broken it to me slowly. Now tell me—how's Mama?"

"Well, last night she was taking a walk on the roof . . ."

The young lady was trying to be nice to the dullest date she'd ever been with, saying, "No, I can't go out with you Sunday night. I'm expecting a severe headache!"

"Who's that ugly man over there?"
"My brother."
"Really? There's no family resemblance!"

talking and talkers

Not quite in the line of orators or the great speechifiers, talkers, of which there always must be one or two at a dinner, should be shown no mercy!

The other day she opened her mouth and a foot fell out.

He can talk out of both sides of his mouth at the same time. He can even give himself mouth-to-mouth resuscitation.

A farmer came home from town very late in the evening. His wife asked what had kept him, and he said, "Well, I picked up Parson Brown, and from then on my mules didn't understand a word I said!"

A customer walked down the row of birds for sale in a pet shop. Passing one macaw, he heard the bird speak. The customer asked, "Hey, can you speak, stupid?"

The bird replied, "You bet. Can you fly, dummy?"

A man bought an expensive parrot. Bringing it home, he spoke to it nicely in hopes that the bird would start to talk. Each morning the man would pass the cage and say cheerfully, "Good morning. How are you?"

The bird refused to respond. It even looked away when it saw the man coming.

After many weeks, the man became discouraged. One day he walked by the cage and didn't say his usual cheerful greeting. The bird looked at him and said, "Well, well! And what's wrong with you this morning?"

A husband answered the phone, "No, I'm afraid she's not in at the moment. Who shall I say was going to listen?"

She'd demand the last word with an echo!

He took her to see *Aïda*. Showing a keen love of music, she talked through every aria, duet, and chorus. After the performance, as they were walking out, she said, "I'd love to see *Carmen* next week."

He said, "That might be nice. I haven't heard you in that yet."

The mother said to the little girl, "You mustn't talk all the time, dear."

The little girl said, "When will I be old enough to?"

He not only holds a conversation, he strangles it!

Speaking of speaking, she's generally speaking!

She's a politician—the speaker of the house!

He has a problem. He has to feed six small mouths and listen to one big one.

He's a man of few words, but he keeps repeating them.

He's got a gift of gab. He should exchange it for a shirt.

After having heard a thousand speeches, I suspect that many people die from elocution.

A nonstop speaker who hadn't heard a word anybody had said for years, Mrs. Calhoun went to the doctor. He examined her and told her that she was going deaf. "What would cause that?" she asked.

The doctor answered, "It could be lack of practice!"

When he speaks, he doesn't know what to do with his hands. He might try putting them over his mouth.

He talks a lot because of heredity. His mother was a woman.

After all is said and done, he keeps talking!

tallness

The bigger they are, the harder they fall. Unfortunately, you're never told who they fall on!

He's so tall, six months a year he goes around with snow on his head!

She was very tall for a woman. She was also tall for a tree!

He's so tall his lap is under him!

He's so tall his shadow has to have a hinge!

It's great to have a very tall friend. I'd want him walking by if I lived on the second floor and the house was on fire!

A visitor went to the circus winter headquarters. He knocked on the door of a trailer. The door was opened by a midget. The visitor said, "I'm sorry. Doesn't the giant live here?"

The midget said, "That's me. I've been ill."

He's so tall he has to stand on his brother to shave!

In his stocking feet he's almost seven feet tall. Without him, his stocking feet are five-six.

A man walked along a beach and saw a strangely shaped bottle. Rubbing it, he was stunned as a genie emerged. The genie said, "You have found a magic bottle. I will grant you any wish you ask for."

The man, rather ashamed of a certain part of his anatomy, asked that it be enlarged. The genie made several motions, said several words, and disappeared. Looking down at his groin, the man watched as the wish started to come true. Unfortunately, the growing member kept growing and growing. The man grabbed at the magic bottle and rubbed it again. The genie reappeared and said, "You can now have a second wish. Think it over."

The man said, "I don't have to think it over."

The genie said, "I know. You want to be returned to the way you were."

"No," the man said, "I just want longer legs!"

He was a big baby. In the delivery room they had to open the window so all of him could come out!

When he walked around with his head in the clouds, they were real clouds!

His mother was tall. His father was tall. His two brothers were tall. He even had a canary with an eight-foot wingspan!

taxes

There are some strong tax jokes in the section titled "Income Taxes and the IRS." Think of the section below as an audit!

I don't understand the government. When I was a kid I walked two miles to school every day. Then the government taxed us for a schoolbus. The bus got us to school in five minutes. Then the government taxed us for a new gymnasium so the kids could get exercise!

The word *syntax* scares my son. How can he pay that tax when he can't even afford to put gas in his car?

I go to a good accountant. He saves me time—five, ten years!

There are tax advantages for people over sixty-five. Now how do you get a woman to apply?

With withholding being what it is, many people are willing to trade their checks for the withholding.

On April 15, you count your blessings and then send them to Washington.

My son thinks "damn" and "taxes" are one word!

A tax auditor went to a home for a meeting. The door was opened by a girl of ten. Seeing who it was, she called up to her mother, "Ma, It's the tax man."

The mother called in, "Give him a chair."

The girl said, "If that's not enough, should I give him the couch and the table too?"

I hate taxes. Every time my ship comes in, the government unloads it!

The owner of a small sandwich shop is brought before the tax people because of certain deductions. The auditor wants an explanation for the deduction of two trips to Greece as business expenses. Going on, the auditor also wants an explanation for a week in Paris, four days in Capri, and a weekend in Bermuda. "You have a small sandwich shop," the auditor protests. "How can you deduct these trips?"

The owner of the shop says, "We deliver!"

The average citizen works six months a year for the government. Government employees don't work six months a year for the government!

On the first page of a tax return are spaces for personal information. I think of them as foreplay.

The government is always looking for ways of making the tax forms easier. Next year, they're coming out with one you can just color in!

Taxation is based on supply and demand. We supply when the government demands!

A woman walked into a tax office and said to the supervisor, "What did you do with the money I gave you last year?"

I just sent the government a big check. Thank heaven, I'm all paid up through 1952!

I just filled out income tax forms. Who says you can't get killed by a blank?

Last year there were two ways of filing your income tax, and they were both wrong!

I know a Christian Scientist who took a strange deduction on his taxes—he took off a speed-reading class as a medical expense!

teachers

As part of a school revue in the Professional Children's School, we did a sketch about a teacher and a class of wild students. I had two big jokes in the sketch:

Teacher: Where was the Declaration of Independence signed?

Me: On the bottom!

Teacher: How can you say that? Don't you go to school, stupid?

Me: Yup, and I come out the same way!

A teacher wrote home to a student's parents, "If you don't believe half of what he says goes on in school, I won't believe half of what he says goes on at home."

The teacher said, "Tom, tell me where you got that gum."

"I don't think I should, Teach."

"I want to know."

"Okay, I got it under your desk."

A teacher was asked to fill out a special questionnaire for the state. One question said, "Give two reasons for entering the teaching profession." The teacher wrote, "July and August."

Some kids want to know why the teachers get paid when it's the kids who have to do all the work!

One teacher recently retired with a half-million dollars after thirty years of working hard, caring, dedicating herself, and totally immersing herself in the problems of the students. That gave her fifty dollars. The rest came from the death of a rich uncle.

The teachers were being feted by a number of business groups in the neighborhood. At the end of his welcoming speech, the head of the Chamber of Commerce said, raising his wineglass, "Long live our teachers!"

From a back table, a voice said, "On what?"

A young boy ran up to his teacher with tears in his eyes. The teacher asked, "What's wrong, dear?"

The boy said, "I just found out I'll be in school until I'm eighteen."

The teacher said, "That's not a problem. I have to stay here until I'm sixty-five!"

A teacher took her class to a museum. As they walked in, one youngster told the others, "Don't look at too much. If you do, we'll have to talk about it in class later!"

The teacher asked, "How many of you children want to go to heaven?"

All but one boy raised their hands. He said, "I can't. I have to go home right after school."

She's an unemployed schoolteacher. She has no class!

Two teachers were sharing class problems. Talking about one specific boy, one teacher said, "I don't know what to make of him."

The other teacher said, "How about a rug?"

In some high schools, teachers have a lot of respect for their students. That's because the students are older than they are!

When I was in school, one of my teachers was crazy about me. I once heard her tell another teacher, "I wish he was my kid for one day!"

I once played hooky from school. My teacher sent a thank-you note!

I just read about a schoolteacher who got hurt. She was grading papers on a curve!

I used to like young teachers. It was fun watching them age!

teenagers

I have the perfect cure for teenagers. Keep them locked up, opening the door only once a day to throw in some raw meat. When they get to be twenty, throw in the usual food ration and a member of the opposite sex. Let them out only if you hear "Oh, Promise Me" coming from inside. Or the "Wedding March" from Lohengrin *being played loudly on a synthesizer!*

It's hard for a teenger to concede that someday he'll be as stupid as his father.

A teenager is a young person who goes steady before his voice does.

Karen's date arrived promptly at eight. Opening the door, Kathy, the younger sister, called up to Karen, getting ready in her room, "Your bird-in-the-hand is here!"

A teenager told his date, "Remember, we have to get out of here at exactly ten dollars!"

A male teenager has problems. He's too old to say anything cute, and he isn't old enough to say anything intelligent!

A teenage girl had been using a beauty cream that was guaranteed to make her lovelier in thirty days. After three and a half weeks, there was no evident change. Her girlfriend said, "Maybe it all happens on the last day!"

A teenage girl said to her mother, "Don't yell at me. I'm not your husband!"

It's amazing. One day you look at your phone bill and realize they're teenagers!

My son never took mind-expanding drugs. I can tell by his grades!

A teenage boy said to a friend, "My pop wants me to have everything he didn't have when he was a kid—like passing grades!"

Marge, aged ten, was showing her friend Marie about the house. Coming to a bedroom, she indicated, "This is my sister's room. It would be a nice room for me, but she's nineteen and she never got married!"

My teenage son took a job aptitude test. The report came back that he was best suited for early retirement!

With teenagers around, it's not having another mouth to feed that bothers a father. It's having another mouth to listen to!

A teenager came to his father and said, "Dad, don't you think it's time I stood on my own two feet?"

"I do."

"I have to face the world and handle my own problems."

"Of course."

"I must make my own way."

"I buy that."

"Well, I can't do it on the allowance I get now!"

There's a new early-warning system for teenage pregnancies. It's called a date!

They now have a teenager doll. You wind it up and it resents you for it!

My teenage niece used to spend the whole day on the phone with her boyfriends. When she finally got married, the phone company retired her number!

Teenagers are something. Their jeans are Calvin Klein. Their shoes are Gucci. They have Louis Vuitton purses. And they yell at their parents, "I want to be me!"

My teenage son is really trying to get a job. Before he goes out on an interview he always shines his sneakers!

My son keeps saying he wants to find himself. The trouble is that he's not lost!

Most airlines let teenagers fly for half-price. That's dumb. The teenagers are the only ones with money!

There's one good thing about having teenagers in the house. Your bathroom mirror will never be stolen!

My wife told me to talk to my son, so last night I had a man-to-it talk with him!

If all the teenagers who slept in class were laid end to end, they'd be a lot more comfortable!

My teenage son has an incredible appetite. We took him to a Chinese restaurant the other night and the owner had to send out for more rice!

Teenage marriages don't last. My nephew and his bride were divorced so quickly, they had to fight over who got the acne lotion!

teeth

I was sixteen. I had the guts of a riverboat gambler. I couldn't wait for a situation where I'd be able to summon up one of my ad libs. One of the first situations was where I'd fumble or mispronounce a word, so I could ad-lib, "How do you like that? I had an eyetooth pulled. Now I can't see what I'm saying!" The moment came. I mispronounced a word, moved ahead, and said, "How do you like that? I had an ear tooth pulled..." Only my mother, in row six, laughed. The joke, or what made a noise like a joke, was retired for years. Of course, by then I'd fallen in love with another ad lib for the mispronounced word or phrase. I'd say, "How do you like that? I had my nose fixed. Now my mouth doesn't work!" Feel free to try either one at your own risk!

Men loved her buck teeth. It gave them a place to hang their hats!

She was so bucktoothed—she could eat corn through a Venetian blind!

She didn't have many teeth. When she smiled, she looked like a graveyard!

She didn't really have buck teeth. Her teeth were straight. She had buck *gums!*

Her front teeth were so far apart they could get severance pay!

His teeth are so bucked, when he smiles he combs his mustache!

She had thirty-two beautiful white teeth—and that was just on top!

She had one tooth, but it came in handy—for opening beer bottles!

One stroke of her lipstick brought out her lips. One good sneeze brought out her teeth!

"How do you get a pair of new teeth like that?"
"You go into somebody's backyard and kick a strange dog!"

She had so many cavities she talked with an echo!

No one knew she had an upper plate till it came out in the conversation!

Her teeth were like stars. They came out at night!

She had so much bridgework, when you kissed her you had to pay a toll!

His teeth look like the front porch when you forget to stop milk deliveries on your vacation!

I went to the dentist because of trouble with my bite. I still want to!

I wonder—is a bicuspid a gay dentist?

She has a mouthful of tooth!

She has one tooth in her mouth. She gives a fellow a hickey with a hole in the middle!

telegrams

My favorite wire came from a President. It said, "Congratulations on your eightieth birthday. If you can read this without glasses, you're only seventy-nine!"

Do you want to drive somebody crazy? Send him a telegram saying, "Disregard first telegram."

I like a girl who only says "stop" when she's sending a wire!

A man phoned in a wire to his partner on vacation, saying, "Business dropped dead. Our loan was called in. The new backers chickened out. We can't even pay the light bill."
The operator said, "Shall I read it back to you?"
The man said, "No, it'll only make me cry!"

I like to send telegrams to aggravate people. On top I write, "Page Two."

A bellboy came to room 120 and knocked on the door. From behind the door, a man called out and asked who was there. "I have a telegram for you, sir," the bellhop said.
The man said, "Slide it under the door."
The bellboy said, "I can't. It's on a tray!"

telephones

Telephoning is like getting married. You don't always end up with the right party!

The first bathtub was used in 1850. The phone wasn't invented until 1875. A lucky guy could have spent twenty-five years in the tub without the phone ringing once!

Two of the cleaning crew were straightening out the airline office when one noticed that there were still some numbers lit on the switchboard. The other cleaner said, "Don't worry about that. When they go home they always leave a couple of people on hold!"

Phone service is terrible. I used to be able to get a wrong number in no time at all!

A man was arrested. He was given the usual courtesy—one phone call or thirty days, whichever came first.

The phone company deserves a rate hike. Who else can pay for those "out of order" signs?

He's rather shy. His answering machine says, "Hello. I'm in right now, but you probably don't want to talk to me."

The new receptionist wasn't brilliant. The operator said, "Long distance from California."
The new receptionist said, "It certainly is." Then she hung up!

They now have a special Dial-a-Prayer number for atheists. You call it and nobody answers!

We'll soon be able to see people at the other end of the phone. The phone company is also working on something that can make us *hear* them, too!

Think of it this way—your telephone is another man's wrong number!

A voice on the telephone said to the information operator, "Zalman! Zalman! No, not Calman! Zalman. *Z*, not *C*. ABCDEFGHIJKLMNOPQRSTUVWXY-Z!"

Mrs. Carter picked up the phone to hear an anguished voice on the other end of the line saying, "Ma, this has been the worst day of my life. I'm going crazy. The kids are all sick and home from school. I haven't a thing in the house. I have a doctor's appointment. I'm going out of my mind!"

"I'll come over," Mrs. Carter said, "but I don't know why Victor can't take care of the kids."

"Who's Victor?"

"Your husband."

"My husband's name is Alan."

"You must have the wrong number."

"Oh, does that mean you're not coming over?"

Joe Grey was furious as the private detective briefed him on what Mrs. Grey had been doing for entertainment. What aggravated Joe the most was the fact that at this very moment his wife was carrying on in his home, in his very own bedroom. Thanking the detective, who ushered himself out, Joe dialed the house. The butler answered. Joe said, "Don't ask any questions. I just want you to get my shotgun. Go into the bedroom and blast the two people in bed. Do it right now!"

Ten minutes later, Joe called the house and asked the butler, "Did you do it?"

The butler said, "Yes, sir."

"What did you do with the gun?"

"I threw it in the pool."

"What pool? I don't have a—Is this 555-0437?"

I knew an operator who had three close calls!

Luft was having trouble getting the long-distance operator to understand him. For the tenth time he tried to get her to hear that he was calling Mrs. Luft. Finally he decided to spell it out, saying, "*L* as in 'long,' *U* as in 'up,' *F* as in 'Frank,' *T*."

The operator said, *T* as in what?"

A man was having a great deal of trouble with his phone. After talking to a dozen people at the company, he finally blew his stack and said to the last party, "Why don't you take your phone and shove it?"

"Sir, you can't talk that way to us! You shouldn't even have a phone. I'm going to see that it's picked up!"

Within an hour, two burly phone company repairmen appeared at his door. The man asked to make one call. Dialing, he said into the phone, "Are you the lady I told to take the phone and shove it?"

"Yes, I am."

"Get ready. They're bringing the phone!"

Alexander Graham Bell worked day and night, night and day, trying to perfect his telephone. Finally he got the currents and voltages perfect. Nervously he rang the first number. A voice answered, "I'm not in right now, but if you'll leave your name..."

I read about a woman who used the phone for the first time in forty years. That's what happens if you have teenagers in the house!

Phone service is getting real slow. I called my house from Las Vegas, took a plane back to California, a cab to my house in Beverly Hills, and got home in time to hear the phone start to ring!

The telephone rings.
"Hello."
"Hello, is this Joe?"
"This is Joe."
"It doesn't sound like Joe."
"Well, it's Joe."
"You're sure?"
"Yes, I'm sure."
"Okay. Joe, this is Tom. I need two hundred dollars."
"I'll tell Joe when he gets in."

They now have a special number for atheists. You dial a number and somebody crosses his fingers for you!

A Scotsman went into a phone booth and called a number. Connected, he said, "Mary, my love, will you marry me? Think it over and call me." He gave her the number of the phone in the booth.

Hours went by and the Scotsman stood around. The phone didn't ring once. Another Scot, watching from a pub across the street, came over and said, "Look, lad. She won't marry you. You might as well come in and have a pint. Not that I'm buying, mind you."

The waiting Scot waved off his friend and continued to wait. Suddenly the phone rang. The Scot said, "Mary's the girl for me, I knew that. She was waiting for the night rates!"

When I come home, I can always tell when my wife just left. The phone is still warm!

How far do you stand from the phone to make a long-distance call?

television

It wasn't too hard to get the name "Mr. Television." I had the only set! Because I was involved with early television and seem to have helped make it popular, one network gave me a lifetime contract. It ran out ten years ago!

I did a lot to help the sales of TV sets. When I went on, my brother sold his, my sister sold hers . . .

They have a great new device for TV weathermen. It's called a window.

Since they've stopped cigarette advertising, my TV set has put on thirty pounds.

If you think TV is bad, go to the movies and you'll see how bad it'll be two years from now!

My TV set just went back to the store for an adjustment. It needed five back payments!

In the old days of TV, there were always lots of lines across the screen. In one football game, I saw a guy get thrown for a twelve-hundred-yard loss!

The day before Noah left in the Ark, the local TV weatherman predicted that it would be cloudy!

Television gets worse every season. It's now ten years ahead of schedule!

When I was a kid, I used to see two movies for a dime. Now I have a six-hundred-dollar color TV set, and what do I see? The same old movies!

I can say one thing for TV—it's dirt cheap!

I used to think my wife and I were perfectly matched, then one day the TV set broke down and we had to talk!

My brother isn't lazy. He gets out of bed every night to watch the late show!

Television is the most effective pesticide for the reading bug!

I know kids who are so dumb they flunked educational TV!

I like pay TV. They *should* pay you for watching it!

Most TV shows are so dull they should have a yawn track!

A man goes to a brothel. He's invited for some free pleasure by the madam. Not a man to insult a free offer, the gent joins a young lady for some pleasure. The next day he returns and is told by the madam, "To-night you will have to pay a hundred dollars."
The man says, "But last night it was free."
The madam says, "Last night you were on television!"

I have an idea. Let's send all of the families used in TV testing on a vacation. When the ratings come in, everything'll be canceled!

The trouble with turning off the TV is that none of us remembers what we used to do before it came along!

Shows are so bad, my TV set listens to the radio!

Television is educational. It helped my repairman's son through two colleges!

Millions wouldn't buy the talent on TV, and I'm one of those millions!

tennis

The way I see it, anybody who wants to jump over a three-foot net should take up track!

There are supposed to be three million tennis players in the United States. Actually, there are nine players. The rest are waiting for a court!

A wife watched her husband play tennis and told a friend, "He's getting in shape. He doesn't turn purple until the second set now!"

My wife loves tennis and anything else that calls for an argument!

"I just adore tennis. I could play like this forever."
"You will, if you don't take lessons!"

"When was the first tennis game?"
"When Moses served in Pharoah's court!"

Tennis champs are getting so young they give autographs in crayon!

Tennis isn't a matter of life and death. It's more important than that!

My wife always hits the ball into the net on her first serve. She doesn't want to get cheated out of a second shot!

I once got the ball over in my first serve. They sent the ball out for drug analysis!

I won't say I played badly, but I lost the last game 800–love!

I play tennis so badly my opening serve is match point!

The Russians took up tennis about twenty years ago. They already play a good game at the *nyet!*

texas and texans

When in doubt and it looks as if the audience is about to attack you, pull out a joke about Texas or a Texan. Should you feel the hot breath of the Texas Rangers on your neck, a simple reworking will let you do the same jokes about rich Arabs, people in Beverly Hills, or stock-market billionaires. That the extreme is funny is proven here again. And Texas is all extremes rolled into one! An extreme is when a Texas kid wants a candy bar, so his father has the corner saloon dipped in chocolate!

It was one of those typical Texas kitchens—seven rooms!

"**I'm** heading for Texas, where men are men and women are women."
"You should fit in there somewhere!"

I just got a "Dear John" letter from a girl in the Panhandle. She can't see me for dust!

A Texan dictated a will to his attorney: "To my son I leave ten million dollars, and he should be glad I didn't cut him off entirely!"

A Texan was escorting an Englishman through one leg of the Englishman's trip through the Lone Star State. Pointing off to one of the endless plains, the Texan said,

"You know, your whole country could fit into one corner of Texas."
The Englishman said, "Yes, and it would do wonders for the place."

What's the use of being a Texan if you're small?

On Christmas, children in Texas sit on Santa's lap and ask him what he needs!

A rich lady in Texas called out to her children, "Get in the car, kids. I'm going to drive you to the backyard so you can play!"

I know a Texan who has his own unlisted telephone company.

A showgirl met a rich Texan and asked, "How much did you say your name is?"

The Rio Grande is so shallow the lifeguards just have to know how to wade!

One Texan asked about buying Hollywood because his son wanted to study the stars!

A Texan went to his car dealer and said, "No new car this week. Just redo the inside of this one. Take out the pool and put in a tennis court."

I know a Texan who bought a Toyota so he could get around in his limo!

One Texan was so sentimental he had his kid's nursery bronzed!

A Texas oilman's wife developed a craving for mints. He bought her Fort Knox!

Texas is one large state. One Texan returned to Brownsville at the southern end of the state and ran into a friend at the airport. The friend asked, "Where you been?"

"Up to Fort Worth."

"Enjoy it?"

"Not much. I never did like Yankees!"

One Texan gave his kid a cowboy outfit—a ten-thousand-acre ranch!

Texas oilmen aren't the biggest spenders in the world. The wives of Texas oilmen are!

I know a Texan who only carries two thousand in cash with him. That's not too shabby for a four-year-old!

I know a Texan who has bookcases just for his bank books!

When a rich Texan was getting ready to go on a trip, his wife asked him for something in silk. He brought her a jockey.

A Texan and his wife were on vacation in Europe. While in Paris they stopped off at an art gallery and bought several paintings for their friends, paintings by major artists like Matisse and van Gogh. Writing a check for nine hundred thousand dollars, the husband said to his wife, "Now that we've got the postcards, let's go buy gifts for everybody."

For a while, Texans fell on hard times, but they refused to concede a recession. One Texan merely explained, "We're having the poorest boom in years!"

You must have heard of the Texan who inherited ten million dollars and ran it into a small fortune!

It gets so cold in the Panhandle, the snow turns blue!

Parts of Texas are so flat you can look farther than you can see!

A Texan's marine detachment was surrounded by a large contingent of the enemy. A bullet smashed into the Texan's leg. When the enemy started to withdraw, the Texan started after them. His commanding officer said, "Hold it, Tex. You got blood pouring out of your wound."

The Texan said, "Don't stop me, Captain. I think I know who did it!"

To get to Texas from California, you head east until you can smell it and southeast until you put your foot in it!

A Texan heard about car pools, so he had one installed in his station wagon!

You don't know how big Texas is until you try to unfold a map of the state in your car!

Texans have a simple formula for success: get up with the birds, work until you fall down, and in between, strike oil!

One Texan named his ranch the Running Lazy Z Double Circle Crossing Trails Ranch. He almost went out of business the first year. None of his cattle survived the branding!

A Texan went to Rome and saw the Fountain of Trevi. He didn't have a coin, so he threw in a check!

One Texan has a property that produces five hundred barrels a day. No oil, just barrels!

Towing a large cabin cruiser, a Texan pulled up to a fancy hotel in a big city. The doorman said, "Sir, what are you going to do with that?"

"Sail it."

"But there's no lake around here."

The Texan indicated back down the street and said, "It's coming!"

A churchgoing Texan thinks that when he dies he'll be allowed to stay in Texas!

The siege of the Alamo was in full swing. Jim Bowie tried to perk up the others, saying, "We're God-fearing folks, and we've been praying to Him and He won't let us down."

One of the other men said, "The Mexicans pray to God in Spanish, asking for help."

Jim Bowie said, "Now, you know God wouldn't understand Spanish!"

thanksgiving

We're having the same thing this year for Thanksgiving dinner as last year—relatives!

Last year we had a frozen turkey. For the first two hours in the stove he enjoyed it!

Last year we had Thanksgiving dinner at a roadside diner. I had to say grace over grease!

The Puritans celebrated Thanksgiving because they were saved from the Indians. Lately I think we've been celebrating because we were saved from the Puritans.

The first turkeys weren't wild. They just went crazy when they found out what we planned to do with them.

Last Thanksgiving, my wife cooked the turkey in a microwave oven. We had to eat at seven-thirty in the morning.

Using a new recipe, my wife put the turkey in aluminum foil. She had to roast it until it was brown. Twenty hours later, the aluminum foil was still silver.

Our last turkey was so tough, when we closed the oven door, it blew out the pilot light!

Our turkey was sick. All day long it had a thermometer in it.

We had a turkey for Thanksgiving dinner. He sat on my right.

Aunt Margaret said to little Alvin, "Would you like some more stuffing?"

Alvin said, "Nope. And I don't know why the turkey eats it either!"

I always eat too much of everything on Thanksgiving. If they have a gas war the next day, it'll be me!

I won't say this has been a trying year, but this is the first Thanksgiving we had a turkey that volunteered!

theater

The first time I walked out on the stage of a theater, I was hooked. That should be obvious from the fact that they can't get me offstage after seventy-five years. No adventure compares to the first laugh from the audience, the first rolling wave of laughter as it rises to the stage and hangs there. It's the real air you breathe. I imagined that it would be nice to retire to a country estate somewhere and smell the new-mown grass. I'll never know!

A man jumps up in a crowded theater and yells, "Is there a Christian Scientist in the house?" He repeats the question several times. Finally, another man stands up and says, "I'm a Christian Scientist."

The first man says, "Would you mind changing seats with me? I'm sitting in a draft!"

It is a typical English music hall. A stuffy master of ceremonies says, "Now we present the beautiful Sonia, who will dance the Dance of the Seven Veils."

From the balcony, a Cockney voice yells, "Sonia is a 'ore!"

The master of ceremonies says, "Nevertheless, she will dance the Dance of the Seven Veils!"

The play was awful. Within ten minutes of the curtain, dribs and drabs of the audience walked out. Soon it was a tidal wave of people scurrying for the exit. Sympathetic, one of the actors, knowing how the play was, said to the audience, "Please remember courtesy—women and children first!"

One Broadway musical tried to save money in a unique way. Instead of installing a rising orchestra pit, the producers had the orchestra just stand up slowly!

theft and thieves

The word thieves *won a spelling bee for me in the third grade. The other finalist spelled it with the* i *and the* e *reversed. It was a tiny victory. The statuette was stolen later, when I put it down on the curb to play ball with some of the other kids. Although this and some of my other adventures with a zinger ending may sound like the workings of a writer's mind, they aren't. I've had many O. Henry moments. They come from living a few years!*

A thief is a man of convictions, and he serves time for most of them!

"That guy there is wanted in Chicago."
"What for?"
"He's a crook."
"Why would they want more crooks in Chicago?"

A good old country boy came running into the tavern and said to his buddy, "Al, they just stole your pickup truck."

Al jumped up, saying, "Who?"

The good old country boy said, "I didn't see his face, but I got the license number!"

A man was a sneak thief. After four years of therapy, his doctor said, "You are now cured. You will not steal anymore. However, if you have a relapse, see if you can get me a nice watch!"

They accused him of stealing a car until he explained, "It was parked outside a cemetery and I thought the owner was dead!

Car thieves have put many a man on his feet!

Two pickpockets were arguing about the weekend football game. One said, "I'll bet you a gold watch my team wins by ten points."

The other pickpocket said, "It's a bet, and if you want to, you can come on the subway with me and pick the one you want!"

"Okay, give me all your money."
"I'll give you all my money if you'll give me your gun."
"It's a deal. Give me your money."
"Okay. Here's my money."
"Here's my gun."
"Okay, now it's your turn to stick 'em up. I want my money back."

"First you'll have to get bullets for that gun!"

thinness

Just when you think you've got every "thin" joke extant, ten thousand new ones show up. We're either all brilliant or cruel!

She's really thin. I've seen more meat under a butcher's fingernail!

If her head had any shape, she could be a cane!

He's so thin his back pockets are in his other pants!

He's so thin the crease in his pants is him!

She's so thin, every time she got her chest sunburned, her back peeled!

He was so skinny, when he went to the beach, dogs buried him!

The last time I saw legs so skinny, there was a message tied to them!

She has no trouble walking the straight and narrow. That's because she *is* straight and narrow!

She's so thin she has no sideways!

He's so thin, when he walks into a pool-room they chalk him up!

She's so thin she took a shower this morning and it missed her!

He was so thin as a kid, his teacher kept marking him absent!

She's as thin as a whisper!

She's so thin she could walk through a harp!

Some men are fat and ugly. He's not. He's skinny and ugly!

She was so thin they once took an X ray of her and it missed!

She was so thin, when she wanted to turn sideways she didn't have to move!

He's so thin it takes two of him to make a shadow!

When he puts on a black suit, he looks like a closed umbrella.

When she drinks tomato juice she looks like a thermometer.

He's so thin he can put shorts on from either end!

She's built like a board, and prays for knots.

She's so thin she could get misplaced in a lumberyard!

She's so thin, mosquitoes miss!

She's so thin she can wear an eyepatch for a bikini!

She's so thin, when she swallows an olive, six guys leave town!

He's tall for his weight. He should be one foot six!

He's so thin his belt has no notches!

He could be the poster boy for Missing!

If she had a filter, she could be smoked!

He was so thin he used his Adam's apple to hold up his pants!

He was so thin he buttoned his double-breasted jacket in the back!

She was so bony they had to X-ray her for meat!

She was so thin she had THIS SIDE UP tattooed on her bosom in case she ever got lucky!

Men liked to needle her. She looked like one!

She was so thin she got a run in her stocking and fell out of it!

time

I'm for helping people slow down enough to have fun. I've never found anyone who can laugh and run at the same time. One or the other has to give. I root for the laughter to stick around. I have nothing profound against joggers, but they're such a somber bunch. I offer a plaque to speakers and performers who can mellow an audience down. "Time" jokes help. They seem to make a neat philosophical point.

The Emersons lived down the block from the church. At two in the morning one time, the church bells went crazy. Instead of ringing twice to denote the hour, they kept ringing. They finally stopped at the hundredth ring. Mr. Emerson nudged his wife. "We'd better get up, dear," he said. "It's later than it's ever been before!"

"What's the longest period of time?"
"One payday to the next!"

A woman asked a neighbor, "Is your husband in favor of daylight saving time?"
The other woman answered, "He's out so much at night, I have the feeling he doesn't like to use any daylight at all!"

He's really laid back. It takes him two hours to watch "60 Minutes."

The trouble is, if you don't use what Mother Nature gave you, Father Time will take it!

It was four in the morning when Mr. Dartle's phone rang. The voice at the other end was pleasant and sweet. "I'm Mrs. Weber, and I would like to tell you that the refrigerator I bought in your store works like a charm."
Mr. Dartle said, "Thank you. But why call me about it at four in the morning?"
Mrs. Weber said, "Because they just delivered it!"

Never put off until tomorrow what you can put off until the day after tomorrow.

A drunk walked over to a man and asked, "Do you have the time?"
The man said, "Eight-fifteen."
The drunk said, "I think I'm going nuts. All day long I've been getting different answers!"

I always know when thirty seconds are up. I'm halfway through my Minute Rice!

A man is walking down the street carrying a grandfather clock. Making a fast turn around the corner, a drunk staggers into him. The drunk looks and says, "This wouldn't happen if you carried a watch like everybody else!"

A farmer walked into the house from doing chores and sat down, his brow wrinkled as he became pensive. His wife asked, "What are you thinking about?"

The farmer said, "I'm trying to figure out where I can find all that daylight I saved when I set the clocks back!"

Time is a great healer, but it doesn't do much for beauty!

Time is money, and the only kind that can't be counterfeited!

Most people don't mind setting their clocks ahead on a Saturday night. They make up the hour's sleep in church!

topless

American men have an awful fetish about a woman's bosom. I find it disgusting, infantile, puerile, and degrading, and I can think of a pair of reasons it shouldn't be!

I know a topless lady ventriloquist. No one has ever seen her lips move!

The topless waitress thought she had heartburn until she saw what was in the soup!

What's the big deal? Once you've seen two, you've seen them all!

A man brought his new client to an agent. The lady was incredibly endowed, with measurements in the sixties. The agent asked, "Is she a topless dancer?"

"Not quite," the man said. "The curtain opens and she tries to stand up!"

They have a new dietetic topless restaurant. The waitresses are flat-chested!

It's an amazing thing—in a topless restaurant, nobody orders milk!

I saw a topless restaurant with a stupid sign: WATCH YOUR HAT AND COAT.

Girls are used to going around topless nowadays. In a department store the other day, I heard a teenage girl ask if they had instructions for her new bra!

toughness

Every day, the people and the neighborhoods get tougher, making the jokes easier. Even my computer is becoming tough. It spilled out the following lines without being asked!

My neighborhood was so tough, they sold Bibles under the counter!

They even have tough kids in rich neighborhoods. In mine, the kids only slash whitewall tires!

My neighborhood was so tough the kids used to surround SWAT teams!

If you wore a clean shirt in my neighborhood, they hissed you!

In my neighborhood, anybody with two ears was a sissy. Especially girls!

I went back to my old neighborhood recently. They were so thrilled to see me, they staged a holdup in my honor!

In my neighborhood, if you want to shake hands with somebody, you have to reach into your wallet pocket!

Talk about tough—the kids in my neighborhood knew the words to the Bronx cheer!

Mine was a tough neighborhood. If you didn't get home by ten, you were declared legally dead!

The city is planning to tear down my old neighborhood and improve it by putting up a slum!

touts

You can't miss a tout at the racetrack. He's the guy with his mouth in somebody's pocket!

A tout ran into a typical pigeon at the track and gave him a daily double that couldn't miss. It missed. The tout proceeded to handicap the next three races for his client. The horses ran last, or as close to last as a horse can run without backing up into the horses from the previous race.

After six losers, the tout ran into another tout and complained about his client's inability to cash a winning ticket. The second tout said, "Dump this guy. He's bad luck for you!"

A man returned to his seat. A friend who had come to the track with him said, "Did you get a big bet on the number-four horse?"

"No, I didn't bet number four."

"You loved him."

"I know, but I ran into this tout who swore that number six was bound to win."

The race went off. The number-four horse won easily. Number six had to be carried back to the paddock.

A few minutes before the second race, the man returned from placing a bet on the second race. He had a ticket on number three, explaining, "I know I handicapped number one, but that tout swore on his mother that number three would waltz in."

The race went off. The number-one horse came in by five lengths. Number three ran next to last.

This went on for five races, with the man unable to collect on one bet. A little disgruntled, he said to his friend, "I'll sit out one race. In fact, I'll just go over and get some peanuts."

"Good idea."

The man went off and returned with popcorn. The friend said, "I thought you wanted peanuts."

"I ran into that tout again!"

A tout is a man, generally in a loud suit, whose father was a bachelor!

A tout is a man who doesn't need a saddle to take you for a ride!

Deciding to give up his checkered career at the track, a tout went to a psychiatrist. After two concentrated years, he felt cured enough to quit therapy. The doctor said, "You've improved greatly, but I'm not sure you're ready. Think about it."

The tout said, "Good idea. I'll think about it on the way home."

The psychiatrist said, "Where do you live?"

"About a mile and a sixteenth from here!"

travel

Travel routines are easy and well received. You pretty much have to tell nothing but the truth. There's a good possibility, if the umbrella for the occasion is a convention, that people in the audience have just gone through a severe travel trauma. A few jokes and stories will unknot that monster in the stomach. Remember—don't start off by being too hard on the ladies and the tonnage they packed. Pick on men first. That's a good rule for almost all routines—go after the men first. When the gals are on your side, unleash the heavy artillery!

An American tourist debarks at the busy pier of a major steamship line. As he walks to the immigration desk, a local in flamboyant colors says, "Can I get you something? A nice, pretty girl? A strong, experienced woman? Many women?"

The American tourist says, "When I'm through here, I want the American consulate."

The local shrugged his shoulders. "It's not easy, but I'll try!"

The tour guide took her own sweet time, not terribly concerned about the exact schedule. Mrs. Kleborn, a stickler for punctuality, kept up a steady barrage of complaints. They'd been a half hour late for Hampton Court. They had been late for the Tower of London. Always late.

The group arrived at Runnymede and the guide said, "On this very spot the historic Magna Charta was signed."

A woman asked, "When?"

The guide said, "1215."

Mrs. Kleborn said, "I knew it. I knew it. We missed it by fifteen minutes!"

"Europe is terrific," Mrs. Kemp told her friend. "If you go there, don't miss it!"

A woman told another, "Last year we took a trip around the world. This year we're going someplace else!"

I took my wife to Italy last summer. You know how it is—you always take something you don't need!

My wife must be descended from Noah. When we travel, she takes two of everything!

With the way those Tahitian girls look, the best time to go to the Pacific is between twenty-one and thirty!

I've seen more strange places than a porno cameraman!

There are only two ways to travel—first-class and with kids!

Big-city people aren't rude by nature. They're just afraid to be taken for visitors!

An American couple went to Europe. In a small town in southern Italy, they stopped for breakfast. Paying for the meal, the husband discovered he'd been charged three dollars for an egg. He asked, "Is there a scarcity of eggs around here?"

"No, a scarcity of Americans!"

Some of those new ocean liners are gigantic. On a recent trip, a woman came out of the elevator that brought her up to the deck and said to a crewman, "Excuse me, but which way is the Pacific Ocean?"

A Russian university student was assigned to escort an American couple around Moscow. While they were taking a break from ogling the beautiful sights, the American husband asked, "What would you like to be after spending your time as an American tourist guide?"

The university student said, "An American tourist!"

The governement tells us to go to friendly countries. I can't find any!

terrific cook. I came home by accident this afternoon and I found a two-hundred-pound truckdriver eating there!"

trust

A small-time comic came to me to borrow two hundred dollars. Not having much money with me, I said, "I can give you a hundred." He said, "I trust you for the rest!" On the other hand, there was a young Scottish boy who lent his friend a few pennies. When his father heard about the loan, he called the boy over and ordered him to stand on the table. Putting out his arms, the father said, "Jump." The boy hesitated. "Jump," the father said, "I'll catch you." The boy jumped. The father let him fall to the floor, then said, "That's a good lesson to learn. Don't trust anybody!"

"Do you remember that umbrella you lent me? I lent it to a friend."
"That's gonna be rough. The fellow who lent it to *my* friend just told him that the owner wants it!"

A young man asked his girlfriend's father if it would be okay if the engagement was announced. The father was very pleased and said, "Remember one thing, my boy, I'm entrusting you with the treasure of my life."
    After the men had toasted the engagement, the young man decided to go home. As he opened the door, rain poured down. The young man asked if he could borrow an umbrella. The father of the bride-to-be said, "Sorry. I don't trust anybody with my umbrella!"

The award for trusting must go to the man who said to a friend, "My wife must be a

twins

My grandmother said once, when we were about to economize, "Going to bed to save candles isn't worth it if the result is twins!" She was a bright lady with a saying for everything. If she couldn't find one in folklore or the Bible, she made it up and claimed it came from an ancient prophet. In those days I never questioned her. I thought she had known a lot of ancient prophets!

Twins, dressed alike, went into a bar for a drink. A man who'd been downing the bourbon with gusto looked at them and blinked. One of the twins said, "Pal, you're not in bad shape. We're twins."
    The wino stared once more and said, "All four of you?"

The doctor told the young lady, "You're going to have twins."
    The young lady said, "That's impossible. I never double-dated in my life!"

A twin came home from a late date and told her sister, "We're not identical anymore!"

It's not too bad when you have twin babies. When one cries, you can't hear the other one!

"How can you tell your twins apart?"
"I put my finger in Billy's mouth. If he bites, I know it's Dennis!"

U

ugliness

Beauty is in the eyes of the beholder. The terrible thing is that ugliness is also in the eyes of the beholder!

She's so ugly, when she goes to bed, she puts her whole body up in curlers!

She's had her face lifted so many times it's out of focus!

She ought to have her face capped!

She went to a doctor and complained, "Everybody says I'm ugly. They say I have a face that could scare a witch and a black cat."

The doctor said, "You're not ugly. But how much would you charge to sit in my window on Halloween?"

The only one who thinks she's a ten is her shoe salesman!

A child came home from school in tears, explaining, "The kids say I look like a monkey."

"Forget it," his mother said. "Now go upstairs and comb your face!"

A woman is walking along with a duck under her arm. A drunk, passing by, says, "Where'd you get that gruesome thing?"

The woman says, "Sir, that happens to be a duck."

"I know. I was talking to the duck!"

When she went camping, the bears built a fire to keep her away!

"Ravage me," said the ugly damsel.
The dragon said, "Don't we dragons have a bad enough reputation?"

There she was, lying on soft white satin sheets. A vampire appeared in the open window. He came to her side. He looked at her face and bit the bed!

"I took my wife to see Frankenstein."
"There must have been a lot of screaming."
"I thought he'd never stop!"

She was some dish—a main dish at a luau!

She was so ugly her face could curdle a cow!

She was so ugly her makeup came in a snakebite kit!

He prayed that his brother would live. If his brother died, *he'd* be the ugliest man alive!

She was so ugly she could scare a saint out of a thicket!

One day she wore feathers. She was attacked by an ostrich!

An ugly woman had a car accident. Police rushed to the scene. One policeman said, "What should we do with the wreck?"

The other policeman said, "We'll get all the details and then we'll drive her home."

She was listed in *The Guinness Book of Yichhh*.

Men looked at her twice. They didn't believe it the first time!

They said she was uglier than sin. Sin sued!

"Mirror, mirror, on the wall. What should I do with my face?"
"Get shatterproof glass!"

She looked like a million dollars—all green and crumpled!

She was so ugly—in those ads showing "before" and "after," she was "during."

She was so ugly, in church they put her behind the curtain even when she wasn't confessing!

They wanted to put her in the ring. She looked just like a boxer!

She was a regular cave woman. That's where they kept her!

"Is that a picture of your fiancée?"
"You bet."
"Gee, I wish *I* knew a rich girl!"

He was so ugly he got into the army as a war atrocity!

If she sued her face for slander, she could collect!

She looked like a character witness for a nightmare!

"Officer, can you see me across the street?"
"Lady, I could see you a mile away!"

She was definitely not two-faced, or she would have used the other one!

Although she looked like a chimp, nobody wanted to monkey around with her!

The ugliest man in the world married the ugliest woman in the world. After a year they had a beautiful baby. The husband looked at his wife and said, "Where did we go wrong?"

She had ten fingers just like any normal person—seven and three!

The last time she heard a whistle, she was hit by a train!

She was so ugly, when she kissed a man she kept her eyes closed so she wouldn't see him suffer!

She was a rare beauty. Nobody could find it!

"Beauty is only skin deep."
"Too bad it's so near and you can't get close to it!"

She went out to sell her body, but she was so ugly they sent her to a rummage sale!

With his wife, he was a man of few words—"Fetch" . . . "Sit" . . . .

When men looked at her, time stood still. She could stop a clock!

He looked like the first husband of a widow!

She was so ugly, when she went on a picnic, ants didn't!

She was so ugly they had towels made out to "Him" and "What"!

He's so ugly, even his answering service won't answer!

He's so ugly, when he goes to therapy, the doctor makes him lie on the couch face-down!

You couldn't find her charms with a scavenger hunt!

She was so ugly, an artist painted her face and his brush broke!

She once asked her mirror who was the fairest of them all. She was so ugly, the wall broke!

Every time he saw her with a broom, he didn't know whether she was going to clean or take a ride!

She was a real rockin' chick. That's what they threw at her!

She was as ugly as three miles of scar!

When it came to looks, she had the seal of approval until the seals objected!

She looked like the den mother for the Dirty Dozen!

She was so ugly she was even ugly in the dark!

It's a good thing for her that a mirror can't laugh!

"Why do they have artificial turf at most Midwestern stadiums?"
"So the cheerleaders won't graze at half-time!"

She was so ugly she entered an "ugly" contest and came in first, second, and third. She would have come in fourth, too, but that went to the judge's sister!

"She didn't invent ugliness."
"I know. But she may be the local distributor for it."

"Look at that ugly girl."
"She's a hooker."
"Who would go with her?"
"Guys who are trying to cut down!"

There was dew on her lips and dew in her eyes. That's what she was—dew-dew!

He went through medical school as a cadaver!

She was so ugly, when she called Information, they told her to get a facelift!

"She's got a face like a rhino."
"Not only that. Once a month she gets an urge to ram a jeep!"

She's so ugly she couldn't lure anybody out of a burning building!

He was the kind who traded on his looks— at garage sales!

"My wife is a cabdriver."
"A lady cabdriver?"
"If you look closely!"

She was so ugly she could make a train leave the track!

She was so ugly, no tide would bring her in!

As a kid he couldn't play in the sandbox. The cat kept burying him!

He was so ugly, in the army his dogtags came with a collar!

He was so ugly he could lift a fog!

He was so ugly his sister was an only child!

She was ugly, even in Braille!

She was a professional blind date.

He was so ugly, even starvation wouldn't look him in the face!

Once they saw her, men couldn't forget her. No matter how hard they tried!

She went to a coming-out party. They told her to get back in!

One day her boyfriend took her to a dog show. She won!

"I wish I had sore eyes."
"Why?"
"You'd be a sight for them!"

Nobody ever saw anything as ugly as he was without paying admission!

She's a treasure—something they dug up!

Her face had everything, including four or five things that a face had never had before!

She looked like death warmed over—in a waffle iron!

When she walked into a bank, they turned off the camera!

She was so ugly they wanted to tar and feather her, but somebody said, "If she wants to improve her looks, let her do it herself!"

Men drank to her face. They had to!

She looked like a great canvas—oily!

She looked like an escaped pimple!

She's so ugly, when she goes to the ladies' room, the attendant asks for ID!

Her face sticking out of a cellar door could start a hockey game!

"Are you attached?"
"No, I'm just put together sloppy!"

She was so ugly, in school she was chosen as the most likely to be the least likely!

She was so ugly she could model for death threats!

"Beauty is only skin deep."
"Good, let's skin her!"

Even the most beautiful woman fades with time. Can you imagine what happens to the ugly ones?

He was born twins, but his mother must have thrown the good one away!

undertakers

Undertaking is a great business. It's easy, keeps going, and you never have to pay a refund!

I wonder—if an undertaker goes to the opera, does he sit in a box?

Do you want to see a hypocrite? Just watch an undertaker at a ten-thousand-dollar funeral!

Don't go into a mortuary that does cremating and ask, "What's cooking?"

The undertaker was describing what he'd done, telling the widow, "I took extra care because your husband was a fine, considerate, giving, and loving person."

The widow said, "Let's open the coffin and take a look. I think you got the wrong man!"

One undertaker tells it like it is—he always signs his letters, "Eventually Yours."

One student flunked out of undertaker school. When he started to work on cadavers, he couldn't stiff it out!

One day a chain smoker died. The undertaker put him into a flip-top coffin.

A girl has to worry about dating an undertaker. He could be after her just for her body!

Then there was the absentminded undertaker who buried himself in his work!

Today an undertaker's prices are stiffer than his customers!

The widow was complaining about the cost of a coffin. After she'd turned down the cheapest funeral, the undertaker said, "If you got a lift to the cemetery, we wouldn't even need a pine box!"

The dying man told his wife, "Don't make a fuss when I go. Just bury me in something that'll snap shut. I don't need fancy brass fixtures."

He died and his wife buried him in cheap luggage!

They ask, "Death, where is thy sting?" It's in the price of the funeral, dummy!

unemployment

I liked the days of slavery. There was no unemployment!

Unemployment isn't all bad. When you get up in the morning, you're already at work!

My brother is dying to get a job so he can go on strike!

Unions have helped workers get many benefits. One man came home recently, blessing the union for having gotten him extra. He told his wife, "I just got a hundred thousand severance pay."

The wife started to jump up and down with joy.

The husband went on, "But wait till I tell you what they severed!"

Some people look forward to the yawn of a new day!

My brother is the family idol. He's been idle for twenty-six years!

I have a nephew who gets unemployment checks in advance!

Unemployment is due to a shortage of money to pay people who work because these people have no money to buy things that could be made if they got paid to make things.

Nowadays, Washington never says that the percentage of unemployed is going up. The government merely announces that there is a downward trend of an upward tendency!

The government keeps saying that there are openings in every field. That's not exactly true. My nephew can't get placed. He's a buffalo hunter!

unions

I belong to six unions. I have a hospitalization plan with four of them. They all agree. If one won't pay the bill, neither will the other three! I actually hold one of the earliest cards in the radio and television performers' union. It's written on a rock!

Every kid born in America has two strikes against it—at least!

A homeowner objected to the price quoted by the union housepainter, saying, "I wouldn't give Rembrandt that much money."

The painter said, "If he does it for a penny less, you'll have pickets around your house in the morning!"

Two representatives from the union visited a manufacturer who didn't want to sign a new contract. One held him while the other pummeled him a few times, kicked him in the groin, and, when he was about to fall in a heap, threw him at the far wall. The manufacturer decided to sign. One of the representatives said, "Why didn't you sign right away?"

The manufacturer said, "You didn't explain it to me before!"

One liquor company pays its employees time and a fifth!

A worker went over to his shop steward and said, "They underpaid me by five dollars this week."

The shop steward said, "What about last week?"

"They overpaid me by five dollars."

The steward said, "We'll have to do something about it. I can disregard an occasional mistake. But two weeks in a row?"

We're a pretty great country. We've got more people striking than other countries have working!

The ushers at a hit musical cheered and stamped their feet at each curtain call. A patron said, "You must be crazy about this show."

One usher said, "Two more curtain calls and we go into overtime!"

A union official told his grandson a bedtime story, beginning, "Once upon a time and a half..."

A good union man believes that time heals all wounds. Time and a half heals them a little faster!

Two union men debated whether or not they should go to the union meeting. One said, "We have to go. We must show these capitalist pigs that we are united in our struggle to attain a living wage that will reflect the dignity of labor."

The other union man said, "You're right. We should go. But we'll have to take your Jaguar. My Mercedes is in the shop!"

They say that unions are mob-controlled, but that's not the case. In fact, at the last meeting I was telling that to our local president, "Knuckles" Barone!

united nations

I think the United Nations is a great idea as long as it doesn't let in too many foreigners!

Things are back to normal at the United Nations. Screaming and cursing have been replaced by just the usual hatred!

Without the UN, some of us would worry about investing in a seven-day clock.

They now have two Chinas in the United Nations—one from Column A and one from Column B!

Every time two countries have a squabble, they call the UN. The UN has finally come up with an answer—an unlisted phone number!

If Noah was alive today, he'd be building a bulletproof ark!

The UN promotes peace. In thirty-five years there hasn't been one war in the building!

The delegate from Bejing wants to be the head of the UN, but he doesn't have a Chinaman's chance!

The UN delegates know a lot about armament. You should see them drive!

The scariest sight in the world is to see an African delegate teaching his wife how to drive!

I think the UN is made of Teflon. Nothing ever sticks!

The UN is made of countries that can't tolerate injustice except at home!

Nations should solve their problems like husbands and wives—yell a little, pout, and stop talking to one another for a week!

The UN has done more to promote peace than a divorce court!

The United Nations, or as we call it, the Tower of Babble!

Arriving in New York, a UN delegate from a Third World country went to a cafeteria for a bite to eat. He sat down at the counter and, not being able to speak or read English, was lost with the menu. He waited until the person next to him ordered and echoed the order, saying, "Apple pie and coffee."

For the next two weeks, each time he walked into a restaurant, his order was the same. "Apple pie and coffee."

The day came when he was unable to face another piece of apple pie or sip another drop of coffee. The menu still a mystery to him, he waited until somebody nearby ordered, and gave his order too: "A cheeseburger."

The waitress said, "How do you want it?"

The delegate stared and said, "Cheeseburger."

"Do you want it rare, medium, well done?"

The delegate said, "Apple pie and coffee!"

A UN delegate went to a speech class to master American speech patterns. In no time at all he was able to say, "Peter Piper picked a peck of pickled peppers." But it never came up in a debate!

unpopularity

Popularity, or the lack thereof, is the Achilles' heel of every guest of honor. As with some other aspects of personality, an audience will believe what is said. The human being is an incomplete creature. He will always believe the unflattering. When I'm being waited on in a shop, another salesperson will sometimes break in on the bond I've formed with the first salesperson. The second salesperson may want information on a matter in no way related to me. Being a devil, I'll blend into a question. I'll indicate the new arrival and ask the first salesperson, "Is he the one you were talking about?" A smart salesperson will play along and indicate that I'm on the right track. Immediately, the second salesperson will feel accused of some dire deed. He or she will want to get to the bottom of it quickly so that a defense can be set up. It's possible that the discussion could have been flattering, but the second salesperson will not come up with that conclusion. The feeling is close to the one that pops up with the delivery of a telegram. When we're not opening in a show, being awarded a Nobel Prize, or getting ready to blow out candles on a birthday cake, we accept telegrams with trepidation. This is important in comedy. It teaches that "bad" stuff will evoke laughter!

Nobody likes her. She once entered a beauty contest and Miss Congeniality bit her.

Her phone doesn't even ring when she's in the shower!

She could commit murder and still not be on a wanted list!

She's so unpopular she had to go to the Sunday tea dance on Wednesday!

His hosts like to see him to the door—as soon as possible.

It's a good thing he has a split personality. He always has a date that way!

He didn't go to his own wedding. Nobody invited him!

She's the kind you bid a welcome adieu!

He's good for people's health. When they see him coming, they go for long walks!

She has no dates. Even the light in her refrigerator never goes out!

When he goes to a football game and the team goes into a huddle, he thinks they're talking about him. And they are!

He's got about as many friends as an alarm clock!

She wouldn't hear a whistle if the teakettle was on!

Unpopular? The other day he had a martini, and the olive stuck its pimiento out at him!

They don't even like him at home. The other day he walked into his house and the canary threw herself at the cat!

unlisted

Unlisted numbers are funny, especially in Beverly Hills, where I live. The fire department has an unlisted phone number. The notion of an "unlisted" something works with almost any rich or powerful component. Rich Arabs can have an unlisted desert. Rich Texans can have an unlisted Stetson size. Any extreme condition can be switched to an appropriate geography. The trick is to reach the conclusion in as few words as possible. If the audience has too much time to think, it will dissect the joke. Dissection is the pneumonia of humor!

The CIA has a list that's so secret it's unlisted!

One fellow loved secrecy. He used an alias, had an unlisted phone number, and kept his money in unnumbered Swiss bank accounts. When he died, they had trouble burying him. They couldn't find him!

I heard of an unlisted gun store. It only sells blanks!

Then there was the fancy jail for the most exclusive inmates. They all had unlisted numbers!

I'm trying to get my unlisted number listed, but I don't know what it is!

urban life

I grew up in the concrete heart of a city. I didn't see a tree until I was fifteen. I remember visiting a neighbor who had two potted plants. I thought I was on a ranch!

Our city has a brand-new plan for the downtown area. It's called neglect!

A tornado went through downtown yesterday and did ten million dollars' worth of improvements!

It's good to live in a city where millions of people who live close to one another spend their time being lonely!

Some cities have large zoos. Others *are!*

The mayor of New York says that he thinks civilization will last for thousands of years in the city. He neglected to say when it would begin!

In one city, the people have terrible slums they're ashamed of. Changes are in order. Next year they're going to put in slums they can be proud of!

They found a strange building in downtown Los Angeles—it's not owned by the Japanese!

Some urban-renewal people want to restore the city to what it once was. But where can you get all those horses?

One urban area had to be rebuilt before it could be condemned!

Some cities refuse to do away with the graffiti on the sides of buildings. The graffiti is what's holding the buildings up!

A man discovered that he had only six months to live. His doctor suggested that he sell his house in the suburbs and move back to the heart of town. The man said, "Will that help me live longer?"

The doctor said, "No, but it'll *seem* longer!"

used cars

A snake and a rabbit met. Never having seen a creature of that type before, each studied the other. The snake said, "You have long ears, two funny front teeth, and you go hippety-hop. You must be a rabbit." The rabbit nodded and said, "You have oily skin, fangs, and a split tongue. You must be a used-car salesman."

"The car doesn't look bad. How about the shocks?"
"You get those when you hear the price!"

I think they turned back the mileage on that car. It was in Roman numerals!

The car was so old it needed both upper and lower plates!

My car is really old. My headlights have cataracts!

This used-car lot had two sections depending on the engines—smoking and nonsmoking!

The used-car salesman sold an Indian an old jalopy. When the Indian complained about the smoke coming from the exhaust, the salesman said, "It's the newest thing in car phones!"

The used-car salesman told me about this one car. It had sleek lines, gorgeous curves, was soft to the touch, and purred. I bought the car and took it to a motel!

A minister bought a used car and returned it the next day, saying, "I couldn't remain a minister and drive this car at the same time!"

The used-car salesman swore by the car. I bought it. The next day I swore too!

The used-car salesman got me to buy the car because he swore that it had only been driven by a little old lady. I didn't know he meant Ma Barker!

I drive a '79. Not the year, that's its resale value!

V

vacations

They have resorts now that satisfy all tastes. In one place, half the girls are looking for husbands and half the husbands are looking for girls!

The doctor gave Jim three months to live. He sent Marge away for twelve weeks!

A man returned to work after his vacation, and his friend asked, "How did you like your trip?"
    The man said, "Did you ever spend a week in a station wagon with those you thought you loved?"

Never go on a vacation in a car unless the windows outnumber the kids!

I just returned from my vacation. I'm still suffering from bus lag!

We were on a Polish vacation—six nights and three days!

Nothing is as dull as a vacation you can afford!

On out last vacation I tried to get away from it all, but my wife brought it along!

I'm going to the same place I went last year—the bank, for another loan!

You can always tell the man who has everything. It's in the station wagon when the family starts the trip!

Vacations are easy. The boss tells you when, and the wife tells you where!

I took a great vacation this year. All summer I looked out the window at the young woman across the street and let my mind wander!

A vacation is a two-week holiday that makes you feel good enough to go back to work—and poor enough to have to!

They're now offering a wonderful tour to Alaska—three glorious nights and then three more glorious nights!

Sid came back to work from two weeks away and asked his boss, "Can I have ten days off?"
    The boss said, "Why?"
    "I'd like to get married."
    "Why didn't you get married during these last two weeks?"
    "And spoil my vacation?"

Harry ran into a co-worker after a two-week vacation. The co-worker asked him about his vacation, and Harry said, "A buddy of mine invited me up to a fishing camp. No booze, no night life, no women."
    "Did you enjoy that?"
    "Who went?"

Here's a blueprint for the best vacation you'll ever have: Buy a new station wagon, put the kids in back, and take a cruise!

We spent the night sleeping with our neighbors. They were showing us slides of their vacation!

I went to a place with sand, sea, and surf. I came back bushed, burned, and busted!

When we left on our cruise, my brothers came down to the boat with candy, cigars, and whiskey. When the boat left, there they were, standing on the pier—eating, smoking, and drinking!

I took a look at my passport picture and decided I looked too sick to travel!

We went to Alaska for two months, then we decided to stay all night!

It always rains in England. I asked an Englishman for directions once, and he pointed off and said, "It's about five miles as the crow floats!"

They eat a balanced meal in Mexico. Every bean weighs the same!

Mine was a voice crying in the wilderness. From now on I'll read the road map!

On my last vacation there was a slight problem. They didn't find any hotel towels in my valise, but they did find a chambermaid in my grip!

I kept an exact expense account on our last trip—my life savings!

When the ship docked, this Scotsman looked over the side and saw a deep-sea diver pop out of the water. The Scotsman said to his wife, "If we'd had outfits like that, we could have walked over too!"

The last place we stayed was the dullest. The first night, the tide went out and never came back!

valentine's day

A nice holiday because it's the first day of the rest of your wife!

My son really has the spirit of Valentine's Day. When he was in college, he used to send his mother a heart-shaped box of laundry.

I like to do things for my wife on Valentine's Day. I open the door for her when she puts laundry in the washing machine!

She was nice to him on Valentine's Day. She gave him a heart-shaped rash!

The only thing that can break a piece of Valentine candy is another piece of Valentine candy!

On Valentine's Day, I wired flowers for my mother-in-law, but she found the fuse!

My wife sent me a Valentine card that said, "Take my heart, take my lips, take my soul." That's just like her. She kept the good parts for herself!

All my wife wanted for Valentine's Day was a little card—American Express!

My wife is a real Puritan. She thinks licking the stamp on the envelope of a valentine is foreplay!

Valentine's Day is like Armistice Day—you declare a truce!

Valentine's Day is the day when you remember that Cupid was a lousy shot!

value

A man's worth is in his deeds, unless he's trying to get a bank loan!

A thief gave his girlfriend a lovely mink coat. Putting it on, she purred, "It's magnificent. It must be worth at least ten years!"

One executive went to Washington as a dollar-a-year man. The next day he was fired because he was being overpaid!

A college coach demanded a pay raise from the dean. He wouldn't return unless he received fifty thousand the next year. The dean said, "Fifty thousand? We can get a good quarterback for that!"

There's an easy way of finding out the value of money—try to borrow some!

It's getting so that there's no money in money!

He who steals my purse steals trash—also my driver's license, my credit cards . . .

He who steals my purse steals trash. What a dumb place to put your trash!

He who steals my purse steals trash. Unless it's Tuesday, when the sanitation men collect it!

vanity

I gave up vanity about the same time my mirror did!

A vain man always keeps looking around for somebody with his ears open!

Vanity is gift-wrapping yourself!

I know a woman who's so vain she even lies about her dog's age!

He speaks to the Lord—on a one-to-one basis!

He once took a walk and was hit by a passing motorboat!

He could pose for a wall in the Vatican!

The size of the balloon isn't important. It goes up because of what's inside!

He's a self-made man. He gave the job to the lowest bidder!

A writer's son and a minister's son were talking about their parents. The writer's son said, "My father can sit down and write a thousand words, and a week later he gets a check for a thousand dollars."

The minister's son said, "My father says ten words to his congregation and it takes ten men to bring the money up to him!"

A beautiful woman, known for her vanity, took her young daughter to a department store. While the mother tried on a dress, the daughter picked up a hat, put it on, and looked at herself in the mirror. "Mother," the daughter said. "Look. I'm as beautiful as you in this hat."

The mother said, "Don't be vain, dear!"

vaudeville

What a training ground! In vaudeville, I learned that there was one rule for a performer like me—anything for a laugh! At the Dutchess Theater in Poughkeepsie, New York, my music was played and I ran out on the stage. I slipped and went kerplunk *into the orchestra. As I brushed myself off, the conductor asked, "Shall I play your music again?" Returning to the stage, I ad-libbed a remark that got a big laugh.*

Bruised, my shoulder a bloody pulp, I considered leaving the whole move in the act because of the big laugh!

An agent called a juggler at his small hotel room and offered him fifty dollars a week to go on a circuit of theaters in the Northeast. The juggler said, "My price is three hundred."

"They won't give anybody three hundred."

"I don't care. I want my price."

"Look, come down, we'll have some coffee and talk."

The juggler said, "What? And get locked out of my hotel room?"

A mimic begged for an opportunity to work a bill. He was sent to Philadelphia and told that he'd receive a hundred dollars for the week.

Onstage, he was brilliant. He mimicked a dozen movie stars and public figures. His singing impressions were perfect. His moves were the exact moves of the person he was imitating. Audiences loved him.

At the end of the week, however, he was only given twenty dollars. He told the boss that he was supposed to get a hundred. The boss said, "Business is so bad, you're lucky to get twenty."

"You don't understand. I was counting on this money to pay my rent, my utility bill, my phone bill, and two months' alimony. Where am I going to get the money?"

The boss said, "You're a great impressionist. Do Rockefeller!"

A vaudevillian is on the road and receives a wire that tells him he has just become the father of triplets. He goes out onstage in a fog and does his act. After the show, the theater owner says, "You dance like a fish. You can't sing. You can't tell jokes. What can you do?"

The vaudevillian hands him the telegram!

Bronson, an ex-circus performer, went to an agent and told him that he could offer the gent an incredible vaudeville act. The agent seemed interested, so Bronson whistled and through the door came a pygmy elephant. Bronson said, "Dumbo, dance for Mr. Klein."

As Bronson tapped out a rhythm, Dumbo started to dance. He did perfect impressions of the great movie dancers. Without stopping for a breath, he went into impressions of the ballet greats of all time.

The dancing over, Dumbo started to do pantomime, each move an exact replica of those done by the great mimes.

When Bronson started to clap his hands together, Dumbo opened his mouth and sang. Caruso came out. Crosby came out. The voice of every great singer filled the room.

Dumbo took a bow.

Mr. Klein walked over and put his arm around the elephant, then said, "Dumbo, you're cute, but let me tell you something about show business—you can't get anywhere doing impressions. Be smart, Dumbo—be yourself!"

A ventriloquist fell on bad times. Unable to find work in the theater, he decided to conduct seances, in which his ability to throw his voice would come in handy. Came the day of his first seance. The table was full as the lights were turned low. A woman asked to speak to her departed husband. Throwing his voice, the medium conjured up a "husband." The wife had a merry time talking with the man she had loved so much. When the "husband" rejoined the spirit world, his wife was thrilled. Then she remembered something else she'd wanted to tell him. She offered the medium a hundred dollars if she could talk to her husband again.

The medium said, "No problem. But for two hundred I can bring him back while I drink a glass of water!"

A vaudevillian was in a plane that crashed. Waking up, he found himself in a warm place with eerie music all around. He asked a man nearby, "Where am I?"

The man said, "Hell."

The vaudevillian said, "Some agent I have. He never booked me in a decent place yet!"

A vaudevillian was called in by a booking agent and offered a week's work on a small circuit. The vaudevillian said, "I'll take it if I can get my price. I get fifteen hundred a week."

The booking agent said, "They're offering a hundred a week."

The vaudevillian said, "I'll take it. I'd never let fourteen hundred dollars stand in the way!"

Hinds and Stone, a vaudeville team, were booked into a small theater in Pennsylvania, but were warned by an act that had recently closed there, "The owner of the theater has an owl. The owl sits high up in the balcony and watches the show. If he laughs at your jokes, you're in. When he makes a face because your jokes aren't getting through to him, you might as well walk off the stage, go to your hotel room, and pack."

Opening night came. Hinds and Stone came out, acknowledged the mild applause, and looked up at the second balcony. Sure enough, an owl sat atop the back of a seat. Hinds whispered, "Keep your eye on the owl. Don't take your eye off the owl."

They went into their opening song and patter and received a good audience reaction. Up in the balcony, the owl smiled.

During the third routine, Stone happened to glance off to the wings, where his wife stood watching the show. Stone noticed that the theater owner was standing near her. The act went on. A few minutes later, Stone looked to the wings again. The theater owner was fondling Mrs. Stone. Another look, a minute later, revealed that the theater owner and Mrs. Stone were making love. Stone whispered to Hinds, "Do you see what that guy's doing with my wife?"

Hinds said, "Never mind that. Watch the owl!"

One vaudevillian had a bad back, just from lifting jokes!

A husband-and-wife juggling act were unable to make the big time. They had to play the cheapest bills in the smallest towns. As a result, they were on the verge of starvation. Their clothes were threadbare. Worn and knocked about, both looked years older than they were. They arrived in a small Ohio town, and even though it was bitterly cold, they were forced to walk the mile to their shabby boardinghouse. As they walked, a well-dressed couple, laughing and enjoying life, went by in a fancy car.

The juggling wife said, "They don't have a bad life."

The juggling husband said, "I bet they can't juggle!"

vegetarians

Jack Sprat could eat no fat, his wife could eat no lean—that explains why Jack is skinny and his wife wears an industrial-strength girdle!

Ugly? She could turn a cannibal into a vegetarian!

"Come, lettuce get married," said Arti.
"Will your celery keep two?" asked she.

"With carrot will do and I think, dear,
Something better will turnip," said he.
So off to old Pars'n Ipps cottage
Onion road, the wedding to stage,
They spud, and it took but a second
In this modern taxi-cabbage.
But you can't beet a taxicab meter;
Appeasing the bill left him broke,
Caused a lump to sprout in his thorax
And nearly made poor Artichoke.
However, they weren't cress fallen;
To the house on the corner they went,
Woke the pars'nip up from his slumber,
On the greensward held the event.
And that is the endive my story
For there isn't much room left to write!

A young boy bit into an apple, saw a worm, and handed the apple to his little brother, saying, "I think I'll be a vegetarian from now on!"

It must be expensive to be a vegetarian. They can't make both ends meat!

We'd all still be in Paradise if Eve had tried to tempt Adam with a brussels sprout!

violins and violinists

I studied violin for about two months. By then, the neighbors were ready to march on our apartment. My love at that time was the trombone. There happened to be an opening for a trombonist in our school orchestra. One day I brought the school trombone home. Curious about how it was played, the kids on the block insisted that I display my talent. Never one to let an audience down, I took out the instrument and blew into it vigorously again and again. I worked the trombone for an hour. When I came upstairs, my uncle Charlie was also curious about the instrument. I took it out of the case and attempted to show him my inborn talent. I'd overworked my gut and lungs with the boys, so when I blew into the mouthpiece in front of my uncle Charlie, my restraint gave way. I upchucked half of my insides. Uncle Charlie merely looked and asked, "Is that how you play that thing?" That day I decided I was a singer!

A man named Plotnick came into a music store. After looking at different objects, he came to the instrument section. Picking up a violin and bow, he started to play. Out came heavenly music. The clerk asked, "Are you a concert violinist?"

Plotnick said, "Nah. I just fool around."

The clerk said, "Please wait here." Going into the private office in back, the clerk called a famous booker and described his experience, saying, "The man in front is a genius."

The booker said, "It just so happens that a big pianist canceled on me today. Could your man be ready fast?"

Plotnick could be, and was.

Plotnick's debut was sensational. He was compared to all the greats of the world. On the basis of this one concert, he was booked into the major concert halls of the world. After his concert in Geneva, the American President and the Russian premier, both in the city for peace talks and soothed by Plotnick's music, settled all their differences. Their mood was so mellow that each gave the other what he wanted.

In Cairo the following month, Plotnick's concert brought peace and brotherhood to all the Arabs and Jews in the area. Plotnick's dulcet tones made even the warring nations of central Africa drop their differences. The night after his concert in the capital of one of Africa's most volatile countries, Plotnick lay in bed, trying to relax. The face of a lioness filled the small window of his room. Pleasantly, the lioness said, "Mr. Plotnick, I heard your concert from afar. It was magnificent. The animals would like to hear you. You know that they won't let us come into town. We have no money to pay you to come to us. Could you see your way, as an errand of mercy, to play one sonata, one concerto, even one etude for the animals?"

Plotnick smiled. Not a greedy soul, he said, "Where is your hall?"

"We have no hall. We made a clearing in the jungle. I have a hundred animals gathered around."

Plotnick picked up his violin. Going to the window, he climbed out and joined the lioness.

As she had promised, a hundred animals of all sorts were sitting around. Plotnick walked to the center of the crowd, put his violin to his chin, and was about to play when a leopard jumped from a perch in a nearby tree. In two bites, the leopard did away with Plotnick. Two more bites and there was nothing left of him and his violin.

The lioness, slightly aggravated, said to the leopard, "Why did you do that?"

The leopard cupped his paw to his ear and said, "Eh?"

A famous violinist was forced to listen to a young boy play. After the youngster had played a whole sonata, his mother asked, "What do you think?"

The famous violinist said, "Your son has a small tone, but it's already very disagreeable!"

After hearing a world-class violinist give a concert at one of the world's famous halls, a man went backstage. Surprisingly, he got into the dressing room and introduced himself. Then he said, "More than anything else in the world, I'd love it if you came to my house and played there."

The violinist said, "My fee is ten thousand dollars."

"I don't have any money. I suppose I could come up with ten dollars. But how happy I would be to have you play in my house, in my living room."

"Since you love music so much, I'll do it."

The next night the violinist came to the man's apartment. Tuning his Stradivarius, the violinist asked, "Are there some selections you'd like?"

The man said, "Play anything. But loudly. I want to annoy my neighbors!"

It was time for Alan's music practice. His mother called to him in the street, where he was playing with the other boys, "Alan, come in and practice on your wonderful violin."

"Be right in, Mom."

Five minutes later, the boy's mother called out once more, "Alan, come in and practice on your wonderful Stradivarius violin."

"Be right in, Mom."

The next summons came after another five minutes, "Alan, come in and practice on your wonderful Stradivarius violin that cost your father ten thousand dollars."

The minutes ticked away and the next call came. "Alan, get in here and practice, or I'll break that lousy fiddle on your head!"

A world-famous pianist and a renowned violinist went to Carnegie Hall for the debut of a new violin virtuoso. The young man played his first selection with fervor and great feeling. His second selection was even better. After the third selection, the famous violinist said to his friend, "It's getting warm in here, isn't it?"

The pianist said, "Not for piano players!"

The violinist finished playing a Brahms violin concerto. A man in the first row called out, "Play a Brahms violin concerto."

The violinist said, "I just did."

The man in the audience said, "I wish I'd known!"

I'd never buy a Stradivarius. I heard he stopped making spare parts for it!

A bad violinist was giving a concert at a college auditorium. As he played, one gentleman in the audience turned to the man next to him and said, "Something seems to be missing."

The other man said, "I think it's his tin cup!"

The citizens of the small town asked the great Krazinski to give a violin concert in their school auditorium. Krazinski was flattered and accepted, saying, "The instrument I shall play is over two hundred years old."

The gent who'd invited him said, "That's okay. No one'll ever know!"

He plays the violin just like Heifetz—under his chin!

virgins

The way I see it, a virgin is a frozen asset!

An eccentric producer demanded purity of the singers and dancers in his shows. They had to swear that they were untouched. One pretty girl, wanting very much to appear in the producer's new show, went to her doctor, and was given a note attesting to the fact that she was a virgin, unsullied and pure.

At the audition the next day, she sang and danced beautifully. The producer chose her as one of the potential players. After the audition, the producer called her over and interviewed her briefly. Finally he got to the important question, asking, "Are you a virgin?"

The young lady whipped out her note and handed it to him. He read it and then threw it up in the air. "What good is this?" he said. "It's dated yesterday!"

She explained that the *V* on her sweater stood for "virgin." But when fellows backed off, she'd add that it was an old sweater!

A virgin is like a parking space. There aren't many, and when you find one, some guy sneaks in ahead of you!

She was really frigid. When she went to the Virgin Islands, they gave her a hero's welcome!

She had to go to the Virgin Islands under an assumed name!

Of course I'll guard my honor
Right up to my final breath;
But strictly between us—
Is it really worse than death?

You can always tell a real virgin. She thinks the sex act is just another way of doing push-ups!

A virgin knows that familiarity breeds attempt!

You're pretty sure she's a virgin if she wears stained-glass contacts!

Virgin wool is from a sheep that can outrun the farmer!

The day she lost her virginity, she had a coming-in party!

She's as pure as the driven snow. And they'll say the same thing next year, when she's three!

A virgin is any young man who buys a car and thinks that backseats are optional!

A virgin is any woman who thinks that all men are created equal!

In some societies they used to sacrifice a virgin to the gods. Now they leave the gods a cookie!

There was a girl named Virginia. They called her Virgin for short, but not for long!

Sir Edmund was about to go off to slay a dragon. Concerned, he put his beautiful young virgin daughter in charge of his young squire, Hilary. As a further precaution, Sir Edmund made certain that his daughter was wearing her chastity belt. Handing the key to Hilary, Sir Edmund said, "The chastity belt must remain on unless there is a dire emergency. Then and only then can it be removed." With those words, the knight rode off.

As Sir Edmund reached the moat fifty feet from his home, he heard Hilary calling to him, "Sir Edmund! Sir Edmund!"

Sir Edmund stopped. Brandishing the key, Hilary rushed over and said, "Sir Edmund, it's the wrong key!"

The hillbilly returned from his brief honeymoon looking less than ecstatic. His father said, "What went wrong?"

"She was a virgin."

"A virgin?"

"Yup. I didn't touch her. If she ain't good enough for her family, she ain't good enough for ours!"

The most precious gift a bride can offer her groom is her virginity. Of course, her father can chip in with a car, a down payment for a house, a trip...

Women say they lost their virginity. That's silly. Most of them know who got it!

visitors

I've solved the visitor problem. We have towels that say "His" and "Get out of Here"!

An out-of-towner visited with an old army buddy and hung around long enough to make it feel as if it was a permanent bivouac. The army buddy said, "Don't you think your wife and kids are beginning to miss you?"

The out-of-towner said, "Probably. I'll send for them next week!"

Aunt Sybil seemed to be planning a long siege. Her nephew Alex and his wife Norma were no longer thrilled with having her around. Alex came up with a plan, saying, "Honey, you'll make a roast. When we sit down to eat, I'll say it's too well done. You'll say it's rare. We'll ask her. The one she goes against will accuse her of meddling and order her out."

At dinnertime, Norma put down the roast. Aunt Sybil sniffed and licked her chops. As Alex cut into the roast, he said, "I can't eat this. Look at this roast. It's burned to a crisp."

Norma said, "It's blood rare."

"It's burned."

"It's rare."

Alex turned to his aunt and asked, "What do you think?"

Aunt Sybil said, "I don't know from anything. I still have three months to stay here!"

The host invited the guests to sit down for dinner. When they were seated, he said, "Shall we pray?"

The small son of the guests said, "In my house we don't have to. My mom's a good cook!"

I don't know how long my uncle's been visiting with us, but he signed our guest book with a quill!

We found a great way for keeping away visitors—we sold the house!

voting

Since all the candidates seem to be the same, the only reason to vote is so we can find out which political analyst was right! The last time I voted, I went into the booth and split the ticket. The man behind me, who weighed 280 pounds, went in and split the booth!

Some late-breaking voting news—with six cemeteries still to be heard from, the election is too close to call!

In some polling places, people stand around and offer money for votes. One party offers five dollars; the other may offer ten. Most of the time the five-dollar party wins. The voter figures it's more honest!

There was a terrible turnout at the last election. There were even two voting machines that didn't show up!

What's nice about Election Day is that seventy-five million Americans take time out to vote, and about four of them do!

In my neighborhood, the people vote because it's a patriotic right. It must be that, because most of them don't need the money!

I remember the motto back home: "Vote early and vote often!"

Since *perestroika* and *glasnost*, the Russians have changed their electoral system. A man went in to vote and was handed a sealed ballot. He started to tear it open. An election official said, "What are you doing, Igor?"

"I'm opening the ballot. I want to see who I voted for."

"You're not supposed to know. This is a secret ballot!"

waiters and waitresses

There must be somebody with a kind word for waiters and waitresses. It's definitely not me! There's no going wrong with jokes about lousy service. Several times, I performed at the annual dinner-dance of the Waiters' Union. They laughed at the jokes I did about abuse heaped on customers. They also appreciated the fact that many of my jokes gave them tips on abuses they didn't know about!

I like to kid around with waitresses. I'm playing for big steaks!

A customer told a slow waitress that her service was miserable. The waitress said, "How do you know? You haven't had any yet!"

In most restaurants today, the food is frozen and the waiters are fresh!

The waiter placed the finger bowls before the two men. Because they were unfamiliar with fine dining, one of the men asked, "What are these for?"

The waiter said, "You wash your hands in them."

The second diner said, "See? You ask a foolish question, you get a foolish answer!"

"Do you have any wild duck?"
"No, but I'll gladly annoy a tame one for you!"

Since the customer seemed uncertain, the waiter suggested, "Our halibut steak is fine."

The customer said, "I'm allergic to fish."

"The London broil is nice."

"My cholesterol is very high."

"We have roast chicken."

"Chicken gives me terrible cramps."

The waiter smiled and said, "Why don't you go to your doctor first? And then you'll order!"

"Waiter, there's a hair in my soup."
"Is it blond? We're missing a waitress!"

"Here's your coffee, sir. It's Brazilian."
"Oh, is that where you've been?"

"Waiter, I'd like some chicken. The younger the better."
"Good, I'll bring you an egg!"

wakes

Most people have some form of wake. Food and drink are served. The atmosphere is gay. The deceased looks down and is thrilled because the group is drinking his whiskey and eating his food. But he does bristle when he sees some relatives in the bedroom trying on his shoes!

The old man lay dying in his bedroom. Gathered around were his children. Suddenly, from the kitchen came the aroma of fresh-baked cakes. One aroma in particular stirred the old man. It was the aroma of his favorite—apple strudel. Gesturing to his oldest son to lean over, the old man whispered, "I'd love to die with the taste of your mother's apple strudel on my tongue."

The oldest rushed out, but returned a minute later empty-handed and said, "Ma says she only has enough for after the funeral!"

Mrs. Padapolis, tears in her eyes, looked down at the deceased lying in the living room, and said, "I hope he didn't die of anything serious!"

The richest man in town had just died. Tom cried sadly into his drink. Seeing him carry on, Al said, "I didn't know you were related to him."

Tom said, "I'm not. That's why I'm crying!"

At Sicilian wakes, people are hired to mourn. On one occasion, two older women, Rosa and Anna, who'd worked as professional mourners all their lives, were hired to keep the tears flowing. They cried, they agonized, they invoked a hundred saints in the name of the deceased, and upped the decibel count to a high pitch. As the invoked the hundredth saint, Mr. Carbatto, an old man, keeled over dead.

A guest rushed over to the professional mourners and said, "Now you have two souls to cry over."

Rosa said, "We can't do that, but we're willing to take off a few lire!"

Arriving at Al Stone's wake, Mrs. Graber looked at the mouth-watering spread on the buffet table. "This is some wake," she said to her husband. "Lila must have spent a fortune on it."

Mr. Graber said, "If Al knew, he would drop dead!"

Connie and Jack walked into the Taylor house for the wake, and were stunned by the richness of the decor. Connie said, "Ellen spent fifty thousand redoing the whole inside."

They worked their way through little pockets of guests and arrived at the piano, on which were pictures of Al. Jack said, "Look at him, the picture of health. What did he die of?"

Connie said, "The silk brocade drapes!"

wall street

The best time to tell jokes about Wall Street is when the market is causing trouble—yesterday, today, tomorrow!

A tailor worked many hours a day, saving every penny he could. He was about to deposit his bundle in the bank when the man who ran the diner next door told him of a great stock. The tailor bought the stock. It skyrocketed. He soon had a nice parcel of change. The man from the appetizer store just beyond the diner told him of a great stock. The tailor walked to his stock brokerage and bought the stock.

Before long, he was able to close his little

shop. He spent his time at the stock brokerage, buying and selling. Just before he became a millionaire, as is too often the case,
his holdings plummeted. In one week he was
worth nothing.

Returning home, he was a sad, defeated
man. His little old mother said, "Look, I
saved up a few dollars from what you gave
me. Open your shop again." The tailor
hesitated, then agreed that the idea was
sound.

Two weeks later the shop was reopened.
Above it was a sign: SAM STEIN, ALTERATIONS
AND CLEANING—FORMERLY MERRILL LYNCH.

"Does the stock market bother you?"
"I sleep like a baby."
"No kidding?"
"Yup. I sleep an hour. Then I get up and cry
    for an hour!"

You know when times are good on Wall
Street. On the ledge there are more pigeons
than brokers!

The other day they found a Wall Street
broker with his pretty filing clerk in Rio. He
claimed he didn't know where she'd filed
him!

Some people do okay on Wall Street. I
know a man who borrowed fifty thousand.
He invested it and lost every penny. He
climbed on a high ledge and jumped off.
Luckily, he landed on the guy who'd lent
him the money!

I made a killing on Wall Street today—I shot
my broker!

I'd think twice about Wall Street. It begins
in a graveyard and ends in a river!

With my luck, if I bought a seat on the
stock exchange, it would be behind a post!

Wall Street is getting more and more like
Las Vegas every day. One big broker just put
in a lounge show!

I left my heart in San Francisco, but everything else went on Wall Street!

When a Wall Street investor says that this is
his bridge night, it could mean either cards
or jumping.

My father did very well on Wall Street until
a broker jumped and landed on his pushcart!

And now a word from Wall Street—Help!!

On Wall Street, they have guys begging
with two hats!

Stand on Wall Street and look at the facades
of all those brokerages. Behind them are
thousands of men on the right side of the
telephone!

Wall Street is where men spend the morning trying to corner the market and the
evening trying to corner a secretary!

When you walk down Wall Street and see
the brokers arriving in limousines, you have
to wonder where the customers' cars are!

The big thing today, they say, is junk bonds.
Big deal. I started that years ago!

One Wall Street broker is taking a big
beating because of a merger, but he insists he
never touched the receptionist!

On Wall Street you have bears, bulls, and, if
you include my stocks, dogs.

They're going after people who trade on inside information. They even arrested a rabbi for his tips.

Every day you read about another Wall Street billionaire going to jail. To tell you the truth, it's getting hard for poor people!

A Wall Street billionaire got into his limo and the chauffeur asked, "Do you want to go to the office first, or should we go right to jail?"

It's hard to get the Wall Street out of a broker. One went to jail. Two weeks later he arranged for the prison library to merge with the laundry.

They fined one insider trader a hundred million dollars. Reaching into his pocket, he said, "Your Honor, you should know you're taking all my cash!"

washington (d.c.)

Can you say anything about the nation's capital that isn't funny? Read the daily headlines to an audience and it will laugh. Later, we'll all cry!

A congressman had a dream that he was making a speech in Congress, and when he woke up, he was!

In Washington, a man gets up to speak and doesn't say a thing, and the other men disagree with him for three hours.

"Did you hear my last speech in Congress?"
"Senator, I hope so!"

"Have you heard the latest joke about the White House?"

"I happen to work in the White House."
"That's all right. I'll tell it slowly!"

Washington is getting scared. There's a rumor that there soon won't be enough poverty to go around.

One time there was a senator who was a dove, until one flew over him!

I figured out a way to balance the budget—tilt the country!

A man ran up and down Constitution Avenue yelling, "No! No! No!" Somebody stopped him and asked what he was doing. The man said, "I'm a yes-man and I just started my vacation!"

They have a statue of the goddess Truth in Washington. It's not a good depiction. She has no stretch marks!

Things must be very bad. The other day the President sneaked into a café and told the bartender, "My country doesn't understand me!"

A man was going through the factory of a company that made plastic shapes. As he arrived, a huge number of horse's heads had rolled off the line. Puzzled, he asked, "What do you do with these horse's heads?"
    His guide said, "We send them to Washington for final assembly!"

The only time when Washington is on its toes is when the ballet is in town!

Mrs. Cameron was bragging to Mrs. Stone about her trip to the White House and how important she was. In recognition of her large contribution to the party's coffers, she was given VIP treatment. Describing the fancy formal dinner, she said, "Right after the salad, the phone rang."

"A call from some world leader?"

"No."

"The Joint Chiefs of Staff?"

"No. No. The President handed me the phone because it was for me!"

A woman called into the Department of Transportation and asked, "Do you have a Sexauer working there?"

The receptionist answered, "Since this new Secretary of Transportation, we don't even have a coffee break!"

The motto of Washington seems to be, "You can't be well informed if you're not confused!"

One senator hired a gorgeous girl and made her the object of a long congressional probe!

A young military officer met a lovely woman at a Washington party. After a few drinks, the couple walked out on the patio of the mansion in which the party was being held. The night air was balmy. The moon shone down, its light dancing off the trees and bushes. Because his ardor had been stirred, the young officer asked the woman if she'd care to join him in an amorous pursuit. The woman barked, "No! Definitely no!"

Her words shook the young officer. Fainting, he slumped to the ground. The woman aroused him and said, "My 'no' might be disappointing, but why did you faint?"

"It wasn't your turning me down," the young officer said, "but I've been in town three months, and this is the first time anybody's given me a definite answer!"

I ate much better when Roosevelt was in Washington. I had my own teeth then!

They just added a new classification to secret papers. "Top Secret" used to be the ultimate. Now you can get "Destroy Before Reading."

When a State Department worker is ill at home, they immediately get somebody to take his crisis.

A new official in Washington doesn't have it easy. One explained, "I feel like an Arabian sheik who has just been given a birthday gift of two hundred wives. I know what to do, but where the hell do you begin?"

A congressman and his wife were fast asleep when a noise from downstairs woke the wife. Tugging at her husband, she whispered, "There's a thief in the house."

Groggily, the congressman said, "Maybe in the Senate, but not in the House!"

A constituent called his congressman and asked, "How long does it take the government to spend ten billion?"

The congressman, busy for the moment on another phone, said, "Just a minute."

The constituent said, "I figured," and hung up.

Officials in Washington divide their time between running for office and running for cover.

One politician just left Washington for good. There's nothing left to steal!

A visitor to Washington asked a local citizen, "Can you tell me which side the State Department is on?"

The local citizen said, "Ours, I think!"

A congressman jumped up and said, "I rise for a point of information."

Another congressman said, "Glad to hear it. Nobody needs it more!"

One agency in Washington asked for eighteen billion last week. This week, another agency asked for twenty-two billion. No wonder the Office of Budget and Management says it's being nickeled-and-dimed to death!

The way I see it, Social Security has as much chance of going bankrupt as Mexico!

In Washington there are a million government workers who see their duty and try to get another million to do it!

With the new budget, we've finally managed to put peace on a wartime footing!

The President is having a rough time nowadays. They're beginning to call it the Oval Bunker!

A congressman was asked what he would do if he was handed a subpoena. He answered, "I'd read it on the plane to Brazil and then come to a conclusion!"

An Indian official came to Washington to plead his tribe's cause. It wanted the right to handle all of its own affairs. The head of the Bureau of Indian Affairs said, "It would be criminal to hand over those rights. Indians aren't smart enough to manage their property."

"Sir, do you think I wouldn't have that much brains?"

"I'm talking about the average Indian. You were sent here because you were the smartest man."

The Indian said, "I'm just an average Indian, sir. We Indians are like the rest of the people of the United States—we never send our smartest men to Washington!"

The architect who designed Washington knew what he was doing. The way he did it, it goes around in circles!

Two birds were sitting on the high fence that surrounds the White House. One bird said, "Are you for the President?"

The other bird said, "Why not? He's for us!"

Did anyone ever worry about what the initials of the Senate Office Building were?

"Did your paper say I was an idiot?" the senator asked.

"No, Senator," the reporter answered. "We never print old news!"

washington (george)

We can't let the father of our country go unmentioned. After all, his birthday is so important to us today, we all go out and buy new sheets!

If George Washington is the father of our country, when did Martha have time to make all those chocolates?

Washington had wooden teeth. That's why he brushed after every meal and saw his carpenter twice a year!

The guide pointed to the Washington Monument and said, "That is dedicated to George Washington. A lie never passed his lips."

A touring Englishman said, "Oh, he must have talked through his nose like the rest of you Yanks!"

Washington never told a lie. Of course, ever since then, Presidents have to hold press conferences!

We've sure come a long way. George Washington couldn't tell a lie. Now we all can!

A kid chopped down a cherry tree. Accosted by his father a little later, the kid was asked if he'd chopped down the tree. The boy said, "I cannot tell a lie. I chopped down the cherry tree."

His father hauled off and smacked the kid halfway across the room. Fighting back tears, the boy said, "George Washington's father didn't hit him when he said he'd chopped down the cherry tree."

The boy's father said, "George Washington's father wasn't up in the cherry tree at the time!"

Washington had the right idea when he stood up in that boat crossing the Delaware. Every time he sat down, somebody handed him an oar!

Washington never forgot a thing. All over the country we have monuments to his memory!

Everywhere you look, there are signs saying, "Washington slept here." No wonder he's the father of our country!

My son is a lot like Washington. He went down in history!

water

Another classic joke that may have helped end vaudeville: "There I was in the desert. Nothing to drink. Water! Water! I didn't pass water for three days!" Obviously, we had no shame in the old days. I'll bet a few bob, however, that it would get a laugh today! The rule is, as I've said time and time again, if they haven't heard it before, it's new!

A boozer from way back poured himself a decent portion of whiskey. Seeing him, the host said, "Let me get you some water for that."

The boozer said, "No need to. I'm not that thirsty!"

My brother gets drunk on water—as well as on land!

The doctor said to the patient, "You have water on the knee."

The patient said, "That's not so unique."

The doctor said, "Hot and cold?"

Our water isn't in great shape. If he were around today, Washington could have *rolled* that dollar across the Potomac!

Our water supply has to be polluted. I walked by the reservoir the other day and heard a fish cough!

I have friends who won't drink water. They know what fish do in it!

I have some stocks that are so watered down, the company had to hire a lifeguard!

Not too knowledgeable about resorts, Mr. Ginsberg ended up in the heart of Morocco. Putting on his bathing suit, he went into the lobby and asked a bellhop how to get to the water. The bellhop pointed and said, "It's about four hundred miles that way."

Mr. Ginsberg said, "Four hundred miles. Oy, is this a beach!"

The small-town doctor paid a house call on Farmer Brown. Before going into the house to examine the farmer's bad back, the doctor stopped at the well for a cup of cold water. The crank backfired on him, the rope pulling him down twenty feet. Luckily, the farmer's son saw this and rescued him.

That should teach somebody a lesson. A doctor should take care of the sick and leave the well alone!

weather

The weather is a perfect starting point for a speaker. We always have weather—too hot, too cold, too much the same. The audience should be measured for what I call the "bug factor." How bugged are those who just came in from the rain or snow? Or heat? If everybody is drenched or patently uncomfortable, laughter ranks about two hundredth in priority. The first ten priorities are to dry off, cool off, or whatever will make up for the outside conditions. I'd begin with self-deprecation. For some reason, people feel better when you are miserable. That may be why soap operas pull an audience. A beat or two after you self-destruct, the audience will be ready to hear about the weather! Additional help can be found in categories about a specific weather condition. Hot? It was so hot an Avon lady got stuck to her samples! Cold? It was so cold, at the zoo I saw a lion gluing himself to a bear! It was so cold "etcetera" hid itself in the middle of a sentence!

A hot summer sun has its advantages. You don't have to shovel it!

The sun's not coming out today. Would *you* come out on a day like this?

They should have known about the recent hurricane. If they'd looked at the barometer, they would have seen that the little hand was on the eight and the big hand was on Louisiana!

The wind does blow in the Texas Panhandle. Yesterday, there was a blow that took away this man's house, wife, and four kids.

He was asked, "Aren't you going to go out and look for them?"

The man said, "With the weather around here, they'll be back in an hour!"

It's going to be a cold winter. I saw a squirrel burying Sterno!

The smog was so bad, I opened my mouth to yawn and chipped a tooth!

A woman who'd moved to the Atlantic coast decided to fix up her new cottage in a typical Early American style. She bought an old-fashioned barometer. Putting it up on the den wall, she noticed that the needle was pointing to "Hurricane." Puzzled, she returned to the general store and told the storekeeper, "That barometer you sold me this morning isn't working."

The storekeeper said, "Let me have it and I'll give you a fresh one, still in the box."

The woman said, "I left it hanging in the den."

"Get it and I'll give you a new one."

The woman sped away from the general store. Ten minutes later she was back. "This is a crazy country," she said. "When I got back, the barometer was gone. And so was my cottage!"

There's a great shortage of water in Arizona. They plan to ration people to one bath a week. My brother wants to move there!

A rustic was sitting on his porch, holding a small piece of rope. His guest, a city man, asked, "What's the rope for?"

The rustic said, "It's my weathervane."

"How can you tell weather with that thing?"

"When it goes from side to side, it's windy. When it's wet—it's raining!"

We now have a topless restaurant in town. Of course, it was a regular restaurant until last night, but then the wind came up!

The English are so noncommittal. When I was in England recently, I stepped out of my hotel into glorious weather. I said to the doorman, "Isn't this a magnificent day?"

The doorman said, "Oh, yes, I've heard it highly spoken of, sir!"

It was so dry the other day I saw an orange sucking a lemon!

A man complained about the hot weather. "This morning," he said to a new arrival in town, "I saw a dog chasing a cat, and they were both walking!"

I have bad news and good news. The bad news is that it's going to drop to zero tonight. The good news is that my air conditioner is working again!

I don't mind freezing sleet and snow, but I wish they'd come in the summer, when the weather is nice!

I like snow. It fills all the potholes.

It was raining so much I saw a sparrow putting sandbags around its nest!

It was so windy I saw Siamese twins looking for one another!

The weather is driving me crazy. On day it's freezing, the next it boils. I don't know what to hock anymore!

If God really cared, he'd have snow fall *up!*

"Where are the snows of yesteryear?"
"Still in front of the house!"

How come a snowbank is never overdrawn?

Last week's storm was the worst in history, unless your name is Dorothy and you have a dog named Toto!

It hadn't rained in months. All the members of the congregation gathered at the church to pray. The minister told them, "I don't know if the Lord will think you're serious. Not one of you brought a raincoat to wear home!"

Last week it only rained twice—once for three days and once for four!

I enjoy this very cold weather we've been having. So does my wife, Nanook!

It was so cold in my house, when you opened the door, the small light in front went on!

A man who lived in a suburb started to drive home one evening and was caught in a vicious snowstorm halfway home. The drifts were so high, he was unable to drive all the way. Leaving his car, he struggled to a small restaurant a mile up the road. He called his house, then bundled himself up and slept sitting up in one of the booths. In the morning he called his office and told his boss, "I won't be in today. I'm not home yesterday yet!"

We get an awful lot of cold waves from Canada. Can't we weatherstrip the border?

It's really cold this winter. When people tell you to go to hell today, it's a suggestion, not an epithet!

It was cold this morning. I put on my coat to take out the garbage, and it didn't want to go!

The weather is great. My car won't start running and my nose won't stop!

weight

Even though obesity has been covered, the computer insisted that the following jokes be added. I have to be nice to my computer. He was turned down by the Xerox machine next door!

Being overweight is a crime. Many women buy a girdle to fit the crime!

We have a small sign on the refrigerator door: "A Word to the Wide Is Sufficient."

She weighed two hundred pounds on the hoof, which is what she had instead of feet!

You know you're overweight when you start to empty your pockets and find out what's in them—you!

I don't mind my extra weight, but when I want to let it all hang out, I have to make two trips.

You know you're carrying a little too much weight if it rains and nothing below your waist gets wet!

You're carrying too much weight if you try to play hide-and-seek and can only play seek!

You're overweight if you step on your cat's tail and the cat dies.

I saw a sadist at a Weight Watchers meeting. She had a dab of gravy behind each ear.

I wasn't an overeater. I was just a do-it-yourself famine!

You know you've got too much weight if you put on a wedding dress and the family goes snow-blind!

I'm carrying too much weight. I've been barred from one-way streets!

Overweight is when you live beyond your seams.

Overweight is when you put on yellow and men whistle for you instead of a cab.

You're overweight if you get out of a metal chair and have to fluff it!

I watch my weight. I have it right out in front of me where I can see it!

You're overweight if you can't get you and the water into the tub at the same time!

No man is an island. But he comes close!

His last picture had to be taken by a satellite!

I know I'm gaining weight. My appendix scar is two feet long!

She has a sunken tub—every time she gets into it!

Her weight keeps going down—and sideways, around, up...

I don't know how much weight she carries, but what's the next size after "truck"?

He's carrying so much weight, each knee has a lap!

westerns

Saturday afternoon, every kid went to the movies. For a nickel, the theater presented three movies, a serial, and a half hour of coming attractions. Westerns were the most popular features. The boys loved westerns because the cowboys were brave, strong, and never kissed the schoolmarm. The girls could never figure out why the cowboy preferred to kiss his horse. Later, "adult" westerns came along. That's where the cowboy's horse kisses back!

One cowboy star became so rich he got himself a Mercedes horse!

I know why some cowboys ride tall in the saddle—blisters!

The cowboy was tied to a stake. Around him had been piled wood and dry brush. The Indians danced around and set fire to the wood. Tied to a tree nearby, the heroine kept screaming, "Help me! Help me!"

The hero said, "Help *you*? Look at the trouble *I'm* in!"

The director laid out the scene for the hero, saying, "All right, John. You are coming down the road in the stagecoach. Suddenly, you're attacked by Indians. Start shooting. A dozen Indians will fall each time you pull the trigger, but don't act surprised."

Off to the side stood a contingent of Indians. They were disgruntled because of the anti-Indian slant of the movie, of which they hadn't been aware when they signed to work in the movie.

The camera crew took positions, the actors were cued, and the shooting started. The hero came barreling along in the stagecoach. The Indians came at him, but decided to attack for real. When the hero whipped out his gun and started to shoot, not one Indian fell. As they neared him, the hero yelled to the director, "They're not falling."

The director yelled back, "*Now* you can act surprised!"

whiskey

The word whiskey *is taken from an Irish word meaning "water of life." When Jews toast one another, they say, L'chaim," which means "To life." I know a few people who got L'chaim from a judge!*

A man walked into a saloon and stationed himself at the bar, saying to the bartender, "Give me a double whiskey. I'm going to have a big fight in a little bit, and I need the courage. It's going to be one for the books."

The bartender served him. The man chugged down the drink, walked over to the phone, and called his physician. "Doc," he said, "stay in your office. In a little bit, I'm going to have a big fight and you may get an emergency call."

He walked back to the bar and asked for a double whiskey with a double whiskey chaser, musing, "I need this whiskey. It's going to be a battle royal. There'll be blood and teeth all over the floor."

He drank the two doubles, returned to the phone, called his physician again, and said, "Stay by the phone. It'll be some fight."

Back at the bar, he said, "Try a triple this time. Some fight, boy!"

The bartender asked, "Who are you going to fight with?"

The man said, "You. I don't have money to pay for the whiskey!"

The other day I had a dozen brandied cherries. I never ate so much to drink in my life!

I must have had a little too much to drink on my birthday. I lit the candles on my cake with one breath!

A man had been reading the life and death statistics put out by the government and said to his friend nearby, "Do you know that a man dies every time I take a breath?"

The friend said, "Try a breath mint!"

For a bad hangover, take the juice of a fifth of whiskey!

Gasoline and alcohol don't mix. But I'd never drink gasoline straight either!

Whiskey won't cure a cold, but it's the best way of failing!

I always start the evening off with a glass of water. That takes care of all the chasers!

My brother lost two of his front teeth trying to drink a pint while falling down the steps!

widows and widowers

We can joke all we dare to about widows, but the fact is that sixty percent of the money is in their hands. That seems a little low, since they had about ninety percent when the husbands were alive!

A widower went to a séance. He wanted to talk to his dear departed wife. After much ritual and dramatics, the medium said, "I hear your wife knocking."

The widower said, "Who's she knocking?"

Many women wish their husbands would leave them just as they found them—widows!

Ruby's husband had been a brakeman with the railroad until an unfortunate accident. To compensate for her loss, the insurance company settled a huge amount of money on her. Making the deposit in the bank, she was still wearing her widow's black. The banker said, "After a decent interval, you will probably marry again."

Ruby said, as she endorsed the check, "It's not likely. But if I do, I'm going to marry a railroad man!"

A city man asked a farmer, "Which are the easiest weeds to kill?"

The farmer answered, "Widow's weeds. Just say, 'Wilt thou?' and they wilt!"

There are two kinds of widows—bereaved and relieved!

Sitting in the park, the old men were appreciating the season. Doberman said, "Spring is so nice."

Cooper said, "When those April rains come down and make everything come up out of the ground."

"Not for me," Patterson said. "I've got three wives down there!"

A widow was fixed up in a blind date with a man of ninety. When she returned home later, her daughter asked, "How did it go?"

The widow said, "I had to slap his face three times."

"He got fresh?"

"No, I thought he was dead!"

An elderly widow made a perfect catch. She married a used-car salesman who could turn back speedometers!

A grass widow is the wife of a dead vegetarian!

When a man is born, they ask, "Was it an easy birth?" When he marries, they ask,

"How did they meet?" When he dies, they ask, "How much did he leave her?"

A young widow went to the stonemason's shop and ordered a stone for her deceased husband. On it she wanted chiseled, "My tears are more than I can bear."

Several weeks later she called the stonemason and asked, "What would it cost to add 'alone'?"

"Why do widows wear black garters?"
"In memory of those who passed beyond!"

He was unable to watch his wife breathing her last and walked out of the house. Returning an hour later, he walked to his dying wife's bed and said, "Do you know who just got engaged?"

The wife shook her head and said weakly, "No. Who?"

The husband said, "Me!"

wife

I'll take my chances with "wife" jokes any time!

A man started to shave. Nicking himself, he started to curse a blue streak. His wife rushed in and asked, "What's the matter?"

The man said, "My damn razor won't cut."

"Don't be silly. You can't tell me your beard is tougher than the linoleum I cut before!"

King Solomon had a thousand wives. That way, the odds were pretty good that one of them wouldn't have a headache!

A woman was telling her friend about a burglary in her house the night before. The other woman asked, "When he saw the burglar, was your husband cool?"

The first woman said, "He was so cool he was shivering!"

My wife buys everything that's marked down. Yesterday she came home with an escalator!

Wives can suffer in silence louder than anybody in the world!

A macho male said to his wife, "We're not going out Saturday night, and that's semifinal!"

A woman noticed that a man was following her. Quickening her pace, she rushed home, bolted the door, and breathed a sigh of relief. She turned to put away her groceries. The man stood in the kitchen. The woman said, "You'd better get out of here. My husband'll be home any second. He'll kill you."

Just then, a car pulled into the driveway. Aghast, the woman went on, "He'll kill you. But I don't want him in jail. Hide in the closet. When he's not looking, you can run away."

The menace hid himself in the closet.

The husband walked in, kissed his wife, looked at the mail, and when his wife had started for the den, he went to put away his coat. Opening the door, he saw the menace and said, "Creep!" He looked closer and said, "Haven't I seen you someplace before?"

The menace said, "Yeah, in my apartment on Fifth Street. This'll make us even!"

On her last safari to a garage sale, my wife bought an old encyclopedia with four volumes missing. I said, "How could you buy an encyclopedia with books missing?"

She said, "I don't have to know everything!"

A woman asked for a divorce. The judge asked how long she and her husband had been married. The woman replied, "Thirty years. But I don't care—I want a divorce."

"Why?"

"My husband has terrible table manners."

"Thirty years of marriage, and you ask for a divorce because your husband has terrible table manners?"

The wife said, "I just found out this morning when I bought the book!"

I bought my wife a mink. She keeps the cage so clean!

A woman went to her physician and complained that her husband talked in his sleep. The physician said, "I'll give you a mild sedative."

The woman said, "Give me something to stay awake. I don't want to miss a thing!"

Whenever a man came home weaving from too good a time, his wife berated him, cursed, and made violent threats. One day she was telling the lady in the next apartment about her troubles and the lady said, "It's not working that way, so try another way. Pretend you don't know that he drinks. As soon as he comes into the house tonight, hug him and kiss him."

Having nothing to lose, the woman waited for her husband that evening. When he staggered in, she embraced him and said, "Honey, give me a little kiss."

The husband was glad not to have walked into a storm, and thought a kiss wasn't too big a price to pay for peace, so he puckered up. He kissed her on the forehead. Trying again for her lips, he managed to kiss her on the nose, then the earlobe. The wife pointed to her mouth and said, "If it was a saloon, you'd find it!"

My wife is a treasure. She's worth her weight in plastic!

Lonely, a man married again after his wife died. When he brought his new wife home, he told her, "You're free to make any changes in the house but one—in the closet there's a hat that belonged to my late wife. Don't throw it out."

The marriage lasted a few months, then the wife was taken away by a sudden illness. Again the man married, brought his wife home, and said, "Make any changes you want but one—in the closet there are two hats that belonged to my late wives. Don't throw them out."

The wife said, "I won't, but let me tell you something—the next hat in that closet'll be a derby!"

A man came home at three in the morning to find his wife in bed with another man. The wife bellowed, "Where were you until three in the morning?"

The husband said, "Who is this guy?"

"Don't change the subject!"

They say that after years of marriage, husbands and wives begin to look alike. I'm getting worried!

"Don't leave me," the wife sobbed to her dying husband. "Don't go. I can't be without you. Don't leave me."

The dying husband said, "Okay, come with me!"

Vera was at the top of her voice as she condemned her husband. "Irv was lazy, a bum, stupid, insensitive, a drunk, a thief, and a liar."

Her girlfriend asked, "Why don't you divorce him?"

Vera answered, "After thirty years of marriage, I should make that bum happy?"

My wife is so frigid, when she opens her mouth a light goes on!

One wife told her husband she couldn't cook, clean, or take care of children. So he went out and hired a woman to be his wife!

What my wife doesn't know about money could fill a checkbook!

A wife cleaned her closet and found things she hadn't seen for years—her vacuum cleaner, her ironing board, her dust mop...

His wife gave him the choice of a new spring wardrobe or a nervous breakdown!

Joe came home after a hard day's work. Plunking himself down in a club chair, he started to watch television. To make him feel better, his wife sat down in his lap. He pushed her away and said, "Stop it. I get enough of that at the office!"

My wife doesn't enjoy running over people. It's too bumpy!

My wife went away for a week. The whole house was empty, except for the kitchen sink!

The wife said, "I have some bad news for you."
    "Shoot!"
    "I thought about that, but a divorce is just as good!"

My wife and I had a little fight the other night. Nothing much—just three police cars!

My wife can find a corner in the middle of the block!

My wife has something that'll knock your eyes out—hair curlers!

My wife knows how to make a long story short—she interrupts!

A woman complained to the marriage counselor, "My husband always tries to push his way in. Even in the beginning, he wanted to be in the wedding pictures!"

"That's a nice coat. Did your husband change jobs?"
"No, I changed husbands!"

A wife had her face lifted, her nose straightened out, her legs shaped, her bosom curved, and then she turned to her husband and said, "You're not the same man I married!"

"Have you been married a long time?"
"Long enough to know that there are lots of things you can't say with flowers!"

My wife complained about not being wanted, so I went to the post office and put up her picture!

Before we got married, my wife used to say, "You're only interested in one thing!" Now I've forgotten what it was.

My wife doesn't clean much. In the living room we have a copy of *Good Housekeeping* covered with dust.

My wife should go into earthquake work. She can find a fault quicker than anybody.

My wife dislocated her jaw and couldn't speak. I called the doctor immediately and told him to come by as soon as he came back from his vacation.

She's an efficient homemaker. After dinner, she gives the kids something to play with in the tub—the dinner dishes!

My wife was going to have her face lifted, but she found out the cost and let it drop!

My wife gets more dirt out of a phone than she can out of a vacuum cleaner!

If my wife dies, I'm going to marry her sister so I don't have to break in another mother-in-law.

I told my wife, "I don't want to go to work. It's a jungle out there."
     She said, "Don't worry. I put a banana in your lunchbox!"

My wife is the light of my life. I put her out ten years ago!

My wife could have been arrested on our honeymoon—for indecent composure!

The last fight was my fault. My wife asked, "What's on the TV?"
     I said, "Dust!"

My wife always keeps a bowl of wax fruit on the table in case a couple of mannequins drop in!

My wife is so afraid of scandal she won't send our laundry out in one bundle!

wife (insults)

When the world runs out of these and "husband" insults, we will be ready for occupation by an alien civilization with a sense of humor!

She's the kind of woman who drove her husband to take lessons in getting a headache!

Her husband loved to take her out on Halloween. He didn't have to explain her!

Her husband took her everywhere he went. It was better than kissing her good-bye!

One night she put on a mud pack. Her husband seeded her!

My wife's a terrible cleaner. She keeps clogging up the dishwasher with paper plates!

He should have been warned when he saw her previous husband in the coffin. The corpse looked relieved!

Her body droops so much, her gynecologist has to wear a hard hat!

She's got so much grease in her sink, the bugs slide to their death!

She got him with soft soap. Now he does the dishes.

He was told he was getting a prize when he married her, but he should have looked at it first.

They knew she'd make him happy. She made six guys happy the week before.

At the altar she promised to love, honor, and obey. She didn't want to make a scene in front of the wedding guests.

She was his secretary before they were married. Now she's his treasurer.

When he proposed, he got a load off his chest—her two brothers!

My wife sent away for a bodybuilding course. Last week she built three men!

She's crazy about him. On Valentine's Day she sends a card to "Occupant"!

Her hope chest was filled with linen. They ran out of silicone.

She must have bought that outfit by accident. It fits her like a bandage.

She gets up early in the morning so she'll have more time to hate her husband!

She badgers him so much he's ready to move to a leaky reactor!

She's thinking about having her hair dyed to its original color, but she can't remember what it is!

She never knows what she wants until the lady next door gets it!

You can't believe her. She told her husband she'd drop dead if he came home early. He did. And she didn't!

Looking for a wife, he didn't leave any stone unturned. He turned one and there she was!

Sex is her way of playing dirty!

She's very happily married. Her latest lover likes her husband!

She's a very entertaining wife, especially when he goes out of town!

His nerve is in her name!

His wife must be from India. She's untouchable!

She gets so excited when she hears four-letter words—like "sale"!

She's an endangered species. Someday he may kill her!

wife's cooking (and cleaning)

Even in jokes, there are specialists today!

She comes up with strange combos. Did you ever eat chili à la mode?

She's such a bad cook she can burn water!

At times I help my wife in the kitchen. I help put out the fire!

Everything she makes is tough. We even have a soup knife!

I once cut my lip on my wife's coffee!

They divide the kitchen chores. She washes the dishes and he sweeps them up.

My wife's meatballs explode on impact!

I shouldn't have bought her a microwave oven. Now I have to eat her food fifteen minutes sooner!

My wife once fed a stray dog and he didn't leave. He couldn't move!

My wife once served snacks on a Ouija board. The Ouija board printed out, "Don't eat the snacks"!

Nobody can cook like my wife, although they came pretty close in prisoner-of-war camp!

My wife doesn't need to call us when dinner is ready. We can tell because the smoke alarm goes off!

My wife keeps buying cheaper and cheaper cuts of meat. Last night we had ankle of veal!

In my house, when you ask, "Guess who's coming to dinner?" it's usually paramedics!

She feeds him so much fish he's breathing through his cheeks!

I defy anybody to find another wife who does the dishes in bed!

When they come to our house, roaches make sure they eat first!

We have the only garbage disposal with ulcers!

My wife never straightens up the house. She doesn't think it's tilted!

When my wife put her finger through her wedding ring, that was the last thing she ever did by hand!

She has no kitchen skills. She opens an egg with a can opener!

Last week, *Bon Appetit* tried to buy back my wife's subscription!

My wife throws away the leftovers. I even want her to throw away the originals!

When my wife gets through burning meat, you can only identify it through dental records!

If my wife ran a restaurant, take-out would be impossible. People would buy leave-there!

wills

I never made out a will. I don't want anybody rooting against me. In fact, only a few weeks ago, I went to my attorney. Instead of a will, I made a won't!

Then there was the lawyer who was up all night breaking a widow's will!

A man died and willed his floating kidney to the aquarium.

She left him because he had a will of his own, and it wasn't made out to her.

Where there's no will, there's no lawyer.

A man told his lawyer the terms of his will. "When I die, I will my body to science. But while I'm still alive, to any chorus girl who'll take me!"

The lawyer read the will and all the codicils that left money to members of the family. Finally he read the last codicil, "And to my secretary, Miss Wilkins, whom I promised to remember even though she resisted all of my advances—hi there, Miss Wilkins!"

windows

"Stockies," as professionals call them, are jokes that belong to the world. Among the oldest is, "I won't say my hotel room was small, but when I put the key in the lock I broke the window!" For that great line alone, I included this category.

A window washer was working his way down from the top floor of a high-rise apartment building. When he reached the sixteenth floor, he was seen by the young lady who lived there. Desiring a little fun, she thought she would see if she could fluster the window washer and turn him on. She took off her clothes and pranced around in the nude, making the most lascivious moves. The window washer just kept on washing the window. The young lady put her act into high and made even sexier moves. The window washer knocked on the window. Smiling, she slithered toward it. When she was close enough to hear, the window washer said, "What's the matter? Haven't you ever seen a window washer before?"

A woman was bathing when there was a knock on the door. From the other side, a man said, "Blind man!"

Because she was charitable, the woman got out of the tub and, without bothering to put on her robe, walked to the door and opened it.

The man said, "All right, lady. Where do you want me to put the blinds?"

My office computer is beginning to act more and more like a person every day. This morning it asked for a room with a window!

winds

This category works beautifully in Chicago and nine-tenths of Texas. It used to work in Montana, too, but the wind blew the state away!

It was so windy, one chicken laid the same egg six times!

You know it's windy when the chill factor exceeds the speed limit!

It'll be in the upper seventies today—that's the wind velocity!

It's going to be windy today. This morning I saw a zebra glueing on his stripes!

These winds are good for driving. This morning I went sixty-five in neutral!

winter

"Weather" just doesn't cover the agonies of a morning when the temperature is zero. This category should help put the season in its place!

You know it's winter when you see a Dalmatian with thermal spots!

You know it's real wintry when you comb your hair outside and it breaks!

It was so cold I saw a hen laying eggs from a standing position!

This has been a terrible winter. So far I've worn out four pairs of galoshes and one pair of shoes.

It was so cold the other night, our snowman was trying to get into the house!

This is the time of year you run to places and pay three hundred a day to get the heat you complained about in July and August.

I'm so thrilled to be one of God's frozen people!

Two feet of snow had fallen and the winds were howling in the street. Mr. Klein walked into the bakery and asked for three Danishes. The baker asked, "Did your wife send you for them?"

Mr. Klein said, "Would a *mother* send her son out on a night like this?"

It was so cold on Christmas Eve, Santa Claus had to jump-start three of his reindeer!

It was so cold my overcoat was wearing a sweater!

It was so cold yesterday, men were wearing their toupees upside down!

It was so cold I saw a robin knitting worm gloves!

It was so cold last night, it took me an hour to get my girl started!

It was so cold I saw a polar bear wearing a grizzly!

wit

Somewhere between bludgeoning and the pointed joke lies the world of wit. For me, wit is the suspended sentence that follows conviction for a nonlethal crime. The first time a caveman said, "To make a long story short," and the first witty cavemen responded, "Too late!" wit was born. Wit differs from a putdown, a squelch, and other responses in humor in that it is brief. In most cases, it is spontaneous, created by people who are intuitively witty. A person can learn to be a comic and even a sort of comedian. Wit is inborn. Yet most of us have a witty streak. Somewhere in our heads are exact sentences, the exact words. If we just let them come out, we'd each score often. We might not have a high average, but that isn't important. If we can stop one fool in his tracks, one snob, one pompous person, we have paid our way. When my mother and I were checking out of a hotel in Albany, New York, after I'd finished my week

at the vaudeville house, a juggler from the same bill, who had spent the seven days boring us and all of Albany with details of his triumphs, looked out the door at the pouring rain and asked, "Do you think it'll ever stop?" My mother said, "It always has!" Her wit saved us the thrill of hearing the juggler describe all the famous rains he'd been through.

A famous French singing star, in the United States to make a movie, was accosted by several dowager types. He answered their questions nicely, ending each response with a smile and a "Mademoiselle" or "Madame." One dowager finally asked, "What is the difference between Madame and Mademoiselle!"

The French singing star said, "Monsieur!"

When the ladies went to work trying to figure out his response, he got away.

A well-known but disliked actor was preparing a one-man show. The director gave him trouble, so the actor walked out. Told about his exit, another actor said to a friend, "I think he quit because he didn't like the cast!"

A Broadway character had a black belt in borrowing. He owed everybody, but there were a few people from whom he cadged money every other day. One of the unlucky victims asked heaven why the borrower sought him out so often. A wit answered, "You're on his route!"

Our Presidents seem to have enjoyed a more than average wittiness. John F. Kennedy, one of my favorite leaders, was asked about his first days in the White House and answered, "When we got into office, the thing that surprised us most was to find that things were just as bad as we'd been saying they were!"

Jimmy Walker, my hero when I was a lad and he was mayor of New York, was caught in a lie. A reporter asked him what he had to say about it. Walker put on his famous grin and said, "Another good story ruined by eyewitnesses!"

A New Yorker, born to the purple, was renowned for his cheapness. He was also a giant in the financial world, always getting what he wanted. At a men's club, two of his acquaintances were discussing some recent maneuvers he'd made with a company. One said, "He gives no quarter."

The other acquaintance said, "He doesn't give any dimes either!"

women

In the western world, there are 1.87 women for each man. I may never get the opportunity to find out, but I'd sure like to know what my .87 looks like! Be forewarned—single women don't laugh as much as those who are married. Forty-five is just about the dividing line. The younger single women may part with a snicker or two. Women over forty-five probably say, "What the hell! Let's have a good time anyway!"

I like a woman with a head on her shoulders. I hate necks!

Women are beginning to wear a lot of makeup again. I saw one fall down the other day, but she didn't hurt herself. She landed on her eyelashes!

The average woman is a good listener when money talks!

Woman is the last thing God worked on. It shows that he might have been a little tired!

If you want to know why they're called the opposite sex, just voice an opinion!

I find it hard to believe that a woman was made from a rib. A funnybone would be more like it!

Women never lose their temper. They always have it!

Women don't believe everything they hear, but that doesn't keep them from repeating it!

Where would woman be without all of her finery? In the bathtub!

There are three kinds of women—those you can't live without, those you can't live with, and those you live with!

A woman has seven ages—the real one and six wild guesses!

Whoever named them the fair sex was a poor judge of justice!

The plural of *whim* is *women!*

If men dressed like women, women would turn around too!

No woman will ever go to the moon. She wouldn't know what to wear!

Intuition is woman's radar!

A woman complained about a man she'd met. "From the first minute, he screamed and cursed."

A friend asked, "How'd you meet him?"

The woman said, "I ran over him with my car!"

Many women are like electric irons. They

start to warm up when there's a new attachment!

A woman forgives only when she's been wrong!

A theater patron sat behind a woman who kept up a steady stream of chatter as the play went on. From behind her, the patron said, "I can't hear a damn thing."

The woman said, "I wasn't talking to you!"

If women are so smart, how come they always dance backwards?

When a woman takes some years off her age, they're not lost. She just adds them to her girlfriends'!

Women have a great weapon—twin beds!

Women are attractive at twenty, attentive at thirty, and adhesive at forty!

A woman is like a gun—don't fool with it!

Women should be allowed to go into combat. Why waste all those years of marriage?

Women put on wigs, fake eyelashes, falsies, fingernails, ten pounds of makeup, and then go around complaining that they can't find a real man.

A man took a woman to a baseball game. They were a little late and he had missed some of the first inning. He looked at the field and said, "We're doing great. We have a man on every base."

The woman said, "So has the other team!"

It used to be hard to find a needle in a haystack. Now it's even harder to find one in a woman's hand!

We never hear about self-made women. They change the plans too often to get the job done.

"Dad, what part of speech is 'woman'?" "She's all of it!"

We'll never have a woman President. She'd have to admit she was thirty-five!

A woman may be taken for granted, but she never goes without saying!

Woman isn't perfect, but she's the best other sex men have!

Women try their luck. Men risk theirs!

Here's to the soldier and his arms,
Fall in, fall in.
Here's to woman and her arms,
Fall in, fall in!

When you don't praise a woman, she thinks you don't care anymore. Praise her and she thinks she's too good for you!

women's lib

It's about time women learned they were our equals. Men have been getting tired of women being their superiors!

Women should stick to their cleaning, washing, ironing, and cooking. There's no reason for a woman to work!

Older women don't understand women's lib. They didn't want to get out of the kitchen. They wanted to get into the kitchen. They wanted to get out of the bedroom!

Too many women get married before they can really support a husband!

Any woman who wants equal rights with men has no ambition!

After the Lord made man, he took a look and said, "I can do much better than that!"

Some women want a man's salary. Don't they get it already?

"Why do you let your wife stay in women's lib?"
"When she's stirring things up outside, it's peaceful at home!"

Everywhere you go, you see signs of women's lib. Last night I was held up by a gunperson!

I have the feeling that when God made man, She was only fooling around!

Women are supposed to be smarter than men. Then why do they wear shirts that button down the back?

Women today are interested in the problems of women. Men are also interested in the problems of women—finding one!

Some of the women in women's lib are so cold they have arctic circles under their eyes!

One woman solved the problem of her husband's philandering. When she left the house to go to work, she hid the maid!

Most women in the women's lib movement think they're so perfect even practice couldn't make them!

I'm glad my wife joined women's lib. Now she complains about all men, not just me!

I'm all for women's lib. I'm tired of dancing backwards!

Two young women went to a women's lib meeting, but left early. It was a terrible place to meet men!

Some women don't want to be liberated yet. First they want to be captured!

A women's libber was yelling, "Free women! Free women!"
A drunk, walking by, said, "Do you deliver?"

One man went all out to help women's liberation. He divorced his wife!

work

Idle hands do mischief make. But they don't get dirty either!

A father told his son, "Hard work never killed anybody."
The son answered, "I'm looking for something dangerous!"

A man saw another digging a trench as the boiling sun beat down. The man said to the digger, "A man with any brains would wait until the sun went down."
The digger said, "If I had any brains, would I have this kind of job?"

My brother just got a great job. He's a lifeguard in a car wash!

My brother went into a new line of work— he's a marriage counselor for the Pope!

I know a garbage collector who lost his job

because he couldn't keep his mind in the gutter!

A worker in a large factory went to his boss and complained, saying, "Mr. Evans, you got me working the boxing machines with my hands, pushing the extracting arms with my feet, biting off the ends of the cords with my teeth, and making sure my eyes look out for imperfections. I'd like a favor."

Mr. Evans said, "What can I do for you?"

The worker said, "Can you push a broom in my rear end so I can clean up too?"

If you hire relatives, you'll have a payroll that won't quit!

"**W**hy are you quitting? The wages are good."

"I know, but I'm keeping a horse out of a job!"

My brother applied for work, but was told by the company that it had more employees than it needed. My brother said, "Don't worry. The little bit of work I do won't be noticed!"

Work is the most unpopular way of making money!

"**C**an you put my son to work?"

"What can he do?"

"If he could do anything, *I'd* hire him!"

worry

I must have been about twenty-two. I was madly in love with this young, innocent girl, fresh from a farm in Ohio. She had taken a small apartment on a hill. I used to worry about her all day long. One day she told me that she wanted to become independent. She didn't want me hovering over her, checking to see if she was all right. I told her that I couldn't help but worry. I loved her so much. She insisted that we stop seeing one another. I told her that I wouldn't be able to sleep at night from worry. She showed me the door. Outside, I got into my car. Already, I had started to worry about her being alone in a big city. How would she survive? How would she remain unscarred? I was so worried. I put my car into gear and started down the hill. I put my foot on the brake. I had no brake. I stopped worrying about that girl in two seconds!

"**I**'d love to bring you to my place, John, but my mother would worry."

"Let's go to my place and let *my* mother worry!"

The Browns were in an utter panic because it was midnight and their teenage daughter wasn't home yet. Knowing that she'd gone to a party at the home of a girl named Jones, they took the number of the first Jones in the phone book and dialed it. If necessary, they were prepared to dial every Jones listed. Connected after about a dozen rings, Mr. Brown said to the Jones on the other end, "I hope you don't mind this intrusion, but are you the Jones who is giving a party?"

Mrs. Jones answered, "No, this is the Mrs. Jones who was taking a bath when you called!"

A friend of mine knows what worry is. He's got a secretary and a note from a bank, and they're both overdue.

If you want to test your memory, try to remember the things that worried you yesterday.

"**D**on't worry about it," the doctor said. "If your husband wants to talk baby talk to your baby once in a while, just let him."

The wife said, "Oh, he doesn't talk that way to the baby. Only to the baby-sitter!"

The boy and his mother stepped up into the bus. The driver said, "How old is that boy?"

The mother said, "Four."

The driver said, "He looks about ten."

The mother said, "If you had his worries, you'd look ten too!"

The doctor tried to be reassuring. "Don't worry," he said. "Many people talk to themselves."

The patient said, "I know, but I'm such a bore!"

Worry is the interest we pay on trouble before it's due.

I worry so much. I wonder what wine goes with fingernails!

I joined a Don't Worry club. I called up and asked, "When's the next meeting?"

A voice said, "Don't worry!"

The man is a born worrier. When he greets you, he says, "Good morning—maybe."

He never worries about tomorrow. He knows that everything is going to turn out wrong.

wrinkles

When you're born, you're wrinkled. Your face wrinkles up when you frown. Your face wrinkles up when you laugh. When you grow old, you become wrinkled. I think God had a one-track mind! I'm not sure I like all those lines on my face. I wish God could have come up with a new wrinkle!

She's got so many wrinkles she can hold ten days of rain!

He's got so many wrinkles on his face he has to dry with a pleated towel!

She's got so many wrinkles she went to a plastic surgeon to get her face terraced!

Wrinkles are hereditary. Mothers and fathers get them from the kids.

She's very neat. Every wrinkle is in place.

With all his wrinkles and blue lines, he looks like a road map his wife folded.

He's got so many wrinkles, an accordion once fell in love with his face.

X

x, the letter

I'm in trouble trying to come up with a witty introduction to this letter. I'm thrilled because I still have Z to look forward to!

A boy came home from school and handed his father his report card. After reading it, the father quietly affixed an X to the line reserved for the parent's signature. The boy said, "Why'd you sign it with an X, Pop?"

The father said, "With the grades on this report card, I'm not going to have the teacher think that the father of the student can read and write!"

In the time of the Caesars, two young lotharios were hanging around the Forum in Rome. A lovely Roman maiden passed by. One lothario whistled and said to the other, "Look at that—a perfect X!"

An Indian went to court and asked that he be allowed to use an O instead of an X when he signed his name. Asked why by the judge, the Indian explained, "It's not so much for treaties, but when I sign a smoke signal, an X is murder!"

xerox

A Xerox machine is a piece of equipment that office workers often pass by on the way to a coffee break. It can be told from other pieces of office equipment by the usual presence of a repairman trying to figure out how twelve paper clips got caught in the feeder!

One company had too much work for its Xerox machine. So a secretary copied the machine and made three more!

A man had fifty thousand shares of Xerox stock. Well, actually it was one share. He copied it 49,999 times!

Washington has a new way of uncluttering the files. They throw out all the files over two years old. But before they destroy them, they make a Xerox copy!

By mistake, a secretary dropped one of her birth-control pills in the Xerox machine, and it wouldn't duplicate!

They now have a Xerox machine with a long top board. It sleeps three secretaries!

New machines can now make a thousand copies a minute. That'll cut down on the paperwork!

x-rated

Appearing in X-rated movies has some drawbacks, but it also has a good thing going for it— when you get up in the morning, you're dressed for work!

One porno star was asked to do a sex scene with three men. She quit—artistic differences!

Men in X-rated films work without clothes. They must be told to take them off. No one could be forgetful enough to leave home without them!

One X-rated picture had to be delayed because of an occupational hazard—a draft!

A drunk wandered into a studio where an X-rated film was being shot. He turned to some of the male stars who were standing around and said, "What are you going to do if the army doesn't take you?"

They performed the sex act for the camera, and kept at it until a star emerged!

You know it's an X-rated film. Instead of saying "Cut," the director says, "Throw water on them!"

inches high. Now they're working on a two-inch shield for the technician to stand behind.

X rays can make you sterile. I didn't believe it until my uncle got overdosed at the doctor's office. Now he's my aunt!

My doctor gives X rays for any complaint. If you have a cough, he'll X-ray your throat; a cramp calls for a body X ray. I was in his office the other day and I saw a nude man in his X-ray room. I said, "What's the matter with you?"
    The nude man said, "I don't know. I just came in to drop off the mail."

They now have an X^2-rated picture. They get it by X-raying an X-rated movie.

x rays

My dentist has a voluptuous assistant. When she takes X rays she wears a heavy lead outfit to keep the rays away. She also wears it for one or two patients!

The doctor in my hometown was really old-fashioned. He didn't have an X-ray machine yet. He used to hold the patient up to the light!

An X-ray technician got married to a woman who'd come in for testing. He must have seen something in her.

One doctor had a great way of treating poor people. If they couldn't afford surgery, he just touched up the X rays.

They have a new X-ray machine that's three

xylophones

One of the great acts of vaudeville, and later of variety, consisted of a man playing the xylophone while, behind him, a woman shed her clothes to applause from the audience. Apparently unaware of the curvaceous young lady, the xylophonist naturally believed the applause to be for him. The act played for years. Nobody in any audience could name one of the songs played! After a show, the audience always went out humming the young lady's wardrobe!

Two dinosaurs passed a xylophone. One said to the other, "She's cute, but she's all skin and bones!"

A nearsighted dentist passed a xylophone and said, "Your folks ought to bring you in for braces!"

Y

yankees

The true Yankee is a New Englander who has never smiled, laughed, or moved his lips while telling a joke. A Yankee out-Englishes an Englishman with a drollery that is part salt spray and part hard rock. The Yankee is unique among ethnic groups in that jokes about him invariably end with him winning. The classic Yankee story tells it all: A tourist is lost in Maine. Approaching a Yankee, the tourist asks, "Does this road go to Mapleton?" "Don't know." "Does this road go to Bracken?" "Don't know." "Does it go to Sylmar?" "Don't know." "Don't you know anything?" "Ain't lost!"

The editor of a small newspaper in New Hampshire sent Daniel Willis a reminder, saying, "Your subscription has expired."

The reminder came back three days later with a note scrawled on the envelope: "So's Daniel!"

A tourist stopped off in a small New England fishing village. At a roadside stand, he looked over some lobsters for sale. He said, "They're very small."

The stand owner said, "Sure are."

However, his appetite whetted, the tourist bought two lobsters and had them boiled in the ever-present cauldron. As he started to eat them, the tourist said, "These lobsters are tasteless."

The stand owner said, "Aren't you glad they're puny?"

A Vermont farmer was asked, "Why do you folks have more cows than people?"

The farmer said, "Prefer them!"

A prospective buyer was looking through a Maine shoe factory. Noticing some older employees, he asked the plant manager, "How many workers do you have heading for retirement age?"

The manager answered, "Seems you can't go any other way!"

Two proper young ladies from Boston, on the way west, stopped at a strange object off to the side. A closer look revealed that it was a homemade tombstone on which was chiseled, "Elbert Brown, Boston."

One of the young ladies said to the other, "Brief, isn't it?"

The other said, "But sufficient!"

"Any speed limit here?"

"Nope, we Yankees don't think you fellows can go through our town fast enough!"

The fair was going full swing. One of the attractions was a five-dollar ride in a small biplane. Aaron and Emma, two elderly Yankees, decided to chance it. The pilot did the usual tricks; then, in order to get a rise out of the passengers, he tried some fancy maneuvers—loops, Immelmanns, and upside-down dives. Not a sound came from the passenger seats.

As they came in for a low landing, the pilot said, "You folks are really the strong, silent type. I've had other passengers scream themselves hoarse."

Aaron said, "Don't believe in public displays, although I admit I almost said something when my wife fell out!"

A touring New Yorker met a Yankee well up in years. The New Yorker said, "You must have seen a lot of changes over the years."

The Yankee said, "Yup, and I've been against every one of them!"

Yankees pride themselves on their weather. They have nine months of winter and three more late in the fall!

A tourist, staying at a Vermont inn, came down to the lobby and asked the cost of the New York paper on the counter. The owner of the inn said, "That'll be seventy-five cents."

The tourist said, "On the front page, it says that the paper costs thirty-five cents beyond Boston."

The owner said, "We're beyonder than that!"

youth

Youth is the first fifty years of your life, and the first nineteen of everybody else's!

"How do you keep your youth?"
"I lock him in my closet!"

The best way to keep looking young is to hang out with old people!

A man was hanging around outside of his house at a wee hour one morning. A passing policeman asked, "What are you doing out at three in the morning?"

The man said, "I forgot my key. I'm waiting for my nineteen-year-old son to get home!"

A man was telling his friend, "I never realized it until now, but my son is the third degeneration of my family!"

Scientists can tell you exactly where each star will be at every minute of the evening. How come nobody knows where my son is at ten-thirty?

"Billy, did you take my car out last night?"
"I went for a spin with a couple of the guys."
"Well, tell them I found two of their lipsticks!"

A woman kept pushing her son to go to the school dance. Finally he gave in, saying, "Okay, if you want me to grow up and become a gigolo, I'll go!"

Youth is always ready to give maturity the benefit of its inexperience!

A lot of young people are getting married today. Their only problem seems to be when her hair curlers get caught in his hair curlers!

A youth with his first cigarette makes himself ill. A youth with his first girlfriend makes everybody else ill!

Z

zebras

They don't talk too often, but when they do, they come up with funny things somehow!

As part of a fact-finding tour for the jungle animals, a female zebra went to the United States. Seeing a cow, she asked, "What do you do?"

The cow said, "I give milk."

Then the zebra saw a sheep and asked, "What do you do?"

The sheep said, "I grow wool. They take it and make clothes."

A moment later, a stallion ran up. The zebra said, "What do you do?"

The stallion said, "Take off your housecoat, I'll show you!"

A man went to a psychiatrist and complained about his feeling that he was a zebra. Everywhere he looked on his body, he saw black stripes. The psychiatrist gave him some mild medication and said, "One of these pills and some rest will help you get rid of the black stripes."

The man returned the next day and said, "I feel terrific. The black stripes are gone. Do you have something for white stripes?"

The female zebra fluttered her eyelashes at this other young striped animal. He said, "I'm not what you think. I'm just a horse, but I sat down on a bench before the paint was dry!"

A drunk, passing a zebra behind a high railing, said, "What are you in for?"

Then there was the male zebra who fell in love with a young female zebra because she had nice lines!

zingers

This is the last chance to fill up before the last entry.

The next time you give your old clothes away—stay in them!

Why don't you take a long walk on a short pier!

You have all the charm of a dirty Christmas card!

Why do I have the feeling she needs a course in remedial sex?

Sir, I'd like to leave a thought with you . . . but where would you put it?

Let's play horse. I'll be the front and you be yourself!

He should get a hobby—he should go home and collect dust!

She looks familiar, and she probably would be if we asked!

God should have mercy on his soul. He didn't on the rest of him!

If I've said anything to insult you, please believe me!

What convention are you left over from?

You have some voice. You sound like a cow who just stepped on her udder!

She's real cool. She works in a meat locker!

Don't go away. I want to forget you exactly as you are!

He shouldn't go to a shrink. He's small enough already!

Don't lose your head. But I can see why you'd want to!

I was told you were down with a virus. I didn't think it stood a chance!

You weren't born yesterday. Nobody could get that ugly in twenty-four hours!

Go out and get a girdle and then pull yourself together!

You make silence such a wonderful thing to look forward to!

I'm warning you. I can lick you with both hands tied behind your back!

She wouldn't hurt a flea. She has so many of them!

Can I have your head for my rock garden?

He's a swell guy—especially around the head!

He's the reason for twin beds!

ZOOS

I like the idea of a zoo. Animals should have a place that protects them from people!

A husband and wife were visiting a zoo where the animals were in compounds rather than cages. Unfortunately, the wife leaned over too far at one of the compounds and was grabbed by a giant male gorilla. As the gorilla was carrying her off, the wife cried, "What should I do? What should I do?"

The husband said, "Do what you do at home. Tell him you have a headache!"

At one zoo, they have a donkey with the IQ of a genius. Unfortunately, he has no friends. Who likes a smart ass?

A female giraffe was talking to another female giraffe about the male giraffe who kept strutting through the compound. The first female said, "Isn't he gorgeous?"

The second female giraffe said, "So he's tall. Who isn't?"

He took his girl to the zoo, but the zoo wouldn't accept her!

At five in the evening, visitors to the zoo go home. Watching them move off, the head ape said to the little apes, "I think they feed them now. We'll come back in the morning!"

I know a waiter who used to go to the zoo often. He loved to watch the turtles zip by!

The peacock strutted in front of the compound where the two platypuses were sunning themselves. One said, "Look at that peacock. Look at all those colorful feathers."

The other platypus said, "You'd put on a front too, if *you* were deformed!"

TRICKS
of the
TRADE

ad libs

An impromptu joke has no "now." Once uttered, it gets its laugh and exits the ranks of the impromptu, becoming part of recorded jokedom. If it's funny enough, by the end of the day it has become part of the language of the office, the party, or gala itself, and, in the case of performers, the act.

Some years ago, when one audience seemed less than awed by my patter, I finished a joke, sighed into the absolute abyss of silence, and said, "Okay, here's *another* you won't like!" The laugh that followed was weighty and welcome. The line itself is now a standard with comedians and would-be comedians. Had I been able to copyright it, my income would have received some delightful padding.

Often, an ad lib is merely an understatement or overstatement of a fact of life. If the audience isn't buying your tidbits, acknowledge the agony of it by saying, in mock anger, "I'm going to remember every goddamn one of you!" That'll get them. Sure, you'll say. You've been at it seventy-five years.

Length of service isn't the sire of the impromptu. We're all capable of ad libs. Funny thoughts form themselves in all minds, especially in times of crisis. One of our neighbors was changing a tire in the middle of summer. The temperature was about five thousand degrees Fahrenheit. The heart attack that ensued was scary, but as the paramedics placed the poor soul on a gurney, he whispered to his wife, "Leave the tire. I'll fix it when I get home!" Even the wife laughed.

Yet, as funny as they think, many people censor out the humor. Not long ago I found myself in a Beverly Hills department store, waiting to one side while two women were dedicating their lives to making a salesman miserable. When the ladies departed, the salesman, a proper and skittish gent seemingly devoid of humor, marched over to me and let off a little steam by saying, "Did you ever have the feeling you were walking up a gangplank and there's no ship?" I feel that this dour-looking gent would have denied being able to come up funny.

I "rented" the line, by the way, and have used it a thousand times.

Grant yourself a funny bone, and the ad libs will come. You need only practice the belief that you're able to get a laugh.

There are two kinds of ad libs. The first is the truly impromptu remark, right off the cuff, with the umbilical cord still attached to the maker. (I love to mix metaphors, or haven't you noticed?) The ad libs will come if you stop censoring your private clown. Will Rogers taught me, "Don't be afraid of your mind. It'll take you to humor."

The second type of ad lib is prepared. It is culled from ad libs of the past or funny thoughts you've been able to come up with when not under pressure.

The prepared ad lib carries with it one caveat: Make it *sound* as if you've just thought of it!

Don't become too good at ad-libbing. I have enough competition already!

blackouts

Blackouts are pure gold in any show. Basically, a blackout is a two-person joke acted out instead of told. Because it has added impact, it brings a special energy. A half-dozen blackouts can juice up your PTA show or the revue put on by your charity group. For shows in which extensive set changes have to be made, the blackout helps to keep the audience's enthusiasm at a high level during what would ordinarily be a slow, tedious activity. Reserve a corner of the stage or even an area off to a side that can be lit up. A set helps, but so does a hand-painted sign that tells the locale of the blackout: "A Doctor's Office," "A Battlefield," "A Street in Paris." A voice can suggest the scene.

Examples: "The Front Lines." A general looks through field glasses as a soldier rushes in. The soldier says, "Sir, the enemy is attacking and we are outnumbered ten to one." The general says, "Tell the men to hold them off for a half-hour, then they can start retreating. I have a sore ankle, so I'll start now." BLACKOUT as he moves off.

"A Perfume Counter." Two women, one a salesgirl. The salesgirl says, "This is a nice perfume: Passion. And Ecstasy is nice too. And how about Seduction?" The customer says, "Do you have something for beginners?" BLACKOUT!

"Justice of the Peace." A justice of the peace works at his desk as a young man and woman enter. The young woman says, "Can you marry us?"

The Justice of the Peace says, "In this state you have to wait seventy-two hours to get married."

The young man says, "Well, could you say a few words to tide us over for the weekend?" BLACKOUT!

Since I love to write and act in blackouts, call me and I'll come running when you do the show for the company picnic!

burlesque

Once an art form, burlesque has fallen on hard times. The few theaters whose marquees boast of GIRLS, GIRLS, GIRLS are relics, filthy, vile-smelling, and often in the ugliest part of town. The stripteasers are old, arthritic, and shapeless. Yet one element of burlesque remains attractive. The comedians and comedy are still funny. They manage to evoke laughter from audiences made up largely of winos and the homeless, an audience light-years away from the desire to laugh.

A good burlesque sketch is worth its weight in comedy gold. True, many of them have been demeaned to fit the decaying curtains of the grind houses, but in their purest form, they are clean and fit nicely in a show being put on by fraternal groups, schools, and even churches. "Slowly I Turned," a piece I would have authored proudly, will work anywhere. "Flugel Street" carries its own guarantee.

Many of these sketches appear in books easily available in libraries. They can also be bought from the same outlets that provide plays for schools and amateur theater groups.

the card game

Or, "Why Index Cards Will Be the Best Friends Your Words Ever Had."

Committing to memory is a valiant exercise. It isn't a necessity in preparing to face an audience. Because I appear and speak at a hundred affairs a year and try hard to use different jokes, jokes that will fit the occasion with precision, I save wear and tear on my memory cells by using index cards.

Four-by-sixes, or the closest you can come to them, are the best size for me. If you use a larger size, you'll need ten companions to help you carry in your material. Smaller sizes don't allow for the fact that your eyes aren't as good as they used to be.

Using dark ink and large lettering to overcome the inadequate lighting often found at a dais, I write each joke on a card. I prefer handwritten cards. The act of writing out a joke helps you learn the joke. I have never become accustomed to typed cards. I suppose that's due to my having broken into the business when quills were still being used. Some of the new word processors have a type size I could get to love. It's about six inches high.

At times I may write only the key words of a joke. I make certain, however, that the punch line is evident. I never go anywhere without a punch line.

Index cards can be more than memory prods. They have the added value of allowing me to juggle the order of jokes while preparing my spot. As I go over the cards again and again, my rhythm is stimulated. My monologue, a key section I always put on cards, gets a flow as I play with the little darlings.

At times, especially when the joke is long, I may even use two or three cards. On each card, however, I put a complete idea so that my reading will seem to be natural. A jarring presentation makes an audience nervous.

Index cards can help your timing, especially if you're inclined, as many beginners are, to rush through your segment. Your brain tells you to hurry so you can sit down in relative safety. The index cards will slow you down.

The cards themselves can be a part of your "act." Look at a card and put it in your pocket, saying, "I'll save this one for a big dinner." Or read a card to yourself and laugh, adding, "Oh, this is so funny!" Then go on to the next joke quickly. When a joke doesn't get a laugh, you can sail the card into the audience as if you wanted to get rid of it.

Audiences won't mind your use of index cards. They may even appreciate the fact that you prepared so well.

Don't *read* from the cards. They're only an aid.

I save all of the index cards I've used. By going through some for a previous show, I may come up with some new jokes. Or find a few old ones that'll serve the cause of laughter.

delivery

A joke is fragile at best. It is, moreover, not necessarily funny in itself. Most often, a joke is a vehicle by which a funny person establishes his or her ability. Otherwise, everybody and his uncle could stand up and get screams. Everybody and his uncle can't. It becomes important for the attempting jokester to give humor all the support that can be mustered.

First, you have to *believe* you'll get laughs. If you don't brainwash yourself into believing your talent, you won't get the desired reaction. People who start the telling of a story with a caveat, a statement of their inability to tell a story, will not tell it well. Why should they make liars of themselves?

Your comedy starts with a pep talk to yourself. You'll do well. You'll do great. They'll hand you the whole world on a plate!

A failure at self-hypnosis, which is really what this is, doesn't mean the end of a promising career. Put aside your fear and perfect a new philosophy—you may not get laughs, but you will have fun with the chore! Life isn't at stake, you're not being paid a million to deliver, and the hell with the knees knocking—all valid supports for your act.

Starting from either pole, your major route home will be your delivery, the way you relate the story, joke, or routine. This is the carpentry of comedy. It has several simple steps.

First, prepare your audience. Set the boundaries of your material. You've no doubt heard comedians and comediennes who start with a premise such as, "The whole world's crazy today. Just look around." The audience is being prepared. If you use index cards, as suggested in the preceding section, let the cards be a wraparound way to prepare: "Let's see what they wrote on these cards." Or, "Well, you didn't like that one, let's try this one."

The next step is to limit the parameters of the jokes even more: "Do you remember how it used to be in the old days? A fellow would meet a girl and ask her for a date and it was a yes or a no." You now can go on to the specific joke area you've aimed for: "Well, today you have to fill out a questionnaire: 'Name all your sex partners in the last eight years. Name all *their* sex partners'!" You've worked into a routine.

Try to give your material the ring of truth in terms of the telling itself. If you want to make it seem as if you're talking off the cuff, each sentence should come out as if you thought of it a millisecond ago. Your fertile mind invented these words expressly for this audience. That's not easy to do if you're using cards. You can still emerge with truth. The audience must know that you are working from prepared material. You're trying to sneak it past the audience as just-thought-of stuff.

Most important, your delivery must reflect your pleasure. You like these jokes. You love them. You are enjoying telling and hearing them. Even when you are obviously struggling, there must be an element of enjoyment coming from the pain. You are really, your selling point says, having fun under the sweat. Some of my biggest laughs come from my "savers."

Prepare the audience, have faith in yourself and the jokes, and enjoy yourself even if your *Titanic* is going down! Remember, too, that the audience is on your side. It'll abandon you only when you exude an uncontrolled fear.

If possible, bring along your mother to lead the laughter and the cheering!

doubletalk

He seemed to be speaking good English. I made out many words I knew. Yet I didn't understand what he was saying. At the tender age of ten, I'd just encountered doubletalk. As children, most of us have some private language we share with intimates. Most often it's a version of pig latin. Sitting at my booth at my club, I still use a private language that can be understood only by one or two people present.

Doubletalk is a giant step past a private language. Using only a few real words, the doubletalker makes it sound as if he were carrying on a normal conversation. The inflections are seemingly normal; the rhythms are those of real speech; yet the language is incomprehensible. Hearing, you are frustrated and wonder if you might not need a hearing aid. An eye chart would make more sense. There is in each of us, however, a streak of false pride that doesn't allow us to admit we don't understand.

Two major tools, among many, help the doubletalker. Most common is to mix words and nonwords in sentences and paragraphs without once departing from the normal tone of conversation. Of equal value is the tone change or mutilation of some sounds to create an effect for the listener of a hearing aid gone awry. Some doubletalkers speak a sort of radio static in which the words may fade and even disappear altogether.

The doubletalker shouldn't betray his gimmick. Just as magicians don't reveal tricks, the doubletalker doesn't admit after a while that it has all been an April Fool's joke. Others at the table may let the unwary in on the tricks. The doubletalker remains aloof.

He may even be insulted at your inability to converse with him.

Doubletalk can also be part of a speech or routine at a roast. As with any comedic technique, doubletalk shouldn't be abused. More is less in doubletalk.

Remember, the snalem of the corginate whenever people get together has a definite effect on the groibes of the tarmel and the way you're perceived! Doubletalk is devanetle and must be pertanned! *What* did he say?

hecklers

A heckler is an unfortunate soul who believes that he or she can go on to glory by interrupting you as you fight for your life at the microphone. Don't become angry with this sorry creature. Feel only sorrow for him.

If your disdain becomes obvious, the heckler has won. The heckler starts out with an advantage. He doesn't have to be funny. He doesn't have to be bright. His function, through disruption, is to make himself important. Bend with his remarks. Enjoy them, or at least make sure you're successfully feigning enjoyment. I hold off doing battle with a heckler until he begins to make the audience nervous; then I'm obliged, as the performer of the moment, to show who's in charge. I don't try to reason with a heckler. Often he has a high alcohol content. Nobody can argue with the third martini. When I do throw a line, I like to start with strength. One line can often squelch the heckler. Moreover, the rest of his party will shut him up if he's in danger of being maimed. My retort is always delivered with a chuckle, as if I know I'm doing battle with an amateur. Lady hecklers, much fewer in number, are harder to cap. In addition, the lady is the ruler of the table or section in which the group sits. A woman can shut up a male heckler with a stare. Men can't stop a lady heckler with an Uzi. I'll often start responding to a lady heckler by being overly nice. I'll say, "And I've always loved you too!" Or, "Please come back again tomorrow." I pull the stops at the third or fourth interruption. When being heckled at a dinner or a roast by peers, I play tough from the beginning. As peers, willing to play the game, they must be prepared to take a few hits.

As with most retorts and jokes, the moment of entry is important. If the audience laughs at the heckler, wait until the laughter is subsiding. Your response will be in the clear. If the audience greets the heckler with silence, get your line in faster, so there is no lull. A pause can erase the reason for an answer. None of the above suggestions work on New Year's Eve! Or at a Shriners' convention!

humor and wit

No matter how easy it looks from the audience, or how good it feels when it's working for you and paying off with laugh after laugh, comedy, for me, requires sweat, spine, and grit. As payment, a titter isn't enough. There is no such animal as a polite belly laugh.

On the other hand, humor and wit try hard not to be too funny. Will Rogers, one of my mentors, often said that humor was comedy with the pinky finger out.

Humor and wit don't go to extremes for material. Raucous comedy depends on the extreme. That may explain why most of the comedians I knew and know lived or live in a world of extremes anyway. Comedians don't go to "good" restaurants. They eat at the "greatest" restaurant, or the "world's best" restaurant. They "kill" an audience; they don't tickle its fancy.

Although my forte is tough comedy, I don't belittle humorists. Humor is an equal art form. With practice, a humorous delivery can be effected. The hardest roadblock is the supposition that a smiling audience isn't as appreciative as one rolling in the aisles. It can be. An audience grinning with its eyes can be having a wonderful time. The droll approach is merely another way of going to pleasure. It may be your way.

I sometimes wish that I lived in humor and wit. Citizenship in the land where pies hit you in the face and seltzer is gushed into your trousers is taxing!

insults

Early on, I learned that insults should be used sparingly. The learning came after I'd been merciless with "fat" jokes at the expense of two heavyset ladies sitting ringside at a club in Chicago. One of them started to cry. The tears were those of hurt. No laughs were worth that price.

Insults, especially those built on physical characteristics, require special care. In using insults, have a smile on your face, as if your comments had no basis in reality. You are throwing lines merely to have a good time, amusement only mildly developed from the blemishes of the target, if at all. As an insulter, you must be aware that there are cross-eyed youngsters who cry themselves to sleep.

An audience will probably laugh at the first insults because of your impudence in daring to deliver them. Some have shock value. Yet, unless you convey the sense that you are playacting or kidding around, the audience will soon abandon you. No audience really wants blood drawn. It hisses

overt malice right off the stage. Its groan lets you know that you've crossed over into dangerous territory.

On a roast, a comedy form built on insults, I won't tell a joke that cuts skin. I'll try to make the line sound untrue enough to be rated only as a joke and not a sworn statement. Comedy isn't the truth; it's the manufacture of almost-truths with a label showing somewhere that says, "Made in Humor"!

introductions

One of the toastmaster's functions is to introduce other speakers. An introduction can be made simply by stating a few ordinary facts about the upcoming speaker. I'd avoid that. Never skip an opportunity to have some fun. The trick is not to appear as if you're reaching for a laugh.

The best introduction sounds as if it were being made up on the spot. I find that a touch of surprise helps, so I let the intro slip in naturally. I'll start by saying, "When I first met our next speaker..." Or, "While I was having lunch with good old Joe, I asked him whom he'd want on his dais. And he said..."

My sentences will never be simply declarative. Most of them will start with a preposition or conjunction. This is a trick great orators use. Winston Churchill made the listener want to hear the next part of his sentence. His phrases and clauses pulled the audience along. Franklin Roosevelt was another who used good old prepositions to lead the audience up the auditory path.

Although many of the introductions that follow are written as declaratives, they should be molded into the second halves of sentences. ("Although we have had a long history of toasting brilliant men in our organization, our honoree tonight...") and move on to the phrase that will skewer him or her. Also, starting in different ways helps create new introductions. In those cases, the intros in this grouping can be used as second and third jokes. Many emcees like to save the name of the next guest or speaker as the button of the whole joke. Most of the time I will mention the name of the person about to be introduced as soon as possible. Knowing that I'm introducing George Washington right off will help to make a joke about wooden teeth or a powdered wig stronger.

I also like alliteration. In introducing an attorney, I will call him a bumptious barrister, a dimpled Darrow, a screwed-up shyster. Always a free laugh.

Alliterative phrases are fun to invent. I appeared dozens of times on a television show of which the star was noted for drinking. I had to come up with thirty ways of calling him a drunk: this Sicilian souse, this Roman rummy, this looped lasagna! I'd just about guarantee alliteration as a laugh-getter.

Whatever the introduction, it should help set a proper stage for the next speaker.

I'm not against working up a short "bit" with the next speaker. At stag roasts, when I'm working with a performer I know, I'll introduce him by saying, "He's not only a bad comic. He's also a lousy lover!"

The performer will jump up and say, "Your wife tells you everything!"

From then on, he's got the crowd.

Our next speaker has risen to every occasion, a fact that amazes his detractors, impresses colleagues, and delights his wife!

Thank you for that nice introduction. I accept it, fully aware of the adage that says, "Flattery never hurts anybody unless he inhales!"

Our next speaker had a terrible experience earlier today. He spoke at a convention of waiters, and couldn't get anybody's attention!

In introducing our next guest, you could say that he was warm, caring, considerate, bright, and giving. You could say all that, but it wouldn't be true!

Earlier today, our guest of honor put on a see-through gown. Nobody looked through it. Nobody wanted to!

I'd like to introduce the world's greatest speaker. I'd like to, but unfortunately I have to introduce ____!

It is said that ____ is one of the greatest men in our field. And here's the man who said it, ____!

I'd like to introduce the next speaker. I'd like to. I'd really like to be home, if you want the truth. But I have to introduce ____!

You'll remember our next speaker for life. If you're run over in the parking lot!

Here is a man who's a legend in his own mouth . . .

Our next speaker is a man of the world. When the waiter brought his vichyssoise, he sent it back because it was cold!

It is not the function of a master of ceremonies to stand up and bore the audience, but to introduce people who will. Our next speaker, ____!

Our next speaker needs no introduction, because nobody cares who he is anyway!

Our speaker tonight needs no introduction. He didn't show up!

Here's a guy who's going places...the sooner the better!

I must apologize for the acoustics here. We will hear every word our next speaker has to say!

If a man is what he eats, tonight we honor a rubber chicken!

Our next speaker needs no introduction. He needs a conclusion!

Our next speaker will talk to us about taking control of life, of mastering one's own fate, and of asserting one's place in the home. That's what his wife told him to talk about, anyhow!

Our next speaker is a remarkable man. Bright—yes. Friendly—yes. Educated—yes. Working—no!

Ladies and germs...I mean, gentlemen!

Our next speaker has never been bored, but he is a carrier!

Our next speaker is going to speak his mind, so here to say three words is ____!

Our next speaker needs no introduction. He knows who he is.

Why should I introduce our next speaker? Why? Why? That's what I want to know—why!!

Now that we've finished our chicken, it's time for some baloney!

Our next speaker will add something to this evening—a half hour!

We've heard so much about our next speaker. Now let's get *his* side of the story!

Usually we bring up a man of integrity, wisdom, talent, and class. Tonight we depart from this tradition!

Our next speaker says that he's known for his intelligence, wit, erudition, and integrity. I know him for his modesty!

introductions (responses)

In testimonials or roasts, never turn the other cheek. If you do, then the other cheek will get it too! In addition, audiences enjoy a good riposte at the expense of the master of ceremonies!

Thank you. As far as introductions go, that one didn't go far enough!

I would call that introduction mediocre, but why be kind?

We all have something in common. None of us knows what I'm going to say!

Thank you for that great introduction. It will always be with me, like the roast beef we had tonight!

It's amazing—twelve hundred of us having dinner together, and we all ordered the same thing!

Thank you for that wonderful introduction. It had all the sincerity of a date with Jack the Ripper!

Isn't it amazing? While you were saying all those fantastic things about me, I was thinking the same thing!

I'm sure I don't deserve an honor like this, but what's my opinion against thousands?

I could be sparkling and funny tonight, but why should I change the mood set by your master of ceremonies?

You people seem to be in a terrific mood tonight. I'll take care of that!

Of all the introductions I've gotten, yours has been by far the most recent!

I'm glad to be here. I'm glad to be anywhere!

Thank you for that very warm introduction—wonderfully restrained, I might add!

Your master of ceremonies knows the secret of how to make people laugh. Tonight he still kept it secret!

Ladies and gentlemen, honored guest and what's-his-name!

I'm not too thrilled at being announced without further ado. I happen to need all the ado I can get!

"k" words

Vaudeville didn't spring full-blown from a set of blueprints devised by theatrical engineers. The shape of an eight-act bill came from trial and error. Thousands of shows had to fail before it was decided that a "flash" act opened. "Flash" acts were noisy and busy; they could get the attention of an audience. They could overcome the rudeness of late arrivals to seats. Among the other great discoveries was the fact that words with "K" in them were funnier than other words. Cabbage is a funnier vegetable than lettuce. So are kale and kohlrabi. This theory was propounded in a brilliant Broadway play a few years ago, the explanation itself evoking huge laughs because it too was loaded with "K" words. The "K" sound comes from a tickle in the throat to start with. Words with explosive sounds are also funnier than those without. Broccoli is funny. Tomatoes aren't. Go for the "K" and the explosive sounds. If you have to name a character in an anecdote, call him Ken Plotnick rather than Sid Lowell. Don't use Gaylord Gonchik. I own that one!

language and languages

I speak five foreign languages. Japanese came my way when my gardener tried to explain why the lawn was dying. I can now say "Tora Tora Tora" with the best of them. I picked up Spanish from our housekeeper. I think it's Spanish. When she tells me that Señora Mayanichoyagola called, I know that she is really saying, "Mr. Hacker called." She conveys great messages from my wife. Her "Señora bankmarkvengacometardelate" tells me that my wife is eating lunch out.

But seriously, folks, the mastery of a foreign language isn't easy. The mastery of an accent is. Telling a story in good dialect starts with the ear. Listen to the music of the different languages. Some are singsong. Others come from different parts of the voicebox. Listen and absorb. Jokes are enhanced with the proper pronunciation of foreign words and names. Some jokes need an accent.

There's more than the sound, however. People speak with their bodies, too. Putting your hands in front of your face and moving them slowly as if conducting an orchestra will pull a French accent out of you. Fling your hands and arms about and you'll enrich your Italian. I've found that I can help an upper-class Yiddish accent by putting one hand on my hip and facing sideways. Keep bowing gently, and you'll do a better Japanese. Whatever your movements, with most accents they should be smooth. Only in Germanic tongues should your movements be jerky, like those of a toy soldier being brought to life. You vill listen, *achtung!*

the man in the box

Loges have gone the way of loose milk and the one-room schoolhouse. In the days of variety and vaudeville, a comedy form called "The Man in the Box" was often the highlight of the show. It couldn't be matched for raw laughter because it pitted a seeming civilian against a highly trained comedian and allowed the comedian to be attacked mercilessly. One of the cornerstones of comedy is in the cutting-dow-to-size of a star. In "The Man in the Box," the star, especially the comedy star, was cut down to size, shredded, diced, and left for dead on the stage. Insult after insult was tossed at him without mercy.

When I started to appear in nightclubs, I modified the form slightly. Instead of a paying customer heckling me from a seat in a plush loge, I'd have an actor masquerading as a waiter. In my television variety show, he became a stagehand. The basic notion never changed. Generally, even the lines didn't have to be changed. "The Man in the Box" was a verbal pie in the face. It was two dozen of them! Today it can be modified to fit a

charity show or a church talent show. No audience is too blasé for the routine. In my college seminars, I'll often demonstrate with a faculty member as the insulter. College students roar at the so-called corny jokes. Most of the jokes are new again, some coming up for the tenth guffaw. The best part is that "The Man in the Box" doesn't need to be punctuated with any of the four-letter words deemed indispensable today!

To start a typical speaker-waiter routine, have the "waiter" drop a tray.

SPEAKER: Please be more considerate of the audience.

WAITER: I didn't mean to wake them!

SPEAKER: These people are awake.

WAITER: Don't bet on it!

SPEAKER: Did you come out here to shut me up?

WAITER: Somebody has to!

SPEAKER: Look, I didn't come up here to have you make a fool of me.

WAITER: You don't need help!

SPEAKER: That's funny. Funny. That's one of my father's jokes.

WAITER: What are you—one of your mother's?

SPEAKER: If you're not careful, I'll give you a piece of my mind.

WAITER: Be careful. You don't have much left!

SPEAKER: I bet you think it's easy for me to stand up here.

WAITER: No, just brave!

SPEAKER: Do you think you could entertain these people!

WAITER: Somebody should. They paid a fortune to get in here!

SPEAKER: I suppose you could tell jokes too.

WAITER: I can be diverting. What's red and goes dingaling?

SPEAKER: I have no idea.

WAITER: A red dingaling.

SPEAKER: Truly brilliant.

WAITER: I have another one. Wanna hear it?

SPEAKER: How could I resist?

WAITER: What's green and goes dingaling?

SPEAKER: A green dingaling.

WAITER: No. They only make it in red! See ya!

monologues

Traditionally a dramatic form, the monologue was borrowed by the comedian and redefined as a grouping of jokes held together by subject or subjects. Some comedy monologues cover a dozen subjects, but there is some kind of epoxy. By declaring that the world is crazy, a comedian can go almost anywhere and cover any area. My forte is to roam from non sequitur to non sequitur. Oddly enough, that approach glues the jokes together. Other comedians can start to tell the audience about a problem he or she had in returning a Christmas gift, and embellish that for fifteen minutes.

Two agents usually help shape the monologue. First, the monologist should have an attitude. He is taking on some institution or institutions. The audience appreciates the attack because it too would like to get even with those institutions. The second agent is the comedian's self-appointment as a representative of a group. He represents the harried citizenry, parents, the poor, minorities—all the helpless who need a defender. For a new comedian, the lack of a constituency can be fatal. Who is there to laugh at his monologue? I have always represented the unstructured, the irreverent. When I do an opening monologue at the roasting of a celebrity, I am compelled to destroy that celebrity. Generally, my opening monologue will be an oral biography of the celebrity with the most outrageous jokes. As one of the world's jesters, I have an attitude. Without an attitude, I wouldn't walk onstage or to the rostrum.

occupations

When I appear before a homogeneous group—one that, for example, has a common professional link—I make it my business to learn some of the language of that line of work. Each trade has a special jargon. In the furniture business, for example, the word "borax" is the key by which shoddy or cheap product is defined. If I can put the word "borax" into my opening joke, I'm indicating that I care enough about the group to tailor my act to it. Familiarity with the jargon helps me, as the speaker, become "one of the boys." Years ago, I entertained at a Tupperware convention. It was held in one of those cities to which senior citizens run to follow the sun. These gatherings usually featured a well-known singer. The crowds weren't easy for comedians. In the back of the auditorium was a gigantic display of the containers sold by the many home salespeople. My opening line was, "It's a thrill to be here with you wonderful people. Especially in this lovely room. The whole auditorium looks like a retirement home for cold cuts!" After that, I could do no wrong for that crowd.

off-color jokes

In comedy, it's all right to be a little pregnant. However, that freedom has resulted in license. Of late, I've watched performers tell scatological jokes that go beyond simple references. Acts of all sorts are described in intimate and loving detail, as if the heavy weight of detail and language made for more meaningful comedy. I feel that the humor is weighted down. Frequent use can lead to addiction that can hurt the performer. If he can get a cheap laugh with filth, why should he bother to learn the craft? Too many are swayed away from learning to do and say things in a funny way. They lose. Comedy loses.

I use a gauge for jokes I consider telling in a regular show: as long as they don't paint an ugly picture, I might use them. If they form pictures that make even a veteran of five thousand roasts cringe, I bid them a fond adieu.

In preparing routines for yourself, feel free to use my gauge. You know what'll make the hair on your own head stand on end. If a strong epithet is to be used, make sure it's indispensable. Shock laughter is temporary laughter. If doesn't stick to the funny bone. I don't believe that there are "dirty" words. I do believe that there are ugly intentions! In the area of off-color humor, a larger danger exists. Evoked laughter can militate against you. An audience may laugh itself sick and hate you as soon as the laughs ebb. You have exposed the prurience of the audience. The audience won't forgive you. Audiences too want to go to heaven!

props, gimmicks, and gizmos

A song from a great Broadway musical hinted that a performer had to have a gimmick. *Almost* gospel. You don't have to have a gimmick, but life is easier with one. Or more.

I was spurred into thinking about gimmicks and props when I assembled the category on cigarettes earlier in this book. I was reminded of the time not long ago that a peer, one of the great straight men of all time and part of the quintessential man-woman team, wanted to start doing personal appearances again. He'd always used a cigar as a prop of sorts, but had never considered using it as an important aid. During lunch one afternoon, he mused about the rustiness of his timing. I suggested that he let the cigar do his timing for him. We drew lines on his cigar. As each one burned, it became a measure of his timing. By now, the cigar has become his symbol. An impressionist must have a cigar in hand before he can attempt to mimic this star. The cigar could probably walk out onstage and get laughs.

Others, myself among them, often use a cigar as a prop. Many won't even light it. A long puff enables the audience to accept a pause. The pause gives the performer time to think of jokes and plan new subjects, and helps prepare the audience. If you study the end of the cigar, lit or unlit, you justify the pause. Otherwise, your silent struggle to find a new joke, a new area, would make for a lull.

Some comedians carry an instrument. They will start to play it a hundred times during a monologue, but never quite get to a meeting of man and music. I know of one comedian who wore a large ring and tapped it against the mike after a joke. The click-click helped prepare the audience for the next joke. A wine or whiskey glass brimming with the hair of the dog has helped many performers. A sip between jokes provides thinking time. One young comedian actually worked onstage with a grocery sack over his head. He may not have become eternally famous, but he did become known.

Physical moves often help. One major comedian today pretends to be nervous and is constantly playing with his tie or preening himself. The actions fill in the spaces between jokes. There have been performers who scratched their heads, tugged at their ears, and just about stood on their heads to fill the spaces.

Most gimmicks are found by accident. After some of my gimmicks from my variety television show caught on, I looked like one great comedy inventor. Imagine—so many expressions, catchphrases, that funny walk. Half of the things that caught on were not planned to win the world. What was deliberate in all of them was an alertness that would recognize something that would catch on. I looked and still look for gimmicks.

When you perform or half-perform at the company luncheon for the retiring night-shift boss, part of you must stand off somewhere in the audience and study yourself. The good moves, the right gimmicks and props, will become obvious. One of the finest down-home comedians of his time, or any time, performed at a luncheon for executives of a giant chemical company. He was unaware of the fact that after a run of jokes on a subject, he'd smile and say, "It wasn't really like that." For some reason, the line got a big laugh. It worked each time he did it. It became almost a slogan for the company. Executives went around saying, "It wasn't really like that." Only after a third affair for the company, this time for the heads of regional offices of the chemical company, did he realize he was building a verbal logo for himself. Unfortunately, a few weeks after that affair, the comedian passed on. You can have the line if it works for you.

Look for a prop, gimmick, or gizmo. It could be the best friend your act or speech ever had.

quotations, a second helping

Made-up quotes can evoke laughs. Putting down a roastee or next speaker, you can

offer, "This man is the man who, when it started to rain, said to Noah, 'It's only a sprinkle!' This is the genius we honor!" "This lover of the truth told a ten-year-old George Washington, 'If you father asks about the cherry tree, tell him your brother did it!' This is the great man we honor." "This adorable woman who said to Jack the Ripper, 'How come you never take *me* out?'—this is our guest of honor!"

If the quotations can be localized or personalized, they can get even bigger laughs. "This is the man who told Mayor X . . ." "It was this man who stood on Fifth and Olive and said . . ."

My attorney's secretary once spent a week ignoring the phones while she prepared ersatz quotations for a brief speech to be made at a shower for a friend. My attorney lost a hundred thousand in business, but his secretary was the hit of the shower. Important things must come first!

Try some quotes. You'll like them!

roasts

Some years ago, I outlined a book on roasts. My agent submitted it to three publishers. All sent it on to their cookbook editors for evaluation.

I wasn't the first victim of a word. Thirty years ago, a famous New York madam wrote a book called *A House Is Not a Home*. The story of her sinful ladies and their gentleman callers, the book was put in the how-to sections, right next to books on electrical repairs.

My roast book is a primer for those who would like to honor someone in that special way invented at the Friars Club in New York some sixty years ago. Enrico Caruso, the great tenor, was "honored" by a dozen of his peers, who stood up and tore him apart with good-natured barbs. They called him every name in the book to show him how much they loved him.

The form caught on, and soon the Friars were roasting every celebrity in sight. Moreover, celebrities were waiting in line to be insulted with a vengeance. Human nature is weird, isn't it?

What the Friars wrought can serve you and any cause you may champion. A roast is a sure-fire, cost-efficient way to honor someone. Outside of mugging, it's the surest way to raise money.

A roast should be prepared down to the last detail.

The hall should be arranged, if possible, so that there are a large number of tables as close as possible to the dais or head table. The head table should be lit adequately, bright enough so that the faces of the speakers and the "stars" can be seen. Only as many tickets should be sold as can comfortably seat the audience and allow each guest a decent view. Mikes should be tested and retested. I sometimes spend hours making certain of the lights and the mike. In each group, there are always knowledgeable people, those who put on PTA shows, those who put together a company party. The entire production, however, must be under the control of one person. Committees bring chaos. Committees are helpful in selling tickets and advertising the event, but the show itself should be under the aegis of one individual. Actors and writers often belittle producers. They don't quite know what a producer does on a movie, for example. Let them be entrapped by a bad producer, and they'll know what a good one can do. A bad producer will make for an unsuccessful roast.

The honoree should be someone who deserves the accolades. The news that he or she will be honored should generate the sale of tickets, as should the publication of the names of the roasters.

For a charity roast, a prominent citizen of the community can help swell the coffers. He or she should be a viable target. To honor Father McBride or the school principal is to invite a tepid roast. Speakers may be uncomfortable joking about a priest's tendency to belt a little; parents of children in school know that the fate of their children is in the hands of the principal. Roast your boss or office manager, but not your kid's boss or office manager. The point is subtle, but I thought I'd offer it.

Since many roasts are part of a larger program, it is important to keep other speeches and testimonials short. Many times I'll suggest that the "business" part of the evening be achieved before the dinner or even during the dinner. There should be no serving of food once the roast starts.

The actual roast should run about an hour. An hour and a half is courting disaster. Some of the roasts held at the Friars last as long as two and a half hours, but the roasters are trained pros who can handle the itchiness of an audience. I would suggest a five-to-ten-minute opening from the master or mistress of ceremonies, five-minute spots from the various roasters, five minutes for a rebuttal by the roastee, and a total of five minutes to introduce nonspeakers who are at the head table. Three- and four-minute spots for each roastee wouldn't be out of line either. Four minutes can be a long time for those not used to the ordeal of performing.

The emcee will have to commit himself to the task. He must accept the responsibility of preparation. Although he should have cards from which to work, he must practice and practice again. As the opening act, as it were, he has a wider range of sources of material. He can joke at length about the crowd, the dinner, the occasion itself. Every aspect of the roastee's life is available to him. In this encyclopedia he will find jokes on most of these aspects. Working with the producer, the emcee should help to apportion categories for each speaker. The honoree has more than enough characteristics to go around. One speaker should be assigned the roastee's work experience. Another should take his home life. A third can take his physical status and his appetite, huge or birdlike. His affection for the bubbly can be the springboard for a spot.

Each speaker should work, if possible, from cards, as suggested earlier. Jokes should be personalized. A joke about a deserted island should reflect the time the honoree was shipwrecked, even if he has never been within a thousand miles of water.

Each speaker is introduced by the emcee with a one-liner or story that could apply to the speaker. When the speaker is finished, the emcee will "kiss him off" with another one-liner. The emcee moves the show. He makes the pace. The fact that a speaker isn't doing well can be turned into a plus with a wry comment.

When the roastee gets up to get even for the wonderful things that have been said about him, he too might have prepared marks. He can have cards. Often I've found that preparing a rebuttal for him, and sealing the jokes in an envelope that is given to him when he stands up, can be a big winner. There are few things funnier than a tyro speaker reading jokes for the first time. The comedy will come, more often, from the way he reads.

A member of the organization should thank the master or mistress of ceremonies to round out the affair.

The following are some roast jokes applicable to all occasions:

That was a lovely introduction. You must write the words for tombstones!

If you were alive, you'd be a very sick man!

These little barbs thrown at our honoree really hit the spot. Now let's listen to the spot hit back!

And now, presenting the case for the defense . . .

He has a ready wit. He should let us know when it's ready!

This has been a weird evening. This is the first time I've ever been to a funeral where I'm the corpse!

After that kind of introduction, anything I do is a pleasure!

Good evening, ladies and gentlemen—and I guess that takes care of most of you!

Thank you, _____. Your talent, like your suit, is always lightweight!

He never did a thing in his life, and he didn't do that well!

Nobody could warm up to her, even if they were cremated together!

She feels like a new woman, and she should be!

For years he was an unknown failure. Now he's a known failure!

He's very familiar with hard work. He's fought it for years!

He always knows where his head is. Until noon it's on a pillow!

He started at the bottom and sank!

I'll say this—whenever we introduce him at these affairs, things pick up speed. That's what happens when you go downhill!

He didn't tell his wife he wasn't good enough for her. He let it come as a surprise!

He just got the key to the executive washroom. When he cleans the stalls, he has to give it back!

He has no prejudices. He hates everybody equally!

She made Phi Beta Kappa—one by one!

She bought that very expensive dress to go with a very cheap husband!

His folks want to know if vasectomies can be made retroactive!

He'd make a great neighbor for anybody with a windmill!

He's here under difficult circumstances. He wasn't asked!

He has a plan for his business. It's called "neglect"!

She's a credit to her cards!

She's always putting him on. Somebody has to!

We think he's a saint. That's because the boss is always crucifying him!

He's looking for a rich woman who's too proud to have her husband work!

The other day he made an obscene phone call to a nudist colony. When a woman came on the line, he told her the kind of clothes he was going to put on her!

She has a tongue that could clip a hedge!

He's the total hypochondriac. He won't eat an ice cube because he can't boil it first!

She hates sex in the movies. She tried it once and the seat folded up!

She uses so much perfume, when she stands still she makes a puddle!

He's been admired for years, none of them recently!

He wanted her in the worst way, and he got her!

The only way she could get a living bra is to set a trap!

He's always putting up a false front. He went to a drive-in movie and for three hours he did pushups in the backseat!

She only likes sex on days that have a *d* in them!

She's a little tired today. She went on a double date last night and the other girl didn't show up!

She recently ran into somebody she knew when they were the same age!

He believes that the greatest joy of fatherhood is getting there!

When they ask him about women's rights, he says he'll take either side!

By the time she gets through telling a man about her past, he's part of it!

She had twins recently—the copier repairman and his brother!

If sex appeal were sunshine, he'd be a snowstorm!

There he goes—the Three Mile Island of dinners!

She's been crazy about boys ever since she found out she wasn't one of them!

He's fired with enthusiasm––every time!

She got her Mercedes the hard way—she bought it!

He came to work early one day and the boss wanted to know if he was having trouble at home!

They offered him a raise if he did good work. He knew there was a catch to it!

He's been fired by everybody but NASA!

He's pooped today. All night long he dreamed that he was working!

She went to work for her new boss and said she'd take any position. They're up to the forty-fifth!

He's no quitter. He gets fired!

He always has the same problems—how to start the car in the morning and his wife at night!

There's no excuse for sloppy work, but he keeps trying to think of one!

If he offers you a deal, see your lawyer. If your lawyer tells you to take the deal, see another lawyer!

Here's a man who went to a masquerade party in the nude. He said he was an unfurnished apartment!

He's head of the membership drive. He's driven out eight of them already!

Now it's time to bring up a man who can start the bull rolling!

He doesn't get many laughs, but the smiles are deafening!

He wants to die with his boots on. He has holes in his socks!

Talk is cheap, and in addition, he gets it wholesale!

We've still got a few minutes to kill, and I don't know anybody who can kill them better!

I wish my future was as bright as his suit!

He's been washing his hair too much. It's shrinking!

There's a guy who can make coffee nervous!

He doesn't know when he's well off, because he never is!

savers

They love to see you in agony. Cover yourself with lines that will let them know you deserve a better fate! I use savers even when I'm getting big laughs. The savers heighten the laughs that follow. Some speakers deliver material with a mock sense of power, daring the audience not to laugh. Most of the power is in the eyes. When delivering a saver, each member of the audience must feel as if the remark is directed at him or her. Behind the dare-you attitude of the audience is its essential warmth. The most hostile-seeming audience has a layer of warmth that can be reached. Savers often find that layer quickly.

Here's another one you may not like!

You're a nice group. Would you like to leave a wakeup call?

We will now pray silently for the joke that just died!

Can you give me a ten-yard head start?

Is this an audience or a jury?

I'd like to see you all again. But not as a group!

Did I see you people at the Nuremberg trials?

Why do you look at me as if I ticketed your car?

I wouldn't give this spot to a leopard! I may give *you* to a leopard!

Are you live or on tape?

I've never worked for an oil painting before!

I've heard of the silent majority, but this is ridiculous!

Silence is golden. I think you're a mine!

How can you people sleep with the lights on?

Look at it this way—I could be marrying your daughter!

Don't panic. I'm almost through. I think I was when I started!

Would it help if I bled?

I'm so glad I didn't give up my day job!

I bet you thought I wouldn't get laughs!

I wish you were here yesterday. I was out of town!

Well, I guess I have to go to the dirty stuff!

Why don't I ever get English-speaking audiences?

This is a new idea—a taped audience!

I wish you'd laugh at my material. *I* laugh at *your* clothes!

Is this an audience? Is this an audience? That's what I want to know—is this an audience?

I knew I was going to go over big by your applau!

I hope the Red Cross gets here in time!

You're a nice audience. The last audience I spoke to hit me!

Don't hate me. I didn't cook the entree!

sketches

A tall, lanky version of a blackout, a sketch—or skit, as the uninitiated call it—is generally one of the highlights of the home-made show.

Wonderful sketches can be found in library collections. Many can be rented from specialized companies. Prices are generally minimal.

While no sketch is foolproof, some come close. I have lent church groups some of the sketches done on my television show forty years ago and found that the laughs are still there to be culled. The surest are those in which a prop is used or some physical comedy is involved. I wrote a sketch called "The Stand-in" that depends for most of its laughs on hitting the main character with a powder puff. The sketch depicts the making of a movie. Every time the word "Makeup!" is called out, a puff loaded down with powder pummels the main character's face. Picture the glee when one of the church elders is the target. I give money-back guarantees on "The Stand-in."

The classic sketches, such as "If Men Played Cards as Women Do" and "Confidential Auto Loan," are timeless. Some first performed fifty years ago are new again.

I find that repetition brings laughter. Think back to the peek-a-boo games played with babies in a crib. We never seem to lose the appreciation for repetition of sounds and moves. A sketch that relies on a move being made over and over again should work well for even an amateur group.

Mess also makes for fun. A television show of some years ago depended on hitting important people with pies. No plot, no special effects, only a pie whooshing into a well-known face.

Those who send in the special form attached to the solid-gold edition of this work can have a "pie" sketch too. I have one in which sixty pies are tossed in eighty minutes. The cost is prohibitive for all groups but the confectionery bakers of the world!

In putting on a company, PTA, or benevolent society show, consider no more than three sketches. Two wouldn't ruin your evening either.

Better to win with modesty than to reach out beyond your grasp! Robert Browning said something like that after he struck out with the annual poets' wingding!

switches

Throughout this book there have been many jokes that can be "switched" or converted to poke fun at things other than the immediate target. A would-be jokester should practice learning how to think "switches." Early in the book was a one-liner about a lonely soul. He joined the auto club for its dances. Obviously, the humor comes from the fact that the auto club isn't a social group and doesn't have dances like the Elks or Knights of Columbus. The notion underlying the joke can be used for other groups that may be closer to the experience of the audience: "He joined the Book-of-the-Month Club for the dances!"

The joke can be switched or converted for other emphases. If, instead of loneliness, the emphasis was placed on illiteracy, a new joke is born: "This man has never read a book. He joined the Book-of-the-Month Club for the dances!"

A joke has many spokes. People who want to learn to live by the funnybone should practice learning where these spokes are. A favorite joke of mine, one I use in my act when I play Atlantic City, is: "Flash! A tornado just ripped through downtown

Newark and did five million dollars' worth of improvements!" This joke can be told about almost any city. It can be based on floods, tidal waves, hurricanes, or the disaster of your choice.

Pick out the most applicable, hurl the barb, and step back as waves of laughter fill the hall.

women in the audience

Women in an audience, I've found, control that audience. If the little lady or girlfriend doesn't think a comedian is funny or a singer gifted, she'll make it uncomfortable for the men to laugh or express pleasure in any way. One "Do you really think he's funny?" can cast a pall three feet thick. Therefore, to win an audience I aim at the ladies. I choose my comedy areas carefully. For some reason, ladies seem to bristle at "son" jokes. They love to listen to husbands and lovers being destroyed, but sons are sacred. So, when there are a telling number of ladies in the audience, I bring out "daughter" jokes. Maybe it's because daughters are the competition in a home. Having studied under Freud for eighteen years, I'd vote for that as a cogent reason for the acceptance of "daughter" jokes by the ladies. The ability to gauge the audience can be mastered to an extent. Once the speaker or performer has "boxed" the audience's taste, the audience is in his hip pocket.

last but not least

Don't overanalyze comedy. If you keep picking at it, it will disappear. Be satisfied with the knowledge that you said something, made some face, or did something mysterious that made everybody laugh!

Remember that Thalia, the Muse of Comedy, was born of the loins of Zeus, the king of gods!